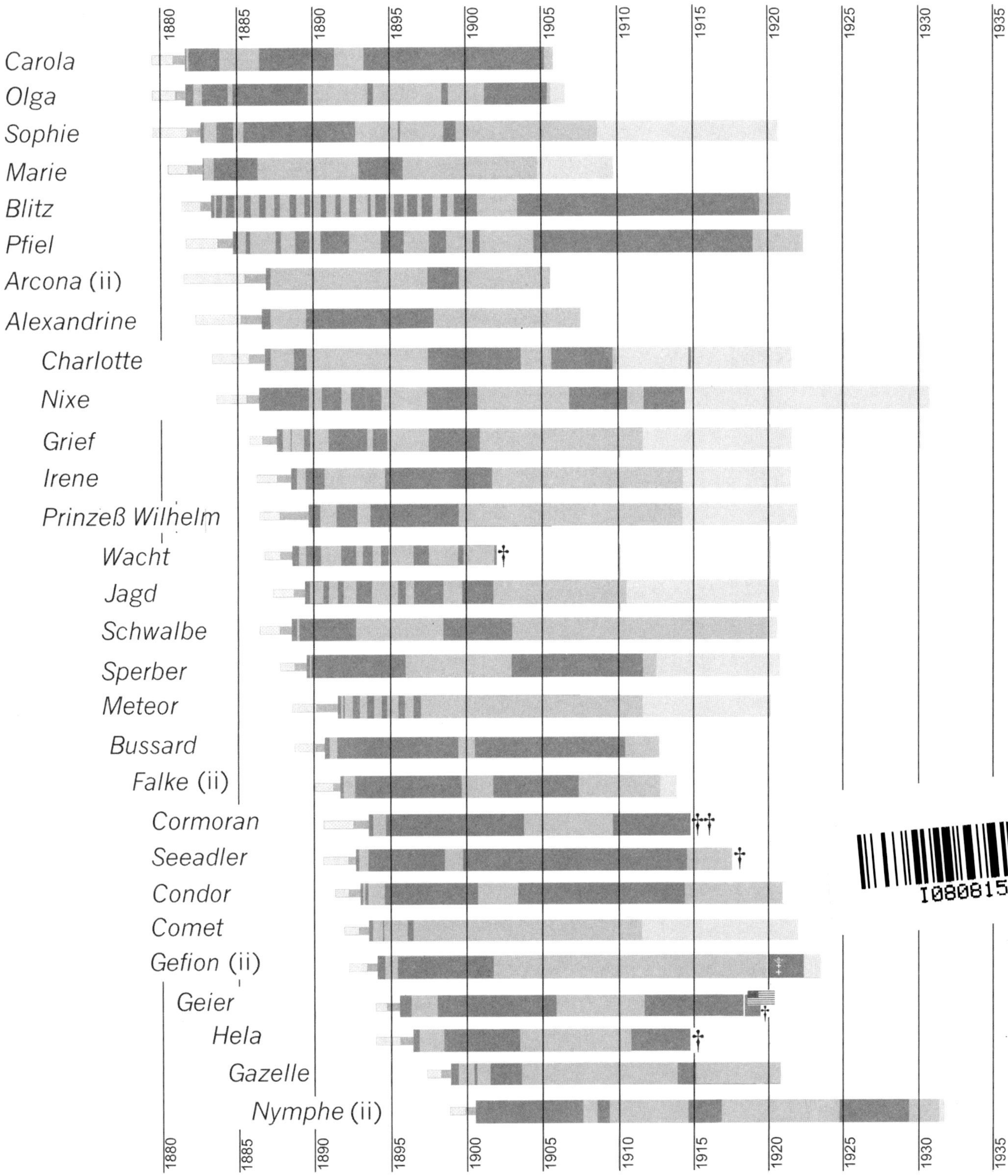

† Ship sunk by accident or enemy action

†† Ship scuttled ↑ Ship refloated

T Ship expended as target

Unless otherwise indicated, ships sold for scrap and broken up at the end of their timelines.

THE KAISER'S CRUISERS

THE KAISER'S CRUISERS 1871–1918

AIDAN DODSON
DIRK NOTTELMANN

NAVAL INSTITUTE PRESS
ANNAPOLIS, MARYLAND

Title page: *Olga* and *Carola* in the Albert dry dock at Singapore during the 1880s. They typified German overseas cruising vessels of the epoch.
(NHHC NH 88777)

First published in Great Britain in 2021 by
Seaforth Publishing,
A division of Pen & Sword Books Ltd,
47 Church Street,
Barnsley S70 2AS

www.seaforthpublishing.com

Published and distributed in the
United States of America and Canada by the
Naval Institute Press,
291 Wood Road, Annapolis,
Maryland 21402-5034

www.nip.org

Library of Congress Control Number: 2021945547

ISBN 978 1 68247 745 8

Printed and bound in India

FSC www.fsc.org MIX Paper from responsible sources FSC® C016779

CONTENTS

PREFACE

THE PRESENT VOLUME is a companion to *The Kaiser's Battlefleet*, published by Dodson in 2016, and also to a series of articles published by Nottelmann in *Warship International* between 2011 and 2020, dealing with the capital ships of the Imperial German Navy (Kaiserliche Marine). Like them, it is intended to tell the story of that navy through the lens of a particular group of warships. In this case, these are the cruising vessels of the fleet – excluding those classified under the 1898 German Fleet Law as 'large cruisers' (Große Kreuzer), which were covered in *The Kaiser's Battlefleet*, as to all intents and purposes capital ships. The ships in question are all those that were – or would have been if still extant – classified as 'small cruisers' (Kleine Kreuzer) under the Fleet Law. This classification brought together, however, a distinctly diverse set of vessels with very different characteristics and employment, ranging from glorified colonial gunboats through full-rigged, composite-hulled, broadside-armed ships, to small, fast, fleet scouts, and modern cruisers intended to make the union of types a practical reality.

These ships have been poorly served in the literature, with hitherto no technical history available in any language. In many ways this book is intended to follow-on from Axel Grießmer's pioneering works on German dreadnought battleships and battlecruisers,[1] employing original sources from German and British archives, including material handed over to Nottelmann by Dr Grießmer when the latter abandoned his plans to produce a volume of his own on small cruisers. Some preliminary material has been presented in the journal *Warship*, but the present work greatly expands on this to produce what we hope will be as definitive a work on the topic as is possible at the present time.

As in *Kaiser's Battlefleet*, a conscious attempt has been made to avoid a dry class-by-class structure in favour a narrative that embraces the political and strategic backgrounds to the various classes and their evolution and modifications. In addition, there are overviews of the ships' operational use, with accounts of the relevant operations specifically highlighting the activities of, and damage suffered by, the battleships and large cruisers, complemented by photographs showing the ships, their modifications and aspects of their operation. Cruisers built for foreign powers are also included to give a fully rounded impression of the German cruiser in its broadest sense, and how German approaches were applied to overseas customers' requirements. A particularly interesting case study is that of a pair of ships building for the Russian navy that were taken over by Germany at the outbreak of the First World War, and what subsequent modifications had to be undertaken to make them fit for service with the German navy.

This core narrative is accompanied by a second part that comprises summaries of the technical details and careers of the ships involved, illustrated with sketches showing the arrangements of armour and machinery spaces, and the evolution of ships' external appearances. It should be emphasised that these are indeed sketches, and do not pretend to be formal technical drawings, some examples of which are, however, provided within the main text.

Our thanks are due to various friends and colleagues for their help in writing this book: Wolfgang Bohlayer; Toby Ewin; Ian Foster; Roland Heidrich; Leon Homburg, Steve McLoughin; the late Hans Mehl; Manfred Meyer; Jean Moulin; Sergei Vinogradov; and Lothar Wischmeyer. Proofreading debts are owed to the Hilton sisters – Dodson's wife Dyan and his sister-in-law Anne – and Reg Clark, but any remaining errors are wholly our responsibility.

Aidan Dodson
Bristol, UK

Dirk Nottelmann
Moorrege, Schleswig-Holstein, Germany

January 2021

[1] *Große Kreuzer der Kaiserlichen Marine 1906–1918: Konstruktionen und Entwürfe im Zeichen des Tirpitz-Planes* (Bonn: Bernard & Graefe, 1996); *Linienschiffe der Kaiserlichen Marine 1906–1918: Konstruktionen zwischen Rüstungskonkurrenz und Flottengesetz* (Bonn: Bernard & Graefe, 1999).

INTRODUCTION

WHEN THE IMPERIAL GERMAN NAVY came into existence in 1871 its largest vessels were, besides three ironclads, a collection of not atypical cruising vessels of the period: three wooden sailing frigates (two laid up and one about to be stricken) and nine wooden, fully rigged screw frigates/corvettes in service, with three more in hand, all capable of worldwide deployment. There were also a pair of paddle avisos (despatch vessels), at least nominally for co-operation in home waters. This distinction between vessels capable of distant service and those for home service would be maintained through to the late 1890s, when a new kind of 'small cruiser' capable of universal service was introduced. These would continue to be built down to the dissolution of the Kaiser's navy at the end of the First World War – although thinking was by then moving towards more specialised types for putative post-war programmes.

That the 'overseas' cruiser should have a full sailing rig to supplement its still uneconomical simple-expansion engines was something that would be maintained through the 1870s. Even after the adoption of compound engines, sails were retained, both to increase range and as training assets, since the ships in question were increasingly used to train cadets and boy seamen. Indeed, the final examples of the breed served out their careers primarily as training ships, although initially still classified alongside ships that retained a primary operational military purpose. Reality was reflected in 1891, when a reclassification made them formally 'training ships'.

Meanwhile, the aviso was becoming a more effective warship, with two outstanding examples laid down in 1881 remaining on active service for three decades. On the other hand, attempts at building diminutives proved – as so often – a false economy, with the resulting ships seeing only limited service. Another line of development was to produce small, rigged cruisers as station ships overseas, essentially as developments of the big gunboats that had begun to be built shortly before the foundation of the Reich.

A move towards new kinds of cruiser began in the mid-1880s, with the construction of the first 'overseas' cruisers without sailing rig, and avisos of much greater size than hitherto. By the middle of the next decade developments were moving towards a new 'large' cruiser aspiring to capital rank, and a 'small' cruiser able to fulfil all other 'overseas' and 'home' roles. All this crystallised in 1898, when the first of Admiral Tirpitz's Fleet Laws legally divided cruisers into these two categories, and in so doing so implicitly made each of them a 'thing', with little or no scope for the creation of specialist sub-types in the context of a legally mandated building programme. Thus, the cruiser-type 'mine steamers' built from 1905 were very carefully *not* placed in the formal cruiser category, although the final pair operated almost entirely in the cruiser role, and are, with their two predecessors, nevertheless included in this book.

In telling the story of these ships, this book will also illustrate the way that the German navy evolved, under Kaiser Wilhelm II and Tirpitz, from an essentially peripheral element of the Reich's military organisation to one that absorbed an increasingly large proportion of the defence budget. As far as the ships themselves are concerned, there is an interesting mix of conservatism and innovation – an example of the former being manifested in the over-long retention of the 10.5cm gun as main armament, leading to the need for an emergency programme of rearmament with 15cm weapons during the First World War. On the other hand, the very existence of the general-purpose small cruiser reflected a recognition of the real need for such ships, rather than spending 'cruising' funds on more glamorous – but much more expensive – big cruisers, as was done especially by France, the United States and, to a lesser extent, Italy. The resulting operational poverty of the French and Italian navies is nicely illustrated by their post-First World War demands for a tithe of ex-German small cruisers, which would form key elements of their fleets throughout the 1920s, with two examples that passed to Italy remaining in service until 1943.

In comparison with British (and French) shipyards, those of Germany produced relatively few cruisers for export, but they played an important part in the growth of the Chinese navy, and provided the Russian fleet with useful vessels, two of which would be sufficiently well regarded to merit the construction of sister ships in Russian yards: one of these would survive to fight in the Second World War. Another pair of ships ordered by Russia would still be under construction in August 1914, allowing them to provide powerful reinforcements of the German cruiser force.

During the First World War, the small cruisers were by far the most active of the major warships of the German fleet, and were involved in operations from the very outset. Those on overseas stations had been eliminated by Allied navies by the middle of 1915, albeit not without having played important roles, with involvement in the sinking of four Allied cruisers and a number of merchantmen, the exploits of *Emden* becoming legendary. Closer to home, they took part in every significant action, although in doing so suffered badly, three being lost at the First Battle of Heligoland Bight, four at Jutland, with three sunk elsewhere by mine or torpedo, and some ships so badly damaged that they never returned to active service.

After the Armistice in 1918, a handful of modern small cruisers were the largest warships Germany was permitted to keep on active service. It had been planned that they would then become the core of the new German navy – but the scuttling of seven of their kind (not to mention eleven battleships, five large [battle] cruisers and fifty torpedo boats!) at Scapa Flow in June 1919 meant that they joined the swathes of German warships surrendered to the victorious powers. Their place was taken by ships of far earlier vintage – indeed among them some of the pioneers of the 'small cruiser' category – which would make up the majority of the cruiser force until the end of the 1920s. A few would survive as hulks down to the end of the Second World War, two even seeing action as unpowered anti-aircraft vessels, and one, surrendered to the USA, not being scrapped until 1954.

This narrative is complemented by tabulated data and sketches that together document the technical data, evolution and service of individual ships, updated according to the most recent sources of information – in particular archival sources, many of which have lain hidden in the files for more than a century. Appendices also include the text of the Fleet Laws, summaries of the organisation of major warships from 1884 onwards, and of the weapons mounted in the ships covered by this volume.

CONVENTIONS, ABBREVIATIONS AND GLOSSARY

IN GENERAL, German terms are translated into their closest English literal equivalents. 'Reich' is not translated, recognising the lack of a straightforward English word for the term (which is perhaps best explained as 'empire without the necessity of an emperor'), the translation 'Imperial' being reserved for 'Kaiserlich'.

This includes ship designations – in particular, 'Große Kreuzer' is translated as 'large cruiser' throughout: unlike the British from 1912, the Germans did not distinguish between pre-dreadnought 'armoured cruisers' and dreadnought 'battlecruisers'. Likewise, it was not until the 1930s that the classification 'destroyer' was first used for fleet flotilla craft: previously they were formally 'torpedo boats' or 'large torpedo boats'.[2]

The only significant exception is that the term 'battleship' is used for 'Linienschiff'. This is because the literal translation, 'ship of the line', is used with the specific meaning of a first- to third-rate wooden fighting ship of the eighteenth/nineteenth century in British naval terminology, with the resulting scope for confusion ('Schlachtschiff' was first officially used in Germany for the *Scharnhorst* class of 1935).[3]

Regarding the ships that are the principal subject of this book, a range of different classifications were employed by the German navy prior to the rationalisation and standardisation of categories under the 1898 and later Fleet Laws (for which, see pp 97-98, 290-295). These classifications and their changes are described in the text, with a graphical summary provided on p 90.

Place names are given as per German usage during the period covered by the book, with modern equivalents in parentheses where appropriate. For other German terms, the following translations/abbreviations are used.

Admiralstab	Naval Staff
Aufklärungsgruppe	Scouting Group
Befehlshaber	Flag Officer (FO)
Gedeckte Korvette	Decked corvette
Geschwader	Squadron
Glattdecks Korvette	Flushdecked corvette
Marine-Inspektion	Navy Inspectorate
Marine-Kabinett	Naval Cabinet
Matrosen-Division	Sailor-infantry Division (naval personnel fighting on Western Front)
Oberkommando der Marine	Naval High Command
Ostasiengeschwader	East Asia Squadron
Panzerfahrzeug	Armoured Vessel
Reichs-Marine-Amt	Naval Office
Schulverband	Training Force
Suchverband	Minesweeping Force
Stammschiff	Parent ship (fully manned vessel within reserve formation)
Verband	Force
Vermehrungsbauten	Augmentation vessel
Vorpostenflottille	Picket Flotilla

[2] Although a series of particularly large vessels requisitioned from or modelled after foreign contracts/boats at the outbreak of the war were referred to colloquially as 'torpedo boat destroyers', they were officially still 'large torpedo boats' – as were even the 2000t, 15cm-armed, *S113* class.

[3] Although frequently erroneously called 'battlecruisers' in English language sources, as are the abortive *Battleship O* class of 1939, which were also actually formally a 'Schlachtschiff'.

SENIOR LEADERSHIP ROLES OF THE IMPERIAL GERMAN NAVY

Chiefs of Imperial Admiralty (Chefs der Kaiserlichen Admiralität)

Albrecht von Stosch	1 Jan 72–20 Mar 83
Leo von Caprivi	20 Mar 83–5 Jul 88
Alexander von Monts de Mazin	5 Jul 88–19 Jan 89

Commanding Admirals of the Naval High Command (Kommandierender Admiral der Oberkommando der Marine)

Max Freiherr von der Goltz	1 Apr 89–8 Mar 95
Eduard von Knorr	8 Mar 95–14 Mar 99

State Secretaries of the Reich Naval Office (Staatssekretäre des Reichsmarineamtes)

Karl Eduard Heusner	1 Apr 89–23 Apr 90
Friedrich von Hollmann	23 Apr 90–18 Jun 1897
Alfred von Tirpitz	18 Jun 97–15 Mar 16
Eduard von Capelle	15 Mar 16–28 Aug 18
Paul Behncke	Acting: 28 Aug–18 Sep 18 18 Sep 18–28 Sep 18
Ernst Ritter von Mann Edler von Tiechler	5 Oct 18–13 Feb 19
Maximilian Rogge	13 Feb 19–15 Jul 19

RANK EQUIVALENCES BETWEEN GERMAN, BRITISH AND AMERICAN NAVIES*

This table reflects the situation during the period covered by this book, which differs significantly from that prevailing at the time of writing.

Imperial German Navy		Royal Navy	United States Navy
Großadmiral	GAdm	Admiral of the Fleet	Admiral of the Navy
Admiral	Adm	Admiral	Admiral
Vize-Admiral	VAdm	Vice Admiral	Vice Admiral
Kontre-Admiral	KAdm	Rear Admiral	Rear Admiral
-		Commodore 1st class*	Commodore (to 1899) Rear Admiral (lower half – from 1899)
Kommodore**	Kdre	Commodore 2nd class***	-
Kapitän zur See	Kpt	Captain	Captain
Fregattenkapitän	FKpt	Captain (with less than 3yr seniority)	Captain (with less than 3yr seniority)
Korvettenkapitän	KKpt	Commander	Commander
Kapitänleutnant	KptLtn	Lieutenant (with over 8yrs seniority – to 1914) Lieutenant-Commander (from 1914)	Lieutenant-Commander
Oberleutnant zur See	Obltn z S	Lieutenant	Lieutenant Lieutenant (junior grade)
Leutnant zur See	Ltn z S	Sub-Lieutenant Chief Commissioned Warrant Officer	Ensign
Fähnrich zur See	Fähn z S	Midshipman	Midshipman
Seekadett	SK	Cadet	Midshipman

* Appointment of Captain leading a formation who is not also the commanding officer of his ship. Commodore did not become a substantive rank in the RN until 1997.

** Appointment (principally in wartime) of the senior Kapitän zur See of a formation not led by a flag officer. Kommodore was only ephemerally a substantive rank in the German navy during 1939–45, and never subsequently.

*** Appointment of Captain leading a formation while still commanding his own ship.

Departments of the State Secretariat of the Reich Navy Office

'A'	General (Allgemeines)
'B'	Shipyards (Bauwerft)
'C'	Administration (Verwaltung)
'H'	Hydrography (Hydrographie)
'J'	Legal (Juristische)
'K'	Construction (Konstruktion)
'M'	Naval Office (Marine Amt)
'N'	Press (Nachrichten)
'W'	Weapons (Waffen)

Chiefs of Admiralty Staff (Chefs des Admiralstabs der Kaiserlichen Marine)

Felix von Bendemann	14 Mar 99–31 Dec 99
Otto von Diederichs	1 Jan 00–19 Aug 02
Wilhelm Büchsel	20 Aug 02–28 Jan 08
Friedrich Graf von Baudissin	29 Jan 08–5 Sep 09
Max von Fischel	6 Sep 09–11 Mar 11
August von Heeringen	12 Mar 11–31 Mar 13
Hugo von Pohl	1 Apr 13–1 Feb 1915
Gustav Bachmann	2 Feb 15–3 Sep 1915
Henning von Holtzendorff	4 Sep 15–10 Aug 18
Reinhard Scheer (1863–1928)	11 Aug 18–14 Nov 18 (also Chef der Seekriegsleitung 28 Aug–14 Nov 18)

ABBREVIATIONS

AA	anti-aircraft
AW	Above Water (torpedo tubes)
BA	Bundesarchiv (in photographic credits)
BA-MA	Bundesarchiv-Militärarchiv
BCF	Battle Cruiser Force (later Fleet: Royal Navy)
BCS	Battle Cruiser Squadron (Royal Navy)
BLR	Breech-loading Rifle
BRT	British Registered Tons
BS	Battle Squadron (Royal Navy)
CinC	Commander-in-Chief
CS	Cruiser Squadron (Royal Navy)
DF	Destroyer Flotilla (Royal Navy)
Div	Division
DK	Denmark
DW	deadweight tonnage
F	Flagship
FF	Fleet Flagship
FO	Flag Officer
HC	Horizontal Compound (double expansion)
HP	High Pressure (in steam turbine installations)
HSE	Horizontal Single Expansion
HSF	High Seas Fleet
JP	Japan
PR	Prussia
QF	Quick-Firing gun
QL	Quick-Loading gun (official German term for QF)
kt	knot(s)
LCS	Light Cruiser Squadron (Royal Navy)
LTB	Leader of Torpedo-boats
LP	Low Pressure (in steam turbine installations)
MG	Machine gun (initially Hotchkiss revolver-type, later Maxim single-barrelled type)
MLR	Muzzle-Loading Rifle
MMS	Motor minesweeper (F-Boat)
MSD	Mine Sweeper Division
NGE	North German Confederation
NHHC	US Naval History and Heritage Command (photographic credits)
nm	nautical mile(s)
oa	overall (length)
OTE	Oblique Triple Expansion
pp	between perpendiculars (length)
RMA	Reich Naval Office (Reichs-Marine-Amt)
RK	Ring Kanone
SG	Scouting Group (Aufklärungsgruppe)
Sqn	Squadron (Geschwader)
SMF	Submarine Flotilla
SNO	Senior Naval Officer
SO	Senior Officer
TBF	Torpedo boat Flotilla
TNA	UK National Archives
TT	Torpedo tube(s)
USNA	United States National Archives (in photographic credits)
UW	Under Water (torpedo tubes)
VTE	Vertical Triple Expansion
wl	waterline (length)
W/T	wireless telegraphy (radio)
2F	2nd Flagship

CONVENTIONS FOR DESCRIBING PROTECTION ON pp 250-289

Armour thicknesses are given from the stern, separated by hyphens. Where they are made up from layers, the thicknesses of the individual layers are separated by a '+' sign.

Deck protection thicknesses are given first on the flat, with those on the slopes given second, following an oblique: e.g. 'Deck 25-20+10-15mm/50mm' denotes a deck 25mm at the stern, 30mm amidships (made up of one layer of 20mm plates and one layer of 10mm), and 15mm at the bow, with 50mm slopes at the side.

DESIGNATION OF NAVAL GUNS

The length of German naval guns, measured in multiples of the bore diameter (calibres), was based on the *overall* length of the barrel (including the breech mechanism), rather than just the rifled element, as in most foreign guns (with the exception of those of Austria-Hungary and Russia). Thus, for example, a German '35cal' weapon would be ~3cal shorter than a UK or US gun of nominally the same length. In a gun designations, the calibre was stated in centimetres, followed by barrel length preceded by 'L/'. Breech-loading guns using bagged propellant were designated 'Kanone' (K; those whose construction was based on reinforcing hoops were 'Ringkanone' [RK]); those with cartridged propellant were 'Schnellade Kanone'(SK) [Quick Loading (QL), equivalent to Anglo-American 'Quick Firing' (QF)]. The model of the entire gun mounting – not necessarily that of the gun/barrel itself – was given in terms of the abbreviated year of introduction, preceded by 'C/'. Thus, a '15cm SK L/40 C/97' gun was a 15cm/40 QL weapon designed in 1897. For a summary of the details of the principal guns employed in ships covered in this book, see Appendix 3 (pp 304-305).

THE NAMING OF GERMAN CRUISERS

IN GENERAL, the naming of German warships followed rules set down for the first time by an order of Kaiser Wilhelm I dated 17 August 1875. For cruising vessels the following paragraphs applied:

> 3) Larger covered-corvettes shall bear the names of the most glorious and decisive victories in wars conducted by Germany. Smaller vessels of this type shall bear the names of eminent German commanders-in-chief, admirals and statesmen.
> 4) My flushdecked-corvettes shall bear the names of female members of German noble houses.
> 6) For my steam-avisos proposals shall be made for names reflecting the special duties of this type either by employing appropriate nouns or adjectives.

These rules were amended and adapted at various times, with an important revision in 1903, in the wake of the Fleet Laws of 1898 and 1900. Deviations occurred mainly with vessels built before this particular order or with vessels whose names followed an earlier tradition.

Perhaps influenced by the British-purchased *Thetis*, mythological females were a staple source of nomenclature from the 1850s until the beginning of the twentieth century. Female names borne by members of the royal and imperial families had been added into the mix during the late 1860s, along with 'names of honour' such as *Frauenlob* ('Praise of Women', referring specifically to a money collection among Prussian females to funding a warship). An outlier was *Arcona*, named after a cape on the island of Rügen. Of the proposed honouring of German victories, only the name *Leipzig* survived as a long-term remembrance for the victory over Napoleon I in 1813, whereas *Sedan*, named for the decisive victory in the war of 1870–71, when Napoleon III had been taken prisoner, was soon changed for political reasons. These political considerations regarding France prevailed for a second time when it came to the naming of the battleships of the *Brandenburg* class. The fourth ship, again originally intended to bear the name *Sedan*, was renamed *Kurfürst Friedrich Wilhelm* before the launch.

The surnames of military leaders and statesmen began to be used after the introduction of the above mentioned Order in the 1870s, and while some (e.g. *Gneisenau*, *Blücher* and *Stein*) remembered individuals of the Napoleonic era, others were those of the current Reich Chancellor (*Bismarck*), Chief of the General Staff (*Moltke*), and Head of the Admiralty (*Stosch*). This latter approach was an unusual one, in that most foreign navies avoided naming ships for living persons other than monarchs or senior members of ruling families. However, it would be continued on occasion throughout the history of the Imperial German Navy, two of the fleet's last large cruisers (battlecruisers) being named for the very much alive generals *Hindenburg* and *Mackensen* during the First World War.

In addition, birds of prey were employed for naming two classes of cruisers built for overseas service during the 1880s and 1890s, reflecting their ancestry among gunboats, which generally received bird and animal names. This theme would be reused for the early destroyers of the Reichsmarine (navy of the Weimar Republic), and fast patrol vessels of the Bundesmarine (navy of West Germany). Avisos were variously named, including for a mythological bird of prey (*Greif* – 'griffon'), meteorological/astronomical phenomena (*Blitz* – 'lightning', *Meteor*), a weapon (*Pfeil* – 'arrow'), a Rhenish siren (*Loreley*), and a peninsula (*Hela*).

While military leaders and statesmen continued to be used in naming large cruisers down to 1918 (and capital ships of the Reichsmarine and Kriegsmarine [navy of the Third Reich], and early frigates of the Bundesmarine), the naming of small cruisers was changed entirely by a decree issued by the Kaiser in 1903. From this point onwards, they were named for German cities, the only exceptions being *Frauenlob* (iii), which remembered the previous ship of the name, sunk at the Battle of Jutland, and *Gazelle* (ii), which remembered the eponymous large corvette. This practice was continued under the Weimar Republic, and also, for frigates, by the Bundesmarine.

From the early days of the Imperial German Navy down to the Second World War, a ship's name would not be revealed until her launch. Prior to this, vessels would be known to the public by a provisional name, whereas, internally, the final name was chosen by the Kaiser from a list of proposals prepared by the RMA. The reasons behind his ultimate choice were never revealed and may well have been just a matter of his personal feelings on that particular day. As an example, the first small cruiser of the 1913 Estimates was originally to be named after the city of Chemnitz until the Kaiser decided – without giving reasons – that its name should be *Wiesbaden* instead.

The provisional name depended on whether the ship in question was being programmed as a replacement for an existing ship – either coming to the end of its 'legal' life (cf.

p 97), or lost – or if she represented an addition to strength (in particular as a result of the Fleet Laws: p. 98). The latter category would be known by a serial letter within its classification – e.g. *Small Cruiser A*. The letter sequence might be restarted even within a class of ship: thus *Gazelle* was ordered as *IV.-class Cruiser G*, but her sisters were *Small Cruisers A* (to be *Nymphe*) through *F* (*Amazone*), the type classification of the class having been changed in the interim (see pp 93-99).

For 'replacement' ships, they were designated *Ersatz-x* (i.e. 'Replacement X'), where *x* was the name of the ship that was being disposed of, reclassified, or had been lost. Thus, four of the *Bussard* class were ordered as *Cruisers C* [*Bussard*], *D* [*Falke*], *E* [*Cormoran*] and *F* [*Geier*], as additions to strength, but the other two were *Ersatz-Adler* [*Seeadler*] and *Ersatz-Eber* [*Condor*], replacing the pair of gunboats lost in the Samoa hurricane of March 1889 (see p 43). As generation followed generation, and with the perpetuation of name-themes, a number of *Ersatz*-names repeated over time, there being two vessels ordered as *Ersatz-Arcona* [*Moltke* (i, 1878) and *Köln* (iii, 1930)], *Ersatz-Ariadne* [*Prinzess Wilhelm* and *Cöln* (ii, 1918)], *Ersatz-Comet* [*Adler* and *Dresden* (i)], *Ersatz-Gazelle* [*Stosch* and *Königsberg* (ii, 1916)]. Only occasionally did a 'replacement' ship actually take the name of the original vessel, the most striking examples being three ships of the *Cöln* (ii) class – *Ersatz-Dresden*, *Ersatz-Leipzig* and *Ersatz-Magdeburg*. This was owing to a desire to immediately replicate the names of ships lost in action early in the First World War.

It should be noted that on their surrender under the Treaty of Versailles, major German prizes were designated by letters, the cruisers being *A* (*Königsberg*), *E* (*Graudenz*), *J* (*Regensburg*), *O* (*Strassburg*), *P* (*Lübeck*), *Q* (*München*), *R* (*Danzig*), *T* (*Stettin*), *U* (*Pillau*), *W* (*Kolberg*), *Y* (*Augsburg*) and *Z* (*Stralsund*); the missing letters belonged to battleships (*B*, *D*, *F*, *G* [*Westfalen* class], *H*, *K*, *L* and *M* [*Helgoland* class]).

Another point to highlight is the revision of spelling that took place in in the wake of the German Orthographic Conference in 1901 with the letter 'C' replaced by an extension of the usage of 'K'. However, the implementation of this was by no means automatic, and the city of Cologne (and the two ships named for it that served during the First World War) remained 'Cöln' until 1919, when it was formally changed to 'Köln', the spelling used for the 1928 cruiser and two later German frigates. Also on the matter of orthography, there is a lack of consistency, even in official sources, over the use of 'ß' versus 'ss' in ships' names – e.g. '*Straßburg*' against '*Strassburg*'. In these situations we have attempted to use the most usual – in the example given, we have used '*Strassburg*' on the basis that it was the spelling used on the ship's own name-board.

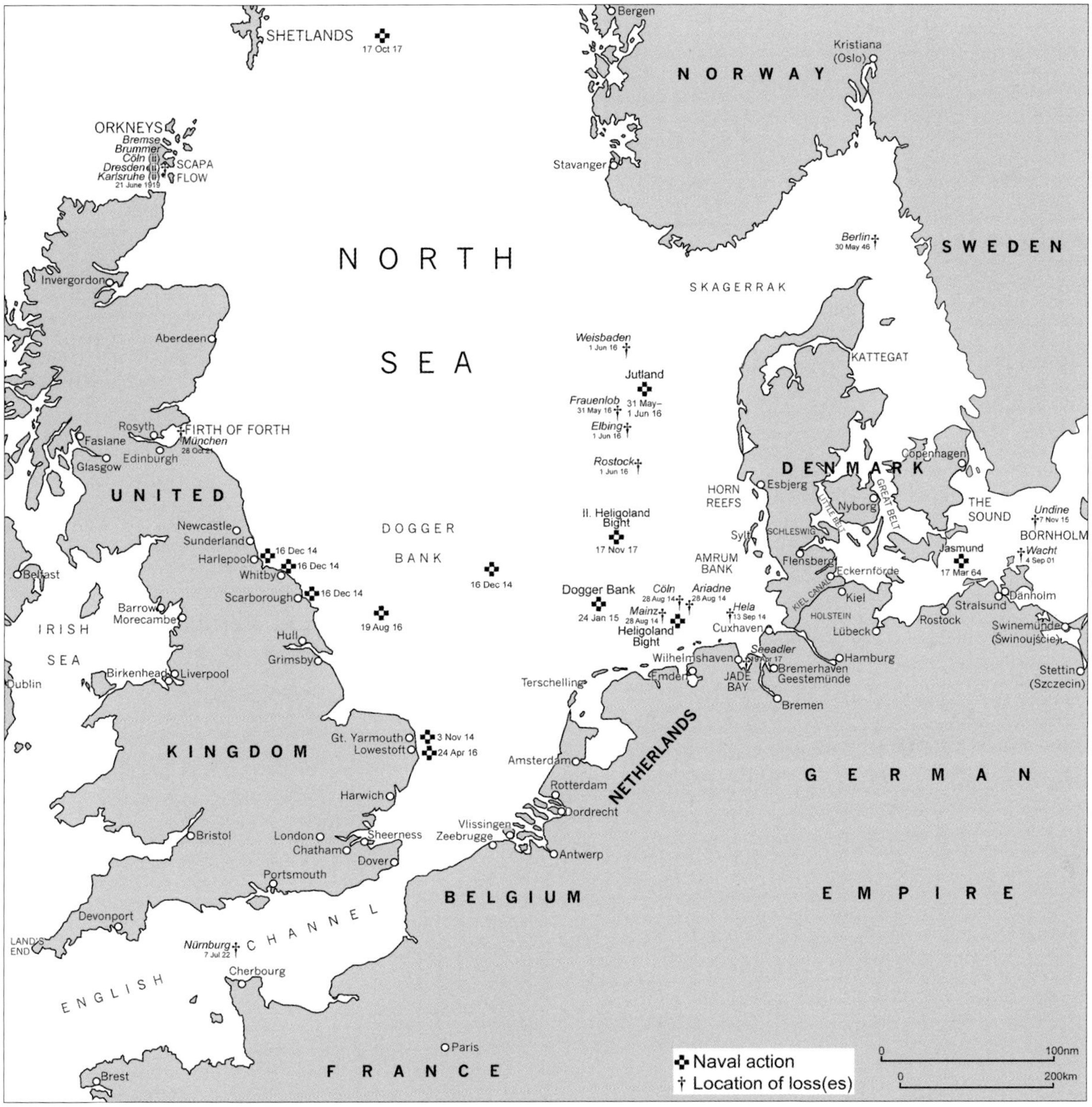

North Sea, showing the locations of the principal locations of actions involving small cruisers and places of loss of vessels covered in this book. *(AD)*

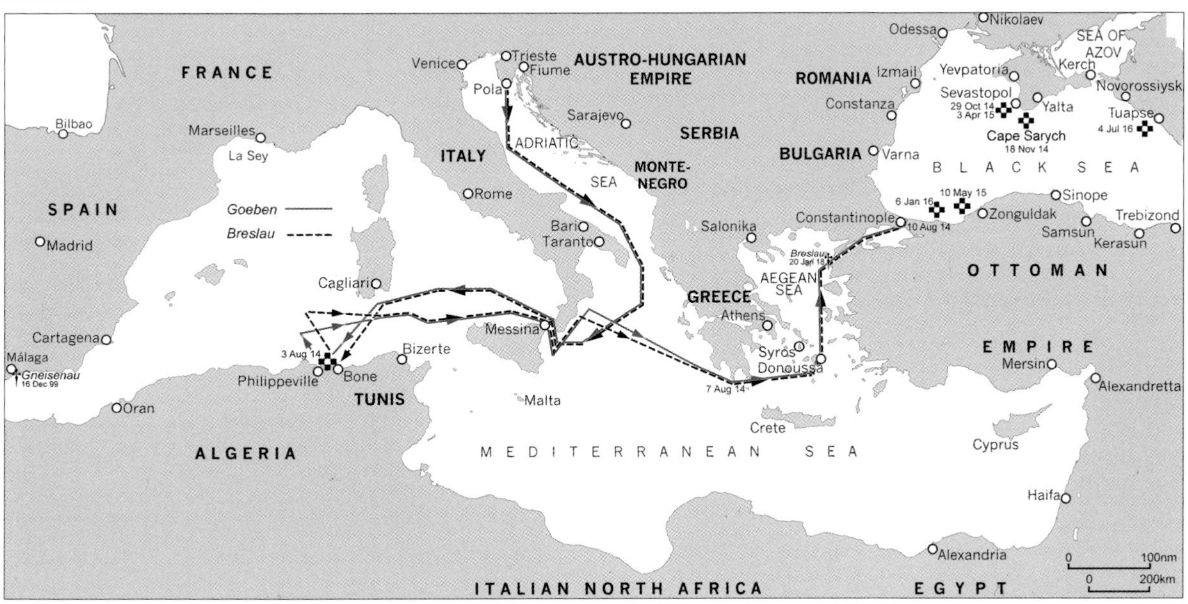

The Mediterranean and Black Sea, showing the tracks of *Goeben* and *Breslau*, and the principal actions involving the latter. *(AD)*

The world showing the German colonies and the navy's overseas naval stations as in 1914. *(AD)*

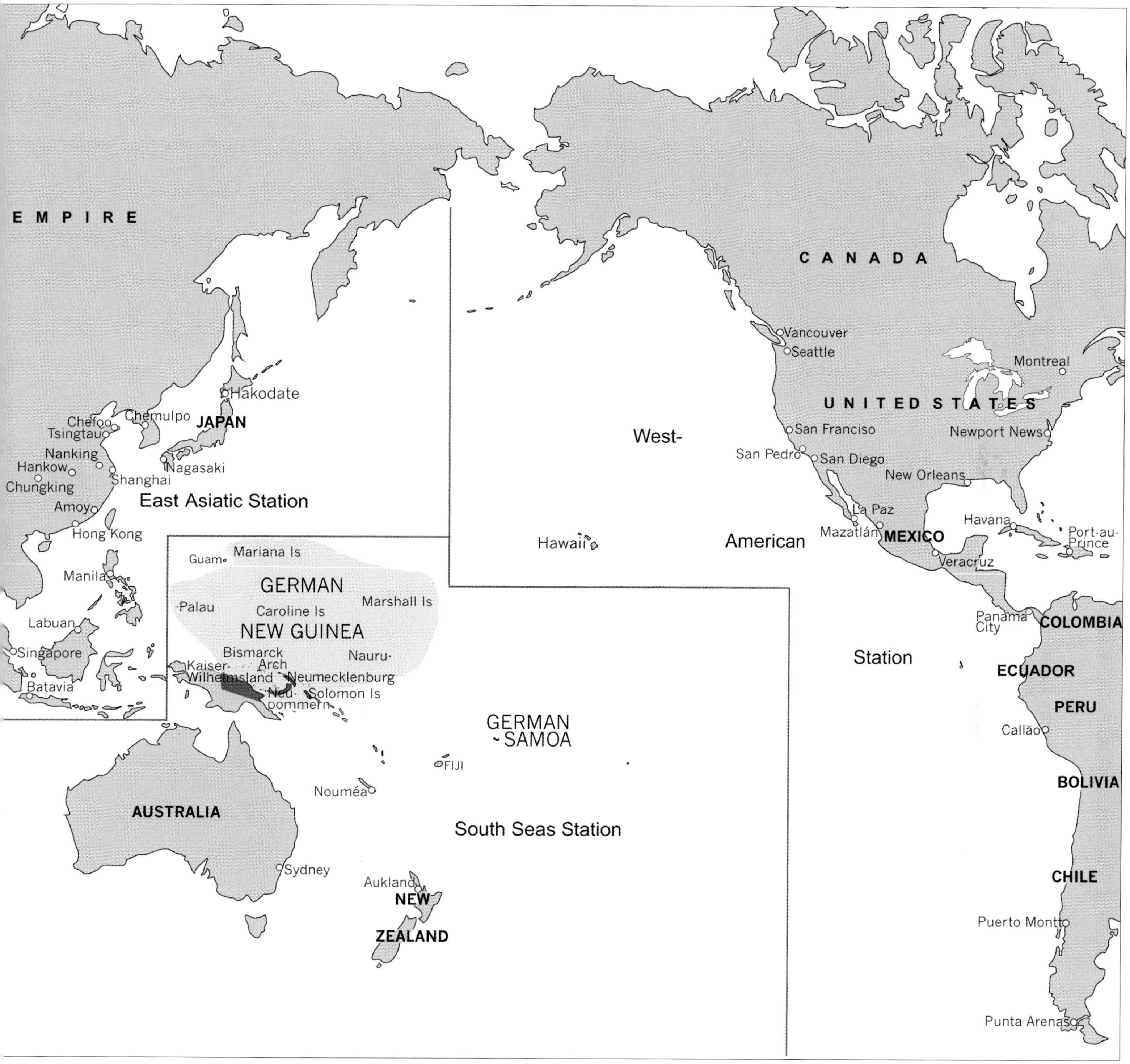
EMPIRE
CANADA
UNITED STATES
Vancouver
Seattle
Montreal
San Francisco
Newport News
San Pedro
San Diego
New Orleans
La Paz
Mazatlán
MEXICO
Havana
Port-au-Prince
Veracruz
Panama City
COLOMBIA
ECUADOR
PERU
Callão
BOLIVIA
CHILE
Puerto Montt
Punta Arenas
West-
American
Station
Hawaii
Hakodate
JAPAN
Chefoo
Chemulpo
Tsingtau
Nanking
Hankow
Nagasaki
Chungking
Shanghai
Amoy
East Asiatic Station
Hong Kong
Manila
Labuan
Singapore
Batavia
Guam
Mariana Is
GERMAN
Palau
Caroline Is
Marshall Is
NEW GUINEA
Bismarck
Arch
Nauru
Kaiser-Wilhelmsland
Neumecklenburg
Neu-pommern
Solomon Is
GERMAN SAMOA
FIJI
Nouméa
AUSTRALIA
South Seas Station
Sydney
Aukland
NEW ZEALAND

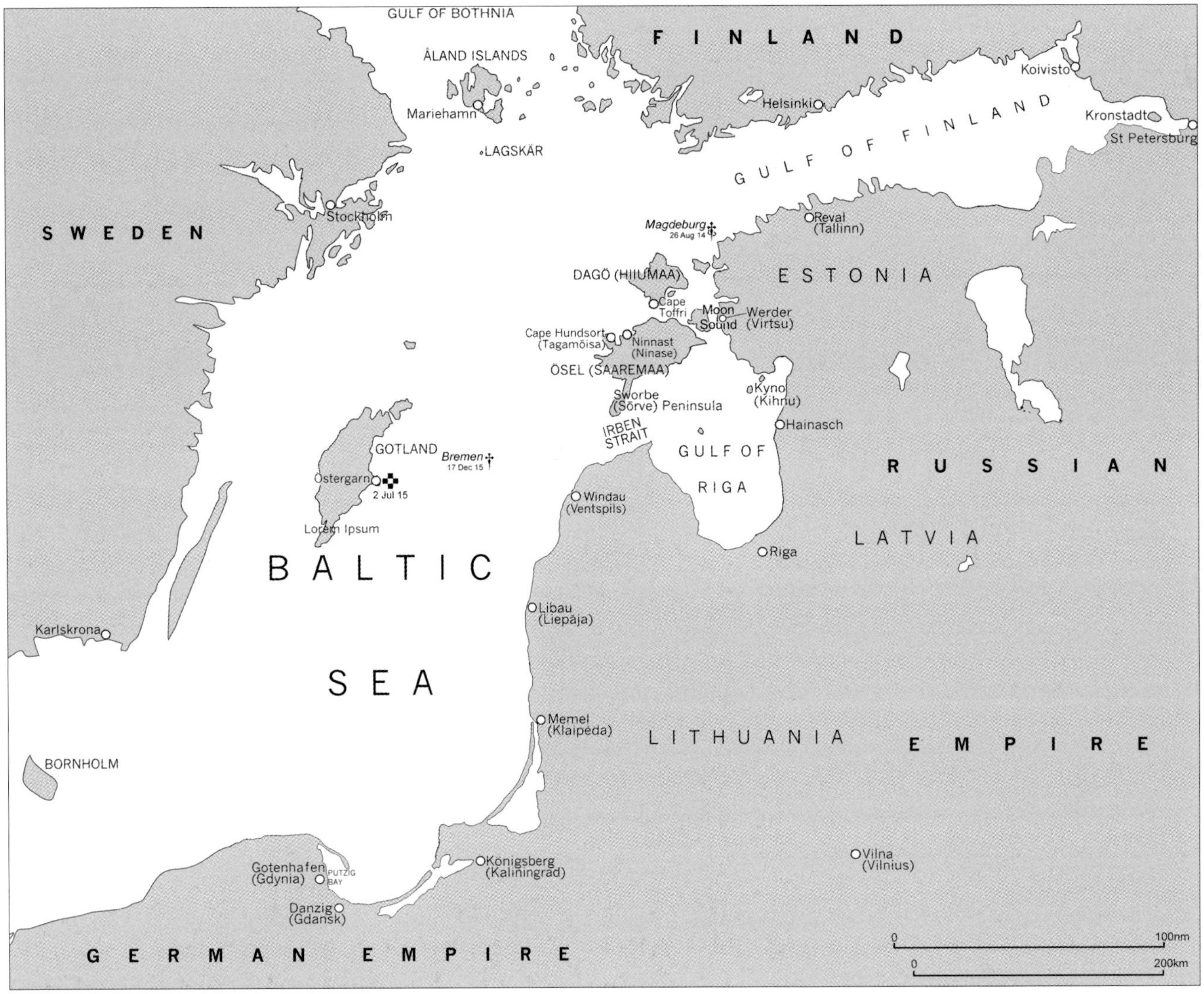

The Baltic. *(AD)*

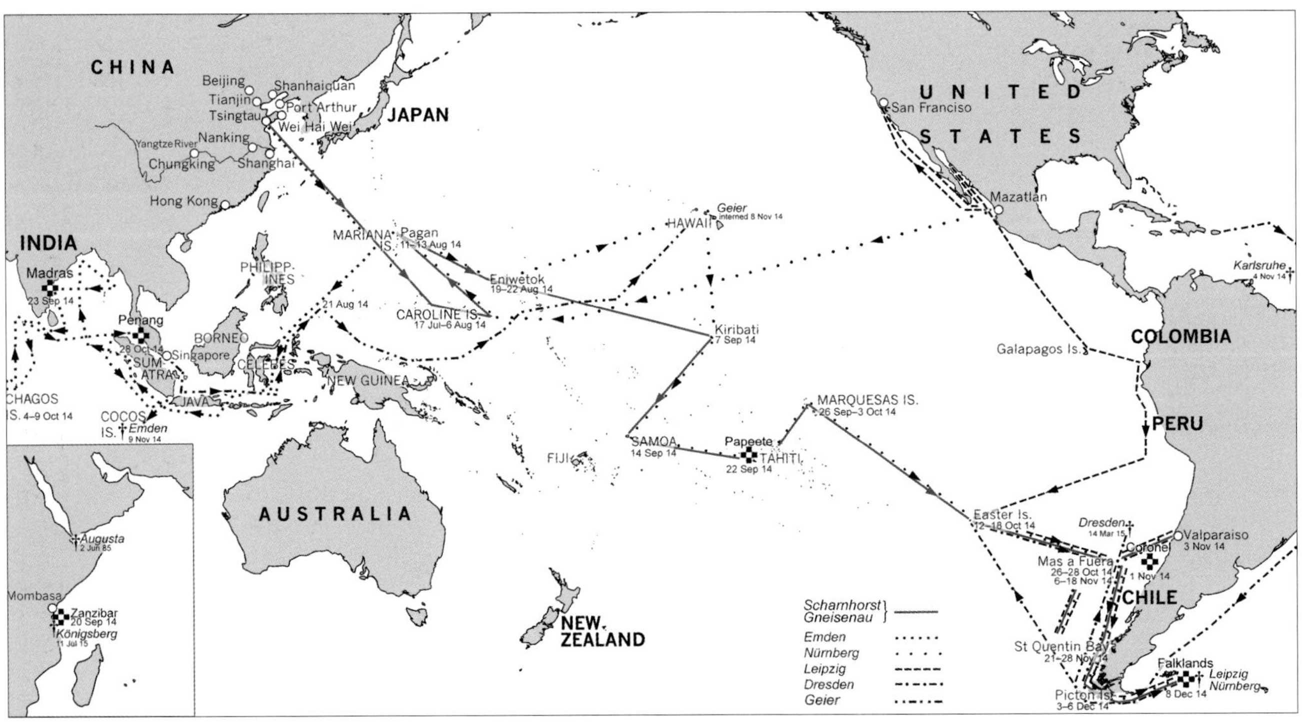

The Pacific, showing the tracks of the ships of the East Asiatic Squadron and *Geier*. *(AD)*

1 BEFORE THE KAISERREICH

UNTIL THE NINETEENTH CENTURY, 'Germany' was simply a large number of separate political entities, whose status and combinations changed over time, and ranged from city-states through to a number of fully fledged kingdoms. Until 1805, most had belonged to the increasingly nominal Holy Roman Empire, which had been replaced during the 1815 Congress of Vienna by a loose German Confederation (Deutscher Bund) of thirty-nine states, to which six more were subsequently added. A progressive customs union (Zollverein) in 1834 gradually brought the states closer together, and the short-lived Frankfurt National Assembly that had been established in May 1848 in the wake of that year's revolutions attempted to transform this into a formal Reich. The failure of this latter initiative, and that of the ephemeral Erfurt Union of 1850, which foundered through Austrian opposition, led the Confederation to continue to exist until 1866.

It is generally agreed that the foundations for the creation of a German fleet were laid in May 1848 by Prince Adalbert of Prussia (1811–73), cousin to King Friedrich Wilhelm IV. In January, the Danish king Frederik VII had proclaimed the union of the duchy of Schleswig with the Danish crown – hitherto it had been, along with the duchy of Holstein, only in personal union, with the king as duke of each of the territories. The German population of Schleswig and Holstein resisted this move and war (the First Schleswig-Holstein War) broke out, the Schleswig-Holstein forces being supported by Prussian and other German troops.

The Danes blockaded the German coasts and estuaries, the consequences for trade being severe, and soon it was realised that there were no means available to even fight the blockaders, let alone to raise the blockade imposed by a comparatively small country. In view of this situation, Friedrich Wilhelm IV established a committee presided over by Prince Adalbert to investigate the options for defending the Prussian coasts and its trade. The commission's initial report would evolve in May 1848 into a 'Memorandum regarding the foundation of German naval forces'. In this important paper Prince Adalbert put forward the idea of a three-stage development for a future unified German fleet that would continue to form the backbone of naval planning until the Tirpitz era.

The proposed first stage consisted of immediate defensive measures to overcome the very recent Danish threat by the construction of up to 120 oared gunboats. Forty of them, of a larger sea-going type inspired by Dutch designs, would be requested for the North Sea, while the remainder – constructed after Scandinavian models – would be employed in the Baltic. The remaining two other possible adversaries in the Baltic – Russia and Sweden – likewise possessed large fleets of this type, so their acquisition seemed well justified. As a novelty, several smaller steam vessels were requested at the same time – not for fighting in line with the gunboats, but rather enhancing their mobility by towing the boats into action before either retreating in the face of a superior force or joining the fight.

The envisaged second stage would employ vessels for an 'offensive defence and the most basic protection of trade'. For the first task, essentially combatting hostile blockading vessels, the prince concluded that the most suitable units would be fast, heavily armed, steamships, which could concentrate in groups should it be necessary to take on more heavily armed adversaries. Being designed for speed, they would be, at the same time, useful as avisos for scouting duties. In these few words, the memorandum anticipates the dualism of tasks for future small cruisers, some fifty years before the latter type formally came into existence under the Tirpitz reforms of the end of the century (see pp 89-102). For trade protection, as well as attacking enemy trade on the high seas, Adalbert recommended the acquisition of several 60-gun sailing frigates, which could be credibly deployed against any second-class navy, provided that crews were well trained and the materiel well maintained.

In conclusion, nevertheless, he stressed that a navy built to the requirements of the first two stages would never be able to act on its own, only in concert with an allied naval power. We find this idea, that the German navy should be of such quality as to be a desirable ally, invoked in Tirpitz's later naval planning as well. It was only when the proposed third stage had been implemented, with the deployment of a significant number of ships of the line, that the navy would be able to act as an independent sea power in European waters, especially as a counter to the Russian navy. The role of the cruising vessels would be altered in this context of this 'ultimate' navy.

Not long after the submission of this memorandum, an act of the Frankfurt Assembly created a short-lived national German

The main units of the 'Bundesflotte' exercising on the River Weser. From left to right these are: *Barbarossa*; *Erzherzog Johann*; *Der Königliche Ernst-August*; *Frankfurt*; *Großherzog von Oldenburg*; *Hansa*; *Bremen*; *Lübeck*; *Hamburg*; *Eckernförde*; *Deutschland*. *(Painting by Lüder Arenhold)*

navy, the Bundesflotte. By August 1849 this included nine paddle steamers: three came from a flotilla that had been acquired previously in 1848 by the Free City of Hamburg on its own initiative, but the rest had been directly purchased abroad. They included the former transatlantic liners *Hansa* (ex-*United States*, 1847), *Barbarossa* (ex-*Britannia*, 1840) and *Erzherzog Johann* (ex-*Acadia*, 1840), now classified as steam frigates.[1] Prince Adalbert was made CinC of this fleet, with active command of the fleet exercised by Kpt (later KAdm) Karl Rudolph Brommy (1804–60). Adalbert's memorandum now became applicable to the potential development of the Bundesflotte – as, indeed, it would be to all later German naval developments until overtaken by the 'Tirpitz-plan' of the 1890s.

In the meantime, the Danish war had been suspended by the Armistice of Malmö in August 1848, but resumed with its expiry in March 1849. Soon afterwards, on 5 April, a Danish force, comprising the sail frigate *Gefion* (launched at Copenhagen Dockyard in 1843), the 84-gun ship of the line *Christian VIII* (1840), the small paddle steamers *Geiser* and *Hekla*, and three yachts, attempted to land 250 troops at Eckernförde in Schleswig. They were opposed by two improvised earthen shore batteries mounting ten guns.[2] At first the Danish ships anchored out of range, but their subsequent attempts to reach the open sea under sail were frustrated by a strong easterly wind, which pushed them towards the lee shore. This allowed the batteries to engage both *Christian VIII* and *Gefion*. Attempts by *Geiser* and *Hekla* to tow the ships back out of range failed, and at 18.00 *Gefion* was forced to surrender; *Christian VIII*, now aground, surrendered some thirty minutes later. The latter subsequently blew up while the ships' crews were coming ashore, but *Gefion* was immediately brought into the inner port of Eckernförde to be taken into service under the German federal flag, renamed *Eckernförde*. On 12 September 1850 she was grounded to frustrate an anticipated attempt by the Danes to retake the ship, and likewise escaped an attempt at burning.

Gefion's acquisition coincided with the demise of the Frankfurt Parliament, and the whole federal experiment, leaving the federal navy in limbo at Bremerhaven. The war was ended in July 1850 by the Treaty of Berlin, under which the port

1. For a solid over-arching history of the navies of Germany down to 1898 in English language, see L Sondhaus, *Preparing for Weltpolitik: German sea power before the Tirpitz era* (Annapolis: Naval Institute Press, 1997); on naval policy and strategy, see I N Lambi, *The Navy and German Power Politics, 1862–1914* (Boston: Allen & Unwin, 1984).

2. North Battery: two 24pdr, two 18pdr, two 84pdr-shell howitzers; South Battery: four 18pdr.

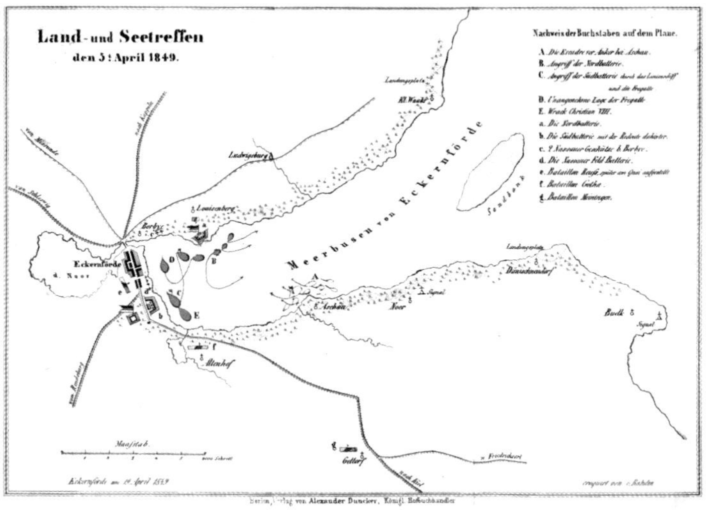

The Danish attack on Eckernförde on 5 April 1849, which resulted in the destruction of the ship of the line *Christian VIII*, and the German capture of the frigate *Gefion*, with a contemporary map. The key translates as: A – The squadron at anchor at Aschau; B – Attack on the northern battery; C – Attack on the southern battery by the ship-of-the-line and the frigate; D – Precarious situation of the frigate; E – Wreck of *Christian VIII*; a – g: information regarding batteries and troops involved, not translated here. *(Vilhelm Pedersen [1820–1859], Nationalhistoriske Museum, Frederiksborg/DN collection)*

Gefion (i) moored in the port of Kiel, sometimes between 1867 and 1869. *(DN collection)*

A model of *Danzig*, formerly in the collection of the Museum für Meereskunde in Berlin, which was destroyed by bombing in 1944. *(DN collection)*

of Eckernförde was to be evacuated by German forces. The frigate was thus sailed with a 'German' crew but under the Prussian flag – the German federal flag was not generally recognised by the major powers – to join the Bremerhaven fleet in November, pending a decision on the fate of the whole assemblage. This finally came in the spring of 1852, when *Eckernförde* and *Barbarossa* were handed over to Prussia as compensation for her contributions to the federal cause; the rest of the fleet was, however, sold to mercantile owners during the winter of 1852–53.

THE PRUSSIAN NAVY

Eckernförde reverted to her original name of *Gefion* under the Prussian flag, and after refit began what would be a series of overseas training voyages. The first was in 1852–53 in conjunction with the corvette *Amazone* – launched in 1843, and Prussia's first significantly sized warship – and the ex-East Indiaman *Mercur* (1847, bought 1850), employed as a transport. However, *Barbarossa* was found to be in poor condition, and served only as a stationary guardship at Danzig until reduced to an accommodation hulk in 1865 at Kiel.

A new paddle-corvette, *Danzig* (1851), was also of limited effectiveness, having rapidly succumbed to dry rot. Nevertheless, she had become famous in August 1856 for her part in the Battle of Tres Forcas, an unsuccessful punitive expedition under the command of Prince Adalbert himself against Moroccan pirates of the Rif tribe. The first Prussian overseas action for a century and a half, this fiasco was much to the disadvantage of the prince's later career.

To supplement the vessels available for training, the British fifth-rate sailing frigate *Thetis* was acquired in 1855, in exchange for two little-used paddle avisos, *Salamander* and *Nix* (both 1850); these served as the British *Recruit* and *Weser* until the late 1860s. Attempts to purchase a further frigate from

Thetis (i) as guardship, moored at Kiel at the end of the 1860s. Astern of her lies a decommissioned *Arcona*-class decked-corvette – either *Hertha* or *Vineta* – while outboard is the armoured frigate *Kronprinz*, housed-over for preservation while in reserve. *(DN collection)*

Sweden were unsuccessful. *Thetis* had been the only ship of her class, and had been laid down at Devonport Dockyard in December 1844, launched in August 1846 and commissioned at the end of 1846, at a cost of £51,926. She was the last vessel of her rate to complete as a sailing ship. Initially used by the British as a training ship, she had served in the Pacific from 1850 to 1854. *Thetis* arrived without her original armament of thirty-two 32pdrs and four 68pdrs, receiving thirty-eight 68pdrs in Prussian service.

The following year, *Thetis*, along with *Amazone*, *Mercur*, a patched up *Danzig*, and the schooner *Frauenlob* (i, 1855) deployed together, before separating on separate missions. A further addition to the fleet, in 1858, was *Grille*, built by Normand in France, classified as an aviso, but with a secondary role as a royal yacht. In her primary role – that of a ship operating in direct support of the fleet – she would be the prototype

One of the earliest images of *Grille*, moored in the Flensburg bight in 1864. Just visible in front of the mizzen mast is the deckhouse for VIPs. *(DN collection)*

of one of the two strands of cruiser development that would run in the German navy through to the end of the century.

Grille was the first screw-powered ship in the Prussian navy, powered by a 2-cylinder horizontal engine, supplied with steam by a pair of boilers, all manufactured by Penn in London, giving a speed of 13 knots. Laid down in 1856, she was launched in the presence of the French Prince Jérôme Bonaparte in September 1857 and commissioned in June 1858. She then proceeded to Dänholm in the Baltic for trials, decommissioning when they were completed on 22 October.

She was briefly recommissioned in early May 1859, as a consequence of tensions between Denmark and Prussia, and then again from August to October. Recommissioned in June 1860 for a prospective Mediterranean cruise that did not take place, she paid off once more in October. Designated a royal yacht on 16 January 1862, she returned to service in July 1863 for the use of Crown Prince Friedrich and his family.

A very early image of the decked-corvette *Arcona* (i) drying her sails, probably taken at Swinemünde. Her hull has yet to be painted with the 'chequerboard' white band typical of warships of the sailing era. *(DN collection)*

The sailing vessels were primarily employed in training cadets and boy-seamen, while also 'showing the flag', with different ships activated each year. In accordance with a proposed 'second step' in Prince Adalbert's 1848 memorandum, the cruising fleet was expanded by the commissioning, in 1859, of the name-ship of the new *Arcona* class screw decked-corvettes, together with the paddle-aviso *Loreley*. On the other hand, *Danzig* was now beyond economic repair and was stricken in 1862. She was sold to British interests and left Danzig in 1864, to be resold a few months later to the navy of the Shogun, one party to the impending Japanese civil war. *Danzig* ended her days by being burned by her own crew during one of the battles off Hakodate in 1869. She was replaced by the former post-steamer *Preußischer Adler*, which, having being requisitioned by the navy twice since 1849 – and having fought in the first ever engagement of the Prussian navy in that year – was now permanently included in the ranks of the fleet.

Amazone had foundered in a storm off the Dutch coast in November 1861, and the year before that had also seen the loss of *Frauenlob*, in a typhoon off Japan. Thus, with *Gefion* and *Thetis* due to become gunnery training ships, another sailing frigate, *Niobe*, together with the brigs *Rover* (1853) and *Musquito* (1851), were purchased from the UK on 9 July 1862 (*Niobe* for £15,892 [£2 million at 2020 prices]) to restore the cadet/boys training fleet. *Niobe*, a member of the three-ship, sixth-rate *Diamond* class,[3] had been laid down at Devonport in May 1847 and launched in September 1849, but never commissioned into the Royal Navy. Designed for twenty-six 32pdr and two 68pdr guns and costing £22,224 to build, in Prussian service she was first armed with sixteen 68pdrs, four 30pdrs, and six 15cm/22 weapons.

During 1862/63, the fleet was further bolstered by the commissioning of the decked-corvette *Gazelle* and the flushdecked-corvette[4] *Nymphe*, although *Gazelle* would suffer significant machinery problems owing to the inexperience of the manufacturer of her engines, AG Vulcan at Stettin. Her sister, *Arcona*, had, however, been engined by a Belgian firm, and seems to have been largely satisfactory mechanically.

Gazelle and *Arcona* each displaced around 2,000 tonnes, and were rated as excellent sea boats. The former carried six 68pdrs and twenty 36pdrs, the latter a uniform battery of twenty-eight 68pdrs; both had them replaced by seventeen 15cm/22 hooped weapons around 1870. *Nymphe*, and her sister *Medusa*, were 1,000-tonne ship-rigged vessels, armed with ten 36pdrs and six 12pdrs. These were replaced around 1870 by seventeen

3. *Diamond* herself became a civilian training ship in 1866 and was broken up in 1885; the third ship of the class, *Tribune*, was reordered as a screw corvette in 1850, launched in 1853 and scrapped in 1866.

4. 'Decked-corvettes' had a closed gundeck; 'flushdecked-corvettes' carried their guns on the open upper deck. The two types would be later reclassified as 'cruiser-frigates' and 'cruiser-corvettes', respectively (see pp 42, 90).

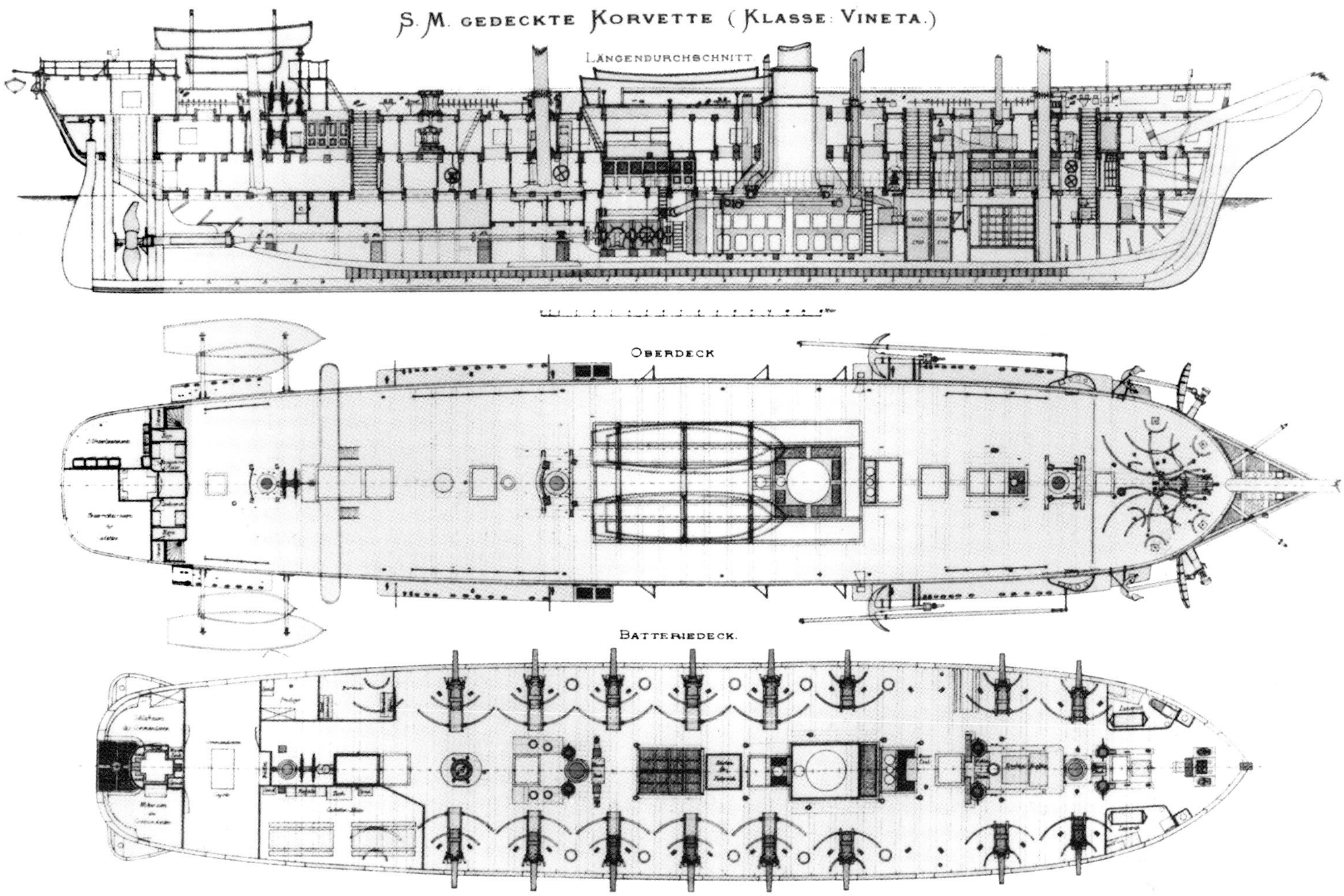

Longitudinal section and deck plans of the decked-corvette *Vineta* (i), taken from a set of similar drawings issued by the Imperial Admiralty at the end of the 1870s. Compared with her initial profile, the addition of a raised poop deck is clear. *(DN collection)*

12cm/23 weapons, two more being added later; their engines came from the UK.

In the meantime, a new Schleswig-Holstein crisis had blown up, with German forces occupying Kiel in late 1863 and a Prusso-Austrian ultimatum issued to Denmark in January 1864. Of the cruising vessels under construction, only the *Arcona*-class *Vineta* would commission in time for the war. Nevertheless, on 17 March 1864, *Arcona* (flag), *Nymphe*, *Loreley* and six gunboats challenged the Danish blockade off the Oder, exchanging fire with the Danish ship of the line *Skjold*, the frigates *Sjælland* and *Tordenskjold* and the corvettes *Hejmdal* and *Thor* off Jasmund, with damage suffered by *Nymphe* and *Sjælland*. On 24 April, *Grille*, previously unarmed, but now carrying two 12pdrs, was leading the Reserve Division of gunboats when they encountered *Tordenskjold* off Hiddensee, and again two days later when they ran into the full Danish squadron. On 6 May, *Grille* and *Nymphe*, the I. Flotilla and the Reserve Division sortied but the arrival of *Sjælland* and

Niobe (i) in 1883, moored off Mount Batten, while visiting Devonport during one of her training cruises. *(DN collection)*

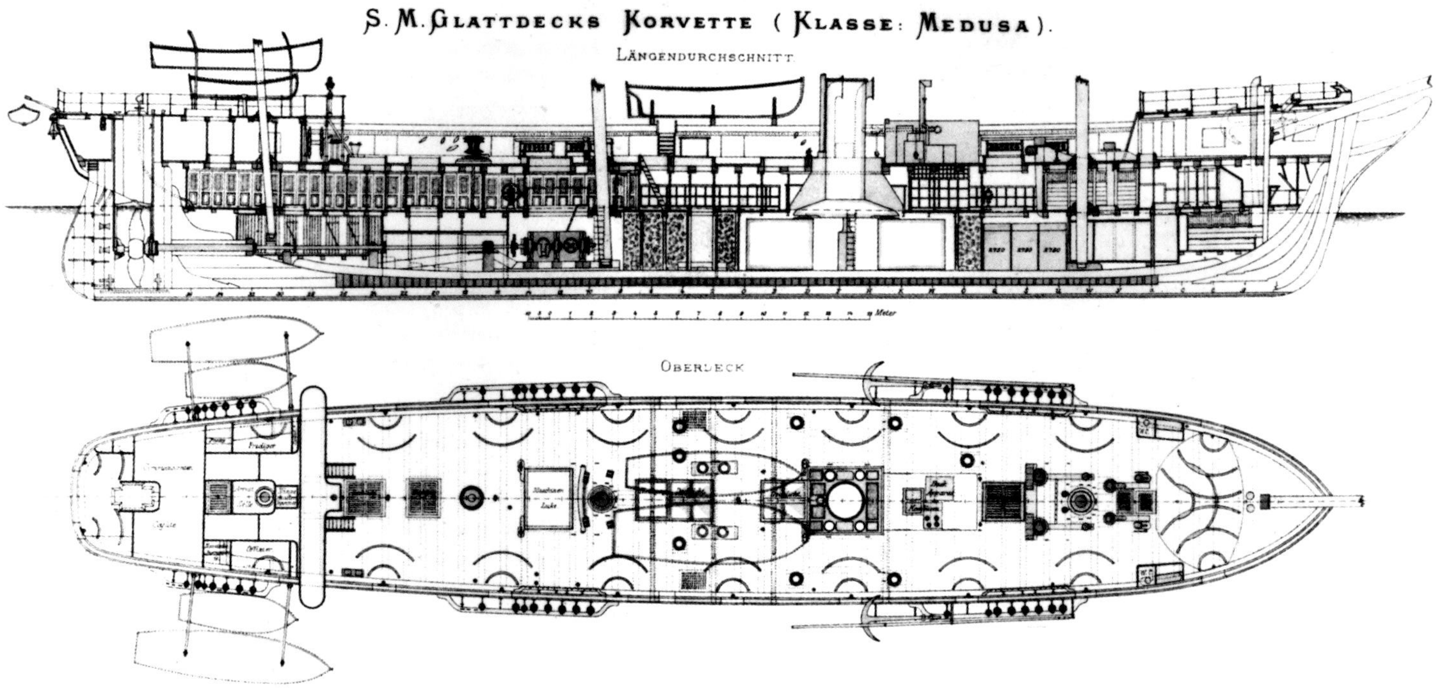

Another of the detailed Admiralty drawings – this time for the flush-deck corvette *Medusa*. *(DN collection)*

the Danish ironclad *Dannebrog* caused the operation to be aborted.

In the North Sea, the Austrian frigates *Schwarzenberg* and *Radetzky*, reinforced by *Preußischer Adler* and the Prussian gunboats *Blitz* and *Basilisk*, engaged the Danish frigates *Niels Juel* and *Jylland*, together with the corvette *Hejmdal*, off Heligoland on 9 May 1864, with both sides suffering damage. In October, Denmark sued for peace, the Treaty of Vienna (30 October 1864) ceding the Duchies of Schleswig, Holstein and Lauenburg to Prussia and Austria.

Prior to the end of the Danish war, Prussia had attempted to reinforce its navy by buying three ships laid down in France for the Confederate navy during the American Civil War.[5] Two were corvettes, which became *Augusta* and *Victoria* in the summer of 1864; the third ship, an ironclad, became *Prinz Adalbert* (i).[6] *Augusta* and *Victoria* had been ordered from the Arman yard at Bordeaux on 15 April 1863 as two of a class of four 2,000-ton vessels. *Mississippi* (later *Victoria*) and *Louisiana* (*Augusta*) were to be built at the Arman yard itself, while *Texas* and *Georgia* were subcontracted to J Voriz of Nantes, but were actually built by the local yards of Jollet & Babin and Dubigeon, respectively.

As with ships ordered in the UK for the Confederacy, there was government concern over breaking neutrality laws, and in October 1863 the French Minister of Marine instructed that the ships could not be delivered armed. Indeed, construction was suspended briefly in November, but then continued and the ships all launched during the first part of 1864, Arman attempting in March to fabricate fictitious sales of *Mississippi* and *Louisiana* to Japan (under the names *Osakka* and *Yeddo*) as a means of delivering the ships to the Confederates. By then, however, the French authorities had decided that none of the ships being built under the Arman contract for the Confederates should be delivered at all. Lucien Arman was thus ordered by Napoleon III to put all the Confederate ships, which also included the ironclads *Cheops* and *Sphinx*, up for sale in May.

Thus, *Mississippi* and *Louisiana* were, together with the ironclad *Cheops*, sold to Prussia on 25 May 1864, the corvettes commissioning in September and July, respectively, and the ironclad in October. Of the remaining ships, *Texas* and *Georgia* were both sold to Peru, as *America* and *Unión*, while *Sphinx* was purchased by Denmark as *Stærkodder*. Her contract of sale was, however, voided in December 1864, and the ship (still in Danish waters) was resold by Arman to the Confederates in January 1865. She served under the Confederate flag as *Stonewall* until surrendered at the end of the Civil War, and was sold by the USA to Japan in 1867; she became *Kōtetsu* and later *Azuma*.

Augusta and *Victoria* entered Prussian service mounting eight 24pdr and six 12pdr guns. In 1872 they were rearmed with four 15cm/22, six 12cm/23 and one 8cm/23 weapons.

In the aftermath of the Second Schleswig War, the August

5. For the Confederate overseas building programme, see D M Sullivan, 'Phantom Fleet: The Confederacy's Unclaimed European-Built Warships', *Warship International* xxiv/1 (1987), pp 12–32.

6. See A Dodson, *The Kaiser's Battlefleet: German capital ships 1871–1918* (Barnsley: Seaforth, 2016), pp 15–17, 178–79.

An early, although undated, image of *Augusta* drying her sails. *(DN collection)*

1865 Gastein Convention between Prussia and Austria gave Schleswig to the former and Holstein to the latter. However, Prussia was granted free passage across Holstein and, crucially, the right to build a naval base at Kiel, and construct a canal to link the Baltic and North Seas. Kiel almost immediately replaced Danzig as the main fleet anchorage, with work on its facilities soon under way, with a shipyard to follow. A North Sea counterpart, Wilhelmshaven, would come into operation in 1869, as a Prussian enclave within the Grand Duchy of Oldenburg, after nearly thirteen years under construction.

A further *Arcona*-class frigate, *Hertha*, joined the fleet in September 1865, a few months before further hostilities broke out, this time between the former allies Prussia and Austria. In April 1866, Prussia agreed an alliance with Italy against Austria, and in June Prussia occupied Holstein. A few days later, she seceded from the Confederation to establish a new North German Confederation, which explicitly excluded Austria. War followed between Austria on one side, and Prussia and Italy on the other, with the smaller German states' loyalties split between the two principal antagonists.

The main naval arena for the war was between Austria and Italy, where the latter's fleet was defeated at the Battle of Lissa. *Arcona*, *Gazelle*, *Hertha*, *Augusta* and *Victoria* were activated alongside the ironclads *Arminius* and *Prinz Adalbert* and some gunboats but, save for *Arminius* and a few of the latter, all remained in the Baltic and saw no action.

A number of Prussian warships were abroad, in particular *Niobe*, returning from a transatlantic training cruise, *Nymphe* in the Mediterranean and *Vineta* in the Far East, but they played no role in the war – although *Niobe* narrowly missed encountering the Austrian corvette *Erzherzog Friedrich* in the English Channel.

The Peace of Prague of August 1866 ended the war between Prussia and Austria and her allies, as a result of which most of the latter (in particular Hanover) were annexed to Prussia, or joined the new North German Confederation, under the presidency of the Prussian king. Only Baden, Hesse-Darmstadt, Württemberg and Bavaria of non-Austrian Germany remained outside. Austria itself would become part of the dual monarchy of Austria-Hungary the following year, and henceforth be excluded from German affairs. As of 1 October 1867, what was now the North German navy adopted the black-white-red ensign in place of the previous Prussian eagle on a white ground.

The 'new' fleet was accompanied by a Fleet Plan, another modification of plans put forward by the Prussian navy since 1855, and ultimately based on Prince Adalbert's 1848 Memorandum – and rejected several times by the Prussian Landtag (State Parliament).[7] The 1867 Plan, however, was approved by the new Reichstag (Reich Parliament), and envisaged by 1877 a fleet of sixteen armoured ships, twenty unarmoured corvettes and eight avisos, plus twenty-six gunboats and auxiliaries, for both home and overseas service. As compared with the 1865 iteration of the Plan, there were four fewer armoured ships and six more corvettes, reflecting what would be an ongoing debate regarding the balance to be struck between building and maintaining a home battlefleet and doing

7. Interestingly enough there was never a true 'Plan' for the development of the fleet; rather, it was a list of the numbers of various types of vessels deemed necessary for the development of the navy. These numbers formed the basis requests to Parliament for the passage of a 'Law for granting a loan for the purposes of developing the navy'.

Elisabeth under full sail (including lee-sails), and funnel down, during 1882. The five decked-corvettes of the *Arcona* class did much to establish the German navy's name worldwide. *(DN collection)*

Ariadne moored to a buoy in an unknown port. Her rather odd 'ram bow' shows very clearly. *(DN collection)*

Pommerania moored off the waterfront of Imperial Dockyard Kiel. Nearly her whole quarterdeck is occupied by the deckhouse for VIPs. *(DN collection)*

the same for a cruising force capable of worldwide deployment. The latter element was influenced by an increasing popularity of the idea of acquiring colonies, and the resulting requirement for more ships to protect them (cf p 64, below).

An early key area of German commercial interests was in the South Pacific, although this was not at first reflected by naval visits. *Arcona* and *Thetis*, together with *Frauenlob* and the clipper *Elbe* (ex-*Columba*, 1857), had undertaken a commercial mission to the Far East during 1859–62, but this went no further than Japan, where a trade treaty was negotiated. The mission also produced a trade agreement with China, as well as undertaking scientific investigations. Likewise, a 1862–64 deployment of *Gazelle* to the Far East concentrated in the same region, as did that of her relief, *Vineta*, during 1865–68, although the latter returned to Germany via the Pacific, calling at Hawaii on the way. *Medusa* arrived on station in March 1869, being joined the following spring by *Hertha*. Cruisers were also deployed to American waters, *Augusta* spending much of 1868 in the Caribbean, *Victoria* also visiting the area the following year. *Niobe* and the gunboat *Meteor* were in the West Indies in 1870, as was *Arcona*.

During the winter of 1866–67, *Gazelle* and the gunboat *Blitz* were deployed to the Mediterranean, but both suffered collisions in February 1867, *Gazelle* being sufficiently damaged to be recalled to Germany. This prevented her from joining, as had been planned, a Training and Exercise Squadron, due to spend the summer in the North and Baltic Seas. *Nymphe* was also excluded, owing to boiler defects, leaving just *Hertha* and the new *Medusa* (commissioned in April) to cruise the Baltic during July and August. They then proceeded to the Mediterranean, en route depositing crews for the new ironclads *Kronprinz* and *Friedrich Carl* (both 1867) in the UK and France, where they were completing. The two corvettes remained in the Mediterranean until they returned home in the spring of 1868.

A final *Arcona*-class frigate, *Elisabeth*, had been laid down in 1866, and would complete in 1869. She was followed on the slip at Danzig by *Ariadne*, the first of a new class of corvettes, laid down in 1868. Looking very different from the earlier ships, with a ram, rather than a knee, bow, and omitting stern

Bearing the unmistakeably shape of an intended Confederate blockade runner, *Falke* is shown now under German flag. *(DN collection)*

galleries, she also marked a technological advance in that she was powered by a compound engine (of German, rather than British, manufacture), giving a speed 2 knots higher than earlier frigates and corvettes.

In 1869, two sister vessels, inconsistently classified respectively as a gunboat (*Ersatz-Crocodil* [*Albatross*]), or aviso (*Aviso A* [*Nautilus*]), were begun. They were 713-tonne wooden-hulled ships, armed with two 15cm/22 and two 12cm/23 guns, with a design speed of 10.9 knots. Carrying a full barquentine rig, and designed specifically for overseas service, they were the first German warships so intended. Their planned role was to act against pirates in Chinese waters, being built with shallow draughts to pursue junks close inshore, although events would mean that their careers took a somewhat different turn (see p 91 and passim).

Elisabeth, *Hertha*, *Arcona* and *Grille* (carrying the Prussian Crown Prince), along with the gunboat *Delphin*, represented the North German Confederation at the opening of the Suez Canal in November 1869, *Elisabeth* then carrying the Crown Prince on to Italy and France. In July 1870, however, France declared war on Prussia, the proximate cause being the ongoing dispute over the future of the throne of Spain. The navy's ironclads were concentrated at Wilhelmshaven, while *Elisabeth* became guardship at Kiel, with *Nymphe* at Danzig, and *Vineta* at Swinemünde (Świnoujście); the latter was also the base for *Grille* and three gunboats. The outbreak of war found *Gazelle*, *Augusta* and *Victoria* under refit at Danzig, the first two returning to service in late July, although *Victoria* remained in dockyard hands until after the war was over.

Of the remaining cruising vessels, *Hertha*, *Medusa* and *Arcona* were overseas, the first two being blockaded in Yokohama by the French East Asiatic squadron, with *Arcona*, caught en route back from the Americas, blockaded in Lisbon. The fleet was reinforced by the requisition of the paddle steamers *Pommerania* and *Falke*, which were armed and commissioned as avisos, as were the hired paddle steamers *Cuxhaven* and *Helgoland*, to serve as guard vessels in the mouth of the Elbe. *Pommerania* had been laid down as a Stettin–Stockholm mail-steamer, while *Falke* had been begun as a potential American Civil War blockade runner, but completed as a passenger and cattle carrier.

The French placed armoured squadrons off the German North Sea and Baltic coasts, but were unable to impose a solid blockade, although more than 200 German merchantmen were seized by the French, all but paralysing German overseas trade. A number of attempts were made by German vessels to engage French ships, but with little success, a sortie by *Nymphe* from Danzig against the much larger armoured *Surveillante* and *Thétis* resulting in her hurried return to port. Likewise, a sortie by *Grille* and three gunboats out of Swinemünde had little effect.

In November 1870, after most of the French ships had departed from German waters, *Augusta* left Danzig and the Baltic for the French Atlantic coast. There, she captured three French ships off the Gironde, burning one and sending the other pair back to Germany as prizes, before being blockaded in Vigo by French ironclads.

The south German states (excluding Austria) had fought alongside Prussia (and the rest of the North German Confederation) from the outset, but agreed to join the Confederation following the defeats of the French armies in August and September 1870. In December, the Reichstag offered an imperial German crown to the Prussian King, Wilhelm I, at same time voting to rename the Confederation as the German Reich, which became effective on 1 January 1871, the formal proclamation being made at German-occupied Versailles in France on the 18th. The accession of the southern states, together with the cession of the formerly French provinces of Alsace and Lorraine, was formalised in the Treaty of Versailles, signed on 26 February, and ratified in the Treaty of Frankfurt of 10 May 1871.

2 THE ERA OF WILHELM I

THE NEW EMPIRE'S CONSTITUTION, promulgated in April 1871, followed that of the North German Confederation in making the navy a federal force (in contrast to the army, built up from state level). The navy's organisational structure was settled in June, to become effective on 1 January 1872. It was based around an Imperial Admiralty that would combine both organisational and operational control. As its first head, Generalmajor (later Generalleutnant) Albrecht von Stosch (1818–96) was chosen, the senior serving admiral, VAdm Eduard von Jachmann (1822–87), being sidelined. Stosch, promoted to the dual rank of General der Infanterie and Admiral in 1875, would serve until 1883; his deputy as Director of the Admiralty was KAdm Ludwig Henk (1820–94).

At the unification, the navy had nine steam corvettes and three avisos in service, with three new corvettes of the *Ariadne* class and the 'aviso' *Nautilus* (albeit identical to the 'gunboat' *Albatross*) under construction or authorised. There were also the three sailing frigates, but of these *Gefion* and *Thetis* were laid up and would never go to sea again: indeed, *Thetis* would be stricken from the navy list before the end of the year. *Gefion* remained on the list until 1880, but only as an accommodation hulk at Kiel. On the other hand, *Niobe* continued in service as a seagoing training ship for cadets and boys until as late as 1890. Accordingly, she, like all other operational vessels, soon had her old smoothbore guns replaced by modern Krupp hooped breechloaders, in her case six 15cm/22 weapons (later superseded by 12cm/23s).

Although Germany had as yet no overseas colonies – a concept opposed for the time being by now Reich Chancellor Otto von Bismarck (1815–98) – the empire's interests in distant waters began to be represented by the regular deployment of cruisers. Thus, in 1872, *Nymphe* became the first German warship to visit the South Pacific, where she called at Samoa, already an important German commercial node in the area. She would be followed in 1873 by *Arcona*, and in 1874 by *Gazelle*, *Hertha* and the new *Ariadne*. Indeed, as early as 1872 it was proposed that a permanent 'flying squadron' of cruisers be established to allow concentrated force to be deployed around the world where required by Germany's interests. However, this was rejected by Stosch and Henk as too costly, as well as likely to cause excessive wear and tear on ships assigned to the squadron.[1]

Hertha had had her machinery replaced during 1873–74, her old boilers and engine being used to replace the old machinery of the gunnery training ship (ex-British ship of the line) *Renown*. They were subsequently taken out to provide the propulsion for the latter's purpose-built replacement, *Mars*, launched in November 1879.

On her way out to the Far East in 1872, *Nymphe* had called at Rio de Janeiro to support local German residents (including the consul), while during the winter of 1871–72, *Vineta* was also in Brazilian waters and *Gazelle* and *Niobe* were in the West Indies. *Gazelle* also applied pressure in Venezuela, in support of the repayment of debts to local German citizens. The two corvettes then spent the summer in the Caribbean, including making a landing in Haiti to ensure the payment of a debt owed to a German. The pair then went back to the West Indies to join *Elisabeth*, the ironclad *Friedrich Carl* and the gunboat *Albatross*, which then undertook further debt enforcement action, this time in Colombia. Although this level of presence was not maintained, *Augusta* was in the region during 1874/75, as was *Victoria* during 1875/76.

After their Colombian visit, *Friedrich Carl* and *Elisabeth*, together with the gunboat *Delphin*, moved to Spanish waters during the summer of 1873, where they joined with British vessels, including the ironclad *Swiftsure*, in protecting national interests in the wake of the disorder that followed the abdication of King Amadeo and the foundation of the First Spanish Republic in the February. The force was commanded by the German Reinhold Werner (1825–1909), as the senior officer present, and led it in the capture of the Spanish rebel ironclad *Vitoria* and frigate *Almansa* off Cartagena at the end of July. The Spanish ships were taken to Gibraltar and handed over to the legitimate Spanish government in September. This action had been undertaken by Werner without the authorisation of the governments of the ships making up the force, resulting in the subsequent ruining of Werner's career.

During the summer of 1873, rather than the usual mixture of

1. Sondhaus, *Preparing for Weltpolitik*, p 119.

The hulk of *Gazelle* (i), moored stern to stern with the likewise hulked *Bismarck* at Wilhelmshaven at the beginning of the twentieth century. She would be broken up in 1906. *(Heidrich collection)*

ironclads and cruisers, the annual manoeuvres comprised *Hertha*, *Vineta*, *Ariadne* and *Arcona*, plus the gunboat *Nautilus*, operating primarily in the North Sea. The deployment also included representing Germany at the Norwegian coronation of King Oscar II, *Grille* carrying the German Crown Prince to Oscar's Swedish ceremony.[2] The next year, 1874, the summer squadron was made up of the ironclads *Friedrich Carl* and *Kronprinz*, supported by *Ariadne* and the gunboat *Albatross*, escorting a visit by the Crown Prince to the UK, and then carrying out exercises in the Atlantic.

The older cruisers continued to play a role through the 1870s, the Russo-Turkish War of 1877–78 bringing a German Mediterranean Squadron, led by *Gazelle* and *Hertha*, to the region. A further example of 'diplomacy with menaces' took place in 1878, following a German demand for reparations following the alleged maltreatment of the consul in Nicaragua. This was supported by the blockade of the latter's Atlantic coast by *Medusa* and her Pacific coast by *Elisabeth*, *Ariadne* and the new *Leipzig*. The ships involved had all been diverted from other deployments: *Leipzig* had been in Japan, as part of a westward circumnavigation, and had to retrace her steps back eastward, *Elisabeth* had been in East Asian waters, on an eastbound route, and *Ariadne* off the Americas while heading west.

However, as new ships commissioned, the 'pre-Empire' vessels were increasingly used as training vessels, in particular supplementing *Niobe* in the instruction of cadets through long overseas voyages. Thus, *Arcona* had become a cadet training ship in 1871, before being reduced to a stoker and engineer training ship at Kiel in 1876. *Gazelle*'s career followed a similar trajectory, both sisters being stricken in 1884, as were their half-sisters *Vineta* and *Hertha*, again after finishing their careers in training roles.

Medusa had been stricken in 1881, directly following the end of a final training voyage to North American ports, but *Nymphe* and *Elisabeth* lasted on the navy list until 1887. *Nymphe* decommissioned for the last time in October 1885 after a long deployment to the West Indies and Central America, while *Elisabeth* had returned from a final two-year cruise in March 1886. She then spent a last winter as a torpedo training ship before being stricken. Although *Arcona* and *Medusa* were broken up soon after being stricken, the other old cruisers were generally reduced to hulks, some surviving into the twentieth century.

THE *ARIADNE* CLASS

As noted above (p 24), the first of a new generation of corvettes had been laid down in 1869. Although built of wood, they were

2. From 1814 to 1905 Sweden and Norway shared a king in personal union.

of a much more modern appearance than their predecessors, had better machinery and would be the first German cruising vessels to carry breech-loading rifled guns from the outset.

Ariadne

Ariadne herself had been launched on 21 July 1871. She commissioned on 23 November 1872, thus becoming the first cruising vessel to actually begin her service in the new Imperial navy. Her first deployment was as part of a training squadron, reviewed by a commission of the Reichstag on 23 May 1873; *Ariadne* then proceeded to Norway in company with *Arcona*. That October she began a refit at Danzig, which included a reduction from ship to barque rig, and in June 1874 took part in exercises in company with *Grille*, the ironclads *Kronprinz*, *Friedrich Carl* and the gunboat *Albatross* (for which see below).

On 5 October 1874 *Ariadne* left Wilhelmshaven for the Far East, arriving at Singapore on 24 December, later replacing *Elisabeth* as station ship at Hong Kong. Later in 1875, *Ariadne*, *Hertha* and the newly re-hulled gunboat *Cyclop* (1860/1874) formed an anti-piracy patrol off the Chinese coast, the group being reinforced by *Vineta* in April 1876. *Luise* arrived on 1 July to relieve *Ariadne*, which arrived at Wilhelmshaven on 20 October.

Following a refit, *Ariadne* recommissioned on 15 October 1877, sailing for South America and arriving at Rio de Janeiro on 16 December 1877, and on 4 February 1878 she was joined by *Leipzig* at Valparaiso; the two then combining with *Elisabeth* to apply pressure to the Nicaraguan government during the so-called Eisenstuck Affair, during which Germany sought an indemnity following an alleged assault on two German traders. *Ariadne* was detached to the Pacific on 7 April, arriving in Samoa on 23 June. She stayed until 16 September, when she sailed for Sydney, before cruising the waters north and east of New Guinea. *Ariadne* returned to Samoa on 16 January 1879, being relieved there by *Bismarck* on 19 May, and arriving at Wilhelmshaven on 30 September. On 14 April 1880, *Ariadne* departed for South America, relieving the ironclad *Hansa* off the Chilean coast in August, protecting German interests during the War of the Pacific of 1879–83 (see p 30, below). She remained on station until relieved by *Moltke* in July 1881, and arrived back at Wilhelmshaven on 7 October.

Ariadne did not recommission until 15 July 1884, initially being used as a training ship, also participating in the annual manoeuvres, before leaving for West Africa on 30 October in company with *Bismarck* (flag), *Gneisenau*, *Olga* and *Sophie* (see below, pp 33-34). She remained in the region until March 1885, when she returned to Germany, to became a training ship for boy-seamen. As such she undertook a cruise to the Caribbean from October 1885 to March 1886. Out of commission between October 1886 and April 1887, and from September 1888 to April 1889, *Ariadne* otherwise continued the round of training duties and participation in manoeuvres, with cruises to the Caribbean in the summer of 1888 and 1889. Following the 1890 manoeuvres, at the end of September she was paid off for the last time, was stricken the following spring, and broken up.

Luise

The construction of *Ariadne*'s sister ship *Luise* had been delayed by the Franco-Prussian War. Her first deployment began in October 1875, to the Far East via South America, relieving *Ariadne*. She served in the region until May 1877, reaching Wilhelmshaven on 1 September for a refit, which included a reduction in her rig. In the Indian Ocean in early 1879, *Luise* relieved *Freya* at Hong Kong in May, and then made various port visits, including a period during March/April 1880 at Shanghai to protect German nationals during a period of local unrest. On her return voyage to Germany in the summer, *Luise* carried out a mission to Madagascar in August, before arriving at Wilhelmshaven on 9 November.

She then followed her sister *Ariadne* in being converted into a boys' training ship. By the early 1880s, the old pre-Imperial cruisers that had been employed in the training role were coming to end of their lives, and thus during the new decade more modern vessels were taking over this role. Indeed, some brand-new ships would be assigned to the task. *Luise* spent June 1881 to August 1882 in American waters, before undergoing an extensive refit at Danzig from 1883 to the beginning of 1885. From June of that year to the summer of 1886 she once again conducted a cruise to American waters. After this she carried replacement crews out to West Africa for the gunboats *Cyclop* and *Habicht*, returning in January 1887. Resuming training duties in the summer of 1887, she then was again used to carry relief crews to West Africa, coming back in February 1888. *Luise* continued to undertake training cruises in home waters, as well as taking part in the annual manoeuvres, until 1891. She was then reduced to a hulk and used in torpedo trials during 1894–96. Stricken on 12 December 1896, *Luise* was broken up the following year.

Freya

The third ship of the class, *Freya*, laid down in 1872 and launched in December 1874, was significantly larger than the earlier pair, displacing an additional 300 tonnes, and some 17m longer. The 12cm guns were replaced by two more 15cm guns, and the machinery had 300ihp more power. Her first deployment began in November 1877, when she joined *Hertha* in the Mediterranean. In August 1878 she left for the Far East to relieve *Luise*, on arrival being refitted at Hong Kong from October to December. *Freya* spent February–April 1879 at Shanghai, and then returned to Hong Kong for relief by *Luise*. She departed for Germany in May and finally reached Wilhelmshaven in September.

Freya returned to the Far East almost immediately, sailing via South America. There, she joined *Hansa* in monitoring events

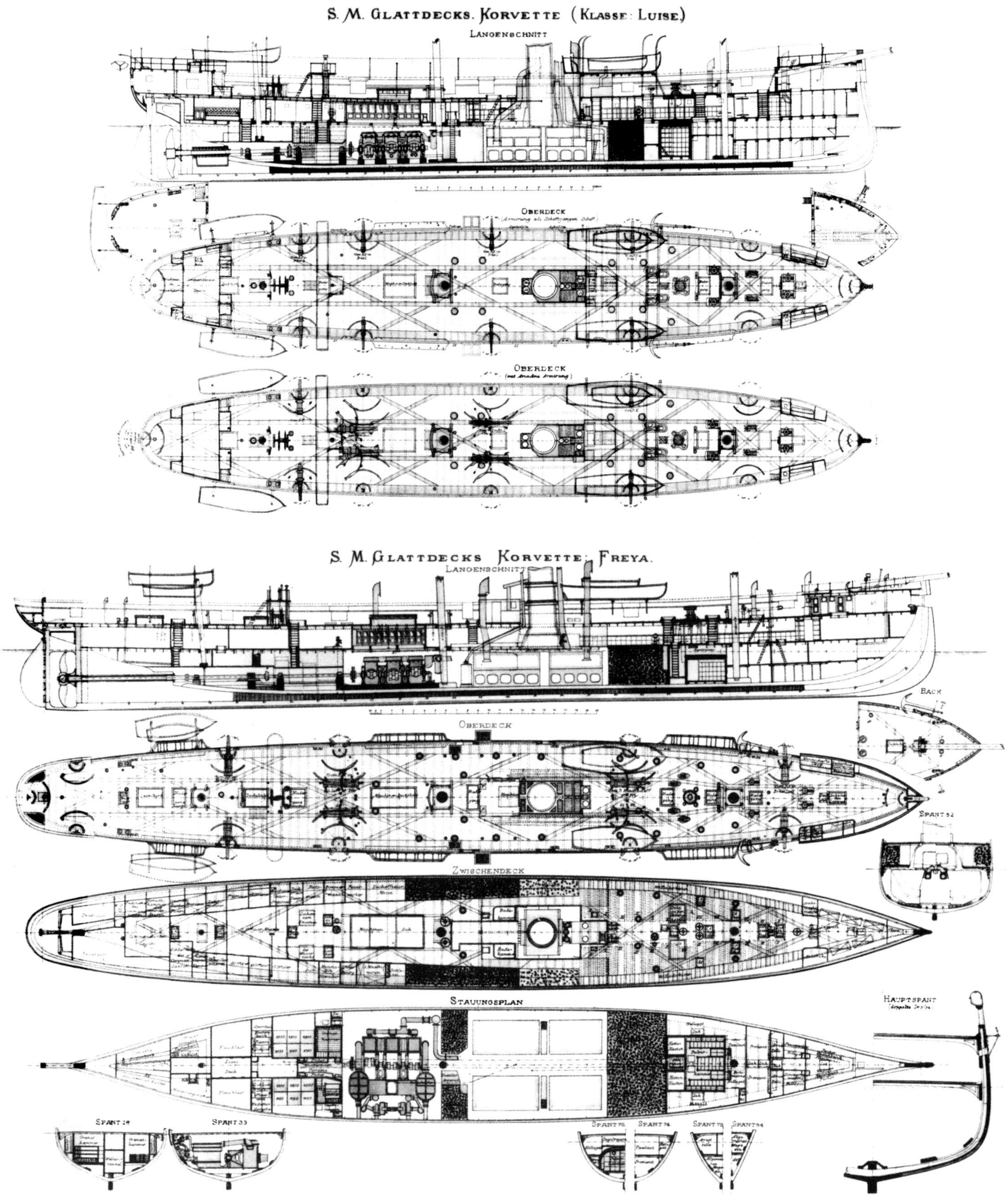

Admiralty-issued sections and plan-views of a flushdecked-corvette of the *Ariadne/Luise* class, and their half-sister *Freya*. The upper *Ariadne/Luise* plan view depicts *Luise* as a training ship, the lower *Ariadne* as built. None of the the class were fitted with a hoistable screw, which must have adversely affected their sailing abilities, even in the case they were able to turn their two-bladed propellers into the dead water behind the sternpost. (DN collection)

during the War of the Pacific (or 'Saltpetre War'), between Chile on one side and Peru and Bolivia on the other, as a result of the internment of a German merchantman by Peru. She then pushed on to the Far East in April 1880, reaching Hong Kong in August to join *Vineta* and the gunboats *Cyclop* and *Wolf*. *Freya* was relieved by *Stosch* in July 1881, arriving at Wilhelmshaven on 6 October.

Like her half-sisters, *Freya* was adapted to become a boys' training ship, the conversion beginning soon after her return from the Far East, including the removal of one 15cm and the addition of four 17cm guns. She also received six 37mm Hotchkiss weapons. She recommissioned in her new role in March 1883, an initial Baltic cruise being followed by one to South America and the Caribbean, returning to Germany in time for the 1884 manoeuvres. Refitted between 1884 and 1887, and reduced to barque rig, she only recommissioned for trials, being subsequently laid up until reduced to harbour service in autumn 1893 and stricken on 12 December 1896.

LORELEY

Also in dockyard hands in 1871 was what was nominally the old *Loreley*, undergoing an extensive refit: in fact, the original ship was being effectively scrapped and a wholly new vessel built around a number of original components, including the machinery. A similar transformation would shortly afterwards be applied to the gunboat *Cyclop*.

The original ship had been ordered in 1857 to fill the gap created in the Prussian navy's steam capability created by the handing over of *Nix* and *Salamander* to the UK in exchange for *Thetis*. To minimise risk, a wooden hull and paddle propulsion were adopted, Danzig Dockyard launching the hull on 20 May 1859, with the ship commissioning on 28 September. The machinery proved to produce less power than contracted for, but little could be done to remedy the problem, and the ship was paid off at the end of her trials.

Loreley recommissioned on 23 July 1860 to protect Prussian and wider German interests during the wars of Italian unification. She was armed with obsolete guns originally carried by *Preußischer Adler* during 1848–49, as her intended armament had not yet been delivered. She sailed from Danzig on 31 July, joining the chartered steamer *Ida* off Naples on 31 August. She undertook various activities until October, when *Loreley* proceeded to Greek and Turkish waters, returning to Germany in August 1862 to decommission.

Reactivated for service as flagship for the gunboat force in the war with Denmark (see p 12), *Loreley* was in service during the summers of 1865, 1866, 1867 and 1868, but by the end of the decade was in poor condition. Taken in hand at Wilhelmshaven in 1870, she was given a new composite hull as part of what was described as a 'new build'. However, the ship remained on the navy list throughout, and was thus 'legally' still the old *Loreley*. Launched on 19 August 1871, she (re)commissioned in April 1873, now armed with one 12.5cm/23 and two 8cm/23 guns.

Loreley at her permanent berth at İstanbul-Tarabya in the 1890s. Her rebuilding with a new hull did not significantly alter her profile, apart from the addition of some extra deckhouses. *(DN collection)*

She became tender to the North Sea naval base, serving as such until January 1879. She was then refitted, including reboilering, to become German station-ship at Constantinople; recommissioning on 1 July, sailing on 20 July, and arriving at the Bosphorus on 30 August 1880. *Loreley* made various cruises as part of her role, sometimes in conjunction with German warships on deployment to the Mediterranean, for example with *Prinz Adalbert* and *Sophie* during the Crown Prince's 1883 visit to Spain. However, by the spring of 1896, *Loreley*'s condition had deteriorated significantly. She was thus stricken on 6 September on her relief by the 1885-built former steam yacht *Mohican* (now classified as a special-service vessel, rather than an aviso like her predecessor), which had commissioned as *Ersatz-Loreley* on 6 August, and became *Loreley* (iii) on 7 September. The old *Loreley* was sold for scrap locally on 23 October.

Sedan (soon to become *Prinz Adalbert*) in home waters during 1877/78, awaiting her first deployment, painted with the old 'chequerboard' scheme of the sailing era. This was abandoned in favour of a simple black hull in September 1878 for newer ships, although surviving for longer in older wooden vessels. *(DN collection)*

THE QUASI-CRUISERS

The two *Albatross* class had been delayed during the war (p 14), but both were launched in 1871, the name ship on 11 March, and *Aviso A* as *Nautilus* on 31 August. However, while *Albatross* was indeed commissioned as an aviso on 23 December, the following year the pair were reclassified as gunboats prior to *Nautilus* belatedly joining the fleet in June 1873. Their later half-sisters of the *Habicht* class were initially classified as gunboats, but became avisos during the design phase, on the basis that their more powerful compound machinery made them (almost) fast enough to have potential as fleet scouts.

The first pair of *Habicht*s continued the letter sequence initiated by *Aviso A/Nautilus*, but became 'gunboats' again in August 1881. The final vessel, ordered in 1882 as *Ersatz-Comet* [to be *Adler*], was explicitly the replacement of an old gunboat of 1860. Nevertheless, the ships' origins among cruising vessels would be recalled when the two classes were reclassified as cruisers in 1884, although this promotion would be short-lived (see p 85, below).

The newly commissioned aviso/gunboat *Albatross*, in the port of Danzig in October 1872. Her heavily raked masts add a touch of the clipper ship to her appearance. *(DN collection)*

THE *LEIPZIG* CLASS

In 1873 Stosch, a year on from his appointment, presented to the Reichstag a revision of the 1867 fleet plan, which now called for fourteen seagoing ironclads, seven monitors, two armoured floating batteries,[3] twenty unarmoured corvettes, six avisos, eighteen gunboats and twenty-eight torpedo 'carriers' of various sizes and types. These targets were to be met within ten years, and were to form the basis for developing the German navy until the 1890s.

The plan required eight additional corvettes to be built, all to be of iron rather than the wood of the existing vessels, and all larger than their predecessors. As regards the building material, it is worth noting that France continued to lay down wooden rigged cruisers for distant service until as late as 1880,[4] the ship in question, *Dubourdieu*, not commissioning until 1887.

The first pair, laid down as *Thusnelda* (but launched as *Leipzig*) and *Decked-corvette A* [*Sedan*] were, indeed, twice the displacement of *Freya*, and similar to the *Bacchante*-class being built at the same time by the UK,[5] and the French *Duquesne* and *Tourville*. Displacing some 4,600 tonnes, the German ships had six trunk boilers and a single-expansion engine, with a lifting screw, giving a design speed of 14 knots, which they exceeded

3. Similar to the Austro-Hungarian *Feuerspeier.*

4. Although the further ship of the type, *Capitaine Lucas*, was ultimately cancelled in favour of *Sfax*, the first deck-protected cruiser in the French navy.

5. Diminutives of the huge iron frigates *Inconstant*, *Raleigh* and *Shah*, laid down between 1866 and 1871.

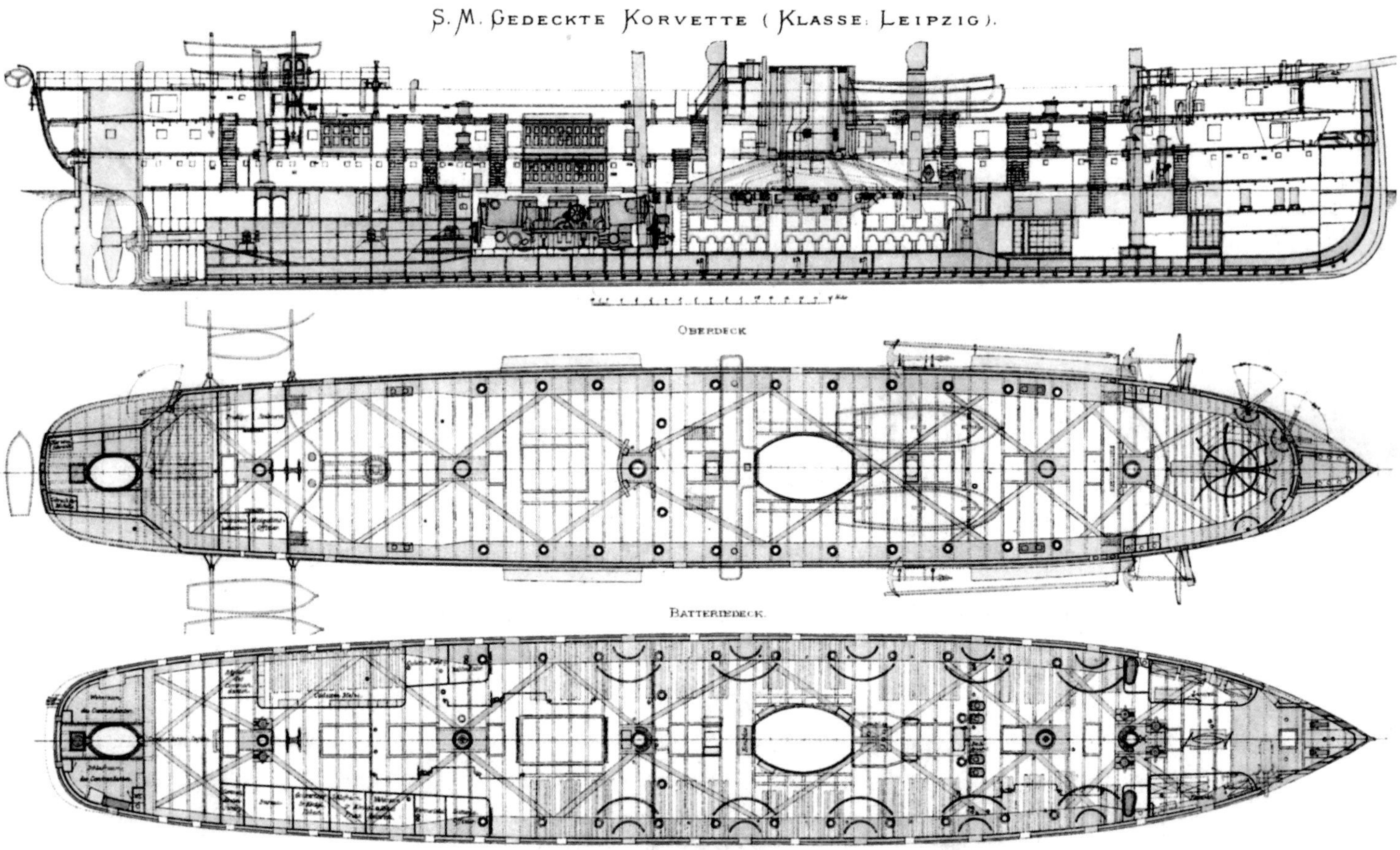

Admiralty-issued sections and plan views of a decked-corvette of the *Leipzig* class. Despite their hoistable screw, the pair have been reported as being quite mediocre performers under sail alone. *(DN collection)*

on trials. They were armed with a dozen 17cm guns, two 25-cal, the remainder being 20-cal.

The original intent was that they should have a dual role, scouting for the fleet as well as undertaking overseas service. However, the 1877 action between the British *Shah* and the Peruvian ironclad *Huáscar* had suggested that unarmoured ships could not currently safely engage armoured vessels; the *Leipzig*s thus served solely on distant stations, for which their size and consequent habitability well suited them.

Leipzig and *Sedan* were named for Prussian military victories, although the latter was renamed *Prinz Adalbert* (ii) before her first deployment, to avoid giving gratuitous offence to the French (cf. p 11, above). This was to the Far East, beginning in October 1878, via the Pacific, the ship remaining in Japanese waters until early 1880. After a period in Chinese waters, she was relieved by *Vineta* and reached Kiel in September.

To begin her service, *Leipzig* made a cruise to Central America and the Far East as a cadet training ship in 1877–78, and undertook a further one to the latter region during 1882–84. During the former, she was diverted back to Nicaragua for operations off that country (see p 27, above). On return, she paid off into reserve.

Prinz Adalbert recommissioned in 1883, carrying the Crown Prince on a series of Mediterranean visits, before continuing to the Far East at the end of the year. On her way back to Germany at the end of 1884, she was diverted to Central America in the spring of 1885, and then again, first to East,

Leipzig in drydock at Wilhelmshaven in mid-1885, during her 1885–86 reconstruction: note the offset bow torpedo tube, added during this reconstruction. *Charlotte* is to be seen on the slipway behind; she would be launched on 5 September 1885. *(NHHC NH 88765)*

The rebuilt *Leipzig* at Cape Town in February 1892, as flagship of the Cruiser Squadron. Flying from her mizzen is the flag of either KAdm Victor Valois (1841–1924), or Friedrich von Pawelsz (1844–1905), who exchanged command at this time. The two funnels are an easy way of distinguishing *Leipzig* after her reconstruction. The ship is now painted in the usual white/buff scheme employed for vessels serving abroad. *(DN collection)*

and then to West, Africa, before finally arriving at Wilhelmshaven in December 1885.

She was then refitted as a cadet training ship, beginning her first voyage in April 1886 in the Baltic, and subsequently in company with the Training Squadron (*Hansa*, *Sophie*, *Stein*, *Moltke*, *Gneisenau*) to the West Indies between October 1886 and March 1887. She began another set of cruises in May 1887, ending back in Wilhelmshaven the following spring. In poor condition, she was stricken in 1890 and became an accommodation hulk until sold for scrap in 1907.

In contrast, *Leipzig* was taken in hand for reconstruction in 1885, to transform her into the long-term flagship for the recently-established German Cruiser Squadron (see below). This included reboilering, giving her henceforth two funnels, which were fixed, as was a new propeller; she also received additional watertight bulkheads and new sheathing of the hull. Although work was completed in August 1886, trials were problematic, with a number of modifications required before she was declared fit to take up her new role in June 1888.

BISMARCK CLASS

The remaining six cruisers of the 1873 plan were built to a smaller design than the *Leipzig*s, but of the same basic concept. Three of the ships (*Decked-corvettes B* [*Bismarck*], *C* [*Blücher*] and *D* [*Gneisenau*]) were additions to strength, the others (*Ersatz-Gazelle* [*Stosch*], *Ersatz-Arcona* [*Moltke*] and *Ersatz-Hertha* [*Stein*]) replacements for old wooden corvettes. In nomenclature, they broke new ground for frigates and corvettes in being named for military and political leaders – including those currently active – rather than mythological and royal ladies (cf p 11, above). More than 1,000 tonnes smaller than the *Leipzig*s, they were also of more 'traditional' appearance with a knee bow. Their four trunk boilers generated steam for 12 knots, the ships also having a full ship-rig, and a designed armament comprising sixteen 15cm/22 guns – fourteen on the gun-deck, with two in the forecastle. However, a number of ships were completed with a smaller number on the gun-deck.

Bismarck

The lead-ship of the class began her first deployment in November 1878, crossing the Atlantic to Montevideo, and then proceeded via the Strait of Magellan to Valparaiso. She then crossed the Pacific, meeting *Ariadne* at Apia in Samoa in May 1879 to relieve her on station. Following the arrival of the gunboat *Albatross* in July, *Bismarck* sailed for Australia for a refit at Sydney. She was then deployed to Samoa following unrest there, later to be joined by *Nautilus*. Although recalled to Germany in January 1880, she was first diverted to Sydney to repair storm damage, and then to the west coast of South America to join the ironclad *Hansa* in protecting German interests. She finally left for home in July, reaching Wilhelmshaven on 30 September. She was then extensively refitted, including the addition of two 35cm above-water torpedo tubes forward, completing trials in August 1883.

In September 1884 *Bismarck* was brought forward as flagship of a new Cruiser Squadron, initially for West African service, which also comprised her sisters *Gneisenau*, *Olga* and *Ariadne*. The year had represented something of a watershed for Germany, in that, although Germans had begun to establish private trading colonies in Africa and the Pacific during the 1850s and '60s, there had been precious little encouragement from the Reich government. Chancellor Bismarck had long regarded colonies as a waste of resources and a political distrac-

The brand-new *Bismarck* shortly before her commissioning in August 1878. She seems to have been the only of her class to carry the old-fashioned 'chequerboard' band along her battery deck for a significant period, although *Stosch* was certainly launched painted in this way. *(DN collection)*

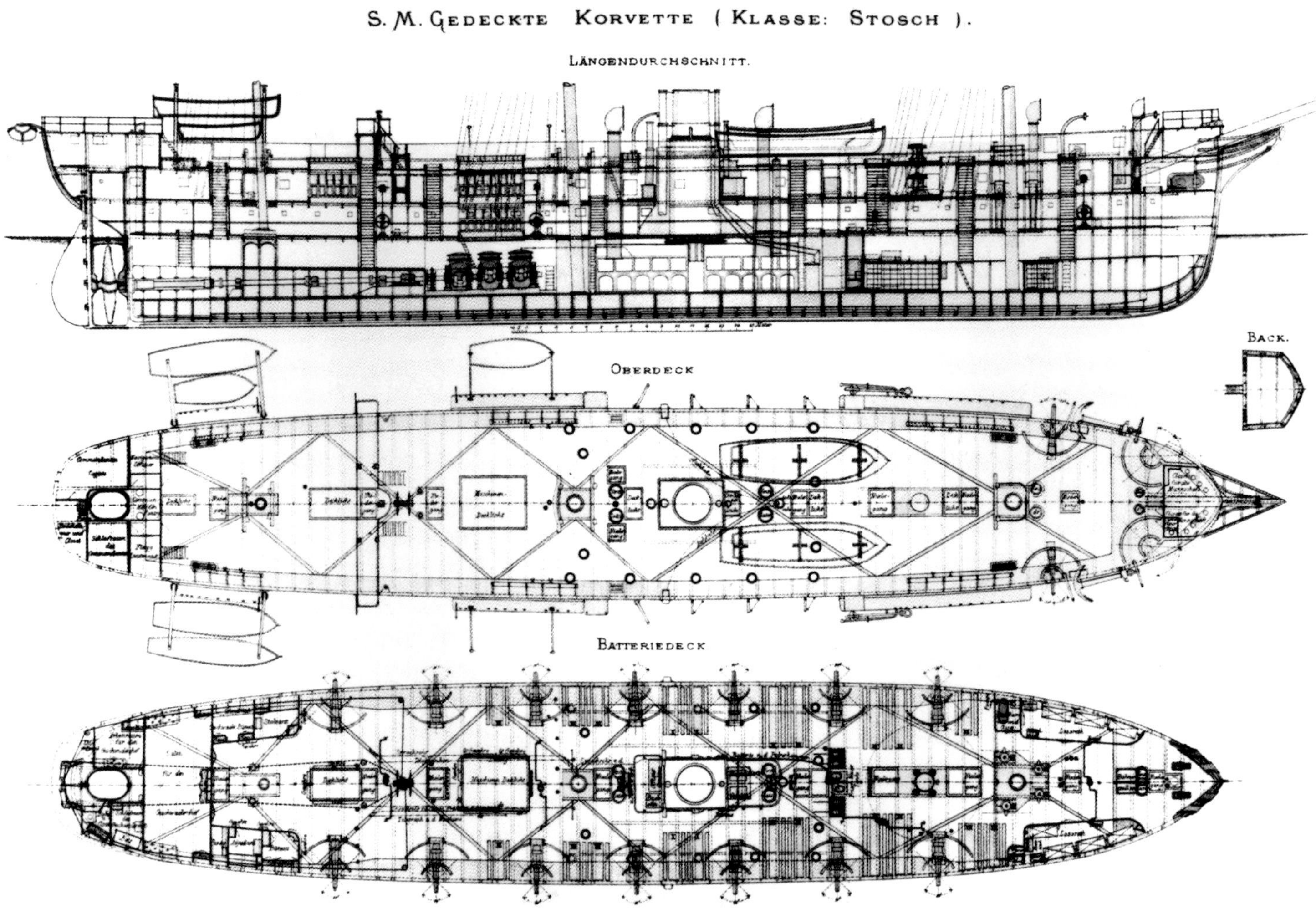

The clean and simple profile of the *Bismarck/Stosch* class is very obvious in these Admiralty drawings. *(DN collection)*

tion, but had reversed his position in 1884. As a result, formal colonies were now established, beginning with German New Guinea (the northeastern part of the island, plus the archipelagos to the north), rapidly followed in Africa by Togoland, Kamerun and German South West Africa. German East Africa became a colony in 1891.

During the preliminaries to these takeovers, *Elisabeth* had been deployed to the coast of South West Africa in June, which was followed by a visit from *Leipzig* and the gunboat *Wolf* in August. *Bismarck*, *Gneisenau*, *Olga* and *Ariadne* operated off West Africa during the autumn, including landing parties to counter those opposing the German takeover. The next year, *Prinz Adalbert*, *Stosch*, *Gneisenau* and *Elisabeth*, later joined by *Bismarck* and the gunboats *Möwe* and *Hyäne*, applied pressure on the Sultan of Zanzibar to acquiesce to German control of mainland territory hitherto regarded as his. This was a precursor of the ultimate formal establishment of German East Africa.

German interests in the Pacific had been advanced in 1884 by *Elisabeth* and *Hyäne* enforcing the German claim to the Bismarck Archipelago, north of New Guinea. The northeastern part of the latter was then seized by parties from *Hyäne* and *Sophie*, to become Kaiser-Wilhelmsland, a key element of soon-to-be German New Guinea. To the southeast, Samoa had for some time been the focus of colonial rivalry between Germany, the UK and the USA, in particular over support for rival factions in the ongoing civil conflict on the islands. This stand-off would be resolved in 1889 (after ships of all three navies had been badly battered in a cyclone that March: p 43, below), through the establishment of a short-lived Anglo-American-German joint protectorate. It was not until 1899 that agreement was reached between the protectors that the western islands of the group should become German Samoa and the rest American Samoa, the UK bowing out in exchange for some adjustments in Africa and to the southern boundary of German New Guinea, plus the ending of German rights in Tonga.

While *Gneisenau* and *Ariadne* were detached en route, the other two vessels reached Kamerun in December, landing parties to deal with 'unrest'. *Bismarck* remained in the area until July 1885, when she sailed to Cape Town for a refit. She left on

5 August, joining *Gneisenau*, *Stosch*, *Prinz Adalbert*, *Elisabeth* and the gunboat *Möwe*, off Zanzibar two weeks later.

It was to further support this colonisation process that formal East and West African naval stations were established in 1885, each with a permanent establishment of two gunboats. This concept was extended around the world in January 1886. At the same time, the 'flying squadron' concept rejected back in 1872 was resurrected, with the formal establishment of a Cruiser Squadron. This provided mobile Reich forces to reinforce local German elements in countering opposition to the consolidation and maintenance of German rule in the new colonies, as well as a wider defence of German overseas interests.

The first iteration of the new Cruiser Squadron comprised cruising vessels already overseas on African service, with *Bismarck* as flagship, leading *Gneisenau*, *Olga* and the gunboats *Möwe* and *Hyäne*. The three corvettes were then sent east, via Australasia, to Samoa, to look after German interests during the civil war.

Bismarck and her squadron then made various visits around the eastern Pacific, *Carola* arriving at Hong Kong to join *Bismarck* and *Olga* as relief for *Gneisenau* in July. The trio returned to East Africa in December to help settle border disputes, being later joined by *Sophie*. They spent March to May 1887 at Cape Town, to be on hand if Franco-German tensions impacted the West African colonies of the two powers.

The Cruiser Squadron then returned to the Pacific, being joined by the gunboat *Adler* at Sydney. It once again proceeded to Samoan waters in August, *Bismarck* and *Carola* then going on to New Guinea in the company of *Sophie*. *Bismarck* was detached from the squadron after a final cruise in East Asiatic waters and a refit at Nagasaki, before being recalled to Germany, arriving in August 1888. A major refit was planned but, in the event, she was stricken in September 1891 and reduced to an accommodation hulk at Wilhelmshaven, remaining as such until scrapped in 1920.

Stosch

Stosch also began her seagoing service as a flagship, for the Far East, relieving *Freya* at Batavia in July 1881, and then joining up with *Hertha* and the gunboats *Iltis* and *Wolf* at Chefoo (Yantai). The vessels then operated in Chinese and Japanese waters, *Hertha* being relieved by *Elisabeth* in the summer of 1882, which was in turn replaced by *Leipzig* a year later; *Leipzig* was then relieved by *Prinz Adalbert* in March 1884; *Stosch* remained as squadron flagship throughout.

In March 1885, *Stosch* was reassigned to become flagship of a new force in East African waters, stopping in Australia on the way, where she aided in the final stage salvage of *Marie* following her grounding the previous December (p 46, below). She met with her new squadron-mates, *Gneisenau*, *Elisabeth* and *Prinz Adalbert*, at Mauritius on 5 July. The ships' first task was the search for *Augusta*, which had disappeared a month earlier after last being seen in the Gulf of Aden while carrying relief crews for *Gneisenau* and the gunboats *Albatross* and *Hyäne* to Australia. Nothing was found, and it was later concluded that she had foundered in a cyclone on 2 June, which had also sunk two other ships off the mouth of the Red Sea.

Augusta had been out of commission since 1878, until recommissioned in April 1885 for her ferry task. Her sister *Victoria* was now serving in a fishery protection role in home waters, and remained as such until 1890, before being stricken the following year.

Its melancholy task having been abandoned, the force then headed on to Zanzibar, where *Stosch* was replaced as flagship by *Bismarck*. *Stosch* now led a new squadron, also comprising *Prinz Adalbert* and *Gneisenau*, originally destined for the Caroline Islands, but then redirected to West Africa. *Stosch* underwent a refit at Cape Town during October/November, and then returned to Germany in company with *Prinz Adalbert* in December.

She was there reboilered and her 15cm guns upgraded to QL weapons, recommissioning in September 1888. She then relieved *Stein* as flagship of the Training Squadron, then comprising *Gneisenau*, *Moltke* and *Charlotte*, which she then led to the Mediterranean. In February 1889, the squadron was earmarked to go to the East Africa station, whose ships were being sent to Samoa, but these redeployments were cancelled by the time that *Stosch* and her companions had reached Alexandria in March. Returning to Wilhelmshaven in April, *Stosch* was then decommissioned until 1891.

On 1 January 1891 *Stosch* was reclassified as a training ship, along with all her sisters save *Bismarck* and *Blücher*. This change occurred in parallel with the beginning of lengthy discussions about which form of rigging the vessels should carry in future. The existing scheme, with large single topsails, was soon felt to overly restrict the number of trainees able to work aloft simultaneously, while the size of the topsails was in any case too large for mainly inexperienced men to easily handle. This discussion intensified in 1894, when KptLtn (later Adm) Wilhelm Lans (1861–1947) proposed the drastic change from ship to barquentine rig, with the main- and mizzenmasts reduced to simple fore and aft rig, with effort shifted from work aloft to more training in boat work, gunnery and engineering.

This was, however, too much for his more traditionally minded superiors and the suggestion was rejected for the time being. Nevertheless, in 1899, it was indeed decided that rigging would eventually be reduced to primarily fore and aft rig, albeit with one topsail left on the fore and main. In the interim, however, square rig would remain, although at Easter 1900 it was decreed that split topsails of reduced size would be fitted. These, as had been anticipated, adversely affected the vessels' sailing capabilities, meaning that those vessels that remained active were primarily steamships, with their rigging now

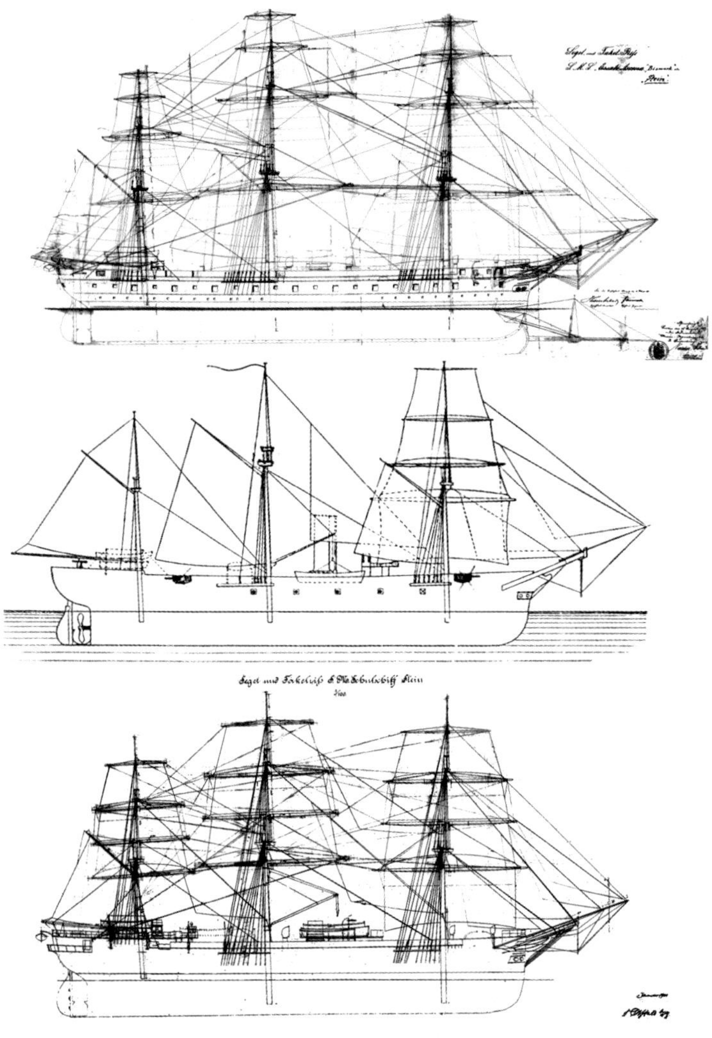

The original sail plan for *Bismarck* and *Stein*, dating to August 1877 (top): even its 2,210 sqm spread of sails (excluding lee-sails) were barely sufficient to make them acceptable sailers. An 1894 proposal (middle) for the future rigs of the training cruisers would have made progress under sail alone all-but-impossible, but this seems to have been the intention of its originator, KptLtn Wilhelm Lans, who wanted emphasis shifted from sailing the ship towards technical subjects. In the event, the ultimate rig (bottom) was something of a compromise, as shown in this official plan 1900 for *Stein*. This involved some 1,700 sqm of sails, but still now required engine assistance for any meaningful progress at sea. *(DN collection)*

very much an auxiliary, and with only a residual training role.

In 1892, *Stosch* was in commission from April to September, including the annual fleet manoeuvres. From April 1893 to April 1897 she undertook a number of cadet (and from 1895 boys) training cruises, as well as with other training cruisers forming part of the III. Division for the August/September manoeuvres. June 1895 saw her take part in a demonstration of power off Morocco, alongside *Marie*, the coast defence ship *Hagen* and the new cruiser *Kaiserin Augusta*, to demand compensation for the murder of two German citizens,

Refitted in 1897, *Stosch* returned to the routine of training cruises, in both northern and Mediterranean, waters from April 1898 onwards. In the autumn of 1902, she went to the West Indies, operating with the East American squadron (the large cruiser *Vineta* [flag], small cruisers *Gazelle* and *Falke*, and the gunboat *Panther*) over the winter, during the Anglo-German blockade of Venezuela. She went again to South American waters in 1904, and to West Africa in 1905, ending her career with a visit to the Mediterranean during 1906–07, being decommissioned and stricken soon after her return to Germany in March 1907.

Gneisenau

Named for Prussian field marshal August Neidhardt von Gneisenau (1790–1831), *Gneisenau* made her first deployment in August 1882, to guard German interests in Egypt during the British intervention there, which had begun with the British bombardment of Alexandria in July. She sailed in the company of *Zieten* and the gunboat *Cyclop* to join *Nymphe* (already in the Mediterranean on a training cruise) and Mediterranean station-ship *Loreley* to reinforce the gunboats *Habicht* and *Möwe*. Returning to Germany in December, *Gneisenau* decommissioned in the New Year.

She recommissioned in October 1884 for service off West Africa, as part of the squadron led by *Bismarck*. However, *Gneisenau* was diverted to Cape Town and then on to Zanzibar, carrying the new German consul, remaining in the area from January until the end of March 1885. She departed for the Far East on 1 April, the intention being that she should meet *Augusta* at Melbourne in August to exchange crews. However, the disappearance of the latter vessel at the beginning of June meant that *Gneisenau* found herself searching for the lost corvette in company with *Stosch*, *Elisabeth* and *Prinz Adalbert*. She then joined them in sailing to East Africa. Although *Gneisenau* was originally to have gone with *Stosch* and *Prinz Adalbert* on to West Africa, she got no further than Cape Town, when she was sent back up to East Africa, serving there until March 1886. She then proceeded, along with *Bismarck* and *Olga*, to the South Pacific, where she remained until beginning her voyage back to Germany in July. She reached Kiel on 27 September, paying off three weeks later.

Gneisenau returned to service in the spring of 1887 as part of the Training Squadron, which played the role of II. Division of battleships during that year's manoeuvres. After this, the squadron went to the Mediterranean, with *Gneisenau* acting as temporary flagship while *Stein* was under repair from November to early January 1888. Returning to Germany in April, *Gneisenau* was refitted, and rejoined her squadron when it escorted the Kaiser (embarked in the ironclad *Baden*) on a tour of Scandinavian ports in July. She subsequently took part in the annual manoeuvres. The squadron then, led by their new flagship *Stosch*, headed to the Mediterranean. *Gneisenau* remained with the Training Squadron until April 1889, then going out of commission until April 1892.

Top: A splendid early image of *Gneisenau*, somewhere in a warm climate, as indicated by the rigged awnings. Quite a long stay in port seems to have been anticipated, as the top-yards have been sent down. **Bottom:** *Gneisenau* is seen refitted as a trainings ship, shortly before her loss. *(DN collection/ AD collection)*

On returning to service, *Gneisenau* undertook training voyages in the Baltic and North Seas, participating in the 1892 manoeuvres before sailing in October for a cruise to the Caribbean. She arrived back in Germany in time for a refit and to take part in the 1893 manoeuvres as part of III. Division, badly damaging the torpedo boat *D2* in a collision. Out of commission over the winter, she then repeated her previous pattern of a cruise in northern waters, the annual manoeuvres, and then a cruise to the Mediterranean.

In 1895 *Gneisenau*'s winter cruise was to the West Indies, and in 1896 to the Mediterranean. In 1897 she missed the manoeuvres to begin a long cruise to South America, paying off for refit on her return in April 1898. She returned to service in April 1899, undertaking training cruises in northern and Mediterranean waters. However, on 16 December, while moored off the mole at Málaga she was driven against it by a gale and became a total loss. After guns and other equipment had been salvaged, the hull was blown up and the remains subsequently scrapped.

Gneisenau lying sunk outside the breakwater of the port of Malaga. Forty-one of her crew did not survive her stranding during a gale on 16 December 1899. *(DN collection)*

Moltke

Named for the Prussian army chief of staff, Helmuth von Moltke (1800–91), whose three-decade career in post had begun in 1858, *Moltke*'s first deployment was to the west coast of America, relieving *Ariadne* at Valparaiso on 14 July 1881. She remained in the region until May 1882, when she departed for the east coast, arriving at Montevideo in June. The following month she carried a scientific expedition to South Georgia, returning to the west coast in September. She was relieved by *Marie* in August 1883, and arrived back at Kiel on 2 October.

Commissioned as a cadet training ship in April 1885, her initial cruises took her to northern and Baltic waters, after which she joined the Training Squadron for the year's manoeuvres and its winter cruise to the West Indies. She remained with the squadron until April 1889, when she paid off for reboilering, the updating of her armament and the rebuilding of her accommodation for boys and cadets; her capacity was now 210 and 50, respectively. She recommissioned on 7 April 1891 in the presence of her namesake – who died seventeen days later – and the Kaiser. She cruised American waters from June, returning to Germany in August 1892, and participated in the manoeuvres prior to decommissioning on 30 September.

In 1893 she was in the Baltic, on manoeuvres as part of III. Division, with her winter cruise taking her to the Mediterranean, and also the Adriatic, where she carried the dowager Kaiserin Victoria to a number of destinations. She then rejoined the Training Squadron for the 1894 manoeuvres and its West Indies cruise, returning in March 1895.

Moltke then undertook a number of independent cruises, first in the Baltic and North Sea, followed by winter in the Mediterranean. This included a period of operational use, protecting German interests at Smyrna (İzmir) during November/January. Her 1896 programme was also interrupted, joining *Stosch*, *Stein* and *Gneisenau* in being diverted from the West Indies to Alexandria, after which she paid off for a refit at Kiel on 14 April 1897. This included the fitting of two searchlights, one atop the charthouse and another on a lattice tower built around her forward main ventilator.

Returning to service in April 1898, she followed the usual pattern of local cruises, manoeuvres and a long-distance cruise, this time to the West Indies, where she spent time at Havana, guarding German interests in the wake of the Spanish-American War. Her 1899/1900 programme took her back to the West Indies, that of 1900/01 to the Mediterranean, 1901/2 to West Indian and North American waters, 1902/3 and 1903/04 to the Mediterranean, and 1904/05 the West Indies. Her final commission, beginning in April 1907, took her to South American waters and the West Indies, before being decommissioned on 7 April 1908, and relieved in the Training Squadron by the large cruiser *Hertha*. Stricken in November 1910, she became the accommodation hulk for the submarine school, renamed *Acheron* in October 1911 to free her name for a new large cruiser, and was broken up in 1920.

Stein

The remaining two vessels of the class spent their entire careers on non-combatant or training duties. *Stein* was named for the

Top: *Moltke* in one of the locks of the Kaiser-Wilhelm Canal at Brunsbüttel during the 1890s. Her list is most definitely the result of her crew being assembled on the port side, watching the ship next to her in the adjacent lock: the imperial yacht *Hohenzollern*, with the 'All-Highest' on board, as shown by the Imperial standard at the head of her mainmast. Clearly visible is the searchlight platform fitted above *Moltke*'s forward ventilator. **Bottom:** In her final role as the accommodation hulk for submarine crews *Acheron* at Kiel. *(DN collection)*

Top: Ensigns flying at the fore and main mastheads, *Stein* returns to Kiel from a long deployment, still bearing her original rig. The flag at the mizzen shows that the commanding admiral is aboard, performing the usual inspection on arrival. **Bottom:** Close to the end of her seagoing career, *Stein* heels under the press of the sails of her already reduced rigging, but with the smoke from her funnel indicates the employment of her machinery – if only as an auxiliary. *(DN collection)*

Prussian statesman Heinrich Friedrich Karl vom und zum Stein (1757–1831). Her first deployment was to Hong Kong, to carry out a relief crew for her sister *Stosch*, leaving Wilhelmshaven in July 1883 and arriving back in January 1884. She did not recommission again until April 1885, when she became a seagoing training ship for boys and, in July, flagship of the Training Squadron (*Moltke*, *Marie* and *Ariadne*). The squadron contributed to the year's manoeuvres before leaving for the West Indies in October, returning in March 1886.

After a refit, in July *Stein* led a revamped Training Squadron of *Moltke*, *Sophie*, *Prinz Adalbert* and the ironclad *Hansa* to the Baltic, followed by the annual manoeuvres, and then on towards the West Indies (not *Hansa*). However, *Sophie* was detached en route to West Africa, with *Nixe* joining in the Caribbean. The squadron returned prematurely owing to tensions with France, reaching Wilhelmshaven at the end of March 1887. The 1887/88 season's squadron continued to be led by *Stein*, accompanied by *Gneisenau*, *Moltke* and *Prinz Adalbert*, and followed the usual pattern of operations, although *Stein* suffered a fire at Naples on 19 November, the flag being temporarily transferred to *Gneisenau*.

After the 1888 manoeuvres, *Stein* paid off to undergo similar modifications to *Moltke*. It was not until April 1893 that she returned to service, her winter cruise being to the West Indies. In 1894, she was flagship of II. Sqn for the manoeuvres, before going to the Mediterranean with *Gneisenau*. The 1895 cruise was to the West Indies, in company with *Stosch* and *Gneisenau*, stopping in Havana to guard German interests in January 1896, and in February *Stein* contributed to diplomatic pressure on Venezuela.

Back in Germany later that month, *Stein* was due to winter in the West Indies with *Moltke* and *Gneisenau*, but they were diverted to the eastern Mediterranean in view of local unrest, spending early 1897 at Alexandria. The 1897/98 cruise did, however, reach the West Indies, *Stein* and *Charlotte* also acting in protection of German nationals during disturbances in Havana. *Stein* was decommissioned in April 1898, but was recommissioned in January 1901 to replace the lost *Gneisenau*. *Stein* accordingly conducted the usual rounds of cruises in northern, Mediterranean and American waters over the next few years, until decommissioned for the last time in April 1908. Stricken the following month, she was subsequently used as an accommodation hulk until broken up in 1920.

Blücher

Named after the Prussian field marshal Gebhard Leberecht von Blücher (1742–1819), *Blücher* not only spent her entire career on non-combatant duty, but, unlike her much-travelled sisters, never left European waters, having been converted into a torpedo trials ship soon after completion. As such, her gun armament was reduced to a few 8cm and light weapons, but with seven torpedo tubes added. Although consideration was given in 1886 to replacing her with *Elisabeth* and rearming her as a combatant warship, she continued in her trials role, including frequently participating in the annual manoeuvres as a makeshift fleet flagship, until 1906. She was then reduced to harbour service, but in November 1907, she suffered a boiler explosion, which killed sixteen men, and was sold out of service the following year, becoming a coal hulk at Vigo.

Blücher as a torpedo trials vessel (and sometime fleet flagship, during manoeuvres) at her buoy at Kiel during 1898/99. One of her torpedo tubes is visible offset to the port of her stem-post. In the distance are the battleships *Wörth* and *Weißenburg*. *(DN collection)*

ZIETEN

An unusual order in 1874 was one placed in the UK for a 'torpedo vessel', intended as part of the small fleet of experimental torpedo craft acquired between 1871 and 1876. Named *Zieten*, for Friedrich II's cavalry General Hans Joachim von Ziet(h)en (1699–1786), her service was initially closely connected with the development of the infant torpedo arm, especially in that of the locomotive torpedo, to replace the spar type hitherto used. Commanded by KKpt Alfred Tirpitz from 1877, *Zieten*'s trials climaxed with her sinking of the old *Barbarossa* during manoeuvres on 28 July 1880. On 16 August 1881 she was reclassified as an aviso, and as such became in many ways the model for the 'true' avisos *Blitz* and *Pfeil* that were laid down that year (pp 50-53, below).

Displacing 1,000 tonnes, she had six cylindrical boilers, providing steam to a pair of 2-cylinder horizontal compound engines, for a design speed of 16 knots, making her the speediest vessel in the fleet. Armament was restricted to six machine guns and a pair of submerged torpedo tubes – one in the stem aiming directly ahead, one in the stern aiming straight aft. The forward tube was re-sited in an upper deck traversable mounting in 1878, when a pair of 12cm guns were also added.

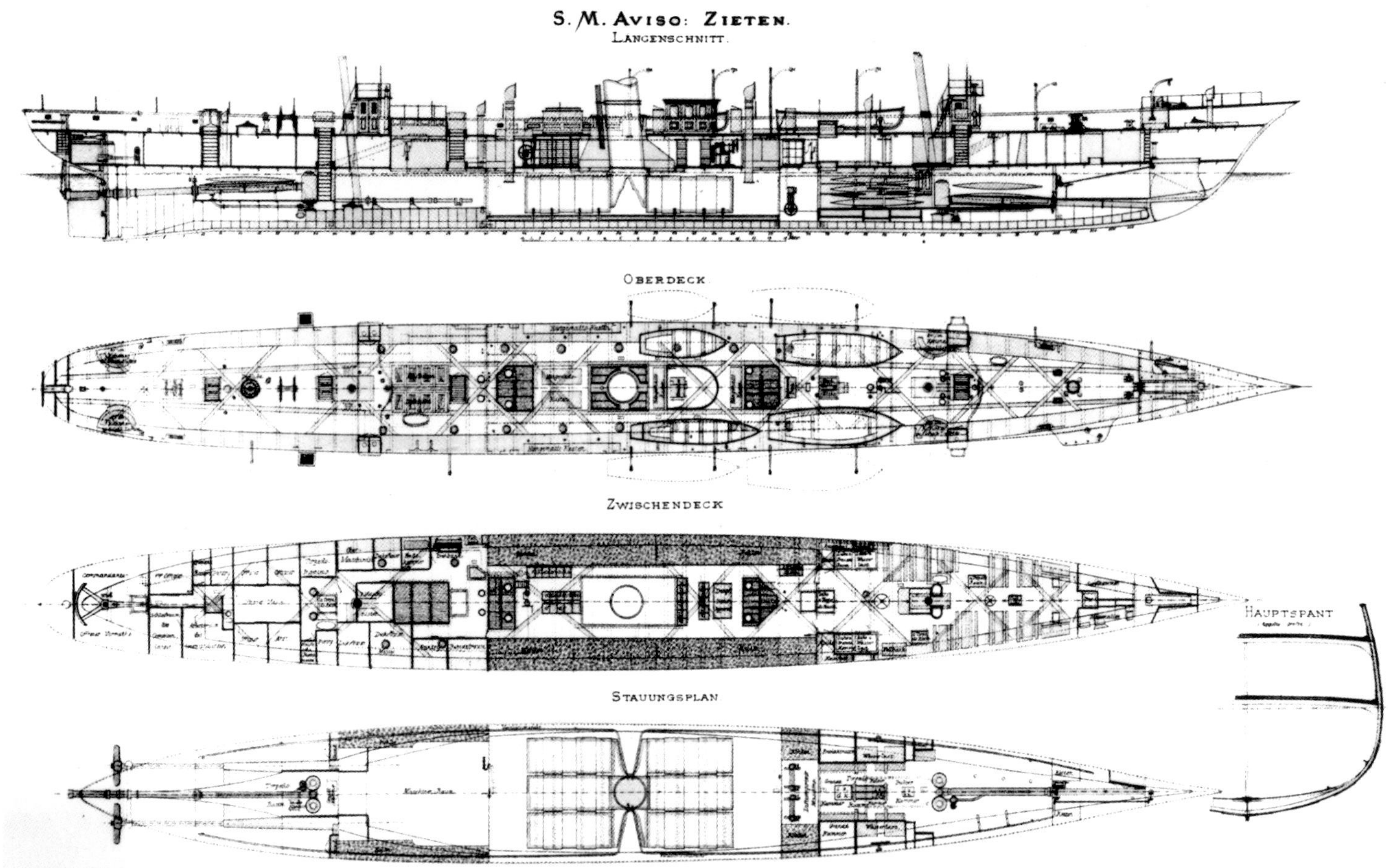

Zieten as built, represented by the Imperial Admiralty drawings and by an early photo, taken in Kiel fjord. Her stern torpedo tube required the splitting of her rudder blade, a detail not uncommon for early torpedo-vessels/avisos. *(DN collection)*

Zieten recommissioned in August 1882, and in her new aviso role deployed to the Mediterranean, accompanying *Gneisenau* and the other vessels reinforcing the German presence in Egyptian waters (p 36, above). Following this, *Zieten* returned to Germany, where she remained out of commission until 1886. She would then commission each summer for scouting duties with the fleet during the annual manoeuvres. Her decommissioning on 30 September 1892 terminated this second period of her service.

Her third period – by far the longest – commenced on 16 March 1897, after a major refit, reboilering and rearmament, during which she lost her torpedo tubes and old guns, receiving six 5cm/40 guns and the ability to lay forty-four mines. She also had a full-width superstructure added amidships, with a conning tower and charthouse, and a shortened funnel. *Zieten* would spend most of her remaining career as a fishery protection vessel in the North Sea, supplemented by some fleet duty during the annual manoeuvres. Out of commission between November 1897 to March 1899, and November 1899 to March 1901, she then remained in constant commission until July 1919.

At the outbreak of the First World War, *Zieten* joined the picket forces for the Jade and Weser rivers, becoming leader of those in the Elbe in July 1918. After the war, her last service was as a pilot vessel, her decommissioning on 5 July 1919 terminating the second-longest service of any vessel in the Imperial navy; *Zieten* was stricken on 6 December 1919 and broken up in Wilhelmshaven from 1921.

The actual record for Imperial navy service was held by *Grille*. Although she had spent most of her previous career as a royal yacht, during the 1880s she was increasingly used as a flag- and training ship, and later as a survey vessel. She was extensively refitted between 1885 and 1888, with new boilers and a new compound engine. On 1 January 1889 she joined the new Baltic Reserve Division, and was employed as a training

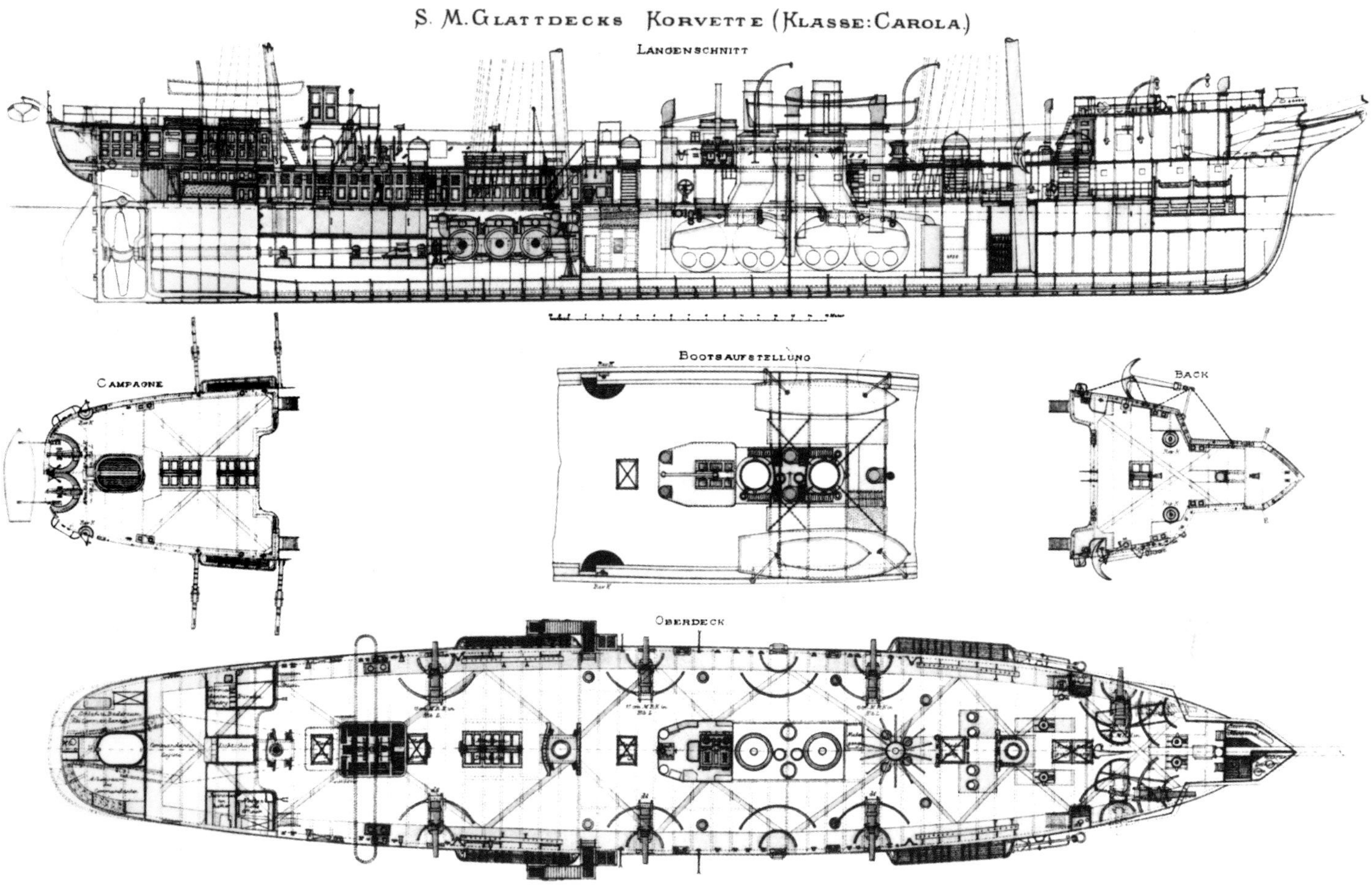

Admiralty drawing representing *Carola* and *Olga*, the two-funnelled units of their class. *(DN collection)*

ship and in the annual manoeuvres, also acting on occasion in her old role as a yacht. She continued in this combination of functions after her reconstruction at Kiel during 1897–98, her rig being reduced to two masts, new boilers fitted and the superstructure extended and remodelled. From the end of 1902 until the end of April 1903 she was attached to I. Sqn, also being used as a fleet tender, a role that, combined with training activities, would take up much of her active time down to 1914.

Grille manoeuvring in the port of Stettin, during one of her regular Admiralty Staff cruises. Her appearance had been changed considerably since her early days (p 20). *(DN collection)*

CAROLA CLASS

By the late 1870s, the wooden-hulled corvettes were in increasing need of replacement, six new flushdecked-corvettes being accordingly procured under the 1873 plan. Of them, *Carola*, *Sophie* and *Alexandrine* were additions to strength (*Flushdecked Corvettes E, F* and *G*), while *Olga* was a prospective replacement for *Augusta*, *Marie* for *Vineta* and *Arcona* (ii) for *Nymphe*. They were reduced developments of the *Bismarck* class, with six fewer main guns.

Marie and *Sophie* had single funnels, their sisters two uptakes, reflecting the two fewer boilers installed in the former pair. The ten 15cm/22 guns were fitted on the upper deck, firing through the bulwarks, with the exception of the forward pair, which were enclosed within the forecastle, with angled embrasures allowing firing on forward arcs. A pair of 8.7cm/24 guns were mounted on the poop.

The final two ships, *Alexandrine* and *Arcona* (ii), were built to a slightly enlarged design, with tandem engines on a single shaft, two extra watertight compartments, a ship, rather than

The earliest known image of *Carola*, while – most probably – swinging her compasses in the entrance to the inner basin of the Imperial Dockyard, Kiel. *(DN collection)*

barque rig, bronze stem-posts, and copper, rather than zinc, sheathing. The armament was also altered, the embrasures under the forecastle being omitted, and the guns formerly mounted there being moved back to the waist. Forward arcs were now covered by two 10.5cm/35 mounted on the forecastle, with corresponding weapons fitted on the poop.

By the time the pair were launched, a reclassification of cruising vessels had taken place, in 1884 (see graphic on p 90). Former 'decked-corvettes' became 'cruiser-frigates', while 'flushdecked-corvettes' became 'cruiser-corvettes'. Thus, the *Carola* class took the latter classification (as did surviving older vessels), while the *Leipzig* and *Bismarck* classes were now cruiser frigates. In addition, the three large iron gunboats of the *Habicht* class (1879–84) became 'cruisers', on account of being above a new 800-tonne upper limit for 'gunboats'.

Although slightly below this displacement, the *Habichts*' earlier wooden-hulled half-sisters *Albatross* and *Nautilus* followed suit. The five vessels' distinction from 'normal' gunboats was underlined by their formal classification as 'Kanonenboot der *Albatross*-Klasse'. The problematic nature of this new 'cruiser' category was further illustrated by the fact that, when an *Ersatz-Albatross* was laid down in 1885, the ship in question entered service as the 'gunboat' *Eber* – and when the latter was lost in 1889, *Ersatz-Eber* became the 'cruiser' *Condor* (pp 7, 71)!

The last and largest of the 'crossover' vessels – *Adler*: gunboat/aviso/cruiser. *(DN collection)*

Carola

The trials of the lead-ship *Carola*, named for the Queen of Saxony (1833–1907), were cut short by a need for her service in the Pacific. The ship sailed on 18 October 1881, and relieved the gunboat *Möwe* at Apia in Samoa on 15 April 1882. She then carried out a number of cruises in the region, refitting at Sydney during February/March 1883. *Carola* returned to Apia in May, where she was relieved by the gunboat *Hyäne*, her voyage back to Germany including the first visit by a German warship to what would become German South West Africa (Namibia) in 1884; she decommissioned at Kiel in November.

While under refit, a torpedo tube was added on a moveable cradle, discharging on the beam through a gun port. *Carola* recommissioned in May 1886 to return to the Pacific, joining *Bismarck* and *Olga* at Hong Kong in August, and sailing for East Africa. Engine defects meant that *Carola* had to undergo repairs at Singapore, meaning that she did not join her squadron-mates off Zanzibar until December. Together with them, she was in South African waters during March/April 1887, before they returned to the Pacific, via refit at Sydney during June/August.

Carola and her companions were ordered back to East Africa in May 1888, although delayed by another visit to Singapore to remedy *Carola*'s machinery defects. Her African sojourn included another visit to South West Africa in July, rejoining the squadron off Zanzibar in November. She refitted at Bombay between November 1889 and February 1890, before returning to station as senior officer's ship, leading the new *Schwalbe* and *Sperber*, until departing in January 1891. On her return to

Carola as gunnery training ship at her buoy in the inner Kiel fjord during the winter of 1896. *(DN collection)*

Germany, *Carola* was rebuilt to supplement the old gunnery training ship *Mars*. Her armament was changed to a mixture of the principal service gun calibres, her torpedo tube removed, and her rig reduced to a pair of military masts. As such, *Carola* served in the gunnery training role until removed from service in January 1905.

Olga

Named for the Queen of Württemberg (1822–92), *Olga* began her career on the South American station, leaving Kiel on 14 October 1882 and arriving in the Caribbean at the beginning of December. She subsequently made various voyages around the region, including a visit to Rio de Janeiro, before returning to Germany, arriving at Kiel on 13 March 1884. Although it had been intended that she now be used for training, she was instead assigned to the Cruiser Squadron, led by *Bismarck*, and also comprising *Ariadne* and *Gneisenau*, that was dispatched to West Africa that October. *Olga* was relieved by the gunboat *Habicht* in April 1885, and returned to Kiel the following month.

Refitted, *Olga* undertook training duties over the summer of 1885, before being deployed to East Africa in late October; rendezvousing there with *Bismarck* at the end of December. Redeployed to the Pacific in February 1886, *Olga* undertook survey work around Neumecklenburg (New Ireland), before rejoining *Bismarck* and the rest of her squadron at Hong Kong in July. *Olga* sailed with them back to East Africa, arriving at the end of December. The squadron was sent back to the Pacific the following year, arriving in Sydney to refit in June. *Olga* then proceeded with it to Samoa. In November she was detached to New Guinea, where she remained until relieved by the gunboat *Eber* in April 1888. Rejoining the squadron at Singapore in June, *Olga* sailed to East Africa with her squadron-mates on the 26th, but was detached back to Samoa on 19 September.

There, together with the gunboats *Eber* and *Adler*, *Olga* represented German interests in the ongoing dispute between Germany, the UK and USA over influence in the islands. Representing the USA were the frigate *Trenton*, the sloop *Vandalia* and the gunboat *Nipsic*; from the UK came the cruiser *Calliope*. All were in harbour at Apia when a cyclone struck on 16 March 1889.[6] *Calliope* managed to steam out of harbour to ride out the storm at sea, but the other vessels were all driven ashore, with *Trenton*, *Vandalia*, *Eber* and *Adler* total losses.

6. For detailed accounts of the cyclone and its impact, see D K Brown, 'Seamanship and Steel: HMS *Calliope* at Samoa 15–16 March 1889', *Warship* XII/48 (1988), 30–36; G Koop, 'The Imperial German Navy and the Hurricane at Samoa', *Warship* XII/48 (1988), 36–42.

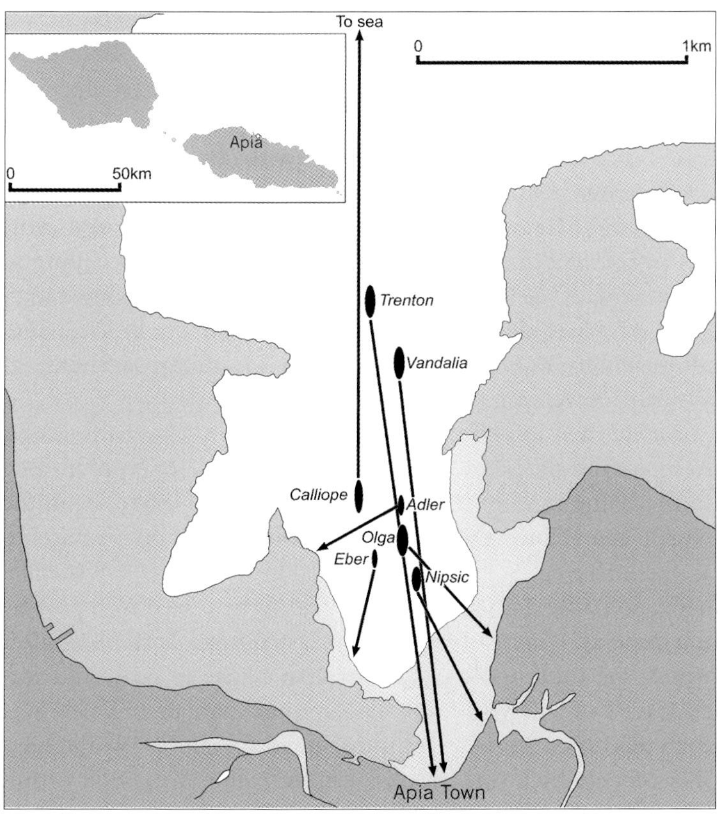

The wrecks of USS *Trenton* and *Vandalia* following the Apia cyclone of 16 March 1889, with *Olga* aground in the background and in the lower-right image. She was lucky only to lose her bowsprit during the night's confusion, her captain steering her to a comparatively safe berth. With the help of North-German Lloyd steamer *Lübeck*, she was refloated on 29 March. The map shows the original and ultimate locations of the ships involved. *(NHHC NH 42289 / DN collection / AD graphic)*

Olga after her conversion to join her sister, *Carola*, as a further gunnery training ship, mainly for light weapons, shown in 1900. *(Heidrich collection)*

Nipsic was refloated in May and repaired in Hawaii; *Olga* was pulled off the beach by SS *Lübeck* on 29 March, which escorted her to Sydney for initial repairs. Patched up, *Olga* left Australia on 20 June, arriving at Kiel on 9 September, before proceeding to Danzig to be refitted as a training ship, with reduced rig, completing in 1891.

Olga commissioned for the 1893 manoeuvres, but was then inactive until brought forward to temporarily replace *Zieten* on fishery protection duties between November 1897 and March 1898. She continued in service even after the latter's return, and carried a scientific expedition to Spitzbergen during June to August 1898. She then operated in the North Sea before making a training cruise to Vigo, in Spain. Paid off on her return at the end of November, the ship was then rebuilt at Wilhelmshaven along the same lines as *Carola* to become an additional gunnery training ship. *Olga* served in this role until relieved by *Nymphe* (ii) in February 1905. She was stricken the following month and broken up in 1908.

Sophie

Apart from a brief period on manoeuvres directly following her trials, first operational service for *Sophie*, named for the Grand Duchess of Saxe-Weimar-Eisenach (1824–97), began when she left Wilhelmshaven in company with *Prinz Adalbert* on 14 October 1883 for the Mediterranean. The deployment included the Crown Prince's tour of Mediterranean ports while embarked in *Prinz Adalbert*. Then, rather than proceeding as planned with the latter to the Far East, *Sophie* was redirected to West Africa to deal with a number of incidents in Togoland, after which duty she returned to Germany, arriving at Wilhelmshaven on 30 March 1884.

Sophie then joined the Training Squadron, alongside *Niobe*, *Nymphe* and the brigs *Undine* and *Rover*, the group proceeding to the Baltic in May 1884, followed by further exercises in the North Sea. However, on 3 September, while on passage to Wilhelmshaven, *Sophie* was in collision with SS *Hohenstaufen*, being so badly damaged that she had to be towed into port by the ironclad *Württemberg*. Repairs lasted until April 1885, after which she undertook a Scandinavian cruise in May, and was then part of I. Division for the summer manoeuvres. She was then placed in the new Training Squadron, alongside the flagship *Stein*, which undertook a cruise to the West Indies from October to March 1886.

While on a training cruise with *Stein* that autumn, *Sophie* was at Lisbon when she was ordered to join the Cruiser Squadron in East African waters. Having swapped her cadets

Sophie in a Chilean port in the summer of 1891, and at the end of her life as a hulk, awaiting the breakers at Hamburg after the First World War. *(DN collection)*

for trained crewmen from *Stein*, she departed on 6 November, arriving at Zanzibar on 14 December 1886. In April 1887, *Sophie* was detached to the Pacific, spending August to November at Apia. She then proceeded via New Guinea waters to Hong Kong to refit, arriving on 6 January 1888. The rest of the cruiser squadron joined her in March and, after time in East Asian waters, was sent back to East Africa in June.

Once there, *Sophie* temporarily relieved *Bismarck* as squadron flagship, but after the arrival of the definitive new flagship, *Leipzig*, in August, plans to send *Sophie* back to the Pacific were abandoned owing to engine defects, *Olga* being substituted. *Sophie* thus remained in East African waters until April 1889, when she was sent to Samoa to replace the damaged *Olga* and sunken gunboats *Adler* and *Eber*. Relieved by

Alexandrine in December, *Sophie* proceeded first to Sydney for repairs and then to the Bismarck Archipelago and East Asian waters, refitting at Hong Kong during April/May. After completion, she met *Leipzig* in Singapore, the two ships then rendezvousing with *Alexandrine* at Sydney before heading to Samoa, where they remained until January 1891.

Sophie went back to Far Eastern waters in February, but she, *Leipzig* and *Alexandrine* were then sent to the Chilean coast to look after German interests during the Chilean Civil War from July to September. The three cruisers then crossed the Atlantic, but *Sophie* was detached at Cape Town to return to Germany, leaving on 18 June 1892 and arriving at Wilhelmshaven on 24 July. She then moved to Danzig, where she was decommissioned on 13 August.

Refitted as a training ship during 1897, *Sophie* recommissioned on 1 April 1898, but only undertook one season of training cruises, to the Baltic, and then to the South Atlantic, before being decommissioned in April 1899. Stricken in 1908, she became an accommodation hulk at Wilhelmshaven, being moved to Heligoland in 1914, and Emden in 1916; she was sold for scrap in 1920.

Marie in drydock at Sydney in 1885. *(DN collection)*

Marie

Named for the Grand Duchess of Mecklenburg-Schwerin (1850–1922), *Marie* was the last of the original four *Carola*s to complete. Her first deployment was to replace *Moltke* in South American waters, doing so at Punta Arenas on 2 August 1883. A month later, she retrieved the scientific expedition left in South Georgia by *Moltke* the previous year, delivering the men to Montevideo for passage back to Germany. She then returned to the west coast of South America until sent to Samoa in September 1884. *Marie* remained there until November, when she relieved *Elisabeth* in Melanesia. She ran on to a reef off Neumecklenburg on 26 December 1884, losing her rudder and leaving her propeller unusable, with significant leakage aft. *Marie* was refloated after three days by shifting and removing weights, and managed to make the island of Nusa on 4 January 1885. Work began there on shoring up the stern. On 6 March the gunboat *Hyäne* began a tow to Keppel Bay on the east coast of Australia, arriving on 6 April. The tow was then transferred to *Stosch*, which took *Marie* to Sydney, where she underwent sufficient repairs to steam home to Germany from 6 May to 29 September. She finally arrived at Wilhelmshaven on 9 February 1886, decommissioning two weeks later.

After repairs, *Marie* remained laid up until l December 1892, when she commissioned to relieve *Sophie* in the Cruiser Squadron. However, before joining, *Marie* was diverted to protect German interests in the wake of the 1891 civil war in Chile, and then continued her deployment in South American waters as an independent command. The Brazilian 'Revolta da Armada' of September 1893–March 1894[7] prompted *Marie* to be directed to join with *Alexandrine* and *Arcona* in February off the coast of Brazil, remaining there until April 1894. The trio were then sent to East Asia in response to Sino-Japanese tensions, but *Marie* had to stop at Puerto Montt to resolve engine defects, rejoining the other two vessels at Callão on 12 July, where they were keeping watch on German interests during a revolution in Peru. She remained there until 15 August.

On 25 November, *Marie*, *Alexandrine* and *Arcona* became the new East Asiatic Cruiser Division (see below), joined by the new *Irene* in February 1895. When the latter's sister *Prinzeß Wilhelm* arrived in June she replaced *Marie*, which took part in the August 1895 demonstration off the Moroccan coast (see p 36, above) while on passage to Germany. Decommissioned at Kiel on 26 September, she remained laid up until stricken in 1904, plans put forward in 1897 to make her a gunnery training ship never having come to fruition.

7. A naval revolt in response to President Floriano Peixoto's refusal to call an election in accordance with the constitution. This culminated in the sinking of the rebel battleship *Aquidabã* by the loyalist torpedo-gunboat *Gustavo Sampaio* on 16 April 1895.

Alexandrine – as yet not commissioned – in the entrance to the inner basin of the Imperial Dockyard Kiel; she was all but identical to her sister, *Arcona*. *(DN collection)*

Alexandrine and *Arcona*

The two ships of the second group were both laid up for some years following completion. *Alexandrine*, named for the dowager Grand Duchess of Mecklenburg-Schwerin and sister of the Kaiser (1803–92), was the first brought forward, in April 1889, to reinforce the German presence in Samoa in the wake of the cyclone there. However, by the time she had reached Australia in July, the situation no longer required her presence. The ship instead cruised in Melanesia, finally reaching Apia in April 1890 and staying until the following month. Refitted at Sydney in July, *Alexandrine* then joined *Leipzig* and *Sophie* in the Cruiser Squadron, proceeding to East Africa with *Leipzig* after *Sophie* was sent home in mid-1892, and then on to the Far East.

In November 1892, *Alexandrine* met up with *Leipzig* at Hong Kong, the two ships then sailing to East Africa, where they were joined by *Arcona* on 6 February 1893. The new arrival had received her first operational commission only in April. She had begun her deployment by heading to Venezuelan waters to protect German nationals during unrest, leaving in October to sail to East Africa via the Mediterranean. The three ships left soon afterwards to refit at Cape Town, although *Leipzig* was sent back to Germany in April, the division disbanding.

Arcona spent April/May in South West Africa, before rejoining *Alexandrine* on 20 May 1893 to proceed to South America, combining with *Marie* for the duration of the Brazilian 'Revolta da Armada'. As already noted, the three ships then went to the Far East, to form the nucleus of the new East Asiatic Cruiser Division in November 1894, with *Arcona* as flagship, relieved as such by *Irene* in February 1895. *Alexandrine* began a return voyage to Germany in March 1895, joining the demonstration off Morocco en route, arriving at Wilhelmshaven on 25 May. A survey having indicated that her hull was in too poor a condition for further seagoing service, the ship decommissioned on 1 June. She briefly recommissioned for her transfer to Danzig the following month, paying off for the last time on 17 July. *Alexandrine* was formally reduced to harbour service alongside a number of other obsolete battleships and cruisers in May 1904, with the nominal wartime role of a floating battery. However, she was stricken three years later, sold and later broken up.

The second ship of her name, *Arcona* arrives at Wilhelmshaven for the final time in her career, on 27 May 1899. *(DN collection)*

Arcona remained in the Far East, including two periods in Philippine waters, while the East Asiatic Cruiser Division grew in size, with the addition of the large cruiser (ex-ironclad) *Kaiser* as flagship to the three smaller cruisers. With them, and *Cormoran*, she participated in the actions surrounding the seizure of Kiaochow (Jiaozhou) Bay in November 1897 (see p 83, below), and aiding in refloating *Kaiser* when she ran aground off the Chinese coast in November 1898. *Arcona* began her return voyage to Germany on 31 January 1899, proceeding via the Persian Gulf, and arriving in Wilhelmshaven on 27 May. Decommissioned the following month and laid up at Kiel, she was renamed *Mercur* in January 1902 to free her name for a new ship launched the following month. Towed to Danzig on 13 August, she was reclassified for harbour service in 1904, and stricken in June 1905; she was broken up the following year.

CHARLOTTE

The last cruisers of the 1873 plan were authorised in 1882, by which time the fully rigged cruiser was a wholly obsolete concept. Nevertheless, *Charlotte*,[8] named for the eldest daughter of Kaiser Friedrich III (1860–1919), and the smaller

8. O Rahardt, *Schiff Profile: SMS „Charlotte" – Segelschiff der Kaiserlichen Marine* (Stengelheim: UNITEC-Medienvertrieb, 2018).

Charlotte leaving Kiel, still carrying her original ship-rig. *(DN collection)*

Nixe were built to designs based on the preceding classes, and were continued with in spite of a change in the leadership of the Admiralty.

Stosch resigned in 1883, and was replaced by Generalleutnant Leo von Caprivi (1831–99). The appointment of another army officer was seen by many as another indication of the generally negative attitude towards the navy. The most qualified candidate, from the point of view of the naval officer corps, would have been VAdm Karl Batsch (1831–98), but he carried the stigma of having been held at least partly responsible for the loss of the ironclad *Großer Kurfürst*, sunk in collision with *König Wilhelm* in 1878, making him unacceptable to the Kaiser. Ultimately, Caprivi was seen as the best choice as being a talented organiser – and apparently not a potential rival to Bismarck: it is thus somewhat ironic that Caprivi would ultimately replace the latter as chancellor.

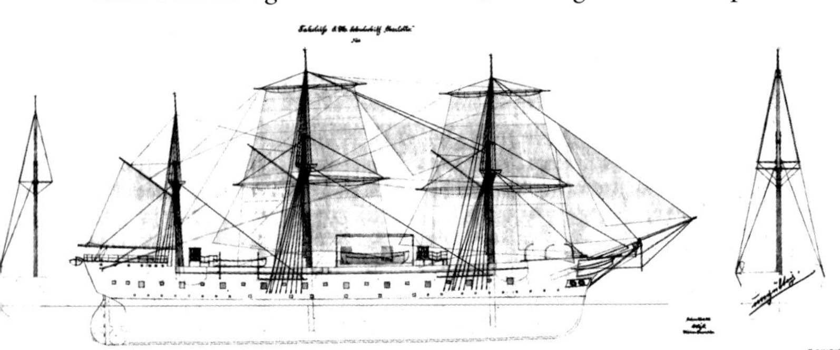

Intermediate rigging-plan of *Charlotte*, applicable only for the years 1898–1900. *(DN collection)*

Charlotte was essentially an updated *Bismarck*, with the tandem engine arrangement of the last two *Carola*s, and was reclassified as a cruiser-frigate while under construction. She was armed with fourteen 15cm/22 guns on the battery deck, with four more in sponsons just forward of the fore and mizzenmasts. A pair of 8.8cm/30s, introduced into service at the end of the decade, were later added just forward of the after sponsons. Commissioned with a ship rig, she was briefly reduced to a barque in 1899, only to receive a rig of a type used in the remaining vessels of the *Bismarck* class in 1900.

The first deployment of the new vessel was as replacement for *Prinz Adalbert* in the Training Squadron, carrying fifty cadets and 230 boys, leaving Wilhelmshaven on 29 September 1888 for the Mediterranean. *Charlotte* returned in April 1889, and was decommissioned. She remained laid up until April 1897, when she undertook exercises in the Baltic, and then escorted *Hohenzollern* to Kronstadt in August. After participating in the manoeuvres, she then began a training cruise to Central America, during which she combined with *Stein* to put pressure on the Haitian government in a dispute over a German

Charlotte, with reduced rig, drying the sails while moored to her buoy in Kiel fjord. *(DN collection)*

national's treatment. Relieved in Haitian waters by *Geier* in January 1898, *Charlotte* returned to Germany, being refitted and then resuming the training routine of a Baltic cruise, annual manoeuvres and a cruise to distant waters. This deployment, to the Mediterranean in company with *Stosch*, was punctuated by a demonstration off Tangier to enforce the payment of an outstanding indemnity, and by courtesy calls to French North African possessions and Spanish ports.

She was refitted after her return to Kiel in March, including the removal of two 15cm guns from the battery and all four from the sponsons, the aftermost pair being replaced by 10.5cm/35 weapons; her rig was also reduced. *Charlotte*'s 1899/1900 long cruise took her to the South Atlantic and that of the 1900/01 to the Mediterranean. During this, while at Corfu, she was sent to Málaga to aid in the salvage work on the sunken *Gneisenau*, in conjunction with the British battleship *Devastation*. This work lasted from 22 December to 12 January 1901. She returned to Kiel on 9 March, where her rig was restored in the way described above. The 1901/02 cruise was again to the Mediterranean, while that for 1902/03 went back to the South Atlantic, and included *Charlotte*'s employment as a support vessel to German ships deployed in Venezuelan waters during the 1902/03 crisis (cf p 73, below). She returned to Kiel in March 1903.

During 1903–05, *Charlotte* was modernised, with new boilers installed, one engine removed, her former lifting screw made fixed, and her armament radically altered to sixteen 8.8cm guns. The fourteen additional weapons replaced the old 15cm and 10.5cm guns one for one. Recommissioned in April 1905, she undertook Mediterranean cruises during 1905/06 and 1906/07, and others to the West Indies in 1907/08 and 1908/09. Decommissioned on 31 March 1909, by then the navy's last sailing ship, she was stricken in May and became an accommodation ship and tender to the commissioned training

Charlotte during the final stage of her career, as a hulk at Flensburg. The upper image shows her soon after arrival, with the stationary training ship (ex-ironclad and large cruiser) *König Wilhelm* on the left and seagoing torpedo training ship (ex-ironclad) *Württemberg* just visible on the far right. In the lower image, *Charlotte* has now been partially housed over. *(Top: AD collection; lower: Bundesmarine Akademie)*

hulk (ex-large cruiser, ex-ironclad) *König Wilhelm* at Flensburg-Mürwik. Following her arrival, she was progressively housed over.

After the outbreak of war in 1914, she was briefly – and uniquely for the Imperial navy – reinstated into the navy list on 20 October to replace *König Wilhelm*, temporarily redeployed as a depot ship in the Elbe. *Charlotte* was stricken once again on 4 November, following *König Wilhelm*'s return. She was sold for further service as a store hulk at Hamburg in 1921, but appears to have been broken up soon afterwards.

NIXE

Like *Charlotte* the last of her line, *Nixe* was wholly outdated even when laid down. It appears that the navy were simply keen to get any possible addition to the fleet that had been authorised by the Reichstag in accordance with the plan of 1873. In addition, the two remaining training brigs, *Musquito* and *Rover*, had now reached the ends of their respective lifetimes, and *Nixe* was certainly an adequate replacement for them.

Nixe under full sail (top), while moored to a buoy in what seems to be a British port, early in her career, and (bottom) on harbour service as headquarters ship for the High Seas Fleet at Kiel between 1906 and 1911. She would later be housed-over as an accommodation hulk at Kiel, and later be transferred to the artillery school at Sonderburg. *(DN collection)*

Indeed, with 500 tonnes less displacement, and less than a third the installed power and 5 knots less speed than *Alexandrine*, *Nixe* was very clearly simply a training ship, with no residual pretentions of being a true warship.

After a brief commission in April 1886 for trials, *Nixe* went into dockyard hands to be refitted as a seagoing training ship for cadets and boys, carrying out her first cruise for the latter during the second half of May 1886. Following this, her first overseas cruise took her to South and Central America, beginning on 15 June. She met *Moltke* and *Prinz Adalbert* in the West Indies, and sailed with them as far as Queenstown (Cobh), Ireland, then proceeding independently back to Kiel via Lisbon and Gibraltar, arriving on 25 July 1887.

Following the next month's manoeuvres, *Nixe* became Wilhelmshaven guardship over the winter, before resuming the training round in April 1888. Short cruises in the Baltic were followed by a deployment to West Indian and Canadian waters, the ship returning to Kiel in September 1889. During 1890–91, she went back to American waters, joining the manoeuvres on her return in August 1891. The subsequent 1892–93 season took *Nixe* to the Mediterranean, and that of 1893–94 to the West Indies – her first cruise with cadets embarked, rather than just boys.

Decommissioned for a major refit at Danzig in March 1894, which included minor modifications to her armament – mainly the addition of two modern 8.8cm QL guns – she recommissioned in April 1897, beginning a cruise to the West Indies in September. On her return she was diverted to Kamerun to represent Germany at a prominent chief's funeral. Her 1898–99 programme took the ship to the West Indies, where she was also responsible for monitoring German interests during disturbances in Venezuela, pending relief in November by *Stosch* and *Moltke*.

In 1900, *Nixe* undertook training cruises in the North Sea and Baltic, but decommissioned on 11 August, owing to a manpower shortage. She did not recommission until November 1906. By this time her rig had been reduced, but a proper modernisation was never funded and *Nixe* never went to sea again. Rather, she was employed as a headquarters vessel for the HSF until stricken in June 1911. She then became an accommodation ship at Kiel, and later attached to the gunnery school at Sonderburg. Sold to be cut down as a lighter in 1925, she was broken up in 1930.

THE *BLITZ* CLASS

The 1873 plan had called for six avisos to be built during the following decade, the first pair being *Aviso D* [to be *Blitz*] and *Ersatz-Grille* [*Pfeil*], provided for in the 1878/79 Estimates. With their preference of machinery over sails – in the tradition of *Zieten* – they marked a major step forward, as lineal ancestors of later small cruisers. They also introduced steel in place of iron for the construction of the hull. Both initially received a light schooner rig, but proved to sail poorly due to the drag of their twin screws. They were, in any case, designed essentially for service in home waters, something emphasised by the fact that their steel hulls were not copper sheathed against marine growth: they thus needed to be docked frequently to preserve their maximum speed of 17 knots, something that could thus not be guaranteed abroad, where docking facilities were lacking.

Their armament was rather unimpressive and initially not very well suited to the likely task of fending off attacking torpedo boats: one slow-firing 12.5cm/23 gun on the forecastle as chase gun, plus four similarly antique 8.7cm/24s on the broadside. Their main weapons against torpedo boats were thus their four 3.7cm Hotchkiss revolver cannon, introduced to the German navy in 1879. The introduction into service of the *Blitz* class established the rule of thumb that any cruising vessel

Top: *Blitz* as leader of a torpedo boat division visiting the Solent during Queen Victoria's Golden Jubilee of 1887. The large flag atop the main mast denotes the presence aboard of Prince Wilhelm – a year later Kaiser Wilhelm II. **Middle:** after her 1891/92 refit, giving her a uniform armament of 8.8cm quick loaders, which – externally – mainly affected the shape of her stern bulwarks. **Bottom:** Longitudinal section of the *Pfeil* as completed. The sisters were two of the earliest ships of the German navy to receive electric searchlights, which can be seen in front of the forward funnel in the drawing and in the upper photograph. *(DN collecion)*

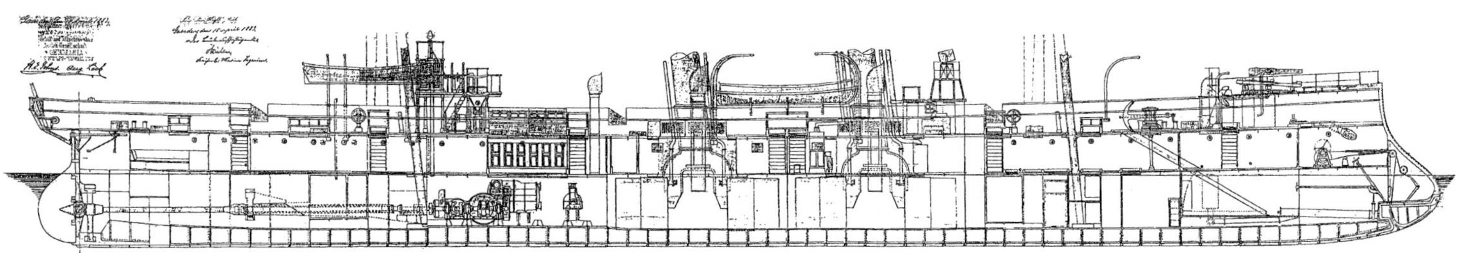

for operation in conjunction with the German fleet should have at least a 2–3 knots margin over contemporary capital ships. This was secured by firetube boilers and a pair of horizontal compound engines in both.[9]

Blitz

The lead ship was laid down by the Norddeutsche Schiffbau AG – later the Germania shipyard – at Kiel during the summer of 1881. She was launched as *Blitz* on 26 August 1882 and commissioned for trials on 28 March 1883. Her commissions during 1883 were reserved for trials, but her recommissioning on 22 April 1884 marked the true start of a long career. Her service down to September 1900 was interrupted by annual winter lay-ups, but following her subsequent recommissioning in 1903 she remained active until February 1919. *Blitz* was initially employed mainly as flotilla leader for the new torpedo boat arm, either as a separate formation or in conjunction with the fleet. The sturdiness of her construction was proven when she collided with a British merchantman in the Kattegat in 1885: the latter sank, but *Blitz* herself was little affected.

9. Previously-published statements that *Blitz* was completed with locomotive boilers is contradicted by the builder's drawings of both: see also C Busley, *Die Schiffsmaschine: ihre Construction, Wirkungsweise und Bedienung* (Kiel: Lipsius und Tischer, 1885), pp 318–319.

In 1892 *Blitz* was modernised. Instead of her antiquated original weapon-fit she received six of the now standard 8.8cm/30 QL guns, three replacing the gun on the forecastle and the aftermost broadside pair of 8.7cm weapons. Two more were installed abreast the bridge and one on the quarterdeck; to mount the latter, the bulwarks aft had to be cut down, giving the ship a markedly different profile in this area. In addition to the existing submerged bow torpedo tube, two more tubes were mounted at the waist on the main deck, in positions originally occupied by the forward pair of the old 8.7cm guns. These new tubes could discharge from 70° forward to 70° aft of the beam. The searchlight in front of the funnels was resited on the foremast, and new bridgework added in the space vacated. The original bridge before the mainmast was also raised and enlarged and a second searchlight added aft. Following with this reconstruction, *Blitz* additionally served as training vessel for torpedo boat stokers, although her new firetube boilers did not reflect the locomotive type still fitted in most small boats of the time.

During the final years of the 1890s, *Blitz* assisted *Zieten* in the fishery protection role but was also, when required, employed as scout for the battlefleet. From 1900 she underwent a major refit at Danzig Dockyard, which lasted until 1903 and included the removal of the broadside torpedo tubes added in 1892. Henceforth her principal task was to serve as a tender to divisions or squadrons of battleships. *Blitz* was thus permanently based at Wilhelmshaven, serving the I. Sqn, in which capacity she served throughout the First World War. It was not until as late as March 1921 that the venerable *Blitz* was finally stricken from the list, to be sold and broken up at Wilhelmshaven.

Blitz was one of the few vessels to outlive her 'legal' replacement, the small cruiser *Nürnberg* (i) [*Ersatz-Blitz*]. Interestingly, and reflecting the vagaries of contemporary German government bureaucracy, it was not until nearly two years after the first commissioning of her 'replacement' that *Blitz* was re-designated as a special duty vessel. Therefore between 1908 and 1910 both *Blitz* and her 'replacement' were carried together on the navy list as cruisers.

Pfeil

The second ship of the class was laid down at the same time as her sister, in her case at Wilhelmshaven, but was launched, as *Pfeil*, three weeks later than *Blitz*, on 16 September 1882. She completed in 1883, but her commissioning for trials was postponed until 25 November 1884 for reasons unknown. The initial trials were very short, and *Pfeil* decommissioned on 9 December. Her first operational commission began on 22 June 1885 and lasted only until October, the pattern being repeated in 1887, *Pfeil* serving as a scout for the Manoeuvre Squadron during the summer months.

In contrast to her sister's service only in home waters, *Pfeil* went as far as East Africa during her next commission in 1889, helping to interdict the region's slave trade, accounting for more than 400 inspections of dhows and other vessels – the most of any participating vessel. During this service, it became increasingly evident that her unsheathed steel hull was – in the absence of local docking facilities – unsuitable for tropical regions, and at the end of September 1889 she was called home to take up her originally intended duties with the fleet.

After a short lay-up, she escorted the Kaiser on a visit to Christiana (Oslo), subsequently serving as a scout for a battle squadron formed by three vessels of the *Sachsen* class, plus *Oldenburg*, during the year's manoeuvres. Later in the year, she joined the training squadron detached to the Mediterranean for the winter months. Her service continued throughout 1891 and

The only known image of *Pfeil* painted in white/buff colours for service abroad, pictured at Wilhelmshaven. Note the electric searchlight on the platform on the quarterdeck. *(DN collection)*

Pfeil after her 1892/94 rearmament refit. Her new chase gun on the forecastle is very prominent, as are her semaphores on the foretopmast. The scrollwork at the bow serves as an easy means to distinguish between the sisters: *Pfeil* always carried her more substantial scroll at a lower level than the narrower decoration on the uppermost strake of *Blitz*'s bow. *(DN collection)*

did not terminate until March 1892, when she paid off for the same major refit as her sister. *Pfeil* returned to service in April 1894 for nineteen months, and in August 1897 for another thirteen months. During the latter period she was employed in various roles: besides her core role of scout, she served as a training vessel for engineers and as a fishery protection vessel. In 1900 she returned to service only briefly, before undergoing a major overhaul.

Pfeil's next commission, from March 1904, became a permanent one, lasting until December 1918. Like her sister, she mainly served as a tender to units of larger vessels, in her case II. squadron. As with *Blitz*, her nominal replacement by the small cruiser *Emden* in 1909 did not initially change her status: it was only in December 1910 that she was reclassified as a special duties vessel, which in turn had no effect on her actual employment. During the war she continued to serve her squadron until its dissolution in 1917, when she was attached to the new IV. squadron. In addition, she served as mother ship for picket formations and as a target vessel for submarine training units. *Pfeil* was stricken in February 1922 and was subsequently broken up at Wilhelmshaven.

Greif lying alongside at Wilhelmshaven during one of her first commissions, still carrying her original – inadequate – main armament of two 10.5cm-RK, visible on forecastle and poop. The lower image shows her after her 1891 rearmament with eight 8.8cm-QL, and now wearing the grey paint scheme. *(DN collection)*

GREIF

As torpedo boats got faster, the vessels intended to lead them, the avisos, had to follow suit. At the beginning of the 1880s, the 16 knots of *Blitz* and *Pfeil* had seemed to be sufficient, but only four years later, when the design of *Ersatz-Loreley* [to be *Greif*] was prepared, a design speed of 18 knots for the proposed new ship was a firm requirement. This meant that several military qualities had to be subordinated to an enlarged machinery plant, which now consisted of six double-ended firetube boilers feeding two compound engines delivering a total of 5,400ihp, twice the output provided in the *Blitz* class. Her hull was made of steel, without any sheathing, and was divided into twelve watertight compartments.

Because of the weight devoted to her machinery, *Greif*'s armament was weak for her size, and inadequate for her intended tasks. Initially, it consisted of two slow-firing 10.5cm/35 guns, supported by ten 3.7cm Hotchkiss revolver-cannon. When the new 8.8cm/30 QL gun became available, her battery was changed (in 1891) to comprise eight examples of this model, supported by four 0.8cm machine guns. Except where the coal bunkers ran adjacent to the boiler rooms there was no protection whatsoever.

Greif's career was uneventful. She commissioned for the first time for trials in July 1887, decommissioning three months later, after an extended cruise up to the Shetlands. In the spring of 1889 she recommissioned, first acting as a fishery protection vessel, later in the year as escort for the Kaiser during his first cruise into Norwegian waters aboard his yacht *Hohenzollern*.[10] This took her as far north as the North Cape, and afterwards to Cowes in the UK. Following another lay-up, *Greif* was employed from the autumn of 1890 by the newly founded Torpedo Trials Command – without being herself equipped with any torpedo tubes! – rarely operating beyond the Kiel Bight. In 1893 she spent nearly six months out of commission for a major overhaul, returning to service for another year, before she was withdrawn from the Torpedo Trials Command in October 1894 to be laid up.

In May 1897, *Greif* was reactivated as a scout and repeating ship for the battlefleet, but after a short-lived employment as flagship of the I. Sqn, substituting for the battleship *Kurfürst Friedrich Wilhelm*, she passed into the hands of Wilhelmshaven Dockyard for a major overhaul of her worn-out boilers. In May 1898, *Greif* returned for another year of squadron work before she became a training vessel for the Artillery Inspectorate. In this capacity, she received in 1899 the first German example of 'ray-telegraphy' equipment, soon to be known as wireless telegraphy (W/T).

During the summer of 1900, *Greif* was employed one more time as escort to the Norwegian summer cruise of the Kaiser – very much an exception to the emerging rule of employing the fleet's newest small cruiser for this duty of honour – before her active career ended on 22 September of that year. *Greif* was then overhauled in 1901, including a complete reboilering and the

10. She would be replaced by a new *Hohenzollern* (ii) in 1892, and be re-named *Kaiseradler*.

exchange of two 8.8cm-guns for four 3.7cm machine cannon, but never sailed again. In 1912 she was finally stricken, but her hull was retained, becoming a storage hulk for mines in the Kiel fjord in 1917. The ship was finally broken up in 1921.

IRENE CLASS

Ersatz-Elisabeth [to become *Irene*] and *Ersatz-Ariadne* [*Prinzeß Wilhelm*] had their origins in the establishment of the so-called 'Admiralty Council' by Caprivi in January 1884. As a soldier by profession, he recognised the need for a team of naval experts to advise him on the future shaping of the navy in general, and its future vessels in particular. For future cruising vessels, the Council produced the following list of essential requirements, which would form – with modifications, of course – the baseline for new vessels:

- Seaworthiness – As intended for worldwide operations, the new vessels should be able to withstand any seaway and climate conditions, while combined with moderate draught.
- Speed – As the most modern merchant vessels were already able to evade recent intended raiders, the new vessels must be given sufficient speed to catch up with such merchantmen, as well as the most likely naval opponents.
- Radius of Action – Because of Germany lacked secure, or even friendly, supply bases around the globe, the vessels would need a relatively high endurance to avoid being located by an enemy.
- Armament – The intended armament must be of a calibre superior to that generally fitted in armed merchant cruisers or other protectors of trade but, on the other hand, total armament-weights should not exceed 5–8 per cent of displacement.
- Rigging – In view of the intended large cruising radius the installation of at least some auxiliary sails still seemed to be required.

These requirements already had the potential to initiate a vicious circle of size and cost growth, but this tendency was further increased by a demand that they should be capable of fulfilling the role of true 'fleet cruisers' if necessary. To make things worse, the German navy was in any case chronically affected by a scarcity of funds and an unwillingness by politicians to grant even minimal appropriations for the navy.

The resulting trade-offs meant that the resulting vessels were neither well suited for fleet work nor for the increasing tasks in distant waters. In recognition of this, Caprivi, facing the Reichstag budgetary commission, urged caution regarding the lead vessel's likely success: 'At the same time, any further progress in the construction of cruising vessels will rather not be advisable until it will be confirmed if the required vessel, preliminarily listed under the name Ersatz-*Elisabeth*, fulfils expectations and is able to serve as pattern for future construction.'

The general design of *Ersatz-Elisabeth* that had emerged was derived from the above mentioned requirements but displayed influences from the privately designed 'armoured deck corvette' *Tsi Yuen*, then under construction for China by AG Vulcan at Stettin (see pp 167-168, below). The Chinese vessel's greatest contribution came in the form of her armour deck, a feature that was now to be installed for the first time on a German

Irene after her launch on 23 July 1887, alongside the fitting out quay at AG Vulcan, Stettin. The sponsons for the guns and hull openings show clearly on the bare hull. *(DN collection)*

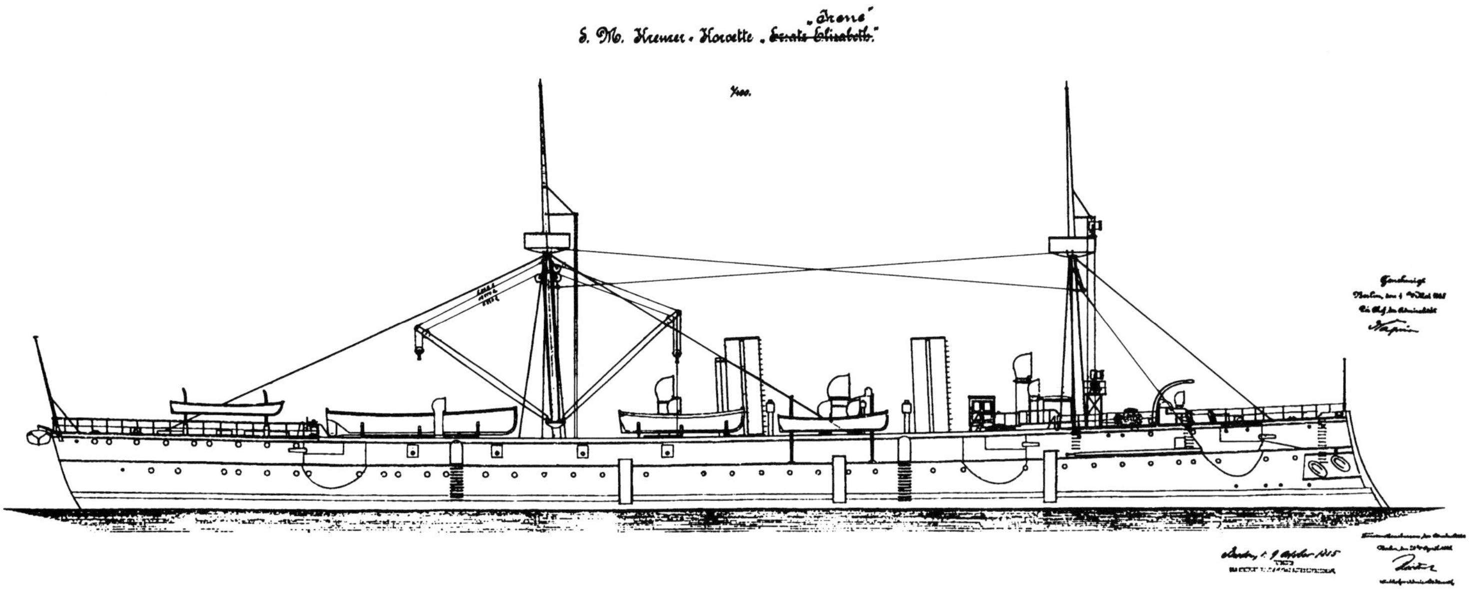

The original rigging plan for *Ersatz Elisabeth* – later *Irene* – signed on 26 April 1885 by Alfred Dietrich and countersigned by Caprivi on 1 May 1885. *(DN collection)*

cruising vessel. Its inclusion was a clear indication of the intended suitability for fleet duty, since this feature had never been regarded as particularly important for service abroad – and a lack of armour had been one of the reasons for the failure to use the *Leipzig* class for fleet service (p 32, above).

A second feature was the absence of even the modest sail plan, which had been regarded essential for cruising vessels only a few months before. However, scepticism about the likely economy of the engine plant as the sole means of propulsion were well founded. Despite an enlargement of the displacement by 700 tonnes compared with the cruiser originally envisaged by the council, the endurance remained only 2,500nm at 9 knots, mainly due to the uneconomical horizontal compound engines: this was quite unacceptable for a cruising vessel with

Irene, as completed with short funnels. Note the bright paint on the inside of the opened gun ports, which would soon disappear (compare with the image below). *(DN collection)*

aspirations for overseas service! Completed with short funnels, these were raised before the ships were first deployed abroad.

The new type's gunnery outfit was superficially impressive: fourteen guns of 15cm-calibre, supported by six 3.7cm Hotchkiss revolver-cannon and three 35cm torpedo tubes. A closer look, however, revealed the weakness of this initial outfit: none of the 15cm guns were quick loaders and only four of them – installed in sponsons – were relatively modern 35-calibre pieces. The remaining ten were antiquated 22-calibre weapons with mediocre ballistic capabilities: but nothing better was available at the time.

Irene

The keel of *Irene*, named for the wife (1866–1953) of Prince Heinrich of Prussia[11] – who would be the captain of the ship during 1889/90 – was laid as late as May 1886, but would be launched on 23 July 1887. Commissioned for trials on 25 May 1888, she was then laid up, and recommissioned for the first time for active service on 1 April 1889, as the first 'modern' cruising vessel of the Imperial navy. Her first deployment was as part of the Manoeuvre Squadron in home waters until September, when she sailed to the Mediterranean to join the Training Squadron, initially as part of the Kaiser's entourage during his visit to Athens to attend the marriage of his sister Sophie to the Greek Crown Prince Constantine in October. *Irene* remained in the Mediterranean until April 1890, when she returned to Germany in company with the Training Squadron. The remaining time until her decommissioning on 18 September was spent as part of the II. Division of the Manoeuvre Squadron in the Baltic and the North Sea.

The next four years were spent decommissioned at Wilhelmshaven, during which time, in 1893, she underwent an

11. Brother of the recently -enthroned Kaiser Wilhelm II.

Irene while deployed to the Mediterranean during 1889–90. Initially equipped with anti-torpedo nets, these were soon removed, as both clumsy and too prone to rusting. *(DN collection)*

extensive refit, including rearmament. The four 15cm/35 guns were retained to provide a lethal punch at short ranges, where the slow rate of fire was of lesser importance, but the ten old 22-cal pieces were replaced by eight of the now-available 10.5cm/35 QL guns, which essentially became the ship's principal artillery. Six 5cm/40 QL guns were also installed, a pair on the poop, a pair in the waist and a pair abreast the foremast. The roofs of the 15cm/35 sponsons were also lowered, the bulwarks between them halved in height, and the hawseholes raised by one deck. The refit coincided with the ship's reclassification as a 'II. class cruiser' (see pp 84-85, below); five years later, she would become a 'small cruiser' (pp 97-98).

In the wake of the outbreak of the Sino-Japanese war in the summer of 1894, the East Asiatic Cruiser Division was formed; its forerunner, the Cruiser Squadron, had been disbanded by the Kaiser in 1893 following tensions with the Reichstag over the annual budget (see pp 86-87, below). Soon, however, it was realised that the available material now consisted of only outdated cruiser corvettes, which were considered inadequate to deal with the emerging events in East Asia. Thus, *Irene* was recommissioned on 1 November 1894 for service in the newly formed division, and arrived at Chefoo on 14 February 1895 to take over the flagship duties from *Arcona*.

After some reconnaissance cruises along the Chinese coast during the final days of the war, *Irene* was relieved of her flagship duties on 10 July, when KAdm Paul Hoffmann (1846–1917) shifted his flag to the newly arrived large cruiser (ex-ironclad) *Kaiser*. Hoffmann had mixed feelings about *Irene*'s value as his part-time flagship: on one hand he saw her as a impressive-looking vessel, well suited for showing the flag abroad; on the other hand, he was concerned about the 'coal-gorging' proclivities of her twin-shaft compound machinery, which made her distinctly unsuitable in the vastness of Southeast Asia and Micronesia with its small numbers of coaling stations.

During the next few years, *Irene* spent her life between the various ports from Hong Kong in the south and Hakodate in the north. Summers saw a customary cruise into the northern areas of the station, with calls at Vladivostok and various Japanese ports, while winters were often spent under overhaul at Hong Kong.

Because of the latter, she was not present during the German occupation of the Kiaochow Bay in November 1897 (p 83). The previous year, *Irene* had been sent to the Philippines, with Tirpitz, the new squadron commander, on board, to observe the rising tensions between the native population and the Spanish administration, which would eventually lead to an uprising and contribute to the outbreak of the Spanish-American war. But at the turn of 1896–97 there seemed to be no need for intervention in support of German interests, and *Irene* returned to Chinese waters. Shortly after the occupation of Kiaochow, with a II. Cruiser Division already on the way from Germany, the existing unit was renamed the I. Cruiser Division, the two together forming the East Asiatic Cruiser Squadron under the command of VAdm Otto von Diederichs (1843–1918).

Soon afterwards, the Philippines came back into focus and *Irene* experienced her share of the antagonism built up between the US and German navies after the Battle of Manila Bay on 1 May 1898. Together with the IV.-class cruiser *Cormoran*, she arrived at Manila on 6 May to guard German interests in the international, as well as the local, conflict. On 27 June she was searched by US blockading forces while entering the bay. Diederichs protested against this measure as the blockade had not yet been recognised by the foreign powers present; nevertheless, the situation was de-escalated by sending *Irene* back to the recently acquired German naval base of Tsingtau (Qingdao: see p 83, below).

The quarrel was, however, revived shortly after her return to Manila in November, when she was accused of not having properly acknowledged the flag of the US RAdm George Dewey, but this dispute was settled soon afterwards. The year 1899 would bring no special excitements, except for the usual summer cruise into northern waters. In contrast, the year 1900 brought the outbreak of the Boxer Rebellion in June, a large-scale anti-foreigner movement in China that focussed on a siege of the Legation Quarter of Peking (Beijing), where foreigners and Chinese Christians had taken refuge.

An eight-nation intervention coalition (US, Austria-Hungary, UK, France, Germany, Italy, Japan and Russia) was established, the key naval action being an attack on the Taku (Dagu) forts, at the mouth of the Peiho (Hai) River and the gateway to Tianjin and Peking, in June 1900. Although a number of coalition warships – including the German *Iltis* (ii) – were damaged by Chinese gunfire, the forts were taken by landing parties, while four Chinese destroyers were captured at their moorings. As a result, the Chinese Empress Dowager declared war on the coalition, leading to Imperial forces joining the irregulars besieging the Legations. Tianjin itself was captured in July, and coalition forces reached Peking and relieved the Legations in August. Hostilities and coalition occupation continued, however, until September 1901.

At sea, the coalition supported the occupation of a number of Chinese ports, as well as patrols off the coast and on major rivers. The Germans were represented by the East Asiatic Squadron, reinforced by ships from other stations including, from the end of August until the summer of 1901, the four *Brandenburg*-class battleships and the small cruiser *Hela* from home waters (cf pp 72, 88). As the oldest vessel on the station, *Irene* was largely employed as guardship at Tsingtau. With the end of the war approaching, she was ordered home in June 1901, together with the newer small cruiser *Gefion* (ii). *Irene* decommissioned at Danzig on 1 October 1901 – never to be recalled to service.

She received a modest reconstruction at Wilhelmshaven Dockyard in 1903–05, comprising mainly of the installation of a searchlight on the foremast, an enlargement of her bunker capacity, and – in compensation – a reduction of the 15cm ammunition outfit by two-thirds. However, she remained in reserve until February 1914, when she was stricken. Already employed as accommodation hulk for submarine crews at Kiel since December 1913, she remained in this capacity throughout the war and was eventually broken up at Wilhelmshaven in 1921.

Prinzeß Wilhelm

The career of *Prinzeß Wilhelm*, named for Augusta Victoria of Schleswig-Holstein, wife of Prince Wilhelm (1858–1921, soon to become Crown-Princess and then Kaiserin), mirrored in many ways that of her sister vessel. Despite being authorised a year later, under the 1886–87 Estimates, her keel was laid at the same time as that of *Irene*, in May 1886, on the slip of the Germaniawerft, Kiel. Christened on 22 September 1887 by her eponymous princess, she undertook extended trials between November 1889 and March 1890. Her first operational commission began only on 16 April 1891, with another spell of trials, before being used as escort to the Imperial yacht *Hohenzollern* during the annual summer cruise to Norway by the Kaiser. Several special duties followed, including serving in the Kaiser's escort during his meeting with the Russian Emperor Alexander III at Stettin in June 1892, and another summer cruise to Norway. Afterwards *Prinzeß Wilhelm* represented Germany at the celebrations for the 500th anniversary of Columbus's first voyage in Italy and Spain, before she decommissioned on 14 November.

During her lay-up, she received her new armament and raised funnels, prior to recommissioning on 10 October 1893 as Wilhelmshaven guardship. Rather oddly for such a modern cruiser, she served as a training vessel for engineers and stokers during the first half of 1894. This was followed by a short stint in the ranks of the Scouting Group of the fleet, and again as escort to the Kaiser, before she returned to her harbour duties at Wilhelmshaven.

However, after the formation of the East Asiatic Cruiser Division, it was just a matter of time before *Prinzeß Wilhelm*, like her sister, would receive her call to the Far East. She thus sailed on 27 April 1894, but this timing proved disastrous, since it took the poorly-ventilated cruiser through the Red Sea as temperatures soared. As a result, several crew members suffered from heatstroke and subsequently died, highlighting the class's unsuitability for duty in the tropics.

On 4 July 1894 *Prinzeß Wilhelm* joined her sister at Shanghai. For the next few years the histories the two vessels matched very closely. One exception was in May 1896, when *Prinzeß Wilhelm* was ordered to ascend the Yangtse river up to Nanking, to suppress insubordination by trainees at the local military school against their German instructors. After staying about four weeks at the waterfront, KKpt Henning von Holtzendorff decided to sail further upstream, reaching Hankow on 11 July, the largest German warship yet to get this far. The remaining months of the year were spent with the recovery of the dead from the gunboat *Iltis*, wrecked on the

Freshly recommissioned after refit, *Prinzeß Wilhelm* lies alongside at Wilhelmshaven in 1893. Besides the lengthened funnels, the reduction in height of the midships bulwarks is clearly visible, as is the change in the position of the hawse pipes forward. *(DN collection)*

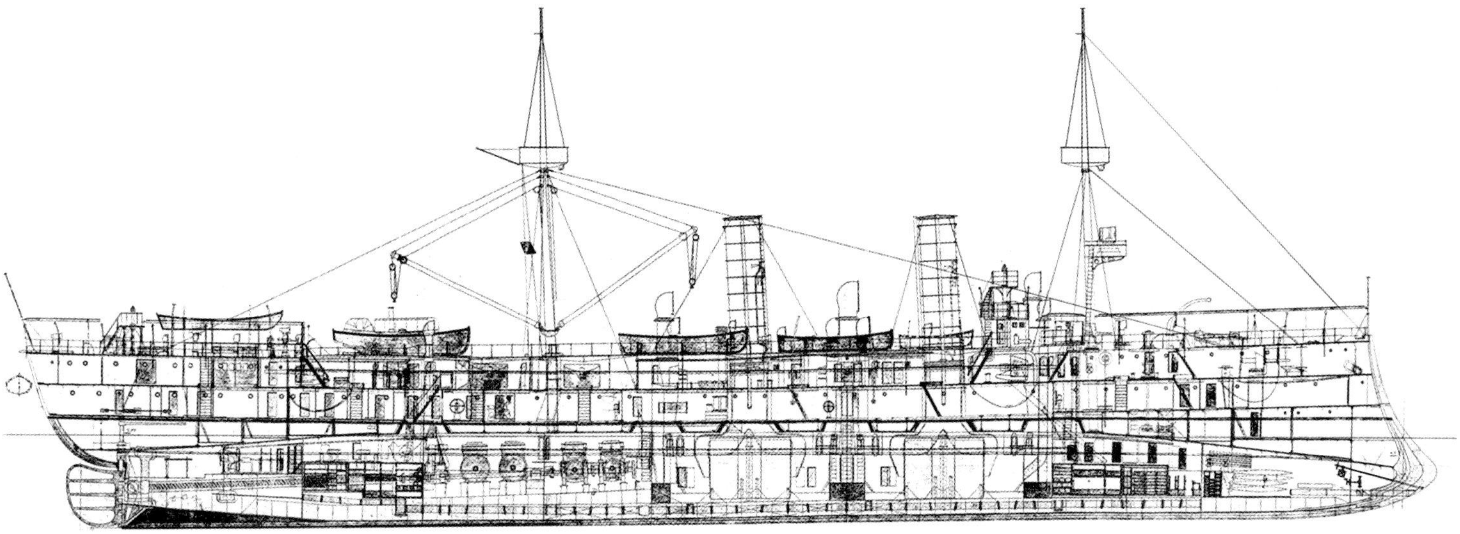

Immediately after their respective returns to Germany from the Far East in 1899 and 1901, *Prinzeß Wilhelm* and *Irene* were still regarded as having future operational value, and thus received a modest reconstruction. This longitudinal section incorporates the work to be undertaken. It is interesting to note the similarity in the profile of their hulls with that of the smaller *Bussard* class (see below). *(DN collection)*

coast of the Shantung peninsula in late July, the first German visit to Kiaochow Bay and an extended stay at Nagasaki for a major overhaul of the engines.

Unlike her sister, *Prinzeß Wilhelm* was present at the occupation of Kiaochow in November 1897; both of them were present during the Manila incidents of 1898. On 26 April 1899, *Prinzeß Wilhelm* sailed for home and reached Wilhelmshaven on 22 July to decommission. In local dockyard hands for modernisation until 1902, like her sister she did not commission again. Stricken on the same day as *Irene*, her hull was used as a floating mine depot during the war. Sold in 1921, she was broken up at Wilhelmshaven the following year.

THE *WACHT* CLASS

Rather than following the leap in size seen in *Greif*, the next batch of avisos reverted to smaller dimensions. While maintaining their function as battlefleet scouts, the role of leading torpedo boat flotillas had now largely passed to the newly introduced 'division boats' – larger torpedo boats that could accommodate a division's staff and thus lead their division or flotilla during an attack. These became models for the flotilla leaders of other navies, but in the German navy they soon became an evolutionary dead end with the introduction of the large torpedo boat in the form of the *S90* class, in which one boat of a series was normally specially equipped as leader.

The lead-ship of the new pair of avisos, provided for in the 1886–87 Estimates, was an addition to strength under the designation *Aviso E* [to be *Wacht*], whereas her sister, authorised a year later [to be *Jagd*], replaced the obsolete aviso *Pommerania*. The new vessels' design was more militarily capable compared with their predecessor *Greif*. Besides the installation of a turtleback protective deck, 20mm thick on the flat, and 40mm thick on the slopes, both received a true ram, despite their small size and their weak scantlings. Three 35cm torpedo tubes were fitted, one discharging forward and two in the waist on swivel mounts, indicating that they were intended to be employed in the melee that was expected to be the culmination of a fleet action, and ram bigger – probably disabled – adversaries. Against the more mobile torpedo craft these weapons were useless.

From the gunnery point of view, they suffered the same shortcomings as *Greif*, since they initially received identical slow-firing 10.5cm/35 guns. Two were positioned abreast forward of the conning tower, while the third was in a rather exposed position on the poop, close to the stern. Like most other pre-1890 vessels, they were re-gunned when quick loaders became available, two 8.8cm/30 guns replacing the forward weapons, another two being fitted in lieu of the single gun aft. The hull below the protective deck of *Wacht* and her

Wacht at Kiel during one of her first commissions. She still carries the old 10.5cm RK as main armament (one of which can be seen at the stern), which would be exchanged to four 8.8cm QL in 1891. Beyond her may be seen the ironclad *Oldenburg* and, far in the distance over her bows, the ironclad *Sachsen*. *(DN collection)*

sister was so narrow that their 3-cylinder triple-expansion main engines had to be stepped longitudinally, and both of the cylinder blocks had to be inclined to fit properly. Locomotive boilers had to be fitted, since there was no room for normal firetube boilers. Sea keeping remained a constant challenge in anything more than calm weather, as was manoeuvrability, due to the high length to beam ratio. Both were notorious as bad rollers for the same reason.

Wacht was laid down on 1 November 1886 by the AG Weser yard at Bremen as their first vessel built from steel. She was launched on 27 August 1887 and sailed on 31 March 1888 to Bremerhaven for a final docking before her acceptance trials could start. These did not progress as intended and additional trial runs had to be inserted into the programme before the vessel was accepted by the navy at the beginning of May. Afterwards, *Wacht* sailed to Wilhelmshaven for the installation of the armament, and finally, on 9 August, she was officially commissioned, for another set of trials, now in the navy's hands, which ended in December. Her first commission, with the Manoeuvre Fleet, began on 1 May 1889 and included exercises in the Baltic as well as a participation at the Kaiser's visit to Cowes Week in the UK. Afterwards, she was transferred to the Training Squadron in the Mediterranean. Back home at Wilhelmshaven, she decommissioned on 6 March 1890: her boilers were already in need of an extended overhaul, which was combined with the abovementioned change of armament.

Her next commission lasted almost exactly one year – from October 1891 to October 1892. *Wacht* spent most of it in the Baltic as part of the II. Division of the Manoeuvre Fleet, whose exercises in spring 1892 extended as far as the southern coast of Norway. After a rather short lay-up, she returned to service on 13 January 1893, first as a training vessel for stokers and engineers, and from April, for the first time, in her originally intended role as a leader of torpedo-boats. This ended with the disbanding of I. TBF for the winter in September and her subsequent decommissioning in October.

For 1894, *Wacht* commissioned as the aviso for the II. Division of the Manoeuvre Fleet; unfortunately she suffered a collision with the ironclad *Deutschland* in July, which resulted in a three-week stay in Kiel Dockyard. After her return she swapped places with *Pfeil*, to serve with the I. Division. This service was terminated prematurely owing to extensive engine defects, which forced her into the hands of Wilhelmshaven Dockyard in December.

In March 1896, she joined the newly designated I. Sqn of the Manoeuvre Fleet for nearly fourteen months, mainly occupied with her usual job as scouting vessel for the squadron. During her subsequent lay-up period, in the wake of the First Naval Law she was redesignated as a small cruiser, and recomm-

A superb image of *Jagd* at Kiel, in her final configuration. *(DN collection)*

issioned as such in April 1899 for the II. Division of the I. Sqn. In September she suffered a boiler explosion in Danish waters that killed four and wounded another five crew members. The ironclad *Bayern* initially towed her to Kiel, prior to *Wacht* being decommissioned at Wilhelmshaven for repairs.

Wacht's last employment commenced on 11 August 1901, when she joined I. Scouting Group in the North Sea. At the end of the month the fleet transferred to the Baltic for the autumn manoeuvres in the Danzig Bight. During the transit, the CinC, Adm Hans von Koester (1844–1928), took every opportunity to exercise his squadrons, and on 4 September, in the waters north of the island of Rügen, he ordered an initial eight-point turn to port for the whole fleet. In doing so, he did not take into account the fact that *Wacht*'s steering engine had previously broken down, and that the vessel was thus being steered by hand, greatly increasing her already large turning circle. She was thus unable to conform to the fleet's movements and crossed the bow of the ironclad *Sachsen*, which was unable to avoid her. *Sachsen*'s ram did its work and tore a large hole in the hull of *Wacht* amidships. She was eventually sunk as the result of progressive flooding, although the whole crew was saved.[12]

Jagd was initially intended to be authorised alongside her sister, but cuts in the 1886–87 budget postponed this for one year. She was ultimately laid down on the same slip used for *Wacht*, and was launched on 7 July 1888 as the first vessel to enter the water during the reign of the new Kaiser Wilhelm II. On 8 June 1889, the vessel was delivered by her builders to the German navy, which initially commissioned her for trials on 25 June. These were interrupted on 6 August and recommenced on 15 April 1890, lasting until the end of June, at which time *Jagd* was included in the Kaiser's escort for his visit to Norway. At the beginning of October, she decommissioned to undergo the same rearmament as *Wacht*.

The ship's 1891 commission was short, from April to October, and included, besides being employed for a period as guardship at Wilhelmshaven, another period as escort to the Kaiser's yacht. *Jagd*'s next commission began in October 1892 and lasted nearly one year. Beginning with another spell as Wilhelmshaven guardship, it continued with use as scout for the fleet during the annual manoeuvres. The following fifteen months were spent in reserve and dockyards hands for reboilering. Back in service in March 1895, the following month she had the distinction of being the first vessel, for test purposes, ever to transit the Kaiser-Wilhelm (Kiel) Canal. The remaining months of the year saw her employment with the Manoeuvre Fleet before the still customary winter lay up interrupted her activities between December and March 1896.

12. There was a story circulating in the German navy that on the very day a despatch vessel arrived on the scene with the spare part for her steering engine. Asking for her actual position and the best way for delivering it to *Wacht* he received the classical response: 'Throw it overboard – *Wacht* is located below you!'

Next followed an uninterrupted employment for two years as scout for the I. Sqn of the Manoeuvre Fleet. *Jagd*'s final commission began in September 1899 as replacement for her sister in the I. Sqn before being employed in the capacity of fishery protection cruiser during October/November 1900. She was part of the German delegation – led by the Kaiser in *Hohenzollern* - attending the passage of Queen Victoria's body from the Isle of Wight to the mainland, and subsequent ceremonies, during January/February 1901. She then continued in service with the fleet until July, when her condition was found to be so poor that she had to be immediately decommissioned on 11 August. Although her legal replacement (which would become the 1907-programmed *Mainz*) was still several years away, no funds were made available for repairs, *Jagd* being relegated to harbour service in May 1904. Stricken in 1910, she remained in existence as a hulk for the torpedo works at Friedrichsort, just north of Kiel, being scrapped in 1920 at Wilhelmshaven.

THE *METEOR* CLASSES

The construction of the follow-on *Avisos F* [to be *Meteor*] and *G* [*Comet*] is difficult to explain on objective grounds. The *Wacht* class were already of marginal utility, yet how the intended capabilities of the aviso type were supposed to be achieved by vessels 20 per cent smaller is nowhere properly explained in the files – although doubtless the ongoing scarcity of funds in combination with a general lack of direction in naval planning played an important role. Contemporary unofficial publications seem nevertheless to have been quite satisfied with the type in general, although influenced by the fact that their speed was grossly exaggerated, reported as either '3-5 knots higher than that of *Wacht* and *Jagd*' or that 'the guaranteed speed will be 21 knots'.

Such speeds may indeed have been intended initially through the installation of engines of 4,500/5,000ihp, now sandwiched between two boiler rooms. Each held two boilers, with two fireboxes each, thus doubling the number of the latter as compared with the *Wacht*s. Installed power was thus significantly above that in their larger predecessors' 4,000ihp, but any expectations of significantly higher speeds seem to have been brought down to earth rather early on, as the new ships' design speed was always recorded officially as the same 19 knots. During trials it was surpassed only marginally (*Meteor*) or not at all (*Comet*). The worst feature of both was their unacceptable endurance of less than 1,000nm at economical speed. In view of this it becomes even less comprehensible why *Comet* was laid down to the very same plans months after *Meteor*'s shortcomings had already been revealed by her trials. The best that probably can be said about these two vessels is that they carried modern QL guns from the beginning and that their shortcomings clearly led to a rethinking of the qualities required in a true aviso, which resulted eventually in the construction of *Hela* (cf p 87,

Meteor, operating together with some boats in Kiel bay. The raised double-cone signal at the gaff indicates the ship to be stopped, while the raised starboard cone (the port cone is invisible) indicates the rudder lying hard a starboard. *(DN collection)*

below) – one of the two ingredients that, a few years later, would produce the German-style small cruiser.

The keel of *Aviso F* was laid in December 1888 by the Germania shipyard at Kiel. Her building proceeded rather slowly so that her launch took place more than a year later, on 20 January 1890. The new vessel received the traditional name *Meteor*, after the gunboat of 1870 fame. A year later, at the beginning of 1891, the first trials commenced. On 15 May, *Meteor* was commissioned for the first time as guardship at Kiel, before even completing her trials. This commission lasted only until the end of July, when it was interrupted for three weeks for necessary modifications. The second commission was even shorter – 28 August–3 October – after which *Meteor* was returned to dockyard hands for even more extensive modifications. These included the extension of the funnels to reduce the amount of smoke being blown on to the quarterdeck in headwinds, as well as strengthening of some scantlings in an attempt to reduce serious vibration at higher speeds.

Meteor's next commission began in May 1892, first as guardship at Kiel again, later as leader of the II. TBF. During this she was joined by the Kaiser in November for a cruise. His interest may have been caused by the fact that officially her trials were still ongoing: only with the ship's decommissioning in December 1892 were these officially terminated. Both subsequent commissions, in 1893 and 1894, would last only for the summer months. In 1893 she was employed as scout for the I. Division of the Manoeuvre Fleet; in 1894 she escorted *Hohenzollern* to Norway but was sent home early because of engine trouble. In 1895, *Meteor* became a fishery protection vessel for the summer months, a task that was repeated the following year when, in May, she had to intervene against British fishermen close to the island of Norderney. The same month saw her take on the additional function of training vessel for engineers and stokers. Briefly employed as scout in the annual autumn manoeuvres, *Meteor* was decommissioned for the final time on 4 October 1896. In May 1903, she was officially reduced to harbour service vessel until being struck from the list in June 1911. The hulk was subsequently used as accommodation for submarine crews until the end of 1918. She was finally broken up in 1919 at Audorf.

Comet as a mine storage hulk in the port of Emden, after 1913. Behind her is the converted minelaying cruiser *Arcona* (iii). *(DN collection)*

This image of the newly commissioned *Schwalbe* shows the arrangement of various sponsons and gun ports of her initial configuration very well, in particular thanks to her fresh white paint for service abroad. *(DN collection)*

The keel of *Aviso G* was laid in November 1891. Its pace of construction is reported to have been slowed down deliberately to gain data from the trials of *Meteor*. Thus, it came that at her launch, on 15 November 1892, all machinery and boilers had already been installed, which reduced her outfitting time significantly. On 9 April 1893 she sailed from Swinemünde for her initial shipyard trials, followed by her commissioning at Kiel for the commencement of the official trials.[13] These lasted until 6 July, when she was decommissioned for the following eleven months. In 1894 her commission lasted for a meagre twenty-five days in June, while in 1895 she was not commissioned at all, although she underwent some modifications in dockyards hands. For the consequent trials, *Comet* was commissioned for one more period, from 22 January until 2 May 1896. After that date she was laid-up indefinitely. In May 1904 she was officially reduced to harbour service until she was stricken, alongside her sister, in June 1911. Her hulk was used as mine depot for the small cruiser/minelayer *Arcona* at Emden until the end of the First World War. She was finally broken up in 1921 at Hamburg.

THE *SCHWALBE* CLASS

The acquisition of a network of colonies by Germany generated a requirement to enhance the long-standing naval mission of protecting German overseas interests: no longer was it sufficient to simply deploy small gunboats, backed up, as necessary, by the Cruiser Squadron. Accordingly, there was a need for larger and more capable vessels to be based permanently in the colonies to supplement the gunboats.

As previously noted, the *Habicht* class gunboats had been reclassified as 'cruisers' in 1884, although only marginally above the new cruiser/gunboat dividing line established in that year. However, the next generation of station vessels for over-

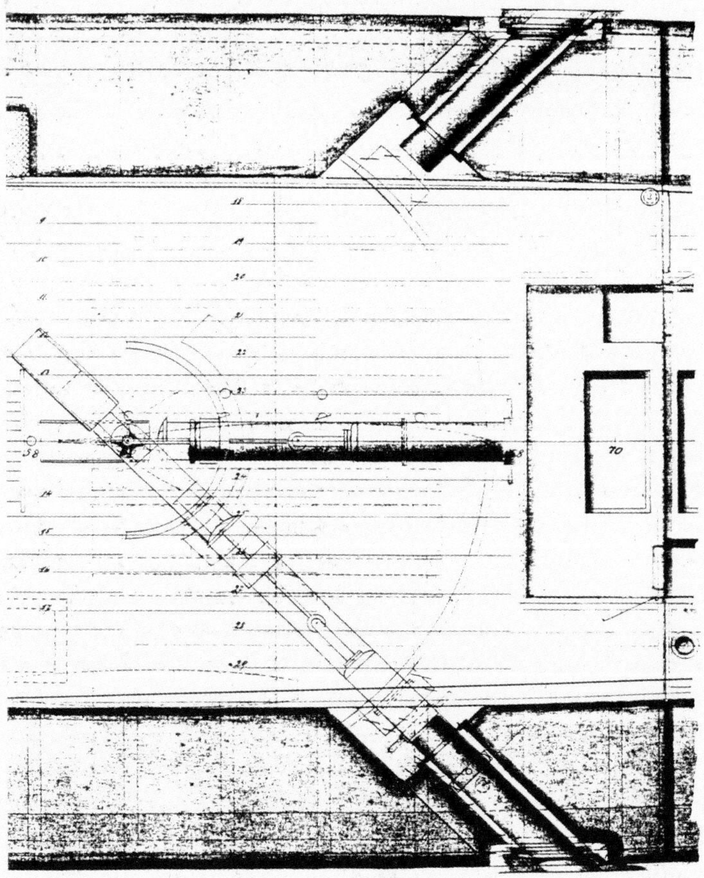

The highly unusual arrangement for mounting a single torpedo tube in the between deck on board *Schwalbe* and *Sperber*, capable of firing on either side of ship. *(DN collection)*

13. Her date of commissioning is given by H H Hildebrand, A Röhr and H-O Steinmetz, *Die Deutschen Kriegsschiffe: Biographien – ein Spiegel der Marinegeschichte von 1815 bis zur Gegenwart* ([Ratingen]: Mundus Verlag, [1997]), vol 2, p 187, as 29 April, with her captain's name unknown. However, a contemporary newspaper reports the date as, rather, 8 May, with a KKpt Jaeckel in command. This seems not unlikely, as this officer had just completed a short trials -commission in the IV.- class cruiser *Condor* on 24 April.

seas service, *Cruisers A* and *B* (to be *Schwalbe* and *Sperber*), provided for under the 1886–87 Estimates, were to be 25 per cent larger, and thus more appropriate to the classification, even if still rather diminutive for true 'cruisers'. They were also to be more heavily armed, with eight 10.5cm/35 guns – the last non-QL guns deployed in German cruisers (with the exception of their immediate successor, *Bussard*) – contrasting with the five 12.5cm/23 guns in the *Habicht*s. The new ships also had a single torpedo tube, rather strangely located in the centre of the between-deck amidships, which could be trained and fired on both sides of the ship at a fixed angle through an extension tube, a feature never previously incorporated into a gunboat. The new type of ship was thus a much more capable first line of defence for the overseas empire.

Nevertheless, they still attempted to meet several contradictory requirements: on one hand, they were to serve as protectors of the trade on the sea lanes. For this purpose, they were rigged as barquentines, to supplement their two-shaft machinery, and had copper-sheathed hulls. On the other hand, their draught had to be sufficiently light for coastal or even riverine service. Finally, their complement was to be large enough – in contrast to that of a gunboat – to deploy a small expeditionary force for local police actions. Although quite modest vessels, the second ship, *Sperber*, would not be funded until the 1887–88 fiscal year, another victim of the Reichstag's unwillingness to fund the navy, particularly in light of the recent start of work on the Kiel Canal.

In general, the pair were a success, and paved the way for the later *Bussard* class. *Schwalbe* herself began her first operational commission on 12 November 1888, sailing for East Africa on 20 November, arriving off Zanzibar on 31 December. She then served with the East African Cruiser Squadron during operations against local rebels until the squadron was dissolved in January 1890. She remained, however, in East African waters, although refitted at Cape Town during March/April. In late 1891, *Schwalbe* moved to Bombay, where she remained until 27 January 1892, before returning to East Africa, with another visit to Bombay in January 1893. She was ordered home in May, arriving at Kiel on 6 August, where she decommissioned on 25 August for an extensive refit.

She recommissioned on 1 April 1898, to relieve *Seeadler* in East Africa, departing on 20 April, and arriving at Zanzibar on 7 June. Refitted at Cape Town during October/November, she was based in South African waters, with *Condor*, from early 1900 to oversee German interests during the Boer War, before returning to Dar es-Salaam in July. Soon afterwards, she was redeployed to East Asia in the wake of the Boxer Rebellion, serving on the Yangtze River from September, with a visit to Tsingtau from 14 February to 3 March 1901. She left the Yangtze on 10 June for Tsingtau, but later briefly returned to the river, before spending September/November at Tsingtau. She

Sperber in home livery shortly after commissioning, and refitting at Tsingtau during August–December 1904; note the changes in her profile since completion. *(NHHC NH 65766/DN collection)*

then refitted at Shanghai, prior to further service on the Yangtze, and another refit at Shanghai.

Schwalbe was ordered back to Germany on 23 July, departing Tsingtau on 16 August and arriving at Danzig on 10 December. Decommissioned on the 13th, she was then given a major refit, but would never recommission again. Reclassified as a special service vessel on 26 October 1911 (her 'legal' replacement, *Cöln*, had commissioned four months earlier), it was planned to refit her as a survey vessel, her armament being removed accordingly in preparation. However, nothing further was done, and in 1912 it was decided instead for her to replace *Grille* in her training roles. However, this refit was cancelled with the outbreak of war in August 1914, *Schwalbe* being instead hulked at Kiel and being used as a target from 1918. Stricken on 6 December 1919, she was sold for scrap on 7 August 1920.

Sperber commissioned on 20 August 1889 to replace the lost *Adler* and *Eber* on the South Seas station, leaving Kiel on 4 September. Nevertheless, when at Aden on 13 October, she was diverted to East Africa to join *Leipzig* and *Pfeil* in quelling a local rebellion, reaching Zanzibar on 26 October. She did not, however, become a formal part of the Cruiser Squadron, although remaining in the area and undertaking operations

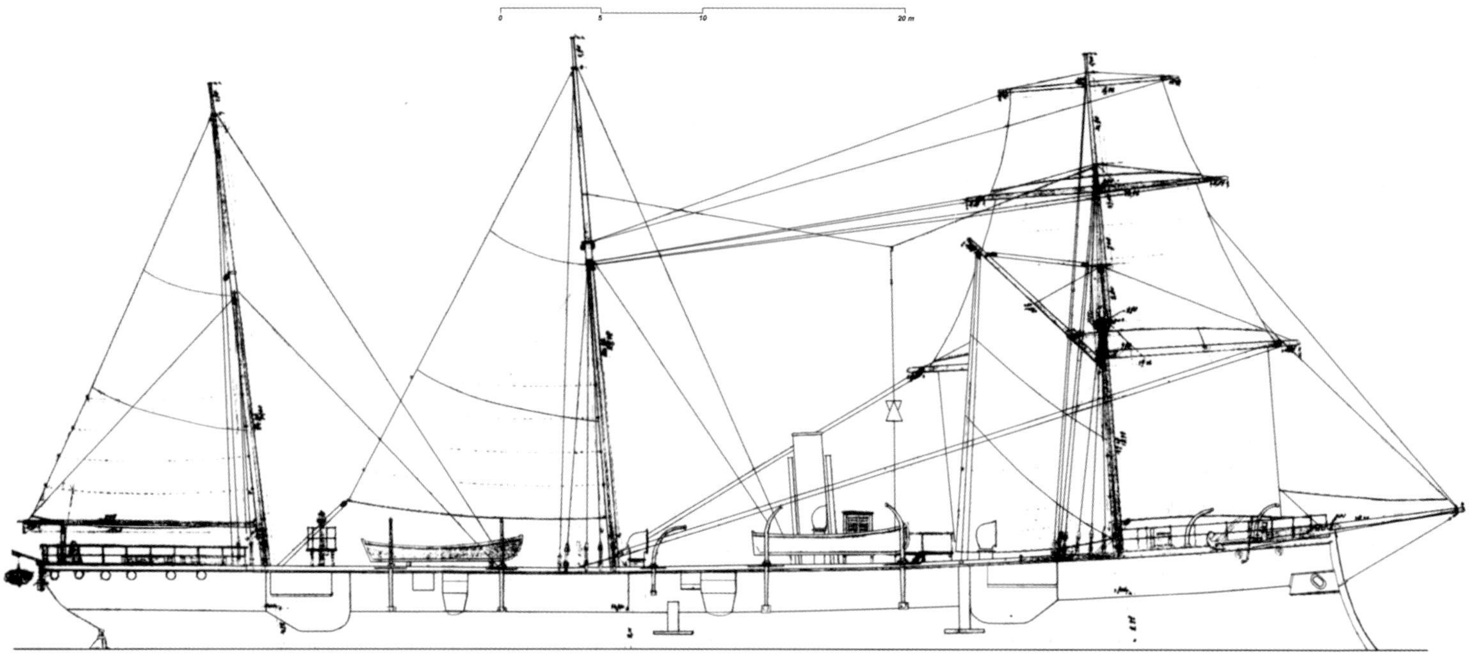

The sail plan for *Sperber* saw changes from the original configuration in *Schwalbe*, as the latter's gaff sails on the main and mizzen have been exchanged for Bermuda-rig. *(DN collection)*

against the insurgents until 22 April 1890, when she was able to continue her voyage to her assigned station.

She met *Alexandrine* at Sydney and underwent a refit before reaching Apia on 30 July. Apart from visits to Sydney to refit, *Sperber* remained on station until 1893, when she carried a Samoan rebel into exile in West Africa. Once there, she swapped stations with *Falke*, sailing for Cape Town on 6 November to refit. *Sperber* served on the West Africa station, with periodic trips to Cape Town for maintenance, until she began her voyage back to Germany on 22 September 1896, arriving at Kiel on 18 November and paying off on 7 December.

Although refitted between the spring and August of 1898, *Sperber* was not recommissioned until 16 December 1902, for the new East American Cruiser Division (p 73), to help protect interests during the current Venezuelan crisis. She left Kiel on 5 January 1903 and rendezvoused with *Vineta* at Willemstad on 3 February. The current crisis was, however, now over, and at the end of February *Sperber* was reassigned to the East African station. She sailed there via the Mediterranean, and arriving at Dar es-Salaam on 1 July. She remained in East African waters until 9 October, when she left to join the East Asiatic Squadron, arriving at Singapore on 23 November.

Deployed to the Yangtze River, *Sperber* relieved the river gunboat *Vaterland* at Shanghai on 15 May 1904. Having undertaken a number of port visits, *Sperber* subsequently refitted at Tsingtau between August and December. Reassigned to West Africa, she left Tsingtau on 24 April 1905, relieving the gunboat *Habicht* at Duala (Douala) on 26 July. *Sperber* remained on station until March 1910, when she was ordered to relieve *Bussard* on the East African station, arriving on 30 May. Refitted at Cape Town from 26 October to 3 December, she was classified as a gunboat on 6 March 1911, a month before she began her final voyage back to Germany. Arriving at Wilhelmshaven on 29 June, she decommissioned on 6 July and was stricken on 16 March 1912, surviving, however, as a target hulk until the end of the First World War. Like *Blitz*, she was still on active service when her legal replacement (*Augsburg*) was commissioned in October 1910.

3 THE UNIVERSAL CRUISER

An era closed with the death of Kaiser Wilhelm I on 9 March 1888. The reign of his son and successor Friedrich III, stricken with throat cancer, would last but ninety-nine days, and on 16 June 1888 his son Wilhelm II ascended to the throne at the age of 29. It is beyond the scope of this book to discuss all the new kaiser's shortcomings that, viewed objectively, made him distinctly unfit for the duty to which he was called, nor his likewise undeniably good qualities, which, taken together, continue to make his place in history distinctly ambiguous. However, one thing seems clear: without his accession at that particular time there would have been a fundamentally different German navy during the coming decades – although exactly what it might have been remains wholly unclear. There is little doubt, however, that none of the decisions taken by Wilhelm II soon after coming to the throne – from the replacement of Caprivi, through the dissolution of the Admiralty in favour of a tripartite system, to the simultaneous construction of four large ironclads together – would have been made by Friedrich III.

It was the intent to implement the second of these that was the proximate cause of the resignation of Caprivi in June. He was replaced by VAdm Alexander Graf von Monts de Mazin (b. 1832, previously the head of the North Sea Naval Station) early the following month who, however, died in January 1889, to be replaced by VAdm Max von der Goltz (1838–1906). The new incumbent transitioned in March to being head of the new Naval High Command (Oberkommando der Marine: OKM), responsible for the operational management of the navy. 'Government' aspects (including procurement) now fell to a new Reich Naval Office (Reichs Marine Amt: RMA), headed by a State Secretary, at first VAdm Eduard Heusner (1843–91), while there was thirdly a Naval Cabinet (Marinekabinett: MK), primarily responsible for personnel matters.

All three of these new bodies – directly mirroring long-standing army institutions – reported directly to the Kaiser, who now became the only point at which all strands of naval policy and management came together. This lack of a single professional focus would lead to numerous squabbles that would undermine the navy's capability over the coming years, and would only be resolved late in the First World War (p 226) – by which time it was all too late. The RMA also got off to a shaky start, with the early retirement of Heusner through ill health in April 1890, his replacement being KAdm (later VAdm and Adm) Friedrich von Hollmann (1842–1913), who would remain in office until 1897.

While Wilhelm II's initial focus lay in the acquisition of the German navy's first superficially modern capital ships, through the order to construct the unprecedented number of four vessels of the *Brandenburg* class,[1] there still existed, underlying

1. See Dodson, *Kaiser's Battlefleet*, pp 37–40; Nottelmann, *Brandenburg-Klasse*, pp 4–10.

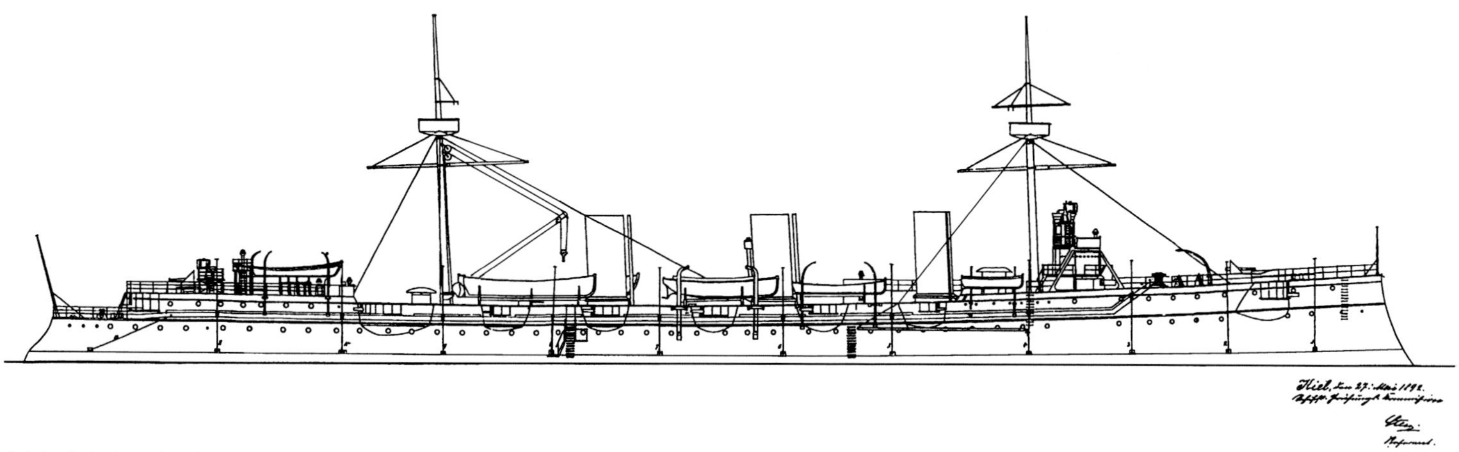

Original rigging plan for *Kaiserin Augusta*, dating to May 1892. At that time, it was still intended to equip the cruiser with anti-torpedo nets, whose booms' locations are shown in the drawing. *(DN collection)*

the planning of naval materiel, Prince Adalbert's doctrine of coast defence in conjunction with cruiser warfare. Indeed, even the acquisition of the *Brandenburgs* and the continuation of building the coast defence ships of the *Siegfried* class, started under the 1887/88 Estimates,[2] was not actually a deviation from this strategy. This was because the intended role all these ships was ultimately to operate in support of coastal defences, thus replacing previous generations of vessels dedicated to the role that were suffering block obsolescence owing to a long-term lack of investment.

At the same time, however, the German navy stood at a crossroads regarding cruising vessels. The construction of a proposed third vessel of the *Irene* class, authorised under the 1888–89 Estimates as *Cruiser-corvette H*, was stopped after Caprivi's departure because of the type's sub-optimal capabilities for fleet work. The ship was thus redesigned and reinstated into the programme as a much larger vessel, which would ultimately fall into the post-1898 category of 'large cruiser', but whose origins were significant for the wider question of the function of cruisers in the German navy.

2. Dodson, *Kaiser's Battlefleet*, pp 33–34, 40.

The debate as to the characteristics of *Cruiser-corvette H* [to be *Kaiserin* Augusta] centred on whether she should be optimised for fleet service (as favoured by the heads of the North Sea and Baltic Sea Naval Stations), or continue the policy employed with the *Irene* class of angling the balance towards a ship suited to overseas service (Caprivi). The latter was initially favoured, but with Caprivi's resignation and replacement by Monts, the 'fleet' option became the basis for further design work by chief constructor Geheimer Admiralitätsrat Alfred Dietrich (1843–98).

A significantly higher speed than hitherto was required for the fleet scout role, demanding 50 per cent more power than the *Irenes*. This was found only possible through adopting novel three-shaft machinery – as had also been the case in France when designing the pioneering armoured cruiser *Dupuy de Lôme* (1890, the first major warship in the world to be so

Top: *Kaiserin Augusta* in her early days moored at her buoy in Kiel bay. *Gefion*'s masts and funnels may be made out beyond. After her 1903–5 major refit, her only service was as a gunnery training ship in Kiel bay during the First World War (bottom). *(DN collection/Heidrich collection)*

equipped). Its success would lead to three-shaft machinery being used in the battleship *Kaiser Friedrich III*, and be a signature feature of larger German warships through to the Second World War. She was also some 1,200 tonnes larger than the preceding pair, but like them entered service with a provisional armament, replaced in the middle of the 1890s with modern guns, after which *Kaiserin Augusta* had a dozen 15cm/35 QL.

In spite of her intended fleet role, the need for wider utility was recognised in her sheathed and Muntz-metalled hull, and indeed she spent almost her whole active career in the Mediterranean and the Far East. This ended in 1902, *Kaiserin Augusta* being only recommissioned in August 1914, to spend the whole of the First World War as a gunnery training ship.

CRUISER-CORVETTE *PROBLEM*

Regarding the intended tactical role of German naval vessels, there is a nearly total void in the official documents from this period. Consequently, one has mainly to rely on secondary sources, which are themselves rather scarce. Fortunately, many of the underlying thoughts of German naval architects regarding the construction of future cruiser-corvettes during these years are well-illustrated in a now rather obscure contemporary work, *Die Kreuzer-Korvette „Problem”*,[3] by the naval architect Marine-Schiffbau Ingenieur Hans Johow (1856–93).[4] In this publication, he firstly promoted a new method of constructing hull lines, developed on his own initiative, and today long forgotten. In devising this new method, he worked from his own first principles, seemingly independent from all 'tradition' regarding shape, profile, rigging, decoration and such like.

Nevertheless, this suggests that his thinking is more widely applicable in considering contemporary more general naval concepts. Johow had been educated and trained in the

3. H Johow, *Die Kreuzer-Korvette „Problem” – eine nautisch-technische Studie* (Kiel and Leipzig: 1889; reprinted Saarbrücken: Fines Mundi, 2009).

4. Johow graduated as a naval architect in 1879 and joined the Imperial Shipyard Kiel in 1881. He rose to the rank of Marine Baumeister before his early death in 1893. Besides this work, he wrote and thus initiated the standard work on shipbuilding of the day: *Hilfsbuch für den Schiffbau* (Berlin: J Springer, 1884). His employment in the Imperial Shipyard allowed thus public insights into the thinking of the naval constructors which otherwise would have remained hidden – even if his '*Problem*' solutions deviated in many aspects from the actual vessels built.

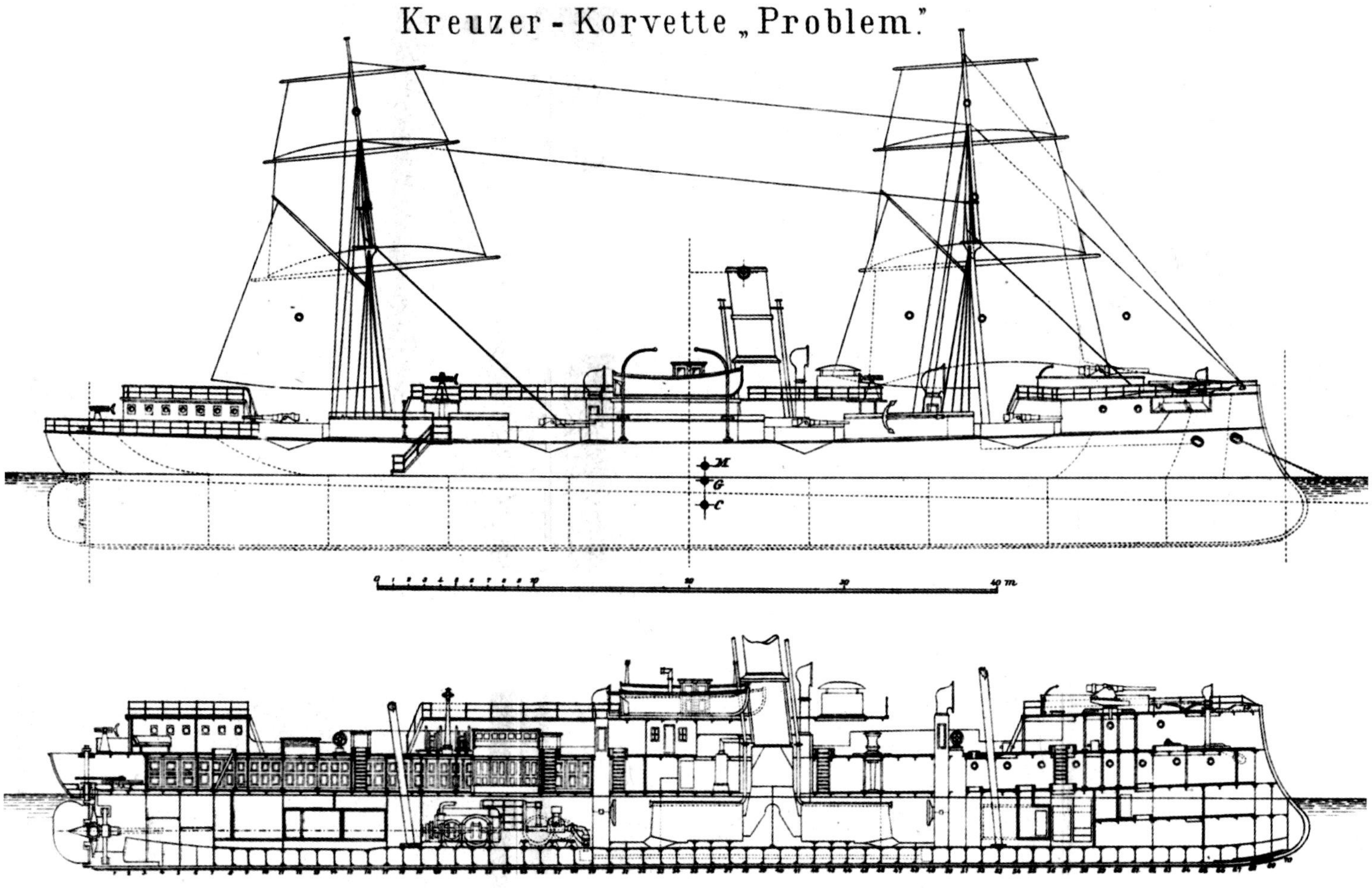

Sail plan and longitudinal section of Cruiser-corvette '*Problem*'. Included in the former are the sails' centre of gravity and the ship waterline's at light displacement, to determine the proportion of the propulsion machinery exposed above the waterline. A careful study of the section shows its similarity to the contemporary official designs. Only the deckhouse aft, instead of a raised poop, attests to some originality on the part of Johow. He adopted locomotive boilers for reasons of protection. A later variant has the simple rudder replaced by a semi-balanced type. *(DN collection)*

construction office of an Imperial Shipyard – employed in the construction of one of follow-on vessels from the *Schwalbe* class, *Falke* (see below), of comparable size to his own design – and was therefore in contact with the prevailing thoughts of his colleagues and superiors during his daily work.

Accordingly, it is no surprise that the requirements to be met in his work were essentially identical with those assumed or known to have been the basis for 'official' ships. Some of them are presented below, as a small indication of the motivations that might also have guided chief constructor Dietrich as well. Johow wrote:[5]

> For a vessel intended to be used as cruiser, one of the chief requirements is high speed at full power, as well as sufficient bunker capacity to keep the seas for long distances at moderate speed. If we set the maximum speed at 16.5 knots at full load and the cruising endurance at 6,000nm at 10 knots speed, we shall fulfil those requirements, which have not actually been fulfilled by many existing vessels so far.
>
> The armament must not, in view of the tasks required, be made excessively strong and will consist mainly of medium-calibre guns … Therefore, to be sufficient for a cruiser-corvette, it shall consist of several 12cm/30 guns whose firing arcs in forward directions must cover 70° at least. As a chase gun, a slightly larger gun, possibly a 15cm/30, shall be mounted near to the bow, whose firing arc must cover 100° from forward to each side. Additionally, several small revolving guns shall not be omitted.
>
> The task of the rigging in this type is a secondary one: it mainly serves as an auxiliary device in case of an engine breakdown or as a stabiliser against rolling; thus, the rigging in general shall not be intended for covering long distances under sail alone – even if this capacity will not be entirely neglected.
>
> For undertaking long cruises on the high seas without the availability of shore supplies, a sufficient amount of provisions must be stored on board; similarly, in case of failure of the distilling apparatus, sufficient potable water must be carried either in iron tanks or boxes. The term 'sufficient' means the storage of provisions for about three months and potable water for four weeks for the whole crew. Spare parts for equipment in general shall last for a minimum of one year.
>
> With regard to the machinery, it has to be mandatory that all its parts have to be installed below the W[ater]L[ine] level in full load condition, while all its major structural elements shall not protrude above WL level even in light ship condition. Spare parts for the engine shall be sufficient for as long as four months at minimum. Coal bunkers must be arranged in such way that they grant maximum protection against hostile projectiles in a fully filled condition.

5. Johow, *Kreuzer-Korvette*, pp 1–2.

It is also interesting to read parts of Johow's prediction of what he thought to be the most likely adversaries for future cruiser-corvettes:

> In recent years a large number of potentially dangerous opponents for older cruising vessels have emerged in shape of the so-called auxiliary cruisers. These vessels, requisitioned in wartime from the merchant navy and, during peace, partly already fitted for warlike equipment with guns, satisfy a large number of those demands, as expected from a high seas cruising vessel adjusted to recent requirements. All of them not only possess the ability to sustain high speeds for long periods, but their large coal bunkers enable them to cover long distances under steam alone. As an example, it may be noted that the French navy requires, inter alia, exactly the endurance of 6,000nm at 10 knots for this type of vessels.

Of course, he also made some suggestions for potential measures to deal with this new breed of adversaries, which in turn explain some of the features to be found in 'real' warships. One of his most controversial views was that:

> for a swiftly manoeuvring vessel the ram is still considered a very important weapon and similarly, especially against a heavily armed but – because of her greater length – slowly responding auxiliary cruiser, an 'ultima ratio', which cannot be dispensed with if no profound arguments from the nautical point of view could be brought up against its employment.

Further on, he supports the prevailing view that a vessel of the intended size must not bear any kind of armour, except perhaps some splinter protection for the gun crews and the conning position. All in all, his ideal vessel had the following main dimensions, which may be compared in the table below with the contemporary *Bussard* class:

	'Problem'	***Bussard***
Displacement	1973t (design).	1,559 tonnes (design); 1,868 tonnes (full load).
Dimensions (l)	77.9 (wl), 80.7 (oa);	79.6 (wl), 82.6 (oa);
(b)	10.9;	10.2;
(d)	4.8/4.2m.	5.6/4.5m.
Machinery	Four locomotive boilers; two shafts; reciprocating (HC) 3,800ihp; 16.5 knots.	Four locomotive boilers; two shafts; reciprocating (HTE) ihp 2,800; 15.5 knots.
Armament	One 15cm/30 six 12cm/30 five 3.7cm Hotchkiss.	Eight 10.5cm/35 five 3.7cm Hotchkiss.
Protection	–	–
Complement	not specified	9 + 152

Johow's vessel remained nothing but a study, without any notable impact on the future vessels to come; the same cannot be said about its real contemporaries.

THE *BUSSARD* CLASS

Like *Cruiser-corvette H*, the *Cruiser C* belonged, legally and conceptually, to the era of Wilhelm I. Not only did she form part of the 1888–89 Estimates, but she was little more than an enlargement of the *Schwalbe* class. However, as the remaining units of the class belonged very much to the reign of his grandson, the whole class will be dealt with here.

Some 450 tonnes larger than the *Schwalbes*, *Cruiser C* [to be *Bussard*] was also 2 knots faster, but had around 300nm less endurance. The armament initially remained the same, except for the addition of one extra torpedo tube, both of them now to be mounted in swivelling cradles on the main deck. Her price would be 1 million Marks higher, but the Reichstag did not object. This easy passage was aided by the fact that *Cruiser C* was initially intended to remain as a single-ship class. Rather than military necessity as the principal rationale for the new vessel, its key purpose was to guarantee a continuous workload for Danzig Dockyard, which was otherwise threatened by unemployment. According to a memorandum accompanying the follow-on Estimates of 1889/90, there was still, however, a long-term intention of building a total of three more cruising vessels, but the subsequent legal letters *D* [to be *Falke*) and *E* [to be *Cormoran*] were pencilled-in for the downstream 1892/93 and 1893/94 Estimates, respectively. In light of this, it would have seemed likely that their designs would have been rather different from that of their predecessors.

However, in the wake of the positive mood displayed by parliamentarians during the debates regarding the Estimates for 1889–90, the navy took the opportunity to bring *Cruiser D* forward into that programme, although the schedule for *Cruiser E* remained initially unchanged. But shortly before the acceptance of the Estimates by the Reichstag, news arrived of the catastrophic Apia cyclone of March 1889. Although the information arrived too late to allow an enhancement of the 1889/90 Estimates, in May the navy took the opportunity to call for the immediate ordering of replacements for the lost gunboats *Eber* and *Adler*.

At this point, it seems apposite to qualify somewhat the generally-negative image of the Reichstag that has generally been given in relation to the demands of the navy. The simultaneous procurement of *Ersatz-Adler* [to be *Kaiseradler/Seeadler*] and *Ersatz-Eber* [*Condor*] was passed without problems, even though both replacements were designated 'cruisers' while their forerunners had been 'gunboats'. Furthermore, *Cruiser E* [*Cormoran*] was also successfully brought forward and included in the 1890–91 Estimates, raising the number of cruisers to three in one year.

However, during subsequent years, times became hard for the navy. An attempt to bring forward *Cruiser F* [to be *Geier*] in the apparently now well-established way failed twice in the next two years – not for reasons connected to the vessel itself, but owing to the general approach of State Secretary Hollmann in dealing with the Reichstag. Consequently, *Cruiser F* remained in the 1893/94 fiscal year, and as a result emerged to a modified design that took into account operational experience with the early ships of the class.

The six vessels of the *Bussard* class represented the standard German cruiser for service on overseas stations through the coming decades. They were an improvement over the *Schwalbe* class in that, rather than following the latter's composite construction, the hull was completely constructed from steel. This made the isolation of the shell plating crucial, as all units were to receive sheathing for tropical waters up to about one metre above the waterline. The isolation thus had to be very elaborate and thorough, consisting of an inner layer of teak planking, clad with a layer of larch, upon which the plates of Muntz metal (a brass alloy made from 60 per cent copper and 40 per cent zinc) would be nailed.

Bussard

The lead-ship of the class, *Cruiser C*, was laid down in August 1888 at Danzig Dockyard, to be launched on 22 January 1890 and be ready for trials on 7 October of the same year. She was unique in her class in mounting the old 10.5cm/35 RK gun, which lacked a quick-loading ability. As an implicit indication of the actual value of a ship's main armament on distant stations, her old guns would at no point be updated during her long career. Following a short lay-up after the completion of her trials at the end of December 1890, she commissioned for active service on 1 May 1891 to be sent, after working up in home waters, to the Pacific station, including Melanesia and Micronesia. She left Germany in August, to reach Apia on 31 December 1891; this would be her main base. Until her recall into home waters in November 1898, she served all tasks required from a station vessel, including cartographic work around Samoa and the Marshall Islands, police duties in Samoa, the Marshall Islands and the Bismarck Archipelago, and various 'flag-showing' cruises encompassing the vast area of the Pacific station – not to mention her annual dockings at Sydney or Auckland. In July 1893 she, along with the corvette HMS *Curacoa*, supported Anglo-German forces against a rebel Samoan tribal leader. Recalled in the autumn of 1898, *Bussard* received on her way home, while at Port Said, orders to divert to Morocco to show the flag and to exert pressure on the local authorities following insults directed at German merchants. On 9 April 1899, she finally arrived at Kiel, from which she was delivered straight into the hands of her builders for a major overhaul and reconstruction. On 20 April she paid off at Danzig.

The most obvious feature of her reconstruction would be a reduction in her rig, the mizzenmast being removed and the

Above: *Bussard* soon after the beginning of her first full commission, awnings rigged, still with a short funnel. She would be one of only two ships in her class never to carry a bow decoration. **Right:** Sailing under the Levensau High Bridge on the Kiel Canal, *Bussard* returns home for the final time on 26 February 1910, flying a 'Heimatwimpel' (paying-off pennant) indicating how long the ship had been away. Clearly visible are the inclined shields of her old-style main armament, retained for the whole of the ship's career. *(DN collection)*

mainmast re-stepped aft of the engine room. On 26 June 1900 *Bussard* recommissioned for service in East Africa, but as a result of the recent Boxer Rebellion in China, she was redirected and left Kiel in company with the four battleships of the *Brandenburg* class (at that time the fleet's I. Division) for Far Eastern waters. En route, on 6 August, she suffered a boiler explosion, which killed three men and severely wounded three more, but nevertheless reached Singapore on 4 September. *Bussard* was assigned the task of patrolling the waters around the port of Amoy (Xiamen), before calling at Tsingtau at the end of the year. The situation in China was still seen as sufficiently precarious to keep her away from her originally envisaged destination, the ship remaining in Chinese waters until April 1904. During this period she performed the usual roles of a station vessel, patrolling the waters of the China station, including regular voyages to northern Japan, as well as the Netherlands East Indies, and a short stint at Chemulpo (Inchon) after the commencement of hostilities between Russia and Japan.

On 26 April 1904, *Bussard* finally departed Tsingtau for Dar es-Salaam, arriving there on 30 June, after exchanging her crew at Colombo. On her new station, *Bussard* was involved in suppressing the Maji-Maji rebellion that raged throughout German East Africa during 1905–7, reinforced by *Thetis* (ii) and *Seeadler* from September/October 1905. *Bussard*'s involvement lasted some six months, during which members of her crew served ashore in the brutal suppression of the revolt. *Bussard* remained on station until October 1909 when, during her annual docking at Cape Town, her commander received alarming reports about the declining structural soundness of her hull. Accordingly, she was recalled to Germany at the end of the year, and arrived at Kiel on 26 February 1910, to be finally decommissioned at Danzig on 12 March. On 25 October 1912 *Bussard* was stricken, and sold to breakers at Bremen in 1913.

Falke

The follow-on vessel, *Cruiser D* [to be *Falke*], was subject of some discussion regarding her armament, as the ship's approval coincided with the introduction of the first quick-loading guns of up to 10.5cm-calibre developed by Krupp. Given that weights available for the armament were limited, the question emerged whether the currently envisaged number of 250 shells per gun could be shipped along with the new mountings, or if other, lighter, solutions needed to be found. Three different distributions of guns were thus proposed: a uniform battery of eight 8.8cm QL; a mixed arrangement of four 8.8cm together with four 10.5cm QL; or eight 10.5cm QL guns combined with a reduced number of rounds per gun. The most telling argument against a lighter or a mixed battery was the insufficient range of the 8.8cm gun, combined with the more complicated ammunition logistics that resulted from the latter alternative. Consequently, the third option prevailed, in which the rounds per gun were ultimately limited to 88 (compared with 103 in *Bussard*). The only obvious external result of this revised armament was the differently shaped shields of the guns installed on the later vessels.

Falke (ii) was laid down in January 1890 at Kiel Dockyard, launched on 4 April 1891, commissioned on 14 September, and was ready for trials on 7 October 1891. These lasted only until the end of the month, after which the cruiser lay decommissioned until August of the following year. *Falke* – unusually for a ship of her type – took part in the summer manoeuvres before being sent to West Africa in October, to relieve the gunboat *Habicht*, joining the other ship on the station, the gunboat *Hyäne*, at Duala on 31 December. They undertook survey work during early 1893 to define borders in the wake of agreements with the UK and Portugal, and to locate a suitable harbour to serve the South West African capital, Windhuk (Windhoek). *Falke* also provided protection for German interests in Liberia

Falke with an impressive spread of sails off Apia, Samoa. The staysails from main and mizzen as well as the square sail on the extra yard on the mainmast were additional to her normal sail plan. *(DN collection)*

during unrest in May/June. In December, she received orders to sail to Apia to reinforce the Pacific station.

There, she joined *Bussard* and *Möwe*, arriving at Melbourne on 8 February 1894 and rendezvousing with her station-mates at Sydney for joint gunnery practice. *Falke* arrived at Apia on 16 April, remaining on station until she went to Sydney in October to refit and exchange crews. She also refitted at Sydney in the July 1895 and from 4 February to 4 April 1896, when she again exchanged crews.

The station's three ships met at Auckland in August 1896, *Falke* undertaking a wide range of tasks over the next three years, again with periodic visits to Sydney to refit; for part of 1898, after the withdrawal of *Bussard*, she was the only ship on station. Relieved by *Cormoran*, *Falke* departed for Germany on 1 July 1899, via Sydney, Batavia, Colombo, Mahé and Lisbon, arriving at Hamburg on 14 October, and decommissioning at Danzig on 3 November for a refit, which included the heightening of her funnel.

Having been thoroughly overhauled by Danzig Dockyard, the small cruiser – as was now her official designation (see pp 97-98, below) – commissioned again on 2 October 1901 for service off South America, to reinforce *Vineta* during unrest in the region. She arrived on 14 November and subsequently operated in conjunction with *Moltke*, *Stein* and *Gazelle*. She ascended the Amazon during March 1902, reaching a point 5,200nm (9,600km) from the Atlantic and only 400nm (740km) from the Pacific coast, at which point a lack of fuel forced her return, reaching the mouth of the river on 30 April. In early May, *Falke* was ordered to the Venezuelan coast to protect German interests during ongoing unrest, and on 30 September went to Port-au-Prince, Haiti, on a similar duty. Continuing trouble in Venezuela took her back to its coasts, running aground while leaving Willemstad in mid-December, and towed off by *Stosch* with some difficulty, albeit without damage. *Falke* joined the East American Cruiser Division on its formal establishment on 16 December, and continued with operations off Venezuela, blockading the Venezuelan coast, alongside *Gazelle* and a British squadron until 21 February 1903.

Falke subsequently carried out a wide range of visits in West Indian and North and South American waters, rounding Cape Horn in October 1904 and visiting Chilean, Peruvian, Colombian and Central American ports before reaching San Francisco on 15 June 1905. After a stay of three weeks, she continued up to Canada and Alaska, before heading back southward, reaching Mazatlán, Mexico, on 25 December. She remained on the west coast of South America until the end of 1906, being damaged in a storm off the Chilean coast in August. At Montevideo in January 1907, she was there ordered home, via Las Palmas and Lisbon, arriving at Danzig on 15 April. Decommissioned on 20 April, she was judged not worth further refitting, but was not stricken for another five years, after which she was broken up by Danzig Dockyard.

Seeadler

Laid down at Danzig Dockyard in September 1890, *Ersatz-Adler* was launched as *Kaiseradler* on 2 February 1892, but as this name was required for the former imperial yacht *Hohenzollern* (i) at the launch of her eponymous successor on

27 June, the new cruiser's name was changed that day to *Seeadler*. Commissioned for trials on 17 August 1892, which lasted until 17 November (during which she was in collision with the ironclad *Bayern* at Kiel), four months later *Seeadler* was designated to relieve *Schwalbe* on the East African station.

However, when recommissioned on 15 March 1893, she was first sent to the USA to represent Germany, in company with the likewise-new cruiser-corvette *Kaiserin Augusta*, at the festivities celebrating the 400th anniversary of Columbus's first voyage. During the crossing of the North Atlantic, *Seeadler*'s limited bunker capacity became evident and *Kaiserin Augusta* had to take her in tow, prior to refuelling at Halifax, Nova Scotia. On 18 April she eventually joined the celebrations at Hampton Roads, at the end of which *Seeadler* crossed the Atlantic successfully, this time calling for bunkers at the Azores.

On 20 June she took over the duties as station ship from *Schwalbe* at Aden, and after a refit at Bombay from 3 July to 21 August, she arrived on station at Zanzibar on 2 September to join *Möwe*. In November, *Seeadler* evacuated German nationals from Lourenço Marques (Maputo) in Mozambique during a revolt against Portuguese colonial rule, by which time *Möwe* had transferred to the Pacific and *Condor* arrived as her replacement. *Cormoran* had also arrived in East African waters en route to the Pacific, but was temporarily attached to the station while *Seeadler* refitted, including major work on her boilers, at Bombay from 10 January to 18 May 1895. She returned to station on 31 May, allowing *Cormoran* to continue her voyage east.

A period on alert during the events surrounding the Jameson Raid[6] at the end of 1895 was followed by refit at Cape Town during February/March 1896, and then service off German South West Africa in conjunction with *Hyäne* during April/May 1896 to support the defeat of the so-called Witboi-uprising, named after a local tribal chief. *Seeadler* returned to East Africa at the end of May, and along with *Condor* carried out a show of force off Lourenço Marques during December 1896/January 1897; *Seeadler* then refitted at Cape Town. She began her return voyage to Germany from Dar es-Salaam on 6 May 1898, meeting her relief, *Schwalbe*, at Aden on 31 May, and arriving at Kiel on 26 June; she was decommissioned at Danzig for a major refit on 9 July.

After having undergone overhaul, which included the same conversion of her rigging as her sister *Bussard*, *Seeadler* commissioned again on 3 October 1899 to relive her sister *Falke* on the Pacific station. Departing Kiel on 19 October, her voyage was interrupted at Tangiers during 27–28 October to apply pressure on the Moroccan government regarding

6. Leander Jameson (1853–1917), an employee of the British South African administration, led an unofficial foray into the Transvaal to trigger a pro-British uprising by expatriate workers there. He was repelled by the Transvaal authorities, leading to the Kaiser issuing a congratulatory telegram to President Paul Kruger, which in turn led to political tensions between Germany and the UK.

Seeadler under sail on trials before being sent abroad in 1893. *(DN collection)*

damages payable to German interests. She arrived on station on 15 November, spending much of the following spring touring German possessions in the region, including the recently acquired Caroline and Marianas Islands (purchased from Spain after the Spanish-American War, and added to German New Guinea), and the now-German Samoa, where she rendezvoused with *Cormoran* for a tour with the German governor and the Samoan chief embarked in *Seeadler*.

In July 1900, *Seeadler* was moved to Chinese waters to participate in the suppression of the Boxer Rebellion, arriving at Tsingtau on 8 August and remaining in the region until January 1903, when she returned to the South Seas station. *Seeadler* was refitted at Uraga, Japan, from 3 August to 14 September, and moved back to Tsingtau after the outbreak of the Russo-Japanese War in February 1904. During the first months of 1905, the ship conducted visits to the Philippines and the Dutch East Indies, before returning to Tsingtau in April. Following the Japanese victory at the Battle of Tsushima 27/28 May, *Seeadler* formally left the Cruiser Squadron on 28 June, but on her way back to Samoa she was detoured to East Africa again, to support the local troops during the Maji-Maji rebellion. On her way back west, she ran aground twice, at Labuan and at Singapore, albeit without damage, *Seeadler* arriving at Dar es-Salaam on 1 October.

What was initially intended as a short-term deployment became permanent at the beginning of 1907, when she officially was transferred to the East Africa station. *Seeadler* spent her remaining active life here, with periodic refits at Cape Town and Bombay, and a detachment to German South West Africa during March/April 1908.

In early 1914, she was called home, departing East African waters on 9 January 1914, with her relief, *Geier*, on passage. By then, *Seeadler* had been abroad for more than thirteen years, the longest uninterrupted overseas deployed period of any major German warship. Having arrived at Kiel on 18 March, she decommissioned at Danzig on the 30th; reclassified as a gunboat on 6 May 1914, she was reduced to a mine storage hulk towards the end of the year (albeit without being stricken), anchored in the Jade estuary off Wilhelmshaven. There, she was sunk by an internal explosion, of unknown cause, on 19 April 1917, fortunately without the loss of life.

Cormoran

Cruiser E was laid down in November 1890 at Danzig Dockyard. Launched as *Cormoran* on 17 May 1892, she was ready for trials on 25 July 1893. After their completion at the end of September she recommissioned on 2 October for East Asia, to replace the gunboat *Wolf*. However, she was temporarily diverted to East Africa to reinforce German forces in the area, sailing in company with *Condor*. The ships arrived at Lourenço Marques on 15 December 1893, *Cormoran* remaining in East African waters until 5 July 1895, when she was relieved by *Condor*. She then resumed her long-interrupted journey to Chinese waters. She called at Muscat en route, also being forced to spend time at Bushehr, Persia, to repair an engine defect that developed on 5 August. She also visited Basra before arriving at Singapore on 13 September 1895. There, she relieved *Marie* on the East Asiatic station, where she would remain the following years. In July 1896, *Cormoran* assisted the rescue of survivors of the gunboat *Iltis*, wrecked off Cape Shantung in a typhoon, and participated in the German takeover of the Kiaochow area in October 1897.

In view of the political situation in what would soon become

Seeadler moored to a buoy on a Chinese river in or after 1900. Except her reduced rigging, the profile is little altered. *(DN collection)*

German Samoa, *Cormoran* was sent to the South Seas station in early 1899 to reinforce *Bussard* and *Falke*, running aground en route on 23–24 March 1899 on the Whirlwind Reef, north of Neupommern (New Britain) in the Bismarck Archipelago. Stuck fast, the ship's steam pinnace and a dinghy were sent to Friedrich-Wilhelmshafen (Mandang) on New Guinea, some 162nm distant, where they found the steamer *Stettin*, which reached the stricken cruiser on 29 March. Drastic lightening and shifting weights (including cutting down the fore and mainmasts, and moving the aft guns forward) were successful in refloating *Cormoran*, which then proceeded to Friedrich-Wilhelmshafen. Taken to Sydney for repairs that lasted until early June, dry-docking revealed remarkably little hull damage.

In the middle of June 1899, *Cormoran* reached Apia to relieve *Falke*. A year later *Cormoran* was back at Sydney to refit and exchange part of her crew, refitting there again in March/May 1901 and, with the large cruiser *Hansa* (ii), representing Germany at the opening of the first Australian Parliament, at Melbourne on 9 May. Ordered back to Germany while refitting at Sydney in March 1903, she departed on 23 May, arriving at Kiel on 13 September, and decommissioned at Danzig two weeks later.

Not being urgently needed, her planned re-rigging (as in *Bussard*) and reboilering were postponed until 1907, and it was not until 1 May 1909 that *Cormoran* finally set sail for the Pacific station once again. Proceeding via the Mediterranean, while in Malta on 8 June 1909 she was ordered to join the small cruisers *Stettin* and *Lübeck* in protecting Armenians against violence in Asia Minor. She departed Port Said for the Far East on 9 July, albeit further delayed at Jeddah to repair boiler defects.

Cormoran in dry dock in Sydney in 1899, with her fore- and mainmasts not yet restepped following her salvage from Whirlwind Reef. Her elaborate bow scrollwork is apparent. *(DN collection)*

In November, *Cormoran* carried the German governor of Kaiser-Wilhelmsland for a tour that included a 183nm (339km) ascent of the Kaiserin-Augusta (Sepik) River, returning to Apia on 8 January 1910. She was badly damaged in a hurricane while en route to Hong Kong in April, requiring temporary repairs at Nouméa, New Caledonia, before arriving at Hong Kong on 3 May. On 15 July *Cormoran* returned to Apia, where she was joined by *Condor* and the East Asiatic Cruiser Squadron's *Scharnhorst*, *Nürnberg* and *Emden*. The five ships operated together until 13 December when, while at Rabaul, Neupommern, they were ordered to Ponape in the Carolines to suppress the Sokehs Rebellion, arriving on 19 December and operating in the area until 22 February with *Condor* and the small cruisers *Emden and Nürnberg*, including the landing of shore parties.

Refitted once again at Sydney during March/April, and at Tsingtau in May 1912, *Cormoran* undertook surveying duties among the German Pacific colonies later that year, returning to Apia on 10 January 1913. Reclassified as a gunboat on 24 February 1913 – her 'legal' replacement, the small cruiser *Stralsund* (p 144, below) had been in commission since 10 December 1912 – *Cormoran* refitted at Sydney from 4 June to 5 July, before landing a shore party to aid in settling unrest in Bougainville, in the Solomons.

On 30 May 1914, *Cormoran* arrived at Tsingtau for a refit, still being in dock at the outbreak of war in August. Accordingly, when the Russian steamer *Ryazan* arrived as a prize of *Emden* (captured on 4 August), *Cormoran* was decommissioned on 6 August, as was the gunboat *Iltis* (ii) the following day, to provide a crew for *Ryazan* – now herself renamed *Cormoran* (ii). Other manpower came from the river gunboat *Vaterland*. Stripped of her guns and other equipment to fit out the ex-*Ryazan* and to reinforce shore defences, *Cormoran*'s hulk, along with the gunboats *Iltis* and *Luchs*, was scuttled southwest of Cape Yu-nui-san at the entrance to Kiaochow Bay on the night of 28/29 September 1914.[7]

Condor

The 'legal' replacement of the gunboat *Eber*, lost at Apia, *Condor* was laid down in June 1891 at the Blohm & Voss yard at Hamburg, being the first new-build order by the German navy assigned to that yard, which would later be responsible for many major vessels. She was launched on 23 February 1892 and left Hamburg on 9 December for Wilhelmshaven, as the effects of a major cholera epidemic, which had hampered her building from the beginning, threatened to delay her outfitting yet further. She was finally ready for trials on 15 December 1892; these lasted – with interruptions – until 24 April 1893.

Her first commission began on 2 October 1894, as the relief

7. One of *Cormoran*'s guns has survived: having been taken from the scuttled wreck of ex-*Ryazan* on the island of Guam, it found its way to an emplacement in front of the county courthouse of De Kalb, Georgia, USA.

Close-up view of the stern of *Cormoran* in dry dock at Hong Kong, sometime after 1909. The sheathing of the hull and the scrollwork at the stern are particularly evident. *(DN collection)*

of the gunboat *Möwe* on the East Africa station. During the following years, she cruised exclusively along the southeast African coast between German East Africa and Cape Town, without encountering exceptional duties. She left Dar es-Salaam for Germany on 3 January 1901, arriving at Wilhelmshaven on 1 March 1901, to be paid off on 23 March for an extended refit.

On 1 April 1903, *Condor* recommissioned to relieve *Cormoran* on the Pacific station, arriving at Singapore on 26 June 1903. Having helped suppress unrest in Samoa between July and September 1904, she refitted at Sydney during April/May 1905, and then carried the governor of German Samoa on a visit to Hawaii from 30 August to 14 September. Further refits at Sydney were undertaken during March/May 1907 and March/May 1908. During September/October 1908, *Condor* operated with the gunboat *Jaguar* against unrest in the Marshall Islands, and in July 1910 joined the large cruiser *Scharnhorst* and small cruisers *Nürnberg*, *Emden* and *Cormoran*, at Apia. She then operated with the three small cruisers in suppressing the Sokehs Rebellion, during December 1910 to 22 February 1911.

Under refit at Tsingtau from 20 May to 1 October 1911, *Condor* was stationed at Yap during November's Agadir Crisis[8] to be able to receive information via the new wireless station there. Refitted at Sydney from 1 March to 18 April 1912, in December she – like her sister *Cormoran* before her – navigated the Kaiserin-Augusta river, this time for about 250nm

8. Caused by a French deployment of troops into the interior of Morocco in April 1911, nominally in support of the Sultan, who was facing a rebellion. Germany reacted by sending the gunboat *Panther*, later replaced by the small cruiser *Berlin*, to the Moroccan port of Agadir. The crisis was resolved by the cession of French territory in Africa to Germany, which was added to Kamerun.

Condor at Apia. *She* was unique among her sisters in retaining three masts throughout her career; all three are rigged with topgallants for WT aerials. *(DN collection)*

upstream. *Condor* was reclassified as a gunboat on 8 January 1913 (her 'legal' replacement, *Strassburg*, having commissioned in October the previous year), but a refit at Tsingtau in May 1913 found major hull defects, which contributed to her recall to Germany in November.

On 25 March she arrived at Danzig, to be decommissioned on 30 March, almost exactly eleven years after her departure from Kiel. Like her sister *Seeadler*, she was not stricken, even after her reduction to a mine storage hulk at Kiel-Friedrichsort in 1916. It was not until November 1920 that *Condor* was finally removed from the list, to be sold for scrap the following spring.

Geier

On 24 October 1895, the last ship of the *Bussard* class, *Geier* [*Cruiser F*] commissioned for trials, marking the end of the cycle of cruisers purely intended for overseas service. As already noted, the start of her construction had not been subject to the same bringing forward as *Falke* and *Cormoran*, and thus it was possible to remedy some of the design defects that had become apparent during the service of the first vessels of the class. The most notable change was the deletion of sponsons for the second pair of 10.5cm guns, installed to intended to give them axial fire. In practice, blast effects made such use problematic, while detracting from the ship's sea-keeping capabilities against head seas.

Geier's second significant variation was in the shape of her stern. Although the reasons appear nowhere to be explicitly stated, it would appear that there was some dissatisfaction with the flow of water aft. Consequently, the lines were improved, resulting in a slightly higher top speed at a comparable power output. Second, the deadwood aft was cut away to allow the installation of a partly balanced rudder, with a view to making *Geier* somewhat more handy. Interestingly, this attempt failed, as her turning circle remained virtually unaltered compared with her sisters.

Laid down at Wilhelmshaven on 2 November 1893, *Geier* was launched on 18 November 1894. Finishing her trials on 21 January 1896, she was then laid up for nearly two years at Kiel, and it was not until 1 December 1897 that she commissioned for the East American station. It had been decided that escalating tensions in Haiti merited a dedicated station ship to guard German interests in the Caribbean, rather than relying on periodic visits by the Training Squadron and other vessels; indeed, the ironclad *Oldenburg* and the large cruiser (ex-ironclad) *König Wilhelm* had been under consideration for deployment to the area.

Geier departed Kiel on 9 December and arrived in the Danish West Indies on 3 January 1898, where she rendezvoused with *Charlotte* and *Stein*, which had by then resolved issues in Haiti. *Geier* thus sailed to Santiago de Cuba, where she remained from 24 March to 6 April, prior to making a tour of Brazilian and Argentinian ports. While at Bahía Blanca in Argentina on 23

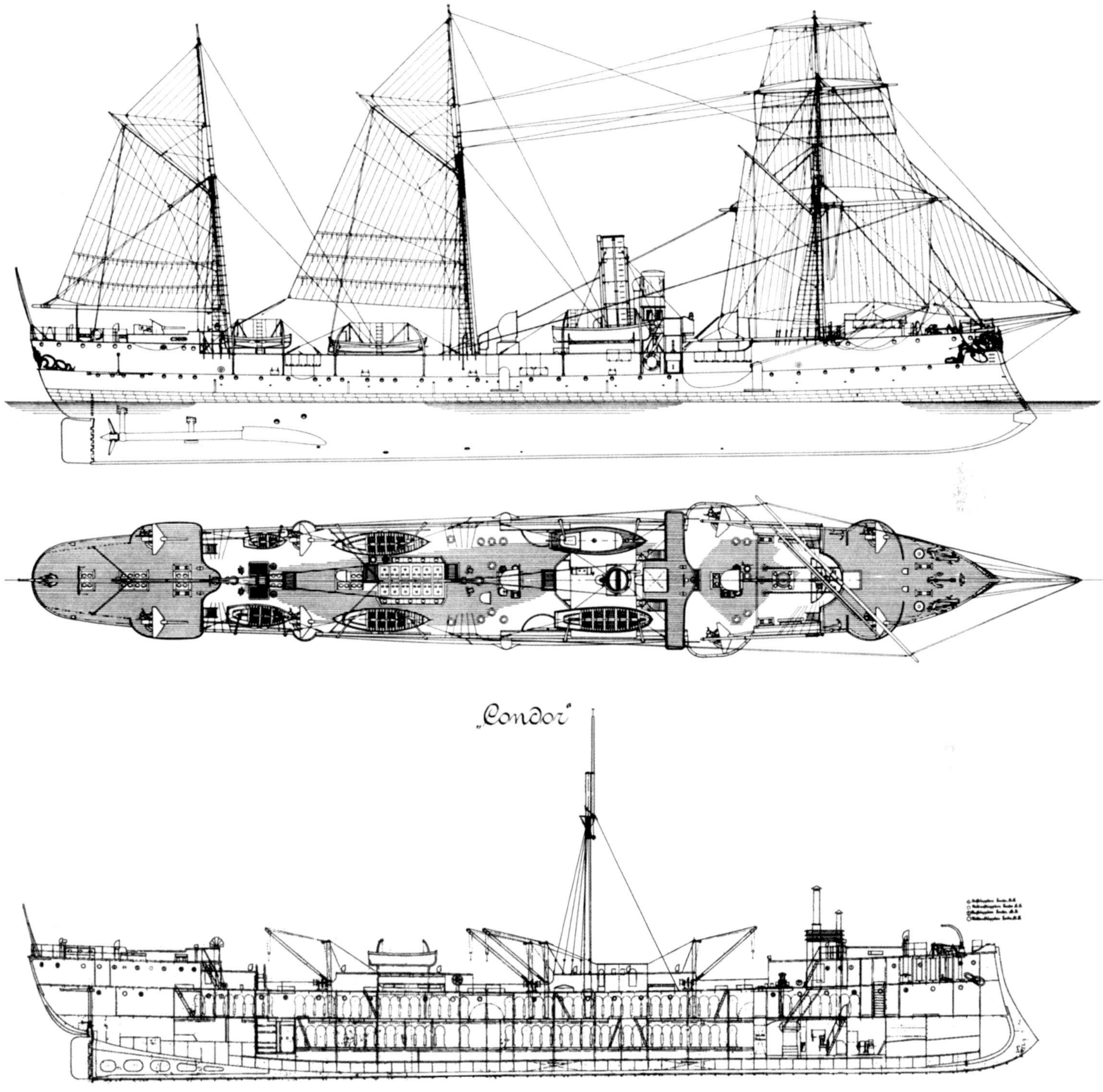

Drawing of *Condor* as delivered by Blohm & Voss in 1892, and (bottom) a longitudinal section of the ship when reduced to a mine hulk for the port of Kiel. *(DN drawing/DN collection)*

April, the outbreak of the Spanish–American War recalled the cruiser to the West Indies; she arrived at St Thomas on 6 May.

During the US bombardment of the Cuban town of San Juan on 13–14 May, *Geier* was permitted to evacuate foreign civilians to Veracruz in Mexico, where she arrived on the 29th. She then returned to Cuba until the war ended, subsequently visiting New Orleans on 14 October. Her tour of South American ports resumed in November and, while at Buenos Aires, she was ordered to the Pacific coast, passing the Straits of Magellan during 20–23 February 1899. *Geier* made numerous port calls, reaching as far north as Vancouver in October, before returning to what was now a permanent West Indies station.

Nevertheless, in July 1900 *Geier* was ordered back to the Pacific to join the forces combatting the Boxer Rebellion in

China, joining the East Asiatic Cruiser Squadron at Chefoo on 29 August. Refitted at Tsingtau in October, she departed for Shanghai on 28 October. She remained there until February 1901, when she ascended the Yangtze to relieve *Bussard* at Chinkiang (Zhenjiang). Back at Tsingtau in April, *Geier* was employed on various duties until refitted at Nagasaki during March/April 1903. Now formally assigned to the East Asiatic Cruiser Squadron, she continued to serve in the region until, in urgent need of a major refit, she was ordered back to Germany at the beginning of 1905. Leaving Tsingtau on 14 January for Kiel, she arrived on 16 March, being decommissioned on the 29th.

Having been refitted at Kiel, including the usual re-rigging with two masts, *Geier* eventually recommissioned on 28 April

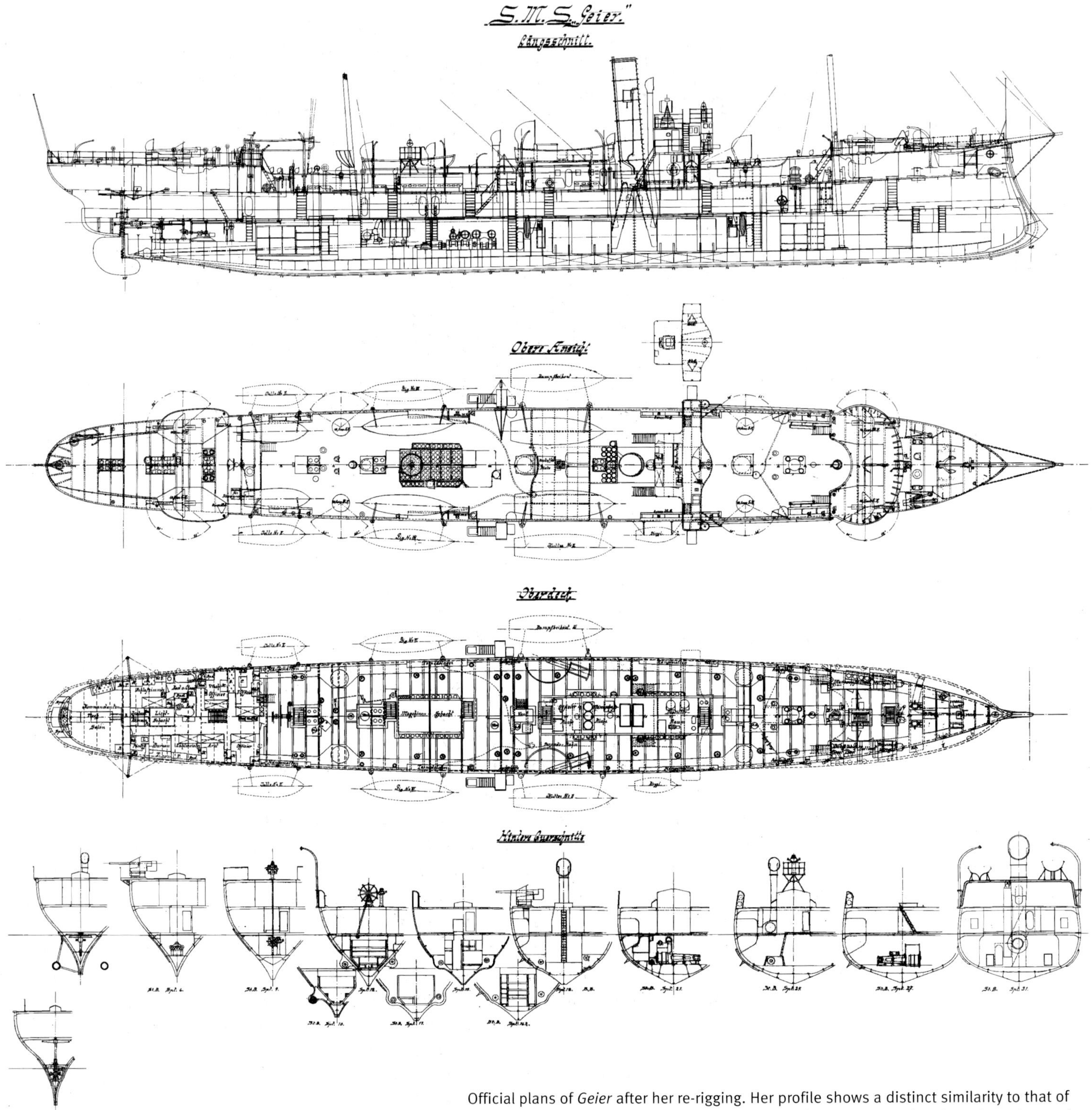

Official plans of *Geier* after her re-rigging. Her profile shows a distinct similarity to that of *Irene/Prinzeß Wilhelm* from a decade previously. *(Courtesy www.dreadnoughtproject.org)*

1911, to relieve *Sperber* in East Africa. Departing Kiel on 8 May, she joined *Seeadler* at Dar es-Salaam on 9 July, but then moved back to the Mediterranean at the end of September to guard German interests during the Italo-Turkish War, arriving at Piraeus on 16 October and remaining there until January 1912. She was then formally assigned to the Mediterranean Division alongside the large cruiser *Goeben*, undertaking various activities between April and July in the Mediterranean and the Red Sea, including accompanying the Imperial yacht *Hohenzollern* to Corfu in early May. From 17 July to 30 September *Geier* was refitted at Trieste, after which she resumed the normal round of port calls, suffering a coal dust explosion at Haifa on 31 January 1913, with two fatalities. On 11 August, she relieved *Breslau* in the international naval blockade of Montenegro during the Second Balkan War, being withdrawn on 14 October for a major refit at Trieste.

On its completion on 4 January 1914, *Geier* was reassigned back to the East Africa Station, and on 6 May was formally reclassified as a gunboat (*Ersatz-Geier* [*Rostock*] having commissioned on 5 February). Now slated to replace the already-departed *Condor* in the Pacific, *Geier* had, however, to wait for her own East Africa relief, *Königsberg*, to arrive on station. Finally relieved by the small cruiser on 5 June, *Geier* sailed east, but she had only just departed Singapore when Austria-Hungary declared war on Serbia, and would spend the coming weeks on an adventurous odyssey that would culminate in her internment in Hawaii, and eventual incorporation into the US navy (see p 204, below).

GEFION

As with a number of vessels begun during the early years of Wilhelm II, the gestation of the cruiser-corvette *Gefion* was by no means a straightforward one. This becomes particularly evident in her initial legal designation, *Cruiser-corvette J*, which neither fits into the letter-sequence of cruisers, nor those of the avisos. In fact, she had been planned as direct successor of the *Cruiser-corvette H*, which ultimately became *Kaiserin Augusta*. Following the approval of the first instalments for the construction of the latter by the Reichstag under the 1889/90 Estimates, the subsequent Estimates for 1890/91 contained no fewer than three follow-on vessels, *Cruiser-corvettes J*, *K* and *L*.

This was one of the first visible effects of a new 'fleet plan', inaugurated by the Kaiser, but prepared under the first head of the newly founded RMA, KAdm Eduard Heussner. In fact, the document was no more than a memorandum issued as an explanatory note to the Estimates for 1889/90, but was regarded – at least by the navy itself – as to some degree binding. Despite the negative impression generally presented as to the Reichstag's position over naval materiel, two of the requested vessels, *Cruiser-corvettes J* and *K*, had their first instalments passed in 1890 without being queried, although the third ship was declined. This was, however, not an unreasonable acceptance:rejection ratio, even if the underlying 'plan' suffered its first hollowing-out through this reduction.

The brand new *Geier*, photographed in October 1895. The main visible difference compared with her sisters is the lack of sponsons for the beam guns. Her new stern shape is largely concealed by shadow. *(DN collection)*

However, the great showdown – which would be one of the key moments of German naval history in relation to the Reichstag – would occur the following year, 1891. Having been granted 4.6 million Marks (2 x 2.3 million) as the first instalments for *Cruiser-corvettes J* and *K*, the navy requested another 1.5 million Marks per ship as a second instalment under the 1891/92 budget. During the following debates one delegate queried how far the two ships had progressed during the past year – which forced the navy to admit that neither had even been laid down. The 'scandal' had hit: the navy was requesting millions for second instalments on vessels that, so far, were nothing but wishful thinking. Unfortunately, this was not far from truth.

Initially, it had been planned to construct vessels closely resembling *Cruiser-corvette H* [*Kaiserin Augusta*]: a displacement not exceeding 6000 tonnes, with an armament of twelve 15cm/30 RK guns, eight 8.8cm/30 QL, and 4 Maxim machine-guns. Also, like *Cruiser-corvette H*, they would be protected by an armour deck. However, as already noted, the navy was on the verge of introducing the quick-loading gun across the board and several RMA sessions during 1889–91 discussed whether, and if so how, the current mixture of outdated 15cm/30 RK guns and 8.8cm QL weapons should best be replaced. The options for a uniform battery were thirteen 10.5cm/35 QL, with current ammunition allowances, or as many as twenty such pieces if the number of rounds per gun were reduced to 150. A major argument against a uniform 10.5cm battery was the introduction of the French armoured cruiser *Dupuy de Lôme* and her successors of the *Amiral Charner* class, whose hull sides were protected by vertical armour of up to 100mm thickness – impenetrable by the 10.5cm gun at anything but point-blank range.

The issue had still not been settled when the 'scandal'

erupted. Consequently, it did not worry the navy excessively when the infuriated Reichstag even decided on the unprecedented measure of retrospectively removing the already approved first instalment for *Cruiser-corvette K* from the 1890–91 Estimates. Indeed, *Cruiser-corvette K* would eventually hold the record of being requested in four consecutive years and being four times denied. Ultimately, the ship would be approved to a completely different design with a 21cm main

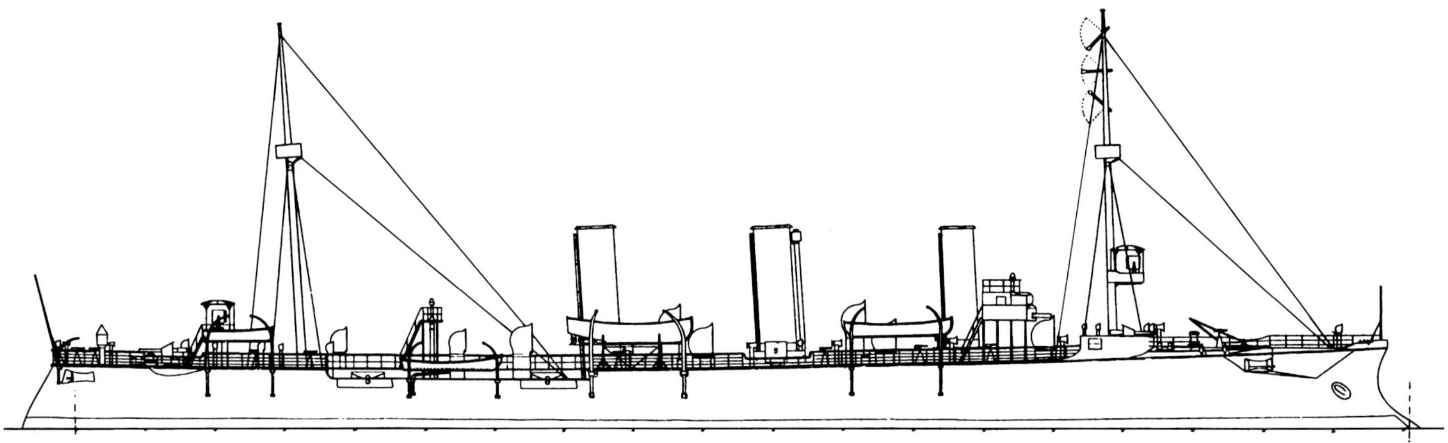

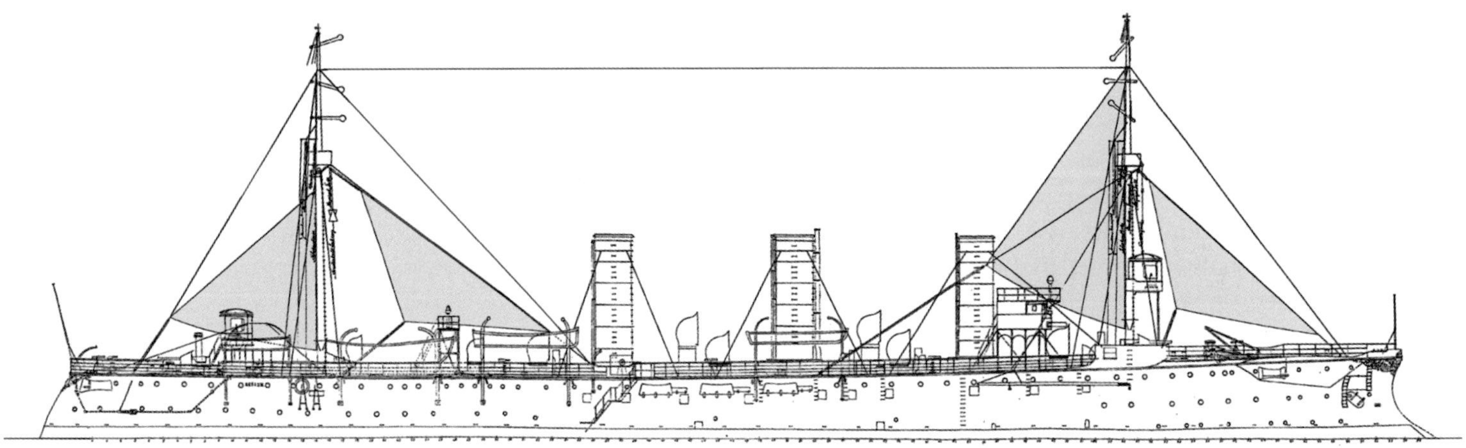

Top: *Gefion* as completed on her measured mile trial on 18 September 1894, during which she attained 20.45 knots. **Middle:** *Gefion* as originally designed, showing the slightly raked masts and funnels, which were later abandoned. **Bottom:** as she emerged from her 1901–04 reconstruction, the main alteration being closure of the after part of the maindeck, to gain additional accommodation, and the moving of the guns hitherto mounted there amidships. She remained in this state until hulked late in the First World War. *(DN collection)*

battery, to be launched as *Hertha* (ii), first vessel of the *Victoria Louise* class of II. class (later large) cruisers (see p 92, below).[9]

It still is not completely clear from contemporary papers what forced the navy to reduce the size of the surviving *Cruiser-corvette J* during the following months, as her first instalment of 2.3 million Marks remained in place and should have allowed the immediate start of construction, even if the second instalment for 1891–92 did not pass. It may have been a measure of atonement towards the Reichstag, especially in light of the rather gloomy financial prospects for 1891: because of temporarily reduced tax incomes, cuts in budgets across the whole Reich had reached unprecedented levels and threatened to require amendments to the funding of the army – still by far the most important part of the armed forces – in the near future. Consequently, it seems, the navy made a point of minimising its demands as far as vessels whose costs were not yet entirely settled were concerned. Thus, the budget for *Cruiser-corvette J* was cut from 6.7 million Marks in total to only 4.5 million, accepting consequent reductions in her military capabilities.

The resulting design thus had a displacement of 3,700 tonnes, with the armament restricted to ten 10.5cm/35 QL, although the inclusion of 'antique' 15cm/30 RKs was debated before being dropped. Of the 10.5cm guns, those paired fore and aft and between the third funnel and the mainmast were deck-mounted in shields, with two more embrasured abreast the forefunnel. They were supplemented by six 5cm/40 QL, embrasured under the forecastle and poop, and in shields abreast the second funnel, intended for anti-torpedo boat use, as were as eight machine guns, capable of being mounted in the fighting tops. So that the bunker capacity and thus the expected endurance could be kept broadly in line with that of *Kaiserin Augusta* (3,240nm at 12 knots), the 25mm armour deck only covered the machinery spaces – with a 100mm glacis over the cylinder heads – with a further patch of 25mm armour over the steering gear. Nevertheless, design speed fell by 2 knots – from 21 knots to 19 knots – compared with her former model. While unanticipated at the time, the reduced 'makeshift' *Cruiser-corvette J* [to be *Gefion*] would become a major influence on the development of later small cruisers.

The Schichau concern having been informed by the RMA in the autumn of 1891 that the order for *Cruiser-corvette J* would be theirs, the future *Gefion* was finally laid down at their new Danzig yard on 28 March 1892, in part to test the ability of the company to construct naval vessels larger than their usual torpedo boats. She was launched on 31 May 1893 and commissioned for trials on 27 June 1894.

These lasted until 2 October and, among other deficiencies, revealed heavy vibration at higher revolutions; remedial work, including strengthening of parts of the structure, was carried out by Kiel Dockyard. On the other hand, *Gefion* had surpassed her design speed of 19 knots by 1.5 knots, reaching 20.53 knots at full power.[10] On 5 June 1895 she began her first and only operational commission, being initially employed, as was becoming customary for newly commissioned cruisers, as escort to *Hohenzollern*. Further trials during the autumn revealed the highly satisfactory fact that her endurance was far better than expected: with her normal load of 770 tonnes of coal, she could steam nearly 7,000nm at 11 knots – making her the first real 'cruiser' able to undertake tasks on the sea lanes. The subsequent two years saw her switching between the duty of guard vessel at Kiel, participation in the manoeuvres of the training squadron and the continuation of her employment as escort to the Kaiser on his cruises.

On 16 December 1897, *Gefion* left Kiel along with the large cruiser (ex-ironclad) *Deutschland* to become part of the newly founded II. Division of the East Asiatic Cruiser Squadron together with *Kaiserin Augusta*, sent from the Mediterranean. This was intended to support the original (and now I.) Cruiser Division, which held the recently occupied Kiaochow Bay. This location had been noted as a possible naval base in the early 1870s by the geographer Baron Ferdinand von Richthofen (1833–1905), and as the Cruiser Division grew, the perceived need for a German base in the region – rather than relying on British (Hong Kong), Chinese and Japanese facilities – also grew. Thus, in June 1896, Tirpitz, now a Konteradmiral and commander of the Cruiser Division, was tasked with finding a suitable location. Four locales were inspected, including Kiaochow, and although no formal decision had been made in Berlin, Tirpitz's successor, Otto von Diederichs, who arrived in 1897, concentrated on Kiaochow.

Offers to purchase were turned down by the Chinese authorities, but an excuse for German intervention was created by the murder of two German Roman Catholic missionaries some 400km to the west of Kiaochow. Thus, on the Kaiser's direction, Diederichs took *Kaiser* and *Prinzeß Wilhelm* (*Arcona* and *Irene* were refitting) from Shanghai, being joined by *Cormoran* from the Yangtze and arriving in Kiaochow Bay, off Tsingtau, on 13 November 1897.

A force was put ashore from the two larger cruisers the following morning, led by Diederichs in person, with *Cormoran* positioned to provide fire support, if required. Within a short time, the outer forts and magazines had been secured – before the admiral discovered that his orders had been rescinded and that operations should be suspended, pending further negotiations. However, he responded that it was now too late: appropriate proclamations had already been issued and could not now be withdrawn. The fait accompli was accepted in Berlin, and

9. For them, see Dodson, *Kaiser's Battlefleet*, pp 44–45.

10. It is difficult of understand the repeated statement within the (admittedly scarce) literature that *Gefion* had surpassed her design speed by 2.5 knots. The only explanation might be that her design speed had initially been set at a rather vague '18–19 knots', which permitted the media to exaggerate on the knowledge of the true results.

Diederichs consolidated his positions, with *Deutschland*, *Gefion* and *Kaiserin Augusta* sent as reinforcements (the latter arriving on 30 December), plus a battalion of marines, who arrived on 26 January 1898. On 6 March 1898, the Chinese government agreed to lease Kiaochow Bay to Germany for ninety-nine years, the treaty being ratified by the Reichstag on 8 April 1898.

Tsingtau was developed as a major town and naval base, including a floating dock, and was henceforth the principal base for the Cruiser Squadron. However, the role of both the base and the Squadron in the event of a general war was problematic at best. In these circumstances the Cruiser Squadron would take over command of all other overseas German naval elements, but its subsequent role was intended principally to be to relieve pressure in home waters through cruiser warfare, rather than achieving any local tactical objectives.[11] As for Tsingtau itself, shore batteries were only installed in 1904, and while including two 24cm, four 21cm and seven 15cm guns, there was little confidence in the ability to resist a prolonged siege (as would indeed prove the case in 1914).

Gefion and *Deutschland* arrived at Tsingtau on 5 May 1898. The old ex-ironclad had been plagued with engine trouble, with *Gefion* having to tow her more than once, and both ships spending much of March and April at Hong Kong while *Deutschland* underwent repairs in dock. The subsequent two years saw *Gefion* fulfilling the typical tasks of a station-ship in East Asiatic waters, including ascents of the Yangtse, and detachments to places as far apart as Bangkok and various Japanese ports.

During first phase of foreign intervention in the Boxer Rebellion, sailors of *Gefion* became part of the abortive expedition led by the British VAdm Sir Edward Seymour to relieve the foreign legations in Peking in June 1900. After re-embarkation of her men, *Gefion* was ordered south, to serve as guard vessel at the mouth of the Yangtse over the coming months. A brief overhaul at the end of the year at Hong Kong was followed by two more detachments, one to Nagasaki, the other one to Shanghai. It was there where she received her order for home at the end of June 1901. On 22 September, *Gefion* arrived at Wilhelmshaven, where she remained, to be decommissioned on 1 October. Initially, it was intended that she would recommission fairly soon, and thus received a general overhaul together with a moderate reconstruction, which lasted until 1904. This work included enclosing the upper deck and fitting embrasures for all of the beam 10.5cm guns, which were now concentrated amidships; the midships 5cm guns were moved aft to abreast the third funnel.

Owing to an ongoing scarcity of manpower, however, she remained laid up after completing her refit, and later transferred to Danzig, where many such out of service vessels were concentrated. It was only with general mobilisation in August 1914 that her recommissioning was put in train, getting as far as the appointment of a commanding officer. But insufficient men were available to man the old ship, with even less to be had as the demands for personnel to man minesweeping and picket vessels increased from the beginning of 1915. By an order dated 5 June 1916, *Gefion* was to be converted to an accommodation hulk for submarine crews under refit at Danzig Dockyard, but lack of manpower resources prevented the work from being completed – although an Allied inspection team in April 1919 noted that *Gefion* was 'housed in overall'.[12] While dry-docked for conversion, it was noted that her bow- and sternposts had been made from bronze, an increasingly rare metal during the war. Nevertheless, her career would take a surprising turn late in 1919 (see pp 234-35).

ALL CHANGE!

In another attempt to clarify the prevailing disorder regarding warships' designations, a decree from the Kaiser, dated 29 August 1893,[13] updated classification criteria for German warships; the relevant part covering cruising vessels ran as follows:

II. class cruisers	vessels carrying a main armament of minimum 15cm or more and an armoured deck.

11. Lambi, *Navy and German Power Politics*, pp 231–35.

12. TNA ADM116/1939, dated 5 April 1919.

13. Published in *Marine-Verordnungsblatt* 20/93, pp 233–34.

Two generations of 'cruisers': *Gefion* in company with the converted ironclad *Deutschland* in Chinese waters. *(DN collection)*

Kaiseradler enters Kiel as the Kaiser's yacht for the last time in 1892, as her successor, *Hohenzollern* (ii), had already been launched and would commission the following year. An interesting array of ships is gathered to greet the Kaiser; from left right: *Beowulf* (commanded by his brother, Prince Heinrich); *Oldenburg* (*Sachsen* beyond); *Siegfried*; and *Baden*, with *Friedrich Carl* behind her. *(DN collection)*

III. class cruisers	vessels carrying a main armament of 15cm or below and an armoured deck.
IV. class cruisers	vessels carrying a main armament of 15cm or below without an armoured deck. Displacement above 1000t.
gunboats	displacement below 1000t.
avisos	[no formal specifications][14]

As far as existing vessels were concerned, three were assigned to the category of II. class cruiser, more owing to their size than any coherence of military capabilities: *Kaiserin Augusta*, *Irene* and *Prinzeß Wilhelm*.[15] Listed as III. class cruisers were *Gefion* and several older vessels due to be discarded in the near future: *Arcona*, *Alexandrine*, *Olga*, *Marie*, *Sofie* and *Freya*. The latter six were subject to the special remark that '[t]hese old corvettes are included in this particular list only exceptionally, notwithstanding their true characteristics' – especially their lack of an armour deck.

The list of IV.-class cruisers comprised *Schwalbe*, *Sperber*, *Bussard*, *Falke*, *Seeadler*, *Cormoran*, *Condor* and *Cruiser F* [*Geier*], while the list of avisos consisted of *Kaiseradler*,[16] *Zieten*, *Blitz*, *Pfeil*, *Greif*, *Jagd*, *Wacht*, *Meteor* and *Comet*. The *Habicht* class lost their 'cruiser' status, reverting to that of gunboats; the *Albatross* class had already been reduced to survey vessels in 1889.

OVERSEAS IN THE 1890s

The beginning of the 1890s already saw the German navy fully occupied by a growing number of overseas commitments. On each of the various 'stations' around the world at least one vessel represented Germany in the concert of nations, while the 'flying' Cruiser Squadron was available to reinforce hot spots in case of need. However, after Bismarck's dismissal as Chancellor in March 1890 and the nomination of the much less experienced former head of the navy, General Leo von Caprivi, as his successor, the orientation of the German foreign politics changed substantially.

Caprivi had never believed in Germany's necessary ascent to 'world power' status, and so stood against not only to the Kaiser's ambitions but most of his advisors as well. Caprivi preferred moderate continental politics with a special focus on securing the German coasts.

Initially the change in the chancellorship had no effect on the navy. The Cruiser Squadron was deployed frequently and widely, beginning in April 1891 with a detachment to Chile, during the developing civil war. This operation was not without internal political implications and set the pace for further feuds between the Reichstag and the Chancellor/Kaiser. Several influential German shipowners had appealed since February 1891 for naval support along the Chilean coasts, only to be informed that no German warships were available. This, in fact, was not true, but the Kaiser wanted to force the Reichstag to grant more money to the navy to fill this alleged 'capability gap'. These issues underpinned some of the debates during which *Cruiser-corvette K* failed repeatedly to gain approval.

In the end, this stratagem having failed spectacularly, the

14. This was partly because the Imperial Yacht *Hohenzollern* (ii) – much larger than any other contemporary avisos – had been given this official designation in an attempt to hide her true purpose from members of the Reichstag.

15. If the terms of this classification had been followed strictly, it would not have been possible to replace the latter pair by the ships in the later-established 'small cruisers' category at the end of their legal lifespan under the later Fleet Laws (pp 97-98) – they would have fallen into that of 'large cruisers'. Consequently, during the subsequent redesignation of cruisers in 1897 they were 'downgraded': parliamentarians had no reason to object as the replacements would be cheaper.

16. *Kaiseradler* was the former Imperial Yacht *Hohenzollern* (i), a paddle steamer, which had been included in the list of avisos to keep her funded, despite only ever being used as a yacht for the Crown Prince. With *Hohenzollern* (ii), her replacement as the Kaiser's yacht, already commissioned, there was no enthusiasm for spending money on *two* large Imperial yachts.

Kaiser and his supporters accepted the deployment of the Cruiser Squadron to South America. In actuality, however, the Kaiser had not been very far from the truth regarding the Cruiser Squadron's actual availability, as would be shown during the subsequent weeks. The three vessels currently making up the squadron – *Leipzig* (flag), *Sophie* and *Alexandrine* – were far from being ready. All required repairs at Yokohama before being ready to sail for Chile, while *Leipzig*'s boilers were so uneconomical that she had to be towed most of the way to San Francisco by her consorts, which delayed the voyage still further. KAdm Victor Valois (1841–1924), in command of the squadron, pleaded for the replacement of his flagship on this and other grounds, in particular her obsolete armament. Nothing was done, however, and despite all the obstacles and shortcomings this – in the end unnecessary – deployment became one of the most successful political actions of the Cruiser Squadron, with far-reaching implications on the future building programme of the fleet. It would, nevertheless, be the Cruiser Squadron's last ride.

It left Chile in December 1891 bound for East Asia, via Cape Horn and the Cape of Good Hope. On the way *Sophie* had to be detached home for repairs, her relief, *Arcona*, going to Chile instead, so that the Cruiser Squadron had now for a period consisted of only two – distinctly worn-out – vessels. Although not a particularly capable force – something that was keenly felt by its crews – and subject to some unrealistic war plans, the squadron continued to be led in East Asiatic waters by *Leipzig* until March 1893 when, after a deployment to East Africa, an examination in dock at Cape Town revealed numerous machinery defects, requiring a return to Germany. Initially it was planned to replace her with *Kaiserin Augusta*, but this failed due to the ire of the Kaiser, whose wishes with regard to

Leipzig (i), seen on 5 October 1919, the day the hulked cruiser had foundered at her Wilhelmshaven berth. In the distance may be distinguished the hulk of *Stein* (outboard) and another unidentifiable hulk. *(Heidrich collection)*

plans for building a 'cruiser navy' (as submitted by Admiral Hollmann) been snubbed by the Reichstag. Consequently, Wilhelm II decreed that the Cruiser Squadron be disbanded in April 1893, in the vain hope of causing a public outcry at this reduction in German naval power and thus shifting Reichstag opinion towards providing funding for the desired new ships.

In any case, it soon became clear that *Leipzig*, which arrived at Wilhelmshaven at the end of March 1893, was beyond economical repair, although her hull remained in good condition. Accordingly, after being decommissioned on 2 June 1893, she was converted under the 1895–96 Estimates into a hulk for training engine room personnel, replacing *Vineta* in the role. *Leipzig* later also housed the first German naval wireless telegraphy school, and also served as a training school for submarine personnel, before foundering at her berth in November 1919.

After *Leipzig*'s departure, *Marie*, *Arcona* and *Alexandrine* proceeded first to Brazil, as observers in the naval uprising there. They then visited a number of ports in South America, before being ordered by the Kaiser to East Asia again in preparation for the expected outbreak of war between China and Japan in the summer of 1894. On the arrival of KAdm Paul Hoffmann at Shanghai on 25 Nov 1894, he raised his flag in *Arcona*, the three vessels now forming the nucleus of a new East Asiatic Cruiser Division, a de facto replacement of the recently disestablished Cruiser Squadron, albeit now focussed firmly on Chinese and Pacific waters (cf p 57, above).

Because of the obsolescence of the current three vessels, it was intended to send out *Gefion* to become flagship but, as her entry into service was delayed by her vibration problems, *Irene* was chosen instead. This decision was challenged by her former commanding officer, Prince Heinrich, on the basis of her habitability and capacity to keep provisions fresh in a tropical climate. Nevertheless, *Irene* was recommissioned and joined the Division as its flagship in February 1895. She was joined by her sister *Prinzeß Wilhelm* in June 1895, replacing *Marie*, which left *Arcona* as the last representative of the former 'sail and steam' Cruiser Squadron. She remained active until the beginning of 1899, when she was ordered home to be decommissioned.

HELA

In the summer of 1896 the last of the projected series of avisos, *Hela*, joined the fleet. Like *Gefion* and some other ships, she was the result of a long odyssey around administrative obstacles, having initially been proposed – and declined – as a sister to *Aviso G* (*Comet*) under the 1890/91 Estimates. Following two more rejections by the Reichstag, *Aviso H* was finally approved under the 1893/94 Estimates; a sister, *Ersatz-Falke* (replacing the old paddlewheeler, stricken in 1890, not the recent IV. class cruiser of the name!), proposed under these Estimates was rejected by the Reichstag, which also turned down the ship the following year.

This delay in the construction of *Aviso H* was, in retrospect, to her benefit as, with the evidence of the poor performance of her immediate predecessors, *Meteor* and *Comet*, now available, the design for the new ship was radically enlarged. This was in particular driven by the German navy's rule-of-thumb that scouting vessels should have a have a speed advantage over contemporary ironclads/battleships of at least 3 knots. The most recent addition to the battlefleet, the *Brandenburg* class, would have a design speed of 16.5 knots, while the preliminary plans for their successor, *Ersatz-Preußen* [*Kaiser Friedrich III*], called for a design speed of 16.5–17 knots. Consequently, the speed of *Aviso H* needed to be at least 19.5 knots, the requirement finally being set at 20 knots. This was, in fact, only slightly more than that of the *Meteor* class, but endurance was tripled, remedying one of worst features of the earlier ships, but at significant cost. While nominal coal capacity was increased from *Meteor*'s 60 tonnes to 310 tonnes, this resulted in more than doubling the displacement, from 992 tonnes to 2,027 tonnes.[17] *Aviso H* thus became an excellent example of how changing only one design parameter can dramatically affect the size of the resulting vessel.

This, in turn, made a *Meteor*-sized armament of four 8.8cm guns appear distinctly unbalanced, even with an addition of six 5cm QL guns to fend off the newly introduced torpedo boat destroyers. Even her armour deck had to remain much the same thickness as that of her predecessors: 20mm on the flat and 25mm on the slopes. However, this was still sufficient against the weapons the ship would most likely face. Another factor, however, was that, as noted above, during the years leading up to the development of *Aviso H*, the German navy had been developing the concept of the 'division boat' for torpedo flotillas, which made the traditional concept of the aviso obsolescent. Thus *Aviso H* would be the type's final representative before its merger into the general-purpose 'small cruiser' type; although *Ersatz-Falke* reappeared in the draft 1897/98 Estimates, she would have been a representative of the new type – had she not yet again been rejected by the Reichstag (see pp 92, 93, below).

Aviso H was ordered from the AG Weser shipyard at Bremen in May 1893. Her keel was laid on 5 December 1893 and the launch was planned for as early as September 1894. However, this soon proved to be overly optimistic, the event ultimately taking place on 28 March 1895, when the new aviso was christened *Hela* in remembrance of the old trainee brig. In the middle of November 1895, *Hela* undertook her initial builder's trials, and then transferred to Wilhelmshaven for final fitting out. Handed over to the navy on 18 January 1896, her first

17. Assuming an average specific weight for the chosen engine plant of 105kg/ihp, as cited from different contemporary machinery manuals, and by keeping the principal constructive features alike, the difference in weight for the enlarged VTE engine plant (6,000ihp vs 5,000ihp; six vs four locomotive boilers) would require an increase of only 100 tons.

The sleek lines of *Hela* on show on the day of her launch; note the submerged bow torpedo tube. *(DN collection)*

commissioning for trials, however, had to wait until 3 May. Various problems with the engines truncated these trials: on her transfer voyage into the Baltic the starboard engine broke down and *Hela* had to continue on her port engine alone. Trials were resumed on 30 May, but had to be terminated again after damage to both high-pressure cylinders. It was found that the thrust blocks of both propeller shafts were insufficiently strong and consequently that the crankshafts tended to move forward, thus affecting the alignment of the cylinders. Later, leaks in the boilers as well as severe vibrations at higher revolutions led to the decision to postpone further trials until after a major overhaul; *Hela* accordingly decommissioned on 19 September. Nevertheless, in general the aviso had proven satisfactory, attaining a maximum speed of 20.4 knots and a calculated maximum endurance of 3,500nm.

Hela in Valletta harbour, Malta, while accompanying the imperial yacht *Hohenzollern* (behind) during the Kaiser's visit to the Holy Land in the autumn of 1898. *(Heidrich collection)*

Hela commissioned again on 10 March 1898 as scout to the I. Division of the I. Sqn (the *Brandenburg* class), which was interrupted twice for the ship to act as escort to *Hohenzollern*: first, for the annual summer cruise to Norway; second, for a cruise to the Holy Land by the imperial couple. In December she finally resumed her duty with the fleet at Kiel. With two exceptions – the first being the detour into the Mediterranean – the year 1899 mirrored the events of 1898, including the participation in the Kaiser's summer cruise. The other exception was the disabling of one engine during berthing at Danzig, after one of her propellers collided with the pier, requiring her to leave the fleet for repairs.

The year 1900 started as usual, but was changed dramatically by an order of 4 July for *Hela* to join the I. Division on its way to the Far East to reinforce German forces during the Boxer Rebellion. Arriving at Shanghai on 3 September, she initially patrolled the mouth of the Yangtse before sailing to the Yellow Sea at the end of the month. Members of her crew took part in the occupation of the forts of Shanhaiquan. After a short call at Tsingtau, she spent most of the remaining months in theatre in the area of the Yangtse.

Hela began her return voyage to Germany on 1 June 1901, again in company of the *Brandenburgs*, now redesignated the II. Division,[18] arriving at Wilhelmshaven on 11 August. *Hela* then resumed her normal fleet duties, now as part of the I. Scouting

18. The main body of the fleet left at home – the brand-new *Kaiser Wilhelm II* and *Kaiser Friedrich III*, plus the old *Sachsen* and *Württemberg* – now bore the designation I. Division.

Hela shortly before the outbreak of the First World War, with the deckhouse for the accommodation fleet staff aft, and as a result no aft guns. It was erected during September and October 1910, immediately before her recommissioning, and thus does not feature in the excerpt from *Hela*'s official booklet of plans, prepared directly after the completion of her reboilering in 1906. *(DN collection)*

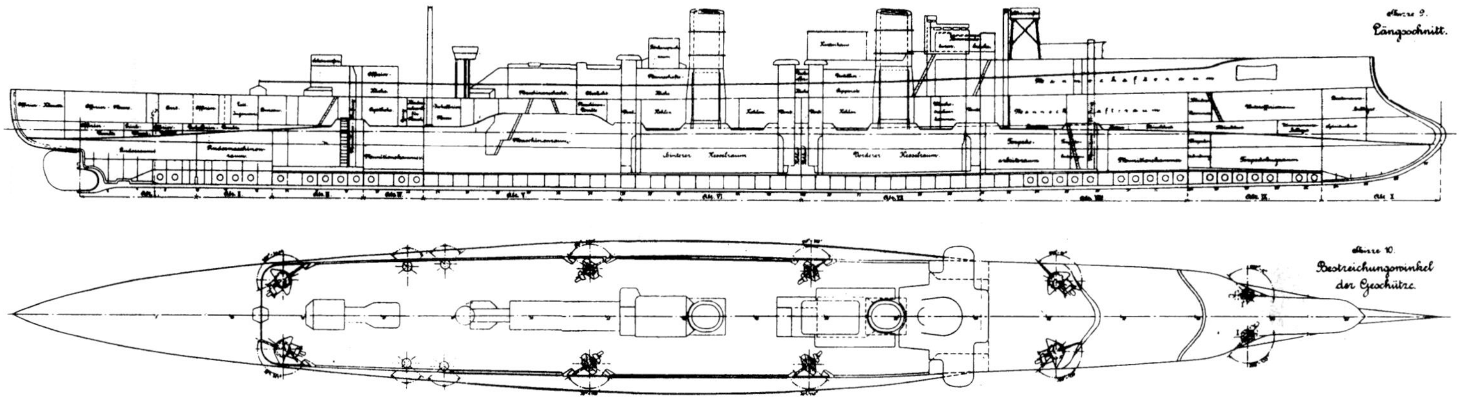

Group. During the year 1902, it became apparent that her present armament was insufficient for her duties as a cruiser with the fleet. Consequently, it was decided to withdraw *Hela* for a major refit, a move further supported by the poor condition of her locomotive boilers. For this purpose, she decommissioned and turned over to dockyard control at Danzig on 25 April.[19]

Her reconstruction was carried out in two stages: first reboilering until 1906 and then, during August and September 1910, the construction of enlarged accommodation aft, to allow her to function as tender to the CinC High Seas Fleet (HSF), as the fleet in home waters had been redesignated in 1907. *Hela* now carried two funnels instead of one, each serving four Schulz watertube boilers. The accommodation aft had been considerably enlarged to provide for fleet staff, displacing the two aft 8.8cm QL, as well as the aftermost pair of 5cm guns. Her deck-mounted trainable broadside torpedo tubes were replaced by two more submerged tubes, just forward of the boiler rooms. This brought her, at least in part, into line with contemporary small cruisers.

She recommissioned on 1 October 1910, and in addition to her fleet tender role, over the following years she sometimes also acted as a target vessel. While so engaged, *Hela* collided with the torpedo boat *S121* in March 1911, albeit without significant mutual damage.

TOWARDS THE GENERAL-PURPOSE CRUISER

Hela was not only double the size of earlier 'fleet' avisos, but also some 500 tonnes larger than the 'overseas' vessels of the *Schwalbe/Bussard* type, albeit with a much lighter armament. A fundamental difference between the 'fleet' and 'overseas' cruising vessels was speed: 15.5 knots in the latter, against the aviso type's 20 knots. The 'fleet' vessel also possessed – partly or completely – a protective armour deck over at least the machinery and the magazines.

The idea that both types of cruiser could be replaced by a merged general-purpose type was first raised in 1893, when the OKM responded to an enquiry by the RMA as to which characteristics, in the eyes of the OKM, were most desirable in future overseas cruiser design. The response was that greater speed had the highest priority. In July 1894, RMA's department 'K'[20] began to consider the demands for further cruising vessels to be included in the Estimates for 1895/96. Initially it was envisaged that they should comprise another III. class cruiser modelled after *Gefion*, and an additional IV. class cruiser *Ersatz-Möwe*, formally replacing the gunboat (and sometime cruiser) of that name.[21] Regarding the III. class cruiser, 'A' was requested to provide 'K' with the necessary requirements; *Ersatz-Möwe* was assumed to be a copy of *Geier*.

Against this background, there appeared memorandum

19. Her final months before (and after) decommissioning are somewhat obscure. Although as it has been reported (in Hildebrand, Röhr and Steinmetz, *Deutschen Kriegsschiffe*, vol 3, p 61) that she was rearmed after December 1902 for use as a training vessel, this is not supported by any other source. Additionally, there is some misleading information within the files concerning a short recommissioning from July to September 1903, which must be a misinterpretation of information in contemporary records, as no confirmation can be found.

20. All departments of the RMA were designated by letter: for a key, see p 19.

21. *Möwe* had been reclassified as a survey ship in 1893; no *Ersatz-Möwe* would ever actually be built.

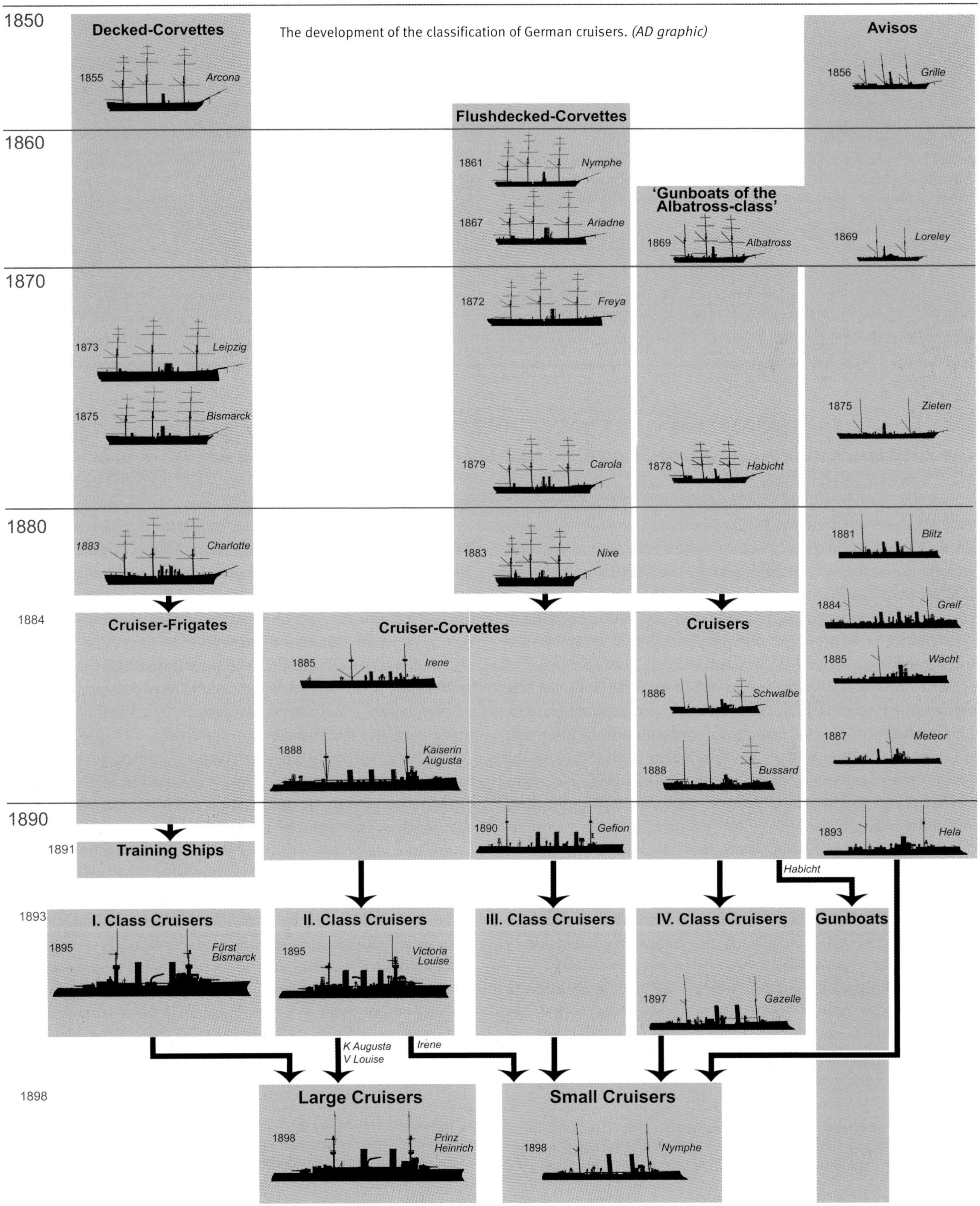

The development of the classification of German cruisers. *(AD graphic)*

prepared in June 1894 by the then-Kpt Tirpitz, Chief of Staff at the OKM, entitled 'General lessons learned from the manoeuvres of the autumn-exercise-fleet' (*Dienstschrift No. IX*). This, for the first time, set out a set of logical concepts for the coherent development of the German navy, making it a key document in German naval history.

A key concept was that meeting the enemy in battle should be the key to German maritime strategy, with cruiser warfare in most cases very much a secondary activity. Thus, the types of ship to be provided in future should be those required by this approach, with battleships of between 8,000 and 15,000 tonnes and a range of around 3,400nm, supported by a large torpedo boat force. Cruising vessels should be restricted to a large type, of some 6,000 tonnes, with a range of around 5,000nm and sufficiently powerful that two could together successfully challenge a battleship, and a small cruiser of 2,000–3,000 tonnes and similar range. Tirpitz's ideas regarding the future shape and the use of the latter type were summarised as follows:

- Speed should be at least such that the small cruiser will be able to break off from an engagement with a battleship. A top speed of 18 to 19 knots at least will be desirable, to be maintained for several hours, but not necessarily indefinitely. It would even enable the small cruiser to hunt for the newest type of torpedo craft successfully on the open seas and to conduct joint operations with large cruisers.
- A sufficient coal bunker capacity is deemed absolutely vital because the consumption during scouting operations is usually excessive and – even if supply by colliers for the main fleet is ensured – the oft-detached scouts will encounter more difficult and rare opportunities to fill their bunkers. Only a comparatively large amount of coal would enable the vessels likewise to be used on foreign stations, which seems most desirable. A true endurance (not based on the results of trials) of 5,000nm at 10 knots must be required.
- The cruiser's fighting ability must be such that she shall be able to fight hostile scouts of comparable size successfully, and that several III. Class cruisers shall be able to resist one single large cruiser, and that she shall be a dangerous adversary for hostile torpedo boats as well. Requiring the small cruiser to be either equal in speed or even faster than a modern large cruiser, or be able to enter a fight single-handedly against a large cruiser, cannot be possible as long as the small cruiser is developed to the extreme in one single aspect, which would render her unusable for normal fleet duties. Nevertheless, it should be required that she shall carry effective weapons for short and long ranges so that several small cruisers acting together will be able to put up an effective resistance to a single large cruiser. The small cruiser thus requires, besides a torpedo armament, numerous and effective medium-calibre artillery.
- The ability of the cruiser to move and to keep afloat has to be ensured by an armoured deck and a suitable form of bottom design, insofar that she will not be lost unless most of the unprotected mounted guns have been disabled and the cruiser thus left unable to continue the fight. It is thus unjustifiable to mount additional dead weight for defensive purposes that could be done only at the expense of other capabilities of the vessel.
- The cruiser requires two complete and independent command posts, of which the forward one has to be protected by a lightly armoured tower against the effect of m[achine] g[un], shells up to 5cm calibre and small debris from explosions.
- The cruiser has to be sufficiently seaworthy such that even during longer voyages away from shore the performance of the crew shall not be diminished significantly while under normal conditions of stress.
- Masts and signal poles have to be of sufficient height to permit either the installation of large semaphores or so that long-distance signal shapes can be used for signalling at long distances …
- One can assume with a certain degree of confidence that a displacement of 2,500 to 3,000 tonnes should be sufficient to fulfil the abovementioned requirements for a III.-class cruiser.[22]

22. Cited in (inter alia) E Besteck, *Die trügerische 'First Line of Defence'* (Freiburg: Rombach Verlag 2006), pp 193–195.

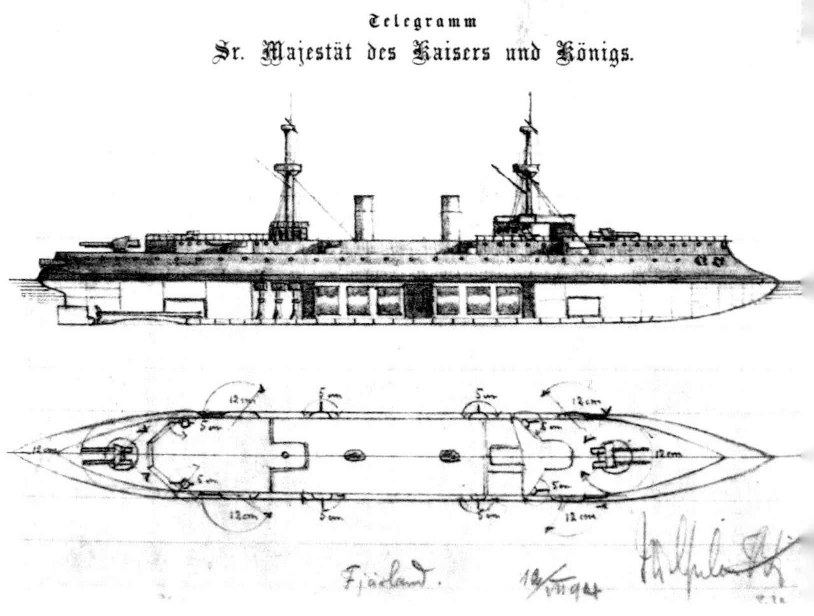

The Kaiser's visualisation of an ideal III.-class cruiser on the basis of Tirpitz's 1894 memorandum, sketched during his annual summer cruise to Norway. As a brainchild of the OKM by origin, it received an enthusiastic response from the commanding admiral, Adm von der Goltz, who used this visualisation as a starting point for the development of submerged broadside torpedo tubes, as the installation of any such tubes had been left open by the Kaiser. *(DN collection)*

Even without hindsight as to the direction of his later career, it is clear that Tirpitz is arguing strongly to make vessels for fleet work the first priority. Foreign stations never played a significant role in his thoughts, as they would drain resources from the expected main theatre of war in waters close to home. There is only the small hint in the proposed endurance of 5,000nm that the vessels should be capable of doing useful work abroad: but this would never be his preference. Another point of interest is Tirpitz's constant reference to 'III.-class cruisers', indicating that he was thinking in terms of something much more heavily armed than the current avisos, but following them as far as protection was concerned.

As it transpired, no provision at all was made for small cruising vessels under the 1894/95 Estimates (when *Ersatz-Falke* was rejected) – nor indeed that of 1895/96. Rather, the much larger type inaugurated by *Kaiserin Augusta* formed the basis of cruiser-construction for 1895/96, comprising three 5,700 tonne vessels of the *Victoria Louise* class – slightly smaller than *Kaiserin Augusta*, but with 21cm main guns – including the long-postponed *Cruiser-corvette* (now *II. class Cruiser*) *K* [*Hertha*] (cf pp 82-83, above), along with the huge 10,700-tonne *Ersatz-Leipzig* [*Fürst Bismarck*], postponed from the previous year. The latter was almost as large as the contemporary *Kaiser Friedrich III* class battleships, with the same four-24cm main armament, but thinner armour and a knot extra speed. *Fürst Bismarck* reflected an international trend towards cruisers of capital rank,[23] and in Germany inaugurated a sequence of such vessels that would culminate in the *Mackensen* class of the 1914 and War programmes.[24]

Two more *Victoria Louise*s featured in the 1896/97 Estimates, but this time a smaller cruiser was included in the proposals issued by the 'A' department on 10 May 1895: *IV. class Cruiser G*. Its letter implied that it would be a follow-on from the *Cruiser F* (*Geier*), launched in October 1894, but a brief remark by Hollmann indicates that something rather different was now envisaged. On 18 May 1895 he wrote:

> Regarding the IV. class Cruiser 'G', I request the design, according to my instructions given earlier, to be of a scheme with an armoured deck roughly similar to the aviso *Hela*.[25]

This was the birth of the *Gazelle* class, and thus of the whole line of small German cruisers down to the 1920s. This hybrid vessel was nevertheless a surprise, and - at first glance - another indication of Hollmann's oft-criticised inconsistency of direction.

However, matters were a little more complicated. It is only recently that it has become clear that the new type can be traced back to an explicit request by the Kaiser himself. He had urged Hollmann to have a vessel designed, 'which, as much as feasible, will combine the features of station vessels with those of a useful scout for the battle fleet at home, generally reflecting the design of *Hela*'.[26] In doing this, certain improvements would need to be worked in, such as a stronger gun armament, a better armour deck and a higher speed: these all combined to demand a greater displacement of about 2,600 tonnes. At least one of this type would now contribute to the roster of station vessels in the 1896/97 fiscal year.

It still remains unclear how Hollmann planned to explain the necessity of a vessel of this novel – merged – type to the Reichstag, which was inclined to think in terms of existing categories. Additionally, according to the official classification scheme, this would actually be a III.-class cruiser, something that Hollmann had himself vehemently rejected during previous discussions with the OKM. He must thus have felt less than comfortable with the decision as, after a prolonged quarrel with the OKM during 1895/96, Hollmann sought in May 1896 the explicit backing of the Kaiser, by explaining to him the design-process and why he had not asked for the consent of the OKM.

His rather weak justification for the latter was that he had seen no use in another approval, as the views of that organisation had amply been made clear through two lengthy statements in 1894 and 1895. Hollmann's own role in this case, as he further explained, had been purely to endorse the wishes of the 'All Highest'. Only in case of the two remaining open questions – the position of the bridge and the possible fitting of a bow torpedo tube – would the views of the OKM be requested. His confidence in the Kaiser's approval of the procedure was justified this time: unsurprisingly, as otherwise the Kaiser would be torpedoing his own demands of the previous year. Curiously, no one in the Reichstag seems to have questioned the type and its specification during the relevant parliamentary sessions, which began in the autumn of 1895.

The fact that the 1895/96 Imperial tax-revenues had been higher than ever before may have eased the passage of some extra spending for the navy during the following, 1896/97 year, with less discussion. However, the 1897/98 Estimates did not fare so well, a third attempt at getting *Ersatz-Falke* approved by the Reichstag failing yet again. Although still referred to as an 'aviso', her specifications were identical with those of *IV. class Cruiser G*, and was linked with it in the table that accompanied the budgetary request. This included the surprising remark that the two ships, allegedly of two different types (a 'IV. class cruiser' and an 'aviso'), were '[t]o be built as III. class cruisers'(!) This clearly shows how the 'IV. class cruiser' and the 'aviso' were now regarded as essentially synonymous in materiel terms, the difference being only as how they would be deployed in service.

23. See Dodson, *Before the Battlecruiser: the big cruiser in the world's navies 1865–1910* (Barnsley: Seaforth, 2018), pp 30–67.

24. For which evolution see Dodson, *Kaiser's Battlefleet*.

25. BA-MA RM3/348, fol. 66f.

26. NARA-Roll T1022-510, PG-66707-NID p. 803

Unfortunately, this approach (which echoed the situation of the 'gunboat' *Albatross* and the 'aviso' *Nautilus* a quarter of a century earlier) did not find favour with the Reichstag.[27]

Also thrown out of the 1897–98 budget were *II. class Cruisers O* and *P* (to be further units of the *Victoria Louise* type), a division torpedo boat and a number of torpedo boats. This debacle further undermined the already deteriorating position of Hollmann, who was now in conflict with the Kaiser over a number of issues. He submitted his resignation in March 1897, which was accepted on the 30th, with Tirpitz, recalled from the Far East, appointed State Secretary in his place the following day, although the formal handover did not occur until 18 June.

GAZELLE

Initially, *IV. class Cruiser G* [to be *Gazelle* (ii)] was envisaged as having an appearance close to her 'overseas' predecessors, although the look of the first three schemes is not wholly clear due to a lack of surviving drawings. What is known, however, is that, as compared with final design, the original concept was intended to be equipped with four cylindrical boilers and a differently shaped stem, without any provision for a bow torpedo tube. Nevertheless, it is evident that *IV. class Cruiser G* matched Tirpitz's ideal cruiser quite closely. She exceeded the displacement of both the *Bussard* class and *Hela* by a considerable margin but, with her declared classification in mind, her main armament was limited to 10.5cm guns. This baselining would become a major burden in the future (see pp 141-142). Tirpitz was certainly aware of the issues involved, since in 1894 he had clearly preferred the 15cm gun, provided that the consequent possible number of mounts would not have been too small on the required displacement:

> A straight reduction of the calibre from 15cm to 10.5cm would appear unwise even for III.-class cruisers because the latter does not possess sufficient penetrative power against armour, while the explosive effects of its shells do not support possible success in a fight against cruisers of other nations which are generally equipped with heavier calibres … To fulfil the requirements …, a main armament of eight 12cm or 12.7cm is considered necessary …[28]

These deviations would very soon become another basis for an exchange between the OKM and the RMA, ultimately calmed only by a decree from the Kaiser himself. This struggle offers a rare insight into the underlying thoughts of chief constructor Dietrich. While *IV. class Cruiser G* had already been laid down in April 1897, on 24 June the OKM requested some modifications to follow-on vessels, which were now to be designated 'small cruisers'. What had happened?

First, the new term 'small cruiser'. Since the preparation of his memorandum of 1894, which would form the basis of the later so-called First Fleet Law, Tirpitz had realised that one of the major keys to obtaining approvals from the Reichstag would be the clarity of the designations of ships being requested – something in which Hollmann had failed, with the ill-fated *Ersatz-Falke* a case in point. Consequently Tirpitz, with the approval of the Kaiser, reduced the existing variety of type classifications for major warships down to simply battleships (literally 'ships-of-the-line'); large cruisers; small cruisers. These would be the types the parliamentarians would have to deal with in the future. With hindsight, one might have seen this amalgamation to have been inevitable – but in practice this could only have actually happened once Tirpitz had taken over.

Second, the underlying rationale of the type. In its 24 June paper, the OKM requested (inter alia) that, in future, the speed of cruisers for fleet service should be raised to 21 knots for a three-hour period, to maintain the requisite 3 knots margin over the new battleships of *Kaiser Friedrich III* class, ultimately designed for a three-hour top speed of 18 knots. Another point was an enlargement of the endurance – as yet unspecified since nobody yet knew the efficiency of the newly introduced watertube boilers that were intended for the new ships. Finally, an augmentation of the main artillery's calibre and numbers seemed desirable. All this, the OKM expected, might probably raise the displacement up to 4,000 tonnes, which nevertheless seemed acceptable. These requirements would apply to any future class of small cruisers.

Dietrich responded about a month later that, according to his calculations, a vessel of 3,000 tonnes would indeed be much too small to incorporate the desired improvements. Rather, it would require a displacement close to 3,400 tonnes and an overall length of 112m, the costs of which would exceed those of *IV. class Cruiser G* by 26 per cent, or 1.18 million Marks.[29] Initially, he was satisfied that this enlarged design would be acceptable, and even produced some sketches, obviously unaware of the financial implications, which could not, unfortunately, be easily overcome. From the accompanying descriptions, it can be seen that he intended a vessel that was something of a cross between the designs of *G* and *Gefion*, with three boiler rooms equipped with Niclausse or Belleville watertube boilers, each with its own funnel. The size of the engines required a glacis to protect the top of the cylinders.

His sub-department 'K II' (boilers and engines) was requested to calculate dimensions and costs, responding a few days later by stating that Dürr boilers had been chosen, since Bellevilles could not be accommodated within the shape of the proposed main frame. A few days later, additional information was given by

27. The approach of requesting two vessels of the same technical type under different designations had been proposed by the then-head of 'A' department, Kpt Friedrich von Baudissin, in 1895 (BA-MA RM3/6690, fol. 85ff); Hollmann's attempt to take this line in 1897 had clearly been equally unsuccessful.

28. Besteck, *First Line of Defence*, p 195.

29. BA-MA RM3/3697, fol. 4ff.

'K II' that would lead the development of the cruiser type in a new direction: by swapping the Dürr-type for Thornycroft-type boilers, an additional 40 tonnes of weight could be gained, which made this option temporarily a favourite.

However, the two key facts – costs and length – eventually buried the OKM's demands for a new design: the 'M' department argued that the greater length would result in inferior tactical capabilities but, in light of the Fleet Law being prepared in parallel, and its unpredictable reception by the Reichstag, the increased costs were the principal problem. The financial calculations presented to the delegates with respect of the required total of thirty small cruisers had been based on the 4.6 million Mark estimate for *IV. class Cruiser G*, which left little leeway for changes. But this outcome could not – and did not – satisfy the OKM, whose head, Adm Eduard von Knorr (1840–1920), wrote a note of protest, aimed at Tirpitz; this must have made an impression on him, since three years previously Tirpitz had himself used similar arguments against the RMA, then led by Hollmann. Knorr wrote:

> Cruiser 'G' has been called inadequate by the OKM since its first appearance in 1894. I was anticipating an equalization of opinions between the two most eminent naval offices after the definition of the Fleet Law. This I did even more so as the views of the OK have not changed since the days when Your Excellency had been member of this institution … If Your Excellency dare to explain to myself … that these demands could only be fulfilled by raising the displacement by 800 tonnes and the costs by 1.2Mill.M, I can only state in return that according to my views it would have been better to make these sacrifices instead of providing the navy with a cruiser type of little usefulness.[30]

Another voice wished to be acknowledged as well – that of KAdm Paul Hoffmann, immediate predecessor of Tirpitz as head of the East Asiatic Cruiser Division. Hoffmann put in his weight as an experienced leader of a cruiser division abroad:

> A 3,000 tonne vessel bearing a 10cm armament represents in reality not much more than an improved *Cormoran* which is, as you admit by yourself, of inferior quality … Sent to any place, a IV.-class cruiser will not suffice because of the small number of men to be sent ashore or because of the inferiority of its armament … an armoured cruiser must be sent in instead then.[31]

In view of these – and further – statements that could clearly not be ignored, Tirpitz wisely assured himself of the backing of the Kaiser, just as Hollmann had done a few years before when faced with opposition within the naval administration. Thus, the new small cruiser would in general remain as originally planned, even if some small improvements could be worked in to pacify at least some of her critics. We will return to this point, especially regarding machinery, in the following chapter.

A marked difference between *Gazelle* and the follow-on vessels would be the omission of the former's forward submerged torpedo tube. This had been a feature of the preceding avisos and contributed to their exaggerated ram bows, particularly noticeable in *Hela*, and now inherited by *Gazelle* at the direction of the Kaiser. In *Gazelle*'s case, it was also a 'true' ram, with an internal casting, designed to fail along a pre-determined seam under excessive stress. However, during the design of the follow-on vessels, Dietrich's successor Johannes Rudloff (1848–1934) – Dietrich had died on 6 September 1898 – deleted this antiquated feature because the supporting structure behind the ram could never be made strong enough for ramming within a lightly built cruiser hull without accumulating excessive weight forward. For reasons of trim, the bow torpedo tube disappeared as well, never again to be reintroduced in a German small cruiser, although the exterior profile of the bow would not be changed significantly until the *Königsberg* class of the 1904 Estimates, when the design reverted to a shape called the 'cutting edge of a hatchet'.

Another not-repeated feature of *Gazelle* was the placement of the navigating bridge between the funnels, as explained by Hollmann in a letter to OKM on 7 February 1896:

> The bridge has been moved aft to between the two funnels in this project to gain a dry command post in a head sea and an improved overview of the artillery; the visibility ahead will only be insignificantly affected by the forward funnel.[32]

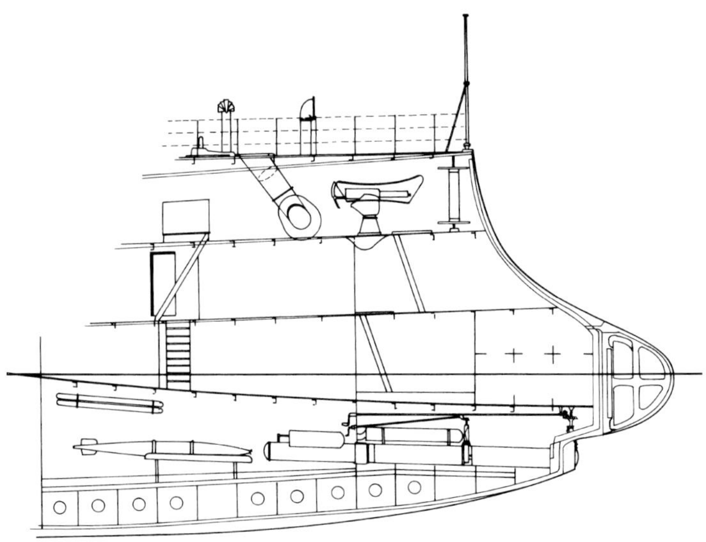

The unique combination of a bow torpedo tube in combination with a proper ram was a distinctive feature of *Gazelle*, and hinted that the ship's balance of capabilities leant more towards fleet service than employment on distant stations. *(DN drawing)*

30. BA-MA RM3/3697, fol. 33ff.
31. BA-MA RM3/2, fol. 6.
32. RM3/3684 fol. 33f.

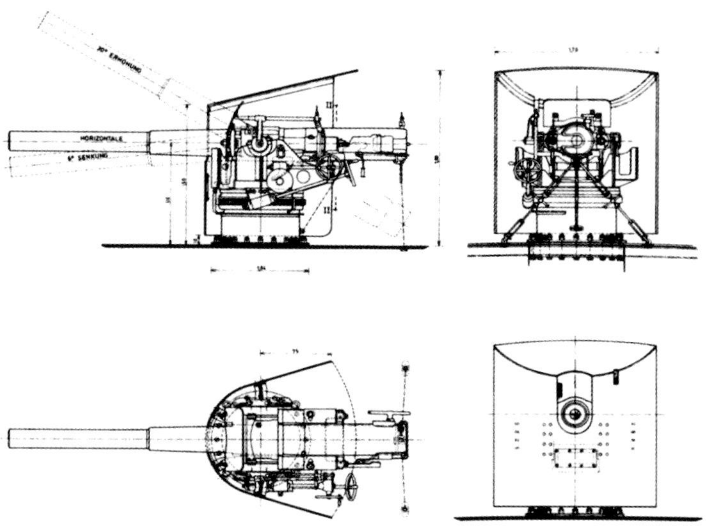

The new 'cruiser gun': the 10.5cm/40 C/97. *(L Wischmeyer drawing)*

The ship nevertheless received an additional small navigation bridge in front of the forward funnel before commissioning (see p 100, below).

IV. class Cruiser G was laid down at the Germania Shipyard on 14 April 1897. She was christened on 31 March 1898 by no less than Tirpitz himself – perhaps as a kind of internal 'demonstration of support' for this new type. As the Fleet Law of 1898 (next chapter) had passed the Reichstag only three days earlier, but had not yet been countersigned and set into force by the Kaiser, *Gazelle* was something of a transitional vessel between two eras – a term which does not seem undeserved in the true sense of the wording.

Gazelle was the first cruiser to mount ten 10.5cm L/40 QL guns of the new C/97 model. This gun used axial recoil, instead of the slope of the preceding Vavasseur system, for the first time. Besides the overall ballistic advantages of the longer gun with its more modern breech, the axial recoil had the benefit of avoiding the large apertures in the protective shields necessary for the older system. During trials, the rate of fire for aimed shots rose from 7.5 to 11.5 per minute. However, the gun performed less than flawlessly during its baptism of fire on board the gunboat *Panther*, while destroying the Haitian rebel gunboat *Crête á Pierrot* in 1902. This, of course, caused some concern among the officials and led to the development of the succeeding C/04 gun.

Initially, the ship received eight watertube boilers of the Niclausse type. These were part of a competitive search for the most suitable model of this type of boiler. Unfortunately for *Gazelle*, the Niclausse type failed in terms of technical reliability in a number of navies[33] – including that of Germany – thus affecting her career considerably from the very beginning. Thus, while the cruiser's trials commenced on 23 November 1898, boiler issues soon became evident. The principal problems concerned the boilers' construction, such as bends and cracks in their tubes, leading to subsequent leakage. On the

An unusual view taken from *Gazelle*'s maintop, showing her unique arrangement of her two navigation bridges, albeit partly covered by awnings. The cruiser was then coaling from the collier *Sibiria* at Puerto Caballo, Venezuela, in February 1903. The triangular structure at the bottom right is the forward section of a target-float, to be towed by the steam-launch for target practice abroad. *(DN collection)*

On a gloomy 31 March 1898, *Gazelle* is launched at the Germania shipyard at Kiel. Her unique bow torpedo tube is just visible. *(DN collection)*

33. The US battleship *Maine* and the armoured cruisers *Pennsylvania* and *Colorado* suffered significant issues with theirs, as did the Russian cruiser *Varyag*, which had many of hers out of service with defects when she faced the Japanese at the Battle of Chemulpo in February 1904.

Gazelle in drydock at Newport News, USA, on 5 May 1903. Note the exceptionally large cut-out to give maximum firing arcs for the aft 3.7cm machine-cannon. *(DN collection)*

other hand, if these particular issues are excluded, their overall performance came out quite comparable to other types. During her six-hour continuous full-power trial *Gazelle* attained an average speed of 20.2 knots at 6,366ihp. Interestingly enough, there is no record of a full-power trial on the measured mile at this time[34] – possibly this had been dropped because of the said boiler defects. This first trial period was terminated on 6 April 1899 for these to be rectified, *Gazelle* remaining laid up until 6 October 1900, when she was recommissioned for a new set of trials. This second period was even shorter – only until 14 November – when the defects reoccurred and she was decommissioned again, for yet further major modifications to the boilers.

It was only on 15 June 1901 that *Gazelle* was finally ready for her third commission, and her first operational one. Initially, she joined the Scouting Force, and became part of the II. SG during the annual manoeuvres, but at the beginning of October she received orders to join the East Asiatic Cruiser Squadron. However, these were soon rescinded, and her half-sister *Thetis* (see next chapter) sent in her stead. Orders were renewed at the beginning of 1902, with a further amendment that *Gazelle* was now to join and reinforce the assembled forces in the West Indies first prior to proceeding to her new long-term station. Thus, on 12 January *Gazelle* left Kiel for the Americas, calling at Port of Spain on 3 February.

Her allocation to the East Asiatic Cruiser Squadron was finally cancelled in the autumn of 1902, in favour of the newly founded East American Cruiser Division. This force immediately joined forces with UK vessels in blockading the

34. There are, in fact, some records of *Gazelle* running a measured mile, but they originate from the second – likewise abortive – trial period at the end of 1900. The recorded maximum power of 4,885ihp is so much below the design criteria that it can hardly be regarded as a full-power trial.

Official plans for *Gazelle*, redrawn September 1907, showing her following reboilering. *(DN collection)*

Venezuelan coast following the Venezuelan President Cipriano Castro's refusal to pay foreign debts and damages claims arising from the country's recent civil wars.

Gazelle took a special part in the operations, when her crew captured the Venezuelan 'cruiser'[35] *Restaurador* on 11 December in a surprise attack by her boats. The following months of spring 1903 were spent refitting at Newport News in the USA, before sailing north to ascend the St Lawrence River as far as Montreal. On 27 October, *Gazelle* was back in the Caribbean – just in time to greet the new division chief, Kdre Ludwig Schröder (1854–1933). Several short voyages around the Caribbean followed until *Gazelle* was ordered home on 19 June 1904. After a short stopover at Kiel on 18 July she decommissioned on 3 August at Danzig Dockyard for a refit, which lasted from May 1905 to October 1907.

Work included the removal of the troublesome Niclausse boilers and during 1905–07 *Gazelle* was reboilered with what had by then become the fleet standard – the Schulz-type 'Navy' boiler. However, always short of personnel, the German navy had no immediate use for the renewed vessel, which would not be employed again in peacetime.

35. The term 'cruiser' is something of an exaggeration for the 750-ton former US pleasure yacht *Atlanta* (1883), armed with one 12pdr and four single 6pdr, making her no more than a gunboat. Nevertheless, it came out afterwards that the captain of *Restaurador* had been prepared to make a desperate surprise attack on *Gazelle* himself, before scuttling his vessel with flying colours to save his honour. *Restaurador* was briefly officially commissioned into the German navy, from 14 January to 18 February 1903, to chase smugglers running the blockade. Afterwards, she was returned to the Venezuelan navy on 23 February and served as *General Salom* until 1950.

4 THE FLEET LAWS AND BEYOND

AT THIS STAGE it is impossible to continue the history of the small cruiser without a closer look at the Fleet Law of 1898, later to be known as the 'First Fleet Law'. Its origins clearly lay in *Dienstschrift IX*, adjusted by Tirpitz to reflect his more recent thinking and – not least – financial realities. The full text of the Law is given in Appendix 1; here, we will consider those parts relevant to the small cruiser.

In *Dienstschrift IX*, Tirpitz had outlined his perceived requirements for a fleet created for 'the offensive' in home waters. The envisaged seventeen battleships (i.e. two squadrons of eight, plus one fleet flagship) would require six torpedo boat flotillas, six I. class and twelve III. class cruisers as support. Not included in these numbers were cruisers required for service on foreign stations – the 'station ships' and those to belong to a widely-deployable 'cruiser-division'. These extra vessels would add-up, as Tirpitz explained in a draft for another memorandum in January 1896,[1] to another nine III. class cruisers. This would be reduced to seven once sufficient I. class cruisers were available for service in the cruiser division .

After his return from the Far East and his appointment as State Secretary at the RMA, Tirpitz became more precise in his prescription of the future needs of the fleet. These were set out in another memorandum, dating from July 1897, entitled *General points of view for determining the outlook of our fleet in regard to classes and types of vessels*.[2] In this he was somewhat ambiguous regarding the value of scouting vessels (cruisers) for the somewhat limited tasks foreseen for the German navy in the North Sea. Despite restressing his conception of building the fleet for the strategic offensive, Tirpitz nevertheless wanted to limit the number of scouting vessels as far as possible, because, 'against England or any other fleet intruding in our waters, the relevance of scouting vessels reduces significantly'. In other words, he expected a fundamentally defensive role for the fleet in the German Bight, to which he wanted 'them [the potential enemies] to come'. Tirpitz continued: 'The other [small] cruisers must accordingly be made only as large as suitable for developing sufficient speed in bad weather.'

[1] BA-MA N 253/3 Nachlass Tirpitz AB 102-105 (cited in V R Berghahn and W. Deist, *Rüstung im Zeichen der wilheminischen Weltpolitik: Grundlegende Dokumente 1890–1914* [Düsseldorf: Droste, 1988], pp 106–7).

[2] BA-MA N 253/4 Nachlass Tirpitz AB 8-18 (Berghahn and Deist, *Rüstung*, p 123).

This time he included in his calculations the numbers of III.-class cruisers needed to act as repeating ships within the fleet, a role hitherto performed by the avisos, giving him a total number of eighteen small cruisers for fleet work. In the later parts of the memorandum he set out his principles as to how the fleet for foreign service should be composed – which would eventually be in force until the end of the Imperial navy:

> The vessels abroad have to be viewed as being simply detached from home waters … This circumstance makes it clear that, for a yet undefined period, we shall employ naval forces abroad on the basis of their qualities as scouting vessels at home. This foundation for identical basic designs becomes reinforced further by the requirement to align the vessels abroad more completely with those coming from home, either by making them fit into the existing vessels there or, the other way around, by fitting in the vessels returning from overseas.
>
> It has to be a basic principle that those vessels ordinarily intended for foreign service have to be designed according to the basic constructive principles applied to the vessels at home until experience has proven the necessity of a deviation from these principles. This has not been the case so far […].

His ultimate conclusion was that for general overseas service nine small cruisers would be sufficient, with another three as materiel reserve, which brought the total number of small cruisers required to thirty. These numbers were fine-tuned in the papers issued to the Reichstag in support of the proposed Fleet Law. The members now had to decide whether to approve sixteen small cruisers for the fleet (including materiel reserve vessels in home waters), ten small cruisers for service abroad and four in reserve. Their service lifetimes – counted from the approval of the first instalment of a ship's construction to the approval of the first instalment of the replacement vessel – was set at fifteen years, which automatically guaranteed – under normal circumstances – the construction of two vessels per year.

The only exceptions were the small cruisers built during the six-year period set for the completion of the first Fleet Law, most of which were to be additions to strength, to bring the overall force up to its new legal level. At the point of implementation of the Law, 1 April 1898, twenty-three 'small cruisers' were extant, the classification bringing together all extant cruising vessels still classified as such, other than *Fürst Bismarck*, the *Victoria Louise* class and *Kaiserin Augusta* (which became 'large cruisers'). The old 'II. class cruiser' category was thus between the two types, the *Irene*s becoming small cruisers.

The oldest of them, *Zieten*, had been begun in 1875, and was thus at least eight years beyond her legal replacement point. However, it was much more important for Tirpitz, within the limited budget, to attain the accepted total number as fast as possible: thus, instead of replacing legally over-age vessels, priority was given in the forthcoming 1898, 1899 and 1900 programmes to building two 'new' small cruisers annually, before commencing the replacement of over-age ships.

To meet the terms of the Law (for whose text see pp 290-93), sufficient personnel would be made available to fully man all active capital ships and small cruisers (except for those serving overseas, where a crew-and-a-half per ship was needed), plus half the torpedo craft and other supporting vessels. For the reserve ships, half-crews would be provided (two-thirds for engineering personnel). The Law also provided for the funding of the programme, including the option of rolling over of any underspend into the next financial year – a novelty in German (and most other countries'!) public finance.

Under the follow-on 'Second Fleet Law' of 14 June 1900 (pp 293–94), the fleet in home waters would be drastically enlarged. As the core of the fleet, battleship numbers were to be doubled by 1917, the numbers of their supporting vessels, including small cruisers, had to be further augmented as well. Now, twenty-four small cruisers would be necessary for service with the fleet, although the numbers for foreign stations and their reserve remained untouched. This would give a total of thirty-eight small cruisers in 1917, of which twenty-nine, extant or under construction, could be counted at the date of the ratification.

THE FIRST SIX ADDITIONAL SMALL CRUISERS

The initial small cruisers built as a result of the First Fleet Law were in due course designated *Small Cruisers A* and *B*, as part of the 1898/99 Estimates, which also included *Large Cruiser A* [to be *Prinz Heinrich*]. The small cruisers were (by a decree of the Kaiser on 24 August 1897) to be full sisters of *Gazelle*, this being reflected in their preliminary plans.

However, the preparation of the necessary documents and definitive plans overburdened the still moderately sized depart-

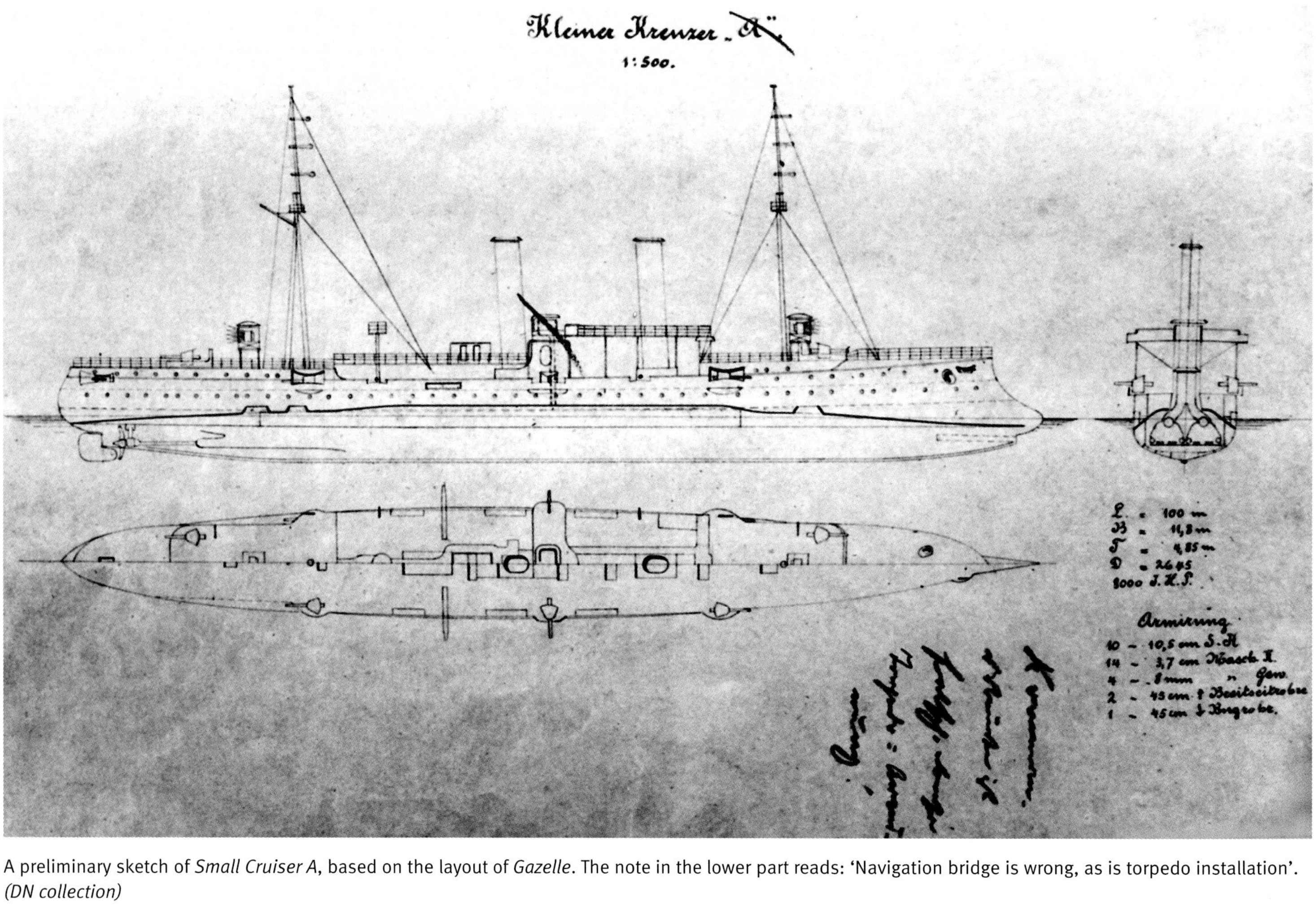

A preliminary sketch of *Small Cruiser A*, based on the layout of *Gazelle*. The note in the lower part reads: 'Navigation bridge is wrong, as is torpedo installation'. *(DN collection)*

ment 'K', and on 23 December 1897, Dietrich reported to Tirpitz that the preparation of the drawings for *Small Cruiser B* (to be built under contract) and their subsequent colouring had had to be contracted out. He expected them to be finished at the beginning of February; on the other hand, documentation and plans for *Small Cruiser A* had already been sent to the Danzig Dockyard for the preparation of an internal proposal.

Interestingly, Tirpitz still seems not to have been entirely happy with the new cruiser type. On 20 January 1898, he informed 'K' of his intention to hold a prize competition among naval dockyards, private yards and interested naval architects regarding a design for a small cruiser. 'A' was ordered to urgently develop the necessary list of requirements, which was done as early as 28 January. Unsurprisingly, its details did not differ significantly from those of the cruisers now under construction: above all, the price was fixed at 4.6 million Marks, which had been the basis for the calculations underlying the Fleet Law. The specified speed was slightly higher than that of the current design, to equal or exceed 20.5 knots on a continuous six-hour run; for twenty-four hours, 17.75 knots should be attained. At 12 knots, the endurance should be at least 5,500nm. All other major features should be equivalent to those of *Gazelle*. It remains uncertain whether or not this competition was ever launched, even if an unsolicited offer from Germania (see just below) may be indicative of some 'leaks' from within the RMA.

Nevertheless, *Small Cruisers A* and *B* were both ordered immediately after the approval of the Fleet Law in April 1898, and laid down in August and November 1898. Owing to an oddity in the ordering process, *Small Cruiser B* [to be *Niobe* (ii)] preceded *Small Cruiser A* [*Nymphe* (ii)] onto the slipway: Tirpitz had decreed on 15 April 1898 that the first cruiser would be built under contract, and would to be fitted – like *Gazelle* – with wood-and-Muntz metal sheathing, but would receive the designation *Small Cruiser B*.

The second cruiser, which, as was noted above, had been planned to be built first by direct award to Danzig Dockyard, was now also to go out to tender, but still retained her originally planned designation as *Small Cruiser A*. The reasons for this change of mind are still obscure: perhaps it was a relic from the abortive competition.

Both cruisers were in some ways transitional vessels, and not exact models for follow-on units – although *Small Cruiser A* came close. In one respect, at least, the OKM's issues with earlier ships were addressed. The Germania yard, which was a competitor for building one of the new pair, and was already building *Gazelle* herself, worked out that installed power could be raised from 6,000 to 8,000ihp without affecting the dimensions of the machinery spaces. This would allow the achievement of the desired maximum speed of 21–21.5 knots by the new pair, principally through substituting different numbers and types of boilers for the Niclausse units being fitted in *Gazelle*. AG Weser who, in the meantime, had won the order for *Small Cruiser B* and had originally planned to install

Niobe on the Jade river off Wilhelmshaven, probably in preparation for *Hohenzollern* escort duty. An early, crude, aerial for W/T has already been rigged; her W/T rig had been updated by the time that the rigging plan below was produced, during her lay-up from 1909 onward, and shows her configuration at the beginning of the First World War. *(DN collection)*

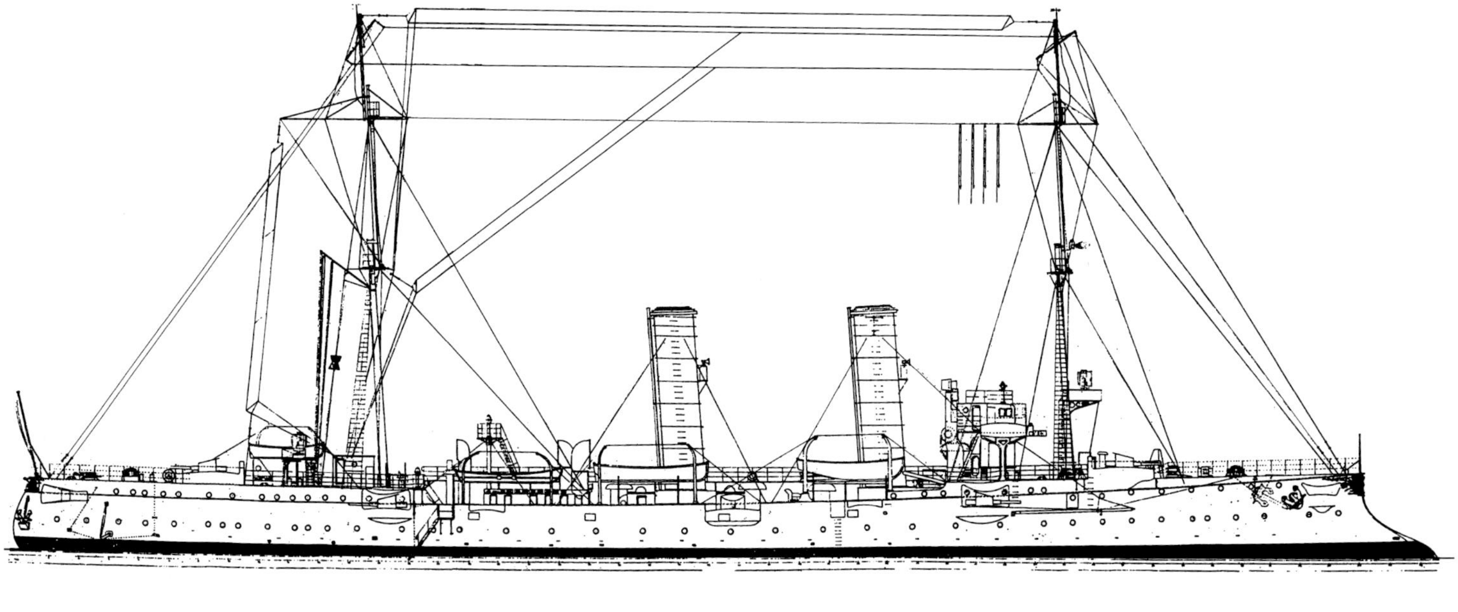

Yarrow-type boilers, was asked to adopt Germania's proposal, and complied by agreeing to fit eight of the Thornycroft type. The maintenance of boiler-numbers would, nevertheless, result in *Small Cruiser B* sharing *Gazelle*'s narrower funnel-spacing, as compared with *Small Cruiser A*, and their later sisters, which would have a larger number of boilers and slightly more broadly spaced funnels.

This further change in boiler arrangements was a result of a view that the expected gains in performance in *Small Cruiser B* would still be insufficient. Consequently, Germania, winner of the second order (*Small Cruiser A*), incorporated further modifications to increase the radius of action while also achieving a higher sustained speed. The former could only be achieved by increasing the capacity of the bunkers, which required weight compensation elsewhere. The solution was found in omitting the wood-and-metal sheathing, a change that had already been proposed by Tirpitz and discussed on 14 January 1898. The small loss of protection against damage by grounding would be compensated for by extending the double-bottom from 40 per cent to 60 per cent of the waterline length, and outward from longitudinal frame I to III laterally. This would, of course, reduce the ship's resistance to hull fouling, especially on overseas stations, but as already seen, Tirpitz's view was that requirements for overseas vessels should not be subordinated to the needs of the home fleet.

Additionally, the stem and the stern, hitherto made of cast bronze in their lower parts, would be replaced by lighter cast steel. The saving in weight was calculated at about 130 tonnes, of which 80 tonnes could be used for additional coal stowage and 50 tonnes for improving the machinery. The resulting output, as calculated by 'K', might, indeed, reach 9,000ihp, another welcome benefit. The department compared the vital statistics of *Gazelle*, *Small Cruiser B* and *Small Cruiser A* in a table, partly reproduced below; elements of secondary importance that did not differ are omitted. It may be noted that the two new ships were originally to share *Gazelle*'s torpedo arrangements but the bow tube was eventually omitted (cf. p 94, above).

	Gazelle	*Small Cruiser B*	*Small Cruiser A*
Normal displacement	2,645	2,645	2,645
Length pp	100m	100m	100m
Beam	11.8m	11.8m	11.8m
Draught (average)	4.85m	4.85m	4.81m
Engine power (max.)	6,000ihp	8,000ihp	8,000–9,000ihp
Type of boiler	Niclausse	Thornycroft	Small-tube
Coal (normal)	300 tonnes	300 tonnes	380 tonnes
- " – (full)	500 tonnes	500 tonnes	580 tonnes
Speed (max.)	19.5–20 knots	21.5 knots	21.9 knots
Sustainable engine power	3,600ihp	3,600ihp	4,000ihp
related speed	16.5 knots	16.5 knots	17.4 knots
related endurance	2,200nm	2,200nm	2,500nm
Engine power for 10 knots	900ihp	900ihp	900ihp
related endurance	4,750nm	4,750nm	5,500nm

Gazelle's central engine control position, showing that there was insufficient space between the main engines for the installation of a centreline bulkhead. *(DN collection)*

The most obvious external difference between the new pair and *Gazelle* would be the relocation of bridge and conning tower and had its origin in a departmental meeting of 6 April 1898. First, it was decided that *Gazelle* should receive another conning position plus small navigation bridge forward of the forefunnel. Second, Tirpitz further expressed his opinion that, in future vessels, the main bridge should be positioned forward of the forefunnel, while a lightly built second bridge should be positioned further aft; however, it was decided to postpone the final decision until *Gazelle* was closer to completion. Eventually, in December, the revised arrangement was approved unanimously, not least because of its greater simplicity. The aft bridge, to be mounted at the forward edge of the poop, was given the designation 'foul-weather bridge', in case the main bridge was washed out by severe weather coming over the bow.

As 'W' had recently designed a submerged broadside torpedo tube suitable for cruisers, additional weight could be saved by reducing the outfit from three to two tubes, omitting the tactically inflexible bow tube. During discussions it was queried whether the saved weight could be employed for mounting two additional 8.8cm QL in the former positions of the deck-mounted tubes, but this was not taken forward.

At the end of 1898, discussions regarding the mounting of a heavier battery were again revived. Initially, Tirpitz supported the idea that a single 15cm QL should replace the paired 10.5cm fore and aft, but was convinced by 'A' that it was not appropriate to raise new uncertainties regarding weights before other open questions had been resolved by experience with *Gazelle*. During this meeting it was further decided to equip *Small Cruiser A* with five boilers of the new Thornycroft-Schulz type (four double-, one single-ender) instead of the eight Thornycroft-single-enders of *Small Cruiser B*, which were expected to guarantee the necessary steam production for the generation of the envisaged 8,000–9,000ihp.

Despite Tirpitz's wishes, *Small Cruiser A* lacked – like *Gazelle* – a longitudinal bulkhead between the main engines, because the engine control positions were placed inboard, which left no space in the narrow hull for the installation of a centreline bulkhead. Tirpitz's desire to include this feature in the new small cruisers was based on the fear of a total loss of propulsive power in case of a lucky hit in the engine room, or a failure of one of the high-pressure steam pipes, as had happened on the battleship *Brandenburg* in February 1894.[3] Consequently, 'K' was ordered to make provision for the feature during preparatory work for *Small Cruisers C* and *D*; this, however, also came to nought.

Another proposal was that the hitherto unprotected openings in the armour deck – such as funnel uptakes and ventilation trunks – should be made splinter-proof in the future. This could be done either by reducing their area to the lowest possible limit, or by introducing armour gratings, which would ironically require the penetrations to be made significantly larger, to guarantee the necessary cross-cut area. Tirpitz decided in favour of the latter, as any kind of unprotected openings could let in splinters, irrespective of their size. The additional weight of the gratings would be compensated for, in part, by a reduction in thickness of the sloping parts of the armour deck from 50 to 45mm.[4] Further compensation was required for an increase in the thickness of the conning tower, which had now been moved forward. Instead of 70mm non-cemented steel, in the future it was to be constructed of 80mm face-hardened steel.[5] 'K' was encouraged to maintain two different orders of construction for *Small Cruisers A* and *B* until the evening of 31 December 1898, in parallel with the drafting of a memorandum to be presented to the Kaiser regarding the constructive details for *Small Cruisers C* and *D*.

The memorandum was presented to Tirpitz on 1 January 1899, summarising the intended deviations of the design of forthcoming *Small Cruisers C* and *D* from that of *Small Cruiser A*. As was now common in the German navy, there was a fight over every kilogramme of weight. While the machinery of *Small Cruiser C* [to be *Thetis*], to be built under direct award by Danzig Dockyard, would remain at a total weight of 566 tonnes, it was expected that the machinery weight of *Small Cruiser D* [*Ariadne*] could be brought down to 530 tonnes in total, e.g. by exchanging the existing 4-cylinder VTE engines with the 3-cylinder type, thus gaining 36 tonnes for further (so far unspecified) improvements.

Thus, on 9 January 1899, the Kaiser not only finally decreed the construction of *Small Cruisers A* and *B* (1898 Estimates) to their now individual specifications, but also issued a joint decree for *Small Cruisers C* and *D* (1899 Estimates), as well. Furthermore, one month later, on 13 February 1899, the 'All-Highest' issued another decree, which authorised the subsequent *Small Cruisers E* and *F* (1900 Estimates [to be *Medusa* and *Amazone*]) to the same specification as *Small Cruiser D*: the implementation of the Fleet law was now truly under way.

However, during the five weeks between the decrees for construction for the two pairs, the first demands for changes were being raised that, consequently, would affect the construction of all of *Small Cruisers A–D*. Department 'A' was concerned

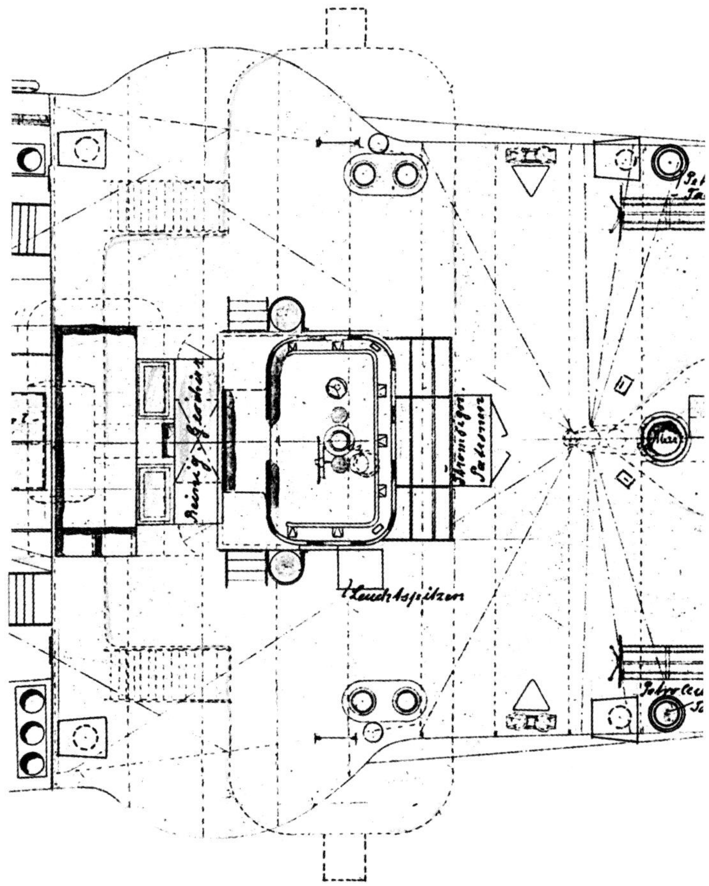

Part of a plan of *Niobe*'s forecastle deck, showing the new arrangement of her conning tower, as compared with that in *Gazelle*. The outlines show the structure of the bridge deck atop the conning tower. *(DN collection)*

3. During a forced power trial of the new ship on 16 February 1894 her starboard main throttle valve burst loose from its flanges and opened the whole cross section of the steam pipe into the starboard engine room. Forty-four people died immediately or shortly afterwards as a result of this accident. It was one of the greatest disasters to befall the German navy in peacetime.

4. The sloped deck armour consisted of the following layers: 10mm mild steel + 10mm mild steel + 30(25)mm armour plate.

5. A thickness of 80mm was usually considered the smallest plate on which the face-hardening process could be applied.

mainly with the number and distribution of the boilers in *Small Cruiser A*, which was now seen as tactically problematic. On longer cruises, the grates needed to be cleaned in turn, meaning that at most times one would need to be off-line. Where a ship had four double-ended boilers, the cleaning regime would deprive the engines of a quarter of potential steam production. However, taking one of eight single-enders off-line would mean that the steam loss only amounted to 12.5 per cent. Accordingly, 'A' proposed the return to the latter type, ending up with eight plus one single-enders in two boiler rooms, instead of four double-enders plus one single-ender. As the proposal neither generated higher costs and weights, nor had any negative tactical implications, the design of *Small Cruisers C–F* was altered accordingly.

Additionally, Tirpitz, in a meeting on 7 February 1899, had raised the question of strengthening the protective shields of the 10.5cm guns against projectiles up to 3in (7.6cm) calibre at anything other than point-blank range. The subsequent discussions, including firing tests to determine the minimum required thickness, lasted well into December. In the course of the trials it had been found necessary to put 50mm armour on the curved front plate, 25mm on the sloped sides and 20mm on the sloping roof plate. (see drawing p 95) Compensation would be provided, first, by restricting armoured shields to the exposed mountings on the forecastle and the poop deck. Second, in *Small Cruisers C–F*, the planned outfit of fourteen 3.7cm machine cannon would be reduced to ten (six firing mainly forward, four mainly aft). The related magazines were converted into additional coal bunkers. The cut in numbers of 3.7cm weapons was later applied to *Gazelle* and *Small Cruisers B* and *A* as well – for reasons of class homogeneity only, as they were now too far advanced to receive the stronger shields.

Niobe

Small Cruiser B was laid down by AG Weser, Bremen, on 30 August 1898 and launched as *Niobe* on 18 July 1899. Her completion was originally intended for 1 November 1899, but although the ship was almost finished, the harsh winter caused damage through lack of care by the shipyard. She finally commissioned for trials on 25 June 1900, which were completed on 22 August. Laid up during the winter, she recommissioned on 11 April 1901 and became flagship of the I. TBF on the 18th, relieving *Blitz*. *Niobe* served as such until 26 June, on 28 June – being the newest small cruiser – becoming escort for the imperial yacht *Hohenzollern* on the customary voyage to Norway. She served with the I. Sqn during the annual manoeu-

Nymphe while serving as escort to the imperial yacht *Hohenzollern*. In contrast to her near-sister *Niobe*, the lack of the 'step' of the upper edge of underwater sheathing is very clear. *(DN collection)*

vres, and then the imperial yacht when the Kaiser met with the Emperor of Russia from 11 to 13 September. After this duty, *Niobe* was refitted at Wilhelmshaven 1 October to 1 April 1902.

She then rejoined the I. TBF in the Baltic, once again serving with the I. Sqn for the manoeuvres and a winter cruise, before again leading the I. TBF from the beginning of 1903. It was intended to send *Niobe* to join the force blockading Venezuela, but this was dissolved before she could set out, the cruiser instead being assigned, on 1 March 1903, to the newly formed Scouting Force, remaining with it until after the fleet manoeuvres of 1904 and decommissioning for a major refit on 29 September. *Niobe* recommissioned on 19 June 1906, for the East Asiatic Cruiser Squadron, leaving Wilhelmshaven on 9 July and meeting the squadron on 8 September. She remained on the station until 31 January 1909, when she began her return voyage from Tsingtau to Kiel, arriving on 21 March. She was decommissioned at the end of the month.

Nymphe

Germania laid down *Small Cruiser A* on 19 November 1898, and launched her as *Nymphe* almost exactly a year later, on 21 November 1899. She was slated to commission on 1 March 1900, but actually commissioned for trials only on 20 September, which were interrupted in January 1901 when she was assigned to escort the imperial yacht, carrying the Kaiser to the funeral of Queen Victoria of the UK. As such, the cruiser lay off Portsmouth from 26 January to 5 February, before visiting Sheerness, and then Vlissingen, Netherlands, and arriving back in home waters on 8 February to resume trials. These were completed in March, after which *Nymphe* joined the Torpedo Inspectorate as a trials vessel. However, in June 1901, she was again detached on imperial yacht escort duties during the Kiel Week regatta. She undertook the escort role for the 1902 and 1903 regattas, visits to Reval (Tallinn) in August 1902, the UK in November 1902, Copenhagen in April 1903, and the Kaiser's cruise to Norway in July 1903. From 16 March to 3 April 1904, she undertook a training cruise to Norwegian waters with her fellow torpedo trials ship *Neptun* (ex-*Friedrich Carl*), including test firings. Each year she also took part in the annual manoeuvres.

In January 1905, *Nymphe* briefly took over the role as primary torpedo trials ship from the battleship *Schwaben*, being relieved by the new small cruiser *München* on 30 March. *Nymphe* now took over from *Olga* as a gunnery training ship in the Naval Artillery Inspectorate. She took part in the cruise of the Training and Trials Ships Force in April and May 1906, and rescued survivors from the torpedo boat *S126* when this was sunk following a collision with *Undine* in the Baltic on 17 November.

During May/June 1907, *Nymphe* was rearmed at Wilhelmshaven, when four of her starboard 10.5cm were replaced with four 8.8cm and two 5.2cm guns to reflect her role as a gunnery training ship. She recommissioned on 2 July, and served with the temporarily created III. Sqn during that summer's manoeuvres. While so engaged she was accidentally rammed by the coast defence ship *Frithjof* on 31 August. Damaged on the port side aft, *Nymphe* went to Kiel for repairs, decommissioning on 19 September. Laid up at Danzig when work was finished, she recommissioned on 23 May 1908, serving until February 1909, on relief in her training role by the *Stuttgart*; *Nymphe* was then placed in reserve.

Thetis

As noted previously, *Small Cruiser C* was essentially the first of the 'standardised' small cruisers. She was laid down at the Imperial Dockyard Danzig on 2 September 1899, launched as *Thetis* on 3 July 1900, and commissioned for trials on 14 September 1901. On 1 December, she was allocated to the East Asiatic Cruiser Squadron, proceeding via the Mediterranean, Suez Canal and Red Sea, stopping at Aden, Colombo and Calcutta, where she met the Austro-Hungarian cruiser *Zenta*; she reached Singapore on 7 February 1902. The commander of the East Asiatic Cruiser Squadron ascended the Yangtze river in *Thetis* from 28 April, visiting Wusung, Nanking and Hankow before returning to Tsingtau on 15 May. After the outbreak of the Russo-Japanese War in February 1904, *Thetis* was sent to Chemulpo (Inchon) in Korea to evacuate German nationals from the country, and cruised the Yangtze once more from October to December.

Following the outbreak of the Maji-Maji rebellion in German East Africa in July 1905, *Thetis* was detached to the area as a reinforcement to *Bussard*, leaving Hong Kong on 28 August. She arrived in East African waters on 26 September, and was there joined by *Seeadler* on 1 October. *Thetis* remained at Dar es-Salaam until 29 March 1906, when she was ordered back to Germany. She was decommissioned at Danzig on 18 June for a major refit, after which she was placed in reserve until recommissioned for war service in 1914. She was thus the Imperial navy's only small cruiser never to have served in home waters in peacetime.

A fine view of *Thetis* during her sea trials on 15 November 1901, already painted white/buff for her intended deployment to the Far East. In contrast to *Nymphe*, and in accordance with regulations, the dividing line between white and buff has been accentuated by a red stripe. *(DN collection)*

Above: 'Change of watch': *Thetis* (inboard) is about to decommission, while her relief, *Niobe*, moored outboard, prepares for her deployment to the Far East. A close inspection reveals the slightly different distances between the funnels of the two near-sisters. *Niobe* bears yet another variant of the theoretically standardised paint scheme. To the right, the bow of the decommissioned *Gefion* is just visible. *(DN collection)*

Below: The port of Kristiansund during the 1904 fleet's annual summer cruise into Norwegian waters: from the left are *Ariadne*, *Niobe*, *Prinz Heinrich* (flag) and *Friedrich Carl*. *(DN collection)*

Ariadne

Small Cruiser D was laid down on 14 December 1899 at AG Weser, being launched as *Ariadne* on 10 August 1900; she commissioned for sea trials on 18 May 1901. During these her port-forward boiler exploded on 11 July, killing three and injuring three more. The cause was traced to be the fact that one feed pump served several boilers at the same time. The system was as a consequence prone to an imbalance of water supply between individual boilers, with the possibility (as in this case) of one boiler being catastrophically starved of feed water. Following repairs, the ship finally completed her trials on 22 October 1902. She then became part of I. Sqn, before transferring to the Scouting Force on 1 March 1903, with which *Ariadne* sailed soon afterwards on a training cruise to Spanish waters. In July, she joined much of the German fleet on a visit to Norwegian waters, followed by the annual manoeuvres in the North and Baltic Seas.

She took part in further fleet exercises in May 1904, followed by a naval review for King Edward VII of the UK during his visit to Kiel; *Ariadne* acted as escort to the imperial yacht on a cruise from 3 to 10 September. In March 1905 she was among the vessels that aided the battleship *Mecklenburg* when she ran aground in the Great Belt, within the Danish archipelago, and in February 1906 *Ariadne* escorted the battleship *Preußen*, which represented Germany at the funeral of King Frederik VIII of Denmark. The cruiser was decommissioned at Wilhelmshaven on 22 September 1906 and placed in reserve.

Medusa

AG Weser laid the keel of *Small Cruiser E* on 22 January 1900, her launch as *Medusa* taking place on 5 December 1900; she commissioned for trials on 26 July 1901. These trials ended on 11 September, but owing to manpower shortages the ship was then laid up until recommissioned on 1 April 1903 to join *Ariadne* in the I. Sqn. Her career down to the summer of 1906 was very similar to that of *Ariadne*, but she then remained with the fleet into 1907 until forced out of that year's manoeuvres on 7 September by a machinery defect. A week later, she was relieved by *Königsberg* and on 19 September became temporary replacement for *Nymphe* as a light gunnery training ship during the latter's collision repairs. *Medusa* decommissioned on 23 May 1908, and was then refitted before reducing to reserve.

Amazone

Small Cruiser F was laid down by Germania on 1 December 1899 and launched as *Amazone* on 6 October 1900, being commissioned for trials on 15 November 1901 and joining the fleet on 21 December, at the start of a career that would last more than five decades. She was initially somewhat accident prone. First, on 24 May 1902, while taking part in a fleet cruise around the British Isles that began on 24 April, she was in collision with the battleship *Kaiser Wilhelm II* off Land's End. The cruiser was hit just aft of her foremast, causing significant flooding, but was able to sail under her own power back to Germany, arriving at Kiel on the 27th. Later, after completing

Images of *Medusa* during her pre-First World War active service are rather rare, because of her comparatively short period in commission. Here she is shown at Kiel in 1906. A number of images of the all-but-identical *Ariadne* have been regularly misidentified as *Medusa* (and as *Undine*). *(Heidrich collection)*

The launch of *Amazone* on 6 October 1900 by Grand Duchess Hilda of Baden (1864–1952) at the Germania shipyard. The launch address had been given by Tirpitz, who may be recognised at the top of the stairs. *(DN collection)*

repairs, she rejoined the fleet, but received damage during the 1902 manoeuvres while coming alongside the auxiliary hospital ship *Hansa*. While earmarked to take part in the Venezuela blockade operation, *Amazone* was instead attached to I. Sqn for its cruise to Norway in December.

On 1 March 1903, *Amazone* joined the newly organised fleet Scouting Force, which accompanied I. Sqn on the Atlantic training cruise that began on 7 May. While approaching Brest on 2 June without a pilot, to pick up post for the fleet, her bad luck struck again when she hit an uncharted rock outside the breakwater and remained aground until high tide. Although sent back to Kiel for docking, *Amazone* proved undamaged, and from 4 to 30 July took part in exercises in the North Sea, followed by the annual fleet manoeuvres during August/September, and a winter cruise from 23 November to 5 December.

Amazone was detached to serve as flagship of the I. TBF for exercises during April/May 1904, before returning to her parent formation, including a cruise to Britain and the Netherlands from 23 July to 12 August. Immediately upon her return to Kiel, she was struck by the Russian barque *Anna*, albeit without injury, the ship going on to participate in the annual manoeuvres. While exercising with the torpedo boat training flotilla on 3 March 1905, the still jinxed *Amazone* collided with the torpedo division-boat *D6*, which she towed to Kiel, before herself being docked for repairs that lasted for most of the month. Following their completion, on 4 April, the cruiser repeated her previous role as exercise-flagship for the I. TBF, which continued until 21 May. At the end of May, she rejoined the Scouting Force for its various exercises and visits, and continued with it until the end of the annual manoeuvres, when she was relieved by *Berlin*; decommissioned at Kiel on 28 September 1905, *Amazone* was then placed in reserve.

Amazone in the Kiel Canal. *(DN collection)*

THE SECOND FLEET LAW

The 1898 Law was, as Tirpitz knew very well from the outset, a 'lex imperfecta'. One of its inherent problems was that, while it provided for a swathe of new construction to get the navy up to its legal strength, once its totals had been reached, and the overage ships replaced, the feast for the shipbuilding industry would be replaced by a famine. This was particularly true as far as capital ships were concerned where, owing to a hiatus in orders during the 1880s, nothing could theoretically be ordered between 1905 and 1912, after which period block-obsolescence would produce up to a dozen orders over five years. Such a build-drumbeat was clearly industrially and operationally unsustainable. Second, even if this problem could be overcome, owing to the still moderate size of the postulated fleet, replacements would be far from becoming automatic: Tirpitz desired 'Äternat', the point at which the first ships built under the Fleet Law became legally over-age and replacements laid down automatically purely by virtue of the Law. As far as cruisers were concerned, he was already close to his legal target of thirty. However, the steady building programme during previous decades meant that the 'tail' of old vessels reaching the ends of their fifteen-year legal lifespans was such that two replacement small cruisers could automatically be built annually.

A further bill to expand the fleet to both increase its strength vis-à-vis the British Royal Navy and fill the order gap was therefore contemplated at an early stage, with a view to bringing it before the Reichstag in 1902. However, the detention and searching of German merchantmen by the Royal Navy during the Boer War provided an excuse for bringing the legislation forward: it became law on 14 June 1900, replacing the 1898 act. The result of the new Fleet Law was that three small cruisers were now to be laid down each year until 1906, when the number would drop back to two.

THE *FRAUENLOB* CLASS

The first trio of small cruisers laid down under the new Law were 1901's *Frauenlob* class. Their development, as further modifications to the *Gazelle* design, had started some time previously. In view of the very early issue of the decree of construction for *Small Cruisers E* and *F* in February 1899, it was clear that there would be a significant gap before the next group of vessels could be ordered. This gave all departments ample time to think about fresh requirements, as well to explore options within the original requirement.

A small diversion emerged in April 1899, when Schichau made an offer to Tirpitz to design a high-speed 3,000-tonne cruiser, incorporating the navy's most recent specifications. The yard was obviously trying to exploit their success in winning the contract for the Russian cruiser *Novik* on 17 August 1898, of exactly that proposed size (see Chapter 6). Schichau's motivations remain somewhat obscure, as *Novik* was at best an amalgamation of Russian requirements and German technical ideas; as such, the offer could be seen as a sort of mixture between technology transfer, covert espionage and an attempt to introducing the yard's own ideas into the construction of German warships. However, the following excerpts from the official specification issued on 23 August 1899 by RMA to provide comparability with German 'official' designs limited Schichau's freedom of movement considerably:

> The cruiser is designated for service abroad, hull and machinery thus have to be designed solidly and sturdy.
>
> | | |
> |---|---|
> | 1) Standard displacement (fully supplied, including 450 tonnes coal and 50 tonnes general margin, draught not exceeding 5m.) | 3,000 tonnes |
> | 2) 6h-speed at minimum (fully supplied, including 450 tonnes coal) | 22.0 knots |
> | 3) Metacentric height (fully supplied, including 800 tonnes coal) | >650mm |
> | 4) Hull | Double-bottom and W/T-outboard compartments along boiler and engine rooms, including aux. engine rooms … Bridge and conning tower forward of fore-funnel with uninterrupted views … |
> | 5) Armour | Armour deck as in small cruisers C and D (50, 25 and 20mm thickness) … |
> | […] | |
> | 8) Engines | At forced draught 22 knots speed for minimum 6h; at least two separated engine rooms. |
> | 9) Armament | As in small cruisers C and D … |
> | 10)Torpedo armament | As in small cruisers C and D … |
>
> […][6]

However, at the end of October, Schichau declared itself unable to design a cruiser within the given parameters. In the yard's own estimation, it would require another 450–500 tonnes displacement to fulfil the requirements set by the RMA. The latter does not seem to have been particularly disappointed at this outcome, as it provided clear evidence that even external designers had difficulties meeting the latest requirements within current displacement limits. It thus confirmed the RMA's arguments that a further increase in displacement was inevitable.

On the basis of a marginal note from Tirpitz in the summer of 1899, departments 'K' and 'A' prepared a study regarding the difference in costs between a cruiser of 3,000 tonnes displacement and the 2,659-ton *Small Cruisers C–F*, which came out at about 1.025 million Marks. The study further considered what would be the outcome if the displacement were increased to 3,200 tonnes, should 3,000 tonnes not suffice to meet the requirement.

At the end of November, 'A' presented a paper regarding the future development of the small cruiser type. Its main focus was on a further increase of the bunker capacity, as trials of *Gazelle* and other vessels equipped with watertube boilers had indicated that the latters' coal consumption under actual conditions had been underestimated. Furthermore, it pointed to experience gained during the Spanish-American War, which showed the greater a ship's radius of action the better. Also, it had become evident that the most recent battleships abroad were attaining speeds in excess of 18 knots, and thus if the small cruiser's required margin of at least 3 knots over battleships was to be maintained, new designs of small cruiser must attain speeds of not less than 22 knots. It would only be through a necessary increase in displacement that this, and other long-standing goals, such as the longitudinal division of engine rooms, could possibly be achieved.

A further interesting proposal by Tirpitz was to install

6. BA-MA RM3/3697, fol. 113ff

armoured twin 10.5cm turrets on forecastle and poop, replacing the two single mounts currently mounted in these positions; such turrets were being fitted in the cruiser *Bogatyr* that AG Vulcan was then building for Russia (see p 174, below). This was rejected by 'A', principally for reasons of weight, even if the two single mounts amidships together with their ammunition were to be sacrificed in compensation: the present hull design definitely had no weight margins whatsoever left. Tirpitz himself officially buried the idea in April 1900 – only to revive it a decade later (see p 148, below).

Although the 1900 funding bill was still under discussion in the Reichstag budget committee, the RMA nevertheless felt confident enough about the outcome to prepare the decree of construction for what would now be three small cruisers to be built under the 1901 Estimates. Because of an existing estimated increase in total costs to 3.075 million Marks, the updated requirements did not reflect many of the desiderata in the original specification for the three 1901 cruisers, which would have to be postponed until the 1902 vessels, as shown in the final construction decree:

> I decree that for the small cruisers *G*, *H* and *J* the terms of construction for the small cruisers *C–F* shall apply. However, the upper deck amidships shall be raised,[7] to improve sea-keeping qualities, as well as increasing the bunker capacity.
> Berlin, Schloss, 7 May 1900
>
> Wilhelm I.R.

Luckily, because of the budgetary rules that meant that orders could not be placed until 1901, this decree would remain only an expression of intent for the remainder of 1900. Its content was thus questioned for the first time when the first results of *Nymphe*'s trials came in. During an October departmental meeting, Kpt Rudolf von Eickstedt (1852–1925), head of 'K',[8] highlighted that her stability was close to being critical. If the upper deck (main deck) were to be raised, as planned for *Small Cruisers G, H* and *J*, the vessels would also have to be widened by around 0.5m. This measure would, on one hand, reduce their top speed for about 0.2 knots, but on the other it would allow the introduction of the long-desired longitudinal bulkhead between the engine rooms. Additionally, bunker capacity could be raised from 560 tonnes to 700 tonnes.

These proposals were unanimously accepted, as would also be, over the subsequent months, modifications to the bridge/conning tower structure. Instead of the rectangular conning tower of earlier vessels, a new model with curved sides was introduced. All three ships were officially ordered at the

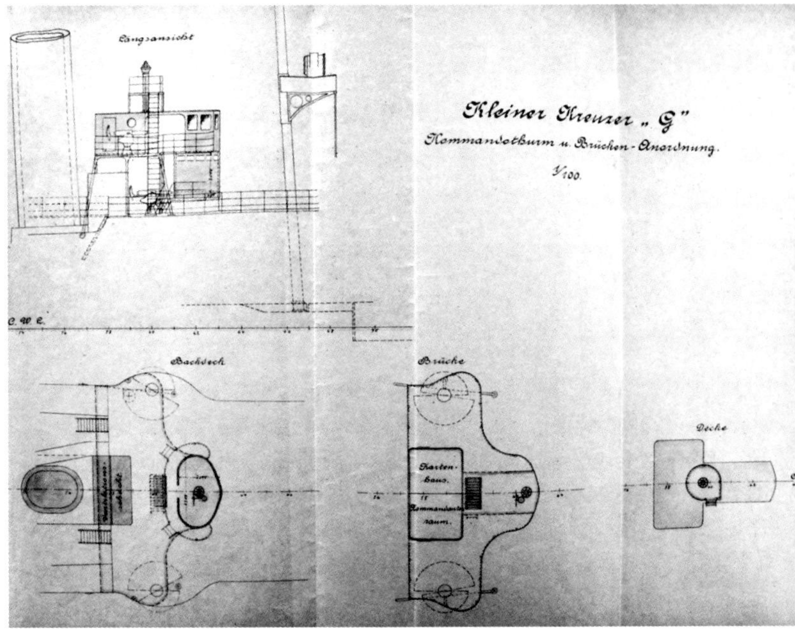

An excerpt from the files regarding modifications to the bridge and conning tower to be applied to the 1901 small cruisers. Most remarkable is the new shape of the conning tower, contrasting with the previous rectangular form. This type would be kept until the 1909 programme vessels. *(DN collection)*

earliest possible date, 1 April 1901, tenders having been received by the RMA at the end of March. AG Weser won a joint contract for the first two, while the third vessel went, as a trial, to a brand-new competitor, Howaldt of Kiel, which had, however, built two cruisers for the Chinese navy back in the 1880s (p 170, below).

Apart from the aforementioned modifications, there were also some changes to the armour arrangements, with the 60mm slopes fore and aft of the flat armour deck thickened to 80mm aft and replaced by a half-deck-height 80mm bulkhead forward; the deck forward of this was thickened to 35mm. This scheme also formed the basis for the protection of the immediately succeeding classes. Externally, a searchlight platform was added to the mainmast and, in *Undine* only, small guns were placed in the captain's cabin in enclosed sponsons. This latter feature would become a standard installation down to the building of the 1905 cruisers.

Frauenlob

Small Cruiser G was laid down on 8 July 1901 on the lower part of an athwart slipway, as was common in AG Weser's old yard, her sister, *Small Cruiser H*, having already been laid down a few weeks earlier on the upper part of the same slip. *G* was launched as *Frauenlob* (ii, named for the schooner lost in 1860) on 22 March 1902: statements that she had been launched earlier than originally planned, owing to congestion in the yard, must be regarded as doubtful, as the part of the slip in question could not be reused until after the launch of *Small Cruiser H* from its upper part – which occurred a month later, on 22 April.

7. It was eventually raised from 7.1m to 7.5m above the keel.

8. The official successor of Dietrich, although not himself a naval architect. After the death of Dietrich, it had been decided that the head of the department should hold a military rank instead of being a civilian. Thus, Dietrich's functional successor, Geheimat Johannes Rudloff, was formally subordinate to Eickstedt.

Frauenlob is launched sideways at the Bremen yard of AG Weser on 22 March 1902; she would be followed a few weeks later by *Arcona* from the upper part of the same slip. *(DN collection)*

Frauenlob commissioned for trials on 17 February 1903, which were observed closely, as those of the first ship of the modified class. During these trials she failed to meet requirements in one particular area: her coal consumption was 0.94kg/ihp/hour instead of the contracted 0.9kg. On the other hand, she attained 21.1 knots on the measured mile and became the fastest of the trio. The cruiser joined the fleet on 5 April with some minor trials still outstanding, but was declared operational for service with both the fleet and abroad two days later. On 23 April, after officially having been released from trials status, she became attached to the I. Sqn as a scouting vessel, and accompanied it to Spain from 7 May to 10 June on her maiden voyage. She served in this capacity and participated in all cruises and manoeuvres of the fleet until her decommissioning on 19 January 1908, by then the last of the *Gazelle*-type still in service; part of her crew transferred to the new *Stettin*.

During 1911/12, *Frauenlob* was reconstructed, initially with the intention that she serve as a light weapons training ship (four guns would be removed to make way for ten 3.7cm weapons), but ultimately to serve as a minelaying cruiser carrying up to 200 mines, to the same scheme as her sister *Arcona* (see below).[9] However, although the work was completed in February 1912, a proposed recommissioning in June 1912 was not carried out, and the ship remained laid up in reserve until August 1914.

Arcona

As already noted, *Small Cruiser H* had been laid down shortly before *Small Cruiser G*, and was built alongside (or, rather, above) her. When launched as *Arcona* in April 1902, she may have gained the distinction of sliding the longest distance down athwart ways of any German warship: 40m in total! She commissioned on 12 May 1903 and, after conducting her trials in June, served with the Scouting Force from 18 July 1903 to 4 April 1907, when she was relieved by, and transferred most of her crew to, the newly-commissioned *Danzig*. *Arcona* was then assigned to the East Asiatic Cruiser Squadron, departing Wilhelmshaven on 27 August 1907 and sailing via the Suez Canal, arriving at Singapore on 23 October; she then proceeded to Tsingtau via Hong Kong and Amoy. She deployed to the East Indies between 8 December 1908 and 21 February 1909, and then to Samoa in the wake of rioting, arriving on 22 March to join *Leipzig*, carrying the station chief, and the gunboat *Jaguar*, by which time the insurrection had largely collapsed.

Accompanied by the supply ship *Titania*, *Arcona* sailed on 6 May via Fiji and Neupommern to Saipan in the Marianas, carrying ringleaders from the Samoan disturbances into exile, before returning to Tsingtau via Guam and then back to Tsingtau. In the autumn of 1909, having sailed via Honolulu, Seattle, San Pedro and San Diego, she represented Germany at the 140th anniversary celebrations of the discovery of San Francisco Bay, and its reconstruction after the 1906 earthquake. Returning via Hawaii, where she towed off the stranded British sailing ship *Celtic Chief*, the cruiser arrived at Yokohama on 24 December 1909.

Ordered back to Germany, *Arcona* sailed from Tsingtau on 17 January 1910, meeting *Leipzig* at Sabang, where they exchanged captains, and *Nürnberg* at Port Said on 4/7 March, with which she exchanged some crew. She arrived at Wilhelmshaven on 24 March and was decommissioned on 30 April. *Arcona* was then rebuilt as a minelaying cruiser during 1911–12, with a mine capacity of 200. Traditionally seen as a weapon deployed by a weaker power, the German navy had acknowledged the utility of the mine and its full potential for the defence of the German Bight only after the events of the Russo-Japanese War, with two specialised fast high-seas minelayers, *Nautilus* and *Albatross*, laid down in 1905 and 1907 (see pp 186-190). However, both would remain the only vessels

Arcona at Kiel, about to leave for the Far East. She was easily distinguishable from her sisters by the unique shape of her engine air intakes. They would be modified before the First World War. Note the open torpedo-loading hatch, which was rather close to the waterline when the ship was under way. *(DN collection)*

9. Curiously, this modification appears to have been ignored by all 'standard works' over the past century.

Stern view of *Arcona* in the outer port at Emden, after her refit as a minelayer but before the outbreak of war, and (below) a longitudinal section and upper-deck plan of *Frauenlob* after her similar reconstruction, showing the stowage of mines in double rows abeam the funnel uptakes and engine-room skylight, with their tracks led together through the poop to the openings visible in the photograph of *Arcona*. *(DN collection)*

of their kind until the commissioning of *Brummer* and *Bremse* in 1916 (pp 190-193), as all cruisers from the 1909 Estimates onwards were built to accommodate dismountable mine rails, with those from the previous three programmes retrofitted to take them (see pp 138-139)

As rebuilt, the most noticeable change in *Arcona* and *Frauenlob* was that the poop now terminated short of the stern, where a minelaying platform was fitted, the mines being transferred aft through the accommodation within the poop. This henceforth served to distinguish the two ships from their sister and half-sisters; both also lost two 10.5cm guns, which were reinstated in 1914.

Undine

The last of her class to commission, and also the last of the *Gazelle* series, *Small Cruiser J* had been laid down at the Howaldt yard on 28 September 1901 – some months after the AG Weser ships. Originally intended to be launched in June/July 1902, her construction suffered from the yard's recent inexperience in building naval vessels. Endless issues arose and had to be resolved between the yard and the building overseers appointed by the RMA. Thus, her launch as *Undine* only finally took place on 11 December 1902. Christened by the President

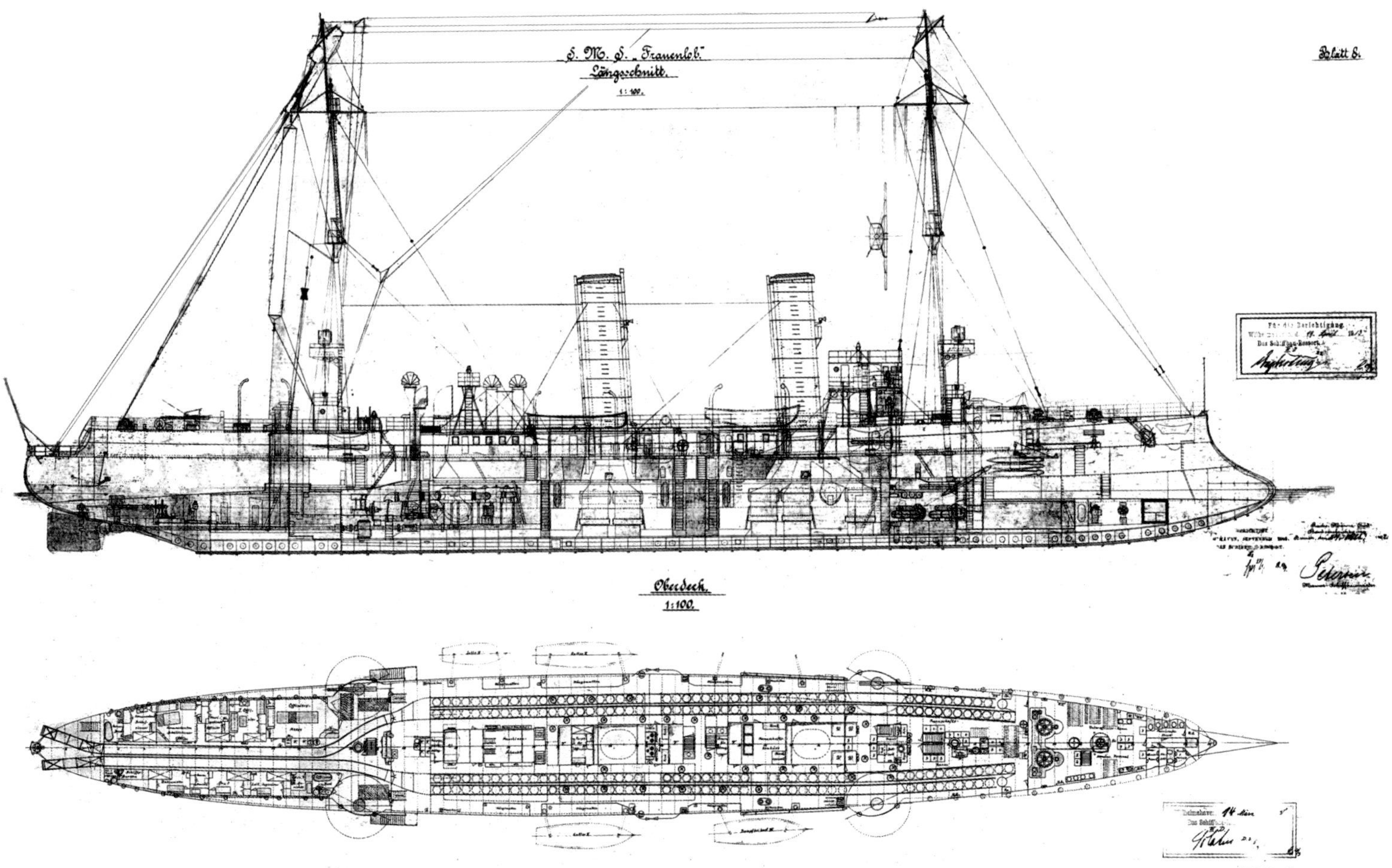

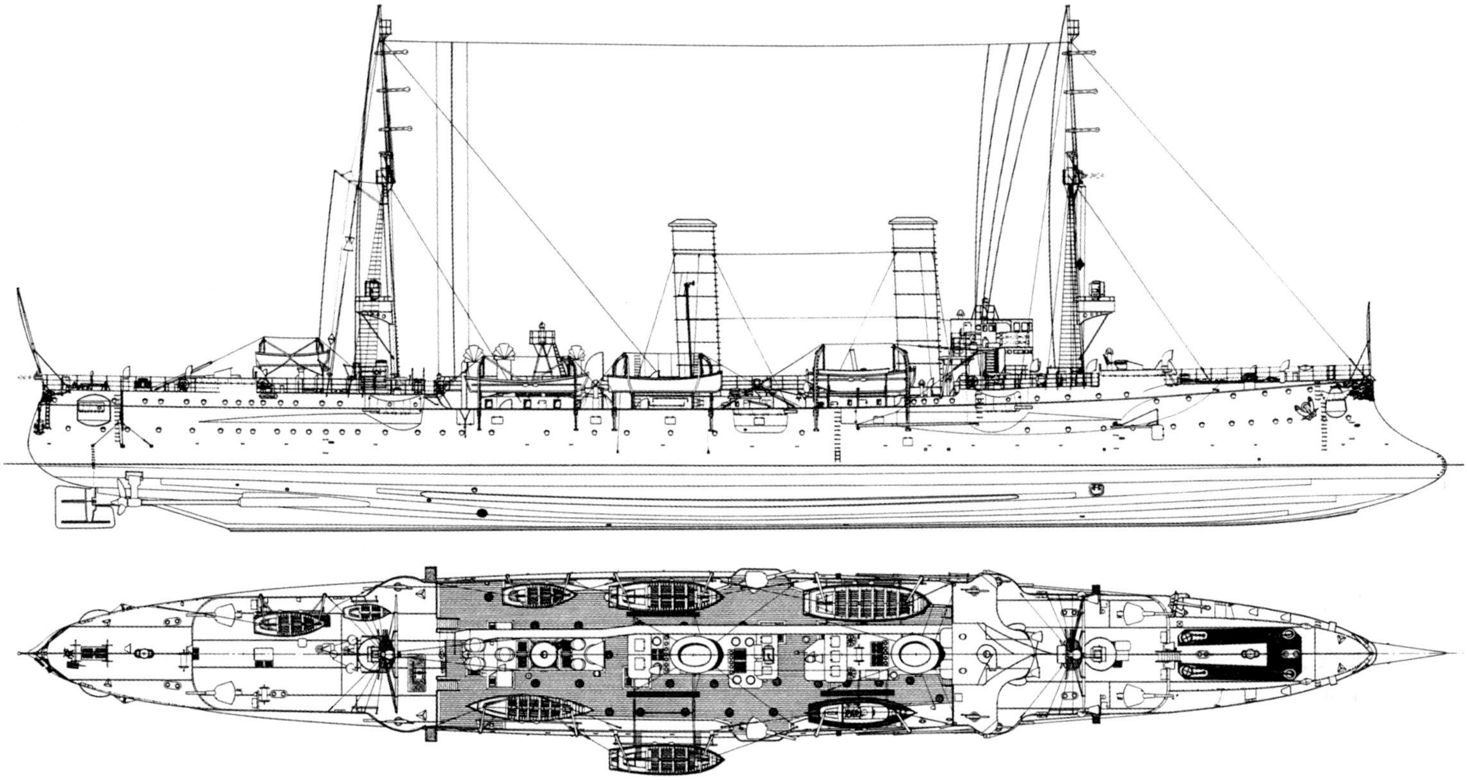

Undine as completed. *(DN drawing)*

of the Navy League,[10] *Undine* thus became 'their' cruiser. She commissioned for trials on 5 January 1904, which ended on 23 March at Wilhelmshaven, when the cruiser was put in reserve for the rest of the year. In view of the worn out state of the former generation of training vessels, *Undine* relieved *Carola* as a gunnery training ship on 5 January 1905.

During night exercises in the Baltic on 17 November 1905, *Undine* rammed the torpedo boat *S126* off Bülk, the latter being cut in two, sinking with the loss of thirty-three lives, although the two halves were later salved, reunited, and the boat returned to service. On 1 July 1908, *Undine* was transferred to the gunnery school at Sonderburg, and refitted at Danzig during September/October 1910. She decommissioned at Danzig on 12 July 1912, when relieved by *Augsburg*; she was then refitted once more before being placed in reserve.

THE *BREMEN* CLASS

The ships of the 1902 Estimates make their first appearance in the files in the autumn of 1899, when 'K' ordered 'K II' to trans-

10. The Deutscher Flottenverein was a pressure group founded on the initiative of Tirpitz in 1898, in particular to agitate in favour of the Fleet Laws, and by 1914 had a million members.

This image of *Undine* belongs to a series of images taken during her trials in Kiel fjord. It has been frequently mis-captioned as other vessels of the *Gazelle*-type, including her sister *Frauenlob*. *(DN collection)*

Part of Sonderburg naval gunnery school, with the two of its ships, *Undine* and, in the background, the battleship *Schwaben*. Note the new topgallants for W/T aerials on *Undine*, as compared to the previous image. *(DN collection)*

form sketchy initial drawings of engine and boiler rooms into a proper design, developing 9,500ihp – better 10,000ihp – in a 3,000-tonne hull. In response, 'K II' reported that the proposed hull was far too small, as the dimensions of the proposed boiler rooms would only allow the fitting of boilers generating 9,200ihp at best. This circumstance ultimately led to the enlargement of the hull to a displacement of 3,200 tonnes.

Negotiations between departments resumed more seriously at the beginning of April 1901, when it had to be decided how this increased displacement might be best used. To increase the top speed by one knot? To strengthen the armament by fitting single 15cm guns in armoured shields on the forecastle and poop instead of current pairs of 10.5cm mountings? Underlying this was the perennial question of the principal role of the small cruiser: a more independently employed unit, fighting against its own kind and, in combination with others, against even stronger units? Or as a pure scouting asset, mainly fending off hostile torpedo boats?

Tirpitz was once again inclined towards the former view, as he explicitly rejected the idea that foreign torpedo services had reached a level of organisation and training that made them a sufficient threat to demand a specific counter. The choice was, in any case, essentially cost neutral. In the event, however, at a meeting on 7 May 1901, Tirpitz gave way to the combined arguments presented by 'A' and 'K' concerning the advantages of the homogeneously armed cruiser.[11] In the new cruiser, bunker capacity would rise to 800 tonnes, top speed to 22–22.5 knots, with a minimum installed power of 10,000ihp; the boilers would now be distributed between three compartments, which would give better ventilation and improve their working. To allow an increase in power of 25 per cent, an additional boiler was installed in the foremost boiler room. This required an extra funnel, giving a basic profile that would be a feature of most future German small cruisers prior to the revolution represented by the *Magdeburg* class (see next chapter).

The maximum thickness of the conning tower would also be raised to 100mm; other changes were also agreed. However, there was still a need to cut weights; accordingly, it was decided to omit shields for the six guns mounted at main deck level, saving weight both directly, and indirectly by cutting the size of the guns' sponsons. Such measures had already been applied in the *Frauenlobs*.

The more powerful engines in the new vessels were larger than those in the previous small cruisers, meaning that the heads of the cylinders now came above armour deck level. They were accordingly protected by a raised glacis of face-hardened armour, 100mm thick. This would remain a feature of German small cruiser design for as long as reciprocating engines remained in use. Turbines, however, had a much lower vertical profile, meaning that the glacis was omitted in vessels powered by this new kind of engine, starting with *Lübeck*. It thus disappeared entirely with ordering of the first all-turbine class, the *Kolbergs* of the 1907 and 1908 Estimates.

Funnels and masts were given a heavy rake in the first five vessels of the resulting series, built under the 1902 and 1903 programmes.[12] All were designed with the same extended 'ram' bow as the *Gazelle* series, but in the event the last 1902 vessel (*Ersatz-Zieten* [to be *Berlin*]) and one of the 1903 vessels (*Small Cruiser M* [*München*]) would receive slightly less exaggerated

11. The Royal Navy had just come to the same conclusion while designing their 'Gem' class: see N Friedman, *British Cruisers of the Victorian Era* (Barnsley: Seaforth, 2012), p 209.

12. This was later reduced in the two of them that underwent major reconstructions: see p 220, below.

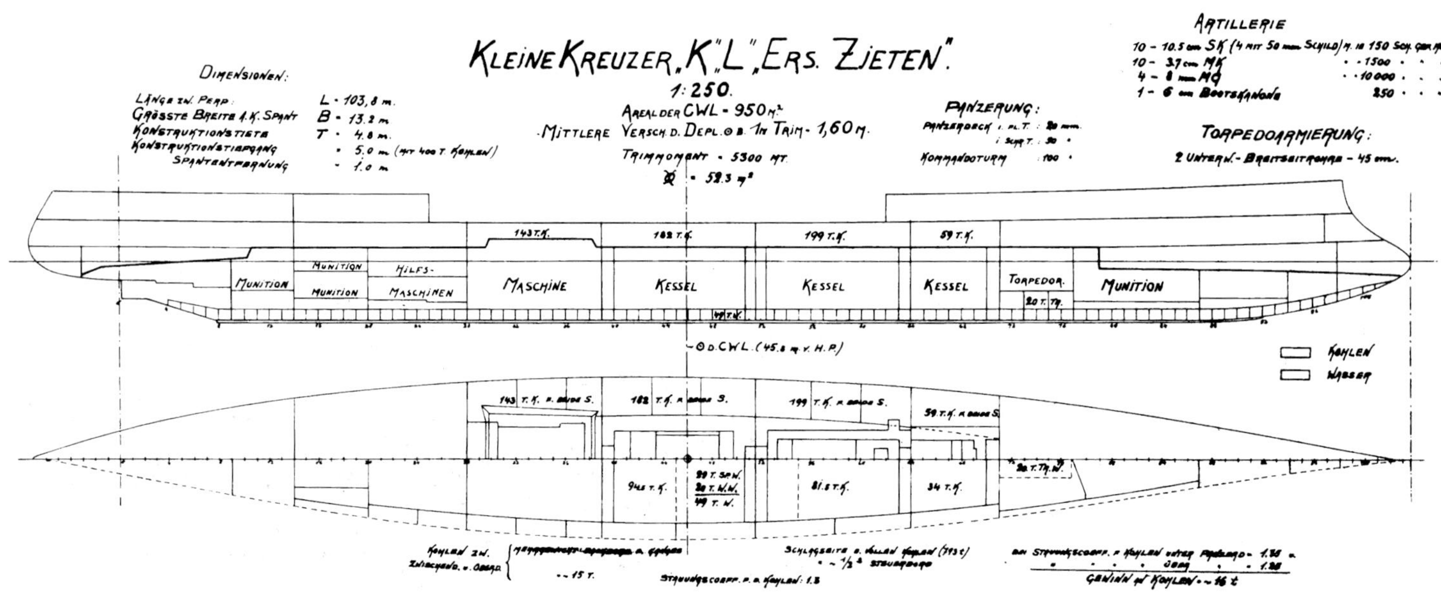

Official profile of the new *Small Cruisers K, L* and *Ersatz-Zieten* [*Bremen* class], showing the main compartments, bunkers and ammunition, together with the armoured glacis over the engine room and principal dimensions. *(DN collection)*

bows than their sisters. The process of redesigning had been started following the sea trials of *Small cruiser K* [*Hamburg*] during the spring of 1904. Everybody had seemed to be happy with the shape of the bows of the *Gazelles*, not the least the Kaiser himself, who had sent an approving note to Tirpitz in August 1901:[13]

> During the voyage from Bergen to Kiel, which I recently concluded within 28½ hours, *Niobe*, in general, fulfilled my expectations, the required high speed of 20 knots was readily maintained; she performed well in the rough seas, the shape of the stem performed especially well against head seas, even in the open ocean while passing Stadlandet [on the Norwegian coast]. This particular shape has to be kept! Regarding the type of the small cruiser we are on the right track, and I am particularly happy expressing this to you.
>
> Wilhelm

This positive verdict became clouded when the Kaiser observed the performance of *Hamburg* under similar conditions in 1904. Virtually invisibly to anyone without an experienced eye, the stem shape of the new class had been altered, adding length forward and making its lines sharper below the waterline, for greater speed, but more voluminous above. The latter measure improved the workability of the embrasured forward 3.7cm guns, as well as that of the anchor gear, but negatively affected performance against head seas. This phenomenon was exacerbated by the new class lacking the stern trim that was a feature of the *Gazelles* when bunkers were full.

It was clear that something had to be done. Two of the new cruisers were already too far advanced to be easily modified at this point (*Hamburg* and *Bremen* [*Small Cruiser L*]), while one (*Lübeck* [*Ersatz-Mercur*[14]]) had been chosen to be equipped with turbine propulsion (see below), and to ensure proper comparison with the reciprocating-engined *Hamburg* her lines needed to remain as close as possible to those of the latter. This only left *Berlin* and *München* [*Small Cruiser M*] as candidates for bow modifications. Both were now fitting out after launch, the former having progressed extraordinarily slowly since her keel laying at Danzig Dockyard in August 1902;[15] the latter had been laid down a full year later. As an immediate measure the stem's inward slope above the waterline was raised, shortened and the remaining part leading up to the upper deck received slightly more flare, although the lines below water remained unchanged. This new shape would be kept virtually unchanged in the succeeding 1904 Estimates' *Small Cruiser N* and *Ersatz-Alexandrine*, while the remaining 1904-cruiser, *Ersatz-Meteor*, just ordered from Kiel Dockyard, would receive a completely redesigned stem (see further below, p 124).

Of interest to 'K' was a comparison between the average values of speed trials of *Hamburg* and *Bremen* and the very similar contemporary British cruisers of the *Topaze* or 'Gem' class (3,048 tonnes, 9,800ihp, twelve 4in [102mm]/40); all but one of them were powered by reciprocating engines. The British results were taken from the British magazine *Engineering*, which was obviously regarded as reliable. Eickstedt's favourable pro-*Bremen* verdict was not without a hint of pride:

> From the relative position of the two speed curves in the diagram it can be deduced that *Bremen*, despite her being 200 tonnes larger, ran about 0.5 knots faster than *Topaze* at identical power to the English vessel and that maximum power had been 2,000ihp and the speed more than one knot higher than *Topaze*'s … The success of the German vessels is to be regarded even greater in that the *Hamburg* class, while being

13. BA-MA RM3/360 fol. 179f.

14. '*Mercur*' being the name bestowed the old *Arcona* (ii), prior to the launch of the new *Arcona* (iii) on 22 April 1902.

15. The reason for the extended building time is not entirely clear, as it had been actually planned from the outset. Most likely the intention was that *Berlin*'s construction should be spread over three fiscal years instead of the usual two, for financial reasons.

Although not perfectly focussed – most probably owing to the weather conditions! – this image gives a good impression of *Niobe*'s obviously-satisfactory sea-keeping qualities. *(DN collection)*

The British third-class cruiser *Diamond* (1904), shown at Venice. She was a member of the 'Gem' class, with whose performance that of *Bremen* was favourably compared. *(NHHC NH 72876)*

Bremen on trials in Kiel fjord; the sharpness of her bow is very evident. *(DN collection)*

6m shorter, incorporates submerged torpedo tubes, while in the English cruisers their launching tubes are positioned above the armour deck. Additionally, the significantly lower revolutions of the engine plant (140 versus 245rpm) must be regarded as clear advantage of the German cruisers.[16]

Towards the turbine

While one ship of the two small cruisers provided for under the 1903 Estimates, *Small Cruiser M* [*München*], was a repeat of the previous year's vessels, except for carrying her 10.5cm guns on the upgraded C/04 mounting, the other was of a modified design. As noted above, *Ersatz-Mercur* [*Lübeck*] was chosen as a test-bed for turbine propulsion in larger vessels than torpedo-boats. The first turbines in the German navy had been installed in 1896 in the coast defence ship *Aegir*, but for driving electric generators only. After acknowledging the progress made in the Royal Navy with its acquisition of the torpedo boat destroyers *Viper* and *Cobra*, commissioned during 1900/01, Tirpitz, at the end of 1901, ordered now KAdm von Eickstedt to evaluate the use of turbines for propulsion on board German warships, with a view to higher output and thus speed. However, it soon became clear that potential German suppliers of turbine sets were not yet in a position to meet the navy's requirements, and thus a delegation from 'K' went to the UK in April 1902 on an information gathering visit to a variety of manufacturers.

'K' concluded in its resulting report, dated 16 May, that only turbines built or licenced from the Parsons company could thus far provide the required performance, but, nevertheless, that there might be scope for competition when the time came to invite tenders later in the year. In fact, there proved to be only one competitor besides the Deutsche Parsons Marine AG 'Turbinia', the German licencee of the British company: this was a joint proposal from Vulcan and AEG, who put forward a turbine system of Riedler-Stumpf design. A careful comparison of both proposals, delivered on 19 September, showed the latter's disadvantages: in particular there stood the fact that no turbines on this system had thus far been built, and accordingly no practical experience had been gained, nor had reliable prices been offered.

On the technical side, the Riedler-Stumpf installation's advantage of only two propeller shafts was more than counter-balanced by the excessively high revolutions of the turbines, which would require no fewer than three small propellers per shaft. The gain in weight compared to a reciprocating plant, allowing for the suppression of the armoured glacis above the cylinder heads, was only 95 tonnes, against Turbinia's 175 tonnes, but it was clear that only the Turbinia proposal would be able to fulfil the requirements. Accordingly, a contract was let on Brown, Boveri & Cie, as a subcontractor to Turbinia, for the delivery of two turbine sets. One was for the torpedo boat *S125*, to be built by Schichau at Elbing, one for the new cruiser.

There remained a problem as to which shipyard would actually build the ship. In a memorandum from 25 September 1902,

16. BA-MA RM3/360 fol. 185ff

Eickstedt foresaw difficulties for the RMA in managing any disputes between the contractors responsible respectively for the hull and for the engine plant. Accordingly, he argued for a formal joint venture: Turbinia had to find a suitable partner among the preferred private shipyards – the Imperial Dockyards were known as be too expensive in delivering just a hull and fittings – to make a combined offer. The choice of hull-building partner was placed entirely in Turbinia's hands, who initially opted for Germania at Kiel.

Eickstedt expected that such a combined offer would translate directly into a 210,000 Mark saving in final costs (the difference between the price of a turbine plant over a reciprocating plant). The RMA additionally required that, if the turbine plant proved to be a failure, it must be automatically replaced by a reciprocating plant at the contractor's expense. However, at the beginning of November 1902, Germania pulled out of the project and although knowing that Schichau, threatened by under-employment, had offered to take over under identical conditions, Tirpitz decided to run a proper competition for the hull and fittings, with the aim of gaining even lower prices. Indeed, Tirpitz's approach proved successful when AG Vulcan bid 3,000 Marks below Schichau's offer, and thus won the contract.

As both vessels, cruiser and torpedo boat, were parts of larger classes, it was expected that there would be ample scope for comparison with the performances of their reciprocating-engined sister vessels. Wisely, the RMA did not demand a higher design speed than the 22 knots of *Ersatz-Mercur*'s sister ships, even though the Turbinia concern was prepared to guarantee an output 10 per cent higher than her sisters' 10,000ihp.

From the outset, the development and installation of the new

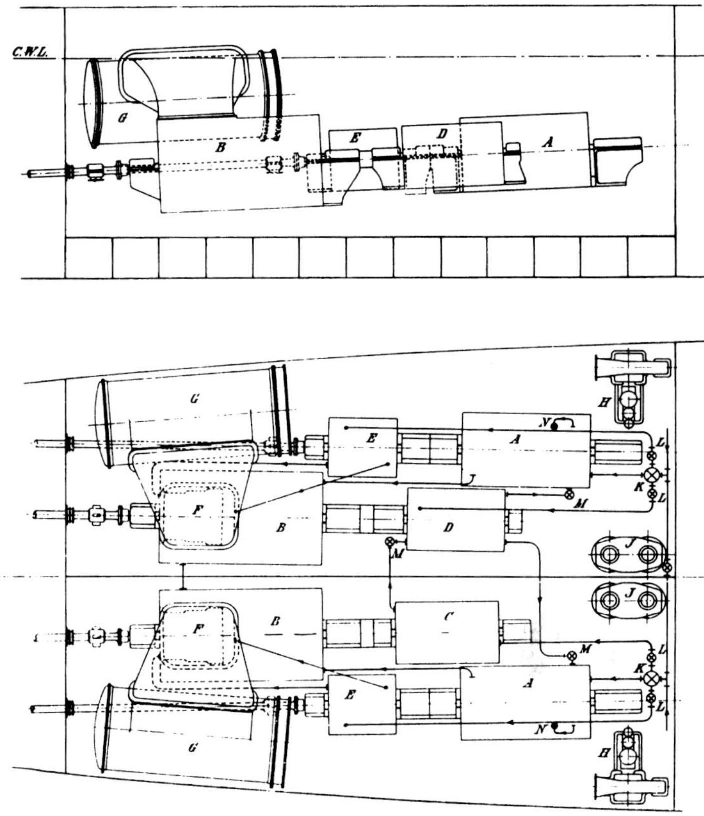

Schematic drawing of *Lübeck*'s engine plant:
A – HP turbine; B – LP turbine; C – HP cruising turbine;
D – LP cruising turbine; E – HP astern turbine; F – LP astern turbine;
G – condensers; H – main cooling water pump; J – air-pumps;
K – main manoeuvring valves; L – manoeuvring valves;
M – non-return valves; N – circulation valves.
(DN collection)

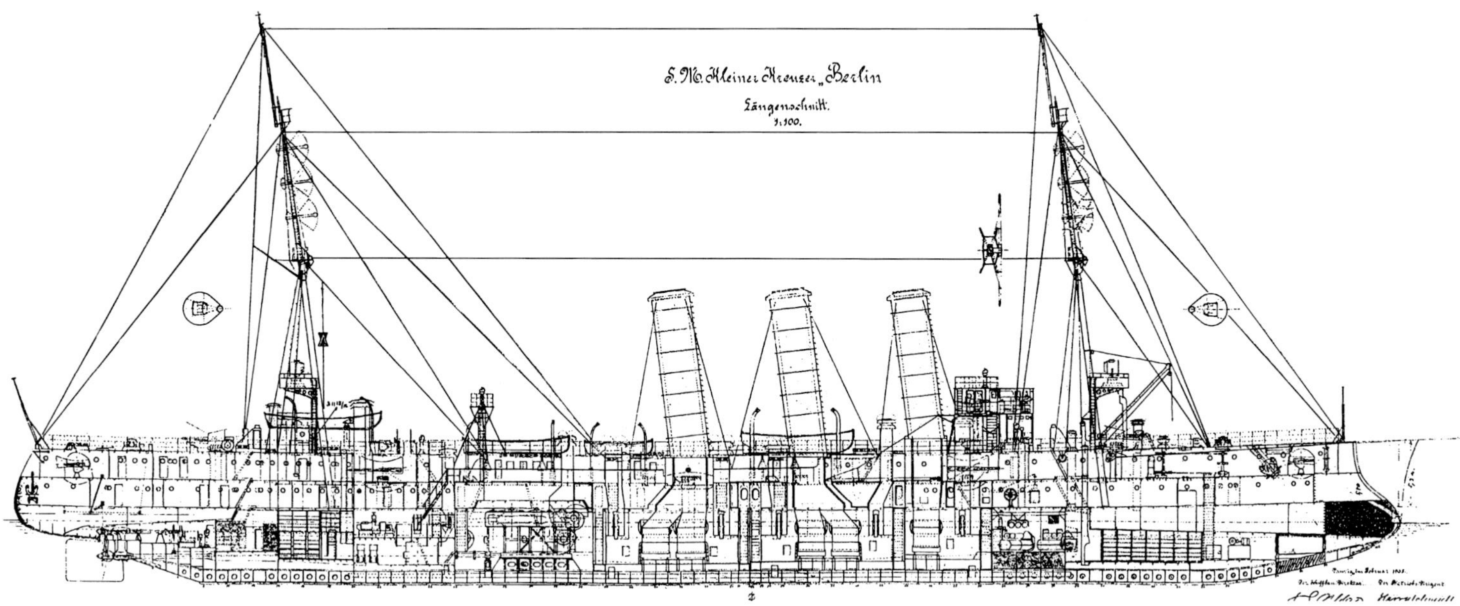

Official longitudinal section of *Berlin*. The bow is interesting in that it shows the three phases of development of her stem profile. Below the level of the lower deck may be seen the original shape, which was enclosed in the revised form applied to *Berlin* and *München* as completed. It also shows an initial sketch for the modification applied to her bow during her 1921–22 Wilhelmshaven refit (p 239), when a new raked stem was fitted over the old one. *(DN collection)*

Lübeck's port pair of shafts during fitting out. Each has two propellers of exceptionally small – 1.372m – diameter. *(DN collection)*

plant was hampered by its novelty and complexity, with no fewer than ten individual (including forward, astern and cruising) turbines powering the four shafts. After the Kaiser's approval had been given on 20 January 1903, the official decree of construction gave a short description of the plant's configuration:

> The turbine engine plant consists of two equal, separated sets of machinery that are symmetrically arranged corresponding with the starboard and port-side engines of common reciprocating steam engines. Each set works on two shafts respectively so that the vessel possesses four shafts in total. Both sets contain one high-pressure and one low-pressure turbine, which drive one shaft each. An astern turbine is incorporated in the exhaust side of each high-pressure and low-pressure turbine. Additionally, a cruising turbine is coupled to the low-pressure turbines, which will mainly come into use during cruising speed. Each shaft is equipped with two propellers, giving a total of eight. The four propellers on port side turn left, the four on the starboard turn right respectively.[17]

It came as no real surprise that the manufacture of the large cast pieces for the turbines fell behind schedule. Krupp for instance, as main supplier, informed Brown, Boveri on 20 January 1904 of the failure of several cast steel pieces for the rotors and their casings, mainly because of issues with the new alloys being tried, as well as the general complexity of the components. Laid down on 12 May 1903, the ship was launched as *Lübeck* on 26 March 1904, with a scheduled delivery date of 1 August 1904. This date came and went without the machinery coming even close to completion.

Finally, on 18 March 1905, acceptance trials were able to commence, which ended with the ship's commissioning on 26 April 1905. However, the eagerly awaited first full speed trial in the measured mile on 22 March had come close to disappointment. Equipped with eight equal-sized propellers of 1.372m in diameter, *Lübeck*'s average top speed was 22.37 knots, while the three-hour continuous-speed trial gave 21.9 knots, thus just missing the 22 knots acceptance speed. But the trials were far from over: they were to be particularly exhaustive because of the entirely new characteristics of the vessel's machinery. These included several direct competitions against *Lübeck*'s sister *Hamburg*, which were not completed until 22 August 1906. During these months a variety of propeller configurations were tested as well, results during the full-power trials including:

Date	Diameter of Propellers (metres)		Number	Speed (kt)
	outer	inner		
22 March 1905	1.372	1.372	8	22.37
26 August 1905	1.700	1.700	4*	22.39
23 December 1905	1.372 (fwd) 1.600 (aft)	1.372 (fwd) 1.700 (aft)	8	22.56
9 June 1906	1.600	1.752	4	22.55

* In this configuration the ship attained her highest recorded speed on the deep water mile at Neukrug, reaching 23.16 knots.

The results of these trials were far from conclusive regarding the efficiency of the turbines, both in themselves, and in their contribution to ship handling characteristics. One major obstacle to explicit comparability had been the impossibility of directly measuring the turbines' output. Rather than the commonly used indicator devices of reciprocating engines, turbines required torque meters for measuring their outputs, and these were still in their infancy at the time of the trials. Thus, all statements regarding the efficiency of the entire engine plant had to remain based on indirect calculations and assumptions. Owing to the comparatively small propellers employed,[18] this meant that not only the maximum speed on the measured mile did not exceed that of her sister vessels – despite a calculated higher power output – but coal consumption was also significantly higher as well. The same could be said about the rates for stopping, acceleration and manoeuvrability in

17. *Endgültige Bauvorschrift für die komplette Maschinenanlage*, 1903. Interestingly, this document was altered by amendments from being an identical copy of *Small Cruiser M*'s decree of construction – with reciprocating engines – to the turbine-driven version, thus giving an indication of the uncertainties existing during the design process.

18. It is generally known that the propeller's efficiency is the better the larger its diameter and the slower its rotation. Thus, a turbine plant on a ship is rather contradictory: the efficiency of turbines rises with increasing revolutions, while that of propellers decreases.

general, in which *Lübeck* was markedly inferior to her sisters.

However, even combined with the above mentioned problems with regard to the manufacturing of the turbine plant, the RMA's intention of introducing turbine propulsion into the German navy remained firm. Tirpitz has often been reproached for being over-cautious in the introduction of new technology but – in the tradition of the former head of the Admiralty, Caprivi – his prevailing view had always been that the German navy could not risk the burden of failed large-scale experiments. Thus, he generally proceeded in small incremental steps: before installing turbines in one of the precious capital ships, prolonged trials should be conducted with small cruisers and torpedo boats.

Accordingly, even before *Lübeck* had commenced her trials in March 1905, it was decided that at least one (if not two – eventually just one)[19] of the three cruisers of the 1905 Estimates would receive turbines; similarly, one of the two small cruisers of the 1906 Estimates was also to be turbine driven. However, Turbinia still remained the only supplier of turbines in Germany, and both vessels, *Ersatz-Wacht* [to be *Stettin*] and *Ersatz-Comet* [*Dresden*], had thus to be equipped with turbines of the Parsons-type without the competition that had originally been planned. Nevertheless, their engine performance would prove markedly better than in *Lübeck,* so that each of them became successively the fastest German cruiser of its time.

The new C/04 mounting of their 10.5cm guns had now become standard, in particular because of incidents with the older model on board the gunboat *Panther* during the Haitian and Venezuelan crises of September 1902 and January 1903. On both occasions, *Panther*'s guns had failed after prolonged live firings due to mechanical defects. The closing words of VAdm von Büchsel, then head of the Admiralty Staff, in his verdict regarding both incidents left no doubts regarding his view, which could of course also be applied to the similarly armed modern small cruisers:

> At the same time, it is recommended that the attention of the responsible departments be directed firmly at these deficiencies. A repeat occurrence of failures of this type in the artillery would mean an unacceptable restriction in the military employment of SMS *Panther.*[20]

Danzig and *Leipzig*

The 1904 Estimates provided for three small cruisers. Two, *Ersatz-Alexandrine* [*Danzig*] and *Small Cruiser N* [*Leipzig*] were modest modifications of the previous two years' reciprocating-engined vessels, with no changes in machinery, speed or armament, and are thus often regarded as belonging to the preceding class. Indeed, the original decree of construction went even further:

> I decree herewith, that for the small cruisers *N*, *Ersatz Alexandrine* and *Ersatz Meteor* the orders of construction determined for the small cruiser *M* shall apply. New Palace, 30 October 1903
>
> Wilhelm I.R.

In the event, *Ersatz-Meteor* would emerge to a significantly altered design (see pp 123-124, below), while the other pair had a number of adjustments made to theirs. The most noticeable external change, implemented during construction, was the shifting of the foremast aft, to the core of the bridge. This measure originated in complaints from the Flag Officer Scouting Force, KAdm Gustav Schmidt (1851–1931), on 24 October 1904, after initial experiences gained with the latest small cruisers during the autumn manoeuvres. In his letter to

19. The number was made dependent on the success of *Lübeck*'s trials, but since only one cruiser with turbines was actually ordered (see below), it is clear that they were not initially regarded as wholly satisfactory.

20. D Nottelmann, *Das Kanonenboot Iltis (II)* ([Düsseldorf]: Arbeitskreis Historischer Schiffbau, 2018), p 98.

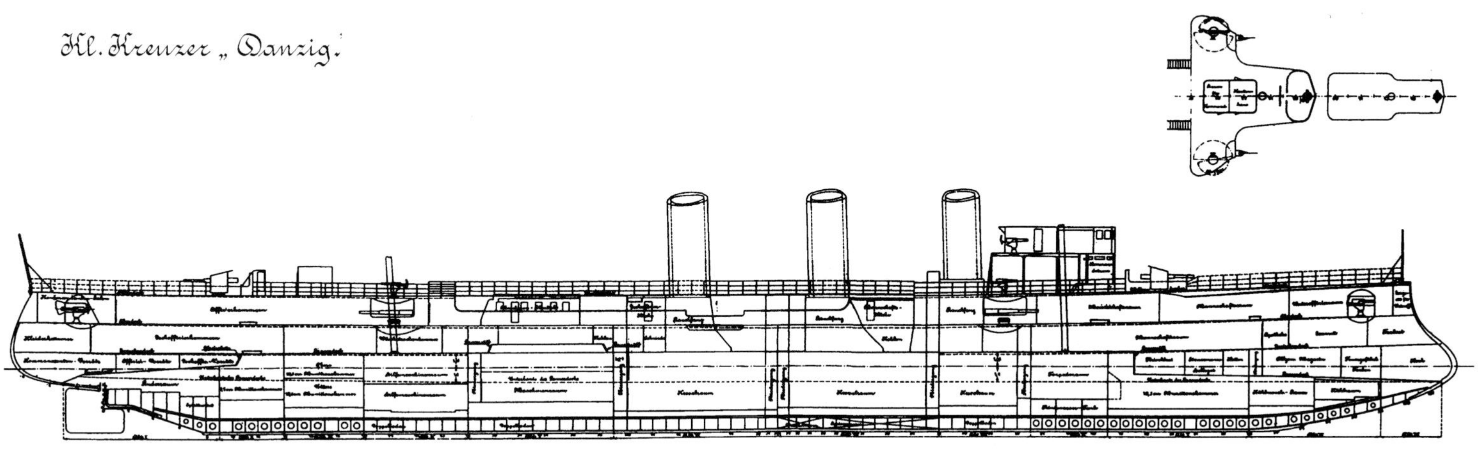

Excerpt from the official booklet of plans of *Danzig*. Her class was essentially a repeat of the previous one, the most obvious change being the resiting of the foremast and consequent modifications to the bridge. *(DN collection)*

Flag Officer Active Fleet, VAdm Hans von Koester (1844–1928), he pointed out the present forward position of the mast was untenable for several reasons. First, the general view ahead from the bridge was much reduced by the mast itself, its searchlight-platform, stays and other rigging. Second, when the searchlight was working and directed on the beam, reflections in the rigging blinded personnel on the bridge. Even the afterglow was still so intense that torpedo boats attacking from forward sectors could not be detected for quite a while. Third, at high speeds and strong winds, no proper communication was possible between bridge and searchlight owing to noise generated by the rigging.

This view was endorsed by Koester in a letter to Tirpitz on 22 November. Koester initially proposed the mounting of two searchlights in the bridge wings, because he feared interference with the central binnacle on top of the wheelhouse if the searchlight were placed on the centreline close to the bridge. Disagreeing with this solution, 'K' saw searchlights in the wings as too exposed to the blast of the forward guns firing on after bearings. Consequently, the platform remained attached to the mast in the 1904 cruisers, but was raised, so that the searchlight's strong magnetic field would not influence the magnetic compass. Koester was accordingly informed on 1 April 1905 that this change of design was indeed possible for *Ersatz-Alexandrine* and *Small Cruiser N*.

There was also a reduction in the rake of the masts and funnels, which originated, in part at least, from complaints regarding the partial invisibility of, and excessive wear to, signal flags hoisted too close to the funnels. This seems a little contradictory, as the foremast was now to be positioned even closer to the forward funnel but, as the halyards were operated from the bridge, their blocks could not be fixed at the yardarms rather than the lines leading aft. Fear of interference with the signal halyards precluded a further – useful – proposed change in design, namely, the moving of the W/T office and the associated aerials from aft of the mainmast to the bridge, where it would have been much closer to the centre of ship management.

In service

Hamburg

The first of the class to commission had been *Hamburg*. She had been laid down by AG Vulcan on 1 August 1902, with the intention of completion by the end of 1903. Despite frequent overtime working by the yard's workers she would only be launched on 25 July 1903, and finally commissioned on 8 March 1904. In June, *Hamburg*, as the most recent cruiser, escorted *Hohenzollern* during her cruise in northern waters. She then relived *Niobe* in the Scouting Force in time for the autumn manoeuvres, and the following year was again escort to *Hohenzollern*, before being used in comparative trials with her turbine-engined sister, *Lübeck*.

In February 1908, *Hamburg* was part of an Atlantic deployment of the Scouting Force, and in May was once more *Hohenzollern*'s escort, this time for a visit to Venice and Corfu, repeating this latter itinerary the following spring. While so engaged, *Hamburg* was diverted from Corfu on 21 April to guard German interests during riots in Anatolia, landing a small force. She returned to Kiel on 28 May, resuming fleet service until decommissioned on 15 September 1909. On 2 July 1912, she recommissioned, becoming flagship of the Submarine Flotilla on 6 August. With the establishment of a second flotilla of submarines on 1 July 1914, under the leadership of *Stettin*, *Hamburg* became the leader of the I. SF, based on Heligoland.

Bremen

Small Cruiser L was laid down by AG Weser on 23 August 1902, and launched as *Bremen* on 9 July 1903, to be commissioned on 19 May 1904. She relieved *Gazelle* on the East American station in late 1904, making a number of visits to the United States, accompanying the large cruiser *Roon* to take part in the International Naval Review that accompanied the opening of the Jamestown Exposition in Chesapeake Bay on 26 April 1907. *Bremen* toured South American ports from late 1908 to February 1909, beginning at Buenos Aires, followed by stops at Rio de Janeiro, Costa Rica, Panama, Guatemala, and the Dutch Antilles.

This was followed by three months of visits to North American ports, while during September and October 1909 she joined the training cruisers *Victoria Louise* and *Hertha*, and the new small cruiser *Dresden*, the latter specially deployed to American waters, in representing Germany at the Hudson–Fulton Celebration in New York.[21] On 30 May 1912, *Bremen* met with the large cruiser *Moltke* and small cruiser *Stettin* on their arrival in US waters for a goodwill visit, accompanying them to Hampton Roads, where on 3 June they were reviewed by the US President, along with eight US battleships.

Bremen remained with them until the visitors sailed for Kiel two weeks later, and continued her activities in American waters until December, when she was deployed to West Africa to support the gunboats *Panther* and *Eber* in protecting German interests in the wake of riots in Liberia. Returning back across the Atlantic in January 1913, she was recalled to Germany in June 1913, proceeding via Kamerun and Togoland in August 1913; however, on arrival at Funchal on 24 September, her orders were changed, since her intended relief, *Dresden*, was not yet ready, and *Bremen* returned to American waters, to guard German interests during the Mexican Revolution. She then proceeded to Haiti, again to look after German interests after rioting, finally beginning her long-delayed voyage home on 13 February 1914 and arriving on 18

21. C L Eger, 'Hudson-Fulton Naval Celebration', *Warship International* 49 (2012), pp 123–51.

March. The cruiser then paid off on 27 March for an extensive refit at Wilhelmshaven.

Berlin

In contrast, *Berlin* spent most of her pre-war career in home waters. Laid down by Danzig Dockyard on 26 August 1902 as *Ersatz-Zieten*, and launched on 22 September 1903, she commissioned as relief for, and with the same crew as, *Amazone*, as late as 4 April 1905. After the usual initial duty for a new cruiser in acting as escort for *Hohenzollern*, from August 1905 she served with the Scouting Force in home waters. On 28 June 1911, she left Kiel to relieve the gunboat *Panther* at Agadir, during the eponymous crisis (p 78 n8, above), remaining there until November 1911 along with the gunboat *Eber*. She returned to Kiel on 14 December and resumed her previous role. On 27 September 1912, most of her crew transferred to the new *Strassburg*, which was to commission two weeks later; *Berlin* decommissioned at Wilhelmshaven on 29 October.

Berlin, photographed during a review, as indicated by the flags atop the masts. Along the poop the two different shades of grey paint may be discerned, which differentiated the hull from the superstructure, although the dividing line differed between types of ship. *(DN collection)*

München

The whole of the pre-First World War service of *München* was spent with the Torpedo Inspectorate, where she replaced *Nymphe* as trials ship in May 1905. *München* had been laid down on 18 August 1903 by AG Weser as *Small Cruiser M*, and launched as early as 30 April 1904. She commissioned on 10 January 1905, having been delivered by the shipyard – less guns

Lübeck during her extended trials; as built, she was indistinguishable from the other early ships of her class. *(DN collection)*

– to Wilhelmshaven on 16 December 1904: *München* was the last naval vessel delivered from AG Weser's 'old yard' close to the centre of Bremen. In 1906 she was chosen for wireless telegraphy trials with the newly erected station at Norddeich, cruising as far as western Norway on this duty. Refitted at Wilhelmshaven from 9 December 1906 to 25 January 1907, she was employed, in the capacity of leader of torpedo-boats, as target vessel for the first attacking attempts of the first true

German submarine, *U1*, with the Kaiser in attendance. The boat succeeded in launching two torpedoes at her unnoticed.

München formed part of III. SG for the August–September 1908 manoeuvres, alongside other trials and reserve vessels, while in February 1910 she rammed the torpedo boat *S122* by way of the engine room during the latter's attempt to pass ahead of the cruiser. While *München* was unharmed, the TB lost two men and had to be secured by two other boats passing hawsers underneath to prevent her sinking. The cruiser remained in service with the Torpedo Inspectorate down to 1914.

München entering the fairway leading to the port of Swinemünde – and later, up the River Oder – to Stettin. The amended shape of the stem is clearly visible. One may note the different outfit of searchlights between *München* and *Berlin* (previous image), despite both images having been taken at roughly the same time. While both carry two searchlights on their foremasts, *Berlin* still carries the original single outfit at the mainmast. *(DN collection)*

Lübeck

As already noted, *Lübeck*'s entry into full service was delayed by her extensive machinery trials, although she was diverted from them on 30 October 1905, when she led seven torpedo boats in the eastern Baltic in the wake of that year's Russian revolution, the cruiser detailed to evacuate the Russian Emperor and his family if so requested, while the torpedo boats kept up the interrupted postal service between Russia and Germany. By mid-November, the immediate crisis had passed, and *Lübeck* returned to her trials programme, although employed between 31 March and 25 April 1906 as leader of the training and torpedo boat flotilla, then transferring to the Training and Trials Force.

Finally, on 22 September 1906, *Lübeck* joined the Scouting Force, unfortunately sinking the three-masted schooner *San Antonio* in collision in the Kiel fjord on 10 June 1908. On 19 April 1909, she was sent to the Mediterranean to strengthen the German presence in covering riots in Anatolia, returning on 2 June and rejoining the Scouting Force on the 17th. The ship decommissioned on 10 October 1911, and was laid up in reserve.

Leipzig

AG Weser laid down *Small Cruiser N* on 12 July 1904, which was launched on 21 March 1905 as *Leipzig* (ii), the first vessel to take to the water from the company's 'new yard'. Delivered in March 1906, she commissioned for trials on 20 April 1906 under a commanding officer of later fame: Kpt Franz Hipper (1863–1932). In June, she acted as the Kaiser's escort on his summer tour, on this occasion aboard the chartered HAPAG steamer *Hamburg* (1900), *Hohenzollern* being under refit. On 19 August, *Leipzig* was detailed to relieve the large cruiser *Hansa*, already on her way home, in the East Asiatic Cruiser Squadron.

Leipzig departed Wilhelmshaven on 8 September 1906, arriving on station on 19 November, to join the large cruiser *Fürst Bismarck* (flag), *Niobe*, four gunboats, three river gunboats and two torpedo boats. In June 1907, *Leipzig*, with the squadron commander embarked, and in company with the gunboat *Tiger* and the torpedo boat *S90*, ascended the Yangtze,

before participating in a squadron cruise in the northern part of its area of responsibility. Over the following eighteen months, *Leipzig* took part in another similar cruise, ascended the Yangtze once again, and made various port visits, culminating in her representing Germany at a Japanese naval review off Kobe on 17 November 1908.

Under refit at Hong Kong from January 1909, riots in German Samoa caused her to sail prematurely, picking up the squadron commander in Manila on 26 February, and reaching Apia on 19 March. There, she was joined by *Arcona*, the gunboat *Jaguar* and the auxiliary *Titania* carrying 100 local police. Matters having been settled the following month, *Leipzig* left on 14 May to Suva, where she arrived on the 17th, disembarking the squadron commander before returning to Apia. On relief by *Condor*, on 22 May, she sailed indirectly to Tsingtau, where she arrived on 29 June.

Over the next few years, *Leipzig* continued the usual round of squadron cruises and port visits, ascending the Yangtze yet again in July 1910, following the outbreak of riots at Hankow. She returned there following the outbreak of the Chinese Civil War in October 1911, to support the gunboats *Vaterland* and *Tiger* already stationed there, later being joined by the gunboat *Iltis* (with the station commander embarked) and *S90*. *Leipzig*, carrying the admiral, was withdrawn in November, rendezvousing with the large cruiser *Gneisenau* at Shanghai. Over the following nine months she made a number of round trips between Tsingtau and the Yangtze until conditions stabilised. Having represented Germany at the funeral of the Japanese Emperor in August 1912, *Leipzig* was present at the heavy fighting around Nanking in July and August 1913, before refitting at Tsingtau during September and October. In May 1914, *Leipzig* was ordered to relieve *Nürnberg* off the west coast of Mexico, arriving on 7 July 1914 at Mazatlán.

Danzig

In contrast to her widely travelled sister, *Danzig*, the last ship of

A distinguished guest visits the brand-new *Leipzig* at Kiel: the Kaiser himself, as denoted by his personal standard atop the mainmast. *(DN collection)*

the class to commission, spent her whole career in home waters. Laid down by Danzig Dockyard as *Ersatz-Alexandrine* on the same day as her full-sister, her construction was again carried on at a rather slower rate than by private industry, the cruiser not being launched until 23 September 1905. Her commissioning consequently occurred as late as 1 February 1907; on the other hand, *Danzig*'s trials were comparatively brief, and completed on 6 March 1907.[22]

At the end of her trials, she relieved *Arcona* in the Scouting Force, taking over most of the crew of the older cruiser, until transferred to the Artillery Inspectorate on 5 June 1910 as a gunnery training ship. In August 1910 she rescued the crews of the torpedo boats *S32* and *S76*, which had collided during manoeuvres in the Kiel Bight. She also took part in the regular cruises of the navy's seagoing trials and training vessels. In 1912

Taken during a fleet review in honour of the heir to the Austro-Hungarian throne, Archduke Franz Ferdinand, on 5 September 1911 in Kiel Bight – note the flag of the Dual Monarchy atop the mainmast – this image of *Danzig* shows her after the refitting of the rigging for extended W/T aerials. *(DN collection)*

Danzig temporarily became part of the newly formed II. SG, before returning in March 1913 to her training role. During the final days of peace in 1914, in the state of raised alertness for war, she first acted as guardship at Kiel, before being sent on 1 August to the North Sea for duty.

THE *KÖNIGSBERG* CLASS

The third small cruiser of the 1904 Estimates, *Ersatz-Meteor* [to be *Königsberg*] was built to a further-updated design. In armament, the previous secondary battery of 3.7cm Hotchkiss machine cannon was superseded by a more modern 5.2cm semi-automatic gun. The reason behind its introduction was once more the increasing size of the possible hostile torpedo craft, on which even multiple hits by the smaller calibre could not guarantee a mission kill. In larger units of the fleet, the standard 8.8cm weapon was still effective, but was too heavy to be carried in sufficient numbers in a small cruiser, leaving aside the closeness of the calibre to that of the 10.5cm main armament and the consequent creation of a rather clumsy mixed battery. A new 5.2cm/55 weapon was thus developed for use in small cruisers, being – for time being – big enough to stop most torpedo vessels. However, the weapon was never very popular in the navy, despite its impressive performance of firing up to 40 (unaimed) rounds per minute, and was discarded when the time came to build the 1909 cruisers.[23]

Königsberg was the first ship to have this new gun, which

22. The date of April 1908 for her becoming operational, commonly repeated in the existing literature, is definitely wrong: see *Nachweisung sämtlicher Seereisen S M Schiffe und der Ablösungskommandos (Seedienstnachweisung) mit Nachträgen.* (Berlin: RMA, 1906, 1913).

23. It was later planned to revive this fast-firing gun, on a new mounting, as the first dedicated anti-aircraft gun in the German navy. However, in the event it was only ever installed in one vessel, and then only for a brief period (see p 152, below).

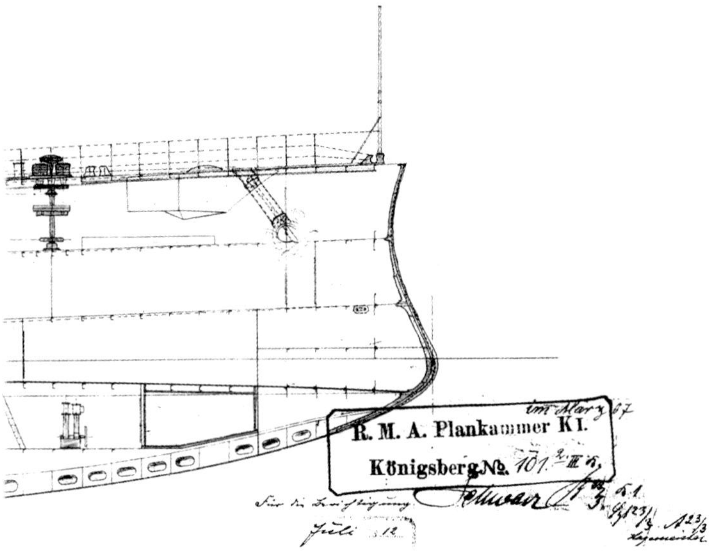

Section of the bow of *Königsberg*, showing the new arrangement very clearly. However, it appears that a final decision concerning the type of anti-torpedo boat gun had yet to be taken at the time this drawing was made, as no detail is provided within the bow embrasure. *(DN collection)*

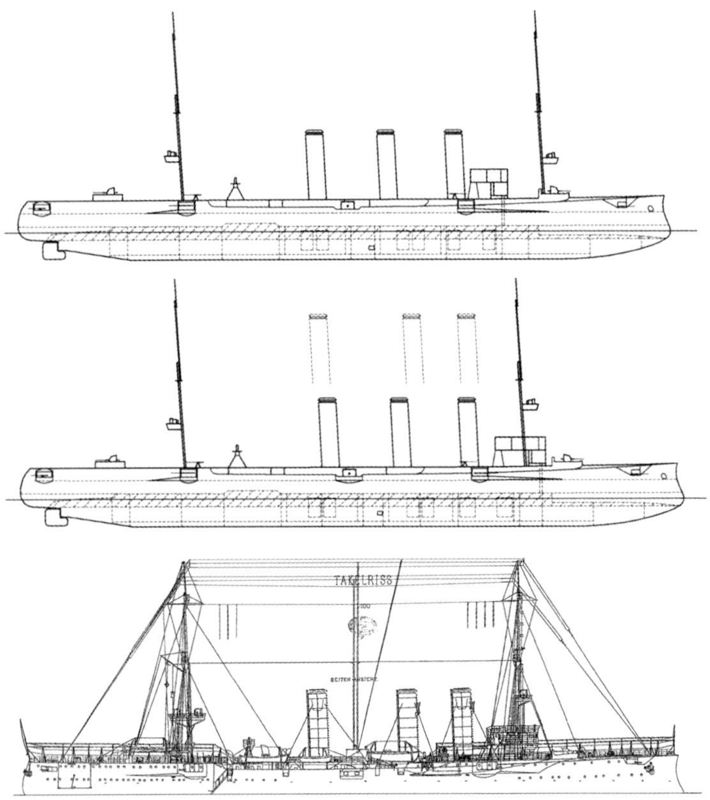

Top: Sketches showing the principal differences between *Königsberg* and *Stuttgart*. The upper shows *Königsberg* in her initial form, with the bridge and mast still separated as in the first group of the *Bremen* class; she was modified along the lines of the *Danzig* while under construction. The lower shows the distribution of *Stuttgart*'s boilers and the planned evenly spaced funnels following the insertion of the extra bulkheads. The broken lines above show the final, optimised arrangement of the funnels. **Bottom:** official rigging plan of *Stettin* after her final pre-war refit. The W/T aerial arrangements have become much more sophisticated during the ten years since their introduction. *(DN drawing/DN collection)*

demanded another change in the shape of the bow. The enlarged working radius at the rear of the 5.2cm mounting, as compared with the 3.7cm installation, required an exchange of positions of the hawsehole and the gun mounting. The former was moved closer to the stem, which generated benefits during anchor handling as well, while the broader deck further aft gave sufficient room for the guns.

In addition, 'K' had developed a new stem, its shape later dubbed the 'cutting edge of a hatchet', which ultimately led the way, via the less pronounced stems of the *Dresden* and *Kolberg* classes, to the 'cruiser bow' of their later successors. The application of the new bow was all the more necessary as *Ersatz-Meteor* would need even finer lines below the waterline forward to meet the now demanded higher speed of 23 knots. This also required another boiler as compared with the immediately preceding vessels and thus an increase of 4.2m in the ship's length. This eleventh boiler was added to the foremost boiler room, meaning that the neighbouring torpedo room had to be moved aft, to a position nearly amidships, between the second and third boiler rooms. To maintain a uniform profile with earlier vessels, with three equally spaced funnels, the gases exhausting from the centre funnel had to sharply change direction twice on the way from the boiler to the funnel – a solution much disliked by engineers.

Fortunately, the construction of the hull had not significantly progressed on the slipway when these changes were decided, so the alterations to the bow were easy to apply. To reduce the generation of spray, the sponsons employed for the 3.7cm guns were replaced by recessed embrasures for their 5.2cm substitutes. The change to the position of the foremast applied in *Ersatz-Alexandrine* and *Small Cruiser N* was, of course, also to be applied to the new ship, although the original sketch-drawings, still showed *Ersatz-Meteor* with her foremast ahead of the bridge.

The three ships of the 1905 Estimates were initially to have been repeats of *Ersatz-Meteor*. However, a report by Tirpitz to the Kaiser on a crucial lesson from the ongoing Russo-Japanese War – the need for more protection against underwater threats – led to modifications. In particular, the second and third boiler rooms of the *Königsberg* design were to be subdivided by two additional watertight bulkheads, thus increasing the total number of watertight compartments from thirteen to fifteen. This required a redistribution of the ready-use coal bunkers, and consequently an elongation of the hull by another 2m compared with the original design.

The new bulkheads made the runs of the boiler uptakes even more problematic, and it was agreed that the middle funnel could be moved forward, and the rear funnel further aft, in order to gain a nearly straight upward flow of gasses for most of the boilers. The 1905 cruisers were accordingly always referred to in the German navy as having a 'detached funnel'.

Besides this major modification, the decree of construction mentioned two more variations from their predecessor – one explicit and one rather vague. The former was an order that the foremast be positioned aft of the conning tower, as now being applied retrospectively to *Ersatz-Alexandrine*, *Small Cruiser N* and *Ersatz-Meteor*. The vague part was once again regarding the possible installation of turbines:

> Depending on the results of the *Lübeck* trials, it is to be considered whether one or two out of the three vessels shall be equipped with turbines instead of reciprocating engines.
> New Palace, 17 December 1904.[24]

As noted above, Turbinia still remained the only German supplier in the field of turbine-propulsion, meaning that there seemed no developmental advantage in constructing two cruisers in parallel with a still unproven engine plant. Accordingly, it was only after the receipt of *Lübeck*'s initial trial results that AG Vulcan received, on 20 December 1905, an order for the turbine-powered *Ersatz-Wacht* [to be *Stettin*]. This was significantly later than the orders for her conventionally-powered sisters, *Small Cruiser O* [to be *Stuttgart*] and *Ersatz-Blitz* [to be *Nürnberg*], which had been placed in April and August 1905, respectively.

Königsberg

Ersatz-Meteor was laid down in July 1904 at Kiel Dockyard, to be launched as *Königsberg* on 12 December 1905 and be commissioned on 6 April 1907. Her trials were almost immediately interrupted to allow her to escort *Hohenzollern* during Kiel Week. Nevertheless, the initial trials held during May gave very satisfactory results, the cruiser reaching 24.1 knots at maximum power and 23.7 knots during the six-hour continuous run. From 3 to 6 June she again escorted the Kaiser, this time to a meeting with the Russian Emperor, and then in July for his annual cruise in Norwegian waters. Having belatedly completed her trials, *Königsberg* joined the Scouting Force, although on 5 November she was once again on imperial escort duty, with the large cruiser *Scharnhorst* and the despatch vessel *Sleipner*, on a visit to the UK and the Netherlands, and then carried Prince Heinrich of Prussia to the funeral of King Oscar II of Sweden at Malmö in December.

Further imperial escort tasks followed in 1910: in March to Heligoland, and from 8 to 27 May to the UK for the funeral of King Edward VII. *Königsberg* was also escort for *Hohenzollern* during the Kaiser's Mediterranean cruise from 8 March to 22 May 1911, and the subsequent visit to the UK. Following her return to Germany, on 10 June she was relieved in fleet service by *Kolberg* and decommissioned on the 14th for refit, which included the removal of the 5.2cm weapons.

Königsberg was temporarily commissioned back into the fleet from 22 January to 19 June 1913 to cover for the absence under repair of *Mainz*, but then returned to reserve. She recommissioned on 1 April 1914 for the East African Station, leaving

24. BA-MA RM2/1613, fol. 37.

Königsberg working up in Kiel fjord after her 1911–12 refit. She is now without 5.2cm guns and has had her bow decoration changed from scrollwork to a simple coat of arms; she also now carries two searchlights on each mast. *(DN collection)*

Wilhelmshaven on the 28th and proceeding via Almería, Cagliari, Naples, Mersin and Alexandretta (İskenderun). Transiting the Suez Canal on 23 May, she visited Aden from 27 to 29 May, before arriving at Dar es-Salaam on 6 June.

Stuttgart

Small Cruiser O was laid down at Danzig Dockyard on 1 November 1905 as the last of the small cruisers to be begun as additions to strength under the 1900 Fleet Law amendment. She was launched as *Stuttgart* on 22 September 1906 and commissioned on 1 February 1908. Rather surprisingly, she fared no better in terms of speed than her half-sister *Königsberg*, despite her greater length, reaching only 24.0 knots at full power and 23.7 knots at about the same power during the six-hour trial. Although she completed her trials on 9 April 1908, manpower shortages meant that *Stuttgart* was then paid off, and it was not until 16 February 1909 that she was returned to service, joining the Artillery Inspectorate as a light weapons training ship, relieving *Nymphe*. As with other vessels in trials or training roles, she participated in the various exercises carried out by the Instructional Unit, standing by the large cruiser *Blücher* when she ran aground off the Danish island of Romsø on 29 May 1913.

Nürnberg

Ersatz-Blitz was laid down on 16 January 1906 by the Imperial Dockyard Kiel, on the slipway just vacated by her half-sister *Königsberg*. Work was pressed forward at an unprecedented rate, with the hull was ready for launching as *Nürnberg* on 28 August of the same year. Nevertheless, her commissioning for trials had to wait about twenty months, until 10 April 1908. The reports regarding her trial speeds are scanty, with power outputs being recorded without indicating the corresponding speeds. Confirmed, at least, however, are the results of the six-hour trial, during which *Nürnberg* attained only 23.4 knots, making her the slowest of the trio.

Stuttgart while serving as a light weapons training ship, as indicated by the absence of funnel bands, which were usually worn by units of the 'active fleet'. Her 'detached funnel' shows very prominently. *(DN collection)*

Unlike her full sisters, whose careers were generally restricted to home waters, *Nürnberg* spent most of her time abroad, although, like *Stuttgart*, manpower shortages led to her being laid up for some twenty months after the completion of her trials. She finally recommissioned on 1 February 1910, to relieve *Arcona* in the East Asiatic Cruiser Squadron, departing Wilhelmshaven on the 14th. She met *Arcona* at Port Said in early March, and exchanged elements of her crew, reaching Singapore on 5 April before proceeding on to Tsingtau.

From 20 June, she escorted the station flagship *Scharnhorst* to Samoa, via Saipan, Truk and Ponape, rendezvousing with *Cormoran* and *Condor*, and then the newly arrived *Emden*. The latter then joined *Scharnhorst* and *Nürnberg* in sailing to Friedrich-Wilhelmshafen on New Guinea, *Nürnberg* then carrying police to Hatzfeldhafen. Back at Friedrich-Wilhelmshafen, *Nürnberg* then towed the survey vessel *Planet*, immobilised by machinery defects, via the Sunda Strait to Singapore for repairs, leaving on 9 September and arriving on the 24th.

Early in 1911, *Nürnberg* joined *Emden* and *Cormoran* in suppressing the Sokehs rebellion on Ponape, and from the autumn was off the Chinese coast during the Chinese revolution, ascending the Yangtze to Hankow with the squadron chief embarked during May and June. At the end of 1912 she was refitted at Tsingtau, and on 16 October 1913, while at Yokohama, was ordered to the west coast of Mexico to protect German and related interests during riots there, arriving on 8 November at La Paz (Mexico), before proceeding to Mazatlán. While based there, she co-operated with the British sloops *Algerine* and *Shearwater*, the US cruisers *Pittsburgh*, *California*, *Maryland*, *New Orleans*, *Albany* and *Raleigh* and, from 25 December, the Japanese armoured cruiser *Izumo* as well.

At the end of May 1914, *Nürnberg* sailed to Panama City to carry out a partial crew change and take on supplies from Germany, and on 7 July was relieved at Mazatlán by *Leipzig*. She then went to San Francisco for docking from 14 to 18 July. The intention had been that she should then sail to Apia, via Hawaii, but this was overtaken by events, and she joined *Scharnhorst* and *Gneisenau* at Ponape on 6 August.

Stettin

The turbine ship *Ersatz-Wacht* was finally laid down by Vulcan on 22 March 1906, her launch as *Stettin* occurring on 7 March 1907. The only turbine-powered 1905 cruiser, her delayed construction allowed the incorporation of a number of lessons from the *Lübeck* trials. Nevertheless, her engines were of essentially identical layout to those of her predecessor, including separate high/low-pressure cruising turbines on two shafts. However, even during builders' trials the yard was proud to announce an extraordinary achievement to Tirpitz, which he immediately telegraphed to the Kaiser at Rominten on 1 September:

Nürnberg moored to one of the visitor's buoys in the Wuangpoo (Huangpu) river off Shanghai. *(DN collection)*

> To the Kaiser's majesty, Rominten. Yesterday, your majesty's small cruiser *Stettin* achieved, during builder's trials on the mile between Hammeren and Christiansoe,[25] a speed of 25.75 knots at about 400 tonnes underweight. Von Tirpitz, Admiral and State Secretary.[26]

Commissioned on 29 October 1907, *Stettin*'s trials were thorough, but not as extended as those of *Lübeck*. Given the incomplete, and very light, state of the vessel when she made the aforementioned record-breaking run, its achievement could not be repeated during the official trials. The figures were, nevertheless, still impressive enough: 25.2 knots at full power and around 24 knots during the six-hour run on 22 November.

Having completed her trials, *Stettin* relieved *Frauenlob* in the Scouting Force on 20 January 1908. Between 17 June and 8 August, she escorted *Hohenzollern* at a number of regattas, on the Kaiser's summer cruise in Norwegian waters, and during a visit to Stockholm. On 19 April 1910, she left Kiel for the Mediterranean, arriving at Corfu on 1 May to replace *Hamburg* in the imperial escort role, after the latter had been diverted to Turkish waters. *Stettin* was at Pola when ordered home on 15 May, and arrived at Kiel on the 26th. During 7 to 30 July,

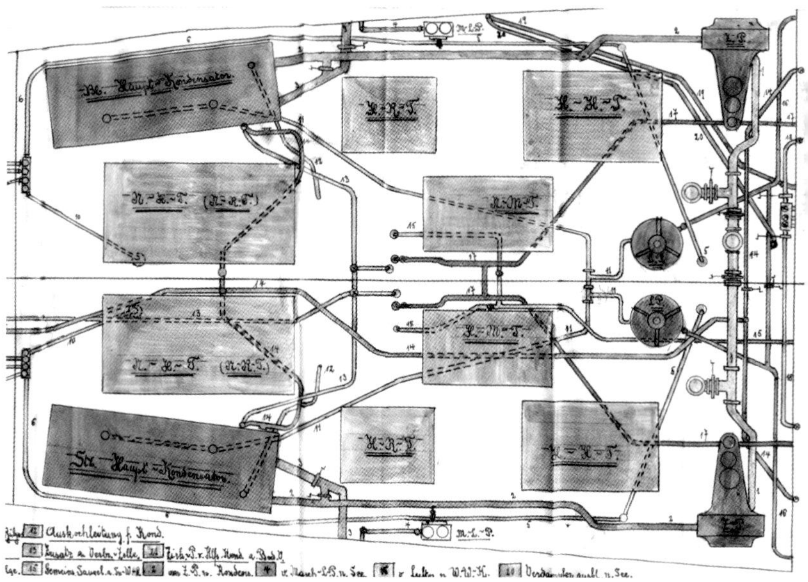

Excerpt from a hand-drawn drawn plan by one of *Stettin*'s engineers for his own use, showing the arrangement of her machinery and some relevant piping in the engine room. The general layout of the turbines and auxiliary machinery is almost the same as in *Lübeck* (p 115). *(DN collection)*

Stettin was once again with *Hohenzollern*, for the summer's cruise to Norway.

From 11 May 11 to 29 June 1912, she escorted *Moltke* to the United States, where they joined the station cruiser *Bremen*, beginning their return voyage to Kiel from New York on 13 June, sailing via Vigo. In early 1914, part of the crew of *Stettin* moved to the new small cruiser *Rostock*, but was made up to full

25. Hammeren is the northwestern promontory of the Danish island of Bornholm, while Christiansoe are two small islands (the 'pea islands') north of Bornholm.

26. BA-MA RM2/1613, fol. 129.

Stettin passing the Grünenthal High Bridge on the Kiel Canal in August 1912. This is one of the rare occasions when a change of position within a division, or a complete change of division, can be observed, as her crew are engaged in repainting the ship's funnel bands. *(DN collection)*

strength again by July, when she became flagship of the new II. SG at Heligoland.

THE *DRESDEN* CLASS

In May 1905, an intradepartmental request by 'K' led to discussions regarding the design of the 1906 cruisers. Eickstedt requested from his subordinates two alternative preliminary designs of 3,500–3,550 tonnes displacement and a speed of 24 knots over the measured mile, specifying the weights and costs for reciprocating machinery with eleven boilers. This was yet another rise in design speed (from 23.5 knots), to be achieved by reciprocating engines as a baseline, with the potential for further increases in turbine-powered vessels, although the true performance of the latter was still rather unpredictable, as seen in the results of *Lübeck*'s trials.

Installed power was set at either 14,000 or 15,000ihp, under forced conditions, on the mile. Given that some 10 per cent less power would be available during the sustained trial, this would equate to 12,600 or 13,500ihp for six hours. The difference between both options came out at about 50 tonnes and 120,000 Marks. Not surprisingly, the higher figure was chosen, even if careful recalculation would show that the enlarged eleventh boiler could be better replaced by two smaller boilers for the same operational reasons applied in the case of *Nymphe* (see p 101).

The now-even number of boilers meant yet another redistribution of boilers/boiler rooms, which was achieved by moving the forward boiler rooms aft, displacing the torpedo room, and allowing the installation of the two boilers athwartships in the foremost boiler room (number 4). This, in turn, required another widening of the hull by 0.2m and, consequently, an elongation of 1.0m, to maintain coherent hull lines. Nevertheless, as the trials would show, the new shape was not as hydrodynamically successful as that of their predecessors (see figures below, p 131).

Briefly discussed was an alternative design with four funnels instead of three, one per boiler room, and a 4+2+4+2, rather than 2+4+4+2, boiler distribution, which resulted in rather odd-looking alternating narrower and wider funnels. The principal argument against this proposal was a need to have coal bunkers outboard of the engine rooms, which would have made the supply of the boilers the more demanding as bunkers were progressively emptied.

The two ships of the 1906 Estimates, *Ersatz-Comet* [to be *Dresden*] and *Ersatz-Pfeil* [*Emden*] thus represented, as built, a 'cleaned-up' version of the previous year's small cruisers. Following the redistribution of the boilers, the displaced torpedo room had to be brought forward again, which further meant that the conning tower and the navigation bridge had to be moved forward as well, ending up entirely in front of the foremast. These measures combined to give the pair probably the most well-balanced look of all 'first-generation' small cruisers of the German navy, even if it was found that the officer of the watch's general overview from the modified bridge was eroded, due to the chart house's proximity to the conning position.

Emden was the first small cruiser to incorporate the outcome of a review of the placement of searchlights in German battleships and cruisers. Hitherto, they had generally been split between the masts and superstructure, the *Stettin* class having one on a platform on each mast (as was the fit in *Dresden* herself as completed), with another pair on platforms above the midships guns, intended to blind attacking torpedo boats from their low position. The employment of additional searchlights had been made possible by adding a third turbo-dynamo of 45kW power to the machinery of small cruisers from *Nürnberg* onwards. However, it was now decided that searchlights should be concentrated on or around the masts. This was implemented in the new battleships of the *Nassau* class in the form of gantries around the masts, which were continued in follow-on capital ships; existing vessels were modified as taken in hand for refit. In the case of small cruisers, the new scheme placed two searchlights abreast on an enlarged foremast platform, while a second platform was added on the forward side of the mainmast, contiguous with the existing platform on the after side. This

Top: Sketch showing how *Dresden* and *Emden* would have looked like in the proposed four-funnel configuration. The second and aft funnels would have had a slightly smaller diameter than the other two. **Middle:** Initial design drawing for *Ersatz-Pfeil* [*Emden*]. The searchlights above the midship 10.5cm guns and the shape of the bow follow the preceding class, as does the arrangement of the foremast and bridge. **Bottom:** Rigging and deck plans of *Dresden* 'as fitted', showing the changes implemented before the ships entered service. *(DN drawing/DN collection/DN drawing)*

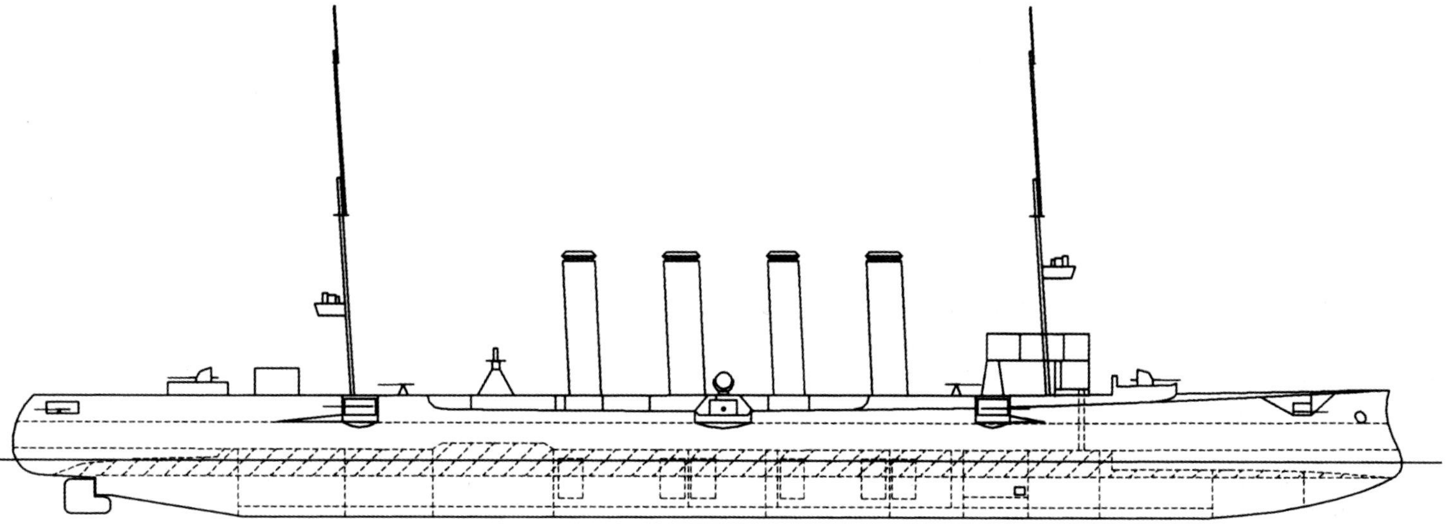

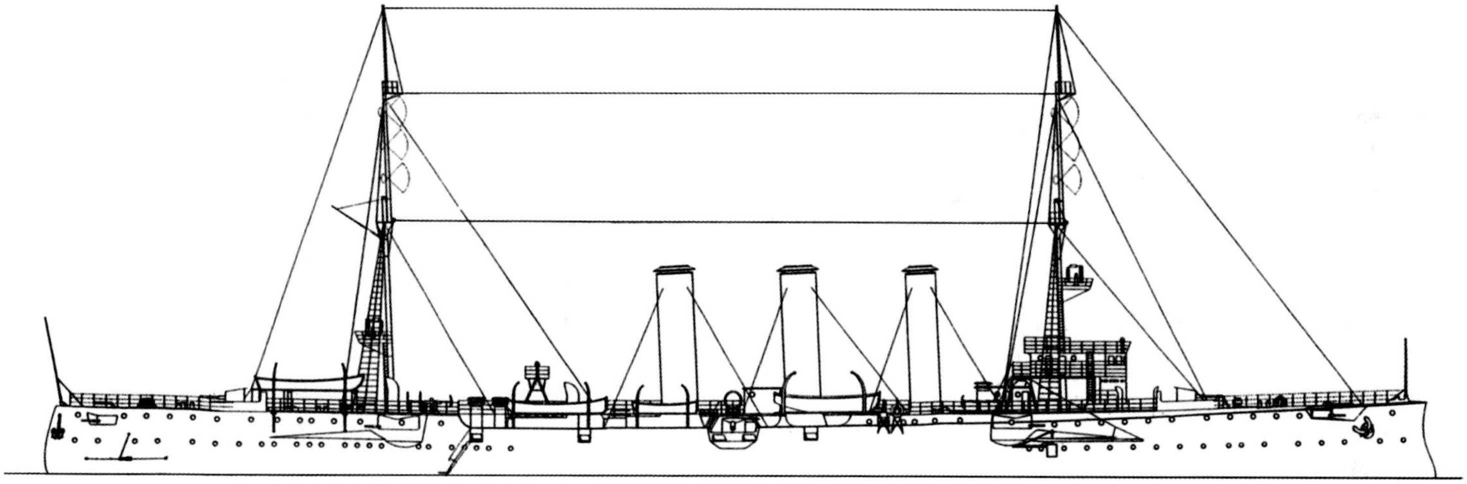

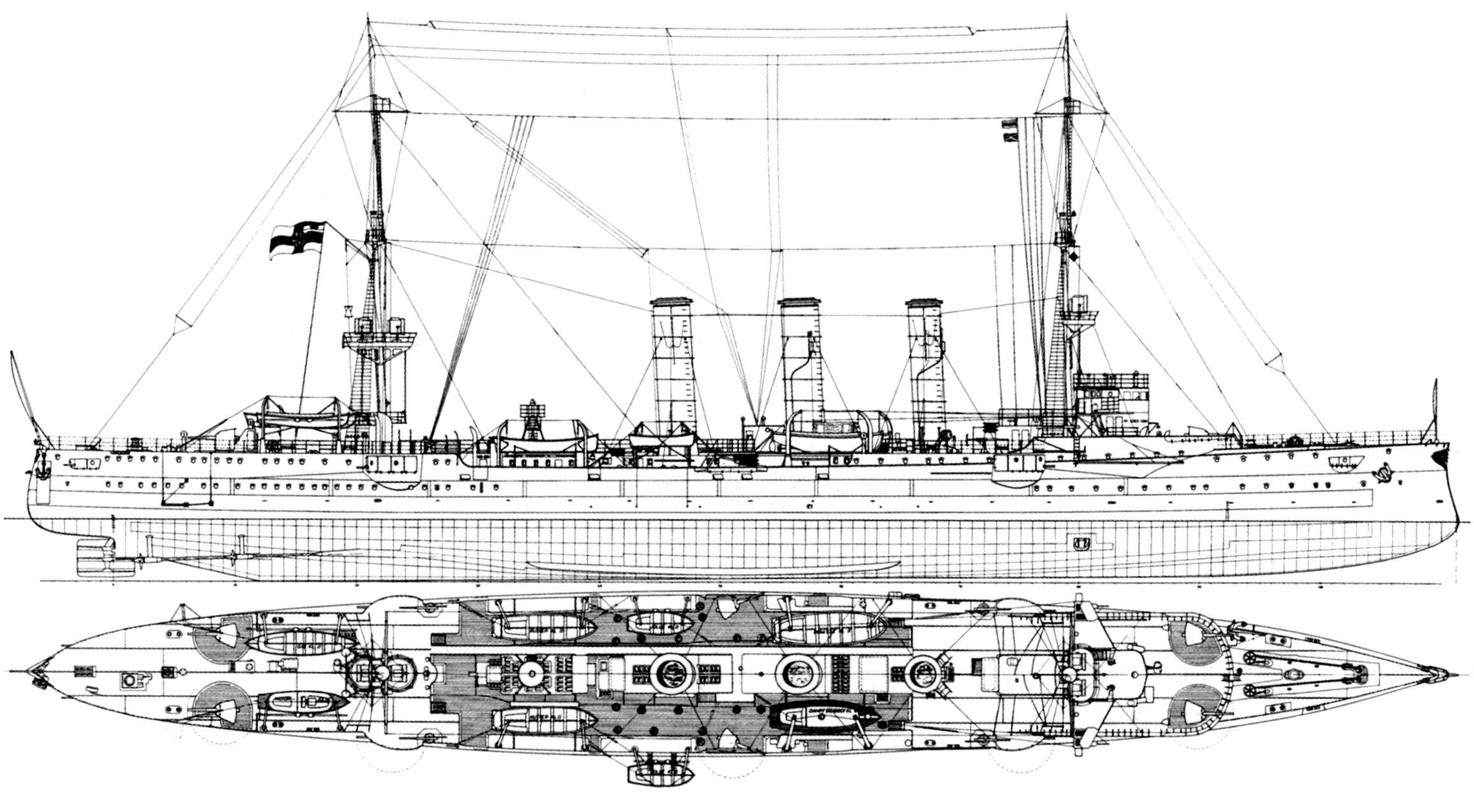

new scheme was implemented in the *Dresden* and subsequent classes, and progressively retrofitted in earlier classes back to *Frauenlob*. *Emden* was initially fitted out in the old configuration, but converted before completion, during winter 1908–09.

The expected performance of the new pair remained rather vague in their joint decree of construction:

> I decree, that for the small cruisers of the 1906 estimates, *Ersatz Pfeil* and *Ersatz Comet*, the specification of the small cruiser *Ersatz Blitz* shall remain valid, with the below-noted deviations:
> [...]
> 12 boilers of the Schulz-Thornycroft system mounted in 4 watertight compartments. Maximum output about 15,000hp. Corresponding speed about 24 knots.
> One of the two vessels is to be equipped with turbine machinery (manufactured by Allgemeine Elektricitäts-Gesellschaft), the other with piston steam engines.
> New Palace, 23 December 1905.

Like in the *Stettin* group, these original plans had to be changed. A new competitor in the field of cruiser construction, Blohm & Voss of Hamburg, had won the contract for *Ersatz-Comet* on 13 October 1906 against Vulcan, Germania and AG Weser. Blohm & Voss thus eventually had to sign a licence agreement with Turbinia on 2 February 1907, when AEG failed to deliver their Curtis-based turbine-design in time.

The RMA had no option but to agree to this change, with the result that, once again, a competition between the two basic concepts of turbine-design (impulse- [Curtis] versus reaction-type [Parsons]), was postponed. Another issue impacting on the broadening of the German steam-turbine market was that Schichau had refrained from participating in the tendering for *Ersatz-Comet*'s engines. The was because the company was engaged in a legal dispute with Turbinia at the time, and thus fearing that it might prove unable to execute any order received. Schichau nevertheless, offered to build a conventionally-propelled cruiser in accordance with the existing specifications 'to demonstrate that a thoroughly constructed [piston-driven] engine-plant will deliver a significantly higher output than a turbine-engine'.[27] The design of *Ersatz-Comet*'s turbine-plant was accordingly a repeat of that already installed in *Lübeck* and *Stettin*. As had now become common, the direct-award order to Danzig Dockyard to build *Ersatz-Pfeil* preceded the tender process for her commercially built sister by six months, having been issued on 6 April 1906.

Dresden

Ersatz-Comet was laid down by Blohm & Voss on 2 March 1907, and launched as *Dresden* after only seven months on the stocks, on 5 October 1907, breaking Kiel dockyard's record with *Nürnberg*. She was handed over to the navy at Kiel on 24 October and commissioned for trials on 14 November 1908. These were abruptly interrupted two weeks later, on 28 November, when the cruiser collided in the Kiel fjord with the brick-laden Swedish galleas *Cäcilie*, which was cut in two and sank, fortunately without the loss of life. The collision was long blamed publicly on a reduced manoeuvrability inherent in turbine engines but, on the contrary, trials reports clearly demonstrate that the authorities were content with the speed of response of the turbines vis-à-vis reciprocating engines.

Parts of the sailing vessel's hull and rigging became entangled with *Dresden*'s starboard outer shaft, moving it about 30mm aft, together with its bossing. The cruiser had consequently to return to Hamburg for six weeks in dry dock for realignment of the shaft and bearings. Trials resumed in January 1909 and demonstrated a maximum speed of 25.3 knots at 18,880shp,[28] while 24.8 knots were attained during the six-hour trial; power for the latter speed is unknown, owing to a defective torque indicator.

Even though she had not yet completed her trials, *Dresden*, as the German navy's latest cruiser, was selected to be one of the ships representing the country at the Hudson-Fulton celebration during September to October 1909, joining *Bremen*, *Victoria Louise* and *Hertha* at Newport, Rhode Island, before proceeding to New York (p 294). She returned to Germany on 22 October, joining the Scouting Force; while serving with the fleet, she was damaged in collision with *Königsberg* on 16 February 1910, requiring a week's repairs at Kiel.

During April 1912, she spent a week temporarily attached to the Training Squadron, alongside *Mainz* and the large cruiser *Friedrich Carl*. In April 1913, *Dresden* and the small cruiser *Strassburg* joined the Mediterranean Division, led by the large cruiser *Goeben*, *Dresden* returning to Germany in September to refit at Kiel until the end of December. Although scheduled to return to the Mediterranean, she was reassigned to the North American station to guard German interests during the Mexican Revolution, relieving *Bremen*. *Dresden* arrived off Veracruz on 21 January 1914, joining *Bremen* – which could now resume her interrupted return to Germany – and the training cruiser *Hertha*.

Various European and North American nationals were evacuated on to ships in co-operation with foreign warships. *Dresden* also provided a landing party to aid the German consul in Mexico City. She also took over German-flagged merchant ship SS *Ypiranga*, using her to carry German refugees, as well as delivering her cargo of arms to the Mexican authorities on 28 May. Once the regime had fallen, on 20 July *Dresden* embarked the deposed Mexican president and vice-

27. BA-MA RM3/865 fol. 4.

28. Other sources claim 25.4 knots at 20,267shp. In general, there is considerable inconsistency in the existing literature regarding the published figures for power output through mixing generally incompatible Indicated Horsepower (reciprocating engines) and Shaft Horsepower (turbine engines) figures in the records – cf. the decree of construction for both 1906 cruisers.

Still under civilian flag, *Dresden* performs her initial trials, still with the original searchlight layout (top). The layout of the steam pipes was the best means of distinguishing between the two sisters (for *Emden*, see page 205). Bottom: *Dresden* while serving with the Mediterranean Division, on a port visit to the Aegean island of Syra, 2–6 September 1913. *(DN collection)*

president, en route to exile in Jamaica. Arriving on the 25th, *Dresden* then rendezvoused with her intended relief, *Karlsruhe*, at Port-au-Prince, Haiti, and swapped captains, the intent being that *Dresden* should now return to Germany to refit. However, the escalating crisis in Europe led to the order being countermanded, the ship now being earmarked to become a raider in the Atlantic.

Emden

Despite her early ordering, Danzig Dockyard laid down *Ersatz-Pfeil* only on 1 November 1906. Her building was constantly beset by delays, mainly caused by the sub-contractors for the armour (Dillinger Hüttenwerke) and the cast-steel bossing for the shafts (Haniel & Cie). Initially planned for launching in August 1907, she actually took to the water as *Emden* on 26 May 1908. The cruiser commissioned for trials on 10 July 1909, but had them interrupted to undertake imperial escort duties in late August. During the initial trials, a mismatch between the generated power and the attained speed became evident, the cruiser being unable to reach the contracted maximum speed of 24 knots. During her subsequent docking at Kiel a disparity in the pitch of both propellers was found; this was corrected and the pitch subsequently reduced on both. During the trials that followed, a maximum speed of 24 knots at 16,350ihp was finally attained, followed by a six-hour trial speed of 'about' 23 knots at 15,683ihp. Given hydrodynamic drawbacks of the class's hull form noted above, a comparison between the *Dresden*s and members of the previous class with the same propulsion systems are instructive:

	Maximum speed/power	six-hour trial Speed/power	Endurance at 12 knots (bunker Capacity)
Stuttgart	24.0 knots/ 13,625ihp	23.7 knots/ 13,745ihp	4,120nm (880 tonnes)
Emden	24.0 knots/ 16,350ihp	23 knots/ 15,683ihp	3,760nm (790 tonnes)
Stettin	25.2 knots/ 21,670shp	24 knots/ 15,448shp	4,170nm (820 tonnes)
Dresden	25.2 knots/ 20,267shp	24.8 knots/ 18,880shp	3,600nm (860 tonnes) [at 14 knots]

Even though the figures are not wholly consistent, the disadvantage of the newer class is clearly evident.

Emden completed her trials on 30 September 1909, only to be laid up due to the chronic shortage of personnel. Entering service for the East Asiatic Cruiser Squadron on 1 April 1910, she sailed on the 12th, with the intention of making South American port visits en route. She reached Montevideo on 10 May, joining *Bremen* in Buenos Aires shortly afterwards to celebrate the centenary of Argentinian independence. She then proceeded via Punta Arenas and Valparaíso, coaling at Talcahuano before departing on 24 June 1910, arriving at Tahiti on 12 July, and rendezvousing with *Scharnhorst* at Apia on the 22nd.

Reaching Tsingtau on 17 September 1910, *Emden* was involved from January to March 1911 in suppressing the Sokehs rebellion, followed by a refit at Tsingtau. She then undertook the usual round of port visits, refitting again at Tsingtau in February 1913. In August, she ascended the Yangtze to Hankow during a rebellion, ending the year at Shanghai. In February 1914, *Emden* was refitted at Tsingtau, but on 28 March was damaged in collision with *S90*, her port screw being bent. July found her the only major warship at Tsingtau, sailing on the 31st to avoid being blockaded in the event of war.

THE LAST OF THE 'FIRST GENERATION': THE *KOLBERG* CLASS

The underlying rationale of the small cruisers of the 1907 (*Ersatz-Greif* and *Ersatz-Jagd*) and 1908 programmes (*Ersatz-Sperber* and *Ersatz-Schwalbe*) is best explained in a summary from Eickstedt:

> In *K Id 10437/05* [a memorandum regarding the design of the small cruisers of 1906] by 'A', dating from December 1905, it was stated as desirable that the speed of future designs should be raised to at least 25 knots. Meanwhile, the speed of large cruisers, foreign as well as our own, has increased considerably. The increase is in fact of such extent that the raising of the small cruisers' speed only to the figure demanded by 'A' is actually no longer desirable: rather, an even higher figure than 25 knots seems to be absolutely necessary. 'K' has initially tried to achieve this increase in speed while staying within the boundaries of the general conditions of construction and keeping displacement below the 4,000 tonnes which had been orally approved by your Excellency …
>
> Compared to the 1906 cruisers these requirements will, nevertheless, demand:
>
> an enlargement of the boiler-plant and consequently of the displacement,
>
> a further lengthening of the vessels […].
>
> The greater length not only results from the fact that the boiler plant must principally be extended in a longitudinal direction only, but also results from several test tank trials using models of different lengths […].
>
> The speed of the new cruiser shall reach about 25 knots during a six-hour trial with forced power and about 25.5 knots during a full-power run on the measured mile, compared to 23.5–24 knots in the 1906 cruiser […].
>
> With regard to the shape of the stem, it is intended to dispense with the ram and replace it with a straight stem with a slight flare at the upper end – comparable to the British scout *Adventure* – because this form is expected to provide the most dry forecastle during the vessel's pitching motion, in conjunction with the provision of the largest deck area forward. If – because of the general outlook – this new form may be not acceptable yet, one of the two 1907 vessels for comparative reasons might be built accordingly with the old form.[29]

Powering the ships

This résumé from 10 January 1907 was the end point of another lengthy design process. This had started in earnest in the middle of 1906 with a pair of sketches for ships of about 4,150 tonnes displacement and 120m length between perpendiculars. Soon it was found that these designs would not work with the required machinery: only thirteen boilers could be installed, incompatible with the intended output, while a new design of turbines would need to be employed, as neither a set of Parsons turbines nor a new 4-cylinder reciprocating plant would fit.

Consequently, a 'Project III' was developed, displacing about 4,300 tonnes and measuring 122m between perpendiculars. The test tanks mentioned by Eickstedt revealed that this hull was hydrodynamically so advantageous that the required minimum of 25 knots on six-hour trial under forced power of 17,500ihp[30] should easily be reached. The only drawback was that a 4-cylinder reciprocating plant of the necessary power would still not fit: the hull would need another 1.5m. The final decision on the powerplant was thus somewhat skewed in favour of turbines, which was reflected in the preliminary decree of construction from January 1907 for that year's pair of ships, that '[b]oth vessels shall, if practicable, be equipped with turbines of different manufacturers (Curtis-AEG, Parsons-Brown-Boveri)'.

It was in this manner that the final shift to turbine propulsion occurred. It was originally intended that each ship would receive turbine installations based on different principles and produced by different manufacturers for competitive purposes. Thus, *Ersatz-Greif* [to be *Kolberg*] received a set of a slightly modified Parsons-type manufactured by the new competitor Melms & Pfenniger (which later became the Schichau turbine), since the types under development by the Zoelly, Germania and Schulz concerns were still not sufficiently advanced. The other 1907 vessel, *Ersatz-Jagd* [to be *Mainz*] received a set of the finally available AEG-Curtis type, whose manufacture was undertaken by the Vulcan shipyard that built her.

29. BA-MA RM3/871 fol. 29ff.

30 This reference to 'indicated power' – not actually applicable to turbines – may be seen as an indication of the obviously still unsettled question as to which propulsion system might eventually be employed.

View straight on to the stem of *Cöln* while manoeuvring in Wilhelmshaven. The minimal flare of her revised bow is quite evident. The cruiser has seemingly lost her port anchor, as its chain is shackled to the spare anchor on the forecastle. *Stralsund* is partly visible in the background. *(DN collection)*

Of the 1908, pair, *Ersatz-Schwalbe* [to be *Cöln*] would initially receive the nominally-now-mature Zoelly-type turbine, manufactured by Escher, Wyss & Cie, of Zurich. However, these proved unsatisfactory and had to be changed even before she commenced initial sea-trials, turbines of a type produced by Germania being fitted in their place. This caused a delay in the cruiser's delivery of some six months. As the Schulz-type turbine did not actually materialise, the final ship, *Ersatz-Sperber* [*Augsburg*] reverted to the 'pure' Parsons type.

The values given for indicated power by Eickstedt stemmed from the calculation of the maximum amount of steam the boiler plant was able to generate in a given space – according to German machinery design criteria not more than the designed 17,500ihp for the six-hour trial – which related to a maximum power of about 19,000ihp during short bursts on the measured mile, giving an as yet unspecified speed. These design criteria demanded the installation of at least fifteen boilers, distributed over four – or five – boiler rooms. Their exhaust gases were initially planned to have been vented through four funnels to minimize the reduction of precious draught through tortuous uptakes. As we have seen above, a similar proposal had previously been scrutinised for the twelve boilers of the 1906 cruisers, but had been rejected. The same happened again here – and, in the end, after a careful comparison between weights and necessary lengths of the boiler rooms, the vessels were given four boiler rooms and three funnels.

Nevertheless, there were different expectations for the trials at maximum power for individual ships: the contract for *Ersatz-Greif* specified a minimum expected speed of 25.5 knots at 515rpm on four shafts, while the contract for *Ersatz-Jagd*, powered by the slower-rotating two-shaft AEG-Curtis turbines, demanded an even better efficiency from the system, generating a minimum of 26 knots at 306rpm. The requirements for *Ersatz-Sperber* reverted back to 25.5 knots at 540rpm, while for *Ersatz-Schwalbe* – due to the troubles with Escher, Wyss & Cie's product – just the standard 25.5 knots was demanded, without any references to the turbines' revolving speed.

Arming the ships

For the first time since the building of *Gazelle*, the main armament was augmented, by the addition of an extra pair of main guns on the beam; these were also upgraded to the 10.5cm/45 gun in an updated C/06 mounting. Nevertheless, this final fit was the result of another long debate. Initially three (probably four) different schemes were worked out, interestingly all under the same heading, 'IIIb':

No. 1	No. 3*	No .4
10–10.5cm QL L/45 MPL	12–10.5cm QL L/45 MPL	12–10.5cm QL L/45 MPL
8–5.2cm QL L/55	4–5.2cm QL L/55	6–5.2cm QL L/55
4–8mm MG	4–8mm MG	4–8mm MG
2–45cm TT	2–45cm TT	2–45cm TT

*It is unknown why there is no 'No. 2'.

Departments 'A' and 'W' opted for No. 3 straight away, because the combined 10.5cm and 5.2cm battery guns could easily be split into two identical groups, fore and aft, as the most recent tactical requirements demanded that two groups of three 10.5cm guns combined on each side should be able to engage one attacking destroyer individually. In either of the remaining alternatives there remained one mounting located right in the middle of the ship, which required a long supply line either from the forward magazines or the aft. Department 'B' agreed, and went even further by requesting additionally the employment of the newly introduced 'heater-torpedo' C/03 of 5.65m length. The proposal was finally approved, even if it ultimately required the lengthening of the cruisers by another 0.5m in way of the torpedo rooms.[31]

31. There is some confusion in the files regarding the designation of these torpedoes. In fact, there was a 'heater-torpedo' under the designation C/03D which, nevertheless, retained the 5.15m length of the original C/03. As 'B' clearly referred to the longer torpedo to be employed, they must, in fact, have been referring to the newly developed C/06D – still of 45cm diameter.

Nevertheless, in spite of these significant changes in the design of the new ships, costing an extra 500 tonnes displacement, the order for construction by the Kaiser emphasised the continuity of the design:

> I decree, that for the small cruisers of the 1907 estimates, *Ersatz-Greif* and *Ersatz-Jagd*, the specification of the small cruiser *Ersatz-Pfeil* shall remain in force with the below noted deviations:
> [as described above].

Thus, the class's external appearance followed that of their immediate predecessors, and radical change was postponed until the 1909 Estimates. Both 1907 cruisers were ordered together on 24 August 1907.

Kolberg

The first cruiser to be built for the German navy by Schichau since *Gefion*, nearly a decade and a half earlier, *Ersatz-Greif* was laid down on 15 January 1908, to be launched as *Kolberg* on 14 November of the same year. She was completed in May 1910 and officially commissioned on 21 June. However, turbine blade failures during her acceptance trials delayed the start of the official trials until 21 November 1910. Scarcity of manpower then caused them to be suspended twice, before their final completion on 13 June 1911. Despite these problems, she attained 26.3 knots at full power of 30,400shp, while during the six-hour trial, at 28,836shp, 25.4 knots was maintained on average. On 14 June 1911, she replaced *Königsberg* in the Scouting Force, having taken over many of her crew (including the captain) at Danzig. Soon afterwards, however, *Kolberg* was detached to escort the Kaiser in *Hohenzollern* on his summer cruise to Norway, before returning to the fleet on 7 August.

Kolberg was again on imperial escort duty from 5 March to 23 May 1912, when *Hohenzollern* went to the Mediterranean, and from 23 June to 9 July was temporary flagship of the Scouting Force following the withdrawal of the large cruiser *Von der Tann* for refit and pending the availability of the new *Moltke*. In July 1913 she served again as imperial escort for a voyage to Norway, before returning to II. SG, with which she was serving the following summer.

Kolberg alongside at Danzig-Neufahrwasser, base port for running the measured mile at Neukrug, during her trials in the Eastern Baltic. *(DN collection)*

Mainz

Ersatz-Jagd was laid down on 4 December 1907, to be launched as *Mainz* on 23 January 1909. She was completed in September 1909, commissioned on 1 October and began her sea trials on the 23rd. However, these were suspended on 24 November in order to allow defects to be remedied. The trials were resumed on 17 January 1910. Before commissioning, Vulcan had undertaken their own full-power trial under light-ship conditions, as in *Stettin* previously. This time, *Mainz* attained an impressive 27.23 knots at 27,115shp. During her official trials in February 1910, she reached 26.9 knots at 27,040shp and kept an average of 26.4 knots at 23,763shp during her six-hour trial. Trials had again to be suspended for shipyard work between 23 February and 19 May, and *Mainz* finally entered fleet service on 6 June 1910 with the Scouting Force, with which she served until the outbreak of war.

Augsburg

The construction of *Ersatz-Sperber* had been allocated to Kiel Dockyard on 8 April 1908. She was laid down on 22 August and launched as *Augsburg* on 10 July 1909. Completed and commissioned on 1 November 1910, she assisted, while still on trials, in rescue and salvage work following the sinking of the submarine *U3* on 17 January 1911 in the inner Kiel fjord. Her trials records show her as the fastest of the quartet, reaching 27.02 knots at 31,340shp and an average of about 25.4 knots at 20,932shp during a five-hour trial. *Augsburg* joined the Torpedo Inspectorate as a trials ship on 24 February, taking part in the cruises of the Training & Trials Ship Force, and also as part of the II. SG during autumn manoeuvres. In July 1912, she relieved *Undine* as a gunnery training ship, transferring to the Artillery Inspectorate and, having again served in II. SG during the year's manoeuvres, refitted at Danzig during September/November. She was again refitted during January/March 1914, and on 20 May visited Dundee. She was assigned to the Baltic Coast Defence Division at the end of July.

Cöln

During the tendering process for the 1907 contract-built ship, Germania had come third. However, as the only remaining known competitor for a further alternative turbine system, RMA took the option of making a provisional order for the 1908 Estimates' *Ersatz-Schwalbe* on 7 October 1907, to avoid any surprises in the 1908 tender round. Accordingly, she was laid down as early as 25 May 1908, the Reichstag having sanctioned the 1908 budget the previous month. She was launched as *Cöln* on 5 June 1909, and was virtually complete – less her machinery – in December 1910. However, her commissioning was delayed by problems with her Swiss-built turbines, as noted above, which were in the end condemned and replaced by a new set built by Germania. Finally completed in May 1911, *Cöln* was commissioned on 16 June 1911, nearly seven months after *Augsburg*. Her propulsion system was unique in consisting of a combination of two main turbines and two cruising turbines, each with its own shaft and working in combination for full power, also employing propellers of two different diameters – 1.78m on the inner (cruising) shafts, 2.55m on the outer (main) shafts.

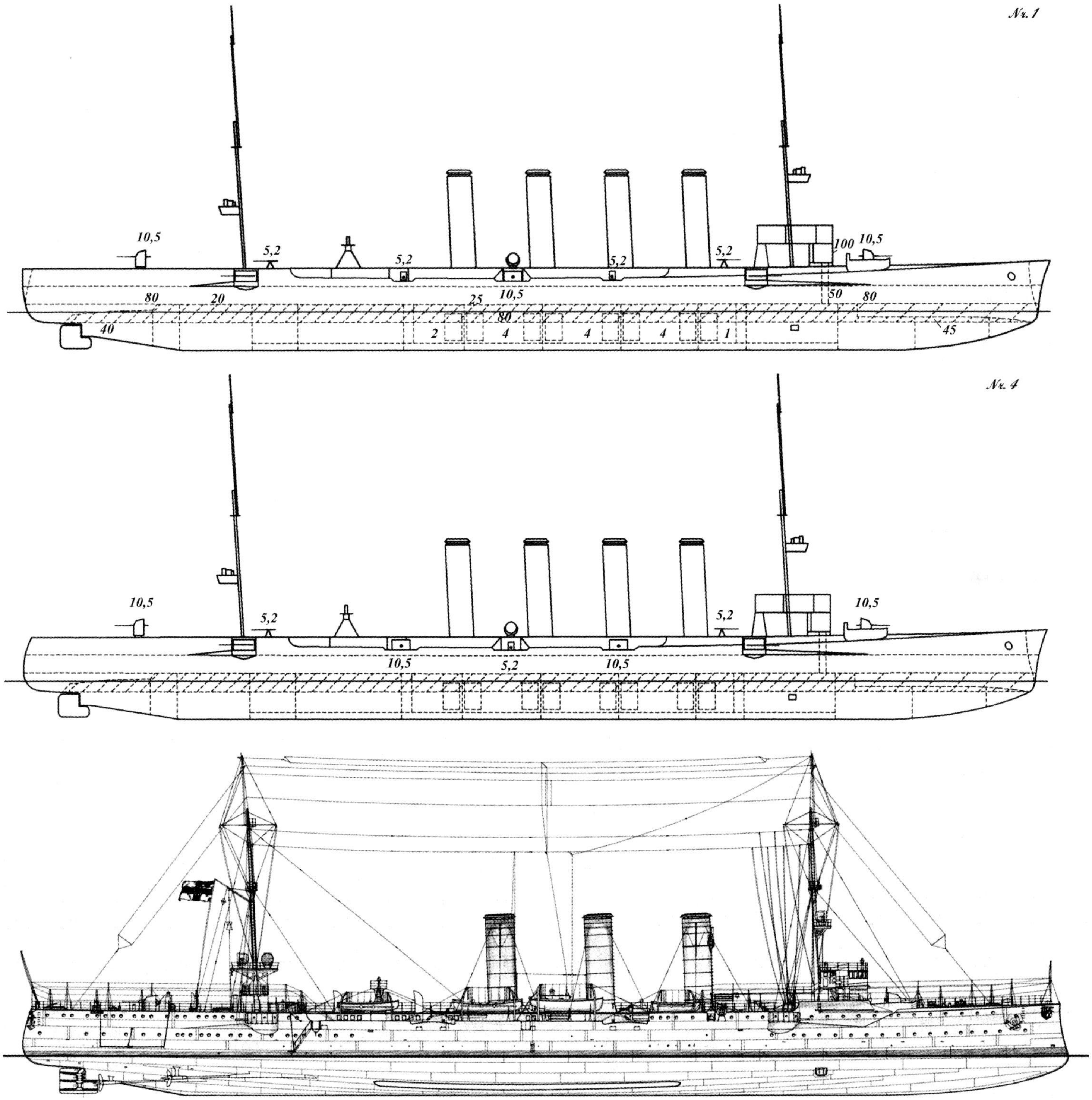

Project IIIb No. 1 (top) retained the ten 10.5cm main battery of previous classes, but proposed new shapes for stem and stern. No. 4 (middle) carried the largest number of most guns of all variants, but was rejected because of the difficulty in supplying ammunition to the central guns on each side. As seen from this rigging plan of *Kolberg* 'as fitted', the final design was far less radical. *(DN drawings/L Wischmeyer drawing)*

Members of the last three classes of 'old-style' cruisers together at Swinemünde. From the right: *Cöln, Dresden, Stuttgart* and *Mainz*. *(Heidrich collection)*

Records of her trials are rather scanty: 26.8 knots were recorded as top speed at 29,036shp, while a four-and-a-half-hour trial gave an average of 26.02 knots at 22,935shp. On 10 October, *Cöln* joined the II. SG, serving as 2nd flagship of the Scouting Force from September 1912 onwards, becoming in addition flagship of torpedo boats in December 1913.

THE SMALL CRUISER ABROAD

Small cruisers akin to the German vessels were only built in significant numbers by the British. The French, US and Italian navies concentrated on big armoured cruisers, with the exception of a trio of scout cruisers constructed by each of the latter two powers. The aforementioned *Topaze* class of the 1902 and 1903 British programmes were designed to be faster than the *Gazelles*, and carried twelve 4in guns as their main battery on a 3,000-ton displacement. One of them, *Amethyst*, was the first cruiser to be powered by turbines. They were followed by a series of scouts for flotilla work of increasing size and capability, the 1907 Estimates *Boadicea* class (3,300 tons, six 4in guns) being the starting point for the next year's 4,800 ton *Bristol* class of five vessels, which were explicitly designed to meet the growing German small cruiser fleet.[32] Originally to be armed with a dozen 4in weapons, two pairs were swapped for 6in mountings fore and aft, the Royal Navy thus taking a different view from the German navy over the desirability of heavier chase guns, even at the cost of a mixed main battery.

On the other hand, the four-strong 1909 *Weymouth* class were enlarged to 5,250 tons to carry eight 6in guns, which became standard until 1911, when the *Birmingham* class (5,440 tons) were ordered with nine 6in. The latter, and the preceding *Chatham* class, introduced side armour into British small cruisers as a result of trials with the old battleship *Edinburgh*, which had shown the weakness of deck-only protection against modern high-explosive shells (cf. p 138, below).[33]

The *Boadicea*s also had successors closer to their own size, the *Blonde* (1909 Estimates) and *Active* (1910 and 1911 programmes) classes being of 3,440 tons and armed with ten 4in guns, making 25 knots on 18,000shp. The 1912 Estimates included further ships of same general size (now 3,750 tons), but beginning a whole new line of development, with armour belts, rather than the traditional armour deck, and with power boosted to 40,000shp, using destroyer-type turbines for 28.5 knots. Eight of these ships, of the *Arethusa* class, were built, armed with two 6in and six 4in guns, and acted as the prototypes for the 'C' and 'D' classes that would be built in considerable numbers under the 1913 and later programmes, and would form the core of the First World War British small cruiser fleet.

32. For the *Bristol*s and the subsequent evolution, see D Lyon, 'The First Town Class 1908–31', *Warship* I/1 (1977), pp 48–58, I/2 (1977), pp 54–61, I/3, pp 46–51.

33. Much as 1887 French trials had led to the reintroduction of side armour in big cruisers (Dodson, *Before the Battlecruiser*, p 41).

5 THE NEW GENERATION

THE *MAGDEBURG*[1] CLASS

The radical changes first mooted during the development of the *Kolberg* class were finally implemented with the small cruisers of the 1909 Estimates. A further increase in the speed of German small cruisers had now become desirable in light of the appearance of the British *Invincible* class of armoured cruisers (soon to be battlecruisers), with a design speed of 25 knots – learned semi-officially in 1907 – which was 2 knots in excess of that of the latest German ships. Indeed, the results of the initial trials of HMS *Indomitable* (the first ship of the class to complete), leaked to the German authorities in May 1908, were even more alarming: although initially no more than rumours, a variety of values between 26 and 28 knots were quoted (she actually made 26.1 knots). The *Kolberg* class had been designed for 25.5 knots, although they had made up to 26.8 knots on trials. Accordingly, the design speed of the next generation of German cruisers (1909 Estimates) was adjusted up to 27 knots – 1.5 knots more than the *Kolberg*s.

This speed required the designers to provide significantly more powerful machinery, a design output of around 25,000shp, versus 19,000shp in *Kolberg*. To provide for this, a further boiler was added to the forward boiler room, bringing the total number to sixteen. To keep trunking to a minimum, this resulted in – at last – the provision of an additional funnel, while the widening of the foremost boiler room to take two boilers athwartships adversely altered the underwater lines, requiring a lengthening of the hull to maximise hydrodynamic efficiency. What would become the *Magdeburg* class would thus be some 6m longer than the *Kolberg*s. In addition, the modified stem considered for the second batch of the *Kolberg* class (pp 132, 136, above) was now finally adopted, while the forefoot was cut away, principally to balance the anticipated deterioration in turning abilities stemming from the new ships' additional length.

To ameliorate the increased stress moments that originated from the extra length of the hull, the designers decided to deviate from traditional constructional practices. Until now, the hulls of German naval vessels had been, like those of most other nations, transversely framed, but following lengthy consideration and calculations, which would eventually delay the keel laying of the first vessels for more than six months, it was decided to construct the hulls entirely on the longitudinal framing system.

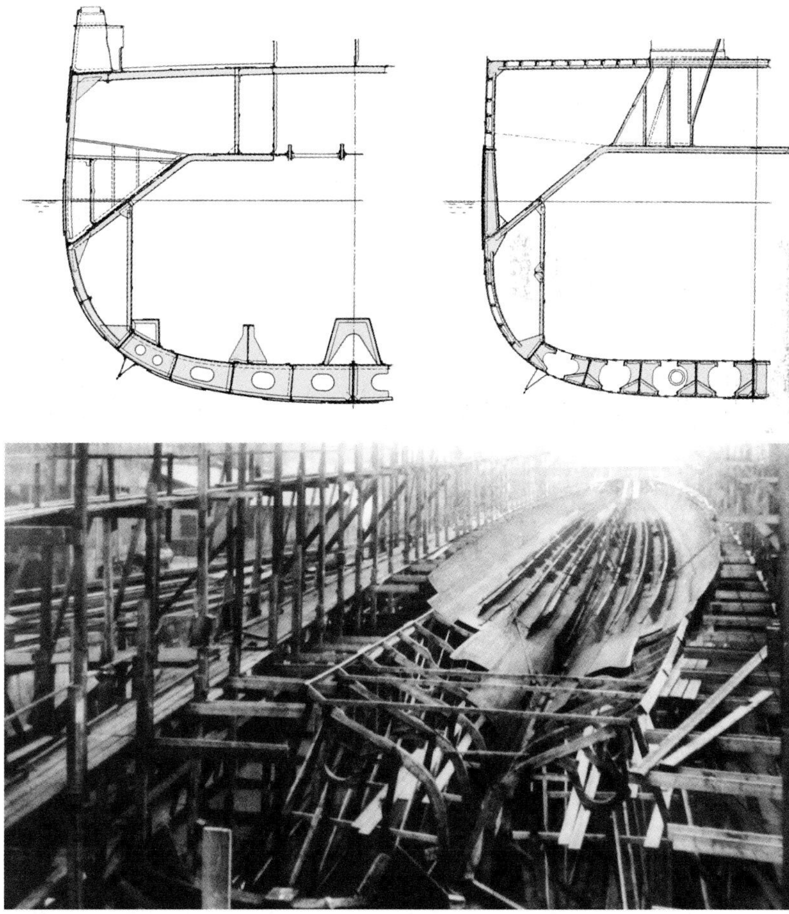

Comparison between the 'classical' framing of *Kolberg* (left) and the longitudinal framing of *Magdeburg*. The difference in the steel work at the bottom structure is clearly evident, and may be seen (bottom) in this December 1916 view of the initial stages of the construction of *Ersatz-A*, the last cruiser begun for the Imperial navy (pp 162-163). *(DN collection)*

The time necessary for these calculations led to another confrontation between Tirpitz and the Kaiser, the latter always eager to accuse the RMA of building too slowly. In response, Tirpitz pointed out that the Kaiser had been kept fully informed by the RMA about the ongoing work, from a first

1. Internally the class was designated the *Breslau* class, but, as *Magdeburg* had been launched three days before *Breslau*, it became known publicly as *Magdeburg* class.

informal briefing on 5 October 1908 to the requested decision in April 1909. This had been in the wake of lengthy negotiations with the prospective shipyards involved, to enable the new structural system to be approved by the 'All-Highest'. Only after this approval, Tirpitz noted, had he been possible to order detailed plans and specifications be prepared, which – according to his preliminary estimates – would take at least six months. The Kaiser's options in April 1909 had accordingly been explicitly between ordering a repeat *Mainz*, to be completed more rapidly, or waiting another ten months for a much-improved type, just as had been his own outspoken desire. As in most of these controversies, Tirpitz's analysis and references to imperial discourses of long ago prevailed over the more subjective position of the Kaiser – to everybody's benefit. The new system proved to be completely successful and was employed in all later German cruisers.

A further constructional innovation came with a decision to provide the new class with side armour, rather than rely on the armour deck, as had been the case in all earlier small cruisers. The weight for this was made available by the savings resulting from the move to longitudinal framing, and met a military need that came from the fitting of 6in (15.2cm) guns in the recent British light cruisers of the *Bristol* (two guns) and *Weymouth* (eight) classes (see above, p 136). Experience during the Russo-Japanese War had demonstrated the destruction that HE shells of such a calibre could wreak on unprotected sides, and as a result the previous German vertical 'protection' of a cork-filled cofferdam, to close up holes torn into the skin plating through the swelling of the cork, was no longer viable. Henceforth, as Tirpitz would argue, holes close to the waterline had to be avoided.

Two options for mounting the side armour were tested on a target representative of the new cruiser's hull at Krupp's proving ground at Meppen. Part of the target followed traditional practice, with the 50mm armour plates separated from the skin of the hull by a 100mm-thick wooden backing. The other made its 60mm plate itself the hull skin, making it an integral part of the structure, with a significant saving in weight. Both sections were equipped with an armour deck behind the side armour, its 20mm slopes meeting its lower edge. The target was fired on with a variety of calibres and projectiles: 8.8cm HE; 10.5cm HE and shot; 15cm AP, HE and common; and 30.5cm HE. A first trial left the coal bunkers above the armour deck slopes empty; a second one had the upper bunkers filled with coal.

The trials indicated that complete protection against nose-fused 10.5cm shells was possible, whereas the immunity zone against nose-fused 15cm shells extended down to a range of about 3,400m. A second series of trials validated these results with regard to the nose-fused HE shells, although 15cm AP shells could be kept out only at ranges over 3,900m. Regarding the effect of 30.5cm common shells, it was concluded that at ranges of over 10,000m it was possible that the armour deck

An illustrious group of officers and civilians pose in front of the cruiser target at the Meppen proving ground in 1909. Among them may be seen Grand Admiral Tirpitz (in civilian clothes, eighth from right) and Gustav Krupp von Bohlen und Halbach, chairman of the Krupp concern (fourth from right). *(DN collection)*

might remain intact following a hit on the belt. The trial results having been considered satisfactory, with the 'integral' solution judged slightly better of the two, as well as saving weight, it was accordingly employed in all subsequent small cruisers. A similar arrangement had also been also introduced in the contemporary British *Chatham* class (p 132).

The full scheme ran the 60mm plating, which extended up to armour deck level, from a 60mm (above water)/80mm (below water) transverse bulkhead just aft of the magazines for the stern guns to just short of the bow. Here, its upper edge sloped up to upper deck level to protect the area affected by the bow wave, and joined 18mm plating that continued to the stem. The point of juncture corresponded with a 40mm transverse bulkhead. The armour deck ran 40mm thick from a 60mm transverse bulkhead aft of the steering gear to the 60mm/80mm bulkhead closing the rear end of the belt, at which point it stepped up to main deck level and continued with a thickness of 20mm (with 20mm slopes down to the lower edge of the belt) to just forward of the bow magazines, where a 40mm slope took it back down to the waterline. Here it reduced in thickness back to 20mm, before increasing to 60mm as it continued to meet the forward transverse bulkhead.

Another significant innovation in the new class was the omission of the poop that had been a feature of all earlier vessels. This change was a result of a requirement that small cruisers should henceforth be capable of laying up to 120 mines, to supplement the new dedicated minelayers *Nautilus* and *Albatross* (see pp 186-190). The *Kolberg* class and some of their predecessors had the ability to stow up to 100 mines, but the presence of the poop made the process of laying them, via the aft gangway ports on upper deck, clumsy. Accordingly, all the new generation of small cruisers would have a flush upper deck aft of the forecastle, for the accommodation of dismountable mine rails leading back to the stern.

In contrast to what had been done with the preceding *Kolberg* and earlier classes, where the builders had been directed – or forced by circumstances – to the turbine installation employed in a given ship, the competing shipyards were now given – at least in theory – much more freedom in their choice of system. In practice, however, they were bound by a network of subcontracts, patent rights and – later on – by renewed interference from the RMA. This freedom extended to the number of shafts: they could offer twin-, triple- or quadruple-screw arrangements at their own discretion. Only one aspect was mandatory: maximum speed over the measured mile had to exceed 27.25 knots, while the average speed during the six-hour trial had to exceed 26.75 knots.

As an example of the complex negotiations that ensued, one may cite parts of the correspondence between Vulcan and the RMA – initially with reference to the yard's offer to build *Ersatz-Bussard*. These discussions were later re-focussed on *Ersatz-Falke*,[2] for whose construction the company had actually received the contract. According to Vulcan's calculations, the most cost-effective option employed four shafts – which would eventually be chosen. The choice of the turbine system in this particular case is quite interesting insofar as the Vulcan-preferred reaction-type AEG-Curtis system was chosen, which normally combined the HP and LP stages in one casing, thus driving only two shafts. In this case, however, the stages were separated, as in the Parsons system, to produce a four-shaft arrangement, with the HP turbines driving the inner shafts, and LP turbines serving the outer pair. Each of the individual turbine casings also contained an astern element at the same pressure level. Despite this splitting, the total weight for this more complex system was less than that of other alternatives, coming in at 33 tonnes below the limit set by the RMA in its preliminary specifications.

Vulcan went even further: as previously in *Mainz*, they dared to guarantee an extra ¼kt above the requirements for the full-power and the six-hour trials. They would indeed keep their promise, with the designed power set at 25,400shp and 22,800shp for each respective trial. However, after receiving the order, Vulcan discovered that they had to adjust the planned run of the shafts, in particular since the available space for the LP turbines had become restricted by the four-shaft configuration.

Ersatz-Falke [to be *Breslau*] was ordered from Vulcan in December 1909, as was *Ersatz-Bussard* [*Magdeburg*] from AG Weser of Bremen. As the latter yard was linked with the Bergmann company of Berlin, they offered as their cheapest option a vessel propelled by three Weser-Bergmann turbines, another derivative of the Curtis type.[3] This was planned to deliver 24,000shp at full power, and 21,600shp for the six-hour trial, and was accepted by the RMA, always open to the most economical prices. But AG Weser was to pay dearly for their choice, as the construction of their turbines lagged badly, and it thus took five extra months to complete the vessel, as compared to her Vulcan-built sister.

At the end of 1909, negotiations began for the second pair of vessels of the class, to be built under the 1910 Estimates. Because of the long delay in ordering the first pair, all four vessels of the class were actually ordered around the same time. Politics also contributed to this, as a worldwide shipbuilding crisis was under way, which had hit many German yards hard. All major yards were accordingly lobbying the RMA for involvement in naval contracts. Tirpitz was initially minded to offer one of the 1910 vessels to Schichau without competition,

2. Now referring to the *Bussard*-class cruiser, rather than the old paddle-aviso that had been subject of the abortive *Ersatz-Falke* of the 1890s!

3. Bergmann's turbine branch would be sold to the Siemens concern a few years later,

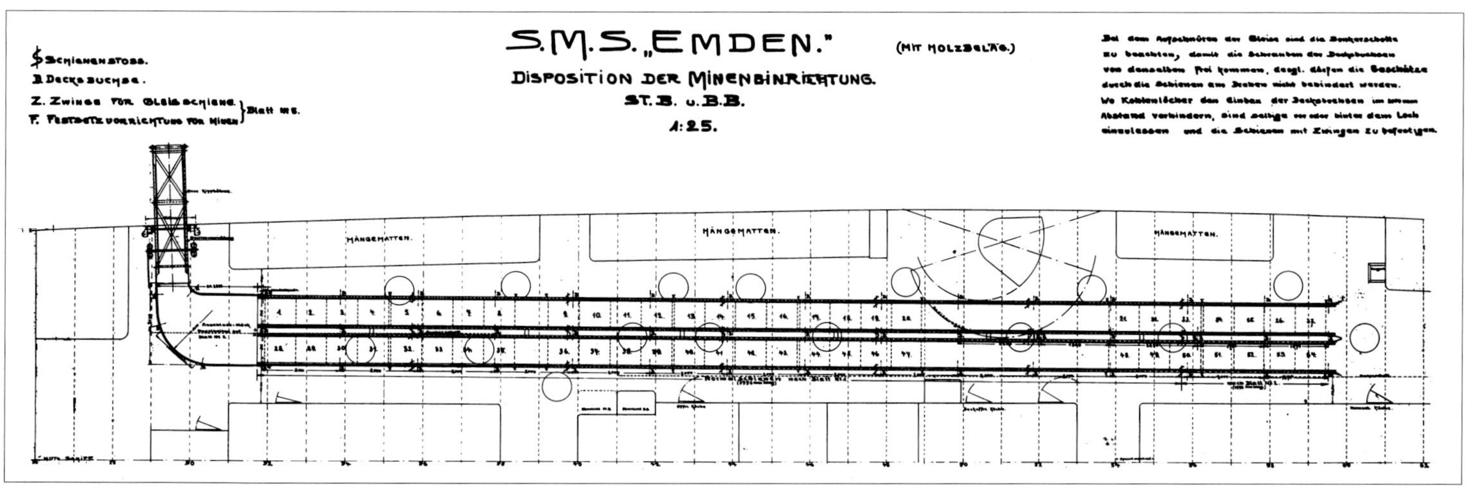

A double row of mine rails could be fitted on the upper deck of older small cruisers, in this case *Emden* (i). The mines were to be laid through the gangway-port. *(DN collection)*

but changed his mind shortly afterwards – probably after intervention by Hunold von Ahlefeld, a former subordinate at the RMA and now Director of AG Weser.

Like other yards, Weser had offered to build a second vessel at a reduced price should the yard receive one of the initial pair. Not involved in the building any of the 1910 Estimates capital ships (unlike Schichau, which had *König Albert* in hand), the Weser yard was in desperate need of work and stood at the verge of bankruptcy. This was an outcome Tirpitz could ill afford, as he needed all the big shipyards to continue his 'plan', if only to keep competition alive and costs down. Tirpitz therefore accepted the Weser offer, and made a direct award of the first of the 1910 cruisers, *Ersatz-Cormoran* [to be *Stralsund*] to them, subject to a significant reduction in its price – down to one which Germania had (unsuccessfully) offered, and actually the same as that of Vulcan's *Ersatz-Falke*.

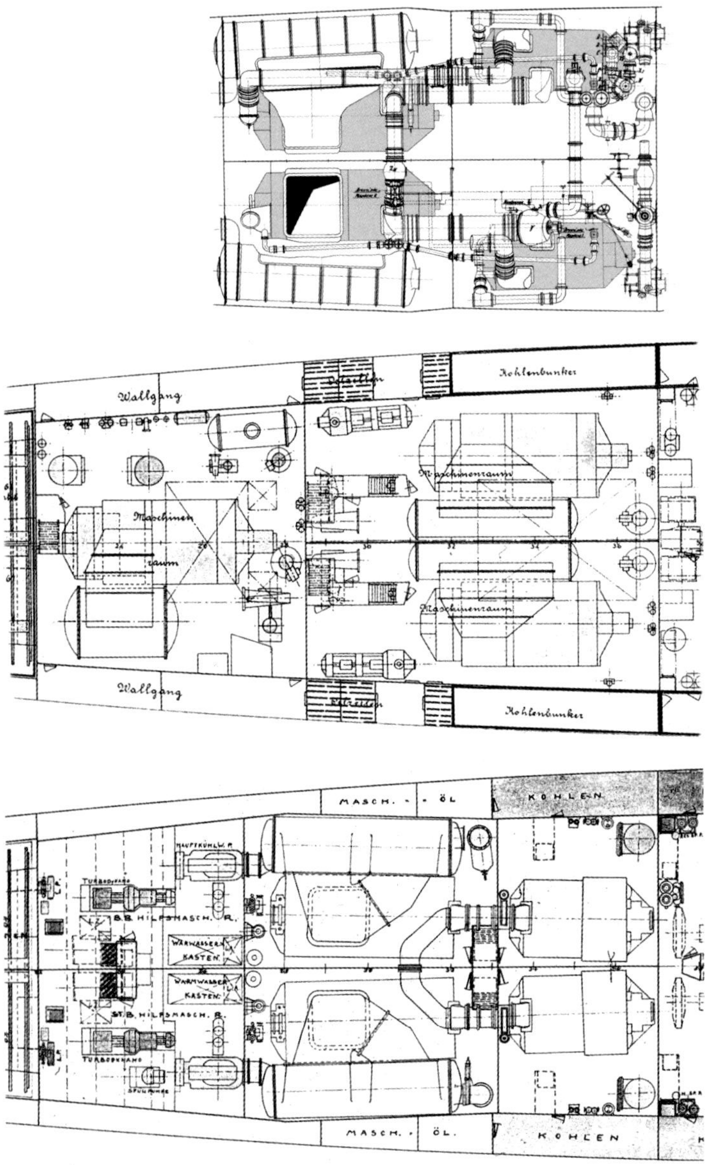

The three different engine layouts of the *Magdeburg* class. **Top:** the main steam piping in *Breslau*'s four-shaft engine rooms, in the 'classical' Parsons configuration, with each HP turbine and each LP turbine (casings shaded) serving its own individual shaft. **Middle:** *Stralsund*'s three-shaft installation (*Magdeburg*'s was identical), with a very different layout from those with even numbers of shafts. **Bottom:** the two-shaft Navy-type turbines of *Strassburg*. *(DN collection)*

There seems to have been an understanding between the RMA and Weser that *Ersatz-Cormoran* would not follow *Ersatz-Bussard* in being propelled by the 3-shaft Bergmann installation, but instead employ a set of Parsons turbines. The reason behind this is not wholly clear, but it seems that the RMA were unconvinced by the cruising mode of the 3-shaft installation. However, the financially pressed shipyard could not afford to pay licence fees to Turbinia for use of the Parsons system – especially after being forced by the RMA to cut their price further – and so retained the cheaper 3-shaft Bergmann installation; no objections were raised by the RMA.

Something of an enigma surrounds the way in which the fourth cruiser of the series, *Ersatz-Condor*, was allocated to its builder, as it was given to Wilhelmshaven Dockyard, taking a precious order away from the hard-pressed private shipyards.[4] The most likely reason for this move is that the ship was to be used as a test bed for a new Navy-type turbine, initially manufactured exclusively by the Wilhelmshaven shipyard. The latter had just expanded its machinery-building plant for that purpose, and was eager to show its capabilities. The Navy-type turbine derived from a design by Brown, Boveri (parent of the Turbinia company), which had been evolved from a pure Parsons-type into a Curtis/Parsons hybrid. In this, the casings for the HP and the LP sections were separated longitudinally in two engine rooms, but worked on one common shaft, providing a two-shaft installation. Power was again set at 24,000shp and 21,600shp for each set of trials.

In addition to the delay caused by the late delivery of her machinery, *Magdeburg* was hampered during her short career by technical problems related to the Bergmann turbines. The closing report of her trials commented favourably in all respects, but just three months later both wing turbines were suffering severe leaks, reducing *Magdeburg*'s maximum speed to 22 knots, and even then, only for short sprints. Twelve months later, in January 1914, her centre turbine failed and had to be removed for overhaul; it had not been reinstalled by mobilisation in August. Her operational speed on her wing turbines was about 22 knots, which prevented her employment with the fleet and limited her to the Baltic theatre; she was lost (pp 208-209) before her missing engine could be reinstalled.

Interestingly, her 'machinery sister' *Stralsund* was initially less affected by such problems, but suffered her own breakdown of her centre turbine in the summer of 1916. During August of that year, first her centre propeller, and afterwards the whole turbine,

4. In the end the navy profited from this choice as *Ersatz Condor* came out cheapest of all the class.

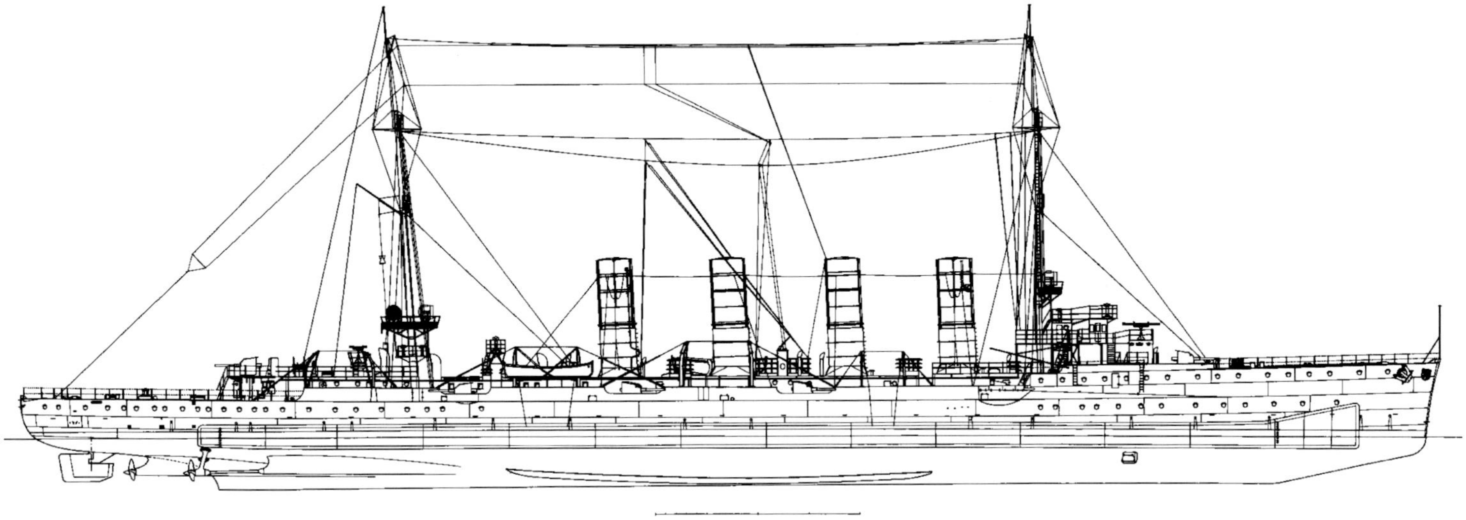

Above: rigging plan of *Breslau* 'as fitted'. Right, the same ship alongside Vulcan's fitting-out pier, shortly before commissioning. *(DN drawing/ DN* collection)

was removed. In this condition *Stralsund* sailed on two shafts until August 1917, when Kiel Dockyard installed the reconditioned centre turbine from *Magdeburg*, restoring her to full power. In spite of this, *Stralsund* became probably the navy's most active small cruiser during the war, albeit operating mainly in the Baltic following the onset of her propulsion problems.

Notwithstanding their machinery difficulties, in the *Magdeburg* class the German navy received a very valuable reinforcement of its cruiser squadrons, which would prove their validity and sturdiness through numerous tasks in peace and war. The design would be the ultimate basis of all German small cruisers down to the *Emden* (iii) in the 1920s.

The calibre conundrum

Although the main battery of the *Kolberg* class had been strengthened by two guns, and more powerful models of the 10.5cm gun employed, there was no attempt to substitute a larger calibre, as was done in the Royal Navy. Tirpitz had favoured a larger calibre on 'his' preferred III. class cruisers back in the 1890s, but the realities of Reichstag politics (and finance) ensured that as the IV. class cruiser evolved into the small cruiser it retained the 10.5cm gun of its ancestral line. During the initial years of the type, neither Tirpitz nor most other naval officers saw this as a major disadvantage. The effect of the comparatively modern 10.5cm gun and its shell, in conjunction with a high rate of fire, seemed sufficient for fighting against any existing small cruisers or torpedo craft in home waters, as well as fighting possible smaller adversaries abroad.

As already noted, the main task of cruisers working with the fleet was to be scouting, either on their own account, or by leading further advanced torpedo boat flotillas. They were not intended to fight it out with hostile flotillas of torpedo class or cruisers: rather, they were intended to garner precious information about the enemy and pass it to the senior officer of the fleet. This had been a major driver in the ongoing quest for additional speed. So, any engagements by small cruisers working with the fleet would be on a small scale only, and be primarily defensive. On this basis, it seems that Tirpitz's earlier concept of a number of small cruisers being able to successfully take on a single large cruiser had now been dropped.

However, likely future battle ranges were now being pushed upwards by the advent of the 'heater' torpedo, significantly reducing the effectiveness of the 10.5cm gun. The size of torpedo craft also continued to increase, meaning that even the main batteries of small cruisers were now becoming ineffective in definitively stopping such vessels. Furthermore, the British navy had, as previously noted (p 136), added 6in chase guns to its larger *Bristol* class (1908 Estimates), and would soon move to a uniform 6in main armament in the subsequent *Weymouth* class (1909 Estimates). The latter's Japanese contemporaries, the *Chikuma* class, had the same eight 6in armament. Against such weapons, the pre-*Magdeburg* German vessels' deck-only protection had become significantly more vulnerable, prompting the addition of side armour to the new class. Yet front-line commanders still wanted to keep the 10.5cm gun, principally because of its higher rate of fire. This is reflected in a statement by KAdm Hermann Jacobsen (1859–1943), long-time head of the Inspectorate for Naval Artillery, after directing a test firing of the new *Mainz*, with the aim of

> determining if the 10.5cm L/45 gun – this calibre's upper limit of effectiveness lies at circa 8,000m – would guarantee a sufficient number of hits and still sufficient effects on the superstructures.... During three passes of the target vessel at between 6500–7900m, 190 rounds were fired and 36 hits obtained .... With regard to the good ability of observing the fall of shot, the failsafe process of getting on the target and the sheer number of hits, the Fleet's High Command thus expected a sufficient effect against unprotected cruisers equipped with open batteries on the weather decks to gain the superiority of fire within a short period ... *This had been a bad fallacy*' [our emphasis].[5]

Additionally, the *Magdeburg* class was the first to lose its second calibre for repelling torpedo craft. The never-liked 5.2cm semi-automatic gun was felt to lack sufficient 'punch' to remain useful in that function, while the increased number of 10.5cm could easily do their job. Interestingly, the space formerly occupied by the 5.2cm magazine was not used to raise the number of 10.5cm rounds carried.

Into service

Breslau

The first ship of the *Magdeburg* class to come into service, on 10 May 1912, was *Breslau*, which had been laid down as *Ersatz-Falke* in May 1910. She was launched on 16 May 1911 and completed in April 1912. Her subsequent trials gave very satisfactory results: at full power of 33,470shp she attained 27.6 knots; during the six-hour trial the figures were 27.2 knots at 28,870shp. As was usual, the new cruiser had to interrupt her trials to act as escort to *Hohenzollern* during Kiel Week and the Kaiser's Norwegian cruise, which ended on 23 August 1912; the cruiser then participated in September's autumn manoeuvres.

Breslau finally joined the Scouting Force on 26 September 1912. However, on 3 November, she was reassigned to the Mediterranean Division alongside the large cruiser *Goeben* (flag), both ships leaving Wilhelmshaven on 5 November 1912 and arriving at Malta on the 13th. There they joined *Geier*, the training cruisers *Hertha* and *Vineta* and the 'gunboat' *Loreley* (iii) on the station. *Breslau* met *Geier* and *Hertha* at Alexandria soon afterwards, and at the end of March 1913 carried Prince Heinrich of Prussia and Prince Ernst August of Cumberland (soon-to-be son-in-law of the Kaiser and reigning Duke of Brunswick) to the funeral of the Greek King Georgios I.

From 10 April 1913, *Breslau* participated in the international blockade of the Montenegrin coast, with a contingent operating ashore, until replaced by *Geier* at the beginning of August. She then sailed to Constantinople, arriving on 10 August and remaining there until 27 October; the end of the year found the cruiser at Messina. In January 1914, *Breslau* returned to the Adriatic, and refitted at Trieste until 18 March, after which she and *Goeben* escorted the Kaiser in *Hohenzollern* from Venice to Corfu. On 4 May she was detached to the Aegean, rejoining the flagship at Alexandria on 5 June, the two ships then proceeding to Albanian waters to protect German interests in the wake of the election of Wilhelm of Wied as that country's prince, with *Breslau* lying off Durazzo from 20 June as part of an international squadron, while *Goeben* refitted at Pola. The squadron began to break up on 27 July, in the wake of the assassination of the Archduke Franz Ferdinand, the British armoured cruiser *Defence* and the French *Edgar Quinet* leaving on the 29th. *Breslau* herself departed at the end of the month, and rendezvoused with *Goeben* off Corfu on 8 July. On 1 August she picked up German personnel, rejoining the flag at Messina the next day.

Magdeburg

The class name-ship, laid down as *Ersatz-Bussard* in April 1910, was launched on 13 May 1911. Her delivery by AG Weser to Wilhelmshaven Dockyard on 9 August 1912 had already been delayed by her machinery problems during the yard's initial alongside trials in June, and during her first builder's trial runs that had commenced on 21 July. She finally commissioned for her official trials on 20 August.

Some of the outputs from *Magdeburg*'s trials may be worth noting, since they generally reflect the performance of the whole class in one way or another. It was found that she easily met the design criteria for her machinery, ultimately reaching 27.6 knots at 29,900shp on the measured mile and 26.9 knots at 25,100shp during the six-hour trial. It was noted, however, that the speed/power curve became very steep at its end, indicating the limitations of the chosen hull form. At high speeds, a significantly large trough developed under the stern, which sometimes drew the aft end of the hull down into the slope of the stern wave, thus flooding the aft end of the main deck and at the same time raising the bow forward. This was to become a signature behaviour of all succeeding cruiser classes as well. Steaming astern, *Magdeburg* attained the remarkable speed of 19 knots and could easily be kept on course. A negative point, however, was that at all speeds in excess of 22 knots – even more so above 26 knots – the after officers' quarters in the between-deck suffered badly from vibration.

A new bridge arrangement introduced in the class also garnered negative comments. Because of the reduced size and

5. H. Jacobsen, *Die Entwicklung der Schiesskunst in der Kaiserlich Deutschen Marine* (Berlin: Reichswehrministerium, 1928). pp 249–50.

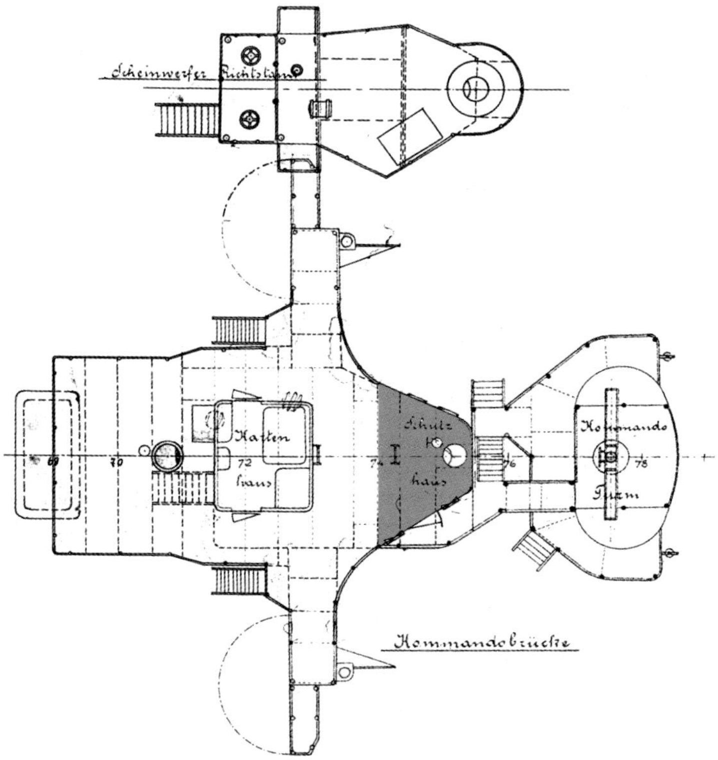

Stralsund's bridge: the shaded part is the small area protected by the windscreen. *(DN collection)*

new shape of the Friedenssteuerstelle (conning position for use in peacetime: in war, the conning tower was supposed to be used), there were hardly any truly sheltered places to protect the watchkeepers from the wind at higher speeds. This was not a negligible issue in anything other than the best summer conditions in northern waters. The small size of the bridge even precluded the fitting of revolution indicator repeaters for the main engines, which were only to be found in the conning tower. This made navigation – especially manoeuvring in ports – rather demanding. On the other hand, one particular military aspect of the trials was found especially satisfactory: mines could be laid over the stern at speeds of up to 26 knots.

In view of the aforementioned problems and the initially intended change of engine plant of the second cruiser built by Weser (see p 140, above), the official verdict regarding *Magdeburg*'s machinery during her trials seems rather surprising: no faults had been detected, the required power and efficiency had been exceeded and even the cruising mode of the turbines had been found more effective than required. It was recommended that the latter be used for speeds up to 17 knots.

But in January 1913 these defects became all too apparent, with *Magdeburg*'s active service hamstrung by continuous machinery problems. As a result, she spent her pre-war service as a torpedo trials ship – except for one short cruise in August 1913 to Madeira and Tenerife, for range-measuring trials of her W/T installations, the Torpedo Inspectorate being in charge of W/T development. Before this voyage, it had been intended that *Magdeburg* be employed as an escort to the new liner *Imperator*, then the largest ship in the world, on a five-day cruise into the Atlantic Ocean in April 1913, with the Kaiser embarked. However, this was ultimately cancelled, a key reason being that *Magdeburg* would be unable to maintain the liner's cruising speed of 22 knots for more than three days without refuelling.

For service as a torpedo trials ship, her forward pair of beam guns, mounted in shallow sponsons because of space restrictions, were replaced by trainable torpedo tubes. Interestingly, the guns were not reinstated at the beginning of the First World War, the torpedoes possibly contributing to the nearly complete destruction of the cruiser's fore part during her subsequent – otherwise only partially successful – scuttling (p 209, below).

Strassburg

Ersatz-Condor was ordered from the Imperial Dockyard Wilhelmshaven in March 1910 and was laid down in October of the same year. She was launched as *Strassburg* on 24 September 1911 and commissioned for trials on 9 October 1912. She attained 28.3 knots at a maximum of 33,740shp – the highest output of the whole class – on the measured mile and 26.9 knots at 25,650shp during the six-hour run in December 1912. *Strassburg* relieved *Berlin* in the Scouting Force on 23 December 1912, but suffered a collision in the Kiel Canal with the Danish freighter *Christian IX* on 6 January 1913; repairs were completed on 23 February. Soon afterwards, in April, *Strassburg* was transferred, together with *Dresden*, to the Mediterranean Division, arriving at Malta on the 13th and proceeding to Constantinople, via Alexandretta, which she reached in May. In June she accompanied *Goeben* to Venice, Pola and Naples, before returning to the Aegean. *Strassburg* and *Dresden* left Alexandretta for Germany on 9 September, arriving at Kiel on 23 September.

On 9 December 1913, *Strassburg* sailed with the battleships *Kaiser* and *König Albert* as a Detached Division for a deployment to South America, via Togoland (29–31 December), Kamerun (2–15 January 1914, rendezvousing with the gunboats *Panther* and *Eber*), German South West Africa (22–23 January), Cape Town (25–30 January) and St Helena, to Brazil. They then proceeded to Argentina, Uruguay and – via the Magellan Straits – Chile (3–11 April), before returning to Brazil. There, *Strassburg* was detached to the Caribbean, to relieve *Dresden* while she was occupied in Mexican waters. On 4 July *Strassburg* met *Karlsruhe*, newly assigned to East American station. She began her homeward voyage on 20 July 1914, sailing via the Azores (27–28 July), with a final high-speed dash through the English Channel, reaching Wilhelmshaven on 1 August, just as mobilisation was taking place.

During the cruise and after her return, the performance of *Strassburg* (and the battleships) was carefully analysed, as this – besides 'showing the flag' – had been the main objective of the extended cruise. *Strassburg* had been the first of the 'modern' cruisers to be exposed to tropical climates and oceanic weather conditions, and her performance would therefore serve as a baseline for the deciding the characteristics of future cruisers for service abroad. Key parts of the report are as follows:

> Behaviour of the cruiser: Less favourable [than that of the battleships] must be regarded the behaviour of the cruiser in higher sea states. At a sea state of 7–8 from the beam and up to 4 points to forward and aft she ships a lot of water and rolls badly (up to 35°), so that she either has to heave to or change course significantly away from the wind. This occasion arose two or three times during the cruise. Because of this effect, her utility as a cruiser is reduced, when she, for example, has to adjust her course to that of an unconstrained enemy while shadowing him, and not taking care of the strength and direction of the seas. Similarly, the radius of action is not sufficient: at a cruising speed of 12–15 knots (the most economical speed) it comes out at only about 2,800nm. On the other hand, the cruiser's good manoeuvrability should be emphasised as compared to the preceding class [...]. The second and third artillery positions on each side become affected by spray and green water easily because of their – too – low mounting. *Strassburg*'s C/O proposes, for future new construction, an extension of the forecastle to the point where both guns can be mounted in an elevated position. Habitability would also be improved by such a measure. The British have chosen this way with the *Birmingham* class already, given that its size has passed the 5,000 tonne mark considerably.[6]

Stralsund

Ersatz-Cormoran was ordered from AG Weser in April 1910 and laid down in September of the same year. She was launched as *Stralsund* on 4 November 1911 and commenced her builder's trials on 18 November 1912, before commissioning on 10 December. She attained trial results nearly identical to those of her sister: 28.3 knots at a maximum of 33,515shp on the measured mile and 27.0 knots at 27,032shp over six hours in January 1913. *Stralsund* joined the Scouting Force on 15 February 1913, and spent her pre-war career uneventfully in home waters.

TOWARDS THE STANDARD TURBINE

Being chronically short of personnel – even in certain parts of the administration – the German navy chose a rather ingenious route in first investigating and finally determining the best configuration for the future propulsion machinery of small cruisers.[7] This took some of the pressure off the responsible officers, and has hitherto been somewhat obscure.

The RMA, as responsible lead institution for shipbuilding and engineering, required from those applying for civilian engineering posts with the navy the successful completion of a number of examinations before appointment to what could be a life of service as a civil servant, initially with the grade of Marinebaumeister (Master Leader of Naval Construction). The

6. NARA-roll T1022-497 PG-67448-NID S. 150ff.

7. Further investigation is needed to determine whether this procedure had been applied to other projects as well.

relevance of these quite elaborate examinations may be taken from the fact that they were set, read and assessed by no less than the head of the department 'K II' (Naval Engineering), Wirklicher Geheimer Oberbaurat Rudolph Veith (1846–1917),

Magdeburg alongside the dolphins at Swinemünde, employed as a trials ship: a torpedo tube has replaced the 10.5cm gun in the foremost sponson. The angled forward part of the belt is clearly visible. *(Heidrich collection)*

Stralsund has the distinction of displaying the highest number of funnel markings ever seen in the German navy: eight red bands, denoting the eighth ship of the II. Cruiser division. *(DN collection)*

together with at least two additional senior officials in the same department and of similar reputation.

One of the known assignments from November 1909 – unfortunately only the task itself has survived in the files – was to explore and discuss the advantages or disadvantages of a possible exchange of *Augsburg*'s exclusive Parsons turbine plant for one that mixed the Parsons and Curtis principles. Another assignment has, fortunately, survived in detail. The presented solution, although missing its accompanying detailed drawings, gives an incomparable insight into some of the thoughts and calculations that would support the German navy's progress towards producing a standard turbine plant for small cruisers. Given to applicant Otto Hänisch (b 1882) on 10 May 1910, the task was completed on 1 November 1910.[8] The problem was presented to him in the following way:

> For a small cruiser … the main engine plant is to be estimated and designed. For the purpose of calculating the necessary engine power, the following values for resistance, taken from tank tests, shall be employed […]. The necessary steam shall be generated by a boiler plant of small-tube watertube boilers of the Navy type of 113.7m^2 grate area. No superheating shall be provided. The prime movers shall consist of steam turbines; the choice of the system and the number of shafts is left open – nevertheless, the result has to be fully justified. The prospective vessel shall attain 27.5 knots during short sprints on the measured mile, while the speed during the six-hour trial run shall be at least 27 knots.
>
> The space between the frames 22–37 below the armoured deck is reserved for the accommodation of the main engine plant and its auxiliaries.[9] […] The turbines' revolutions must be as low as possible, so that even at full power a reasonable efficiency of the propellers and an adequate impulse is to be expected. The design of the ahead turbines shall be such that at moderate power a high degree of efficiency will be attained; the hourly coal consumption of the main turbines, in combination with their necessary auxiliaries, during the 24-hour trials at 12, 17 and 22 knots shall, in particular, not exceed 2,300, 4,800 or 10,100kg respectively.

Here is not the place to recapitulate the whole solution of the problem, for which Hänisch required some eighty-five pages, but a few relevant issues may be repeated here in some detail, in particular the choice of the number of shafts. As a basic principle, Hänisch stated that the diameters of the turbines would be as great as the hull permitted, for reasons of efficiency, by attaining the highest possible circumferential speed at the tip of the turbine blades. Further, he stated that, to attain comparable results, the respective load on the propellers should be equal in terms of combined propeller-area and circumferential speed at the tip of the propeller blades, whether there were two, three or four of them. Using the accepted standard formulas of the day, this resulted in the following basic values:

Number of screws	Revolutions per minute	Diameter of screw
2	350	3.30m
3	428	2.70m
4	495	2.35m

Unsurprisingly, these figures closely resembled those actually to be employed on the *Magdeburg* class. From a purist view, the choice would have been simple: the higher the circumferential speed, the higher the efficiency of the turbine. But this nominal advantage is more than offset by the hydrodynamic disadvantages of multiple propellers rotating at high revolutions. Hänisch then goes on to discuss the pros and cons of the individual shaft arrangements, beginning with the quadruple-screw system. In doing this, he had to be careful insofar as, when discussing the triple-screw system, he was touching on the German navy's long-preferred (cf pp 68-69, above) arrangement for capital ships; therefore, he had to find good reasons to set it aside:

> 1) quadruple system
> It seems doubtful whether the higher efficiency of the turbines in the quadruple system offset the disadvantages of the propeller's efficiency. One of the significantly negative effects of the turbines' sequential arrangement is that, at low power,

8. *Entwurf der Turbinenanlage für einen Kleinen Kreuzer*, 1910.

[9. These numbers reproduce exactly the dimensions for the machinery-spaces of the contemporary *Magdeburg* class, then under construction.]

> the turbine plant's load may be unequally distributed among the propellers – up to the point when the propellers driven by the LP turbines are running idle, and not generating any power at all. A greater complexity of the engine plant is a consequence of the necessarily more complex piping, which similarly makes the plant heavier. Thus, the comparative light weight of the individual components, designed for higher revolutions, is offset in the plant's total weight, compared with the competing systems. The four shafts and their bossing will cause a more complex form of the stern, thus generating more drag. [...]
>
> 2) triple system
> The triple system possesses all the advantages inherent in triple-screw vessels, insofar the shafts and their prime movers are designed as individual systems. All three turbine sets, in combination with their auxiliaries, are totally independent of each other. At low power the vessel may sail economically on the centre shaft alone, or on both wing shafts, despite dragging along the idle shaft(s). [...] The advantages of the system's better efficiency may, however, be counterbalanced in the future by greater demands for space and weight, combined with a certain awkward arrangement of the engine plant. Nevertheless, it must be emphasised again at this point, that any sequential cross-connection of turbine sets [required at economical speed], especially if they are – under normal conditions – separated of each other and operate independently, may be considered an emergency measure, if not a clear disadvantage.
>
> 3) twin system
> The twin-shaft system seems to be ideal for small cruisers. As soon as the struggle for raising the plant's efficiency is successful, its ubiquitous introduction in the type is unlikely to be hindered. Nevertheless, a sequential connection (working the LP turbine of one side with the exhaust steam of the other side's HP turbine), should be avoided because of the shafts' consequential dependence of each other. [...] Adding to the problem [of sequential connection] to a very significant degree is the imbalanced delivery of power to the propellers by turbines at varying rates of power, which cannot be avoided. Despite this, the twin-shaft system prevails in simplicity, reliability and manoeuvrability over each of the competing systems.
>
> Because of the results of the foregoing considerations the last-named arrangement will be chosen.

Hänisch next discussed the choice of the turbine system itself. His investigations were limited to a certain degree insofar as, at the time, no operational experience had been gained with (e.g.) the Bergmann turbine. Nevertheless, he writes in favour of

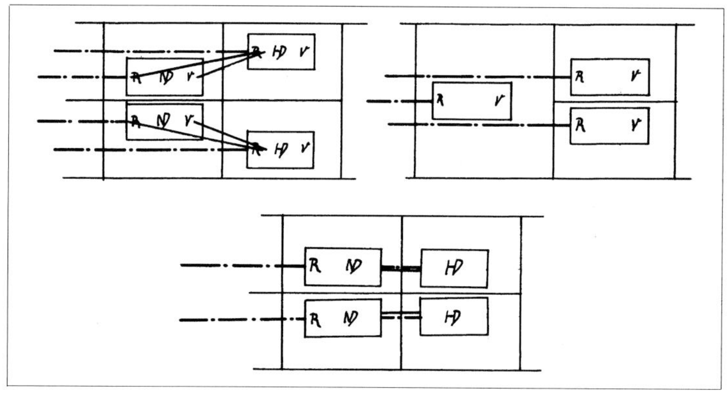

The only surviving sketch-drawing from Hänisch's report. Here, he shows the necessary connections between even numbers of turbines. *(DN collection)*

combined systems, which coupled a partially charged impulse HP turbine of several single-vane wheels with either a second impulse LP turbine or a Parsons reaction turbine. These combined sets were mainly promoted by AEG-Curtis, Zoelly and Germania, and were seen as more or less equal in efficiency by Hänisch.

Nevertheless, he favoured the system chosen for *Ersatz-Condor* [*Strassburg*], which may suggest that he may have been part of the design-team at Wilhelmshaven Dockyard. As noted above, this turbine was built under licence from Brown, Boveri in Wilhelmshaven's own engine shop. Constructively, it was mainly on the Parsons principle, but possessed a Curtis wheel coupled to the rotor, which reduced its length considerably and thus – mainly because of the missing greater number of sectional divisions by the stators – made the system lighter and simpler. In the following sections of his dissertation, Hänisch presented his detailed calculations. Interestingly, his main references to real values and experience gained during trials thus far were mainly from those of *Mainz* and, to a much smaller degree, of *Dresden*.

It is interesting to compare Hänisch's theoretical findings with the actual values attained during the trials of *Strassburg* two years later, even if the values for speed requested from him were 0.25 knots higher (the actual trial results shown in brackets): Hänisch predicted a maximum speed of 29.4 knots (28.3 knots) at 39,000shp (33,740shp) and 27.9 knots (26.9 knots) at 29,300shp (25,650shp). The specific consumption he calculated to 2,300kg/h (?)[10] at 12 knots, 4,630kg/h (6,042kg/h) at 17 knots and 8,880kg/h (9,500kg/h) at 22 knots. Obviously, his superiors agreed in general with his calculations and assumptions, as 'his' preferred twin-shaft turbine plant became standard in the small cruisers of the German navy, beginning with the *Karlsruhe* class.

10. No comparative figure for 12 knots has been published; both other published sources differ slightly regarding sustained speed – 17.6 knots and 21.3 knots – and thus may only be compared to Hänisch's calculations with caution.

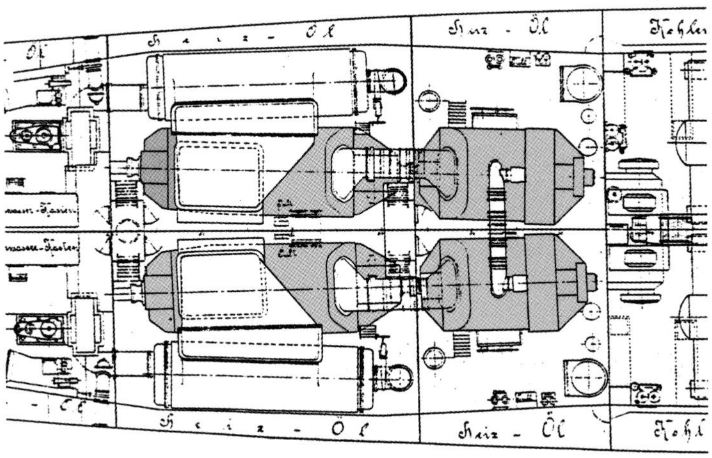

Karlsruhe's engines, showing the future standard installation for German navy's small cruisers. *(DN collection)*

THE *KARLSRUHE* CLASS

On 6 May 1910, members of the relevant departments assembled at the RMA to discuss the requirements for the 1911 small cruiser. Initially, Tirpitz was willing to grant an increase in displacement of only 100 tonnes, as he had just been informed that the money available for small cruisers was only sufficient to cover the average cost of the 1909–10 ships. However, at the same time, there were some pressing demands from the military side that had not been possible to work into the previous class. The main issue was the narrowness of the belt. As already noted, Tirpitz felt that it was imperative that flooding through large holes close to the waterline must be avoided at all costs. Accordingly, the protective scheme was modified to significantly heighten the belt. The second issue was whether any approved higher displacement should be used to improve the armament.

As usual, opinions were far from unanimous. One fraction, led by KAdm Gerhard Gerdes, head of department 'W', advocated a mixed armament, consisting of two fully enclosed 15cm QL twin mounts fore and aft, supported by six 8.8cm anti-torpedo boat guns on the beam. Another fraction, led by Kpt Friedrich Schrader, head of department 'A', supported a uniform installation of twelve 12cm QL guns instead. A third option for change was the mounting of both forward and aft 10.5cm QL in twin mountings. All of these proposals would have had the disadvantage of delaying the construction by several months, as department 'K' would have to be involved to a greater degree than current resource levels permitted. In particular, over the following months, 'K' would primarily be concerned with the development of diesel propulsion for battleships. This was, according to Tirpitz, intended to avoid Germany losing the 'lead we have among the nations' during this anticipated revolution in propulsion engineering.[11] Thus, in the end, only marginal improvements were worked into the 1911 cruiser, which is apparent from the phraseology of the official order for construction:

> I decree that the small cruisers *Ersatz-Seeadler* and *Ersatz-Geier* shall be constructed according to the plans of *Ersatz-Bussard*, incorporating the following deviations: Displacement shall be about 4,880 tonnes, waterline length shall be 139m, the height of the waterline belt shall be extended up to 2.05m above design waterline, whereas the horizontal part of the armoured deck shall be levelled at 1.45m above design waterline. The freeboard is to be increased to 3.625m amidships and 7.8m at the stem. Bunker capacity is to be increased to 1,350 tonnes of coal. The choice of turbines and the number of shafts is left to the discretion of the state secretary of the RMA.
>
> Wilhelm I.R.[12]

Another new feature derived from the flexibility granted by this comparatively open decree was the introduction of oil-fired boilers into cruisers. The advantages of oil as a combustion material had not gone unnoticed in the RMA: indeed, it had been first employed as early as 1870, before it descended into obscurity for more than two decades. Shortly before the end of the nineteenth century, trials were renewed, first through mixed firing, later as oil firing alone. However, it took over another decade to develop a reliable boiler–burner combination, which, in 1910, coincided with an offer made by the Allgemeine Erdölindustrie AG, granting the German navy oil at a price around twice that of coal – which was seen as a favourable deal.

It was accordingly decided to equip every large vessel with a mixture of coal- and oil-fired boilers – employing a ~6:4 ratio of output for cruisers. Cautious as ever, however, the RMA did not apply as high a ratio to *Ersatz-Seeadler* and *Ersatz-Geier*. In them, the total number of boilers was thus reduced to fourteen, twelve of them coal burning, with the remaining (oil-fired) forward pair made twice the size and equipped as double-enders. This was possible only because there was no need to leave space for stoking equipment. Bunker capacity was enlarged to 1,300 tonnes of coal plus 200 tonnes of oil.[13] The designed power of the two Navy turbine sets working on two shafts – which would be employed in all future German small cruisers of RMA design – was raised to 26,000shp, resulting in a slightly higher design speed of 27.8 knots.

However, as trials would reveal, there had been a miscalculation regarding effective power of the twelve coal-fired boilers,

11. Tirpitz was also particularly attracted by the forecasts of the diesel's fuel consumption; a pilot installation of a cruising motor in the *Kaiser* class *Prinzregent Luitpold* never, however, went to sea, and although such a cruising motor was intended for the *Baden*-class *Sachsen*, this was also abandoned, owing to the exegeses of war – see Dodson, *Kaiser's Battlefleet*, pp 85–86, 90, 98; Nottelmann, 'From Ironclads to Dreadnoughts: The Development of the German Navy 1864–1918, *Warship International* 54/3 (2017), pp 216–20; 55/4 (2018), p 283–86, 291–92; 56/4 (2019), pp 300–03.

12. BA-MA RM2/1614 – fol 52.

13. Another official source states as much as 260 tons of oil.

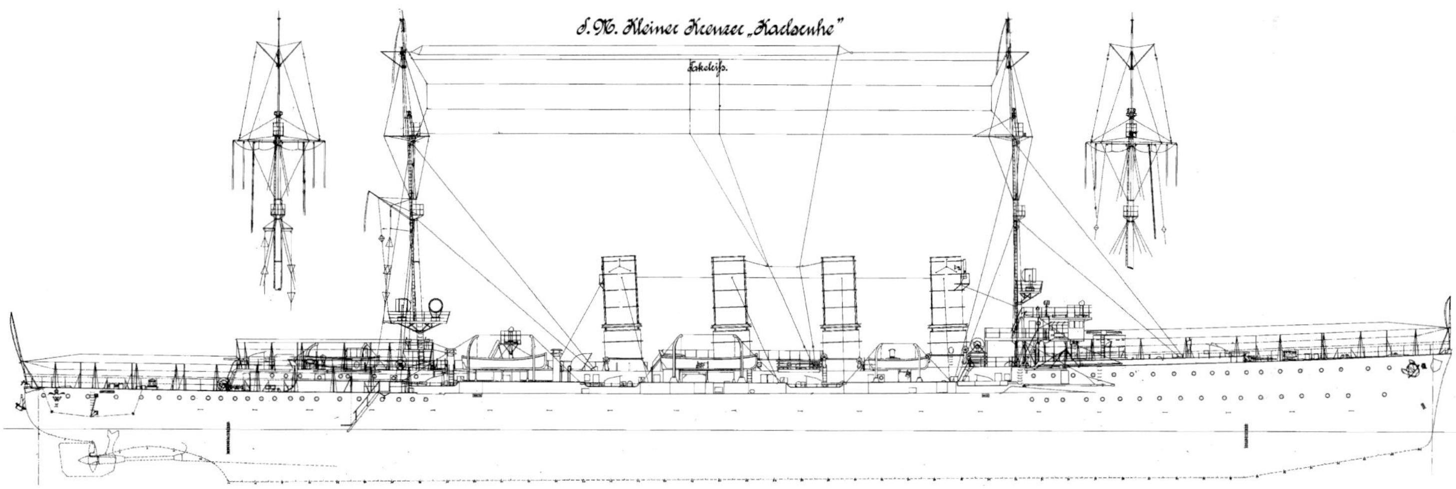

Top: *Karlsruhe* departing Kiel for the Caribbean on 15 June 1914, having passed *Blücher* to starboard and the fleet flagship *Friedrich der Große* to port. The latter flies the flag of CinC Admiral Friedrich von Ingenohl at the head of her mainmast. **Bottom:** rigging plan of *Karlsruhe* 'as fitted', with the addition of views from fore and aft of the fore- and mainmasts. Compare the height of the forecastle with that of *Breslau* on p 141. *(DN collection)*

and to compensate for an insufficiently sized grate area extra coal had to be fed into the furnaces. This in turn affected the overall efficiency of the propulsion machinery, resulting in the endurance of the new class being smaller than that of the *Magdeburg* class (5,000 versus 5,800nm), despite the latter's smaller bunker capacity. Apart from this drawback, the machinery worked satisfactorily. The new pair would be the last small cruisers to be completed and run their trials in peacetime.

Karlsruhe

Ersatz-Seeadler was ordered from Germania in May 1911, who laid her keel on 21 September of that year. She was launched as *Karlsruhe* on 11 November 1912 and commissioned, after some delays, on 15 January 1914. During her trials, *Karlsruhe* reached 28.4 knots at 37,450shp and an average of 27.6 knots at 34,680shp during her six-hour run.

She sailed from Kiel on 15 June 1914 for the East American Station, with the intention that she relieve *Dresden*. The assassination of the Austrian Archduke Franz Ferdinand on 28 June found her coaling at St Thomas in the Virgin Islands, from which she was directed to join *Dresden* as a matter of urgency. On 4 July she met *Strassburg*, and then *Dresden* at Port-au-Prince on 26 July, as noted above, exchanging captains with the older cruiser. On the 28th, *Karlsruhe* was notified of the break in diplomatic relations between Austria-Hungary and Serbia, and diverted to Havana to take on stores, before putting to sea to await events.

Rostock

While her sister's ordering process progressed comparatively smoothly, *Ersatz-Geier* was eventually ordered in September 1911 from Howaldt after stiff competition. The call for tenders has been issued only after *Ersatz-Seeadler* had been ordered, and Howaldt had had to compete with the full range of possible competitors: Germania (again), Schichau, Vulcan, Weser and at least one of the Imperial dockyards. It seemed initially that Vulcan would win, but Howaldt's offer – submitted on 6 September, the last possible date - was even lower. Howaldt received the order the following day, and finally laid the keel for *Rostock*-to-be (the name had already been chosen by the Kaiser, unusually early, on 14 October) on 7 December. Nevertheless, she was launched only one day later than her sister, on 12 November 1912. Delivered on 17 January 1914, she commissioned on 5 February. During trials, *Rostock* exceeded her design power by 18,000shp, attaining 29.3 knots in the measured mile, and an average of 27.4 knots at 31,348shp during the six-hour run.

On 3 May 1914 her trials ended, and she relived *Stettin* in the Scouting Force. *Rostock* then acted as escort to the imperial yacht during the Kaiser's final cruise to Norway in July, returning to Kiel on the 27th. On mobilisation four days later, she became the flagship of the II. Leader of Torpedo-boats.

THE *REGENSBURG* CLASS

The 1912 small cruisers again differed very little from the preceding class – even if, at first glance, their profile suggests otherwise. They were ordered during the difficult days of the introduction of another amendment to the Fleet Law (for which see pp 293-294), which was ultimately successful, but not without having to accept reductions in overall funding levels. Thus, the price of all the vessels of the 1912 Estimates, in particular battleships, large cruisers and small cruisers, had to be kept down as far as possible. As a result, deviations from the *Karlsruhe* design were largely cosmetic. There was a further reduction in the number of boilers, from fourteen to twelve, giving the opportunity to reduce the number of funnels from four to three, while maintaining the requirement of mainly straight exhaust leads. The ratio between coal- and oil-fired boilers also changed in favour of the latter, as the 'lost' boilers were coal burners, while both double-ended, oil-fired units were retained. The installed power nevertheless remained set at 26,000shp, for 27.25 knots.

The most striking difference between the new pair and their immediate predecessors, except for the number of funnels, was

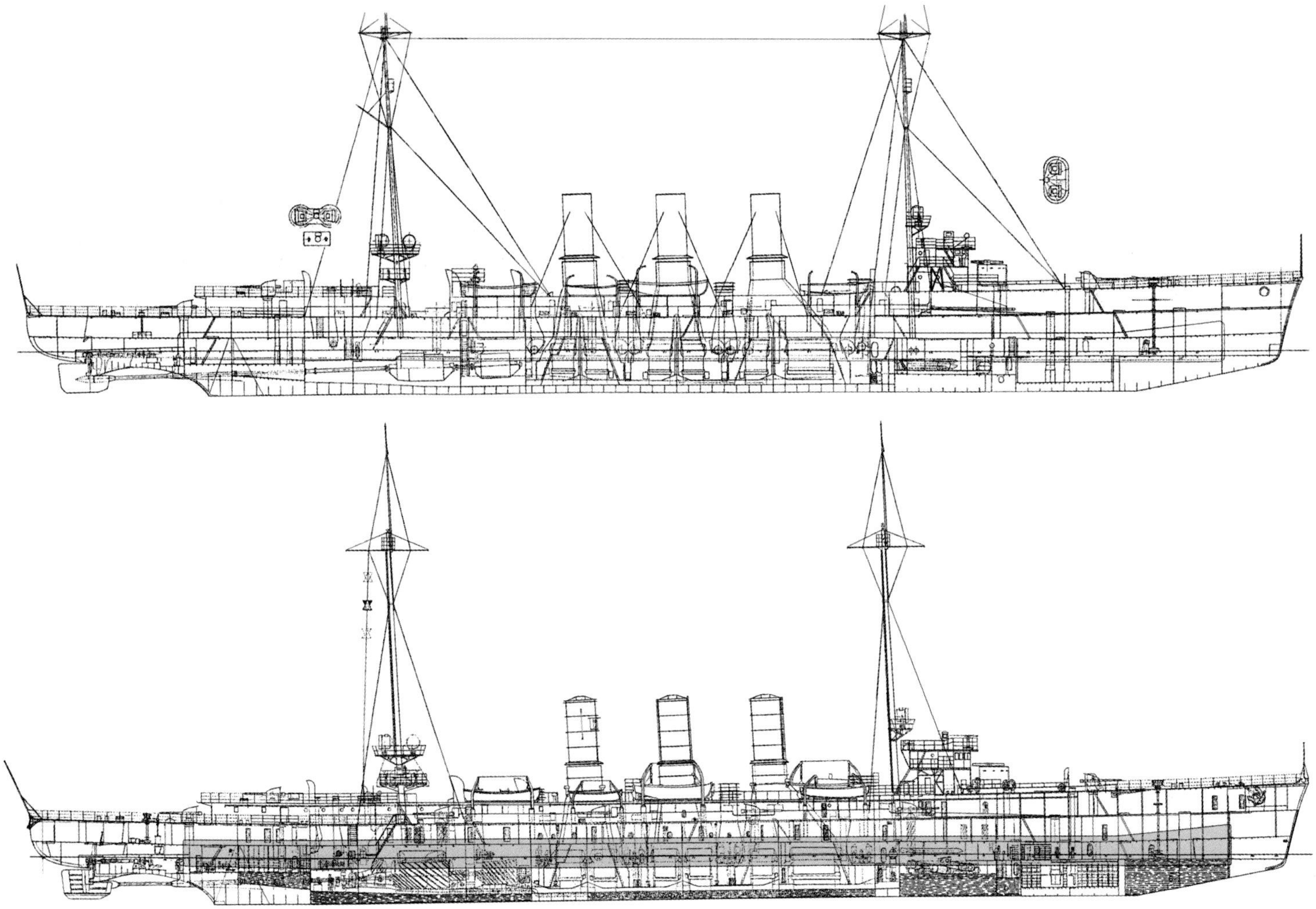

Comparison between rather simple preliminary plans for *Ersatz-Prinzeß Wilhelm* (top) and the more elaborate semi-final 'as fitted' plans for *Graudenz* (below). *(DN collection)*

the height of their masts. *Regensburg* and *Graudenz* were both intended to be flagships for the commodores of torpedo boat flotillas. The German navy had given up on the construction of a separate class of 'leaders', with flotillas led tactically by boats of the standard series. To allow the commodore to communicate with the latter, long-range wireless telegraphy was required, secured by the masts of both new cruisers being heightened by 7m compared with the 'standard' masts of earlier ships.

Another modification would serve as a stepping stone towards the next major innovation: the superimposition of the after 10.5cm guns, achieved in practice by moving one of the guns down from its former position atop the after superstructure to the main deck. This was a leftover from informal discussions that had suggested that the vessels might either be equipped with ten 13cm[14] or eight 15cm guns. In case of the eight-gun variant, superimposition was seen as mandatory, to provide a sufficient number of guns on the broadside. Although this up-gunning came to naught for the time being, it nevertheless set the stage for a more effective distribution of main artillery, with better things to come.

Ersatz-Prinzeß Wilhelm was ordered without competition from Kiel Dockyard in April 1912. She was laid down on 23 October of that year, to be launched as *Graudenz* one year later, on 25 October 1913. She was on builders' trials when war broke out. Since these were delayed due to defective machinery-components and her builders' excessive workload, she was commissioned on 10 August 1914 on a preliminary basis. During the forced trial she attained 42,470shp for 29.2 knots on the measured mile, while the speeds achieved during the six-hour trial on 2 September in the Kiel Bight varied. For one hour, at 32,000shp, 27.3 knots were attained, while the average for the remaining five hours was 25.6 knots, at an unrecorded power. As these latter values had been assessed by dead reckoning only, without proper reference to the bearings of landmarks, and in depths of water barely exceeding 20m, the results cannot be regarded as of any great significance.

The order for *Ersatz-Irene* [*Regensburg*] went to AG Weser in May 1912. She was laid down on 14 November, and took to the water on 25 April 1914. After the outbreak of war her fitting out was speeded up and she commissioned on 3 January 1915. Like her sister, *Regensburg* exceeded her designed power on trials, making 28.0 knots at 38,500shp on the measured mile; reported results of 27.1 knots at 30,200shp over six hours should, however, be viewed with the same caution as her sister's performance under similar conditions.

THE *WIESBADEN* CLASS

The development of the 1913 small cruisers (*Ersatz-Gefion* and *Ersatz-Hela*) marked a significant waypoint in the history of the German navy that has gone rather unnoticed by most historians. Since the introduction of the small cruiser, the fundamental nature of the type had been settled, and improvements had been made in small increments only. Indeed, at the beginning it was far from clear if these ships would differ significantly from their predecessors: initially, 'K' stated that '[c]hanges in displacement and costs compared to the type *Ersatz-Irene* shall be kept, as much as feasible, to small amounts'.[15]

But events moved rapidly, especially as the 1913 estimates gave a little more financial freedom, given that the Fleet Law required only two battleships/large cruisers to be laid down under the 1913 Estimates. Thus, in May 1912, the Kaiser had ordered Tirpitz to report, inter alia, concerning the intended future armament of small cruisers. The subsequent report was drafted by KAdm Reinhard Scheer (1863–1928), then head of 'A'. He now opted openly for the 15cm solution, already discussed

This image offers a very interesting comparison between the heights of the masts of *Stralsund* (outboard) and *Graudenz* (inboard), as they lie alongside in Wilhelmshaven after their wartime rearmament with 15cm guns. In the background may be seen *Prinzregent Luitpold*. *(DN collection)*

Regensburg entering Wilhelmshaven's Grosser Hafen, having just completed her trials in spring 1915. *(DN collection)*

14. The 13cm calibre had originally been developed by the army for use in fortifications.

in previous years (pp 141-142, above), not the least sparked by the first reliable information regarding the most recent British cruisers, to become the *Chatham* class, which were reported to be equipped with a waterline belt of so far unknown extent and thickness (it actually extended along the whole waterline and was 3in [76mm] thick).[16] Initially, this solution was rejected by the Kaiser and the fleet command, arguing for the resulting unhandiness of the necessarily enlarged vessels. In their view an outfit of ten 13cm QL guns would suffice, which was roughly equal in weight to an outfit of eight 15cm QL guns.

However, in Tirpitz's view, the 13cm calibre did not possess sufficient 'punch' against any form of side armour. During the design process there had been a further small discussion, whether there should be only one 15cm gun mounted on the forecastle, reducing the overall number to seven, but Tirpitz ultimately decided on the larger number. Thus, the 13cm variant would not, apart from a brief oral mention, even be presented to the Kaiser during the annual autumn audience at his Rominten hunting lodge. This mention was apparently not even noticed, the 15cm variant being accepted.

In addition to the up-gunning, four 5.2cm AA (officially 'Ballon-Abwehr-Kanonen' [BAK – anti-balloon guns]) were proposed for the first time to deal – prospectively, as the British did not yet possess operational dirigible airships[17] – with the anticipated dangers from above. These guns were to be mounted in pairs on a common platform between the bridge and the forward funnel. During the design process, 'A' (Scheer) had queried whether one guns on each side might actually be enough to fend off slow-moving airships. For the time being, however, his proposal to cut numbers was rejected – although *Ersatz-Hela* would actually commission with only two AA guns – albeit of 8.8cm calibre; in any case, the four 5.2cm were never mounted.

There were other innovations included in this rather ground-breaking class of vessels. The first was a return to traversing deck-mounted torpedo tubes in cruisers, of a kind last seen in *Gazelle* and soon to be trialled aboard *Magdeburg*. Nonetheless, submerged broadside tubes were retained, resulting in a doubling of the torpedo armament. The upper-deck mounts were installed as far forward as possible, in order not to interfere with the mine rails aft, in case the full load of up to 120 mines were to be taken aboard. Searchlight arrangements were slightly altered from previous practice, the units on the foremast being placed en echelon, rather than abreast, to increase coverage.

Another innovation was the introduction of the geared turbine in *Ersatz-Gefion*. As already noted, the efficiency of the turbine and the propeller stood diametrically contrary to each other. The solution to the problem had long been known as well: decoupling the two elements through the mediation of a gearbox. Unfortunately, the development of such equipment was still in its infancy, at least for the transmission of high powers, mainly due to a lack of precision in the gear-cutting process. Other solutions therefore had to be investigated, and an employee of the Stettin yard of the Vulcan combine, Dr Hermann Föttinger (1877–1945),[18] came up with the idea of mounting two rotary pumps in a common casing. The primary

15. BA-MA RM3/3698 – fol 11ff.

16. War experience (eg the *Emden*/*Sydney* action [p 205]) would show this belt to be impenetrable by the German 10.5cm gun.

17. The prototype HMA *1* ('*Mayfly*') has been lost in September 1911, with the succeeding HMA *9* not flown until 1916.

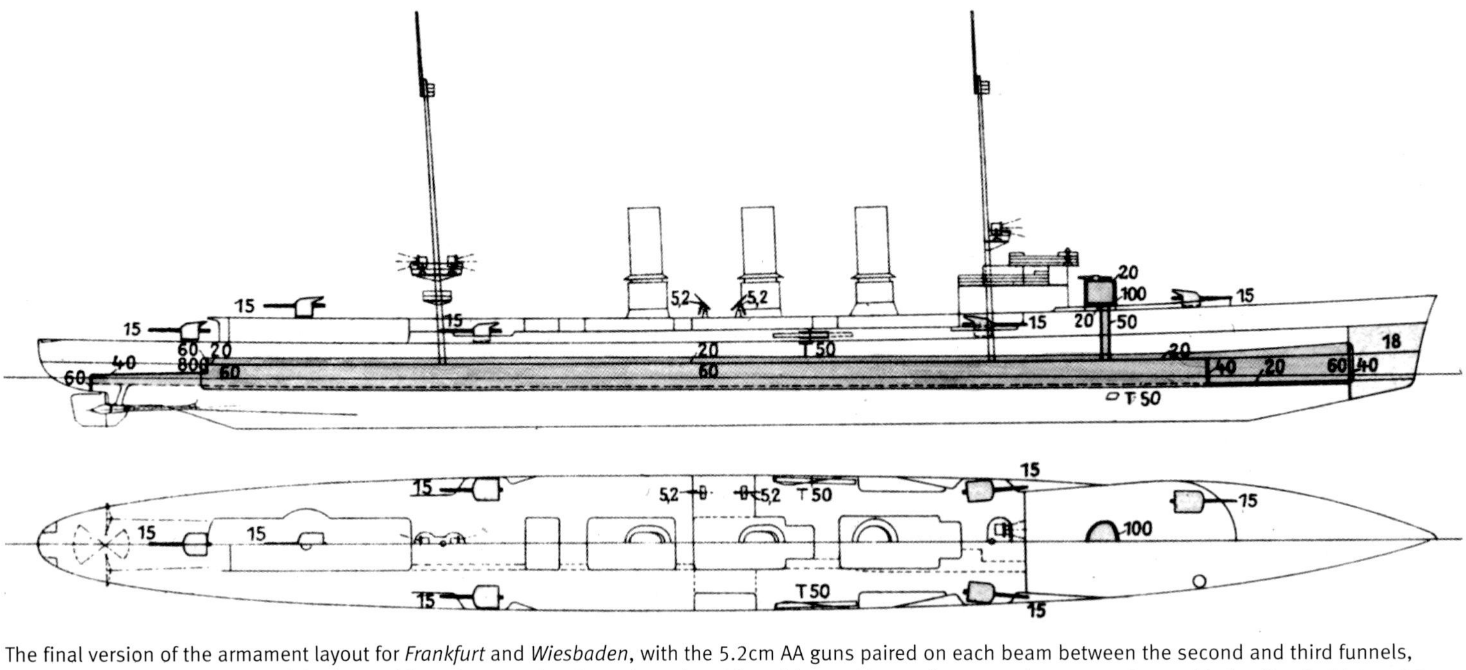

The final version of the armament layout for *Frankfurt* and *Wiesbaden*, with the 5.2cm AA guns paired on each beam between the second and third funnels, rather than between bridge and the forward funnel, as previously envisaged. Neither ship would actually mount these guns, instead being fitted with two 8.8cm as soon as they became available. *(DN collection)*

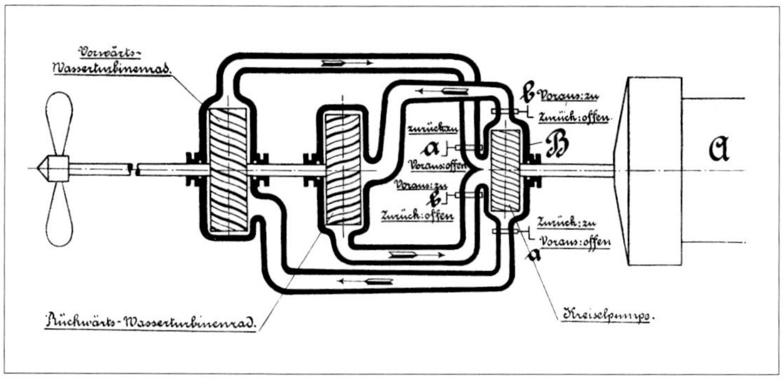

Schematic sketch showing the principle behind the Föttinger system: driven by the turbine 'A', water becomes accelerated by the rotary pump 'B', and is then either led through the valves 'a' to the left impeller, and back again, for moving ahead, or through the valves 'b' to the right impeller for moving astern. *(Neuerungen im Schiffsbetrieb)*

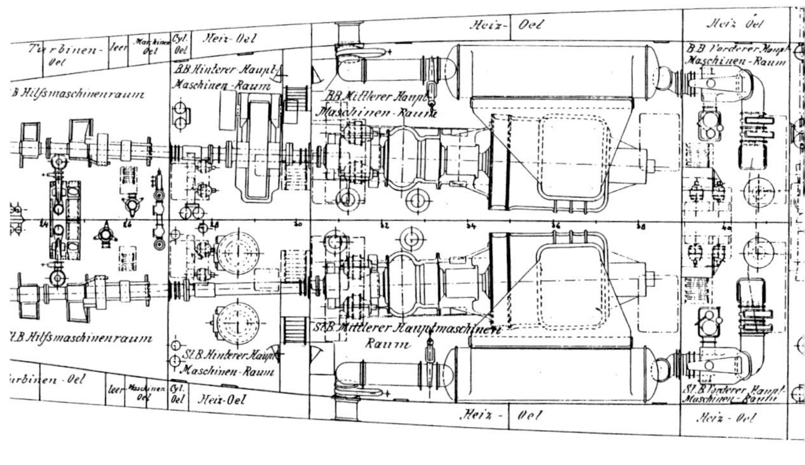

Wiesbaden's after machinery compartments, with the Föttinger transformers coupled to the turbines in the main engine room, and a geared cruising turbine coupled to the port shaft. The whole installation met Tirpitz's desire for extensive subdivision and may have contributed to *Wiesbaden* remaining afloat for a considerable time after severe damage at Jutland. In view of her thorough subdivision, the one hit that immobilised her was extremely unlucky. *(DN collection)*

side, driven by the turbine directly, delivered fluid with high velocity to the secondary side, where the principle of the rotary pump was inverted by forcing the generated velocity down to nearly zero and thus transforming the energy into rotation, driving the tail shaft and ultimately the propeller. As the system worked unidirectionally, a second rotor had to be mounted on the secondary shaft for supplying astern power.

The principle, later patented, was systematically tested, first on a small stationary installation of only 100hp, and afterwards in a small tugboat, named *Föttinger Transformator* after the inventor. This used a simple Curtis turbine of 500shp as prime mover, its trials being sufficiently encouraging to be demonstrated to Tirpitz, who visited the Vulcan shipyard on 3 July 1909 for that purpose. However, the subsequent full-scale test installation was in a merchant vessel, the small Hamburg-Amerika-Line passenger vessel *Königin Luise*,[19] which received a two-turbine set of 7,800shp. This was thoroughly tested before installation, even under overload up to 10,000shp, and confirmed the experience gained thus far. The efficiency of transmission, set at a ratio of about 5:1, was as high as 90 per cent under certain conditions, which was seen as highly successful. During a fourteen-day sustained trial no breakdowns occurred and the vibration- and noise-free performance was highly praised.

As a result, *Ersatz-Gefion* [to be *Wiesbaden*], already assigned to the Vulcan shipyard, was chosen as test bed for the first installation in the German navy. The designed power at the secondary side was set at 29,800shp, to compensate for the increased displacement of 5,150 tonnes (the anticipated transmission losses of the Föttinger transformer were expected to be compensated for by higher propulsion efficiency), with the design speed maintained at 27.5 knots. Additionally, the port shaft was equipped with a cruising turbine of 1,165shp for up to 14.5 knots speed, which was geared to the main shaft on the transformer's secondary side, while the low-pressure steam would serve the main low-pressure turbine on the starboard side. Another benefit of the new propulsion system would be astern power was as high as 75 per cent of ahead power, in contrast to the conventionally driven *Ersatz-Hela* [*Frankfurt*], which would have only 33 per cent. Other ships that received the Föttinger transformer included the liner *Tirpitz* (later RMS *Empress of Australia*).

Ersatz-Gefion was ordered on 29 June 1913, and was laid down on 10 November of that year, to be completed, according to the contract, on 29 August 1915. She was launched as *Wiesbaden*[20] on 30 January and commissioned on 23 August 1915. On the measured mile in the Little Belt, *Wiesbaden* attained an output of 39,531shp, which gave, however, a speed of only 27.4 knots. Corrected for deep-water running, however, this would correspond to a maximum of around 29 knots. During her six-hour trials, she maintained an average of 26.4 knots, owing to shallow (17–35m) water.

Since the sisters ran their trials roughly in parallel, comparisons could be made between their respective machinery plants. In general, the trials commission was impressed by the perform-

18. Föttinger had been head of Vulcan's turbine department since 1904, from 1909 to 1924 Professor at the Technische Hochschule at Danzig, and from 1924 until his death Professor at the Technische Universität Berlin.

19. Laid down in 1912, launched on 8 May 1913 and completed on 28 September 1913, she was of 1,846 revenue tons, 88.4m long, 12.4m broad and 3.1m draught. Capable of 20 knots, she was employed as a minelayer at the outbreak of the First World War, and was sunk by the light cruiser HMS *Amphion* (which was shortly afterwards sunk by one *Königin Luise*'s own mines) in the company of the 3rd DF on 6 August 1914.

20. Until shortly before her christening, she was destined to bear the name *Chemnitz*, but was changed for yet unknown reasons. Possibly, somebody from Saxony had caused the ire of Wilhelm II., who was ultimately responsible for ships' names.

ance of the Föttinger plant, emphasising its superior economy, which would more than offset the transformer's transmission losses. Another benefit was seen in the significantly smaller associated turbines, which revolved at much higher speeds. This meant that the required length of the engine rooms was reduced from 19.5m in *Frankfurt* to 15m in *Wiesbaden*. The final verdict was a clear recommendation to employ the new system in future examples of the much larger and much more powerful large cruisers. Accordingly, *Ersatz-A,* fourth ship of the *Mackensen* class, was planned to receive transformers.

Ersatz-Hela was ordered on 19 May 1913 from Kiel Dockyard. She was laid down on 1 December of that year, scheduled for completion in 'summer 1915'. She was actually launched as *Frankfurt* on 20 March 1915 and commissioned three days before her sister, on 20 August 1915. During her trials she is reported to have achieved a maximum output of 42,500shp, although her maximum speed is not recorded. Her highest recorded and confirmed speed (26.7 knots) derives from a run at deep draught on 22 September 1915 in shallow water, but at an unrecorded power. This generally corresponded to her sister's performance, but not necessarily to her own maximum power capability. Her trials ended on 12 October, after which she joined the II. SG.

Frankfurt on 22 September 1915, making 26.7kt during her full load trials. Her full-mantled centre funnel of larger diameter distinguished her from *Wiesbaden*. *(DN collection)*

A SECOND *KÖNIGSBERG* CLASS

The contracts for the 1913 small cruisers had not even been signed when 'K' approached 'A' in May 1913 regarding potential changes to the 1913 design that might be desirable for the 1914 small cruiser. 'K' had already put forward several proposals, of which the most notable were the enlargement of the accommodation for both officers and men, an increase in the size of the engine rooms to accommodate a larger (60kW) third generator – to be diesel powered – under armour, and an improvement in the torpedo installation. The latter would include quick-loading arrangements for the torpedo tubes and, consequently, a higher number of spare torpedoes. They were possibly to be mounted – rather surprisingly, if not bizarrely – as *submerged twin* mountings.

The option of a larger calibre for the AA guns was briefly mentioned but left vague, to be addressed in a separate later discussion. In total these proposals would require a further enlargement of the vessels by 100–150 tonnes. 'A' was quick to respond that, in general, the 1913 type should be retained, although small variations, such as the extension of the deck-houses, or the replacement of the four 5.2cm AA guns by two of 8.8cm calibre might be possible. However, 'A' rejected the

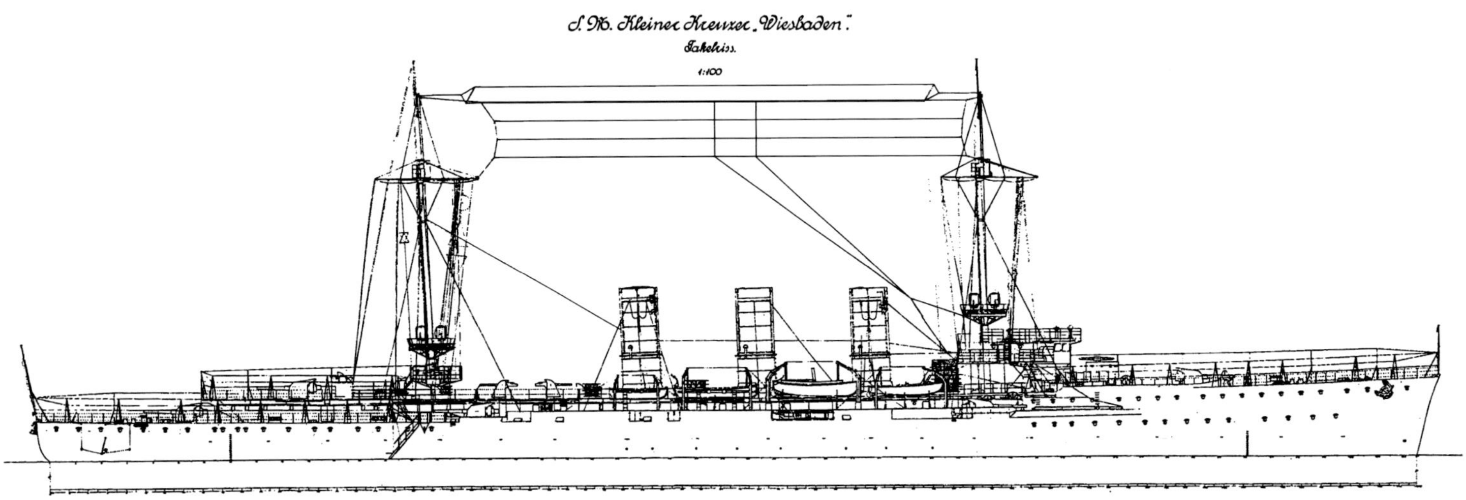

Wiesbaden as completed and her 'as fitted' rigging plan. *(AD collection/ DN collection)*

need for protection for the third generator, since it seemed hard to believe that 'in a case where the generator had been shot to pieces in a fight, the searchlights that it powered would still remain unharmed'. However, 'A' was outvoted in this case and the generator was protected within a lightly armoured box on top of the armour deck, on the starboard side.

Regarding the proposed twin torpedo mounts, 'A' also expressed caution; nevertheless, the necessary weights and space for additional tubes should be reserved. Other objections came from 'W', which stated that the proposed substitution of the AA guns was unnecessary: in their view the AA mounts were ineffective as anti-torpedo boat guns, and the greater number of 5.2cm mounts, together with their higher rapidity of fire, might even have better effect against airships.

The subsequent discussion between the two departments reveals the true nature of the question of AA calibre: as long as the main armament of the small cruisers had been the 10.5cm gun, this had been seen as able to deal with faster-moving targets from the air, due to their higher rate of fire. This possibility would be lost with the adoption of the larger 15cm gun. On the other hand, there was a surplus stock of semi-automatic 5.2cm guns, which were no longer being installed for use against surface vessels, and 'W' had decided to adapt these as AA weapons as a cost-saving measure. However, this stratagem did not work, as 'K' would successfully urge Tirpitz to decide in favour of the newly developed 8.8cm AA, intended to be the standard weapon for that purpose on every major warship in the future.

After the usual hiatus during the summer, the entire project was presented to Tirpitz for his consent, before being taken to Rominten in September 1913 to get the approval of the Kaiser. Tirpitz endorsed the decision to adhere to the existing general design, although the above mentioned amendments (which were not yet fully agreed) would raise the displacement up to the maximum noted. Shortly before final approval was given in April 1914, another proposal brought the agreed design to its limits, when 'K' opted for the replacement of the linoleum cladding of the weatherdecks with wood for reasons of maintainability, linoleum having been found very susceptible to excessive wear during coaling. Its substitution by 55mm teak, even though only on the main deck, added an extra 40 tonnes in weight and extra 40,000 Marks in costs. A further 25 tonnes, to clad the forecastle and the roofs of the aft superstructure, was rejected for stability reasons. In April 1914 the Kaiser accordingly signed the order of construction for the last German cruisers designed in peacetime, once more in a rather summary way:

> I decree that for the small cruisers *Ersatz-Gazelle* and *Ersatz-Niobe* the plans of the *Ersatz-Gefion* class shall be retained, subject to the following deviations: waterline length shall be 145.8m, maximum width shall be 14.32m, design draft shall be 5.28m aft, 4.83m forward, displacement shall be about 5,300 tonnes.
>
> Depending on the results of the recently begun tests either 4–5.2cm or 2–8.8cm AA shall be mounted.
>
> The choice of the turbines and the number of shafts is left to the discretion of the State Secretary of the RMA.
>
> Bunker capacity shall be 1,340 tonnes of coal and 500 tonnes of oil.
>
> Given at Achilleion, Corfu, 24 April 1914.
>
> Wilhelm I.R

Just two months later these specifications would be changed as, during the trials of *Karlsruhe*, it had been discovered that, at high loads, the boilers generated steam that tended to condense at the turbine nozzles, which endangered the engines. This meant that the new vessels needed superheaters to dry the steam and thus avoid the problem in the future. As this required another 20 tonnes of displacement, which was beyond approved design limits, oil capacity had to be cut back.

Other differences from the *Wiesbaden* class included more extensive bridgework, a heightened forefunnel as completed and a revised searchlight layout, with units placed on individual platforms, one above the other, on each mast. A final redesign took place in July 1915, when it was decided to raise the 15cm mountings abreast the bridge from main to forecastle deck level. This was partly a result of the experience gained by *Strassburg* during her cruise with the Detached Division to South America during the winter of 1913–14 (pp 143-144, above), and partly from experience gained during the first year of the war. This had shown that main deck guns, especially the foremost ones, could be very wet, exacerbated by their being sponsoned out. Additionally, it was observed that the foremost beam guns of the *Wiesbaden* class would be unable to fire straight ahead.

Königsberg (ii)

The first pair of ships were ordered in June 1914, just two months after their approval. The contract for *Ersatz-Gazelle* had been won by Weser under competition against the usual panel of bidders. The cruiser would be laid down in the beginning of August 1914, for completion during 'summer 1916'. An interesting part of the competition was that Vulcan had included an option to incorporate a Föttinger transformer, as in *Wiesbaden*.[21]

Like all vessels in hand during the initial months of the war, the ship's construction was delayed, but not excessively. She was thus launched as *Königsberg* (the previous ship of the name having been lost five months earlier) on 18 December 1915 and commissioned in the shipyard on 12 August 1916, even though her order transmission system was still inoperable. Her transfer to Kiel for trials thus had to be postponed until 24 August. These were truncated, since to the cruiser was urgently needed

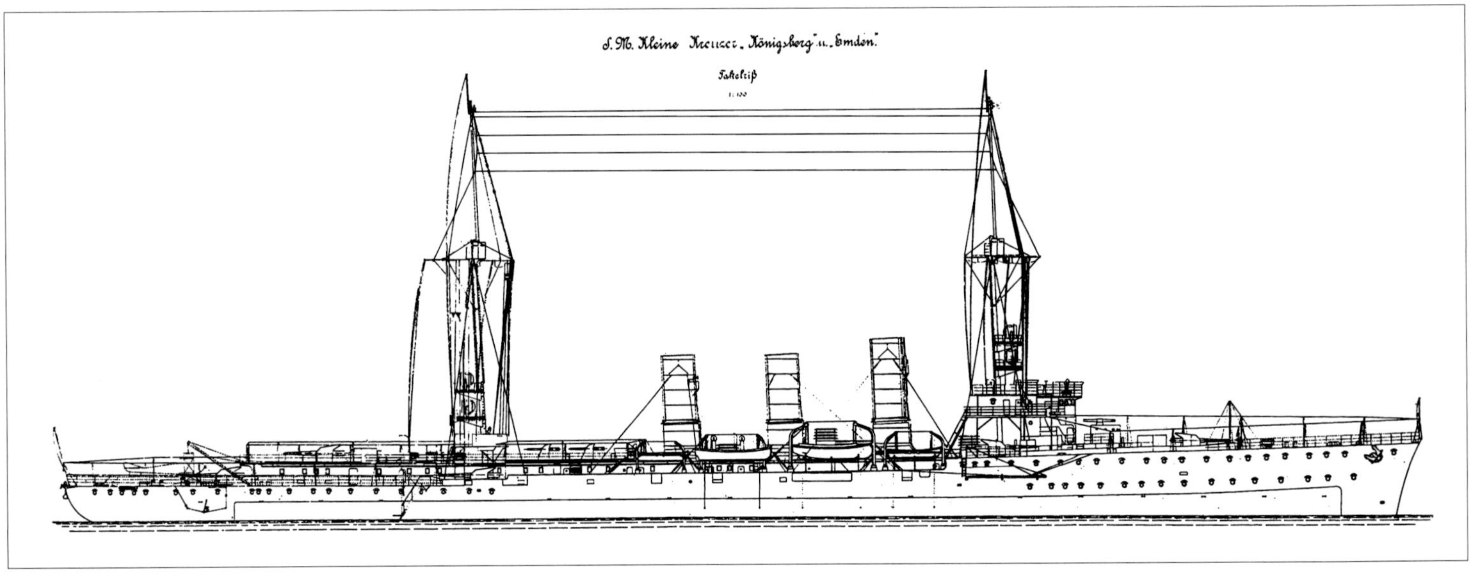

Königsberg (ii) running the measured mile, her high speed and the shallow water contributing to her trim and wave profile, together with an 'as fitted' drawing applicable to her and *Emden* (ii). Except for the enlarged bridge structure and the raised forefunnel, there are few deviations from their immediate precursors. Note the provision for embarking a seaplane on the quarterdeck. *(DN collection)*

to help make up the losses suffered at Jutland (pp 216-217, below), and ended on 14 October.

This was but one of the reasons why there were never official speed trials on the measured mile. Nevertheless, her performance during the trials was recorded, giving her a maximum of 45,000shp, while the highest recorded speed was 28.1 knots. The six-hour trial was affected by the same conditions as had prevailed for *Frankfurt*, running over depths between 25–35m, during which *Königsberg* attained an average of 34,400shp. The related speed would have been around 26.6 knots, according to appropriate resistance curves. Again, it was observed that at high speed and shallow water the stern was dragged under; at speeds above 24 knots in depths below 20m the aft part of the main deck flooded.

The trials report contained several interesting points. One noted insufficient space in the forward conning tower, while the view from inside was barely sufficient in daytime; at night, it was wholly inadequate. For this reason, the gunnery control position – normally located inside as well – had to be moved to the upper bridge for night fighting. While the report regarding the artillery and its auxiliaries was favourable, the ship's speed was seen as insufficient for a small cruiser. Survivability through watertight integrity was regarded as good,[22] even if doubts were raised regarding the submerged forward torpedo room: its flooding would take away a large part of the vessel's reserve buoyancy.

Karlsruhe (ii)

Ersatz-Niobe, whose contract had been directly awarded to Kiel Dockyard, was not laid down until 5 May 1915, owing to the excessive workload at that yard, which was responsible for mobilisation-related activities in the Baltic after war had commenced. She was launched as *Karlsruhe* (ii) on 31 January 1916 and commissioned at Kiel on 15 November of that year, even though the initial trial under her own power in the port of Kiel had to wait until 1 December. *Karlsruhe*'s machinery was innovative insofar as she had gearing fitted to her high-pressure turbines, the first such installation in a larger German warship.

To increase flexibility, and thus make working more economical, two HP turbines (two-stage Curtis wheels) of 2,500rpm worked, via 7:1 gearing, on one common shaft on each side, both delivering their exhaust steam into a common LP turbine. The HP turbines could be decoupled individually, thus making a separate cruising turbine unnecessary. This principle seems to have worked well, although no special trials regarding the resulting economy were carried out owing to the demands of the war.

21. Vulcan-Werke: 'Projekt Nr. 1612/31, S.M. Kleiner Kreuzer "Ersatz Gazelle" – Anlage mit Turbo-Transformatoren', Mai 1914.

22. This verdict was well founded, given the experience of *Wiesbaden* at Jutland (p 216), and following the mining of *Breslau* and *Stralsund* (pp 201, 226).

Regarding her sea trials, carried out until 11 January 1917, as in *Königsberg* no true tests on the measured mile were performed, the highest recorded power being 54,711shp, while the highest recorded speed was 27.75 knots, circumstances unrecorded. The final verdict of the trials commission mirrors, unsurprisingly, many aspects of the report on *Königsberg*. The trials were hampered in many ways by *Karlsruhe*'s still unfinished condition: e.g. the forward conning tower was unusable because of the ongoing fitting out of the newly introduced central direction pointer system for the main armament. Nevertheless, its cramped nature was already being noted in this early stage. Despite the armament's first trial firing on 18 December, its order transmitting system was finished only shortly before the termination of the trials period on 31 January 1917.

Top: *Karlsruhe* (ii) at anchor in Schillig Roads while on picket duty. As compared with *Königsberg* and *Emden* she had an extended lower bridge deck, similar to that fitted in *Nürnberg* (bottom). Her experimental angled recess for her port anchor is visible; for the vertical one on the starboard side, see p 232. In the background is the auxiliary minelayer (ex-ferry) *Deutschland*. *(DN collection)*

Emden (ii)

The ordering of the second pair, *Ersatz-Nymphe* [to be *Emden* (ii)] and *Ersatz-Thetis* [*Nürnberg* (ii)], is shrouded in an obscurity that is exacerbated by deficiencies in the extant files. The ships were ordered in August 1914, in spite of not legally being 'due' as replacements for the old *Nymphe* and *Thetis* until 1915: the regulations of the Fleet Laws were very explicit that a vessel could only be replaced after its determined lifespan, or in case of its loss.

As the German navy had by then already lost four small cruisers (see pp 198-199, 203, 208-209, below), their immediate replacement would not legally have been an issue: but why then were only two vessels ordered, and then under designations that referred to ships not yet legally replaceable, rather than two of the lost cruisers? There is, however, some indication that the August 1914 'order' was only a 'promise' to the yards, since *Ersatz-Nymphe* would not actually be laid down by AG Weser before December – which could easily be held to be 'almost' 1915. *Ersatz-Thetis* had to wait even longer, until 8 May 1915, to be laid down at Howaldt, her actual contract not being signed before 13 January of that year. The matter becomes even more confusing after looking at the financial aspect. As the funds for both cruisers were eventually taken from the so-called 'war-fund', there would have been no financial objections against ordering them immediately. Exactly what happened will probably remain forever obscure.

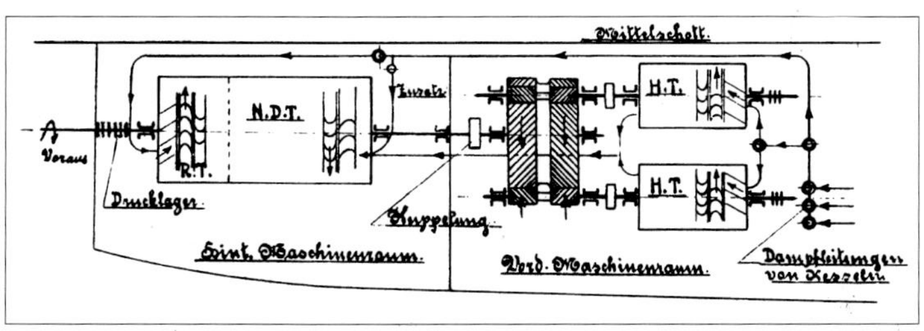

Schematic drawing for *Karlsruhe* (ii)'s geared turbine installation. For maximum economy each of the HP turbines could be decoupled by clutch, as could the connection between reduction gear and the LP turbine. *(Neuerungen im Schiffsbetrieb)*

Ersatz-Nymphe was launched as *Emden* (ii) on 1 February 1916 and commissioned at Bremen on 16 December of the same year. Quite revealing regarding her actual condition at that point, however, are two remarks in the trials report: 'The vessel left the shipyard on 26 December in more or less complete condition'(!) Further on we read: 'The circumstances regarding health were negatively affected by the fact that the vessel had been commissioned while the accommodation was still incomplete, so that the crew was insufficiently protected against rain and cold.' During the trials *Emden* attained a maximum of 50,200shp and a maximum speed of 27.75 knots, at a sea depth of 35m. During the six-hour trial she attained an average of 32,400shp while running at 26.5 knots. It was explicitly noted that this speed could have been kept up for even longer, due to the new cooling system of the furnace grates and the reintroduction of supplementary oil burners in the coal-fired boilers. She finally joined the fleet on 12 March 1916.

Nürnberg (ii)

While *Emden* had been built to exactly the same plans as

Königsberg – building in the same yard – *Ersatz-Thetis* would differ in being fitted with experimental hawseholes at the bow, with a semi-recessed type (which would be employed in the follow-on class) to port, and a completely recessed vertical type to starboard. These which made her easily distinguishable from her sisters. She had also been intended to serve abroad in peacetime, and had thus been built for tropical climes, which mainly affected the design of the ventilation system, berthing arrangements and the insulation of store rooms.

As noted, the ship had a rather late start and was thus even more affected by delayed deliveries from subcontractors, who had lost some of their employees to the army. In March 1916, *Ersatz-Thetis*'s launch was forecast for the beginning of April, while completion was planned for 15 December of that year. In the event, while the launch indeed took place on 14 April 1916, at which the cruiser was christened *Nürnberg* (ii), her commissioning had to be postponed until 15 February 1917.

Most of her crew came from *Berlin*, which had decommissioned on 11 February (cf p 222, below). Her sea trials began on 27 February and culminated on 22 March 1917 with a high-speed run at maximum draught, during which *Nürnberg* attained a maximum of 53,763shp and a corresponding speed of 27.64 knots, at a sea depth of 35m. During the six-hour trial she attained an average of 32,700shp, although no record of the related speed survives. Of special interest to the trials commission was the inefficient distribution of the coal bunkers. In particular, boiler room 2, equipped with the most powerful coal-fired boilers, was found to have direct access to only 190 tonnes of coal, before having to tap the bunkers arranged for protective purposes. The 190 tonnes would last, under operational conditions, for little more than nineteen hours.

After this, coal supply would become much harder to obtain and, most probably, be insufficient to properly feed the boilers in question; additional crew would be required to compensate for the problem of coal access. Therefore, in the view of the trials commission, the arrangement of the bunkers in future vessels needed to be altered, and the oil-fired boilers placed between the coal-fired ones. This comment seems to have been anticipated by the RMA, as the distribution was already being changed in the next batch of small cruisers (see below). On 1 May 1917, *Nürnberg* finally joined the fleet.

SMALL CRUISER 1915

In the meantime, between the first presentation of the draughts for the 1914 cruisers at Rominten, and their final approval in April, 'K' had in January already pressed for work to begin on outlining the design for the 1915 small cruiser. The reason for this haste is hard to see, as the department was not overly busy with new designs at the time, and the 'storm clouds' of the summer of 1914 could not yet be anticipated. However, the main point of concern was the current small cruiser design's speed deficit in relation to the cruisers and battlecruisers of other nations, principally the UK, although ships of similar kinds were also now being built for Russia and Japan.

The rule of thumb, as laid down by 'A', remained that 'the small cruiser must possess at least the same speed as the modern large [battle] cruiser, while carrying the highest possible amount bunkerage'.[23] Now, however, the German navy was confronted with anticipated figures of 30 knots for the British *Tiger*[24] and 29 knots for Russia's *Borodino* class.[25] The situation was exacerbated by an understanding that the latest British light cruisers (the *Arethusa* class) would be significantly faster than previous vessels.[26]

Accordingly, 'A' proposed increasing the design speed of the future cruiser to at least 28.5 knots. Since, for budgetary reasons, a major increase of the size of such vessels had to be avoided, the necessary extra power output would have to be achieved by an increase in the proportion of oil-fired boilers. However, it was felt that this substitution of fuels should not go as far as in the navies of the UK, Italy or Russia, which relied entirely on oil in their newest small cruisers. It was argued that a certain proportion of coal-fired boilers should be retained, sufficient for cruising at around 15 knots, for the following reasons:

1 Not to lose the extra protection provided by coal bunkers.
2 The danger arising from the flammability of oil.
3 The danger of loss of liquid fuel through holes caused by hits either above or below water.
4 The excessive cost of oil for peacetime operations.
5 The possibly restricted availability of oil during overseas service.

Nevertheless, the advantages of oil were clearly noted, in particular the much lower manpower requirement of oil-fired boilers, based on *Breslau*'s experience in the Mediterranean and later that of *Strassburg* in the Atlantic. *Breslau* had in particular reported the frequent need to employ sailors to support the stokers and trimmers in supplying the necessary amount of coal to the boilers, even at medium speeds. In wartime this kind of supplementary manning would be untenable. Additionally, a higher ratio of oil-fired boilers would be advantageous to allow 'smokeless' cruising at higher speeds than the present limit of about 21 knots using the oil-fired boilers alone. To validate the arguments for and against greater oil stowage, it was felt necessary to perform flammability tests on oil bunkers using 15cm (and larger) HE shells.

Also still not settled was the question of the substitution of

23. BA-MA RM3/3698 – fol 61.

24. Actual design: 28 knots; trials: 29 knots.

25. Actual design: 26.5 knots (28 knots forced).

26. They were designed for 28.5 knots, rather than the 25.5 knots of the preceding *Birmingham* and *Chatham* classes.

two 8.8cm AA guns for the four projected 5.2cm weapons, as the new larger-calibre gun had only been ready for initial trials since November 1913. Although still seen as desirable, it was noted that this measure would probably add yet another 40 tonnes to the design.

During the subsequent interdepartmental discussions, in July 1914 'K' questioned the necessity of an increased speed, as all the relevant information from abroad had come from unconfirmed oral sources.[27] Even more seriously, owing to the size of the vessels, a switch in emphasis towards speed would significantly degrade habitability and the suitability of the type for the dual fleet/overseas role that had underpinned the small cruiser type since its inception. The only solutions to this dilemma would be either to introduce a special smaller 'fleet cruiser' along the lines of the British *Arethusa* class, or increase displacement by about 1,500 tonnes for the standard cruiser.

In any case, the verdict was that – even without major modifications – the 1915 cruiser would at least need another 100 tonnes of displacement just to compensate for the already acknowledged shortcomings of the 1914 vessels. Another 50 tonnes would be required for the proposed change in the ratio of coal- and oil-boilers, and further 50 tonnes in case a vessel would be required as flagship – which was expected to be the case for at least two of the forthcoming ships. This rather simple calculation was overshadowed by the results of an alternative redesign of the armour layout, which eased the handling of coal in the upper bunkers by making the armour deck flat and deleting its traditional slopes. This would require vessels of at least 6,000 tonnes displacement, by offsetting the loss of deck slope protection by a thicker belt of 80mm, without any gain in speed or habitability.

'K' therefore put forward three options, embracing variations in the boiler-options and necessary changes in the configuration of the bunkers. Variant I would be the 'natural' follow-on design, incorporating only the 'necessary' changes; Variants II and III would have eight coal- and six single-ended oil-fired boilers, II with oil bunkers arranged alongside the boiler rooms, III with the 'classical' stowage of oil in the double bottom:

Variant	Displacement (tonnes)	six-hour trial (knots)	forced trial (knots)	cost (million Marks)
1914 type	5,300	27.25	27.5	8.7
1915 – I	5,400	27.25	27.5	8.8
1915 – II	5,600	27.75	28.0	9.2
1915 – III	5,700	27.75	28.0	9.3

27. 'K' could, however, be more confident with its statements regarding the planned Russian cruisers, as the turbine plant for the two *Svetlana* class being built by the Russo-Baltic Works at Reval had been designed with the assistance of Vulcan, and both turbine sets were actually under construction at Vulcan and its subcontractor Blohm & Voss (cf p 190, below).

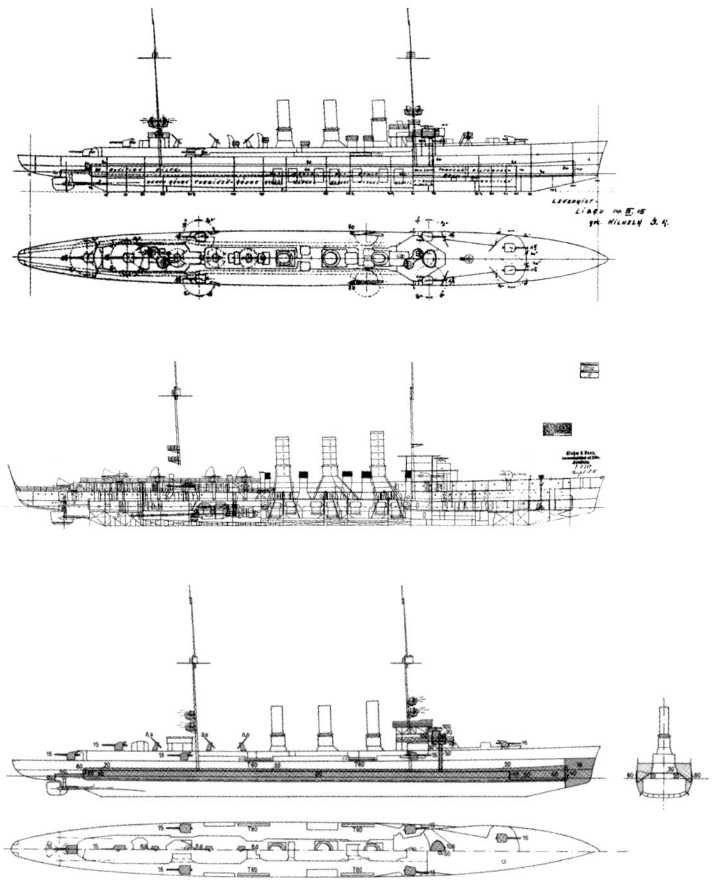

Ersatz-Leipzig [*Leipzig* (iii)] was the original lead ship of the final class of small cruisers to be built, the upper sketch showing its original sketch, with the Kaiser's approving endorsement, given at Libau on 14 December 1915. The mainmast is positioned exceptionally far aft, to gain room for three AA-guns between it and the aftermost funnel. Consequently, the mother-compass binnacle had to be positioned before the bridge in rather unusual way. Another odd feature is the heightened forefunnel casing, resulting from a different bridge configuration, not included in the final design. The middle drawing is taken from the official booklet of plans for *Ersatz-Ariadne* [*Cöln* (ii)], the first of the only two ships to be completed. This shows some continuing uncertainties as to her final configuration, as while the submerged TTs had already been given up, the position of the mainmast has yet to be finally fixed. The armour deck over the boiler rooms is also shown as slightly raised, suggesting problems with the height of the boilers. Invisible in this profile are the newly introduced anti-rolling tanks. The bottom drawing shows the definite form of this ultimate small cruiser type. *(DN collection)*

In every other aspect the vessels would have mirrored the preceding class quite closely. However, no 'official' 1915 cruiser would actually be built: everything was changed by the outbreak of war in August 1914.

RENEWAL

The major losses of the first months of the war were reflected in the names actually assigned to the pre-war-programmed *Ersatz-Gazelle* class: *Königsberg*, *Karlsruhe*, *Nürnberg* and *Emden*; the latter's connection with the lost cruiser was made explicit by the placement of an Iron Cross on her stem.[28] However, on 22 March 1915, Tirpitz presided over a meeting of the RMA's departments at which physical replacements were discussed. The discussions mainly concerned numbers, rather than the design of the ships themselves, as any major deviation from the 1914 cruiser would lead to a loss of precious time. In the end it was decided that, of the nine replacement vessels, six would be ordered immediately to the same general specifications of the 1914 ships, with a few modifications – none of which would exactly match any of the three '1915' proposals noted above. The orders for the – originally – remaining three would be held back for around three months, for the possible inclusion of the latest lessons from the war. The fourth ship – *Ersatz-A* – was added sometime in between: there is no explicit statement in the files as to exactly when. The final schedule was as follows:

Provisional name	Definitive name	Shipyard	Ordered	Laid down
Ersatz-Leipzig	*Leipzig*	Weser	10 Apr 15	Aug 15
Ersatz-Emden	–	Weser	10 Apr 15	Aug 15
Ersatz-Cöln	–	Weser	10 Apr 15	Aug 15
Ersatz-Nürnberg	*Wiesbaden*	Vulcan	10 Apr 15	Oct 15
Ersatz-Mainz	*Rostock*	Vulcan	10 Apr 15	Nov 15
Ersatz-Ariadne	*Cöln*	Blohm & Voss	14 Apr 15	Aug 15
Ersatz-Dresden	*Dresden*	Howaldt	7 Aug 15	May 16
Ersatz-Magdeburg	*Magdeburg*	Howaldt	7 Aug 15	Jun 16
Ersatz-Königsberg	*Frauenlob*	Kiel DYd	20 Aug 15	Dec 15
Ersatz-A[29]	–	Kiel DYd	20 Aug 15	Sep 16

The actual process of ordering the two new batches of cruisers was unusual, to say the least, for the otherwise legalistic German navy. On 23 February 1915 Tirpitz had informed the Kaiser for the first time of the RMA's intention to continue, in general, with the 1914 design, subject to a few alterations. The Kaiser gave his oral consent and, on the basis of this, the first batch of six vessels was ordered by the RMA in April, followed by the second batch of four in August, while detailed design work was still going on. Finally, on 14 December 1915, the Kaiser signed a formal order of construction that covered all ten vessels. It would be the Imperial navy's final order for small cruisers.

Of the changes compared to the *Königsberg*s and earlier vessels, two were particularly noteworthy. Both added to the already good survivability of the new cruisers: first by a further separation of the boiler rooms, and second through the deletion of the submerged torpedo tubes, and their replacement an additional pair of revolving mountings on the upper deck. The second measure was a result of war experience, especially a fear of sympathetic detonations of the torpedo warheads in case of an underwater hit by mine or torpedo. Although practical experience in this matter was generally mixed, the torpedo flat's deletion was demanded in February 1916 by the chief of the Scouting Force, VAdm Hipper, following the losses of the large cruiser *Prinz Adalbert* by sympathetic detonation after a torpedo hit and the small cruiser *Bremen* by mine – albeit without sympathetic detonation (see below, p 212).

The upper-deck tubes were later changed from the 50cm G/7 type to ones suitable for the newly introduced 60cm H/8 'battleship torpedo'. This did not initially have any negative impact on stability, as long as the mountings' optional armoured hoods were omitted. The alterations to the machinery spaces added one more bulkhead to the boiler rooms, raising their number from four to five. This had become necessary when the former two double-ended, oil-fired boilers were swapped for four single-enders. This was accompanied by the exchange of two further coal-fired boilers for two more oil-fired units, which resulted in the following distribution of boilers between boiler rooms: 2 oil/4 coal/2 oil/4 coal/2 oil. This gave an oil:coal ratio of 6:8; maximum oil bunkerage was doubled, but that for coal was reduced by 18 per cent. In these changes, the issues that would be raised during *Nürnberg*'s trials (p 158) had effectively been anticipated. There was no change, however, in nominal installed power.

Another modification was the increase in the originally envisaged number of two 8.8cm AA guns from two to three. In the event, only two were actually carried in service (possibly with a brief exception in the case of *Ersatz-Dresden* [*Dresden* (ii)[30]], reflecting a common pattern in the German fleet, due to constant shortages of mountings owing to the insatiable demands from the 'front'.[31]

28. *Emden* (i) was one of the few vessels that had been 'posthumously' decorated in her own right with this order; her tradition was maintained in subsequent warships of the name by the placing of an Iron Cross at her stem – most recently the frigate *Emden* (v), decommissioned in 2013. Her award was surpassed only by the decoration of the gunboat *Iltis* (ii) with membership of the Pour le Mérite order after the action against the Taku forts in 1900.

29. *Ersatz-A* is sometimes referred to in print as *Ersatz-Karlsruhe*, but this is not reflected in the relevant files. There is no indication of her being ordered as an addition to strength, although this might be implied by her letter-designation, although its combination with the '*Ersatz-*' prefix is somewhat odd. Among the *Mackensen* class large cruisers of the same period there is a similar case of '*Ersatz-Friedrich Carl*' versus '*Ersatz-A*'.

30. One of a very few vessels that took the name of the ship they were legally replacing; other examples include the large cruiser *Freya* and the gunboat *Iltis* (ii).

31. Seen at its extreme in the *Bayern*-class battleships, which were fitted for no fewer than eight, but completed with none, and eventually only carried two at most.

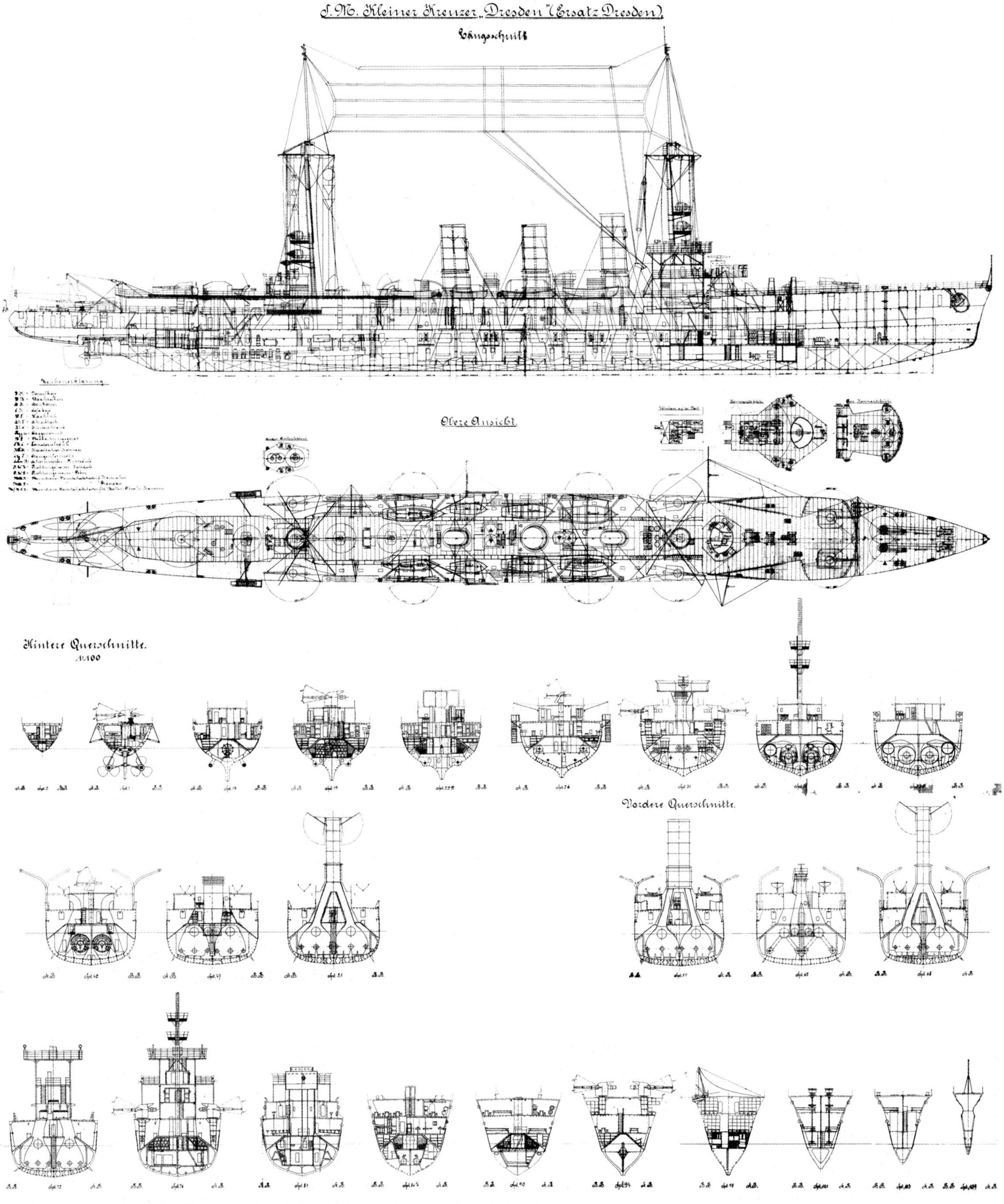

Official drawings of *Dresden* (ii) as completed. *(Courtesy www.dreadnoughtproject.org)*

Close-up view of *Dresden* (ii) in drydock at Kiel, showing the definitive configuration of her class, with the new-style conning tower and the forward beam guns lowered to upper deck level. *(DN collection)*

An important change from the point of view of actually operating the new ships was a re-designed conning-tower, which now resembled the form employed in contemporary battleships and large cruisers, including becoming raised and integrated into the bridge structure. Although the reasons behind this change of approach are not entirely clear, it was, at least in part, a reaction to the raising of the forward wing-mounted 15cm guns to forecastle deck level to render them less wet in a seaway. While advantageous in one aspect, the guns' new location had caused concern regarding flash and blast effects on the personnel within the conning tower when firing straight ahead. While blast screens were mounted as an initial measure, these, in turn, adversely affected the view from inside the conning tower. Consequently, after the first trials of *Königsberg* in September 1916, Hipper, as well as 'W', requested yet another change for the new-builds, in this case the shifting of this pair of 15cm guns back to main deck level. Although this had improved the command of the guns, the knock-on effects on the conning tower, and thus the running of the ship, could not be neglected either. During a decisive inter-departmental meeting on 24 September, it was almost unanimously agreed that, despite the theoretical advantages of the raised position of these guns, the operators' arguments should prevail.

However, the three still-unfinished *Königsbergs*, were already afloat, with *Ersatz-Ariadne* of the new class only two weeks from launch, and thus too far along to be modified. On the other hand, the remaining five vessels ordered in April 1915, although still scheduled to be completed during 1917 (having been assigned Priority I), were still far enough from launch to be altered. A decision on the four vessels of the August 1915 batch was left open. The resulting status of *Ersatz-Ariadne* [to be *Cöln*] as an 'odd man out' was not of major concern to the RMA, as it would allow direct comparison between the two configurations in otherwise-identical ships. No-one expected at that time that only two of these vessels – one of each configuration – would eventually be commissioned.

All vessels of the class were to be delayed by the diversion of increasingly scarce resources towards the submarine force and away from major surface warships; the latest official report regarding their progress dates from December 1917 (amended to 1 July 1918):

Name	**anticipated completion (as at Dec 17)***	**actual/anticipated launch (as at Dec 17)**	**(as at July 18)**
Leipzig	undefined	Jan 18	28 Jan 18
Ersatz-Emden	undefined	undefined	undefined
Ersatz-Cöln	undefined	undefined	undefined
Wiesbaden	undefined	3 Mar 17	3 Mar 17
Rostock	undefined	undefined	6 Apr 18
Cöln	Jan 18	5 Oct 16	5 Oct 16
Dresden	Mar 18	25 Apr 17	25 Apr 17
Magdeburg	undefined	17 Nov 17	17 Nov 17
Ersatz-Königsberg	undefined	undefined**	(Sept 18)
Ersatz-A	undefined	undefined	undefined

* In July 1918, the following statement applied to all ships: 'This build is either continued to keep the yard's company engaged in times of idleness, or is suspended, as the shipyard is entirely engaged in the construction of submarines or torpedo boats, as well as working on already commissioned naval forces'.

** Launched as *Frauenlob* on 16 September 1918.

Of those that *did* come into service, *Cöln* finally commissioned on 17 January 1918, employing the former crew of *Hamburg*. Her trials at Kiel were rather basic, lasting from 5 February to 18 April, during which only the output of her machinery has been recorded with certainty, giving 48,700shp at full power and 33,200shp for sustained running. Some sources state that her maximum speed had been recorded at 29.3 knots, but this is unconfirmed – and rather unlikely.

Dresden commissioned on 28 March 1918. Her trials at Kiel, although rather extended in time, were also only summarily recorded, but include a maximum output of 51,000shp, and one of 35,100shp sustained. The latter value was significantly higher than the 29,000shp required by the order of construction for the machinery (dated 28 August 1915),[32] but not exceptionally so, compared, for example, with the results of *Karlsruhe*'s trials. It is probable that the high value for sustained power was a function of the higher proportion of oil-fired boilers in the *Cöln* class. That *Dresden*, launched in April 1917, had been fitted out in less than a year, redounds to the credit on her builders, Howaldt of Kiel. They also had *Magdeburg* fairly well advanced by November 1918, with her machinery nearly finished, except for her low-pressure turbines and condensers.[33] *Wiesbaden* had been launched at Stettin some six weeks before *Dresden* had taken to the water, but the end of the war found her still in her builders' hands. Although nearly complete, with funnels up and bridges erected, she was actually little further

Cöln (ii) is moved by tugs in the basin of her builders Blohm & Voss in December 1917, shortly before her commissioning in January. Some of her boilers had already been lit. *(DN collection)*

Top: the dark hull of *Magdeburg* (ii) lying alongside the fitting out pier of the Howaldt yard at Kiel in December 1917, having been launched the previous month. Behind her may be seen the funnels of *Dresden*, launched in April, and only a few months from completion. **Bottom:** *Wiesbaden*, seen afloat at Stettin, was closest to completion of any of the ships still under construction when war ended. However, she was still months from being ready for sea. *(DN collection)*

advanced than *Rostock*, launched in the same yard over a year later. *Leipzig* had been launched by Weser, and had had her machinery installed and decked-in when work stopped. Of the rest, *Frauenlob* was launched only in September 1918, while *Ersatz-Cöln*, *Ersatz-Emden* and *Ersatz-A* were all still on the stocks when the First World War ended.

PHANTOMS AND FUTURE

In addition to the 'real' *Cöln* class, reports reaching the UK during 1918 alleged that she and an alleged sister *Mannheim* were of a much-enlarged type.[34] This was supposedly of 6,300 tons, 520ft x 49ft x 17½ft in size, and armed with two 21cm and six 15cm guns, plus four torpedo tubes, with a range of some 12,000nm. These rumours led to the British sketching a 7.5in-gunned version of the 'E' class to match it. Less extreme reports dating to 1916 suggested that new construction German cruisers would be armed with ten or eleven 15cm weapons, and this had contributed to the construction of the new British 'D' class.[35]

It was long thought that no such vessels had ever been actually contemplated in Germany, but, as quite common with rumours, they contained a grain of truth. As early as the winter of 1915, a questionnaire had been circulated to the commanding officers of the larger vessels of the fleet – including cruisers – regarding the experience gained so far during the war, and the potential lessons for the future. The responses were, unsurprisingly, diverse, with little unanimity as to desiderata. However, focussing on those that potentially impacted the future development of cruisers, one extremely detailed proposal came from FKpt Heinrich Retzmann, then CO of *Strassburg*, who felt that the events of the war indicated that the present small cruiser was something of an evolutionary dead end.

In particular, he believed that none of the current vessels were capable of waging commerce warfare west of the British Isles – the only kind of maritime warfare that he saw as endangering to the British war effort. In his view, a split was necessary in future development. One line should comprise a smaller-sized true 'fleet cruiser' or 'flotilla leader', principally capable of

32. 'Bauvorschrift für die Hauptmaschinen (zwei Turbinensätze auf zwei Wellen) und Kessel mit zugehörigen Hilfsmaschinen, Zubehör und Inventar des Kleinen Kreuzers 'Ersatz Dresden' – M I'.

33. For a contemporary report including the state of the incomplete small cruisers in November 1918, see Dodson and S Cant, *Spoils of War: the fate of enemy fleets after the two World Wars* (Barnsley: Seaforth, 2020), pp 89–90.

34. N Friedman, *British Cruisers: Two World Wars and After* (Barnsley: Seaforth, 2010), pp 339–40 n.30; on the other hand, by the time that the July 1918 Admiralty Confidential Book covering German cruisers was issued, the *Cöln* class had been correctly identified as similar to the *Königsbergs*, along with the names *Wiesbaden, Leipzig* and *Magdeburg* for vessels under construction. On the other hand, another of the latter was believed to be a '*Bremen*', with all provisional names wrong. British intelligence had assumed that *Ersatz*-names after *Cöln* (correctly noted as '*Ersatz-Ariadne*') would then continue the sequence of replacements under the Fleet Laws, rather than war-losses, as was actually the case (*Cöln* confused matters, as *Ariadne* was *both* one of the first war-losses *and* due to be replaced directly after *Thetis* – the last of the *Königsbergs*, *Nürnberg*, having been *Ersatz-Thetis*). Thus, *Dresden* is listed as '*Ersatz-Amazone*' and *Wiesbaden* as '*Ersatz-Medusa*'. The later vessels are cited as having the provisional designations '*P*', '*Q*' and '*R*' – continuing the small cruiser sequence last used for *Stuttgart* (N. Friedman [ed.], *German Warships of World War I: The Royal Navy's Official Guide to the Capital Ships, Cruisers, Destroyers, Submarines and Small Craft, 1914–1918* (London: Greenhill Books, 1992), p 114).

35. Friedman, *British Cruisers: Two World Wars*, p. 54.

fighting British destroyers that, he anticipated, might some day be equipped with 12.7cm (5in) guns.[36] The other line would develop into a cruiser intermediate between small and large cruisers in capability, which he dubbed an 'armoured cruiser'. The key characteristics of the two proposals are given below:

	Fleet cruiser/ Flotilla Leader	Small armoured cruiser
Displacement	4,000 tonnes	8,000 tonnes
Length	137.9m	160.9m
Beam	14.1m	18.3m
Draught	5.0m	5.9m
Armament		
main	five 15cm	eight 19cm
secondary	–	four 8.8cm
torpedo tubes	four (2 x 2, armoured)	four (2 x 2, armoured)
Speed		
sustained	32 knots	30 knots
maximum	35 knots	32 knots
Power (turbines)	42,000shp	60,000shp
Armour		
side	40mm	80mm
conning tower, shields, &c	–	yes, unspecified

A similar opinion was voiced by the temporary leader of the IV. SG, Kpt Karl von Restorff (1871–1944), who stated that the small cruiser had not proven its worth in action thus far. Accordingly, it should be developed into a true cruiser for distant stations, while the type for service at home must be developed into a small armoured cruiser.

Both (and further similar) opinions were initially rejected by FO II. SG, KAdm Georg Hebbinghaus (1866–1944) because he foresaw that the development of the newly proposed 'armoured cruiser' would ultimately end in the logical culmination of the 'battlecruiser', as had been the case with large cruisers.[37] However, he saw some merit in the smaller 'flotilla leader', explicitly referring to the British 'C' class in comparison.

36. The 4.7in [120mm]-gunned 'Modified W' class would be laid down during 1918.

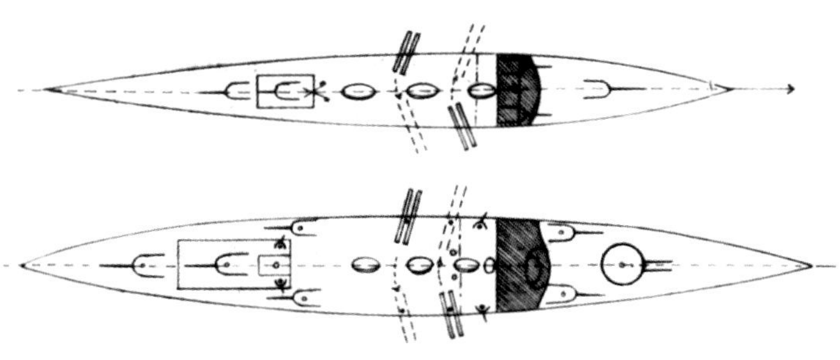

Sketches for the 1915 concepts for a flotilla leader (top) and a small armoured cruiser (bottom). *(DN collection)*

On the contrary assumption that the existing division of cruiser types should be maintained and continued, several proposals came in – none of which were new. For example: design speed should be raised to at least 30 knots; protection should be raised to 100mm in some areas (unspecified); an enlarged forward conning tower, giving good visibility aft, plus an additional command post aft should be fitted; ten 15cm guns should be mounted; the forward torpedo flat should be omitted, with four torpedo tubes (four singles or two twins) mounted on the upper deck under protected shields instead; the manual steering position should be brought under armour protection.

The – preliminary – closing verdict came from VAdm Hipper, commander of the Scouting Force, in August 1915. For the time being, he did not agree with the dissenting voices, seeing the recent small cruiser not replaceable by other types. Nevertheless, the seed was sown, and the discussion would re-emerge during 1915. Perhaps surprisingly, sometime during the second half of that year, Hipper would change his mind and also become a promoter of the 'flotilla leader' design.

In May 1916, Tirpitz's successor as State Secretary at the RMA, Adm Eduard von Capelle (1855–1931), was summoned to brief the Kaiser regarding the future development of the fleet in the context of the existing Fleet Law. In his review, topics other than the development of future battleships and large cruisers were dealt with only very briefly. But regarding small cruisers, the main requirements for future types for service abroad were seen as settled, although any detailed design work would have to be postponed indefinitely, for the lack of personnel. The same applied to designs for 'fleet cruisers' (FK) that had been worked out as pure studies during the initial months of the year. One issue already apparent was that all of their design speeds were inadequate for working in conjunction with the modern torpedo boats that they were intended to lead.

These studies for FKs clearly originated from the desiderata of a number of the front-line commanders, now with support from Hipper. The Kaiser was apparently[38] impressed enough by some of these sketches to have ordered in November and December 1915 – via Tirpitz – their development by 'K', under the direction of Baurat Alfred Blechschmidt, into true design studies. Numbered in an 'FK' sequence, these ranged in size from 3,000 tonnes (FK 1), through 4,500 tonnes (FK 2) and 6,000 tonnes (FK 3) to 7,500 tonnes (FK 4). Some of their known – not totally consistent – vital statistics are noted opposite.

The logic behind studies FK 3 and FK 4 is hard to see, as they were contrary to the request for a smaller flotilla leader type,

37. Probably with some justification one is similarly inclined to see this as the road leading the future 'light cruiser' and 'heavy cruiser' categories. Besides this, it may be interesting to note that both protagonists, Retzmann and Hebbinghaus, were soon promoted to posts in the RMA.

38. Whether he really was inspired by the reports, or got the initial spark by other means, remains obscure.

instead growing to a size well beyond the latest 1914–15 small cruisers. Quite probably they were simply studies of what was possible, and would most unlikely have been chosen to be actually built. Blechschmidt himself would call them in 1931, 'material to choose suitable requirements for design from, in case new buildings of this type could be afforded'. Further support for this statement may be taken from discussions during the winter of 1916, when several options were tabled at the RMA. One originated from the question of whether it would really be necessary to build expensive cruisers (costing some 20–25 million Marks) for 'service abroad' (code for cruisers intended for commerce raiding), when their potential effectiveness seemed dwarfed by the successes of auxiliary cruisers: for example, *Möwe* had sunk vessels with goods worth some 60 million Marks during her first cruise during 1915–16, compared to her conversion costs of about 0.5 million Marks!

The true death knell of the existing type, however, came in the wake of Jutland, when the leaders of tactical units and captains of individual ships were once more invited to share their recent battle experiences with senior officers, guided by another questionnaire. Of special interest regarding cruisers were, of course, the responses of the leaders of the II. SG, KAdm Friedrich Boedicker (1866–1944), and of the IV. SG, Kdr Ludwig von Reuter (1869–1943), to the questions raised by their direct superior, Hipper. He wanted to know:

1. In which way may the existing type to be improved in new construction?
2. In which way may the existing vessels be improved through the lessons learned in battle?
3. Has any type of vessel been proven worthless for further development?

Assuming that the two senior officers had not conferred before submitting their individual answers, their opinions proved to be very similar.

If the existing type of small cruiser was to be continued, both of them required a higher continuous speed in new ships, preferably by employment of a higher degree of oil firing. Further, as one lesson learned from battle, splinter protection must be improved in existing vessels as well as new-builds. Third, protection against underwater weapons must be improved: since the installation of anti-torpedo bulkheads would be futile, because of the lack of beam to provide enough depth for the protection system, the subdivision of the hull must be further elaborated.

In their response to question 3, Boedicker and von Reuter made it very clear that they did *not* recommend the continuation of the existing type of small cruiser. They saw it as outdated for several reasons. First, the existing type had already become too large and expensive to be easily risked against anything smaller than themselves. Regarding a ship's value as a fighting unit, the protection (for example) was regarded as too weak compared with the size of the vessel, yet the cruiser was already too slow and unhandy to perform its intended tasks of either leading torpedo boat flotillas in battle,

CHARACTERISTICS OF THE FK-SERIES

	FK 1	FK 1a	FK 2	FK 2a	FK 3a	FK 3b	FK 4a	FK 4b
Displacement (design)	3,000 tonnes	3,450 tonnes	4,500 tonnes	4,500 tonnes	5,500 tonnes	6,100 tonnes	7,500 tonnes	7,500 tons
Length (wl)	128.0m	131.0m	139.0m	139.0m	155.0m	155.0m	170.0m	170.0m
Beam	11.6m	12.4m	13.0m	13.0m	14.2m	14.2m	15.4m	15.4m
Draught (aft/fwd)	4.9/4.1m	4.6/4.6m	5.5/4.8m	5.5/4.8m	5.8/5.2m	5.8/5.2m	6.0/5.4m	6.0/5.4m
Armament								
15cm guns	five	five	five	five	six	seven	eight	eight
8.8cm guns	two	two	two	two	two	two	three	three
60cm torpedo tubes	four	four	four	four	four	two	two	four
Speed								
design	30 knots	33 knots	30 knots	30 knots	30 knots	30 knots	31 knots	31 knots
maximum	32 knots	?	32 knots	32 knots	32 knots	32 knots	32 knots	32 knots
Power (maximum shp)	32,000	52,000	46,000	59.500	66,000	69,100	71,900	74,140
Shafts	2	2	2	2	3	3	3	3
Endurance (@ 17 knots)	2,800nm	3,070nm	2,800nm	3,560nm	2,410nm	?	?	?
Armour								
side	0–40mm	0–40mm	0–50mm	0–50mm	0–50mm	0–50mm	0–50mm	0–60mm
deck	0–15mm	0–15mm	0–15mm	0–15mm	0–20mm	0–20mm	0–20mm	0–20mm
shields	50mm	50mm	50mm	50mm	50mm	50mm	50mm	50mm
conning tower	20–80mm	20–80mm	100mm	100mm	100mm	100mm	100mm	100mm

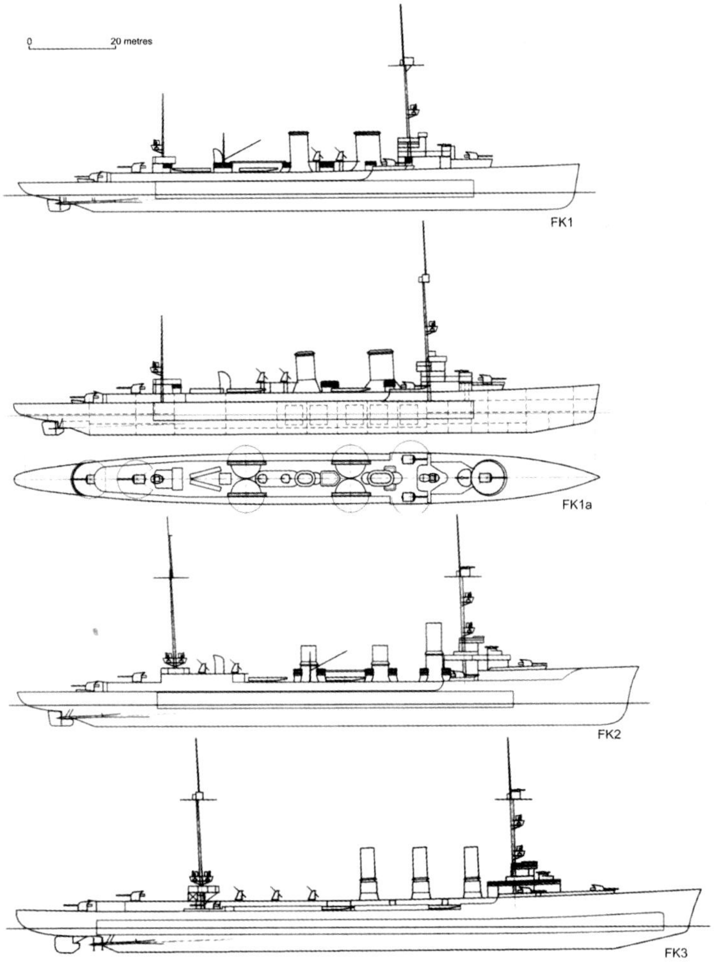

Sketch drawings of FK cruisers were, except for FK1a, long thought to have been lost. However, a number of others have now come to light, as shown here. FK1 and FK1a owe much to destroyer design, especially the 1918 Mob type, while FK3 shares the profile of the post-*Graudenz* 'standard' small cruisers fleet cruisers. (*DN drawing*)

or reconnoitring enemy forces. With explicit regard to the latter, both officers stated that the effective controlled range of heavy guns had become so great that the small cruiser was unable to gain any visual information on the enemy fleet before entering the danger zone and presenting an easy target. In addition, von Reuter saw the beginning of another arms spiral, as he – rightfully – expected the Royal Navy to counter the most modern German cruisers with a super-type of their own, armed with 19cm (7.5in) guns (as would actually emerge as the *Cavendish* class, although their genesis actually lay in providing trade protection in distant waters).

In the opinion of both officers, the only solution was the creation of a force of smaller-sized fleet cruisers, armed with five 15cm guns, to counter the growing number of British 'C' class cruisers, and be capable of high-speed raids. The ships should not, however, be equipped for minelaying, since this task could be done more effectively by submarines.

In his report to the CinC, Adm Scheer, on the results of the questionnaires, Hipper gave qualified endorsement to the views of his two most important subordinates. Like them, he would postpone any decisions regarding the 'cruiser for foreign duties' until after the war, when Germany's political situation would have become clearer. Regarding the 'fleet cruiser', however, he held back from a definite decision against the current type of small cruiser. In his view, the prevailing negative mood against it was, at least in part, influenced by the loss of four such vessels at Jutland which, however, were only partly the result of enemy action or design issues. Nevertheless, he also saw the deficiencies of the type, which could be partly solved by the introduction of a smaller 'fleet cruiser' or 'flotilla leader', a type whose utility, he admitted, he had not initially been persuaded.

However, he still had his reservations, particularly in view of discussions regarding future battleships and large cruisers, which would be able to wage war on the oceans and thus would need adequate escorts, over and above the current small cruiser. In conclusion, Hipper, saw the design 'FK 2' as probably the best, but queried whether the situation really required a completely new design. Might it not be sufficient to simply reduce the armament of the existing type and use the weight saving to improve their other capabilities? It is unlikely that an answer was forthcoming. In his subsequent report to Capelle, Scheer supported Hipper in his reluctance to abolish the 'standard type' entirely, not the least because there were still ten cruisers of that type under construction, but warmly endorsed the decision for a special 'flotilla leader'.

At this point in the summer and autumn of 1916, the discussion began to move in circles. On one hand, the creation of a new type was strongly recommended; on the other, its creation should have to be postponed until after the war. Yet by this time, the 'flotilla leader' role would have begun to be taken up by the *S113*-type 'large torpedo boats' that were just being begun in 1916, armed with four 15cm guns, displacing well over 2,000 tonnes, and designed for 34.5 knots.[39] The development of cruisers had come to a halt for the time being. However, it seems certain that the 'unification' of the two lines of development in the 1890s was about to be split again. The story of the 'classic' German small cruiser therefore ends with the end of the German Imperial navy itself.[40]

39. The first vessel of the type, *V116*, was commissioned in July 1918, followed by *S113* in August 1919 – just in time to be surrendered to the Allies. As the French *Amiral Sénès*, the latter was used as leader of Mediterranean torpedo craft down to the 1930s.

40. The subsequent *Emden* (iii) has often been seen as a final continuation of the 'classic' small cruiser: but see p 240, below, for her true background.

6 CRUISERS FOR EXPORT

CHINA

Tsi Yuen

Although German yards were never able to challenge British shipbuilders, especially the River Tyne's Armstrong's, in gaining overseas orders, they were nevertheless able to make a number of foreign sales. The first of these arose from an 1875 decision by the Chinese government, reacting to the emerging threat from Japan, to establish a Sea Defence Fund, and order an initial tranche of British-built Rendel gunboats.[1] In 1880, it was proposed to acquire four modern armoured vessels for the Northern (Peiyang) fleet; plans to buy from Britain (as with the gunboats) having been stymied by Russian objections to the British government (and reportedly concerns at the ability of British yards to deliver in a timely manner), the orders went to AG Vulcan at Stettin. A contract was placed on 2 December 1880 for an 'armoured corvette' (battleship), based on the German *Sachsen* class and with the explicit permission from Stosch to freely copy the plans of the German class.[2] It was followed by an order for a second vessel of the same type, together with one for a cruiser-type vessel in August 1881.

The latter became a 2,363-tonne protected cruiser ('armour deck corvette') named *Tsi Yuen* [*Jiyuan*],[3] with a 75mm 'turtle-back' deck located entirely below the waterline and a conning tower with 30mm splinter protection.[4] Launched on 1 December 1883, she was armed with two 21cm/35 guns on a common turntable forward, protected by a fixed barbette of 250mm armour, resting on the armour deck, plus one 15cm/35 in an open mounting aft. Six 37mm Hotchkiss revolver cannon and four 381mm torpedo tubes completed her armament. As noted above (p 54), *Tsi Yuen* had a significant impact on the development of future German cruisers, in particular by introducing the complete armoured deck to cruising vessels built in German shipyards. Except for the principal dimensions, the armament and general layout, the Chinese gave Vulcan carte blanche for the design, so the ship's final form must be regarded as a reflection of the views of the Vulcan yard's director of naval construction, Rudolph Haack (1833–1909). There can be little doubt that Haack brought the experience gained during the construction of *Tsi Yuen* to the construction a few years later of the Vulcan-built lead ship of the *Ersatz-Elisabeth* [*Irene*] class, although the latter's design had been produced by the German navy's chief constructor, Alfred Dietrich.

Tsi Yuen began her initial trials on 19 August 1884, before returning to the shipyard to complete the final stages of fitting out. However, her delivery, like that of the two armoured corvettes, *Ting Yuen* [*Dingyuan*] and *Chen Yuen* [*Zhenyuan*], was affected by the enforced halt of military exports to belligerent countries after the outbreak of hostilities between China and France in August 1884. Consequently, it was only after the end of the war in April 1885 that the cruiser could leave Stettin, en route for Kiel, on 22 June, concluding her final trials on passage. Running the measured mile in the Kiel Bight, *Tsi Yuen* ultimately surpassed her design-speed of 15 knots by one knot.

All three Vulcan-built vessels left Kiel for China on 8 July 1885. *Tsi Yuen* had, however, to stop at Malta for three weeks, when problems with the feedwater supply for the boilers were detected, an engineer being sent from Stettin to supervise repairs. The cruiser departed Malta on 20 August, touching at Hong Kong on 25 October and ultimately arriving at Shanghai's Taku Roads on 31 October.

After a rather uneventful career of some nine years in Chinese service, *Tsi Yuen* had the doubtful distinction of receiving/firing the first shots of the Sino-Japanese war on

1. For a history of the Chinese Navy in the late nineteenth and early twentieth centuries, see R N J Wright, *The Chinese Steam Navy, 1862–1945* (London: Chatham Publishing, 2000); see also Chen Yue, 中國軍艦圖誌 1855–1911 [*Chinese Warships Atlas 1855–1911*] (Hong Kong: The Commercial Press, 2013).

2. R Haack, 'Ueber die in Deutschland gebauten chinesischen Panzerschiffe', in *Sitzungsberichte des Vereins zur Beförderung des Gewerbefleisses* 1896, p 55; A Mach, 'The Chinese Battleships', *Warship* VIII (1984), pp 9–18; Wright, 'The Peiyang and Nanyang Cruisers of the 1880s', *Warship* XX (1996), pp 95–110; Dodson, *Kaiser's Battlefleet*, pp 27–30, 237.

3. Conventions for transliterating Chinese into Roman script have changed over time. At the time of her construction, the Wade-Giles system was commonly used, yielding *Tsi Yuen*, but since the 1950s the Pinyin system has increasingly been used and is now the official standard: according to this, the ship's name is usually transliterated today as *Jiyuan*, although occasionally found as *Chiyuan*. Thus, here, and elsewhere in this chapter, Chinese ships' names are given first in Wade-Giles form, as the form by which they were usually referred to by westerners during their service lives, with their Pinyin forms in square brackets.

4. Haack, *Sitzungsberichte* 1896, pp 62–63; J Chunxiao, *Mit Barbaren gegen Barbaren: Die chinesische Selbststärkungsbewegung und das deutsche Rüstungsgeschäft im späten 19. Jahrhundert* (Berlin: Lit Verlag, 2002), pp 92–94.

25 July 1894, during the Battle of Pungdo against the Japanese cruisers *Akitsushima*, *Naniwa* and *Yoshino*. While the conning tower's weak 30mm armour was easily pierced by an initial 6in shell from the Japanese flagship *Naniwa*, another hit was defeated by the armour deck, thus proving its worth. Nevertheless, the Chinese cruiser was hopelessly outgunned and, following several more hits, fled to the shelter of the Weihaiwei forts, albeit not without scoring one hit on the new *Yoshino* in exchange. The subsequent Battle of Yalu on 17 September was no more encouraging: after receiving a few hits during the opening phase of the battle, *Tsi Yuen* once more fled the battlefield and retired to Port Arthur. She was captured by Japanese forces at Weihaiwei in February 1895 and subsequently became the Japanese navy's *Saiyen*. She was ultimately sunk by mine on 30 November 1904, during the siege of Port Arthur in the Russo-Japanese War.

King Yuen and *Lai Yuen*

Two other ships of the same general type as *Tsi Yuen* had been envisaged, but nothing was done until after China's humiliating defeat by France.[5] Then, immediately after the termination of hostilities in 1885, the Chinese court directed viceroy Li Hongzhang (1823–1901) to acquire four cruisers on the model of *Tsi Yuen* in Europe. This was done through the Chinese ambassadors in Berlin (Xu Jingcheng [1845–1900]) and Paris (Zeng Jize [1839–90]). Vulcan in Germany and Armstrong in the UK were requested to improve on the already evident shortcomings of *Tsi Yuen*, Armstrong even receiving her plans for that purpose. Two very different schemes were evolved by the two shipyards to meet the same basic requirement, Armstrong's offering being more offensively oriented, while Vulcan placed more emphasis on defence. In the end, Li Hongzhang decided to split the order in order to maximise Chinese experience of modern designs.[6]

The German pair, *King Yuen* [*Jingyuan*] and *Lai Yuen* [*Laiyuan*], were essentially enlarged versions of *Tsi Yuen*, with side-armour added abreast the machinery spaces and forward magazine. At 2933 tonnes design displacement, their 241mm compound-armour belt extended about 0.6m above the waterline: at full load it is reported to have been almost entirely submerged. The belt was topped by a 40mm compound plate armour deck, with a 75mm compound-armour turtleback fore and aft.

The twin 21cm/35 mounting rested on the upper deck, and was protected by 203mm compound plate. An armoured trunk of the same thickness connected the mounting with the magazines below. The conning tower was protected by 159mm plate. As compared with *Tsi Yuen*, the pair had an extra 15cm/35 gun, these guns being now installed in sponsons, thus giving the potential for fire both forward and aft. They also had 18in rather than 15in torpedo tubes, more powerful compound

5. Wright, *Warship* XX, pp 102–10.

6. Chunxiao, *Mit Barbaren gegen Barbaren*, pp 118–21.

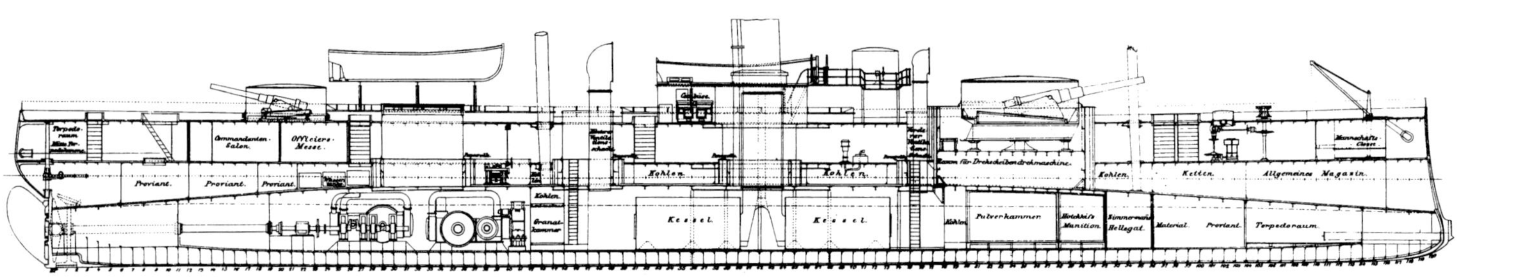

The top-left photograph is the only known image of *Tsi Yuen* under the Chinese flag, at her builders' yard at Stettin, wearing the 'Victorian' paint scheme. Compared with published drawings (middle) she has sloping shields over her main guns, rather than cylindrical ones; in any case, she rarely carried shields in Chinese service. The foremast shown in the drawing was only rigged for her delivery voyage, during which she also sported a mizzen. The novel – for German-built cruisers – complete armoured deck is evident. At the top-right the ship is seen in Japanese service as *Sai Yen* (the Japanese reading of the characters of her name), little altered. *(DN collection/DN collection/ NHHC NH 101774)*

A rather detailed fold-out 'model' of *King Yuen*, which was used to show the German public the features of an armoured cruiser, while ships of this type were still missing in the German navy. *(DN collection)*

engines of 3,400ihp at natural draught (4,400ihp forced),[7] and two funnels.

According to their designer,[8] the ships were not designed to fight modern heavy-gunned vessels: rather, they were meant to deal with lightly constructed cruisers against whose guns their armour would provide sufficient protection for the crews, the guns, the engines and the boilers. Interestingly, owing to the lack of modern German cruisers at the time of their construction, they fulfilled the role of examples for the public as to how modern armoured cruisers were supposed to look: a 'pop-out book' was produced at the time, in which the interior of the vessels could be shown by folding away the hull plating and further sections, and actually shows them wearing the German ensign.

On 13 February 1886 the contract was signed between Vulcan and the Chinese ambassador, both ships being laid down in early 1886, launched on 3 January (*King Yuen*) and 25 March (*Lai Yuen*) 1887. Completed in July 1887, they were formally delivered in the presence of the Chinese ambassador on 11 August, about a year in advance of the parallel-built *Irene*.

During trials in the Kiel Bight, both cruisers exceeded their contracted speed of 15.25 knots by about 0.5 knots; both were nevertheless slower than *Tsi Yuen*.

The British-built pair, *Chih Yuen* [*Zhiyuan*] and *Ching Yuen* [*Jingyuan*], also completed in the summer of 1887, differing from the German vessels in having only deck protection, but an extra 21cm gun; they also looked very different. All four ships sailed to China together, arriving in November, and joining the Peiyang (Northern) Fleet the following spring. The simulta-

Lai Yuen or *King Yuen* fitting-out on the Stettin waterfront. *(Heidrich collection)*

7. There is a common misunderstanding regarding the machinery of these two vessels. In the majority of the literature it is repeated that they were equipped with two triple-expansion engines (HTE) working on two shafts. According to her supervising designer, Rudolph Haack, however, they actually had two three-cylinder compound engines, in which the low-pressure cylinder was split into two of lesser diameter; this is, however, contrary to the model.

8. Haack, *Sitzungsberichte* 1896, p 64.

Taken from one of the German cruisers in Far East, this undated image shows either *Nan Thin* or *Nan Shui*, dressed overall, near Chinkiang. *(DN collection)*

neous delivery of the two pairs led to an early 'propaganda war' in the press, particularly between Chinese-based British and German newspapers, demonstrating how intense industrial competition between the UK and Germany already was. In particular, William White, then Armstrong's chief constructor (later the Royal Navy's Director of Naval Construction) was cited as saying that the few good features of the German design had been liberally copied from his own design by Vulcan. The latter's representatives were furious but, in the end, the Chinese were very satisfied with the quality of the cruisers, leading to a number of further orders.

King Yuen and *Lai Yuen* were present at the Battle of Yalu, where the former was sunk after being battered for several hours by the Japanese Flying Squadron of modern cruisers. Her sister survived the battle, although hit several times and burned out on and above the upper deck, but with her machinery apparently remaining largely intact. She was, however, present at Weihaiwei when the anchorage was attacked by Japanese torpedo boats on 5 February 1885, and sunk by a single torpedo abreast the port engine room.

Nan Thin and *Nan Shui*

For the Southern (Nanyang) fleet, the local commissioner, Zuo Zongtang (1812–85), had initiated a programme for five 'fast' cruisers in 1881. The ships were to be of 2,100 to 2,200 tons, and armed with two/three guns of 190–210mm calibre, plus seven of 120mm.[9] Three, *Kai Chi* (1883), *King Ching* and *Huan Tai* (1886), were built in China, with composite hulls (the frames for the later pair being purchased in Germany), but the remaining pair, with steel hulls – but still without armour[10] – were ordered from Howaldt at Kiel. This yard had hitherto lacked any significant international profile, but obtained the contract via a Hamburg trading house. The negotiated price was 270,000 Chinese Taels (1,035,000 Marks) apiece – significantly less than the Chinese-built vessels' 386,000 (*Kai Chi*) and 366,000 Tael (others) each – excluding armament. The latter would be supplied by Armstrong's after delivery – perhaps rather curiously, since *Kai Chi* had been fitted with Krupp weapons. On the other hand, *King Ching* and *Huan Tai* also received Armstrong guns.

Begun in 1883, *Nan Thin* [*Nan Chen*] was launched on 12 December 1883 and *Nan Shui* [*Nan Rui*] on 8 January 1884, and completed in March 1884. Displacing 2,200 tons, they had a one-shaft compound engine of 2,400ihp and a design speed of 14.5 knots, with an auxiliary barquentine rig. The armament consisted of two 8in (10 tons) BL and eight 4.7in BL guns and two 37mm Hotchkiss revolver-cannon. They could be distinguished from the Chinese-built ships of the programme by having two funnels, rather than just one.

Both sailed from Kiel in March 1884, allowed to do so, despite the looming Sino-French war, principally owing to their unarmed state, but possibly also owing to their much lower capability than the armoured corvettes and *Tsi Yuen*, which were detained at Stettin. However, on arrival on the Tyne to embark their armament, the British authorities were initially nervous about allowing them to proceed. In the end, the pair were allowed to depart, albeit without having fired their guns. As a result, on arrival on the Yangtze in July, it was discovered that the gun supports were insufficiently strong, and thus *Nan Thin* and *Nan Shui* had to be immediately taken in hand at the Kiangnan Dockyard for remedial work. Reports that up to four sister ships were to be built locally were without basis.[11]

After the attack on the Chinese naval base of Foochow (Fuzhou) by a French force under Adm Amédée Courbet (1827–85) on 23/24 August 1885, the main vessels of the Nanyang fleet, including *Nan Thin* and *Nan Shui*, sought shelter under the guns of the Kiangyin forts on the banks of the Yangtse river, defending Nanking, but returned to Shanghai when the French turned to blockade Taiwan. On 18 January 1886 the force sailed from Shanghai for an attempted relief of Taiwan, but had to flee for shelter at Zhenhai, where they were blockaded for the rest of the war. Ten years later, during the Sino-Japanese war, both cruisers were based on Taiwan, to control the Taiwan straits.

Following the disastrous end of the war, *Nan Thin* and *Nan Shuin* were sent north to begin the reconstitution of the Peiyang fleet, which had been annihilated by the Japanese. Although one of their 4.7in weapons had been replaced by a QF weapon of the same calibre, *Nan Shui* was stricken in 1903 and broken

9. Wright, *Chinese Steam Navy*, pp 55–57.

10. Curiously, however, the German pair are alleged to have armour decks by *All the World's Fighting Ships 1900* (London: Sampson Low, Marston, 1900), p 42, and listed alongside a phantom Chinese-built sister, '*Fu Ching*' (see next note).

11. Allegedly named '*Hi-ying*', '*Yung-pao*', '*Foo-sing*' *and* '*Fu-ching*' (Wright, *Chinese Steam Navy*, p 57). The latter's existence as a sister of *Nan Thin* and *Nan Shui* was maintained not only by *Jane's* (see last note) but also into the 1970s in R Gardiner, R Chesneau and E M Kolesnik (eds), *Conway's All the World's Fighting Ships 1860–1905* (London: Conway Maritime Press, 1979), p 396. In reality, *Fu Ching* was a 1,000-ton torpedo gunboat, probably laid down under the name *Kuang Ting*, and launched in 1893 (Wright, *Chinese Steam Navy*, pp 70–73.

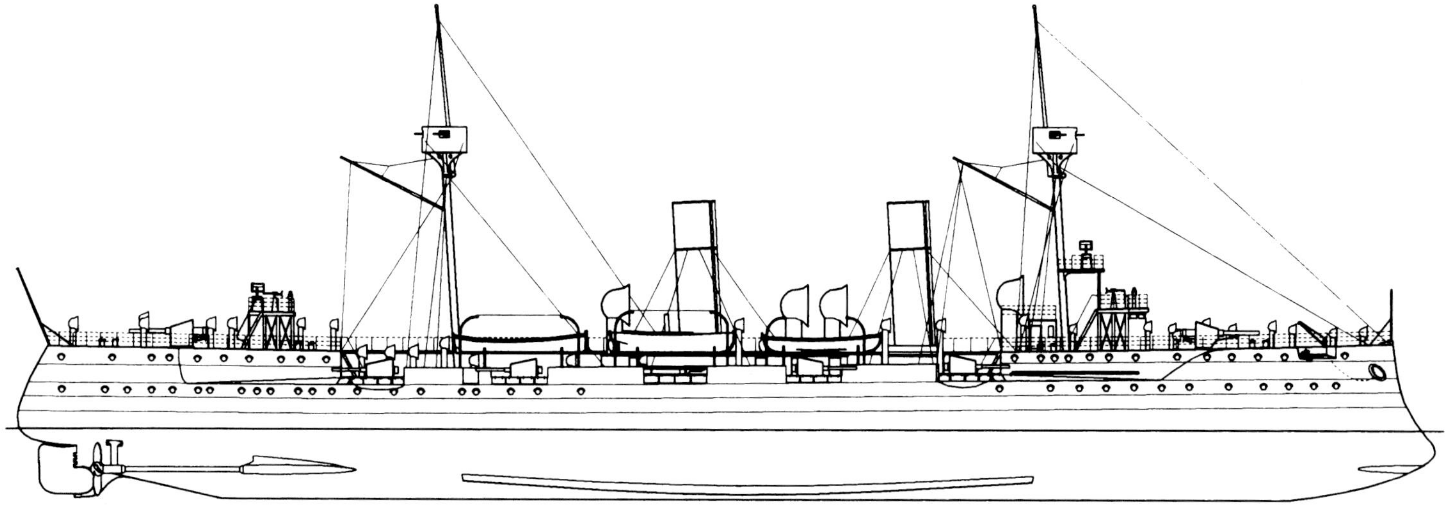

Top: 'As fitted' drawing of one of the *Hai Yung* class; all ships were identical. **Right:** *Hai Yung* with *Gneisenau* in the background just before the First World War. (*DN drawing/DN collection)*

up in 1906, while her sister had become a training hulk before 1900 and was scrapped in 1919.

The *Hai Yung* class

Soon after the termination of hostilities between China and Japan by the Treaty of Shimonoseki of April 1895, European firms saw a great potential market in once again rearming China. As early as the summer of 1895, the Vulcan yard sent two emissaries, the two technical directors Carl Jüngermann and Robert Zimmermann, to the Far East, to 'be there'. This pertinacity would indeed pay off the following year when, in May 1896 the former viceroy Li Hongzhang – now responsible for national military matters – announced a renewal of ship-building activities for the navy.[12]

At this time Li was in Europe as a special envoy to the coronation ceremonies of the new Emperor Nikolai II in Moscow on 14 May 1896, but found time to place a direct order for three protected cruisers with Vulcan's representatives Justus Flohr (1855–1933) and Louis Schwartz, who were 'coincidentally' also in the city. This oral order was eventually confirmed by an official written one from the Chinese government, which arrived at Stettin on 8 June. This required the first ship to be ready within fifteen months, the other two to follow three months later. The vessels were to displace 2,950 tonnes (full load), have a design speed of 19.5 knots and carry three 15cm/40 and eight 10.5cm/40 guns, plus four 45cm torpedo tubes.

The true origin of the specification remains somewhat obscure. It is likely that the Chinese government were simply accepting existing proposals from the shipyard, which may have been on a 'design to cost' basis to meet an available budget. This would explain why they were 1,300 tons smaller and more weakly armed than a pair of further cruisers, *Hai Chi* [*Haiqui*] and *Hai Tien* [*Haitian*]), which were ordered a few weeks later from Armstrong in the UK.[13]

In the – admittedly scanty – literature on this particular class of cruisers one finds the assumption that the design of the German-built ships might have been based on the Dutch *Holland* class, which, in turn, had been inspired by the British *Apollo* class.[14] However, this does not work chronologically, as both the Dutch and Chinese classes were built roughly in parallel and, in any case, apart from a generic resemblance, which they shared with a wide range of protected cruisers of the period, they only really had a main armament of 15cm Krupp guns in common – and even their respective numbers of guns was different. The Dutch ships were also nearly 1,000 tonnes larger. Rather, it is much more likely that Vulcan were aware of the prevailing thoughts and ideas within the OKM (i.e. those of Tirpitz) regarding the 'ideal' III. class cruiser, carrying as much armament as possible on a somewhat limited displacement.

The Chinese navy did not envisage any kind of 'true' cruiser

12. Contemporary sources indicate an aspiration for a five-year plan, to ultimately deliver six battleships, a dozen armoured cruisers and twenty second- and third-class cruisers.

13. The three German-built ships came out at a price of about 10 million Marks in total, while the two British ships came out at a total of about 13.7 million Marks (at the 1901 rate of exchange between the Mark and the Pound Sterling).

14. J Mulder and W F Ruygrok, *De Nederlandsche Zeemacht – Pantserschepen, Pantserdekschepen, Monitors* (Emmen: Lanasta, 2004), p 191.

warfare, only a small radius of action (2,100nm at 10 knots) being provided, with the machinery based around four heavy, but reliable, double-ended firetube boilers. The external profile of the *Hai Yung* class was distinctly German, with a nearly identical stern profile to *Hela* and *Gazelle*, but with a less pronounced stem than their German contemporaries, despite the fitting of a similar underwater bow torpedo tube. The abreast mounting of the forward pair of 15cm guns reinforced this impression. The vessels carried an armour deck 56mm thick fore and aft, thinning to 40mm amidships where, however, it was given 70mm slopes. A cork-filled cofferdam was seemingly intended to be provided, but not actually installed, above the deck slopes, while, as in the *Gazelle* class, armoured coamings were provided around hatchways. Additionally, the conning tower received 30mm nickel steel splinter protection, and the gun shields 50mm plate.

An interesting comparison between these privately designed vessels and the contemporary *Gazelle* and *Small Cruisers A* and *B* [*Nymphe* and *Niobe*] was prepared by Department 'A' at the behest of Tirpitz, and submitted on 14 May 1898. Key conclusions were that:

- The armament is slightly stronger, but consists of two different calibres.
- The armoured deck is slightly stronger, but no cork-filled cofferdam is provided. [sic!]
- Maximum speed is about 1.25 knots less.
- Accordingly, the overall military capabilities of *Hai Yung* are inferior, despite having a 305 tonnes higher displacement.[15]

While the exact keel laying dates of all three cruisers have apparently been lost, *Hai Yung* [*Hairong*] was launched on 15 September 1897. Her trials started on 14 April 1898 in the Pomeranian Bight, and ended on 4 May with the customary full-power trial, during which she attained a speed of 20.7 knots at 8,000ihp, which was well in excess of her 7,500ihp design power. After a final docking, the cruiser left Stettin for Swinemünde, where her hired German civilian crew boarded her for the voyage to China, which ended at Shanghai on 27 July.[16]

Meanwhile *Hai Shew* [*Haichou*] had been launched on 11 December 1897, although it was not until 15 December that she was free of the slip, as the grease on the slipway had become frozen. She commenced her trials at the beginning of June 1898, attaining 20.4 knots at full power. Her delivery voyage began on 15 June at Stettin, the ship arriving at Shanghai on 24 August.

Hai Chen [*Haichen*], the last of the trio, was launched on 12 February 1898. She commenced her trials one month later than *Hai Shew* and left for China on 22 July, arriving on 21 September. The delivery crews of all three vessels complained on their return about the exceptionally bad provisions provided and warned future crews against similar enterprises. One trimmer had died in the Red Sea of heatstroke.

All three cruisers shared their country's troubled history during the first four decades of the twentieth century. At the beginning of their career, during the Boxer Rebellion of 1900, they remained 'in the shade' and thus avoided capture, albeit closely watched by the interventionist powers. Then, on 25 May 1901 the commander of the Russian Pacific Ocean Squadron, VAdm Evgeni Ivanovich Alekseev (1843–1917), reported that he had received news from the naval attaché in Japan, Kapitan 2. ranga Aleksandr Ivanovich Rusin (1861-1955), that the Chinese government wished to secretly sell its five most modern cruisers – the *Hai Yung* and *Hai Chi* classes.[17] When this was reported to the Emperor Nikolai II, he suggested to his Minister of Finance, Sergei Iulyevich Vitte (1849–1915) that, rather than buy them for cash, Russia might be able to prevail on the Chinese to transfer the *Hai Yung* class as a means of paying off some of the indemnity owed to Russia as a consequence of the Boxer Rebellion. One assumes that the preference for the German-built trio (only) may have been owing to their relative ease of assimilation into the Russian fleet, given that German yards (including Vulcan) were already in the process of delivering cruisers to Russia.

On 4 June 1901, Rusin reported from Japan that the Japanese had purchased the *Hai Yung* class from China, but on 28 September telegraphed that the transaction had not occurred after all. Having been informed that the asking price for the three German-built ships was £680,000 Sterling (about 6.5 million Roubles), Vitte, following consultation with the Director of the Russian Naval Ministry, proposed to the Chinese authorities that Russia pay 4 million yuan (about 5.6 million Roubles), including commission, with half to be paid in cash, half credited against the outstanding indemnity. Alekseev, whose fleet they would join, was content that this was a fair price, given their condition. However, the Chinese responded with a demand for 5 million yuan in cash, plus a 0.25 million yuan commission, amounting to more than 7 million Roubles, which was rejected by Russia as excessive, especially in view of the need to refit the ships to allow them to be integrated into the Russian navy.

Hai Yung was sent on an extended cruise around East Asia in 1906, to show the flag to the many Chinese living in that area. All three ships were employed to some degree during the 1911 civil war, when *Hai Yung* being flagship of Admiral Sah Chen-

15. RM3/3697 fol. 70f.

16. Norddeutscher Lloyd (NDL) provided the three captains (Woltemas, Pollack and Krebs) for the delivery voyages, while the crews were hired by agents in the normal manner.

17. V Ia Krest'ianinov, *Kreisera Rossiiskogo imperatorskogo flota 1856–1917 gody*, I (St Petersburg: Galeia Print, 2009), pp 198–99.

ping [Sa Zhenbing]. She shelled rebel positions along the Yangtze on several occasions, albeit with little effect, before defecting to the victorious rebels. During the second revolution in 1913, all three cruisers bombarded positions of the Kuomintang party at the Woosung forts near Shanghai. On 24 April 1916, *Hai Yung* made headlines when she collided with the troop transport *Hsin Yu* in the South China Sea and sank it with the loss of some 1,000 lives.

The ageing cruisers continued to serve in the navy of the Republic of China after the First World War, *Hai Yung* initially taking a small part in the support of White Russian forces at Vladivostok in 1919. Overhauled and slightly modernised during the 1920s, the vessels were ultimately earmarked as potential blockships in the Yangtze river should Japan attempt to assault China's then capital, Nanking [Nanjing]. On 25 August 1937, when the Japanese threat became a reality, all three cruisers (plus their surviving Armstrong-built contemporary *Hai Chi*) were scuttled at Jiangyin, 150km northwest of Shanghai, joining the eight small warships, twenty-three merchantmen and 189 junks, sampans and pontoons that had been sunk there on the 12th. The wrecks remained in the river for more than twenty years, until they were finally cleared. The salvage of *Hai Yung*'s wreck was completed on 25 April 1959, that of *Hai Chen* in 1960 and *Hai Shew*'s in 1964; *Hai Chi*, whose wreck had been blown up by the Japanese in 1940, was raised and scrapped during 1959–60.

RUSSIA[18]

The accession of the Emperor Nikolai II on 1 November 1894 led to a new impetus towards increasing Russian naval strength in the Far East, in particular in the wake of China's defeat in the Sino-Japanese War, and the destruction of much of its navy at the Battle of the Yalu. Although Japan's triumph had been blunted by the 'Triple Intervention' of Russia, Germany and France, which had reversed a key territorial element of the Treaty of Shimonoseki, this was in exchange for the Chinese paying an even higher indemnity than had originally been imposed. Nearly half of the money was allocated to an expansion of the Japanese navy,[19] already swelled by the surviving remnants of the Chinese fleet, including *Tsi Yuen* and *Chen Yuen*.

Therefore, although the Russian 1895 programme focussed on strengthening the Baltic Fleet against Germany, it included the long-range, hybrid battleship-cruisers of the *Peresvet* class and the big armoured cruiser *Gromoboi* – the third of its kind – all capable of Far East/Pacific operations, and aimed at a potential conflict with the UK. Nevertheless, pressure grew for the acquisition of ships specifically to confront the emerging Japanese fleet, in parallel with arguments that Baltic defences might be better served by torpedo craft and coastal defence installations, rather than big ships, thus freeing resources for the Far East.

The seizure of Tsingtau by Germany in November 1897 raised stakes in the region. As a result of China offering them basing facilities for the duration of the crisis caused by the seizure, on 27 March 1898 the Russians secured a twenty-five-year lease of the Liaotung peninsula, including Port Arthur (which had been denied to the Japanese by the Triple Intervention). In parallel, discussions towards the next Russian naval programme concluded that the balance of resources should indeed be shifted towards the Far East, with a fleet originally planned to be headed by no fewer than ten battleships and twenty-five cruisers (some redeployed from the Baltic) by 1903 (later pushed back to 1905). The prevailing doctrine at the time was that each battleship would be supported by two or three scouting craft (first and/or second-class cruisers). After considerable discussions, the 1898 naval programme 'for the needs of the Far East' was established. This was refined in early 1899 down from the originally envisaged eight new construction battleships, six first-class and ten second-class cruisers to five, four and four of each type, respectively. Owing to insufficient Russian yard capacity, the first cruisers could be built abroad, although follow-on vessels would be built at home.

To this end, basic requirements for such ships were developed. The first-class type was envisaged as being of a protected cruiser of no more than 6,000 tons, with a dozen each of 6in/45[20] and 75mm/50 guns, six 15in torpedo tubes, 23 knots speed at forced draught, 20 knots at natural draught, using Belleville boilers, and with a range of around 5,000nm at 10 knots. In essence it was a faster and more heavily armed version of the three Russian-built *Diana* class, laid down in July (*Pallada* and *Diana*) and October 1896 (*Aurora*). As a general model, the British-built Japanese cruisers *Asama* and *Tokiwa* were cited (although these both had side armour, four 8in guns, and were nearly 4,000 tons larger!)

Its second-class counterpart would have the same range, displace 3,000 tons, and carry six 4.7in and six 75mm guns, plus six torpedo tubes at 25 knots. Invitations to tender were issued in April 1898 to foreign and domestic shipbuilders for both types of cruiser, although the second-class competition was an 'unofficial' one, with specifications issued to a range of yards, but there was no formal announcement of a competition.

The US firm of William Cramp at Philadelphia had been in informal discussions with the Russians over prospective construction work for some time when the specification was issued, and managed to obtain the direct award of a contract

18. For these ships, see in particular S McLaughlin, *Russian and Soviet Cruisers to 1960* (Barnsley: Seaforth, in preparation); we are most grateful to Mr McLaughlin for the provision of draft copies of the relevant chapters, and Sergei Vinogradov for additional material and comments. During the period in question, Russia remained on the Julian calendar, then some two weeks behind the Gregorian used elsewhere in Europe: to avoid confusion, all dates are given in Gregorian terms.

19. H Lengerer, 'The Genesis of the Six-Six Fleet', *Warship* [XLI] (2019), p 46.

20. Initially, it was planned to include a pair of 8in chase guns, but General-Admiral Grand Duke Alexei Alexandrovich (head of the Naval Department) ordered them to be removed, in favour of a mono-calibre main armament.

against the first-class specification on 23 April 1898, for what became *Varyag* – along with a battleship, *Retvizan*.[21] Interestingly, when ranked against the other bids submitted (for purposes of comparison only) the Cramp design was placed fifth out of six.

Of the other proposals, the first one to arrive, in May 1898, was from Ansaldo of Italy; they were prepared to use Belleville boilers, although their own preference was for Niclausse. Next came that from Germania, and then Schichau and Howaldt on 3 July. When formally assessed on 15 July 1898, first place was awarded to the Germania design, as having the smallest displacement, providing the greatest cruising range, of up to 6,500nm with a coal supply of 1,100 tons, and the greatest thickness of the deck armour.

Schichau came second,[22] Ansaldo third, Howaldt fourth, with sixth place going to the Nevskii Works of Russia. Following this ranking, a contract for the Germania design (to become *Askold*) was signed on 16 August 1898. However, seventeen days after the selection had been agreed, two more designs arrived, one from Vulcan, and one from London & Glasgow. The latter was soon rejected, but the Vulcan vessel was placed ahead of the recently ordered Germania offering. Accordingly, a contract was agreed on 17 August for what would become *Bogatyr*, just one day after that for *Askold*.

As far as the second-class cruisers were concerned, the first bid received came from Howaldt, followed in June by ones from Ansaldo, Germania and Schichau, and in July from London & Glasgow and the Nevskii Works. At the 15 July assessment meeting, the Schichau offering was placed first, followed in order by Germania, Nevskii Works, Howaldtswerke, and Ansaldo; London & Glasgow had already been ruled out. A contract was thus signed with Schichau on 17 August 1898, with the ship to be ready for trials within twenty-five months. Although Nevskii's bid, a design prepared by the former British chief constructor Sir Edward Reed (1830–1906), had been rejected, they appealed to be allowed to submit a revised design; nevertheless, the award of the contract to Schichau went ahead.

However, as no deadline had ever been announced for the competition, further tenders arrived in early 1899, from Laird Brothers, Chantiers de la Gironde and Burmeister & Wain. Although these firms were informed that the contract had now been let, the Russian navy was directed to order a ship from the Danish Burmeister & Wain yard, generally assumed to be the result of lobbying by the Empress-Dowager Maria Feodorovna (née Princess Dagmar of Denmark). The move may also, however, have been to avoid having all of the new cruisers built in Germany. *Boyarin* was ordered in April 1899, although the design, inferior to that of the Schichau vessel in numerous ways, including speed, was more expensive.

21. For which see S McLaughlin, 'Retvisan: An American Battleship for the Tsar', *Warship* XXIII (2000), pp 48–66.

22. Complimented for its strong armament of two turreted 8in, eight 6in, four 4.7in and sixteen 47mm guns.

Bogatyr

Early in the conversion of the Vulcan bid into a workable design, and as a result of changes required by the Russians, it was clear that the vessel would be heavier than originally envisaged, early compensation including the reduction of the planned military masts to poles, moderate thinning of vertical armour and the omission of the aft conning tower. In the end, despite all weight reductions and compensations, the displacement necessary to produce a viable design rose from 6,000 to 6,750 tons. Delays were occasioned in particular by changes in the deck armour and confusion over who should design the ship's turrets, finally resolved by their being provided by the Russian authorities. Inevitably, the contractual delivery date slipped from early 1901, first to the end of the year and then to the spring of 1902. Having been laid down in December 1899 and launched on 30 January 1901, *Bogatyr* ran her first steam trials in December 1901, being finally handed over in May 1902. Her official trials commenced on 20 June, during which the cruiser attained an average speed of 23.45 knots on the measured mile, developing 20,161ihp.

The ship was of conventional form for a cruiser of the time, with a raised forecastle and poop, and in some ways an enlarged version of the *Hai Yung* class. However, the four embrasured main guns were enclosed in armoured casemates and her chase guns were mounted in twin armoured turrets, leaving just four in open shields. The 75mm guns were widely distributed in the hull and superstructure, as were eight 47mm/43 Hotchkiss weapons. Contrary to the original specification, only four torpedo tubes were fitted, the bow and stern ones being omitted, leaving two trainable above-water and two submerged broadside tubes. Protection was provided by a full-length armour deck (35mm thick, 70mm on slopes), with the tops of the engine cylinders protected by an 85mm glacis. There was also a waterline cofferdam, intended to be filled with cellulose, but completed empty, owing to its reported ineffectiveness, and coal bunkers over the armour deck slopes.

Although Belleville boilers had been specified, it was agreed that Normand units could be used, sixteen of them exhausting through three funnels, one for each boiler room; the forward one contained only four boilers, the others six each. These supplied steam to two 4-cylinder vertical triple expansion engines, which comfortably made the contracted speed of 23 knots on trials. In service, *Bogatyr* was regarded as a reliable steamer, and it was her design (rather than that of the Germania or Cramp vessels) which was used for the Russian-built follow-on first-class cruisers (for which see below).

Bogatyr went to the Far East on completion, and was based at Vladivostok during the Russo-Japanese War. Unfortunately, she was damaged by running aground on 15 May 1904, not being

Bogatyr as completed (right), and a set of drawings first published in the journal *Zeitschrift des Vereins deutscher Ingenieure*, who later licensed it to other publications, including *Engineering*. *(AD collection/DN collection)*

salvaged until a month later, and was under repair until June 1905. She then returned to the Baltic, arriving in March 1906. She spent much of the next few years on cadet training cruises in the Baltic and further afield, including to the Mediterranean. Early in the First World War *Bogatyr* was fitted to carry mines, and was rearmed during the winter of 1916–17, emerging with sixteen 130mm guns, with all smaller guns (except four 7.62mm weapons) and above-water torpedo tubes taken out.

Following the Bolshevik seizure of power, she was placed in reserve at Kronshtadt in May 1918, and later disarmed to free her guns for use on river vessels. She was sold for scrap to the Soviet-German firm Derumetall on 1 July 1922, and towed to Germany to be broken up at Bremen at the end of the year. Engine components had previously been removed to repair her Black Sea sister *Komintern* (ex-*Pamiyat Merkuriya*, ex-*Kagul* – see below).

The Russian-built sisters

The original plan was that one sister would be built for the Baltic, plus two for the Black Sea Fleet, which at that time possessed only one cruiser, the 3,000-ton unprotected *Pamiat Merkuriya*, launched in France back in 1879. However, a flaw in the contract with Vulcan meant that the Russians were not permitted to share *Bogatyr*'s drawings with other shipbuilders, meaning that negotiations and an additional fee to the German firm were necessary to make construction in Russia possible.

In the meantime, the Baltic Works had developed their own alternative design to the planned repeat *Bogatryr*s, which was, however, rejected, and on 12 January 1900 the building of a ship of the Vulcan design at the Galernyi Island yard was authorised. Around the same time, the construction of the Black Sea vessels at the Lazarevskoe Admiralty (Sevastopol) and Nikolaev Admiralty yards was formally proposed. However, it soon became clear that modifications would be needed as a result of converting measurements from metric to the system of British Imperial feet and inches (used in Russia since the time of Peter the Great) and matching structural items to those available from Russian suppliers, resulting in a complex process to provide the three Russian yards with workable drawings. This was exacerbated by changes in the detailed design of *Bogatyr* herself.

Any new drawing produced by Vulcan was first handed over to the Russian resident constructor at the Stettin yard, who transmitted it to the resident commanding officer of *Bogatyr* for approval. He would then send it to the Technical Council of the Russian Main Administration of Shipbuilding (MTK) at St Petersburg, which then sent the drawing, via the Main Administration of Shipbuilding and Equipment (GUKiS), to the head of the St Petersburg naval port. The latter eventually passed it to the New Admiralty shipyard for copying. Copies then went back to the Naval Ministry, who forwarded them to CinC Black Sea, at Sevastopol. He, in turn, distributed copies via the respective chief constructors at Sevastopol and Nikolaev to the constructors responsible for the construction of the Black Sea pair. All involved in the process were invited to make comments or propose alterations to the drawings. It is thus little wonder that several complaints arose regarding the precision of the final drawings, not least regarding translations from metric to Imperial units.[23]

It was accordingly not until 3 November 1900 that the construction of *Vitiaz* could be begun at Galernyi Island (officially laid down 3 June 1901, although actually begun on 3 November 1900), with *Ochakov* (Sevastopol) and *Kagul* (i – Nikolaev) begun in March 1901 (officially laid down 26 August [actually begun 12 March] and 5 September 1901, respectively). However, on 13 June 1901, a fire broke out in the wooden ship house within which *Vitiaz* was being built, and the hull (already 40 per cent complete) was damaged beyond repair. A replacement, to be named *Oleg*, was ordered only ten days later from the New Admiralty yard, but could not be begun until after the launch of the battleship *Borodino* on 14 November. The use of drawings and materials assembled for the unfortunate *Vitiaz* (including the casting for her stem-post) allowed work to move forward quickly, the official laying down occurring on 19 July 1902. Modifications being incorporated into *Bogatyr* by her designers at Stettin were built into the Russian-built ships, which also had their above-water torpedo tubes deleted and the spaces under the forward turret rearranged to improve ammunition stowage, and to install two of the ship's dynamos. Other changes from the prototype included the use of steering gear of the type previously used in the *Diana* class, some modifications to the casemate armour, a slight enlargement of the conning tower, a modified drainage system, improved magazine ventilation and more extensive voice piping.

Oleg was launched on 27 August 1903, after which her machinery was installed by the Franco-Russian Works. Fitting out was accelerated after the outbreak of war with Japan, with basin trials run in May 1904. Sea trials began in September, and were completed in October, albeit abbreviated owing to machinery defects, in particular a cracked cylinder. She sailed for the Far East on 16 November 1904, in company with the likewise new cruiser *Izumrud*, the destroyers *Groznyi*, *Gromkii* and *Rezvyi*, and the auxiliary cruisers *Rion* and *Dnepr*. They joined the main force at Madagascar in February 1905. On passage, *Oleg* suffered further machinery problems, which would only be resolved after her return to the Baltic in 1906. At the Battle of Tsushima in 1905 she suffered a number of hits, and was one of the three cruisers that sought internment at Manila on 3 June. She returned to the Baltic in March 1906.

The two Black Sea ships were launched on 2 June (*Kagul* [i]) and 4 October (*Ochakov*) 1902, and in spite of giving up some material to speed the completion of *Oleg*, were approaching completion during 1905. However, on 24 November, *Ochakov*, while still on trials, was seized by mutineers at Sevastopol during the final phase of the 1905 Revolution, becoming the 'flagship' of the uprising's leader, Pyotr Petrovich Schmidt (1867–1906). During the suppression of the revolt on the 28th, the cruiser was badly damaged by gunfire from shore batteries, supplemented by a few rounds from the battleship *Rostislav*. The cruiser was hit fifty-two times and burned for two days. She was renamed *Kagul* (ii) on 7 April 1907, her sister receiving the name *Pamiat Merkuriya* from the recently decommissioned old ship of the name.[24] Extensive repairs lasted until the ship finally entered service on 23 June 1909, delayed by a shortage of resources and funds.

23. H Pinl, *Deutsch-russischer Schiffbau vor 1914* (Langenhagen: BoD, 2002), p 147.

24. The name itself recalled the sailing brig *Mercuria*, which had in 1829 held her own against two Turkish ships-of-the-line. Emperor Nikolai I had made the ship a 'guards' vessel and ordered that there always be a '*Pamiat Merkuriya*' on the navy list, a tradition that lasted until 1917.

Pamiat Merkuriya's entry into service was also delayed, proposals being made in the interim to add two 6in and four 4.7in guns in lieu of six 75mm weapons; these were finally rejected in September 1907 to avoid further delays. Later suggestions for improving the class by removing all unprotected guns and adding a 90mm belt were also not taken forward. Conversely, *Oleg* lost four 75mm and four 47mm guns during her 1906–08 refit, when her bridgework was also modified; a plan to add a belt was frustrated by a lack of funds. She spent much of 1909–10 in the Mediterranean, an enlarged conning tower being then fitted during 1910–11; the ship was also reboilered.

Modifications during the First World War began with *Oleg* receiving mine rails, followed by the replacement of her 75mm guns with six 130mm/55 in June 1915. Her 6in guns were taken out during January/March 1916, and replaced by ten 130mm weapons, her AA battery being increased to two 75mm and two 47mm, while some of her boilers were retubed. *Kagul* (ii) had been due to be rearmed in 1914, but it was not until March/April 1915 she had four 75mm guns replaced by 6in weapons, a change also made in *Pamiat Merkuriya*. A proposal that the twin turrets be replaced by single 8in mountings was overtaken by a full rearmament with 130mm guns, although only *Kagul* had been altered (during September/October 1916) before the 1917 Revolution; in contrast to the Baltic ships, the turrets were replaced by single guns.

Oleg was taken over by Red forces in November 1917, and served with them until torpedoed off Kronstadt by the British motor torpedo boat *CMB4* on 17 June 1919. Some guns were salvaged, the wreck being finally refloated in 1938 and broken up.

Pamiat Merkuriya was briefly under the Ukrainian flag in November 1917, before opting for the Reds in February 1918. Laid up at Sevastopol in March, she was captured by the Germans on 1 May and used as an accommodation ship. In November she was taken over by Anglo-French forces and stripped of all guns other than those of her twin turrets in February 1919. Her engines were disabled with explosives by the British on their evacuation between 22 and 24 April. *Pamiat Merkuriya* was then captured successively by Red and White troops, and left behind when the latter evacuated the Crimea in November 1920. She became part of the new Red Fleet in 1921 and was used as an immobile training ship for petty officers from the summer of 1922, although in poor condition, and significantly waterlogged, including the machinery spaces.

Docked for repairs in September 1922, *Pamiat Merkuriya*'s engines were repaired using cylinders from *Bogatyr* and material from the battleships *Evstafii* and *Ioann Zlatoust*, with ten boilers made serviceable and her previous main armament reinstalled; two submerged torpedo tubes were removed. Renamed *Komintern* on 31 December 1922, she ran trials in June 1923 and returned to service on 7 November as a seagoing training ship, making a number of cruises.

Her forward boiler room was converted to classrooms in 1930, reducing her to six working boilers, although the redundant forefunnel was for the time being retained. Her turrets were replaced with single 130mm mountings, and six other 130mm guns replaced by four 75mm weapons, giving her eight main guns. Now purely a training ship, she served as such until 1941, when she was refitted as a minelayer, carrying up to 160 mines, finally losing her forefunnel, and gaining an enhanced anti-aircraft battery.

On active service after the German invasion, her AA armament was further improved in May 1942, but after German bomb damage at Novorossiisk on 2 July and Poti on the 6th, she was disarmed at Tuapse during August/September, before returning to Poti and being sunk as a blockship at the mouth of Khobi River on 10 October. Stricken on 2 February 1943, the hull was used to mount an anti-torpedo boat battery in 1946; the wreck remains in situ.

Kagul (ii) became the White *General Kornilov* in September 1919, sailing with the bulk of the White fleet from the Crimea on evacuation on 14 November 1920. She was interned with her companions at Bizerte on 29 December, and although her return to the Soviet Union was discussed, along with that of the battleship *General Alekséev* (ex-*Volia*, ex-*Imperator Aleksandr III*), in 1924, she remained in French hands and was sold for scrap at the end of the 1920s, being broken up at Brest in 1933.

Askold

Construction of the Germania vessel began before drawings had been approved by the Russians, and was well advanced on the slip by November 1898. Thus, when concerns were raised in a number of areas and major revisions required, significant dismantling would have been needed for their implementation. However, compromises were reached by the end of January 1899 and the drawings approved, including placing the forward gun on an extension of the superstructure to reduce wetness, which did indeed prove to be a problem in service.

A shipyard fire in April damaged equipment, and slipped the delivery date to 18 April 1901, with the yard adding manpower after her launch on 15 March 1900 to ensure on-time completion. Builders' trials began on 24 April 1901. This showed vibration that required reinforcement of the superstructure and hull plating aft, although vibration towards the stern remained an issue in service. Interestingly, as Germania then lacked docking facilities to investigate the problem and finish the bottom painting, *Askold* had to transit the Kiel Canal under the German merchant flag for dry docking at Blohm & Voss at Hamburg in June 1901.

Her trials continued for several months, during which she ran the mile in September 1901. After a first unsuccessful result, reaching only 21.85 knots at average, on a second attempt on 19 September – employing specialist stokers and specially ordered Welsh steam coal – she managed an average of 23.39 knots, having touched 23.83 knots. The marginal nature of such speeds and their achievement is shown by a discussion between Germania and the Russian trials commission, who had requested an extension of the ship's rigging prior to the trials, which Germania successfully refused by arguing that the resulting extra wind drag during the high-speed trials might have sufficient negative impact on speed to make penalties possible! *Askold* finally commissioned on 25 January 1902, and arrived at Libau on the morning of 11 February 1902.

Unlike *Bogatyr*, *Askold* carried all her twelve 6in guns – one forward, one aft, and the rest on the beam – in mountings with a 25mm splinter-protected shield only. Her twelve 75mm/50 weapons were all on the battery deck, the four at the bow and the stern in sponsons, with the eight 47mm guns distributed around the superstructure and the pair of 37mm just abaft the fifth funnel. There were fixed submerged bow, stern and beam 381mm torpedo tubes – the latter pair installed between the boiler and engine rooms – plus a pair of trainable ones at battery deck level, and the ship had the capacity for thirty-five mines, laid via a raft that was stored dismantled. Protection was based around a 40mm deck, with 75mm slopes, with a 100mm glacis over the cylinder heads, with cofferdams along the sides; as in *Bogatyr*, their intended cellulose filling was not actually installed.

The nine boilers were placed in five boiler rooms (the foremost holding only one boiler), each with its own funnel, giving her a unique appearance. Originally designed with four funnels (like *Varyag*), the fifth was added as a result of a rearrangement of boiler rooms. Three engines were installed, with the option of economical cruising on the centre shaft only; the wing engines were installed in the forward of the two engine rooms. As noted above, initial trials showed vibration problems, but the ship exceeded her contract speed and proved reliable in service. Her actual range came out at 4,100nm at 10 knots.

Askold arrived at Kronstadt in April 1902, and left for the Far East on completion of final fitting out on 16 September, arriving at Port Arthur on 26 February 1903 in company with the battleships *Peresvet* and *Petropavlovsk*. During the outbound voyage, *Askold* called at several ports in the Persian Gulf, legend having it that the local inhabitants were so much impressed by her five funnels that the British Admiralty decided to send out a cruiser with a higher number of funnels (enhanced by 'dummies') to restore its own reputation. During the siege of Port Arthur by the Japanese during the last months of 1904, two 75mm and two 47mm guns were removed, the ship then taking part in the Battle of the Yellow Sea on 10 August 1904. Engaged by the Japanese armoured cruisers *Asama* and *Yakumo* (the latter also Vulcan-built), she received four underwater and six above-water hits, with the aft two funnels badly damaged, having eight main guns disabled, and eleven crew dead. Loss of boiler draught reduced *Askold*'s speed to 15 knots, requiring the ship to seek internment at Shanghai.

She remained in the Far East after the war, departing Shanghai on 11 October 1905, reaching Vladivostok on 1

Askold running builders' trials in Kiel fjord in 1901 before her delivery to the Russian navy. *(DN collection)*

November, where she spent 1906 under repair and refit, with the above-water torpedo tubes removed. In 1908 she became the flagship of the Siberian Flotilla, but machinery defects restricted her service until her boilers were retubed and her engines overhauled during a major refit at Vladivostok from January 1911 to November 1912, during which her remaining torpedo outfit was reduced to just the two submerged tubes. Another major part of the refit was the installation of trim tanks, formed from the cofferdams outboard boiler rooms 4 and 5. Until then, any heeling moment could only be compensated for by adjusting water levels in either the port or starboard boilers. This procedure might have been moderately effective in firetube boilers, which contained a large amount of water, but would have been ineffective and dangerous with watertube units.

With the departure of the German cruiser squadron to the eastern Pacific and capture of Tsingtau in late 1914, *Askold* was transferred to the Mediterranean in November of that year, operating in Syrian waters under British and French control, and then in the Dardanelles, where she served as relay ship for communications with the Russian Black Sea Fleet, as well as engaging in bombardments. She began a refit at Toulon on 3 February 1916, during which, at 03.00 on 1 September, she suffered an explosion in the 75mm magazine, followed by a fire that, fortunately, did not detonate the shells and propellant. This was assessed as sabotage, with four sailors sentenced to death and the ship's captain dismissed from his post.

Askold was transferred to the Arctic Flotilla on 9 December 1916, whence she sailed on 8 January, via a two-week stay at Gibraltar, and hull and boiler tube work at Devonport. She finally arrived at the Kola Inlet on 30 June 1917. During these refits, two 47mm guns were removed and two French 47mm and two British 6pdr AA guns fitted.

Murmansk was occupied by British forces in March 1918, and on 12 June *Askold* was taken over by them. She commissioned as the depot ship HMS *Glory IV* (the battleship *Glory* being the British station-ship in the White Sea) at Murmansk, being moved to Archangel on the 19th, and remaining there until 31 October, when she returned to Murmansk; she then proceeded to the UK and paid off on the Clyde on 16 April 1919. In 1921 the ship was inspected by a Soviet commission and handed over to the Soviet authorities; she was immediately sold to Derumetall for scrapping at Hamburg.

Novik

The design of the second-class ship, which was soon named *Novik*, resembled in many ways that of a huge destroyer with, as in such vessels, half of her length taken up by machinery. It also meant that accommodation space was tight, especially for the ordinary seamen. Her armament was to be supplied by the Russians, the six 4.7in/45 guns being arranged fore and aft and on the beam. The forward gun had its shield removed following delivery to help remedy a lack of visibility from the conning tower, which had been fitted aft of the bridge. Four of the 47mm guns were located on the upper deck in the waist of the ship, the other two on the forecastle abreast the conning tower, with the two 37mm weapons on the wings of the after bridge. The original requirements had called for six above-water torpedo tubes, but in April 1899 the bow tube was deleted from the specification. The broadside tubes had limited training arcs.

The armour deck extended over the whole length of the ship, the slopes extending to 1.25m below the waterline. The cylinder heads extended above the armour deck, and so were protected by a glacis. *Novik*'s three engines were arranged in two separate compartments, separated by the aft boiler rooms, the wing engines being in the forward compartment. They were fed by a dozen watertube boilers, in six boiler rooms, each pair sharing a funnel.

Work began immediately, albeit slowly at first, owing to delays in steel deliveries, but by the official keel-laying ceremony on 13 March 1900, the hull had already been completed up to the armour deck. During construction, minor changes were made to the design at the direction of the Russian supervising constructor, who was also unimpressed by attempts to hurry trials following delays caused by the harsh winter of 1900–01. These were subject to a number of problems, with four of the eight sea trials during May to September 1901 being cut short as a result of engine breakdowns or propeller damage. During a trial run in October, the plating of the upper deck was seen to undulate at high speed, a symptom of chronic vibration issues. Blistering was also noted at the propeller shafts, which therefore had to be replaced over the winter of 1901–02. Several attempts were made to reduce vibration by making changes to the propellers, success being achieved by reducing the diameter of the centre screw and increasing that of the wing examples, to harmonise the revolutions of the three engines. During her acceptance trials on 6 May 1902, *Novik* achieved an average speed of 25.08 knots, at 17,789ihp, making her the fastest cruiser in the world. The original contract deadline of September 1900 was extended to 18 December 1900 owing to Russian change requests, but even so, the ship was delivered three months late; however, no penalties were imposed, the ship being judged a success.

Novik arrived at Kronstadt on 31 May 1902, and left for the Far East on 27 September, arriving at Port Arthur on 15 April 1903. During the Russo-Japanese War's Battle of the Yellow Sea on 10 August 1904 she was hit three times, became separated from the Russian squadron and went to Tsingtau for coal, stopping to top up at Korsakovsk on Sakhalin, while attempting to make Vladivostok. She was, however, caught there on 20 August by the Japanese cruiser *Tsushima*, which hit her five times, including thrice below water, damaging her rudder. Although *Novik* thus managed to make *Tsushima* temporarily break off the engagement, the latter was soon joined by *Chitose*, forcing *Novik* to scuttle at Korsakovsk.

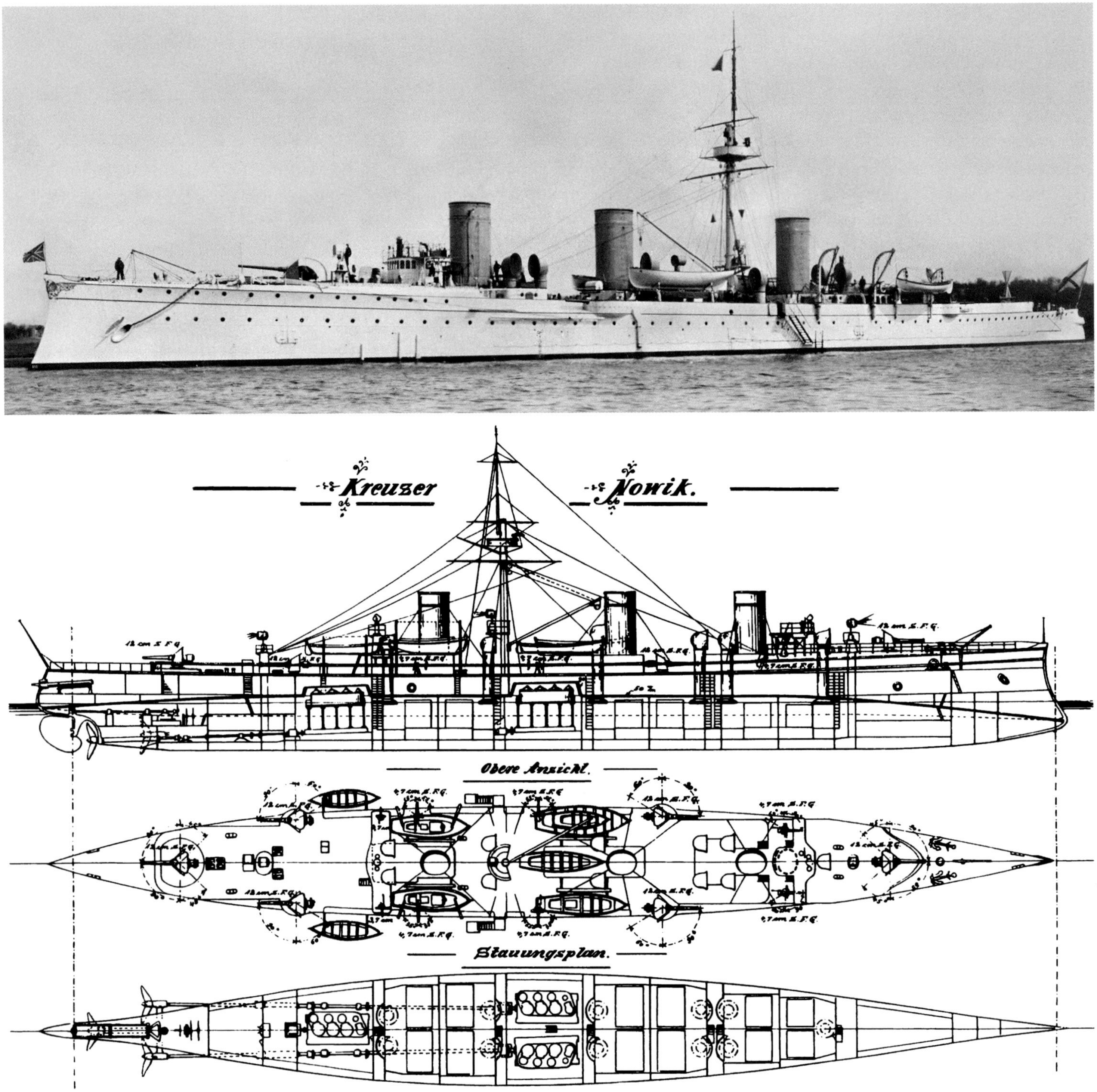

Novik as completed, and a set of drawings from the German journal *Schiffbau*. This gives a good impression of the major characteristics of the ship, in particular how much of the hull's volume was taken up by machinery. *(AD collection/DN collection)*

Captured by the Japanese on 21 July 1905, the wreck was raised on 16 July 1906 and repaired at Yokosuka, being renamed *Suzuya*. The original boilers were replaced by Miyabara units, the forward two boiler rooms and their funnel being deleted, as was the central engine, reducing her speed to 20 knots. New Armstrong-pattern 6in/50 weapons initially replaced the fore and aft guns, and the waist guns by 4.7in examples of the same pattern. In 1908, soon after recommissioning, she was rearmed again with 4.7in guns fore and aft and four 3in/40 in the waist. She was stricken 1 April 1913 and scrapped.

The Russian-built sisters

While *Novik* was still under construction, the Nevskii Works had continued to press their second-class cruiser design, again revised, on the Russian authorities. This remained unacceptable, but delays in the 1898 programme meant that the early ordering of further vessels was needed to achieve the target fleet strength. Accordingly, it was decided to have the under-employed Nevskii Yard build a pair of repeat *Novik*s. Obtaining drawings suitable for this purpose proved a problem, however, as these were in part being developed as *Novik* was built; also, the Russian and German versions of the contract differed over the contractor's obligations as to the provision of constructional drawings to the Russian authorities for repeat vessels.

Negotiations dragged on through 1900, with Schichau proposing to release the drawings if they received the order for the machinery for the two Nevskii ships, or a second ship – or a number of torpedo boats. This was rejected by the Russians in the autumn, but at the same time a set of drawings was brought to Russia by one of the Russian constructors working on the ship at Schichau. These, together with copies of drawings sent to the Russian authorities by Schichau for approval, were the basis for the two repeat *Novik*s that were ordered from the Nevskii Works on 20 April 1900. However, a draft contract was not issued until 9 February 1901, and final agreement not reached until 5 October. By then, 'proper' drawings had finally been extracted from Schichau, albeit without a compensatory order, in spite of press reports in July 1901 and February 1902 of a repeat or improved *Novik* having been ordered from the German yard.

The two Nevskii ships, *Zhemchug* and *Izumrud*, would not, however, be exact copies of *Novik*. While working through the drawings, it became apparent to the Nevskii constructors that the ships would come out 100 tons under design displacement; a number of modifications were therefore proposed to utilise the 'spare' tonnage. One was to increase the beam by 0.6m to allow the extension of the double bottom up to the armour deck, at the cost of 1 knots in speed. This was not, however, taken forward.

Sixteen Yarrow boilers replaced the dozen Schichau-Thornycroft units fitted in *Novik*, requiring significant internal rearrangement and slight reduction in maximum bunkerage. The two forward boiler rooms each held two units, the after pair three; in-service experience in *Novik* required additional ventilation fans to be fitted. In addition, the issues revealed during *Novik*'s trials resulted in a number of structural enhancements, adding 55 tons, while disconnecting couplings were fitted to the wing shafts, allowing the propellers to windmill when steaming on the centre engine alone, thus theoretically enhancing fuel economy – although in practice this was not the case. Fitting wood rather than linoleum on the upper deck added 24 tons, while increasing the protection of the uptakes added yet further weight, as did the fitting of fore and mizzenmasts to enhance flag signalling, following in-service experience with *Novik*. All this resulted in around ⅓ knot loss of speed, an extra 30cm immersion and degraded sea-keeping. Another early modification was the deletion of the torpedo tubes and stowage for mines – although the forward pair and stern tube were reinstated in April 1904.

Construction was accelerated following the outbreak of the Russo-Japanese War, as well as an enhancement of the ships' armaments. The addition of two more 4.7in guns had already been proposed during 1903 by *Zhemchug*'s prospective captain, and this was approved on 17 April 1904, although more radical changes were also considered. The weapons needed were sourced from those taken out from the armoured cruiser *Dmitri Donskoi* during her current rearmament; they replaced the midships 47mm guns, which were moved to the wings of the aft bridge, replacing the 37mm weapons in this location, which were shifted to the upper deck.

Zhemchug and *Izumrud*, launched in August and October 1903, respectively, had been contracted for delivery by 14 July and 14 September 1904. In view of the needs of the now ongoing war, trials were truncated and a plan to install bilge keels, to remedy excessive rolling experienced in *Novik*, dropped, but in the end only *Zhemchug* was ready to leave with the 2nd Pacific Squadron for the Far East on 15 October, still with shipyard personnel aboard and some unresolved machinery defects. *Izumrud* sailed in a similar condition on 16 November, along with *Oleg*, the destroyers *Groznyi*, *Gromkii* and *Rezvyi*, and auxiliary cruisers *Rion* and *Dnepr*.

Both *Zhemchug* and *Izumrud* fought at Tsushima. *Izumrud* escaped at the end of the battle, but ran aground on the night of 29 May, and had to be blown up when refloating proved impossible. *Zhemchug* was one of a number of cruisers that sought internment at Manila. Post-war, she remained in the Far East, in increasingly poor condition, having only half her boilers working and one engine inoperative by late 1908. She was finally given a proper refit at Vladivostok between December 1909 and October 1910, which included reduction to a single mast (the main), and the loss of two 47mm guns. She was sunk by *Emden* at Penang on 28 October 1914 (p 205, below).

The *Muravev-Amurskiy* class

The origins of these two ships[25] lay around the end of 1911, when the Russian Naval Ministry received an offer from Vulcan, through 'Wossidlo & Co.', their representative in St Petersburg, to build them a 4,600-tonne cruiser. However, as no funding was available in the current Russian programme for additional ships, it was suggested that Vulcan be invited to participate in a forthcoming international competition for a new small cruiser for Far Eastern service that had been

25. N N Afonin, 'Kreisery "Murav'ev-Amurskii" i "Admiral Nevel'skoi"', *Sudostroenie*, 1989/2, pp 49–52; id. 'Malye kreisery "Murav'ev-Amurskii" i "Admiral Nevel'skoi"', *Gangut* 26 (2001), pp 31–42; Krest'ianinov, *Kreisera* II, pp 129–34, 175; I D Spasskii (ed.), *Istoriia otechestvennogo sudostroeniia*, III (St Petersburg: Sudostroenie, 1995), pp 326–36; S B Trubitsyn, 'Kreisery "Elbing" i "Pillau"', *Gangut*, 26 (2001), pp 42–48.

included in the large Russian 1912–16 programme.

A pair of these new ships were intended to replace the old *Askold* and *Zhemchug* on the Siberian station. They were to enter service as soon as possible so that they could also be used to train engineering personnel in the management of turbine propulsion, which was just coming into general Russian service. To facilitate early completion, foreign yards were to be invited to compete, in contrast to the rest of the 1912–16 programme, which was to be wholly of domestic construction. Indeed, the urgency was such that consideration was given to buying ships of the Italian *Nino Bixio* class (launched during 1911–12) off the shelf. The specification called for a displacement of 4,000–4,600 tons, eight 130mm and four AA guns, two submerged torpedo tubes, a 50mm belt, a 20mm deck, ten boilers, turbines on either the Curtis or Parsons principle, or a combination of both, and a speed of 29–31 knots.

In May 1912, the requirements were circulated to both Russian and foreign shipyards, with responses received from the Nevskii and Putilovskii yards at St Petersburg, the Russo-Baltic Works at Reval, Vulcan (Stettin) and Schichau; the latter both offered designs based in the recent *Kolberg* class. Evaluation was completed in September 1912, with none judged satisfactory. The options of buying the plans for the *Bixio* class, or fulfilling the engineering training requirement through a separate vessel were considered, but as funds for the two cruisers had now been voted, the procurement was continued.

Accordingly, the two better submissions (Vulcan and Nevskii) were reviewed with a view to issuing a revised specification. This included a somewhat larger displacement and a somewhat lower speed, and would form the basis of a new competition, launched on 28 September 1912, with submissions due on 4 October 1912. One extra competitor, Lange & Sons, of Riga, was added to the list of those invited to tender. However, it became clear that none of the Russian yards would be able to meet the required delivery dates for the ships, and when Schichau (through their St Petersburg representative, Rudolf A Ziese (1850–1933), brother of the yard's owner) submitted their own design on 15 October 1912, with an offer to deliver the first cruiser by 28 July 1914, and the second four months later, it was circulated for comment to the interested bodies.

The fuel stowage arrangements were deemed completely unsatisfactory, while the machinery specifications were 'brief and very vague'. They were in any case unacceptable, providing as they did for separate coal-fired and oil-fired boilers, rather than providing mixed firing for some boilers. There were also three shafts, which the Russians saw as adversely affecting manoeuvrability. Issues also existed regarding the siting of the main battery, the location of the magazines and mine stowage. The slopes of the armour deck were seen as too thin, although there was no criticism of the lack of belt armour, which had formed part of the Russian specification.

Revisions to meet the comments were incorporated by Schichau into a new version of the design, which was again circulated, and formally considered by the MTK on 12 December 1912, which deleted torpedo tubes from the requirement. In parallel, political concerns at placing such an order with Germany had been expressed, but now Schichau applied some pressure of its own. The company owned the Mühlgraben Shipyard at Riga, who had won a contract to build nine *Novik*-type destroyers with a price lower than any competitor: the Russian navy was now intending to use this price as a baseline in agreeing prices with other yards for the

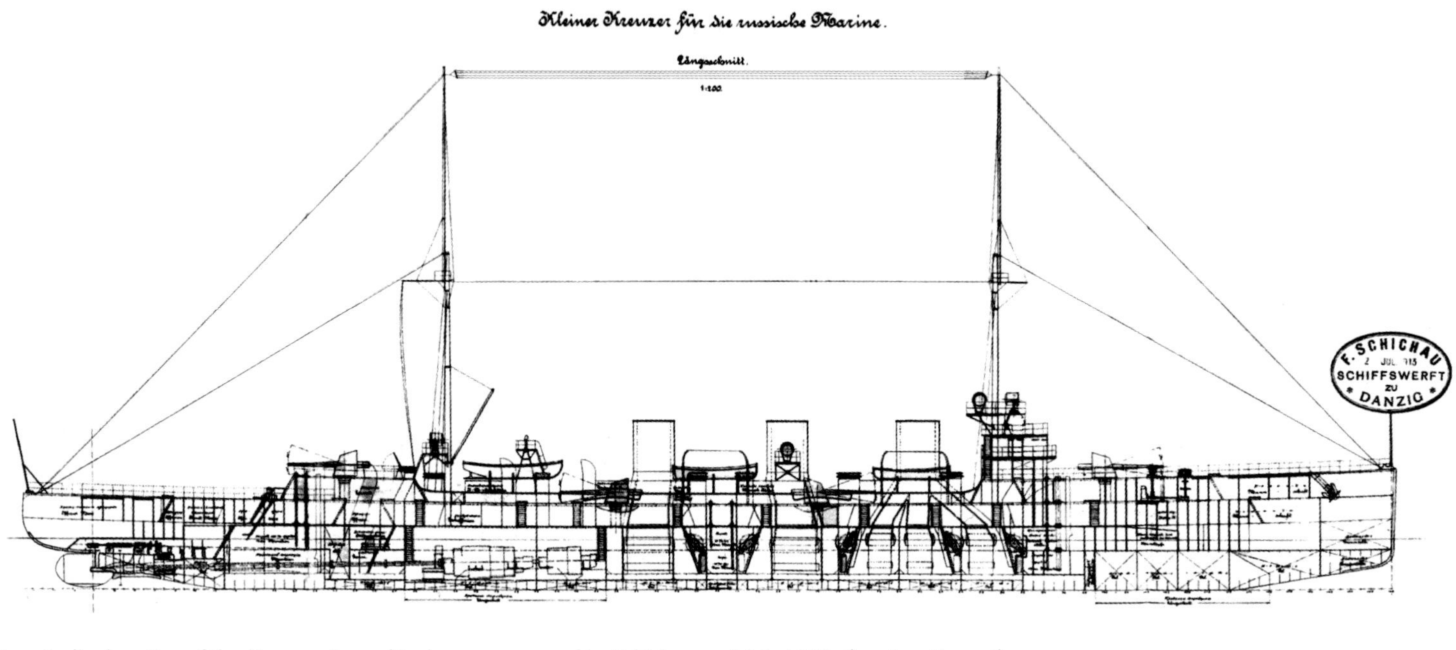

Longitudinal section of the *Muravev-Amurskiy* class, as prepared by Schichau on 2 July 1913. *(courtesy* Gangut*)*

construction of the other twenty-seven destroyers of the programme. However, Schichau let it be known if they lost the cruiser contract, they would decline the Mühlgraben destroyer contract, thus directly and indirectly pushing up the cost of the destroyer programme.

Faced with this prospect, the Council of Ministers ultimately agreed to award the cruisers to Schichau, the contract being signed on 17 December 1912. Under this, the first vessel was to be presented for trials no later than 28 July 1914, the second by 28 October, with delivery within three months. However, revisions to the design continued, with 'corrected and additional specifications' issued by the Russians on 3 January 1913, and final approval given on 19 February 1913.

The ships were to be armed with eight Russian 130mm/55 guns, paired on the forecastle and aft superstructure, and on the beam amidships, with Russian fire control equipment and supported by four 63.5mm AA guns. From the outset, the ability to lay mines had been part of the requirement, the initial idea being that at least fifty should be stored amidships on removable rails and to be dropped on the beam, leaving the quarterdeck free for the stowage of aeroplanes. Now, a double row of rails was envisaged on each side of the middle deck, of which the inner pair would lead to the stern for dropping up to 150 mines.

The armour deck was 20mm on the flat, thickening to 80mm over the steering gear, and 40mm on the slopes (thickened from the original 20mm at Russian request), thinning to 15mm at their lower edge, 1.1m below the waterline, over most of their length. The conning tower had 75mm sides, a 50mm roof, and a 25mm communications tube, gunshields and hoists being also protected by 25mm plating.

Five boiler rooms each housed two boilers, the three forward compartments containing mixed-fired Yarrow double-ended boilers, the after two having four Yarrow double-ended, oil-fired boilers, all to be constructed by Schichau. Uptakes were led to three short, widely spaced, funnels, matching the same programme's other cruisers and destroyers, and in many ways going back visually to *Novik*.[26] Two turbine sets were distributed between four compartments, the high-pressure turbines in the forward pair, the low-pressure and astern turbines in a single casing in the after compartments. Designed output was 28,000shp at 345rpm, providing a speed of 27.5 knots; astern power was 10,000shp at 270rpm. There were two turbo-generators, each with an output of 100kW, and a 50kW diesel generator for use in harbour.

Keels were laid in April to May 1913, the Russian traditional silver plaque bearing the ship's name and other details being subsequently affixed to the keel amidships on 23 September, with the Russian Naval Minister Ivan Konstantinovich Grigorovich (1853–1930) in attendance. However, subsequent progress was deemed unsatisfactory by the Russians, who alleged that the two vessels were being given less priority than German navy orders at the yard (which included the large cruiser *Lützow*), with other delays caused by strikes. Nevertheless, by the end of 1913 the lead-ship, now named *Muravev-Amurskiy* was 31.2 per cent complete, while the second vessel *Nevelskoi* (since January 1913: *Admiral Nevelskoi*) was 13.8 per cent complete. Both ships were added to the Russian navy list on 19 February 1914, and the lead ship launched on 11 April. However, neither ship would join the Russian navy (pp 195-197, below).

URUGUAY

In December 1905, the Uruguayan government announced a competition among twenty-four shipyards from the major shipbuilding countries for a small protected cruiser of about 800–1,000-tonne displacement and a draught of no more than 3m. Steam was to be generated in conventional single-ended firetube boilers, capable of generating steam for 18 knots with forced draught, 14 knots with natural draught. Protection would be sufficient to ward off firearms and light artillery, with an armament of two 12cm and four 7.5cm QF guns plus several machine cannon and guns.

Sheathing of the lower hull was originally envisaged, but later dropped from the requirement. Vulcan's initial design was well received by the Uruguayans, but demands for a higher speed led to the cancellation of the process and a reissue of the invitations to tender in summer 1907. This time, the desired speed had been raised to 22 knots, with a minimum endurance of 3,000nm at 12 knots. To accommodate these requirements, the displacement was raised to a minimum of 1,150 tonnes.

Uruguay returning to the shipyard from one of her trial cruises. This image has sometimes been reproduced with an Uruguayan ensign flying aft, but this is certainly the result of retouching. *(DN collection)*

26. Indeed, it had become something of a Schichau trademark, to be found in their submission to the Kaiser's 1906/7 battleship design-competition (see Nottelmann, 'From Ironclads to Dreadnoughts: The Development of the German Navy 1864–1918. Part VII: "Political Enforcements"', *Warship International*

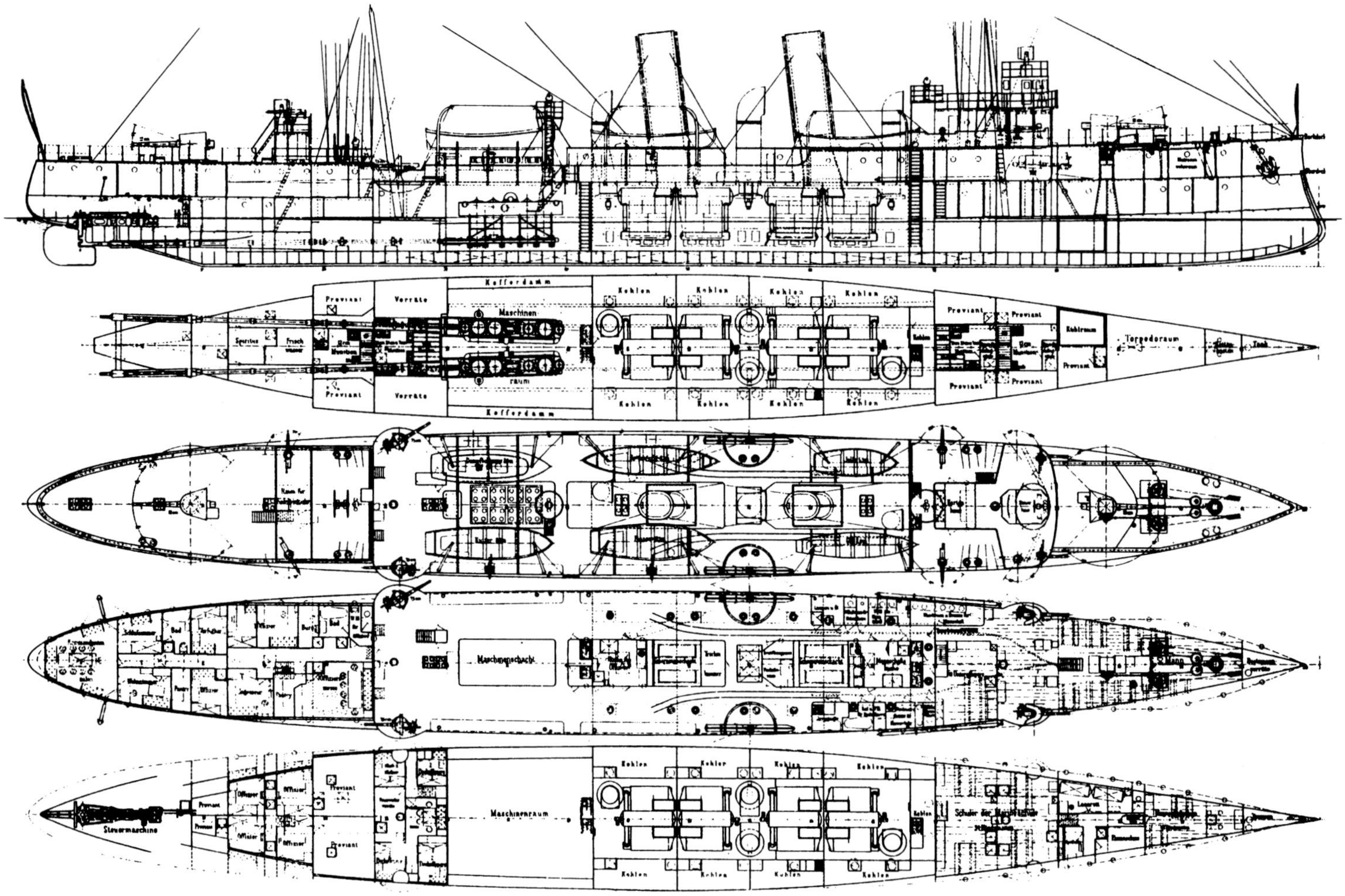

A set of drawings of *Uruguay* first issued in *Zeitschrift des Vereins deutscher Ingenieure*, a journal that enjoyed close links with the Vulcan yard. *(DN collection)*

Invitations were sent to the shipyards originally contacted, and in April 1908 it was reported that the Uruguayan design commission had recommended the Vulcan design to its government. Four months later confirmation came, when the yard received the order for a vessel to be named *Uruguay*, of 1,400 tonnes normal, armed with two 12cm L/45 QF and four 7.5cm L/45 QF guns, to be supplied by the Škoda works in Austria-Hungary. Additionally, six 37mm machine cannon and six 7mm machine guns would come from Vickers in the UK; two single 45cm Whitehead torpedo tubes would be mounted in revolving mountings on the upper deck. Protection against small arms fire would be given by 17mm nickel steel side plating, reaching from 1m below the waterline to the main deck, abreast the boilers, engines and magazines, topped with the 15mm nickel steel main deck. Cofferdams flanked the engine room, the machinery comprising two balanced 4-cylinder triple expansion engines delivering a total of 8,250ihp, fed by four Normand watertube boilers in three boiler rooms.

Uruguay was launched on 12 April 1910, and was completed in July. On her initial trials on 7 July, the ship maintained an average speed of 23.1 knots at 8,550ihp in Sea State 6, which was calculated as corresponding to about 24 knots in calm seas. During a trial on 13 July, her endurance was calculated to be 4,480nm at 12 knots. On 23 July the Uruguayan flag was raised and *Uruguay* departed Stettin on 26 July, arriving at Montevideo on 25 August. Employed mainly as a training vessel, *Uruguay*, served until May 1951, when she was stricken, to be eventually sold for scrap in August 1962. As already noted, the ship's size was rather small for a cruiser of her era, and as a result she has often been dubbed a 'torpedo gunboat'. This, however, does not fully fit with her actual design, which was indeed essentially that of a cruiser in miniature.

7 THE MINELAYERS

AS A GENERAL POINT, it must be noted that the ships covered by this chapter were never classified as 'cruisers' in the German navy: they were formally 'Minendampfer' (mine-steamers). On the other hand, the last pair to be built were almost exclusively operated as ordinary fleet cruisers during the First World War, which is in itself sufficient justification for their inclusion in this book, along with their lineal ancestors.[1]

Originally viewed as a weapon of a minor or 'defensive' power, the utility of the sea mine was recognised at an early stage by as-yet-ununited German coastal states. It was first employed in the First Schleswig-Holstein War of 1848, when Professor Carl Himly of Kiel University proposed that a row of mines should be deployed for the protection of the inner Kiel fjord and its then small commercial port. He secured the aid of the then Prussian artillery lieutenant Werner (von) Siemens (1816–92),[2] who seems to have been responsible mainly for the electrical triggering of this early controlled minefield. The field's deterrent effect was successful: during their blockade, the Danes would not attempt to penetrate the inner Kiel fjord.

Mines were subsequently employed during the Franco-Prussian War of 1870-71, albeit mainly in the form of weapons improvised from wine casks, and under the control not of the navy but the Matrosen Artillerie Abteilungen (Marine Artillery Divisions). Luckily, those defences were never challenged during the war, with the French navy's early retirement in the wake of the catastrophe suffered by French land forces.

Having apparently proved successful in war, this approach to mine warfare was maintained subsequently, with responsibility for mine defences remaining under the supervision of local 'fortresses' (Festung). As a consequence, minelaying capacity was initially concentrated in small vessels, the self-propelled ones aptly named 'fortress mine-planting vessels', carrying one or two mines each, together with non-propelled barges of greater capacity. In each case the mine(s) had to be laid individually by cranes or derricks – a time-consuming and tedious job, not designed for quick reactions to external threats.

A new momentum in the development of a special mine service was engendered when Caprivi took office as head of the Admiralty in 1883, with a particular focus on coastal defence. In 1877 a standard specially designed mine, the C/77, containing 40kg of gunpowder, had been introduced, with 1884 updates allowing it then to be laid further offshore. The navy-owned transport *Rhein* was converted in 1883 to plant so-called 'stray mines'[3] during a series of trials that lasted until 1887. *Rhein* was then converted into a permanent mine-training vessel, serving as such from April 1888 onwards.

She soon would be supported by a new-build vessel, *Pelikan*. Her origins were rather curious: for many years the navy had aspired to owning its own ocean-going transport vessel, especially for exchanging crews on overseas stations. The necessary funds had been denied by the Reichstag for some ten consecutive years until, in 1888, they were finally granted. Unfortunately, by this time, the requirement for such a specialised vessel had all but evaporated, common practice now being for crews to either be carried by outgoing warships or in commercial steamers. Nevertheless, it was decided that the vessel should be constructed anyway, given the difficulty the navy had in prising money out of the Reichstag.

It has often been stated that the result was a vessel for which the navy had to actively seek a role once in service.[4] However, this view can only be partially supported, as the vessel's original design drawings, dating from November 1888, already bear the designation 'mine steamer'. Nevertheless, it seems that *Pelikan*, launched on 29 July 1890 at the Imperial Dockyard Wilhelmshaven and commissioned on 15 October 1891, was not actually employed in a mine-related role until as late as November 1895, after several years of fulfilling assorted subsidiary tasks. This coincided with the establishment of a

1. In this, it follows in the long-established wake of the doyen of German warship studies, Erich Gröner, who placed them amongst 'true' cruisers in his classic compilation of German warship data (*Die deutschen Kriegsschiffe 1815–1936* [Munich/Berlin: J F Lehmanns Verlag, 1937]), and subsequent revised and enlarged editions. However, Gröner's alleged 1914 reclassification of *Nautilus* and *Albatross* as mine cruisers (pp 119, 133) appears not to be reflected in surviving contemporary documents.

2. German inventor and founder of the Siemens (& Halske) company, today Siemens AG.

3. The term 'stray mines' (Streuminen) means mines planted irregularly or in small rows, in contrast to larger 'fields' or 'barrages'.

4. See, e.g., Hildebrand, Röhr and Steinmetz, *Deutschen Kriegsschiffe*, vol 5, p 43.

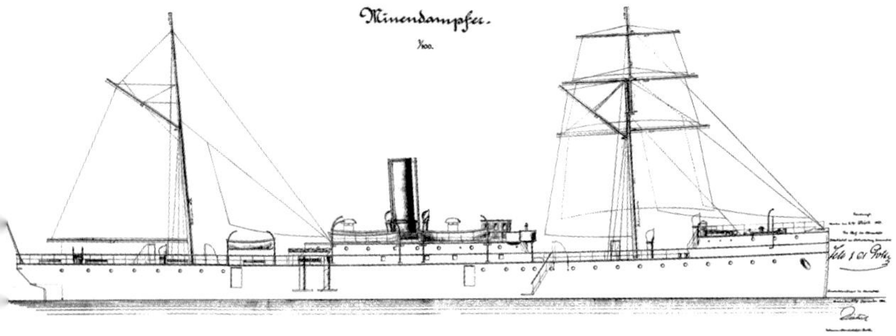

Rigging plan for a 'mine-steamer', approved on 24 March 1889, and later named *Pelikan*. The plan is signed by chief constructor Dietrich and countersigned by the Head of Admiralty, Adm von der Goltz. *(DN collection)*

new section within the – still land-based – Naval Depot Inspectorate (Marine Depot Inspektion), which was responsible for the development of minelaying and minesweeping.

The real impetus for pushing this development on to another level came with the news of the impact of mines on the Russo-Japanese War at sea. The Russians had demonstrated to the world the effectiveness of thoroughly planned and executed mining operations, especially by employing their specially designed ocean-going minelayers *Amur* and *Yenisei* – the first of their kind in the world. Mines laid by *Amur* were responsible for sinking the Japanese battleships *Hatsuse* and *Yashima* in May 1904, reducing the Japanese battle line by a third.

Thus, as early as the spring of 1905, following discussions concerning the current naval estimates, it was announced that '[e]xperience gained during the Russo-Japanese War has led to the creation of a special corps for mine warfare, for the planting and sweeping of sea mines. The resources for the creation of a special mining division, numbering 300 people, have been made available [and] the planned construction of a mine-steamer has been easily justified by the experience gained during the Russo-Japanese War.'[5]

NAUTILUS

In parallel with the Reichstag debates over the introduction of *Mine-steamer A* [to be *Nautilus*] into the forthcoming programme, 'K' had begun design work for a specialised minelaying vessel of 20 knots speed and a capacity of 200 mines, to be stored entirely within the vessel's hull. Although there is no documentary proof, it seems likely the Russian vessels served as general models. However, the most remarkable external feature of the new design would be its clipper bow, contrasting with both the ram bows of the Russian vessels and usual German navy practice.

This was a combination of attempting to disguise the vessel's warlike nature, and a consequence of a special strengthening of the hull against ice pressure by reducing the spacing of the transverse frames fore and aft from the usual 1.2m to only 0.6m. This feature underlines the intended area of operation of the new vessel: the Baltic, where ice-breaking capabilities would be crucial in allowing the winter navigation of its eastern extremity for several additional weeks.

5. *Nauticus: Jahrbuch für Deutschlands Seeinteressen* 1905, pp 22–23.

Nautilus running her trials in 1907, showing her first configuration. *(DN collection)*

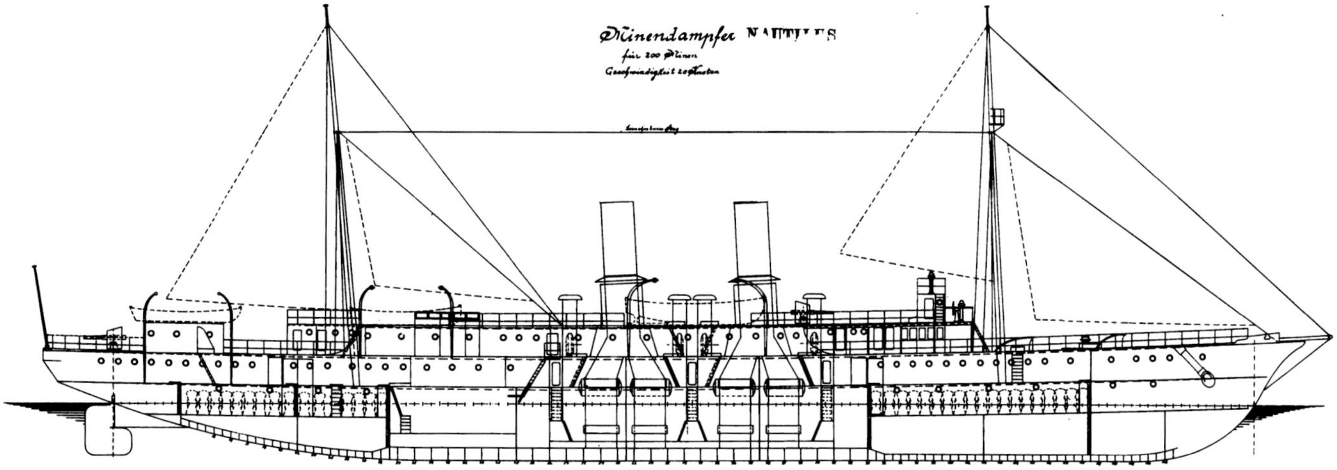

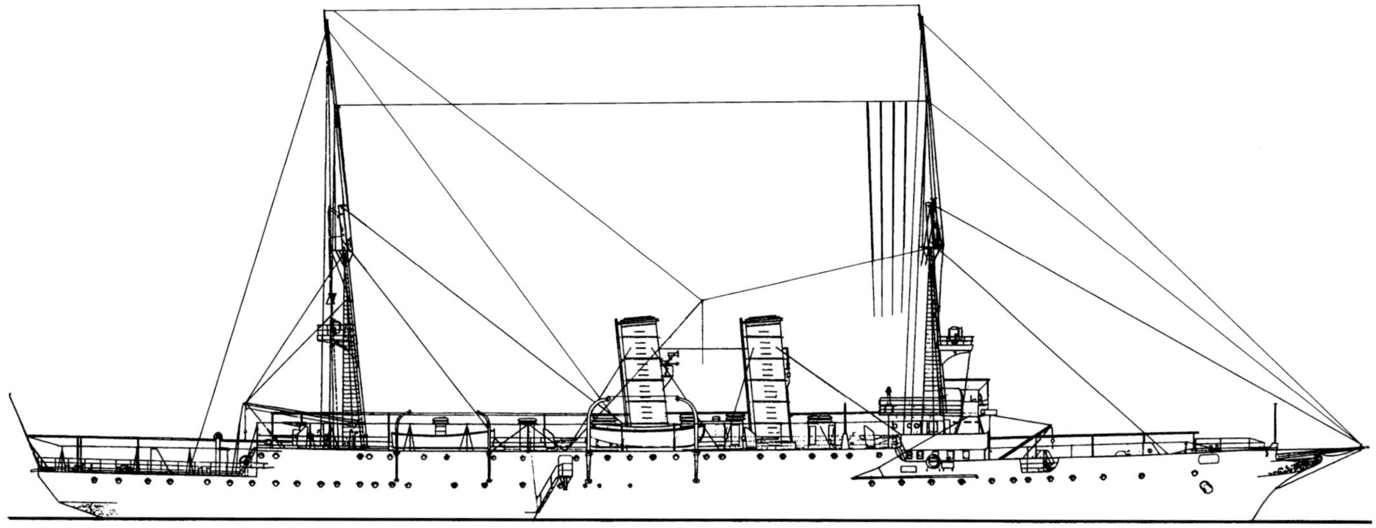

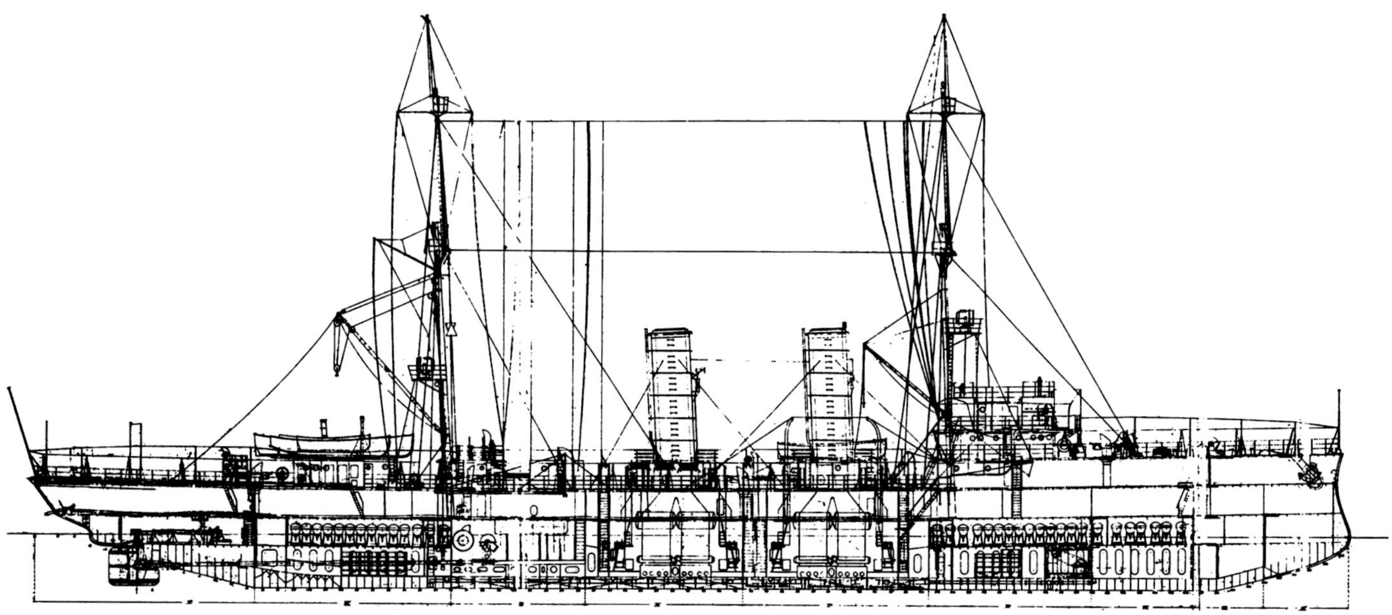

Top: This preliminary project of a minelayer, later to be named *Nautilus*, has a distinctly mercantile look, but nevertheless incorporated all the features of the future minelayer. These included stowage capacity for 200 mines and the speed of 20 knots, but only four 8.8cm guns on the upper and shelter decks.
Middle: *Nautilus* after reconstruction, with a doubled armament and no superstructure on the quarterdeck, to permit the installation of four parallel mine tracks.
Bottom: Longitudinal section of *Albatross*, showing the general similarity of the internal arrangements of both minelayers, in spite of their rather different external appearance. *(DN collection)*

Mines were stowed in parallel rows as low in the hull as possible, on the so-called mine deck, at around waterline level, separated into two sections fore and aft of the machinery spaces, with 108 mines aft and the remaining ninety-two forward. Initially, it was planned to lift the mines up to the between deck, from which they were to be laid, using eight manually powered individual lifts. However, this was redesigned shortly after keel laying, when the hand winches were replaced by single hydraulic cylinders underneath the mine cages. The mines of the after stowage could then be placed directly on to one of the four parallel launch tracks on the between deck, while those of the forward stowage had to be conveyed on two tracks leading aft, narrowing to only one track abreast of the engine casings. Mines would then be laid through stern doors. As defence against small craft, eight 8.8cm/35 QL guns were mounted, while as passive protection the bunkers along the boiler rooms extended from the double bottom to the level of the main deck.

Weser won the order to build *Mine-steamer A* on 22 May 1905. Although the subsequent building contract was agreed during June/July, preliminary drawings were not finished until as late as 11 August, meaning that the laying of the keel had to be postponed until 19 December. Her launch nevertheless took place on 20 August 1906, at which she was named *Nautilus*, perpetuating the tradition of the successful and long-lived gunboat of the name.

Commissioned on 19 March 1907, *Nautilus* initially operated only briefly from her new homeport of Cuxhaven, which would be the German navy's centre for mine-related training until 1969. Experience gained during the first eighteen months of the ship's service indicated that the minelaying installation was unsatisfactory. This led to the ship being taken in hand for reconstruction as soon as she could be relieved by her new half-sister *Albatross* in 1909. The work was a reflection of the value placed on the ships by the then-CinC, Adm Henning von Holtzendorff, who also saw them as welcome additions to his scouting forces, despite their comparatively low 20 knots maximum speed, light armament and lack of armour.

Nautilus refitted at Kiel from May 1909 to January 1910, during which the transfer of mines from the forward mine deck was speeded up by the addition of a second track outboard of the port engine casing. Furthermore, it was decided to add additional launch tracks by moving the main launch area, consisting of four tracks, to the upper deck, leaving two of the original tracks on the between-deck, thus increasing the total number to six. Although most sources state that this measure required a redesign of the stern area, adding 2.7m in total length and requiring a removal of the small deckhouses on each side of the aft upper deck, the ship's drawings show that the modified overhang added just 1m to her length.

The ship rejoined the fleet on 23 January 1910, refitting again at Wilhelmshaven during December 1910/January 1911. *Nautilus* officially transferred to Kiel on 4 April, to serve with the Mine Experimental Commission; she was replaced at Cuxhaven by *Albatross*. The move of *Nautilus* to Kiel did not mean that her service was restricted to the Baltic, as the trials she conducted with minesweepers mainly took place in the North Sea. She participated in the 1912 manoeuvres before decommissioning on 30 October 1912, on relief by the newly converted *Arcona* (pp 109-110, above). *Nautilus* recommissioned in June 1914 to relieve *Pelikan*, which was going into refit.

ALBATROSS

The history of *Mine-steamer B* was rather more complicated than that of her half-sister, despite her funding being passed in the estimates for 1906 without any objections. The contract had again been won by Weser, on 5 September 1906, but the keel-laying was deferred until initial experience has been gained with *Nautilus*. This faced the RMA with the problem of having already bid for the second instalment of funding for *Mine-steamer B* into the 1907 estimate, yet the ship had not even been laid down. Just such a procedure had caused a public outcry fourteen years before – when two annual instalments for *Cruiser-corvette K* had been demanded from the Reichstag, without any keel being laid – or even any construction drawings completed (pp 81-82, above). However, the practice was accepted on this current occasion, given the novelty of the new type and desirability of building any lessons from the first ship into the second vessel.

Keel laying finally occurred two months after *Nautilus* had commissioned, on 24 May 1907. Progress was, however, rapid, the ship being launched as *Albatross* on 23 October, strongly suggesting extensive prefabrication in the period between ordering and laying down. Her chosen name recalled a gunboat of 1871, as did that of *Nautilus*. *Albatross* was delivered on 21 April 1908, less than a year after keel laying, and commissioned for trials on 19 May, which would last until 20 July.

No records survive to indicate whether the original plan was for *Albatross* to be a repeat of *Nautilus*, or whether significant differences had been intended from the outset, perhaps reflecting an intention for one ship to be primarily for Baltic and one for North Sea service. Thus, while *Albatross* had the same strengthened scantlings fore and aft as *Nautilus* for ice navigation, she also has a raised forecastle and cut-away stem, suggesting a desire for improved sea-keeping qualities in the rougher North Sea, and significantly changing her overall appearance as compared to her half-sister. Otherwise the design of the vessel was essentially the same as that of *Nautilus*, with the same arrangements for laying from four tracks on the between-deck, albeit with the double-track leading past the engine-casings from the forward mine-elevators from the outset.

One of the mysteries surrounding both minelayers – but

Albatross alongside at Wilhelmshaven, early in her career. *(DN collection)*

particularly *Albatross* – is their true mine capacity, a range of different figures existing, with little consistency even between official files. In the case of *Nautilus* the problem appears initially straightforward, as the preliminary drawings call her a 'Mine-steamer for 200 mines'. This would match with the figures in her 'as-fitted' plans that, as already discussed, give 108 mines aft and ninety-two mines forward.

For *Albatross*, however, the numbers in the 'as-fitted' plans are eighty mines aft and seventy-five + twenty-one mines forward, giving a total of only 176 mines, despite the officially announced load of 200. Other figures also exist, ranging from the '196' in the official 'Directive for the conduct of a naval war' to the 'about 600', estimated by British naval intelligence.[6] In 1918, the former CinC, Adm Friedrich von Ingenohl, stated that in 1914 '[t]he fleet's only modern minelayers had been *Nautilus* and *Albatross*, of 20 knots speed and a maximum capacity of 400 mines, of which only 200, however, could be kept ready for dropping instantly'.[7] Based on the 164m (220m after conversion) total length of mine tracks in the ship, one may calculate, on the basis of the dimensions of the then current Carbonit mine (length of carriage: 1.04m, weight of mine + carriage: 760kg), the maximum theoretical capacity would come to 157/211 mines. This calculation leaves open the question of whether both would have been able to carry the extra weight of 160 tonnes, mainly at upper-deck level, following their reconstruction.

Albatross began her career in July 1908 supporting trials with

6. N Friedman (ed); *German Warships of World War I*, p 372.

7. O Groos (ed), *Der Krieg zur See – der Krieg in der Nordsee*, vol 1, (Berlin: Mittler, 1920), p 64.

minesweepers, as a short-term replacement for *Pelikan*, as well as participating in the autumn manoeuvres, being part of a very heterogeneous division, acting a place-holder for a future 'real' III. Sqn: the old battleship *Kurfürst Friedrich Wilhelm* (flag), the coast defence vessels *Frithjof* and *Aegir*, plus *Nautilus* and *Albatross*, and the former small cruisers (now special-duty vessels) *Blitz*, *Pfeil* and *Zieten*. After termination of the manoeuvres *Albatross* became a mine warfare training ship, based at Cuxhaven. Her minelaying arrangements were modified at Kiel Dockyard, between the autumn of 1910 and spring 1911, before the ship returned to her ongoing role in April 1911. She remained in service until the outbreak of the First World War.

THE *BRUMMER* CLASS

Two final 'true' mine-steamers, *C* and *D*,[8] were ordered on 23 December 1914. They have been the subject of a number of myths, the most persistent and pernicious being that they had been built around turbines allegedly then under construction at Vulcan's Hamburg works for the Russian battlecruiser *Navarin*, building at New Admiralty Shipyard, St Petersburg.[9] The precise origin of this myth remains a mystery, as the relevant files are quite clear as to the true origins of the ships.

These reveal that 'at the end of September 1914, the Vulcan works informed [the RMA] that in its shops at Hamburg it had 4 turbines presently under construction, *intended for a Russian small cruiser* (authors' italics), and proposed to employ them for the construction of two torpedo(boat) catchers. At the same time, they presented two designs of 2,000–2,350 tonnes displacement.'[10] It was in *these* 'spare' turbines that the true origins of the new minelayers can be found.

Reference has been made (p 182) to the huge Russian rearmament programme of 1912-16 as the origin of the Schichau-built *Muravev-Amurskiy* class, which would become the German *Pillau* and *Elbing*. As well as these small cruisers, the programme also included the 'armoured cruisers' (redesignated battlecruisers in 1915) of the *Borodino* class, intended primarily for the Baltic fleet. As usual, their final design followed a competition between a number of domestic and overseas shipyards,[11] one of the latter being Vulcan – the only German firm participating. Although the winning design came from Russia's

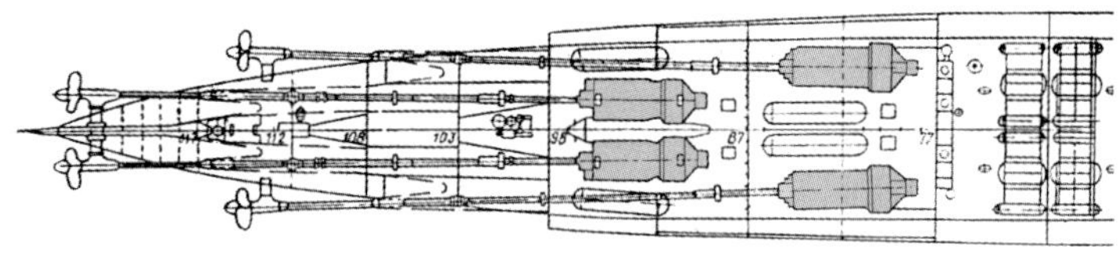

Sketch of the proposed layout of the turbines of *Svetlana*, showing her four turbines of identical type. *(Courtesy* Sudostroinye*)*

own Admiralty Works, there remained a public perception of a link between these vessels and Vulcan, which may be one reason for later misunderstandings.

The final design for the *Borodino* class was a combination of the Admiralty Works design with one submitted by the Baltic Works, as directed by the Russian Navy Minister I K Grigorovich, who also required that the ships adopt a standardised turbine engine plant *on the Parsons principle* (authors' italics). This information should have sown doubts regarding the possibility of dividing *Navarin*'s four-shaft engine plant between two German minelayers, as each Parsons turbine set traditionally consisted of one HP turbine in combination with one LP turbine. Thus, each minelayer would have either have an HP turbine on one shaft and an LP turbine on the other, or one ship would have two HP and the other vessel two LP turbines. These facts alone should have made the idea of the minelayers employing *Navarin*'s engines impossible, as there is no doubt whatsoever that the minelayers were each powered by two individual HP/LP turbines *on the Curtis principle*. In any case, it is also quite clear from Russian official records that the engines for *Navarin* were ordered from the Franco-Russian Works at St Petersburg on 22 April 1913![12]

Vulcan were, nevertheless involved in the production of turbines for the Russian programme. On 28 February 1913 the Russian Navy Ministry contracted with the Russo-Baltic Shipyard, Reval (Tallinn), for the construction of two cruisers of 6,800 tonnes displacement, a design speed of 28 knots and of 50,000shp design power on four shafts. The contract allowed the shipyard to 'order the turbine plant and half the boilers for the first cruiser from abroad'[13] to gain experience with the equipment. The Russo-Baltic shipyard did just this, concluding a subcontract with Vulcan for a set of Curtis-AEG-Vulcan turbines,[14] not least owing to the success of similar machinery in the Vulcan-designed (but Putilovskii [St Petersburg]-built) destroyer *Novik*, launched in 1911.[15]

This was the machinery still in the Vulcan workshops in

8. Several auxiliary minelayers were designated before the war, divided between the North and Baltic Seas, which also had the local official designations 'A' through 'D'. At the commencement of hostilities in 1914 these were, in the North sea: 'A' – *Kaiser* (1905); 'B' – *Königin Luise* (1913); 'C' – *Silvana* (1897); in the Baltic: 'A' – *Prinz Sigismund* (1899); 'B' – *Prinz Adalbert* (1895); 'C' – (temporarily, as the definitive 'C' - now 'D' – was not yet ready) *Deutschland* (1909); 'D' – *Prinz Waldemar* (1893).

9. e.g. Gröner, *Deutschen Kriegsschiffe*.

10. This, and other quotations below, are to be found (if not otherwise noted) in BA-MA Ma 473, Akten des R.M.A., Geh. Arch. K I, Entstehungsgeschichte der Minendampfer C u. D.

11. See S McLaughlin, *Russian & Soviet Battleships* (Annapolis: Naval Institute Press, 2003), pp 244–49.

12. McLaughlin, *Russian & Soviet Battleships*, p 253; the same firm would also build the turbines for the other Admiralty Works ship (*Borodino*), while the Baltic Works themselves would build those of their pair (*Izmail* and *Kinburn*).

13. I D Spasskii (ed), *Istorija otechest-vennogo sudostroenija*, 3 (St Petersburg: Sudostroenie, 1995), p 378.

14. Pinl, *Schiffbau*, p 325, quoting the original contract in the Russian archives: RGAVMF f 401, op 1, d 370, l 122–24.

15. *Novik* was initially designated as 'mine cruiser of 36 knots speed'.

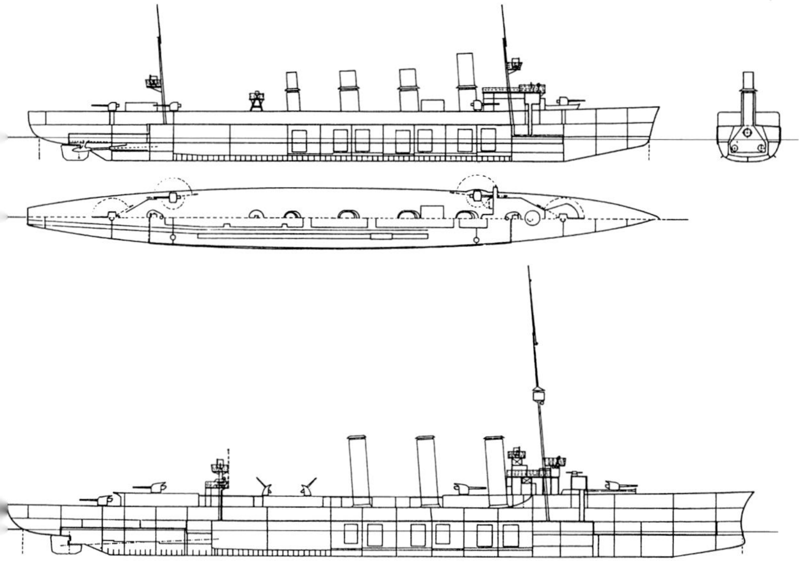

Two sketches showing the two stages in the development of the minelayers. The only common feature of both is – unsurprisingly – the length of the engine rooms, to contain two ex-*Svetlana* turbines. The later variant is still missing the torpedo tubes included in the final design. *(DN drawing)*

August 1914,[16] and the subject of their offer to the RMA. Accordingly, the first of these Russian cruisers, although laid down at the end of 1913, was not launched as *Svetlana* until 12 December 1915, replacement machinery having had to be ordered from the UK. She was still incomplete at the time of the revolution, and was not finally completed until 1928, under the new name *Profintern*.

'K' rejected Vulcan's proposals for 'torpedo boat catchers' in October 1914, proposing that the machinery be applied to fast mine-steamers instead, in view of the existing lack of specialised vessels of this type, and the fact that 'the small cruisers could not be employed for laying mines because of their small numbers'. On 11 November, a decisive interdepartmental meeting was held at the RMA, during which 'K' presented its initial proposals. It was agreed that these vessels should be built, even if their construction might take around a year. Their specifications are given in the table opposite.

Initially, Tirpitz was not convinced: he would rather build specialised minelaying submarines, but finally gave his consent on 5 December 1914. Six days later Vulcan received initial drawings from which to develop their solution – albeit without a guarantee of receiving an order. This rather nebulous situation would be corrected at a meeting on 23 December, when Vulcan was given an official order to construct both vessels to a fixed price, for completion by 1 December 1915 and 1 February 1916 respectively. The yard would be responsible for producing the detailed specifications and drawings themselves, conforming, of course, to the general requirements received from the RMA. While the design work would be carried out in Vulcan's new main office in Hamburg, both minelayers would be built in the old yard at Stettin.

At the beginning of January 1915, the Admiralty Staff became involved in the discussions for the first time – and objected to the plans. As far as they were concerned, the proposed endurance was far too low, with 4,000nm the absolute minimum necessary. On 19 January, RMA consented to the request, even at the prospect of completely redesigning both vessels. Vulcan was informed of the decision four days later.

On 2 February 'K' had new sketch drawings prepared and presented those in another meeting, this time with the participation of the Admirals Staff. The new specifications were indeed quite different from the initial ones, as shown below:

	11 Nov 14	**2 Feb 15**
Length (wl)	115m	135m
Beam	11.4m	13.2m
Draught (average)	4.4m	4.8m
Displacement	2,800 tonnes (approx)	4,300 tonnes (approx)
Armament		
Guns	Six 10.5cm	Four 15cm/45 C/14 Two 8.8cm/45 AA
Torpedo tubes	–	– (Two 50cm added later)
Mines	200	300+
Armour		
Side	40mm	40mm
Deck	15mm	15mm
CT	80mm	80mm
Boilers	5 (oil) + 2 (mixed)	4 (oil)+ 2 (mixed)
Bunkers (coal+oil)		
normal	400 tonnes (total)	300+500 tonnes
full	800 tonnes (total)	600+1,000 tonnes
Speed (max/six-hour/sustained)	30/28.5/ 25–26 knots	28.5–29/27.5–28/ 25.5 knots
Endurance (at 21 knots)	1,800–2,000nm	3,200nm

From these figures it may be seen that even though bunkerage had been doubled, endurance was not increased in proportion. This is clearly attributable to the updated design's increase in size: more fuel was needed to simply move a bigger vessel. The proportion of oil-burning to coal-burning boilers was significantly larger than seen in contemporary German cruisers, but this was not necessarily a result of new thinking at the RMA. Rather, it was the inevitable outcome of the fact that the design was so tight that it was simply impossible to accommodate enough stokers to service the number of coal-fired boilers that

16. The surviving files hint that Vulcan had also received the order for the turbines for the second cruiser (*Admiral Greig*), and had subcontracted these to Blohm & Voss. *Greig* would never be completed as a cruiser, being converted to a motor tanker under the name *Azneft*.

would normally have been employed. As an incidental consequence the two ships would benefit from a higher average speed during their intended sorties.

Freeboard amidships was slightly reduced as compared with the original scheme. The new design not only required the addition of a forecastle for sea-keeping purposes, but the minelaying deck had to be moved from the between to the upper deck. This required the installation of hydraulically driven lifts to bring the mines up from below.

Two additional statements regarding more general features are equally noteworthy: 'If possible, similarity with recent British cruisers shall be attained.' Additionally, however, it was underlined that 'even after their enlargement, the vessels shall be constructed as mine steamers solely; their construction and their fittings shall be adjusted only to serve this particular purpose'. Their high speed was mainly intended to allow them to lay offensive minefields, but the vessels were also to be suitable for assisting in the laying of defensive barrages. The approval of not only Tirpitz, but also ultimately the Kaiser, for the new specifications was obtained during 12–23 February 1915, but with Vulcan receiving them in parallel. Thus, 15 February 1915 was officially fixed as the start date of construction. *Mine-steamer C* was laid down on 24 April; her sister, *D*, followed three days later.

The minelayers' construction was impacted by several special requirements. All material already prefabricated or on order for the initial design was to be employed as much as was feasible. In general, the construction was also to be simplified and lightened to the maximum possible extent, based on torpedo boat constructional principles. This meant, for example, a deviation from the purely longitudinal framing now in use in cruisers of this size; instead, a mixed system was employed, avoiding the time-consuming fabrication of the large numbers of intersectional stiffeners. For greater rigidity, a spacing of only 0.5m was chosen for the transverse frames, although this was still barely sufficient for the foundations of the turbines.

The upper deck was employed as the strength deck, further supported by the fixed mine-rails and additional girders below. Mines were mainly to be stowed under cover on the between-deck, which was also the armour deck – fitted without any slopes, contrary to normal German practice – to save weight. Another deviation from usual German cruiser practice could be found in the drainage system of the hull, which had hitherto consisted of a central main drain, into which all auxiliary piping was led. Now, each large compartment had its own drainage system.

Only a single signal mast was provided that, in conjunction with the fully cased funnels, was intended to help disguise the vessels' true identity (see above). Nevertheless, a retractable spar could be rigged aft as well, supported by a very short fixed tripod, for a proper spreading of W/T aerials. The three funnels themselves were unusually strongly built, to withstand the usual static or dynamic forces without needing the support of stays. These would otherwise have restricted the firing arcs of the second 15cm gun, which was mounted between the forward pair of funnels; auxiliary stays could, however, be rigged in the case of exceptionally bad weather.

Other simplifications employed to speed up construction included the use of two armoured tubes captured from the French to make up the communication tube below the conning tower; the anchor capstans were of the type already being produced for the *Königsberg* class. A revealing note is one directing that all water piping should be constructed from steel owing to the shortage of copper, even at this early stage of the war.

On 11 December 1915 – only ten days late – *Mine-steamer C* was launched as *Brummer*, taking the name of a long-stricken armoured gunboat of 1884: this choice may be seen as another indication of the non-cruiser status of the new class. She commissioned on 2 April 1916, less than one year after laying her keel, although she would not actually be ready for her first trials until 18 April. On 27 April she transferred to Kiel, to be handed over to the trials commission, the official trials beginning on 6 May. Her sister's constructional pace was not been kept up to schedule to the same degree, the ship being launched as *Bremse* (again, the name of an armoured gunboat) only on 4 March 1916, instead of 15 January, as originally envisaged.

Owing to the ever-present fear of spies, especially in the Kiel area, both vessels were given a measure of disguise to hide their true profile. Their unusual (for Germany) cutaway bow – mirroring that of the British *Arethusa* class – was temporarily disguised by steel plating, thus creating the appearance of a straight stem. The measure was only partially successful: the plates were constantly bent by sea forces during the trials, and in any case British intelligence would eventually become aware of the ships' basic characteristics. There were, however, some areas of misinterpretation: for example, the British were unaware that the ships had belt armour; the design speed was

Brummer at Kiel, about to commence her trials, as is indicated by the gauges mounted along her hull, to determine of her wave profile. She is still missing her AA guns and torpedo tubes. *(DN collection)*

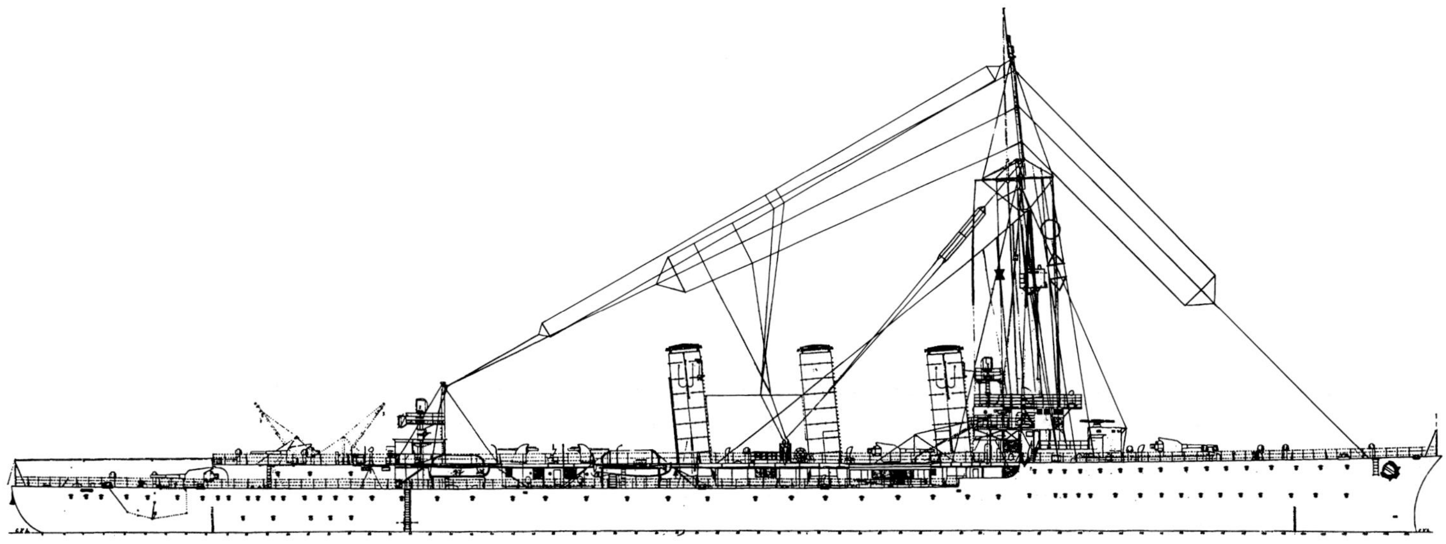

'As fitted' plan of *Bremse*. It is interesting to note that this did not include the extended spar that could be rigged as decoy at the position of the mainmast. *(DN collection)*

believed to be 'about' 34.0 knots; and there were repeated reports of phantom sisters under construction.[17]

Trial-results were affected by the limited depths of water available in the Kiel Bight, but in terms of speed they fell only slightly short of expectations. Another drawback would be that, during the second set of *Brummer*'s trials at full load, the torque indicator for the port engine failed, meaning that no power measurement was possible. Previously, at design draught, 28.05 knots at 42,797shp had been attained, while the three-hour run resulted in an average speed of 27.8 knots at 42,305shp. In full load condition, the vessels' speed dropped by an average of 0.6 knots. In general, the trials commission was satisfied with the results of the machinery trials and the performance of its components, even though some minor details required improvement.

Regarding sea-keeping qualities, it was noted that it would be hard to keep the vessels on an even keel, due to the comparatively large free surface area within the oil cells, which tended to amplify any slight inclination, such as might be induced by the force of the wind. Regarding their military capabilities, it was noted that it might be hard to supply the guns with sufficient ammunition during an action – especially to the second amidships mounting – as the hoists ended on main deck level. This would require extra manpower – which might well not be available in battle – to transfer it up one more deck. Happily, their capability as minelayers was regarded as good, with laying possible at any required speed. A total of 250 mines could be stowed with ease, with sufficient room for another sixty, without affecting gun firing arcs or the efficiency of ventilators.

The final verdict is significant: 'SMS *Brummer* surpasses the earlier mine steamers significantly in terms of speed and armament. The number of mines to be stowed permanently under cover is slightly larger: 250 against 200, recognising that the stowage in special holds in the earlier vessels must be regarded as advantageous in terms of protecting them against coal dust during bunkering. *For a further-going employment as cruiser the vessel is unsuited, referring to the principles of construction laid down by RMA on 29 January/11 March 1915* (authors' italics).' Ironically both ships would spend their active careers employed mainly as cruisers, and they were rarely employed operationally in their intended role as offensive minelayers.

Bremse was launched with her turbines already fitted; nevertheless, she would not commission for trials until 1 July 1916. These mirrored those of her sister, although the results were even more scantily published. A maximum attained power 47,800shp is recorded, but without indication of the corresponding speed. Her highest published speed was 28.12 knots, although without further reference to the prevailing conditions. The trials commission once more highlighted the inadequate number of rounds provided for the main guns. Originally designed for eighty rounds per gun only, this had already been raised to 110 rounds during construction and would ultimately be raised to 125 rounds by reducing stowage for AA ammunition.

After a little more than a year's service by both ships, the RMA summarised the experience gained as follows: 'Even if the vessels had not been built as cruisers, they had to be employed as such, given the small number of (heavily armed) small cruisers. Thus, with regard to the necessities of war, everything possible must be provided for making them fulfil this role accordingly, which presently is striven for …'

17. Friedman (ed.), *German Warships of World War I*, p 114; this erroneous assessment continues to crop up in the literature, e.g. K Jakobsen, *Die Seeschlacht vor dem Skagerrak* (Thyborøn: Sea War Museum Jutland, 2018), p 302, a work that also claims (p 303) that *Bremse* could be distinguished from *Brummer* by a missing row of scuttles amidships at between deck level. In fact, both vessels were all-but identical.

8 WAR – I

MOBILISATION

Germany declared war on Russia on 1 August 1914 and on France on the 3rd; the UK declared war on Germany on the 4th. At this point, cruiser strength in home waters comprised the large cruisers of I. SG and the small cruisers of II. SG: *Cöln* (flag), *Mainz, Stralsund, Kolberg, Rostock* and *Strassburg*, the latter just having returned from South America. Mobilisation brought forward to active service various small cruisers that had been in service as trials vessels, or laid up. Thus, the III. SG (redesignated IV. SG on 25 August)[1] was led by the former torpedo trials ship *München*, and contained the ex-gunnery training ships *Danzig* and *Stuttgart*, along with *Frauenlob*, recommissioned from reserve on 2 August, and the former tender to the HSF, *Hela*. The latter received another 8.8cm gun atop of her aft accommodation and was detached to act as leader of vessels on picket duties in the German Bight.[2]

Most other ex-trials, training and reserve vessels joined the various coastal defence divisions: *Arcona* was in that of the Ems; *Ariadne, Berlin, Niobe* and *Blitz* in the Jade/Weser; *Nymphe, Medusa* and *Pfeil* in the Elbe; and *Amazone, Augsburg, Gazelle, Magdeburg, Lübeck, Thetis* and *Undine*, with the large cruiser *Freya*, in the Baltic. Owing to a shortage of personnel, a few reserve vessels were not brought forward in time to join the initial formations. In the event, some of the oldest and least capable of the ships actually mobilised had begun to be withdrawn to secondary duties before resources became available to bring forward this residue.

As a result, *Gefion* remained laid up until she became an accommodation hulk in 1916. The old *Grille* finally recommissioned in July 1915, becoming tender to *Freya*, now again a training vessel, based at Flensburg-Mürwik, until the end of the war. The ex-small cruisers *Blitz* and *Pfeil* soon reverted to their long-standing pre-war roles as tenders to the battlefleet, split between North Sea and Baltic, attached respectively to I. and II. (later IV.) Sqns.

1. The IV. (renumbered III. on 25 August) and V. SG comprised older large cruisers.

2. The chief of staff High Seas Fleet ordered that *Hela*'s additional VIP accommodation aft – although unnecessary for her revived active role – should be left in place, in view of the short expected duration of the war. Nevertheless, at the special request by her CO, FKpt Paul Wolfram, she had the additional 8.8cm installed on her quarterdeck from 13–16 August, to give her some astern fire.

Of the Baltic vessels, it had originally been intended that, on mobilisation, *Magdeburg* should lay and protect a mine barrier in the List Deep, north of the island of Sylt. However, the breakdown of the cruiser's centre turbine in December 1913 had affected her manoeuvrability as well as speed, because of the lack of propeller wash around the rudder, and as a result she was placed on more general Baltic duties. Accordingly, with *Augsburg*, the brand-new torpedo boats *V25*, *V26* and the older *V186*, she initially became part of the Baltic Coast Defence Division under KAdm Robert Mischke (1865–1932). The vessels were, however, soon afterwards placed under the command of the Detached Admiral for the Baltic, KAdm Ehler Behring (1867–1918), a separate command established on 23 August 1914. This relatively weak force was all that the German navy could muster for offensive action in the eastern Baltic at this time, priority being given to the North Sea. Both cruisers had been so-allocated owing to defects that limited their top speeds (see p 140 for *Magdeburg*), but this was not felt to be an issue in the Baltic, since the Russians had no modern small cruisers in service[3] and, of their powerful armoured and protected cruisers, only the 21 knots *Rurik* was potentially fast enough to catch them.

Overseas, the largest grouping was the East Asiatic Cruiser Squadron, with the large cruisers *Scharnhorst* and *Gneisenau*, and the small cruisers *Emden*, *Leipzig* and *Nürnberg*, the latter pair having just exchanged duties as the vessel guarding German interests in western central America during the Mexican Revolution. On Mexico's Caribbean coast were *Dresden* and *Karlsruhe*, the latter in the process of relieving the former on the East American Station. On the East African Station was the newly arrived *Königsberg*. She had relieved *Geier*, freshly reclassified as a gunboat, and which had now been reassigned to the South Seas Station to replace *Condor*. The latter had been sent home early owing to her poor condition, and had arrived in

3. In addition to the two *Muravev-Amurskiy* class, which would now be completed for the German navy, four 6860t *Svetlana* class vessels had been laid down by Baltic yards in 1913 (pp 190-191). Launched during 1915/16, only one would eventually commission as a warship, in 1927, with two more finished in 1926 as mercantile tankers, and the fourth ship scrapped incomplete after languishing for more than three decades. Four 7,700-ton *Admiral Nakhimov* class vessels were building in the Black Sea, but only two were ever completed, in 1927 and 1932, the others being scrapped on the slip.

Probably the last known image of the intact *Magdeburg* in the Baltic, seen from her consort *Augsburg*. Torpedo tubes still occupy spaces intended for the foremost beam 10.5cm guns. *(DN collection)*

Germany in March 1914. Finally, in the Mediterranean were *Breslau* and the large cruiser *Goeben*. They had been due for relief, but were still on station when war broke out.

NEW CONSTRUCTION

While the lead-ship of the *Graudenz* class joined the III. (soon to be IV.) SG at Wilhelmshaven on 9 September 1914, her sister *Regensburg* would not be ready until the beginning of 1915. The follow-on *Ersatz-Gefion* [*Wiesbaden*] and *Ersatz-Gazelle* [*Königsberg* (ii)] classes would not be ready until late 1915 and late 1916, respectively.

Luckily, however, there were the two vessels under construction by Schichau at Danzig for the now enemy Russia (pp 181-183, above). By early May 1914, *Muravev-Amurskiy* had six boilers aboard, while the remaining four oil-fired boilers had just been delivered from the builder's boiler shop at Elbing. By the beginning of July, it was noted by Russian construction supervisors that quality control was falling short in the yard's efforts to meet its delivery schedules. The following month, work was nearing completion on many of *Muravev-Amurskiy* internal spaces, as well as on her superstructure, while *Admiral Nevelskoi*'s stem- and stern-posts had been set up, the bottom framing was complete, as were six strakes of the hull plating one each side.

Following the declaration of war on 1 August, the more advanced cruiser was provisionally requisitioned (under a Reich law dating back to 1873) for the German navy on 5 August 1914. This took the form of a simple telegram from the RMA: 'To Schichau Danzig: *Amursky* [sic!] to be completed for us with great expedition. Decision regarding armament will follow – RMA.' The telegram was confirmed by letter the following day.

It is important to note that, even under the said law, the cruiser could not be simply 'taken' or 'requisitioned' as war booty by the Reich, as it was still legally owned by Schichau, even though Russia had already paid several instalments towards its purchase. The German navy accordingly had to buy the ship from Schichau, the yard offering *Muravev-Amurskiy* for a basic price of 7.56 million Marks – which corresponded to the price of 3.5 million Roubles per vessel negotiated with the Russians in 1912. One week later, Schichau sought confirmation from Tirpitz that the Reich would actually pay for both cruisers.

To this, department 'K' objected, arguing that the second cruiser was so little advanced that the war might be over before its completion. In this case the vessel would be of little use, since after the war better cruisers of navy design would be available. Consequently, only the legal ownership on *Amurskiy* was transferred on 27 August 1914, in return for a first payment by the RMA. However, the question of adequate payment would become a serious and long-lasting issue. Tirpitz was, as always, keen on saving money, and tried to link the price to be paid for the ex-Russian ship to that agreed – after fierce competition – with Weser for *Ersatz-Irene* [*Regensburg*], two years earlier.

Schichau protested against this approach, as its own (allegedly cost-neutral) bid for the 1912 cruisers had been considerably higher. Consequently, the yard stubbornly insisted on a basic price of at least the equivalent to that which would have been paid by the Russian navy. On top of this would be any changes to the design necessary to take it from Russian to German standards. Matters would become even more complex, as Schichau wished to keep the instalments already paid by the Russians, as security against any requisitions by the Russians against Schichau-owned resources in Russia – e.g. the Mühlgraben yard at Riga (cf p 183).

The dispute escalated to such a degree that the State Secretary of the Treasury threatened Schichau with seizure of the Russian funds by the local military authorities.[4] Finally, at the end of November, both parties agreed on a price of 7.305 million Marks for *Amurskiy*, now renamed *Pillau*. This price would also be applicable to *Nevelskoi* but, as more deviations from the original plans were possible owing to her less-advanced state, the final price eventually paid for the latter ship would be different.

Back in August 1914, Schichau had been asked how far continuation of the work on *Nevelskoi* might affect the high-priority completion of not only *Amurskiy*, but also the large cruiser *Lützow* and a number of torpedo boats that the yard had in hand – and when *Nevelskoi* might be completed taking this other work into account. Schichau had replied that *Nevelskoi*'s construction would not affect the timely completion of the

4. The legal basis for this threat was that, since payments made for the two vessels to date could, obviously, not be repaid to Russia, Germany, by international law, was now Russia's temporary legal successor. According, the money entirely belonged to Germany, notwithstanding any further contracts concluded between (e.g.) the RMA and the shipyard.

other vessels, and that the yard should be able complete the second cruiser by May 1915 – provided no major changes to the design were requested by the RMA.

In any case, during an interdepartmental meeting on 17 September, Adm von Capelle, deputising for an absent Tirpitz, ordered that the second Russian cruiser should now be bought and completed for the German navy. Already, the Battle of the Marne a week earlier had halted the German army's early advance and initiated long-term trench warfare on the Western Front. This ended any hope of a speedy end to the war, and made longer-term thinking necessary regarding military materiel. Interestingly, the RMA did not inform the Admiralty Staff of the decision until 2 December.

At the September decision point, it was hoped to launch the hull of ex-*Nevelskoi* in early December. Large quantities of material had already been delivered, and apart from two oil-fired boilers – ready for delivery but still in the workshop at Elbing – everything needed was present at the Danzig yard. The four turbines were due to be delivered on a monthly basis between October and January, auxiliary machinery following afterwards.

While *Muravev-Amurskiy* had been renamed *Pillau* on 16 August 1914, *Admiral Nevelskoi* did not become *Elbing* until as late as 9 January, which indicates that her launch on 25 November 1914 had been without ceremony. Further friction between the RMA and shipyard arose when the former insisted on fitting bilge keels to both ships, which prompted the yard to decline to guarantee making the originally specified design speed of 27.5 knots.[5]

Both cruisers were completed with 15cm/45 guns in lieu of the planned Russian 130mm weapons, *Pillau* becoming the first German small cruiser in service carrying the long-debated heavier calibre, beating *Wiesbaden* into service by several months. *Pillau* also received the four 5.2cm AA weapons planned for (but never fitted in) the latter and her sister (see pp 152, 155), mounted in a rather cramped manner on top of the aft superstructure, which also accommodated both aft 15cm guns. The 5.2cm weapons were removed from *Pillau* as quite useless early in 1915, with the intention that they be replaced with two 8.8cm/45 mountings. However, although the first examples had been mounted in the large cruiser *Derfflinger* in September 1914, and were fitted in *Elbing* on her joining the fleet, *Pillau* did not get hers until January 1916 owing to supply difficulties. Two single 50cm torpedo tubes were added on the upper deck amidships in rotating mounts, while taller, part-cased, funnels were installed, the forward one further raised to clear the bridge of smoke. *Elbing* could be distinguished from her sister by having 1m-higher funnels, but lower casings. Also, as much less advanced when taken over, *Elbing* was rigged with masts of the latest German style, with crossed yards. Bridgework and deckhouses were also extended in both as compared with the original design.

Pillau commissioned at Danzig on 14 December 1914 and ran her initial trials on her transfer from Danzig to Kiel on 20/21 December 1914. Hand-over to the German navy had been scheduled for 11 January, but while the initial hour's run showed a maximum power of 35,500shp and an average of 34,103shp, this fell off during the later hours as the oil filters became repeatedly clogged by bad-quality fuel. Unfortunately, until her final release from trials on 16 March 1915, there is a significant gap in *Pillau*'s records, apart from a small unconfirmed note that she ultimately attained a maximum power of 44,900shp; no speed records have survived.

Initial plans had *Elbing* due to complete for preliminary trials on 19 July 1915, with trials starting on 31 July, but Schichau were unable to keep to this schedule. Even the next target of 29 August was missed, the cruiser finally commissioning at Danzig on 4 September. Her transfer to Kiel for official trials was carried out on 12–13 September, and on 19 October, she ran the shallow-water mile at design draught, attaining 27.64 knots at 43,716shp. The trials commission was

5. As an interesting comparison between Russian priorities, as enshrined in their contract, and those incorporated in the subsequent German one, the Russians would impose penalties on not fulfilling speed requirements, while the Germans concentrated on achieving the contracted power.

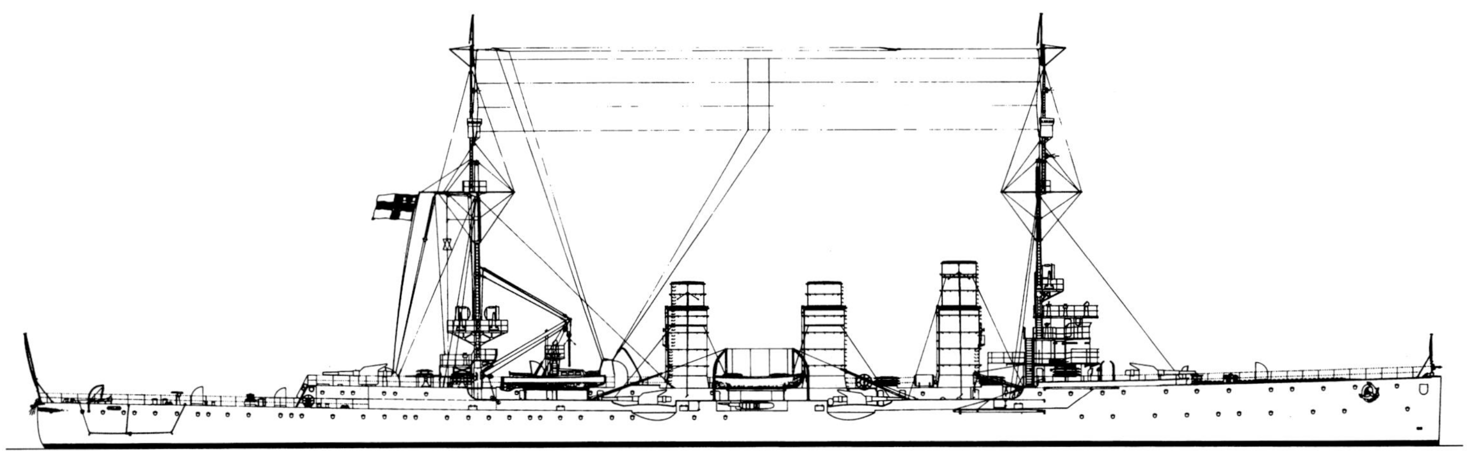

Rigging plan of *Pillau*, as completed. The two starboard 5.2cm AA guns may be seen just aft of the mainmast. *(B Abramowski drawing, courtesy M Biedermann)*

Above: *Elbing* returning to port during her trials. She still lacks her AA guns, while the spar often rigged over the stem during trials appears to have been retouched out. Compared with her sister, she has forecastle extended further aft, to just forward of the first beam guns, while her differently cased funnels are clearly visible. **Right:** *Pillau* on 4 January 1915, running preliminary trials at high speed. Note – contrary to expectations – the minimal volume of smoke generated by the coal-fired boilers of the forward funnel. *(DN collection)*

not particularly impressed with *Elbing*'s performance, calling her, inter alia, extremely unhandy and hard to manoeuvre.[6] In addition, in anything other than calm weather, and at high speeds, the two 15cm guns on the forecastle were badly affected by spray, due to the lack of flare on the very sharp bow. On the other hand, after *Elbing* was finally released from her trials on 4 November, the German navy had now received two well-armed 15cm cruisers, which it would use to good effect.

Brief consideration was given to employing *Pillau* as a commerce raider. This was, however, dropped, as the high proportion of her power derived from oil-fired boilers meant that her need for a proper oil supply was too critical: colliers might be regularly captured, but not oil tankers, still less those from which oiling at sea might be possible.

FIRST BLOOD

German doctrine had assumed that the British would impose a close blockade, thus giving ample opportunities for British numerical superiority to be whittled away by coastal mine and torpedo warfare. However, this had in reality long since been abandoned as a concept by the British in favour of distant blockade, which nullified the German strategy.[7] Thus, there was a need to take a more proactive approach, beginning with an operation on 17–18 August 1914, when *Strassburg* and *Stralsund*, supported by *U19* and *U24*, were to surprise British destroyers in the Broad Fourteens, between Yarmouth and the Netherlands. Distant cover was to be provided by *Kolberg*, with three large cruisers at high readiness in Schillig Roads off Wilhelmshaven in case of emergencies.

At 06.18 on the 18th, HMS/M *E5* and *E7* were sighted by

6. These issues may have contributed to *Elbing*'s loss following a collision during the Battle of Jutland (see p 217 below).

7. For an overview of the first months of the war at sea in home waters, see J Goldrick, *Before Jutland: the naval war in northern European waters, August 1914–February 1915* (Annapolis, MD: Naval Institute Press, 2015). See also the official British narrative, *Naval Staff Monographs* 1–18, available at www.navy.gov.au/media-room/publications/world-war-i-naval-staff-monographs.

Strassburg 20nm off the Norfolk coast, already on the return leg of the Broad-Fourteens sortie, which in turn mistook her for a British armoured cruiser of the *Cressy* class; she fired on them, without scoring a hit. Twenty minutes later, some 30nm further east, *Stralsund* sighted British destroyers of the Harwich-based 1st DF, and part of the recently organised British Southern Force. Fire was exchanged, but the German cruiser was then misidentified as a large cruiser of the *Yorck* class by Captain (D) in the light cruiser *Fearless*, leading to a temporary withdrawal by the British force. Kpt Victor Harder initially followed but, suspecting a trap, and believing he had spotted a second cruiser, turned away and retired at 07.40. The British, now satisfied that their opponent was only a small cruiser, followed, but it was too late to resume the action. This had been the first surface action by a German small cruiser during the war. *Stralsund*'s war diary reported several hits on British destroyers, and being missed by torpedoes, but British sources report neither hits nor torpedo discharges.

In retaliation for this raid, the British planned a sweep against German patrol vessels off Heligoland, to be carried out by *Fearless* and her destroyers, the 3rd DF, the new light cruiser *Arethusa*, flagship of the Harwich Force, plus eight submarines. They would be supported by the battlecruisers *New Zealand* and *Invincible*, to the north, together with the 7th CS to the west. The 1st BCS and 1st LCS were later added as further support.

When the operation was carried out on 28 August 1914, the German patrol line comprised nine torpedo boats of the V. TBF. They were supported by a number of small cruisers: *Stettin* and *Frauenlob*, lying at anchor east of Heligoland; *Hela* to the east, between Heligoland and the Eider estuary; *Ariadne* in the Weser estuary; and *Mainz* in that of the Ems. *Cöln*, flagship of the II. SG and HSF torpedo boats, was coaling at Wilhelmshaven. The first contact was between *G194* and a number of British destroyers at 07.53, the former falling back and being joined by *G196*, *V1*, *V6*, *G9* and *S13*. *Stettin* intervened and, at 08.58, opened fire on one group of British destroyers, thus saving *V1*, which had already been hit twice, and *S13* from probable destruction, before breaking off at 09.10 to raise steam on all boilers.

This allowed the British to push deeper into the Heligoland Bight and attack the III. MSD of old torpedo boats, a number of vessels being badly mauled and saved only by the arrival of *Frauenlob*, which opened fire on *Arethusa* at 09.08, hitting her some thirty times and leaving her badly damaged, receiving ten hits in exchange. She then retired to Heligoland, towing the badly damaged *T33*, hit by three shells, and then on to Wilhelmshaven, arriving at 11.30. Meanwhile, *V187*, leader of the V. TBF, had become heavily engaged, being sunk around 10.00, just as *Stettin* returned to the fray, to herself receive a number of hits from British destroyers. *Hela* had headed towards the action, but was at 11.15 diverted to support the northern part of the patrol line.

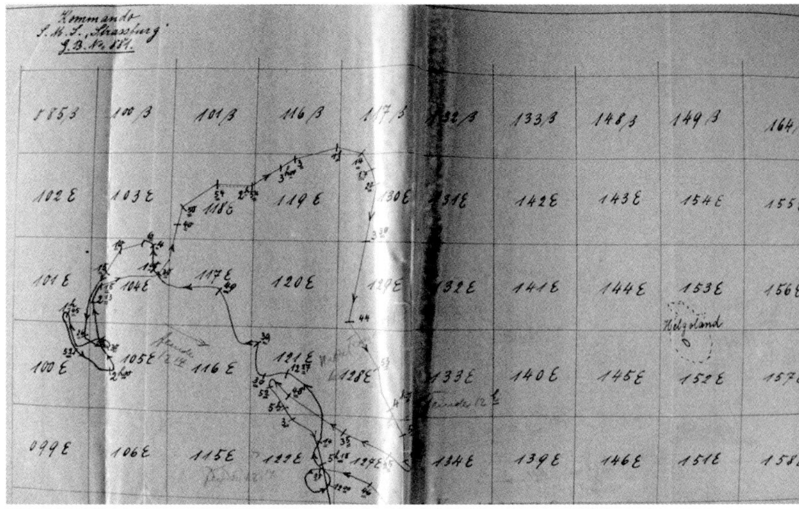

Strassburg's rather chaotic track during the Battle of Heligoland Bight, as plotted on the North Sea grid map. It may serve as a general indication of the action's generally confused nature. *(DN collection)*

At Wilhelmshaven, *Cöln* and *Strassburg* put to sea at 09.10 and 09.30, *Stralsund* being ordered to the roadstead, where *Kolberg* was to raise steam. *Danzig* and *München*, at Brunsbüttel, were directed to Elbe estuary, while *Mainz* was to remain at readiness on the Ems. The I. SG of large cruisers were ordered to raise steam, although they would be unable to cross the Jade bar until after 12.00, and the II. Sqn of battleships went to one hour's readiness.

By 11.30, *Cöln*, *Strassburg* and *Stralsund* were on their way to the area of the action, as was *Mainz*, with *Kolberg* to follow, *Strassburg* being the first to engage, at 11.55. *Mainz* ended up in action with *Fearless* and six destroyers around 13.00, having her steering jammed by a hit aft, and as a result coming under fire from much of the British light cruiser and destroyer force. *Mainz* was largely disabled by 13.20, at which time she was also hit by a torpedo from the destroyer *Lydiard* on the port side amidships. Scuttling measures were ordered at 13.35, and around 14.00 the British destroyer *Lurcher* came alongside to take off survivors, ten minutes before *Mainz* rolled over and sank.[8]

During *Mainz*'s final ordeal, the balance of forces was totally altered by the arrival of the five British battlecruisers. *Cöln*, which had initially engaged *Arethusa* and accompanying destroyers, came under their fire soon after her arrival on the battlefield, being badly hit and her admiral killed. Initially able to retire, following the appearance of *Ariadne* from the Weser around 14.00, *Cöln* was again caught by the battlecruisers and rapidly reduced to a sinking condition, capsizing to port at 14.25.

Ariadne was herself soon under fire, losing her forward boiler

8. One of her survivors was Tirpitz's son, Obltn z S Wolfgang von Tirpitz, the news of whose survival was secretly transmitted to his father by British First Lord of the Admiralty, Winston Churchill via diplomatic channels.

room due to a severe bunker fire caused by a heavy hit and suffering other damage before the British ceased fire around 14.15. She was now burning fore and aft, with the forward magazine flooded and ready-use ammunition exploding on deck. An hour later, *Danzig* and *Stralsund* were able to take off her survivors, but the ship herself capsized and sank at 16.25, in spite of an attempt by *Stralsund* to take her in tow.

Other German cruisers were more fortunate, *Strassburg* escaping by virtue of her resemblance to a British cruiser, and *Stralsund* suffering only minor damage in her exchange with the battlecruisers. The large cruisers *Von der Tann* and *Moltke* sailed at 15.00, arriving near the sinking *Ariadne* at 15.25, and were joined by *Seydlitz* at 16.10, and still later by *Blücher*. By then, the British had withdrawn, and the big ships were back in Wilhelmshaven roads by 21.30. The German home cruiser fleet's wretched start to the war was exacerbated little over two weeks later when, on 13 September 1914, halfway between Wilhelmshaven and the island of Heligoland, *Hela* was torpedoed by the British submarine *E9* and sank within twenty-five minutes. Fortunately, with the exception of two men, the whole crew was saved.

Mine warfare would be an important part of the conflict, *Nautilus*, which had recommissioned on 5 June 1914, being placed under the direct command of the HSF on the outbreak of war for service in the North Sea. As such, she laid the first defensive fields outside several inlets and river estuaries north of the Elbe river. A planned offensive use of both minesteamers against the British east coast in mid-August had to be postponed, due to fear of detection during the still-too-bright summer nights. Only at the end of August, it was expected by fleet command, would the first raids be possible. On 25 August 1914 *Nautilus* finally sailed, escorted by *Mainz* and torpedo boats, to lay fields off the Tyne and Humber, the vessels sinking six British fishing vessels on their return journey. In the meantime, *Albatross*, in company with *Stuttgart*, laid another field off the Tyne during 22–26 August.

On 9–10 September 1914, *Nautilus*, *Albatross* and the auxiliary minelayer (ex-passenger steamer) *Kaiser* ('A') laid a defensive minefield in home waters, as first leg of the enclosure of the inner German Bight, supported by the cruisers *Prinz Adalbert*, *Roon*, *Kolberg* and *Stralsund*. On 14 October, *Nautilus* and *Kolberg* made an abortive foray into the North Sea, when plans for a field in the Firth of Forth were frustrated by the presence of British ships, only 40nm short of her destination.

Nautilus remained assigned to the North Sea until April 1916, although detached on occasion to the Baltic (including laying a field from the Gjedser Riff lightship to Darsser Ort [covering the 'Kadet-gutter' between Denmark and Germany]). She was also used as a target ship for submarines in training, colliding with the submerged *U70* in the autumn of 1915 while so employed, damaging herself considerably, with a 4m gash in her hull and a flooded compartment.

The first major fleet operation came in early November 1914, when the I. SG, (*Seydlitz* [flag], *Von der Tann, Moltke* and *Blücher*) undertook a bombardment of Yarmouth, supported by the II. SG (*Strassburg, Graudenz, Kolberg* and *Stralsund*), of which *Stralsund* would also lay mines there and off Lowestoft. This was part of a broader strategy to deploy the Scouting Force on operations that could draw out parts of the British fleet, which would then be destroyed by the main body of the HSF, lying in wait further to the east. On this occasion, little was achieved, save the loss of HMS/M *D5*, apparently sunk by a mine laid by *Stralsund*, and three British trawlers, for the accidental loss of the large cruiser *Yorck* on a German defensive minefield of the inner Jade barrage. It was only after this accident that the various inner mine defences, under the guns and supervision of the fortifications along the coast, were properly assessed.

A further operation of the same type was begun on 15 December, against Hartlepool, Scarborough and Whitby, with I. SG now reinforced by the new *Derfflinger*. Bad weather meant that all the small cruisers except *Kolberg* (carrying mines) and torpedo boats were detached from the raiding force to return home early on the morning of the 16th. The I. SG successfully carried out its bombardment and retired around 11.00, but the main fleet had in the meantime missed its chance to come to grips with the very detachment of the British Grand Fleet that had been a key objective of the operation.

At 05.15, the fleet's vanguard, *Roon* and *Prinz Heinrich*, had run into the advanced destroyers of the British BCS and 2nd BS – ten capital ships in all – plus four armoured and six light cruisers, accompanied by destroyers. Against them were ranged thirteen modern and eight old German battleships, the two aforementioned armoured cruisers, the seven small cruisers of the IV. SG, and supporting torpedo boats. While by no means comprising overwhelming force (especially since most of the British capital ships mounted 13.5in [34.3cm] guns, rather than the lighter German 28cm and 30.5cm pieces, and were faster) the chances of some success were reasonable, especially in light of the deficiencies in British explosives safety that became all too clear during the Battle of Jutland eighteen months later. However, concerns at exceeding standing orders regarding avoiding action with potentially superior forces meant that it was decided at this point to withdraw the HSF: the chance would never come again.

WAR IN DISTANT WATERS

The Mediterranean and Black Sea

On 2 August 1914, as war was beginning, the two ships of the Mediterranean Division, *Goeben* and *Breslau*, were coaling at Messina. It had been envisaged that in the event of hostilities, the division would disrupt the movement of French troops from the North African colonies, and/or break out through the straits of Gibraltar and return to Germany. In accordance with the former concept, on 3 August, *Breslau* shelled Bone (Annaba), while *Goeben* fired on Philippeville (Skikda).

Orders were then received to sail for Constantinople, a journey that could not be undertaken without coaling, which was planned to take place once again at Messina. En route, at 10.15 on the 4th, the German ships encountered the British battlecruisers *Indefatigable* and *Indomitable*, but as the UK's ultimatum to Germany would not expire until later that day, no hostile moves were made, although *Goeben* and *Breslau* were now shadowed by the British ships – which had, however, been eluded by the time that the Germans reached Messina on the 5th.

Although part of the Triple Alliance with Germany and Austria-Hungary, Italy had declared her neutrality on 2 August, but permitted the German cruisers to remain for half a day over the normal limits for a belligerent power while receiving coal from a German collier. However, by the time they sailed, not enough coal had been transferred to them to reach Turkish waters, now the ship's intended destination after brief consideration had been given to diverting the ships to the Adriatic, to join the Austro-Hungarian forces, or to the Atlantic. *Breslau* and *Goeben* left for the east on the 6th and, although shadowed for a time by the light cruiser *Gloucester*, the latter was soon shaken off.

The idea that the German cruisers might head for Turkey was not easily grasped by the Anglo-French commanders, the French fleet remaining in the western Mediterranean on the assumption that the German ships would either attempt to break out into the Atlantic, or retire to the Adriatic. The three British battlecruisers in the Mediterranean (the third was *Inflexible*) were also far away when the German force sailed from Messina, although, the British 1st CS (armoured cruisers *Defence*, *Black Prince*, *Duke of Edinburgh* and *Warrior*) was in the vicinity but, misled by the Germans' initial course, first sought to intercept the German ships at the mouth of the Adriatic.

The error having been realised, the British light cruiser *Dublin* and two destroyers attempted to intercept, but were foiled by the darkness. The armoured cruisers continued the chase until early on the 7th, when the British commander, RAdm Sir Ernest Troubridge, concluded that *Goeben* represented too superior a force against which to risk the British ships and withdrew – a decision that earned him a court martial (at which he was acquitted). Thus, *Goeben* and *Breslau* were able to find a secluded location, off the Greek island of Donoussa in the Cyclades, to coal once again on 9–10 August, and on the afternoon of 10 August enter the Dardanelles unmolested. On 16 August, they were 'sold' to the Ottoman Navy, *Goeben*, ostensibly to replace the battleships *Sultan Osman I* and *Reşadiye*, requisitioned while completing in UK shipyards on 31 July (to become HMS *Agincourt* and *Erin*, respectively). *Goeben* became *Yavuz Sultan Selim* and *Breslau* became *Midilli*.

Midilli (ex-*Breslau*) as leader of the Ottoman cruiser division at anchor during exercises in the Sea of Marmora. In the distance the ex-German battleship *Torgud Reis*. *(DN collection)*

Nevertheless, they retained their German crews, albeit now dressed in Ottoman uniform, the German Flag Officer Mediterranean Division (KAdm Wilhelm Souchon [1864–1946]) becoming double-hatted as simultaneously CinC of the Ottoman Navy a month later.

Beginning on 27 October, *Midilli* took part in operations, initiated by the personal order of the Ottoman War Minister, Enver Pasha (1881–1922), that were intended to draw the Ottoman Empire into the war on the German side. While *Yavuz* bombarded Sevastopol on the 29th, and two Ottoman destroyers raided Odessa, *Midilli* and the Ottoman torpedo cruiser *Berk-i Satvet* were to attack Novorossiysk, and the Ottoman cruiser *Hamidiye* Feodosia and Yalta. *Midilli* and *Berk-i Satvet* set oil tanks on fire, and sank one merchant ship and damaged damaged seven others. As a result, Russia declared war on 2 November, followed by the UK and France on the 5th.

In early November 1914, *Midilli*, while covering transports, was detached to shell Poti, and on 17 November she and *Yavuz Sultan Selim* sailed with a view to intercepting the Russian fleet on its return from a bombardment of Trebizond. This led on 18 November to the Battle of Cape Sarych with the Russian Black Sea Fleet Battle Brigade (*Evstafii*, *Ioann Zlatoust*, *Panteleimon*, *Tri Sviatitelia* and *Rostislav*), which was returning from a bombardment of Trebizond. While the small cruiser did not open fire, mainly because of poor visibility, damage was suffered by both *Yavuz* and *Evstafii* before the action was broken off.

Midilli was then employed on escort duties to Trebizond. On 5 December, she escorted the small coastal steamer *Zafer*, transporting a small cavalry force intending to attack railway facilities at Akkerman, Bessarabia. On the return leg she undertook a reconnaissance of Sevastopol, during which the cruiser had a short engagement with minesweepers, damaging one of them. On 24 December, *Midilli* sank the Russian transport *Oleg*, en route to be expended as a blockship in Zonguldak, but was forced to retire by the approach of *Rostislav*. Nevertheless, she was then able to force another intended blockship, *Athos*, to scuttle. Ottoman coast batteries forced the Russians to scuttle the remaining blockships as well. The cruiser undertook a series of operations during early 1915, including one alongside *Hamidiye* in January, during which they encountered the Russian fleet. *Midilli*, despite being heavily under fire, was not hit and did not herself open fire before withdrawing into the covering darkness.

During the following months, *Midilli*'s serviceability became problematic. She was immobilised during the critical days of the Anglo-French Dardanelles operations owing to defects with her starboard HP turbine, which also restricted her speed during several short raids against the ports of Yalta and Feodosia on the Crimean coast. On 3 April, the Ottoman fleet sailed to interdict Russian transports off Odessa, with the two Turco-German cruisers acting as a covering force for the attack. *Midilli* came directly from duty as a fast transport along the Anatolian coast, meeting *Yavuz Sultan Selim* near Sevastopol. However, during the operation the cruiser *Mecidiye* was mined off Odessa and foundered in shallow water: she was later salved and commissioned as the Russian *Prut*.

On 10–11 June, *Midilli* engaged the Russian destroyers *Derzki* and *Gnevny* off Zonguldak, crippling the latter with her first salvo, in exchange for three hits that, however, did moderate damage. The lessons from this minor engagement included further evidence in favour of up-gunning the German small cruiser force: it was becoming all too obvious that modern Russian destroyers were a match for the cruisers, which were armed with nothing bigger than 10.5cm guns. On this occasion the 'hail of fire' at short range (1nm) had prevailed, but the damage received in exchange from only two of the three hits was alarming. *Midilli*'s firepower issues were further exacerbated by having given up two 10.5cm guns consecutively to the defences of the Dardanelles.

Midilli hit a mine under number 4 boiler room on 18 July 1915 while outbound from Constantinople, taking on 600 tonnes of water and killing eight men, although she was able to make İstinye under her own power. Her survival owed much to her longitudinal framing system, which absorbed the detonation's bending forces close to amidships without failing. Complete repairs lasted until February 1916, even though the cruiser would have been able to sail on ten boilers on 24 October 1915. The main reason for the extended refit period was that it included the replacement of the forward pair of 10.5cm guns with a single 15cm weapon, and the placement of another example of the latter on the quarterdeck. Although the repairs would have been an ideal time for the complete up-gunning of a ship whose services were normally in constant demand, a backlog at Krupp's and the low priority accorded to the German-Ottoman ships meant that only two guns could be spared at this point in time.

On 27–28 February 1916, *Midilli* acted as a transport for military reinforcements to Trebizond, evading the Russian destroyers *Pronzitelni* and *Bespokoiny* en route, making further

Two of the various iterations of *Midilli*'s armament. The upper image shows the single 10.5cm left atop the superstructure deck aft after the second gun had temporarily been handed over for use ashore at the end of May 1915. The lower image shows not only the missing gun returned to its place, but also the addition of a 15cm weapon to the quarterdeck. *(DN collection)*

runs on 11–13 March and 3 April. The latter was followed by an attack, along with the submarine *U33*, on Sürmene Bay, east of Trebizond, where they sank the Russian minesweeper *T233*. *Midilli* then sank a Russian sailing vessel off Tuapse before encountering the Russian battleship *Imperatritsa Ekaterina Velikaya* on 4 April, escaping in spite of being more than once straddled and hit by splinters.

Early in May 1916, *Midilli* laid minefields off Izmail and Cape Tarkhankut in the Crimea, the second lay being followed by a bombardment of Eupatoria. She transported troops to Sinope and Samsun on 30 May, returning with a cargo of grain and tobacco. In July, she and *Yavuz Sultan Selim* supported an Ottoman counterattack at Trebizond, *Midilli* sinking three Russian ships off Sochi on 4 July. On the 21st, *Midilli* was nearly trapped by the Russian battleship *Imperatritsa Mariya* while attempting to lay a minefield off Novorossiisk, escaping with splinter damage and a number of wounded personnel.

Midilli's withdrawal had been hampered by several factors.

Midilli in the autumn of 1916 at İstinye, moored alongside *Yavuz Sultan Selim*, while temporarily immobilised by coal shortages. She has had now landed all 10.5cm guns, leaving just a 15cm weapon fore and aft, pending the arrival of additional pieces of the latter calibre. At this period the upper parts of her funnels had been painted a dark colour for camouflage purposes. *(DN collection)*

Before being able to reply against the escorting destroyers, several mines had to be jettisoned to clear the arcs of the aft 15cm gun. The extra weight of the remaining mine load may be one of the reasons for the exaggerated speeds later attributed to *Imperatritsa Mariya*, when she was seen to be gaining on the overloaded *Midilli*, which was making revolutions normally adequate for 24–25 knots. The experience of this rather lucky withdrawal would reinforce the need for the already planned complete up-gunning that, together with other necessary modifications, finally began in the late summer of 1916 and would last until the spring of 1917.

This was an upside of the coal shortages that would limit operations for much of the following year. Thus, *Midilli* had her machinery overhauled, the remaining ten 10.5cm weapons landed and replaced by six more 15cm guns on the broadside. Additionally, director firing for the guns was installed, supported by additional rangefinders fore and aft. Work was completed on 30 April 1917, the ship being left with a completely different arrangement and number of weapons as compared with her two surviving sisters back in Germany. The removed 10.5cm guns were redeployed, some of them on rafts for riverine use in Mesopotamia.

In May 1917, *Midilli* laid a minefield off the mouth of the Danube, also destroying the wireless station on Fidonisi Island off Izmail. While returning, she ran into a Russian force led by *Svobodnaya Rossiya* (ex-*Imperatritsa Ekaterina Velikaya*), once again managing to escape. On 1 November, she sailed to conduct a sweep that was detected by the Russians, but a potential interception by *Svobodnaya Rossiya* and the new battleship *Volya* (ex-*Imperator Aleksander III*) was frustrated by a mutiny aboard the former vessel.

The end of hostilities with Russia on 15 December 1917 freed the Ottoman navy to undertake operations to the west. Thus, on the morning of 20 January 1918, *Midilli* accompanied *Yavuz Sultan Selim* on a raid against British forces off the islands of Imbros and Lemnos. However, not long after their departure, *Yavuz Sultan Selim* struck a mine, allegedly in spite of the force's possession of a captured British sketch map of the minefields in the area.[9] However, damage was minor, and the ships pushed on, finding the Aliki anchorage empty, but bombarding the radio station at Kephalo en route to the anchorage at Kusu Bay.

There, they first sighted the patrolling destroyer *Lizard* and then the 14in-gunned monitor *Raglan*, the only big gun ship present, the battleship *Agamemnon* being at Mudros, on Lemnos, and her sister *Lord Nelson* having gone to Salonika four days earlier. A shell from *Midilli* wrecked *Raglan*'s fire control, while further hits from the cruiser penetrated the engine room. Also hit by *Yavuz Sultan Selim*, *Raglan* was eventually sunk by a magazine explosion. *M28* was hit amidships by *Midilli*, blowing up and sinking twelve minutes after *Raglan*.

The Turco-German ships then sailed to attack Mudros, under ineffectual attack by British aircraft. However, due to *Midilli*'s overtaking of *Yavuz Sultan Selim* – only the large cruiser had AA guns capable of firing on an aft bearing – the former soon found herself unexpectedly at the edge of a minefield. *Midilli*, having narrowly avoided the nearest mine, then exploded it with one of her starboard screws at 07.45, blowing off both starboard propellers and leaving the ship all but unmanoeuvrable. While attempting to pass a tow, *Yavuz Sultan Selim* struck a mine on the port side amidships, causing sufficient flooding to cause a list. Now, helplessly entrapped in the mine-

9. This sketch map is still one of the major mysteries surrounding events of First World War. It was reported – according to the war diary Mediterranean Division – to have been found on a grounded British drifter named '*Kim*' (in fact *Annie*, Admiralty drifter no 2118, stranded on 19 December 1917 [TNA: ADM 137/400, cited in D J Hepper, *British Warship Losses in the Ironclad Era 1860–1919* (London: Greenhill Books, 2007), p 113]) off Enos (Edez), in the Gulf of Saros, and brought aboard *Yavuz* immediately before her departure. A key question is why this particular vessel had a 'secret' sketch map on board that in fact contained erroneous information regarding the British minefields' positions off Gallipoli. Because of *Annie*'s reported task on that day, landing agents, one is tempted to suspect that the map was left behind as deliberate deception, especially as it was reported that all 'secret' materials had been burned.

Karlsruhe coaling at San Juan, Puerto Rico, on 9 August 1914. *(DN collection)*

field, *Midilli* subsequently struck four more mines in quick succession around 08.00, and sank at 08.07.

The Western Atlantic

The wartime mission of *Karlsruhe* was to carry out cruiser warfare in the Atlantic and, to bolster this task, on 6 August she met the German liner *Kronprinz Wilhelm* off the Bahamas to transfer two 8.8cm guns and ammunition, to allow the latter to act as an auxiliary cruiser.[10] As such, *Kronprinz Wilhelm* would capture fifteen ships between September 1914 and April 1915, when she was interned in the USA.

The two ships were surprised by the armoured cruiser HMS *Suffolk* while transferring stores, *Karlsruhe* being pursued, but able to escape owing to her much higher speed than the (at best) 23-knots armoured cruiser. An attempt to call at Newport News for fuel was frustrated by the appearance of HMS *Bristol*, there being a brief exchange of fire before *Karlsruhe* once again escaped. Running extremely short of fuel, the German cruiser now made for Puerto Rico, arriving at San Juan on 9 August 1914 and taking on 550 tonnes of coal from the German steamer *Odenwald*, before sailing the next morning, making her way into the Caribbean. Here, she met with the HAPAG steamer *Patagonia*, which had been sent with supplies and 2,000 tonnes of coal.

Karlsruhe was thus able to start her raiding career, taking her first prize on 18 August. From 21 to 23 August, she coaled from *Patagonia* near Maraca Island (Amapá), taking aboard 1,300 tonnes of coal, 130 tonnes of which was stowed on deck. Further fuel supplies arrived aboard other German merchantmen over the next few weeks, allowing *Karlsruhe* to capture seventeen ships between 3 September and 26 October 1914.

Coaling from *Farn*, captured carrying 7000 tonnes of coal, at the São João Islands on 29 October, and from another prize, *Indrani*, on 1 November at Maraca Island, she then sailed towards Barbados, to raid not only the island itself, but also its shipping. However, at 18.30 on 4 November, *Karlsruhe*'s forward magazine exploded, the bow, with the conning tower, bridgework and forefunnel, sinking immediately. The remainder of the ship foundered twenty-seven minutes later, with the loss of 263 men, including the captain. The 146 survivors were picked up by the accompanying supply ship *Rio Negro*, which reached Kiel on 6 December. The loss of *Karlsruhe* was successfully kept secret until April 1915.

Although no definitive conclusion can be reached over the cause of the explosion, several potential causes have been proposed over the years. A simple magazine explosion seems unlikely, as the break in the hull seems to have occurred considerably aft of the forward magazines. It is perhaps more likely the disaster was triggered by the forward transverse oil bunker, at that time containing an unusually light and volatile oil, rather than the more usual tar oil. The high ambient temperatures could have led to the build up of vapour in the bunker, the combustion of which would have affected the adjacent torpedo room (slightly aft of the bridge) before eventually causing a sympathetic explosion of the magazines further forward, under and before the bridge.

The other cruiser in American waters, *Dresden*, had just left the Virgin Islands en route home when her orders were changed to cruiser warfare off the east coast of South America. The Hamburg-Süd steamer *Corrientes* was allocated as *Dresden*'s first collier, and having coaled from her, *Dresden* made her first capture on 14 August 1914, another following on the 26th. Two more supply vessels having now joined, repairs, supplies and further coaling took place on 5 September in Orange Bay near Cape Horn, at which point *Dresden* was redirected to the Pacific to join *Leipzig*. The cruisers made radio contact on 3 October, while in the Juan Fernández Islands, the two ships meeting the East Asiatic Cruiser Squadron on 12 October at Easter Island.

The Far East and Pacific

On 2 August 1914, *Leipzig* had left her Mexican base and sailed to Magdalen Bay on the west coast of Baja California, where she received news of the outbreak of war with the Entente powers. Having unsuccessfully sought British merchantmen in the area, she went to San Francisco on 17 August to coal, but the cruiser was permitted to receive only 500 tonnes. Returning to Mexican waters, she was able on 10 September to acquire 930 tonnes of coal at Guayamas, allowing *Leipzig* to sail to the Galapagos Islands. There she met the German ships *Amasis* and *Abessinia*, which provided her with enough coal security to meet *Scharnhorst*, *Gneisenau* and *Nürnberg* on 14 October off Easter Island.

Leipzig coaling in the port of Guayamas, Mexico. *(AD collection)*

10. *Karlsruhe* (and *Königsberg*: see below) had been the first small cruisers sent abroad carrying two extra 8.8cm guns for the possible outfit of auxiliary cruisers. This was a precursor to a proposal by the Admiralty Staff that selected non-liner merchantmen sail with dismantled guns, ready to be quickly mounted should hostilities break out. One of the prevailing arguments for this approach was that the UK already suspected that this was German policy.

The third small cruiser of the East Asiatic Cruiser Squadron, *Emden*, had, together with the auxiliary cruiser *Prinz Eitel Friedrich*, also from Tsingtau, joined *Nürnberg* and the two large cruisers of the squadron, *Scharnhorst* (flag) and *Gneisenau*, at Pagan on 12 August. However, the following day *Emden* and *Prinz Eitel Friedrich* had been detached to act as commerce raiders. The latter, armed at Tsingtau with guns from the gunboats *Tiger*, *Luchs*, *Iltis* and *Jaguar*, would sink seventeen ships before seeking internment at Newport News in the USA in March 1915.

Emden and *Geier*

Geier had headed for Batavia after leaving Singapore on 29 July, to minimise the danger of being located by potential enemy forces. While off the former port she was ordered on 3 August to join the East Asiatic Cruiser Squadron at Yap, while also carrying out cruiser warfare. She coaled from the German steamer *Elmshorn* at Jampea on 6 August, before passing through the Buton Strait and rendezvousing with SS *Bochum*, which was to be her collier – and also acted on occasion as her tug, to save fuel.

On 21 August, *Geier* met *Emden* and her collier *Markomania* at sea west of the Philippines, after which *Geier* steamed to Angaur, where she coaled from the German steamer *Tsingtau*. With the intention of meeting the East Asiatic Cruiser Squadron in the central Pacific, *Geier* proceeded through the Bismarck Archipelago, before turning north. On 4 September, off Kusaie, *Geier* captured the British steamer *Southport*, but did not sink her, merely disabling her engines; after effecting repairs, *Southport* made Australia and gave the alarm. *Geier* reached Majuro on 11 September, but had missed the East Asiatic Cruiser Squadron by nearly a fortnight, and was now suffering from increasing machinery defects.

Nevertheless, it was decided that *Geier* would continue east, being towed by the German steamer *Locksun* to the Romanzoff Islands, where repairs were undertaken from 17 to 20 September. But by now it was clear that the fuel and water situation would not allow *Geier* to proceed any further than Hawaii. The ship arrived at Honolulu on 15 October 1914, where she was interned on 7 November – much to the frustration of the Japanese battleship *Hizen* and armoured cruiser *Asama*, which were by now waiting offshore for her to emerge.

Geier under the US flag as USS *Schurz*, at San Diego during November to December 1917. *(NHHC NH 94909)*

With the US entry into the war on 6 April 1917, *Geier* was seized by the American authorities. On 22 May, President Woodrow Wilson signed Executive Order 2624 officially authorising the US navy to take possession of the vessel. She was then refitted, including rearmament with four 5in guns, incorporated into the US navy as USS *Schurz* on 9 June, and commissioned on 15 September 1917. Departing Pearl Harbor, she escorted Submarine Division 3 from Hawaii to San Diego, arriving on 12 November, and then shepherding the submarines *K-3*, *K-4*, *K-7* and *K-8* through the Panama Canal. *Schurz* subsequently operated off the US east coast and in the Caribbean until she collided with SS *Florida* off the North Carolina coast on 21 June on passage from New York to Key West. She sank three hours later in 35m of water, with one dead and twelve injured.

Having taken leave of *Geier*, *Emden* continued southwest through the Molucca and Banda Seas, being prevented from coaling off Jampea Island, just south of Celebes, by the Dutch coast defence ship *Marten Harpertzoon Tromp*. She then passed through the Lombok Strait and sailed along the coasts of Java and Sumatra to enter the Indian Ocean.

The cruiser entered the Bay of Bengal on 5 September, taking her first prize on the 10th – a Greek collier that became a further support vessel for *Emden*. Five more ships were taken shortly afterwards, with two more added on the 13th. News of the captures resulted in a suspension of Allied sailings in the area, with the cruisers HMS *Hampshire* and HMS *Yarmouth* and the Japanese cruiser *Chikuma* directed to search for Emden, and the armoured cruiser HMS *Minotaur* and the Japanese battlecruiser *Ibuki* to cover likely coaling stations.

On evening of 22 September 1914, *Emden* bombarded the port of Madras, damaging a merchant ship, setting fire to two oil tanks and damaging three more. This was followed by a suspension of shipping in the Bay of Bengal, thus further paralysing local trade. *Emden* then headed west of Ceylon (Sri Lanka), where she sank two British merchantmen on 25 September, and two days later sank two more ships and subsequently captured a British collier, which was added to the German cruiser's support network. She coaled in the Maldives on 29–30 September, and then cruised the Aden–Australia and Calcutta–Mauritius trade routes before sailing to the British possession of Diego Garcia in the Chagos Islands – which was unaware of the outbreak of war. This allowed *Emden* to remain under maintenance, including bottom cleaning, until 10 October. She then returned to her hunting area.

Emden at anchor on Tsingtau's outer anchorage, shortly before the First World War. *(DN collection)*

Having picked up British radio traffic from HMS *Hampshire*, she sailed from the Chagos Islands on 13 October to the area just north of the Maldives, where *Emden* made six captures between the 16th and 19th, before shifting her area of operations back east. These began, following coaling in the Nicobar Islands, with an attack on Penang at 03.00 on 28 October, again sporting her dummy fourth funnel. The Russian (German-designed!) cruiser *Zhemchug* lay anchored in the roadstead for repairs, *Emden* firing her guns and a torpedo at a range of only 270m, a second torpedo being fired during a further pass against the already burning hulk, causing the Russian ship to blow up and sink immediately, with only her mast left above water. The French aviso *D'Iberville* and destroyer *Fronde* were also in harbour and fired on *Emden*, but were left unharmed as the latter decided to withdraw. However, in the process she met the French destroyer *Mousquet*, which was rapidly sunk. The attack yet further dislocated Allied shipping, convoys from Australia to Europe being delayed while escorts capable of fighting the German cruiser were organised.

After coaling, it was now decided to destroy the British wireless station in the Cocos Islands, *Emden* arriving off Direction Island at 06.00 on 9 November, and sending ashore a landing party. However, in spite of attempts by *Emden* to jam transmissions, a signal from the wireless station was picked up by the Australian *Chatham*-class light cruiser *Sydney*, on convoy duty less than 100km away, which immediately headed for the islands. Her signals were detected by *Emden*, but their strength (and so *Sydney*'s distance) was underestimated, and thus *Emden* was still inshore when the Australian vessel was identified around 09.30.

The eight 6in guns of *Sydney* outgunned *Emden* significantly, but the latter hoped that she might be able to disable her assailant by sheer volume of fire before suffering significant damage herself. *Sydney* was indeed hit twice in the early stages of the action, but soon began to hit the German cruiser, which was attempting to get into a torpedo-firing position at 09.50 when *Emden*'s steering gear was put out of action. A hit soon after 10.00 caused a fire among ready-use ammunition, and by 10.45 most guns had been disabled, with the foremast and the after two funnels collapsed. Accordingly, *Emden* was run aground on North Keeling Island at 11.20, with breech blocks and torpedo aiming gear thrown overboard, and all confidential material burned; 136 of her crew were dead. *Sydney*'s post-action report[11] noted that no shell from *Emden* had made any impression on her armour belt, bearing out the concerns raised when news of the *Chatham* class had reached Germany, and which had contributed to the switch to 15cm guns in the *Wiesbaden* class (p 152, above).

The wreck was examined, and bodies and equipment (including torpedoes) recovered by the sloop HMS *Cadmus* two weeks later. Three 10.5cm guns were removed and are now on display in Australia, along with the ship's bell and other relics. During the early 1920s, the wreck began to break down, including the loss of the stern, and during the 1930s a Japanese company began to dismantle what was left of the hulk, continuing in the 1950s. A storm in 1954 demolished everything left above water, although parts of the keel and machinery, plus one of the propellers, remain in situ, and have been legally protected since 1982.

Coronel and the Falklands

In the meanwhile, *Nürnberg* had accompanied *Scharnhorst* and *Gneisenau* to Eniwetok Atoll in the Marshall Islands, arriving and coaling on 20 August 1914. On 8 September *Nürnberg* was sent to Honolulu with despatches and to gather news, the squadron then sailing to the recently captured German Samoa in the hope of catching an isolated British warship. However, nothing was found there on the 14th, although better luck was had at the French harbour of Papeete, on Tahiti, on 22 September, where the gunboat *Zélée* was sunk, and the town bombarded by *Scharnhorst* and *Gneisenau*.

On 12 October, the German ships reached Easter Island, where they were joined from American waters by *Dresden* and *Leipzig*, together with three more colliers. A week later, the squadron pushed on to Mas a Fuera, and then towards and down the Chilean coast, seeking the British light cruiser *Glasgow*, which was known to be in the area. At 16.20 on 1 November, the squadron encountered not just *Glasgow*, but also the armoured cruisers *Good Hope* (flag) and *Monmouth*, together with the armed merchant cruiser *Otranto*. When fire was opened around 1900, beginning the Battle of Coronel, *Scharnhorst* engaged *Good Hope*, which was dead in the water by 19.50 and sank around 20.00. *Monmouth* was badly mauled by *Gneisenau*, and then found by *Nürnberg*, which opened fire at 20.50, also firing a torpedo, which missed. The British cruiser capsized and sank less than ten minutes later. *Glasgow* had been engaged by *Leipzig* and *Dresden*, but escaped with five hits. Following the battle, the German squadron proceeded to the Chilean port of Valparaiso, neutrality rules allowing only

11. Quoted in Lyon, *Warship* I/3, p 47.

three ships to enter port at the same time, for a maximum of twenty-four hours. *Scharnhorst*, *Gneisenau* and *Nürnberg* came in on 3 November to coal, sailing the next morning for Mas a Fuera, arriving on the 6th, and more coaling. On the 15th, *Scharnhorst*, *Gneisenau* and *Nürnberg* sailed for St Quentin Bay in the Gulf of Penas, on the southeast coast of Chile, being joined en route by *Dresden* and *Leipzig*, which had travelled via Valparaiso, arriving on the 21st. There, they prepared to break back to Germany across the Atlantic.

The squadron departed St Quentin Bay on 26 November, rounding Cape Horn on 2 December, stopping at Picton Island, at the very tip of South America on the 3rd. While there, it was agreed to undertake a raid on the Falkland Islands before pushing on homeward, the squadron sailing on the 6th. In the interim, two battlecruisers (*Invincible* [flag] and *Inflexible*) had been dispatched from the UK to hunt down the German ships and, as *Gneisenau* and *Nürnberg* approached the Falklands on the 8th, had been in harbour there since the previous day, together with the armoured cruisers *Kent* and *Carnarvon*, plus the Coronel survivor *Glasgow* and the battleship *Canopus*, grounded as a battery. A 12in hit from the latter on *Gneisenau* dissuaded the Germans from pressing home what might have been a successful assault on the British force while it was confined in harbour, the German force instead steaming away, initially unaware of the presence of the 25-knot battlecruisers that could outpace the German ships' best speed of 22 knots.

Within three hours, *Invincible* and *Inflexible* had sailed and caught up with the Germans, *Scharnhorst* and *Gneisenau* accepting action at 13.20 in the hope that the small cruisers might escape: *Scharnhorst* sank at 16.17, *Gneisenau* at 18.00. Nevertheless, *Leipzig* was intercepted by *Glasgow*, which opened fire at 14.40, hitting the German vessel for the first time twenty minutes later. A short pause was followed by *Leipzig* being struck again, although *Glasgow* took two hits, after which battle was joined by the armoured cruisers *Cornwall* and *Kent*, hits from the latter causing damage that eventually knocked out one of *Leipzig*'s boiler rooms, before she moved on to pursue *Nürnberg*. *Leipzig* continued to take more damage, although scoring eighteen hits on *Cornwall*. From 19.15 three torpedoes were fired successively by *Leipzig*, but all missed, and soon afterwards the order was given that the German cruiser should be abandoned and scuttled. Nevertheless, *Glasgow* closed and opened fire again, *Leipzig* finally sinking at 21.23, with only eighteen survivors.

Nürnberg, with boiler defects restricting her speed to 18 knots, was engaged by *Kent* at 17.00, the latter having broken off from the attack on *Leipzig* twenty minutes earlier. Some thirty minutes later, *Kent* scored her first hit, with damage mounting as the range closed, *Nürnberg* being almost wholly disabled soon after 18.00, although she had herself hit her much larger opponent thirty-seven times. Orders were given to abandon and scuttle around 18.30, but as *Nürnberg*'s ensign remained flying, *Kent* reopened fire at 18.45 until the German cruisers colours were struck at 18.50. She sank at 19.27, with only seven survivors.

Only *Dresden* escaped, managing to steam southwest and round Cape Horn, reaching Punta Arenas on 12 December, where she coaled from a German ship. For the next few weeks she remained among the islands of the southeastern Pacific, until 8 March 1915, when she reached Mas a Tierra with only 80 tonnes of coal remaining. On the 14th, *Kent* and *Glasgow* arrived, and opened fire, in spite of *Dresden* being in Chilean territorial waters. Her after guns were soon knocked out, and a white flag raised as a cover for the scuttling of the ship, which was achieved by detonating the forward magazine, *Dresden* sinking at 11.15.

Africa

Königsberg arrived at Dar es Salaam on 5 June 1914 to begin what was intended to be a two-year stint on the station. In view of the rising tensions in Europe, she left the port on 31 July to avoid being blockaded by the British cruisers *Astraea*, *Hyacinth* and *Pegasus*, shaking them off, and she was at sea off Aden when notified on 5 August of the outbreak of war. Detailed to attack Allied commerce in the area, SS *City of Winchester* was seized the following day. However, replenishing fuel was a problem, only 14 tonnes being left when she managed to meet SS *Somali*, which had slipped out of Dar es Salaam, with a cargo of 1,200 tonnes of coal on 14 August. The 850 tonnes taken aboard the cruiser allowed *Königsberg* to make an unsuccessful search for enemy merchantmen as far south as Madagascar; the remainder of *Somali*'s coal was taken on board on the 23rd.

The cruiser then retired up the Rufiji river to allow defects to be remedied, after which she sortied on 19 September to raid Zanzibar, where *Pegasus* was believed to be coaling and undergoing maintenance. Arriving the next morning, *Königsberg* opened fire at 05.10; forty minutes later, outranged and badly damaged, with thirty-eight dead and fifty-five wounded, *Pegasus* surrendered; in spite of attempts to beach, she foundered in 10m of water that afternoon. The German cruiser then bombarded the wireless station and damaged the ex-German tug *Helmuth*.

Plans to continue raiding were frustrated by engine defects, so *Königsberg* retired back to Salale in the Rufiji delta, from which components were sent overland to Dar es-Salaam for repairs. The ship was camouflaged and troops and field guns deployed, while a minefield was also laid to prevent the approach of British vessels. Nevertheless, she was located by the British at the end of October, and the mouth of the delta blockaded by the light cruisers *Chatham*, *Dartmouth* and *Weymouth*.

On 3 November, a bombardment was begun, but failed to hit *Königsberg*, which withdrew further upstream. A British collier, *Newbridge*, was successfully sunk across one of the delta mouths on 10 November, although *Königsberg* could still have made her

The sunken *Königsberg* resting in the mud of the Rufiji River. The middle funnel was felled by British gunfire, while all guns, searchlights and other reusable equipment has been stripped by German forces. *(DN collection)*

way out via other channels. In response, the cruiser was taken yet further upstream. The British blockading force had now been reinforced by the cruisers HMS *Pyramus* and HMAS *Pioneer*, but it was not until later in the month that *Königsberg* was relocated by aerial reconnaissance. However, attempts at reaching the ship with 12in gunfire from the battleship *Goliath* were foiled by the shallowness of the waters around the delta.

Königsberg was now, on 18 December, moved even further upriver, although by now her crew had been so reduced by the transfer of crew members to duties with the German army that she was no longer capable of going to sea. On 23 December, two British shallow-draft craft got within range, but only managed to hit *Königsberg*'s supply ship *Somali* once before defensive fire forced them to retire. Nevertheless, the morale and health of the remaining crew of the cruiser was deteriorating, an attempt to resupply from Germany via SS *Kronborg* (ex-*Rubens*) in March 1915 being frustrated by HMS *Hyacinth*.

In June, the 6in-armed river monitors HMS *Mersey* and HMS *Severn* arrived from the UK, which could navigate the river and get within range of even *Königsberg*'s latest location. In spite of German fire from the river banks, they reached what was thought to be a suitable firing position on 6 July, although faulty navigation meant that they had placed themselves within range of *Königsberg*'s guns: *Mersey* was hit twice and the two monitors were forced to withdraw after three hours.

A fresh attempt was made five days later, the cruiser opening fire on the approaching British ships at 12.12 with four guns, which replied at 12.31, knocking out all but one of the cruiser's guns within twenty-five minutes, and causing mounting damage and casualties, final casualties being nineteen dead and forty-five wounded. At 13.40, *Königsberg*'s crew were ordered to abandon ship, and the cruiser was scuttled, sinking in shallow water with a starboard list.

The hulk was later stripped of reusable equipment, the guns being repaired at Dar es Salaam and adapted for shore use, except for one that went into the former ferry *Graf von Goetzen* on Lake Tanganyika. The wreck of *Königsberg* had by 1940 rolled on to its side, and although some material was removed in the 1960s, by the 1970s it had become completely submerged in the mud of the river.

9 | WAR – II

WAR IN HOME WATERS

The Baltic

From the outbreak of war, the Baltic-based cruisers were mainly employed in observing and securing the central Baltic against expected Russian raids, e.g. by offering protection for offensive minelaying operations. A secondary role – which only consumed minimal resources during the early months of 1915 – was to lend some support to the German army during its initial retreat and subsequent northwards advance along the coastline. *Magdeburg* fired the first shots in the theatre when she bombarded Libau (Liepāja) while so engaged on 2 August, albeit with little effect, while *Augsburg* laid a minefield outside the port.[1]

1. Unbeknownst to the Germans, nearly all important Russian military and naval units had long since left Libau, the General Staff having recognised its dangerous proximity to the German border (about 75km) and its rather weak landward defences.

To deceive the Russians about the true strength – or, rather, weakness! – of the German Baltic forces, further bombardments of Russian positions followed, including a shelling of the Dagerort lighthouse on the western tip of the island of Dagö (Hiiumaa) by *Magdeburg* on 12 August. On the 17th, *Magdeburg*, *Augsburg*, three destroyers, and the auxiliary minelayer 'C' (ex-rail ferry) *Deutschland* ran into the Russian armoured cruisers *Admiral Makarov* and *Gromoboi*, but were not attacked, the Russians' assuming that the Baltic force's armoured cruisers *Roon* and *Prinz Heinrich* would be nearby in support.

However, *Magdeburg*, which had been relegated to Baltic duty owing to her propulsion problems (p 140, above) was less fortunate ten days later. She and *Augsburg*, with destroyers, had been sent into the entrance of the Gulf of Finland in search of Russian forces, but early on the morning of 26 August she ran aground in dense fog on the island of Odensholm

Augsburg coaling in the port of Swinemünde on 4 August 1914, following the initial raid against Libau. *(DN collection)*

Above: a view, taken from the stern of the grounded *Magdeburg*, of the torpedo boat *V26* coming alongside, having already been hit by one of the Russian cruisers, as indicated by the steam engulfing the mainmast. **Right:** *Magdeburg* after the detonation of her forward magazine. *(DN/AD collections)*

(Osmussaar), off the Estonian coast. The destroyer *V26* was unsuccessful in towing her off, and started to take off some of the cruiser's crew. At this point, the Russian cruisers *Bogatyr* and *Pallada* came on the scene and opened fire, prompting a decision to destroy the stricken *Magdeburg*. The forward magazine was accordingly detonated, but the destruction of confidential documents was not carried out thoroughly, with the result that – among other valuable documents, including grid charts and W/T logs – two copies of the German navy code book were recovered from the seabed adjacent to the wreck. One was passed to the British, which ensured that the Royal Navy could read most German signals from October onwards. The Russians also recovered guns from the wreck, these being used to rearm the gunboat *Khrabryi* and fit out the two new gunboats *Korshun* and *Kopchik*.

On 2 September 1914, *Augsburg* exchanged fire with the Russian destroyer *Novik*, and participated in a sweep from the 3rd to the 7th that included the IV. Sqn (*Braunschweig*- and *Wittelsbach*-class battleships) and the large cruiser *Blücher*; this included a sighting of the Russian cruisers *Pallada* and *Bayan* by *Augsburg*, although she was unable to draw the Russians under the superior German guns. She was, however, more fortunate on the 7th, when *Augsburg* and the torpedo boat *V25* steamed northward and sank a Russian steamer in the Gulf of Bothnia.

On 17 November she and *Thetis* stood by the large cruiser *Friedrich Carl* when the latter was mined and sunk off Memel on the Russian minefield No 7. *Thetis*, together with *Amazone*, *Augsburg* and *Lübeck*, supported an operation in the Åland Islands during 15–18 December, to scout the area of the island of Utö and the surrounding skerries. This was rightly suspected to be used by the Russians as an advanced base for ships up to cruiser size. *Augsburg* was herself mined on the night of 24–25 January 1915 in the Russian minefield No. 11 east of Bornholm, killing eight stokers in the third boiler room; however, she reached Swinemünde under her own power, and Blohm & Voss completed repairs at Hamburg in April.

Gazelle was also mined on 25 January 1915. She had recommissioned on 4 August 1914 at Danzig, and joined the Baltic Coast Defence Division on 18 August, allocated as required to the force of the Detached Admiral for the Baltic. *Gazelle* therefore joined the forces that proceeded to the Gulf of Finland in support of the grounded *Magdeburg*. However, she soon fell astern of the force, to be left behind entirely once it was discovered that her maximum continuous speed did not exceed 16 knots. This was much too slow even against the Russian cruisers, and still less their destroyers. Despite her shortcomings, *Gazelle* was nevertheless still deployed as part of the next operation, an attempt to lure units of the Russian fleet out of their defended bases. However, *Gazelle* was stationed on the far left wing of the German force, to allow her to withdraw into Swedish waters in case of an attack by stronger Russian vessels. It then became necessary to send her to Danzig Dockyard to remedy loose shaft bearings, which were reducing her speed yet further.

During one more operation in September 1914, *Gazelle* served as flagship for the supply vessels of the main force, before reverting to the coastal defence forces defending the minefields in the Great Belt and south of the Sound, based on Kiel. In this capacity *Gazelle* was ordered on 24 January 1915 to patrol the waters between the Sound and Cape Arkona, the northern tip of the island of Rügen. On the next day, 9nm NNW of Arkona, an explosion occurred aft, which was initially assumed to have been caused by a torpedo. It was actually a mine, part of Russian minefield No. 12, comprising ninety-eight mines, laid on 14 January 1915 by the armoured cruiser

Top: *Gazelle* safely alongside at Swinemünde, albeit considerably down by the stern. Since the beginning of the war she has received a charthouse on the forebridge. In the lower image, taken in autumn 1916 at Danzig, she has already been stripped down to a bare hull for service as a mine store: even the spur of the ram has been removed to recover the now-scarce bronze (cf. p 100). To the right may be seen the rear part of *Gefion*. *(DN collection)*

Rossiya during her most extended foray into German waters. *Gazelle* took on water rapidly, but was initially still able to move under her own power until both propellers fell off. The torpedo boats *G132* and *G134* eventually took the stricken cruiser in tow to Swinemünde. Dry docked at the Stettiner-Oderwerke yard, it was decided that restoration to operational status would not be worthwhile, and the cruiser decommissioned on 22 February for the last time, freeing her company to man more modern units. Her hull was then used for mine storage, first at Danzig, later at Cuxhaven, and finally at Wilhelmshaven.

From 21 to 24 March, the II. SG, led by *Graudenz* and comprising *Rostock*, *Stralsund* and the brand-new *Regensburg*, was temporarily deployed to the Baltic to bombard potential Russian escape routes leading north from Polangen (Palanga) and Pappensee on the Latvian coast to Libau. The cruisers were ordered back to the North Sea on the evening of 23 March. At the same time, *Strassburg* undertook a short raid against commercial trade into the Bothnian Gulf, without result.

In April, a major push by the German army began, one of the objectives being the seizure of Libau, to be supported by the coast defence ship *Beowulf*, the armoured cruisers *Prinz Adalbert*, *Prinz Heinrich* and *Roon*, and the small cruisers *Augsburg*, *Lübeck* and *Thetis*, plus torpedo boats and minesweepers, together with the IV. SG (*Danzig*, *München*, *Stettin* and *Stuttgart*) and twenty-one torpedo boats, detached from the HSF.

The IV. SG and the torpedo boats were intended to guard against any intervention by Russian forces coming undetected from the Gulf of Finland, while the other vessels bombarded the port. As a result, *München* was involved in a brief exchange with the Russian cruisers *Admiral Makarov*, *Bayan*, *Oleg* and *Bogatyr*. The German formation was recalled to the North Sea once Libau had fallen, but *Danzig* returned for a sweep by the IV. Sqn toward Gotland that lasted from 8 to 10 May.

Augsburg and *Lübeck*, now forward-deployed to Libau with a number of torpedo boats, were detailed late in May to lay a minefield near the entrance to the Gulf of Finland, but this was cancelled following a submarine attack on *Thetis*. On 20 June *Albatross*, newly transferred to the Baltic, undertook the first in a series of lays off Bogskär, south of Mariehamn in the Åland Islands, escorted by *Roon*, *Prinz Heinrich*, *Prinz Adalbert*, *Augsburg* and *Lübeck*, returning to Danzig on the 22nd. A further operation took place three days later, when *Albatross* was escorted by *Prinz Adalbert*, *Prinz Heinrich* and *Thetis*, together with eight torpedo boats, returning on 26 June.

On the 28th, a bombardment of Windau (Ventspils) by *Beowulf* was accompanied by a skirmish between *Augsburg* and *Lübeck* and Russian destroyers. No substantive damage was inflicted on either side, but at 19.45 *Augsburg* was missed by two torpedoes from the Russian submarine *Okun*.

A further operation began on 30 June, intended to complete the current minefield, with *Albatross* escorted by *Augsburg*, *Lübeck*, *Roon* and seven torpedo boats. *Augsburg* was to provide close escort, with the other two cruisers providing more distant cover. The lay took place successfully, but signals notifying its completion, and giving ships' positions, were intercepted by the Russians (and read owing to their possession of *Magdeburg*'s code books), who had sailed a force of cruisers and destroyers twenty-four hours earlier to carry out a bombardment of Memel. Accordingly, this could be vectored on to the unsuspecting German ships, of which *Albatross*, *Augsburg* and the torpedo boats *G135*, *S142* and *S141* were now off the coast of Gotland, en route to Danzig, while *Lübeck* and *Roon* and the remaining torpedo boats had been detached towards Libau.

Around 06.30 on 2 July 1915, *Augsburg* spotted the leading ship of a Russian force comprising *Admiral Makarov*, *Bogatyr*, *Bayan* and *Oleg*, plus four destroyers. The latter correctly identified *Augsburg*, but at first mistook the *Albatross* for the similarly two-funnelled *Undine*. Outgunned and outnumbered, *Augsburg* and the torpedo boats were ordered at 06.53 to try and break away, while the minelayer was to seek refuge in the nearby Swedish territorial waters. At first fired on only by *Bogatyr* and *Oleg*, *Albatross* nevertheless received her first hit at 07.20, at which point the other Russian cruisers switched target from the retreating *Augsburg* to the minelayer. *Augsburg* and the torpedo boats found themselves shortly afterwards in a position to briefly fire on the Russians, but the range then opened and contact was lost.

On board *Albatross*, damage mounted, although as the range closed, her own 8.8cm guns were able to claim hits. Nevertheless, by the time she entered Swedish territorial waters at 07.45 the foremast and bridge had been wrecked, with damage to the steering gear, but not to her machinery.

Russian shooting continued until *Oleg* ceased fire at 08.07; by this time *Albatross* had been hit by six 8in and twenty 6in shells, with twenty-seven dead. Listing heavily, she was run ashore on the Kuppen Bank near Östergarn.

Meanwhile, *Lübeck* and *Roon* had been recalled, the latter exchanging shots with *Bayan* soon after 09.00, hitting her once, while *Lübeck* duelled with *Bogatyr* and *Oleg*, without effect, before the Germans broke off at 09.22. Around 09.30, *Lübeck* ran into the big Russian armoured cruiser *Rurik*, which had earlier been separated from the rest of the Russian force by fog. The German vessel was not hit by any of *Rurik*'s 10in and 8in shells, and managed to make ten hits on her much larger adversary during the fifteen minutes that elapsed before *Roon* closed and herself opened fire, scoring one hit; *Augsburg* also soon joined the fray. Nevertheless, the action was broken off at 10.21, the Germans concerned at the likely appearance of the rest of the Russian force, and *Rurik* by the sighting of an apparent periscope.

Prinz Adalbert and *Prinz Heinrich*, with *S138* and *S139*, had sailed from Danzig at 10.00, in the hope of joining with the other three German cruisers, and returning to Östergarn to salvage *Albatross*. This aim was frustrated by the torpedoing of *Prinz Adalbert* by HMS/M *E9* around 14.00. *Albatross* was thus left to be refloated by the Swedish authorities on 23 July and towed to Fårösund. She was then taken to Oskarshamn, where she was interned until she returned to Kiel in January 1919.

Bremen had been in dockyard hands for an extensive refit at the outbreak of war (pp 119, 220). She recommissioned on 27 May 1915, joining the Baltic Scouting Force, transferring from Kiel to Libau at the beginning of July. As such she took part alongside IV. Sqn and III. SG in sorties into the eastern Baltic in support of the German army's advance towards the Gulf of Riga.

Close-up view of *Albatross* amidships, taken after she had been beached on Gotland. The effects of hits from Russian cruisers are evident, as are the effects of her zigzagging, as some holes are a mixture of entry and exit damage. The partly dark-painted shields of the 8.8cm guns are an unusual feature perhaps intended to resemble casemates for camouflage or deception purposes. *(DN collection)*

Accompanied by two torpedo boats, *Bremen* cruises the eastern Baltic, shortly before her loss. Her profile had been considerably altered by her 1914–15 reconstruction, but not as much as would be the case with her sister *Lübeck* (see p 220). *(DN collection)*

She also joined *Augsburg*, *Kolberg*, *Graudenz*, *Regensburg* and *Pillau* in forming a large force (also comprising the battleships *Nassau*, *Posen*, *Braunschweig* and *Elsaß*, the large cruisers *Moltke*, *Seydlitz*, *Von der Tann*, *Roon* and *Prinz Heinrich*, and fifty-six destroyers) that made a number of penetrations into the Gulf of Riga during August 1915. *Kolberg* shelled the island of Utö along with *Von der Tann* as part of the first attack on the 8th, while *Augsburg* (which had been missed by a torpedo on the 13th) joined *Nassau* and *Posen* in the attack beginning on the 16th. *Augsburg* and *Posen* sank the Russian gunboat *Sivutch* on the 19th, and on the 25th *Regensburg* and *Pillau* bombarded the island of Dagö.

On 19 August *Moltke* had been torpedoed and damaged by HMS/M *E1*, another of an increasing number of attacks by Baltic-based British submarines on German warships. The large cruiser *Prinz Adalbert* was then sunk on 23 October, followed by *Undine* on 7 November. The latter had been escorting the passenger-railway ferry *Preußen* from Trelleborg to Sassnitz when, about halfway between Sweden and Cape Arkona, she was hit by two torpedoes from HMS/M *E19*, and sank rapidly in 48m of water – luckily with only twenty-four casualties. Little more than a month later, on 17 December, *Bremen*, while standing by the mined torpedo boat *V191*, herself struck two mines, sinking with fifty-three survivors.

On the morning of 8 August 1915, *Thetis* had been mined off the Gulf of Riga, being towed to Libau and then on to Danzig and Kiel, arriving at the latter on 21 August and decommissioning on 3 September for repairs. *Danzig*, which had only returned to the Baltic on 13 November, hit a mine on the 25th, and was badly damaged; again towed in, by *Berlin* and torpedo boats, she was under repair at Danzig and Bremen until 12 July 1916. On 13 January 1916, *Lübeck* struck a mine on passage from Libau to Kiel, north Rixhöft, damaging the rudder and screws, the shock also collapsing the foremast onto the bridge, seriously injuring the cruiser's captain. With 240 tonnes of water aboard, she was initially towed by *V189*, which then handed her over to the tug *Weichsel*; this this brought her into Danzig-Neufahrwasser. On 28 January 1916, *Lübeck* was decommissioned and taken to her builders at Stettin for repairs and reconstruction (for which see p 220, below). These incidents convinced the navy that the regular deployment of major warships into the eastern Baltic was too risky, most being withdrawn by early 1916. The older of the ships in question were soon reduced to subsidiary roles.

Showing already signs of wear and tear, *Undine* enjoys a quiet moment moored to her buoy in the inner Kiel fjord in 1915. *(DN collection)*

A VI. SG had been established on 15 January 1916, with the brand-new *Elbing* as its first flagship, having previously been involved in mining sorties with *Augsburg*. She was, however, soon relieved by *Kolberg*, which served alongside *Augsburg* (which would operate aircraft on an experimental basis during the summer, and on occasion replace her as flagship), and *Strassburg*, which joined in March. However, *Augsburg* touched ground in the Gulf of Riga during the attempt to force the Irben Strait on 12–15 September, and had to be sent to Kiel for repairs, during which she was rearmed and modernised (see p 220). *Strassburg* had replaced *Kolberg* as group flagship in September, and in December 1916 *Kolberg* was withdrawn for her own refit and rearmament.

Kolberg and *Augsburg* rejoined *Strassburg* in the VI. SG in April 1917, which, during October, took part (with *Kolberg* as flagship, and with the addition of *Blitz* as a tender) in Operation Albion, the occupation of the West Estonian Archipelago. They were accompanied by a large force detached from the HSF, including the II. SG (*Königsberg* [flag], *Karlsruhe*, *Nürnberg*, and *Frankfurt*, plus *Danzig* detached from submarine target duty), and the III. and IV. Sqns of battleships. On 21 September, *Emden* rendezvoused with *Nautilus* (which had formally transferred to the Baltic on the commissioning of *Brummer* in April 1916) at Libau, where all the torpedo boats available for the operation had assembled, in order to cover army landings from 9 October. *Emden* then undertook bombardments in conjunction with the battleship *Bayern* against the island of Dagö in support of the landings there, engaging Russian vessels in the process.

The VI. SG proceeded to Libau on 14 October 1917 as escort to the minesweepers due to work in the Gulf of Riga as a key part of Albion. On the 16th, *Augsburg* took part in the occupation of Arensburg, having entered the Gulf in the company of the battleships *König* and *Kronprinz*. Along with her two groupmates, *Kolberg* engaged a Russian coastal battery at Woi on Moon Island, before anchoring with *Strassburg* and sending a

Kolberg, now rearmed with 15cm guns, moored in the inner port of Helsinki during the summer of 1918. Directly ahead of her is the former Imperial palace, which had recently been the headquarters of the short-lived Helsinki Soviet, and would become the Finnish Presidential palace. *(Heidrich collection)*

landing party to capture Woi's guns. *Nautilus* was intended to lay a minefield on 21 October, but this was frustrated by overly shallow water.

Following the end of hostilities on the Eastern Front in December 1917, *Kolberg* sailed from Libau to Kiel for refit on 29 December.[2] *Strassburg* went back to the HSF on 10 January 1918, *Augsburg* being transferred the same day to the Submarine Inspectorate as a submarine target, remaining until 20 July, when she relieved *Stettin* as minesweeper flagship, based at Cuxhaven. *Stettin* had fulfilled this role on a temporary basis since May, and now returned to a submarine target role with the Submarine Inspectorate.

On 24 January 1918, the Baltic Scouting Force had been disestablished, and its tasks passed to Flag Officer Baltic Defence (FOBD). *Stettin* had been flagship of the latter's Western Division from September 1917 (when she relieved the battleship *Deutschland* in that role) until she went into refit at Wilhelmshaven on 8 December 1917. On her return to service, *Stettin* went to the Submarine Inspectorate, although consideration had been given to converting her into a seaplane carrier, as was actually done with her sister *Stuttgart* (see pp 220-221).

Kolberg became flagship of the FOBD Western Division on her return to service on 17 March 1918, but ten days later she was detached to the Special Force for the Baltic Sea. This had been established to support German intervention in the Finnish Civil War, and as such *Kolberg* took part in the attack on Hanko on 3 April. The force also included *Nautilus*, assigned to it in February, and which served as flagship from 30 April. *Kolberg* subsequently took the place of the battleship *Rheinland* in the Åland Islands after the latter ran aground there on the 11th, being relieved by *Stralsund*, newly repaired after mine damage (p 226), on 19 May. *Stralsund* had became Force flagship on 16 May, later hoisting the flag of FO Baltic Waters (formerly Baltic Defence – FOBW) on 7 June at Helsingfors (Helsinki). She was back in the North Sea from 24 June to 8 August, but then returned to the Baltic. *Kolberg* had left Mariehamn in the Åland Islands on 20 May, arriving at Kiel on 22 May and being returned to her original formation. A short deployment to the Little Belt was followed by a return to the eastern Baltic on 18 June, now as flagship FOBW, replacing *Stralsund*. *Nautilus* remained in the northern Baltic, patrolling off the Åland Islands, until the end of the war.

Stralsund and *Kolberg* were attached to IV. SG for the purposes of Operation Schlußstein in early August 1918. This was a proposed amphibious occupation of Kronstadt and Petrograd, with the objective of securing the strategic railway line north to Murmansk. Preparations were ordered on 4 August and mine clearance begun in the Gulf of Finland on the 12th. *Kolberg* was earmarked to form part of the main force, comprising the battleships *Ostfriesland*, *Thüringen* and *Nassau*, with *Blitz* as their tender, also supported by V. TBF and the seaplane tender *Answald*.

2. Reportedly, the refit – and likewise that of *Augsburg* – included the fitting of a pair of 8.8cm anti-aircraft guns; this is very doubtful, as photographs taken of both in 1918 still show them without such weapons. It may have been a case of 'fitting for but not with'.

The operation staff were embarked in *Stralsund* on 16 August, and proceeded, via Libau and Helsingfors, to Koivisto (Björkö/Primorsk), 137km west of Petrograd, in preparation for the operation. However, this was postponed early in September, *Stralsund* leaving on the 9th to return the staff to Wilhelmshaven, with *Strassburg* replacing her at Koivisto. *Stralsund* then returned to Koivisto, taking over from her sister on 16 September, *Strassburg* returning to the North Sea on 1 October.

Kolberg had in the interim been transferred back to FOBW, to become station ship at Helsinki. However, on 25 September 1918, while at Reval, she was ordered back to Kiel to pay off, arriving on the 29th. Part of her crew was then transferred to the Crimea in early October, although formal decommissioning of the ship did not occur until 17 December, along with many other German warships.

Stralsund was relieved at Koivisto by the coast defence ship *Beowulf* on 22 September, Schlußstein being finally cancelled on the 29th in light of the collapse of the Central Powers on the Macedonian Front. *Stralsund* was back at Reval on 11 November, when the local soldiers' council demanded that her naval ensign be lowered and replaced by the merchant flag, under threat of bombardment. The cruiser's captain acquiesced, but sailed early the next morning, via Libau and Swinemünde to Kiel, where she arrived on 14 November 1918. She decommissioned there on 17 December.

With the Fleet

The year 1915 opened with the follow-on operation to the Hartlepool, Scarborough and Whitby raid. This was intended to probe the Dogger Bank and attack the fishing fleet that was suspected of being a key source of British intelligence on German movements: that German naval codes had been compromised was as yet unsuspected. On this occasion there was no intent to use the operation as a means of drawing out and ambushing a section of the British fleet (as had been the case with previous year's raids, and would be later, since the most modern battleships of the HSF, the III. Sqn, were unavailable. Accordingly, the raid would be carried out by just the Scouting Force: four large cruisers of the I. SG (*Seydlitz, Moltke, Derfflinger* and *Blücher*: *Von der Tann* was under repair), the four small cruisers of the II. SG (*Kolberg, Stralsund, Rostock* and *Graudenz*) and eighteen torpedo boats.

Pre-warned by signals intelligence facilitated by the '*Magdeburg* trove', the British BCF (five battlecruisers and four light cruisers) and Harwich Force (two light cruisers and thirty-five destroyers), with other formations as distant cover, were directed to intercept. The first contact was between HMS *Aurora* and *Kolberg* at 08.10 on 24 January, the latter hitting her opponent three times; *Aurora* made two hits in reply, killing two men. However, the battle was essentially between the big ships, with *Blücher* sunk, and *Seydlitz, Lion* and *Tiger* suffering significant damage. Two days after the battle, *Kolberg* became flagship of the II. Leader of Torpedo-boats (II. LTB), a role in which she continued for the rest of the year.

Following the Dogger Bank battle, the fleet carried out various short sorties: on 29/30 March and 29/30 May 1915 to the north of Terschelling; on 17/18 April and 17/18 May to cover mining operations by the II. SG; on 21/22 April towards the Dogger Bank; on 10 May to cover the return of the auxiliary cruiser/minelayer *Meteor* (which had, however, been sunk the previous day); on 11/12 September to cover a minelaying operation west of Terschelling; and on 23/24 October as far as the Horns Reef. In no case was there any potential contact with British forces.

Five new small cruisers had now joined the fleet since the outbreak of war. *Graudenz* had originally been planned to relieve *Mainz* but, having commissioned on 10 August 1914, underwent a truncated series of trials, which terminated on 6 September. On the 10th, she was allocated to forward defence duty in the German Bight, and then temporarily detached to the Baltic from 20th to 26th, before returning to the North Sea. A further stint in the Baltic from 7 to 17 November was followed by a definitive return to the fleet, becoming flagship of the II. LTB on the 27th, the type of role for which she had been designed (pp 150-151, above).

Her sister *Regensburg* commissioned on 3 January 1915, completing her trials on 10 March and joining the II. SG. She was then part of the large detachment that went to the Baltic later that month (see p 210, above). The ex-Russian *Pillau* was next, joining the II.SG on 16 May. *Frankfurt* commissioned in August 1915, and *Wiesbaden* at the beginning of September, completing her trials on 12 and 23 October, respectively, and joining the II. SG. A sixth new small cruiser, *Elbing*, was added to the Group on 16 November.

In addition to the ships operating with the fleet, a number of old small cruisers had been on coastal defence duties in the west since the outbreak of war. However, although *Arcona* would remain in the Ems until the end of the war, *Niobe* and *Medusa* were withdrawn from active service in the Jade/Weser and Elbe in September 1915. The latter vessel then went to the Baltic as

Wiesbaden at full speed, in company with other units of the II. SG; it may be the last photograph ever taken of her. *(DN collection)*

Photo taken from the north side of the Kaiser-Wilhelm Bridge at Wilhelmshaven, showing *Niobe*, already disarmed, employed as headquarters ship for the I. SG. *(DN collection)*

replacement for the sunken *Undine*, while *Niobe* relieved the coast defence ship *Siegfried* as HQ ship for the local torpedo boat flotillas on 14 January 1916. She wore the flag of FO IV. SG, from 6 June to 3 July 1916, before becoming HQ ship for the I. SG on 20 August in Wilhelmshaven (and later FO North Sea Defence as well). She remained in a headquarters role until January 1919, being disarmed in 1917 and her guns redeployed ashore, as was the fate of weapons from many older German warships.

Graudenz was relieved as flagship of the II. LTB by her sister *Regensburg* on 14 October 1915, and was refitted at Kiel from the 26th. This included rearming, work being completed on 18 February 1916, and her admiral's flag rehoisted on the 20th. Her return to the fleet coincided with the appointment of Adm Reinhard Scheer as CinC HSF, who instituted a more active operational policy for the fleet. However, *Graudenz* was not part of the first fruits of this, as she struck a mine on the night of 21–22 April off the Amrum Bank; towed into Wilhelmshaven by *S51*, she would be under repair until September 1916.

On 24 April 1916, I. SG, under the temporarily command of KAdm Boedicker, FO II. SG, substituting for KAdm Hipper, sailed to undertake a bombardment of Lowestoft and Great Yarmouth, supported by the II. SG, which was temporarily being led by Kdre von Reuter (leader of the IV. SG). The II. SG currently comprised five of its formal strength of seven units (*Regensburg* [temporary flag], *Frankfurt*, *Wiesbaden*, *Elbing* and *Pillau*; *Graudenz and Stralsund* were in dockyard hands), plus two torpedo boat flotillas, led by *Rostock*. The main fleet would, as usual, provide distant cover. The British were aware of the sailing of the German fleet, a decrypted signal indicating that

Part of the II. SG at anchor, shortly before Jutland; from left to right we have *Frankfurt, Wiesbaden* and *Pillau*. *(DN collection)*

an objective was Yarmouth. At 19.50, the Grand Fleet was thus ordered south, while around midnight the Harwich Force was ordered north.

At 03.50 on the 25th, *Rostock* sighted the Harwich Force to the southwest, which attempted to lure the German force away. It was unsuccessful in this, and I. SG fired on Lowestoft between 04.10 and 04.20, but fog hindered the follow-on firing against Yarmouth, which was broken off, since the force's cruisers and torpedo boats were now in action with the Harwich Force, with *Rostock* and *Elbing* attempting to lead the British towards I. SG. The latter badly damaged the light cruiser HMS *Conquest*, but the action was not pursued further.

A few days later, soon after dark on 4 May, *Rostock* encountered HMS/M *E31*, which had just surfaced. The cruiser attempted to ram, also firing some twenty rounds at the crash-diving submarine, scoring a hit on the forward casing. The shell did not, however, explode and the submarine escaped.

Jutland

The next bombardment sortie was planned to be against Sunderland, with the usual objectives, with an elaborate deployment of 'ambush' submarines and reconnaissance airships. First planned for 17 May 1916, departure eventually slipped to the 31st owing to defects and overrunning repairs. As a result, the bombardment was postponed in favour of a sortie by I. and II. SGs, plus three flotillas of torpedo boats, to attack Allied shipping in the Skagerrak as the bait for British forces, which would be dealt with by the main German fleet, waiting over the horizon. As before, signals intelligence revealed the fact of a sortie to the British, with the Grand and Battlecruiser Fleets deployed on the 30th.

The small cruiser element of the German force was split between supporting the large cruisers of I. SG and working with the main fleet. With the former was the II. SG, comprising *Frankfurt* (flag), *Pillau, Elbing* and *Wiesbaden*; *Regensburg* had now returned to her task as flagship of the II. LTB, but she and her torpedoboats worked tactically with the I. and II. SG. The IV. SG was with the main fleet, and comprised *Stettin* (flag), *München, Frauenlob* and *Stuttgart*. *Rostock* carried the I. LTB, while *Hamburg*, serving as the flagship of the Leader of Submarines, was attached tactically to the IV. SG.

Elbing, holding the westernmost position in the cruising screen of the large cruisers, made the first contact with the British, in the form of the light cruiser *Galatea*, flagship of the 1st LCS, part of the Battle Cruiser Fleet. Both cruisers had spotted the Danish steamer *N J Fjord* and, while approaching to investigate, sighted the opposing force, leading to the first exchanges of fire between the two sides, at 14.32 (all times given are British Summer Time) on 31 May. *Elbing* succeeded in hitting *Galatea* below the bridge; *Frankfurt* and *Pillau* also fired a few rounds, without any hits.

The German small cruisers and their British opposite numbers played little part in the first phase of the battle between I. SG and the British battlecruisers, which began at 15.50, during which HMS *Indefatigable* and *Queen Mary* were both sunk, and significant damage inflicted on other ships. The II. SG struggled to overtake the I. SG on its lee-side to regain their designated position in the van of the large cruisers. It was only as the British 5th BS (detached to the BCF) were coming into action that the II. SG were fired upon briefly; although shells came as close as 50–100m, no hits were received.

It was with the meeting of the battlefleets after the 'run to the north' by the two battlecruiser forces that things began to change, as II. SG engaged the light cruiser HMS *Chester* at 17.38 at an initial range of 8,000m, hitting her seventeen times and causing her severe damage. However, *Chester*'s engines remained intact, and in withdrawing she led the German vessels under the guns of the newly arrived British 3rd BCS (detached to the Grand Fleet), led by *Invincible*, which opened fire at 17.55. *Pillau* received a 12in shell through the casing of the forward funnel into boiler room 4's uptake, which exploded and wrecked the exhaust ducts of boiler room 5, as well as surrounding structures. This required the six coal-fired boilers to be shut down, temporarily reducing the ship's maximum speed to 24 knots; three of the boilers were, however, later brought back on line.

Much more serious damage was inflicted on *Wiesbaden* by one or two 12in hits, possibly from *Indomitable*, but more probably from *Invincible*, herself sunk thirty minutes later. The crucial hit disabled *Wiesbaden*'s engines, rendering her unable to follow her fellow cruisers' turn away, and leaving her immobilised between the opposing fleets, thus receiving a blizzard of shells from passing ships and taking a torpedo from the destroyer *Onslow* around 18.20. In exchange, however, at about 18.43, the crippled cruiser was able to fire one last torpedo as a wild shot which, by pure coincidence, hit the battleship HMS *Marlborough*, flooding a boiler room.

An attempt by torpedo boats of III. TBF to reach *Wiesbaden* and rescue the crew around 19.00 failed owing to British fire, and a later effort failed to locate her. The cruiser was further damaged by two salvoes fired by *Marlborough* around 19.03, but the burning wreck was then gradually left behind as the battle moved away. She eventually drifted around 8nm northward, to capsize and sink around 01.45 the next morning, with just one survivor.[3] The rest of the II. SG continued their withdrawal, although *Frankfurt* took two 6in and two 4in hits from HMS *Canterbury* during 18.26–18.29, albeit without critical damage; the ship then remained unengaged until after sunset.

IV. SG also saw little action until dusk, by which time both the II. and IV. SGs were respectively near or at the head of the German line. Both encountered the 3rd LCS around 20.00, but the II. SG was sighted by the British battlecruisers that lay beyond and turned away after *Pillau* had been the target for salvoes from *Lion* and *Tiger*. On the other hand, the IV. SG managed to engage the enemy, although owing to issues of range and visibility only *Stettin*, *München* and *Hamburg* were able to come into action, albeit without scoring any hits (*Hamburg* only getting off one salvo). On the debit side, *München* was hit by 6in shells twice around 20.20–20.25, one causing little damage by exploding in the port-side cutter, but the blast of the other, in the upper part of the aft funnel, damaged the casings of four boilers, and made it difficult for the ship to work up to full speed. *München* also suffered a steering defect, owing to splinters from the first hit. An attempt was made to lure the 3rd LCS towards the German main fleet, but this was unsuccessful.

During the night, the German fleet worked its way across the wake of the Grand Fleet, and during this phase the II. and IV. SG had a number of encounters with British warships. First, at 21.58, *Frankfurt* and *Pillau*, at this time the sole remnants of the II. SG – *Elbing* having now lost contact with her formation – sighted the light cruiser *Castor* and part of her 11th DF, and fired two torpedoes at them, but without result or detection. The IV. SG, now with *Elbing* and *Rostock* in company, also fell in with *Castor*, opening fire around 22.13, before turning away five minutes later. *Hamburg* was hit by three 6in shells, but with only minor damage. *Castor* had been hit about ten times (one 15cm, the rest 10.5cm), but with negligible damage.

Around 22.00, things had become congested, as the German ships steered to break through the rear of the Grand Fleet, also engaging with British ships in that location. Indeed, *Stettin* was forced to reduce speed to avoid being run down by *Moltke* and *Seydlitz*, leading to the rest of the IV. SG becoming more crowded together, just as they encountered the British 2nd LCS. The ensuing action also involved *Elbing* (currently restricted to 20 knots by a leaky condenser), *Rostock* and *Hamburg*, and was brief (lasting around three-and-a-half minutes) but fierce. *Stettin*, *München*, *Elbing* and *Rostock* all fired on *Southampton*, starting fires (she suffered two 15cm and around eighteen 10.5cm hits), *Dublin* also being set alight by five 15cm and eight

3. Her wreck was discovered, upside down, in 1983 (I McCartney, *Jutland 1916: the archaeology of a naval battlefield* [London: Conway, 2016], pp 126–35).

10.5cm shells from *Elbing* and *Stuttgart*, the latter being herself hit twice. *Nottingham* and *Birmingham* were also firing on the German cruisers, *Frauenlob* being badly hit aft, and suffering an ammunition fire.

Almost immediately afterwards, round 22.35, *Frauenlob* was struck in the port auxiliary engine room by a torpedo from *Southampton*; immediately brought to a halt, the ship capsized to port and sank around 22.45; there were only eight survivors.[4] *München* fired a torpedo at *Southampton*, which failed to hit, herself being hit by one more shell in the middle funnel. *Stettin* received two hits (one gun disabled), and *Elbing* and *Hamburg* one each, with minor damage.

In the wake of this skirmish, the German cruisers became disordered, only *München* remaining with the flagship *Stettin*, later firing in error on the torpedo boats *V1*, *V3* and *G11* of the V. TBF around 00.20. *Stuttgart* attached herself to the I. Sqn, where she was joined by *Rostock*, *Elbing* and *Hamburg*, which, together with *Westfalen*, *Nassau*, *Rheinland* and *Posen*, engaged the British 4th DF around 23.30, *Rostock*, *Elbing* and *Hamburg* contributing to the destruction of the flotilla leader HMS *Tipperary*. However, in the melee, the German cruisers were forced to cross the main German line to avoid torpedoes, and while *Rostock* just managed to avoid the oncoming battleships, *Elbing* was rammed just aft of midships by *Posen*. Despite a last-minute evasive manoeuvre by the latter, the impact was still such that enough damage was caused to flood both engine rooms, leaving the cruiser immobile. As nothing could be done to restore movement, *S53* of the III. TBF took off most of *Elbing*'s crew, leaving a small party aboard in case she could be saved: experiments included rigging a sail. Nevertheless, by 02.00 it was clear that nothing would work, and when British ships were spotted nearby, scuttling charges were fired and *Elbing* was finally abandoned before she sank bow first.[5]

Having narrowly avoided the fate of *Elbing*, *Rostock* reached the other side of the German line, but around 23.50, while engaging the flotilla leader *Broke*, and having received three or four 4in hits, she was struck by a shallow-running torpedo, fired by a British destroyer, either *Contest* or *Ambuscade*. The forward two boiler rooms were flooded with some 930 tonnes of water, and power temporarily lost. *Rostock* was soon, however, able to steam at 13 knots, but gradual salting of the remaining boilers, whose cause was never established, gradually reduced her speed. As a result, *S54* of the III. TBF took the cruiser in tow, attaining 10 knots at one point. Progress was nevertheless slow, and when HMS *Dublin* was sighted around 03.55, followed by the receipt of a report by the airship *L11* that enemy vessels were approaching, *Rostock* was abandoned and sunk by a combination of scuttling charges and torpedoes from *V71* (two) and *V73* (one) of III. TBF at 04.25.[6]

The surviving vessels of the II. and IV. SGs took no further active part in the continuing battle, during which the armoured cruiser HMS *Black Prince* was sunk by gunfire at 00.10, and the battleship *Pommern* sunk by a British destroyer torpedo at 02.10. *Frankfurt* and *Pillau*, which had met around 23.30, took station starboard of the fleet around 01.30, where they were later joined by *Hamburg*, with *Stettin* and *München* to port, whence *Hamburg* moved later on. By 03.00, *Regensburg* and *Stuttgart* headed the German line, along with such torpedo boats as remained with it. *Stuttgart* was acting as navigation pilot for the I. Sqn, and would later do so for the III. Sqn and the fleet flagship, *Friedrich der Große*. The II. SG was directed to the rear of the fleet at 03.38, where they were joined by *Regensburg*.

As the German fleet approached home, *Pillau* was detached at 08.30 to stand by and pilot the badly damaged *Seydlitz*, joined by the I. MSD and *S36* of the IX. TBF. The cruiser attempted to take her charge in tow during the late afternoon, but without success. Salvage vessels arrived at 17.30 and began the task of pumping out water to aid the stricken large cruiser's return to Wilhelmshaven.

ALTERATIONS AND ADDITIONS

As already noted, (pp 151-152), the decision had been taken to complete the *Wiesbaden* class with 15cm guns. Early war experience had made it clear that the 10.5cm gun was inadequate against British and Russian opposition, and as early as December 1914 the question of up-gunning was being considered by the Admiralty Staff. This was initially in the context of a proposal to employ the almost-complete *Regensburg* as a commerce raider; an idea to so-use *Pillau* was soon dropped (see p 197, above). The choice of the latter had been based on her 15cm guns, to provide adequate offensive power against screening British light cruisers, and Adm Hugo von Pohl (1855–1916), soon to be appointed CinC HSF, strongly argued for the up-gunning of *Regensburg* for the same reason. In her case, the original proposal was to replace the forward two, midships and aftermost 10.5cm guns with a total of four 15cm weapons. A few days later, Tirpitz agreed to an alteration, but with only the fore and aft pairs of 10.5cm guns replaced by single 15cm mountings.

This decision caused a wave of disagreement from the various responsible departments and front-line commands. All were united in their concerns regarding the control of such a mixed armament, which was seen as much more disadvantageous than the putative benefits of possible single hits by the larger calibre.

The most productive and far-sighted critique came from FKpt Retzmann, CO of *Strassburg*. He proposed the removal of

4. The wreck lies upright, but listing to port; it is now badly collapsed (McCartney, *Jutland 1916*, pp 152–61).

5. The wreck lies upright (McCartney, *Jutland 1916*, pp 190–99).

6. The wreck also lies upright in 45m of water, but in two halves, about 55m apart, with the intervening 15m missing; some of her guns have been recovered and are on display in the Sea War Museum Jutland (McCartney, *Jutland 1916*, pp 208–15).

all 10.5cm guns and the arming of his cruiser with seven 15cm instead, directly replacing the foremost and aftermost beam weapons, with a single 15cm substituting for the forecastle pair, and two guns superimposed aft. The remaining two beam positions on each side could possibly be used for 5cm QL weapons. In one of his last statements as CinC HSF, Adm von Ingenohl supported Retzmann's proposal as 'very remarkable'. *Stralsund*'s commanding officer, FKpt Harder, added another perspective: to remove the need for the unpopular forward 'swallow's nests', he proposed the extension of the forecastle further aft, to allow the mounting of the forward beam guns on each side one deck higher (cf pp 155, 160, above).

Pohl's original proposal was withdrawn and, after being appointed CinC of the HSF the following month he aligned himself with his new subordinates and immediately requested that the RMA undertake a complete rearmament from 10.5cm to 15cm of all of the 'fast' small cruisers (i.e. the *Kolberg* class onwards). Of earlier vessels, only *Bremen* and *Lübeck* would receive 15cm guns – and then only two as chase guns, replacing their forward and after pairs of 10.5cm weapons – owing to weight limitations and the ships' exclusive use in the Baltic. Even in these latter exceptional cases, 'W' maintained its position against mounting only two 15cm, but as the four 10.5cm guns to be removed from these two cruisers had already been reallocated, restoring their original uniform 10.5cm batteries was not a short-term possibility.

Eventually, the RMA responded positively to Pohl's proposal, proposing a six-gun 15cm fit, supplemented by two 8.8cm AA guns on the centreline amidships. However, it was pointed out that each cruiser would need to be taken out of front-line duties for around four months for the conversion and subsequent working up. Additionally, Tirpitz rejected Pohl's generalised assertion that German cruisers were quite defenceless against their faster and more heavily armed British counterparts. Indeed, he noted that only the *Arethusa* class had the speed to overtake the newest German cruisers – and that they had exactly the mixture of gun calibres that had been universally rejected by the German service.[7]

In his March 1915 reply, Pohl argued for the addition of a seventh gun aft, omitting the less important 8.8cm AA mountings. In this, he was strongly supported by the leaders of the I. and II. SGs and all their commanding officers. Accordingly, at a meeting on 22 March, the RMA (with almost-universal stakeholder agreement) finally endorsed the seven-gun fit. The main obstacle to a quick conversion of all relevant vessels was the limited number of guns available. As of February 1915, the delivery schedule of 15cm guns would provide full seven-gun outfits for just two cruisers during 1915: which vessels should be chosen?

7. The British were, however, coming to the same conclusion over mixed batteries, the 1914 programme *Centaur* class receiving a uniform 6in main battery, with earlier classes back to the *Arethusa*s retrofitted.

In view of keeping a balance between the individual characteristics of the most recent cruisers, it was decided that the conversion of *Stralsund* and *Strassburg* should be undertaken first, as the oldest and slowest of the side-armoured ships. In addition, 'W' agreed to divert as many 15cm guns as possible from new construction to speed up conversions. Accepting extra weights of 50–60 tonnes, which would give an additional draught of 4–5cm, the rearming of *Stralsund* and *Strassburg* was seen positively from both technical and military points of view. The practical order of these initial conversions would depend on when each vessel was due for a major overhaul, or needed repairs in the normal course of operations.

In response to an enquiry by Pohl at the end of March regarding an anticipated schedule for conversions, 'B' gave the following assessment from Wilhelmshaven Dockyard, which would carry out the work:

- each vessel's conversion would require about 9 weeks of labour
- guns would be available as follows:
  - 7 guns at the end of July 1915
  - 7 guns at the end of August 1915
  - 7 guns at the beginning of October 1915
  - 7 guns at the end of January 1916
  - 7 guns at the end of February 1916

In July 1915, KAdm Hipper endorsed a proposal from the CO of *Rostock* to strengthen ahead fire by mounting a second 15cm gun on the forecastle – on the larger vessels at least – giving a total of eight 15cm guns, following the pattern employed in the new *Wiesbaden* class. However, as noted by 'K', this would be impossible in *Rostock* herself, as she had come from her builders already 100 tonnes overweight; in the end, all but one rearming would be limited to seven guns.

A wealth of detail is visible on this image of *Strassburg*, lying in the harbour canal at Libau. Looking forward, one may see the (loaded) newly installed port above-water torpedo tube. Forward of the tube one may note the open locker for spare torpedoes, with the monorail for loading overhead. Some of the cruiser's boats have already been replaced by floats, mounted on the former boat-skids. *(DN collection)*

Refits began with *Strassburg* in July 1915, a pair of 50cm torpedo tubes being installed on deck amidships, effectively replacing the midships 10.5cm mountings. *Stralsund* and the *Graudenz* class were similarly altered during 1915–17, *Stralsund* and *Regensburg* also losing their submerged torpedo tubes, the latter getting a second pair of deck tubes in lieu. The side plating of the forecastle was extended aft, as proposed by Harder, to cover the areas previously occupied by the foremost beam 10.5cm guns and gain more room for accommodation. The searchlight platforms of *Stralsund* were also altered to match the new *Königsberg* class, a modification also made to *Frankfurt* after Jutland; *Strassburg* retained her old platform on her mainmast. *Wiesbaden* was lost before any modifications could be applied to her.

Rostock would have been rearmed had she not been lost at Jutland. As noted above (p 201), *Midilli* (ex-*Breslau*) was also rearmed with 15cm guns, but in phases and in a different

Strassburg, in dry dock in Libau, after her conversion to a 15cm armament. Uniquely, she retained the old double searchlight platform on the mainmast. The standard white-circle aerial identification mark is visible on the quarterdeck. *(DN collection)*

Graudenz seen from directly overhead, late in the war. This image clearly indicates the lack of space between the aft funnel and the mainmast, which prevented the fitting of two AA guns. *(DN collection)*

arrangement from her sisters and half-sisters. Anti-aircraft guns were installed in *Frankfurt* and later ships, two 8.8cm/45 AA between the funnels and the mainmast being the usual fit by the end of the war. While a similar fit is recorded in standard published reference sources regarding *Strassburg*, *Stralsund*, *Graudenz* and *Regensburg*, no photographic evidence seems to survive that they ever carried such guns.

The surviving *Kolberg*s were also rearmed with 15cm guns and the addition of 50cm deck tubes, but without a superfiring gun aft. The bridgework was extended and foremast searchlight platforms were altered to match the *Königsberg*s, but they retained the old double platform on the mainmast. As already noted, most remaining pre-*Kolberg* ships retained their old 10.5cm armaments, with the exception *Bremen* and *Lübeck* when rebuilt during 1914–15 and 1916. *Lübeck* also received 50cm deck torpedo tubes in lieu of her submerged installation.

These reconstructions also included alterations to the ships' foreparts, with the curve of the stem moderated in *Bremen*, while the *Lübeck* had a complete new bow-section, with a raked stem, fitted. *Bremen* and *Lübeck* also had their foremasts – which in the latter case had collapsed when she was mined – moved aft of the conning tower and the bridgework rebuilt around them. New funnels were installed, half-cased in *Bremen*, fully cased in *Lübeck*, at a significantly reduced rake compared to that previously used; the masts were now rigged at the same angle. *Lübeck*'s appearance was in part intended to mimic that of the *Brummer* class, and she thus had her forward searchlights placed above the back of the bridge, rather than on the foremast.

Of the rest of the *Bremen* class, *Hamburg* was reduced to six 10.5cm guns after 1916, before being completely disarmed in 1918; *Berlin* and *München* were also completely disarmed while on harbour service. Most of the *Gazelle*/*Frauenlob* group also lost their guns; only *Thetis*, recommissioned on 19 October 1917 as a gunnery training ship (now armed with nine 10.5cm/45 guns), the training ship *Medusa* (six 10.5cm/40) and the minelayer *Arcona* (ten 10.5cm/40) kept guns. *Arcona* also had her submerged torpedo tubes replaced by a pair of deck-mounted units. The most extensive modification to the series had been applied to *Frauenlob* herself after the damage received at the Battle of Heligoland. She not only had her outfit of searchlights doubled, but additionally received a W/T cabin between her funnels, as had been installed in the *Dresden* and later classes from the outset.

Frauenlob in her final days before Jutland. A number of modifications are evident, such as her reconstructed searchlight platforms, the W/T cabin between the funnels and, on close inspection, her cutaway poop. *(DN collection)*

The most drastic wartime modification to any small cruiser was that applied to *Stuttgart*, which was rebuilt as a seaplane carrier at Wilhelmshaven between February and May 1918. A large hangar was constructed aft of the funnels, with space for two seaplanes; a third aircraft could be carried on the aft end of the poop deck. The foremost four broadside 10.5cm guns were retained, with the pair on the forecastle replaced by 8.8cm AA weapons; the submerged torpedo tubes were kept. There were also proposals to convert *Stettin* and *Danzig* along the same lines, but these were not carried forward given the limited number of aircraft that they would deploy. Accordingly, the much larger cruiser *Roon* (to have four aircraft) and unfinished liner *Ausonia* (up to twenty-nine aircraft) were substituted; however, no physical work was undertaken on either project.

8. For an overview of the naval war during the second half of the War, see Goldrick, *After Jutland: The Naval War in Northern European Waters, June 1916–November 1918* (Barnsley: Seaforth, 2018).

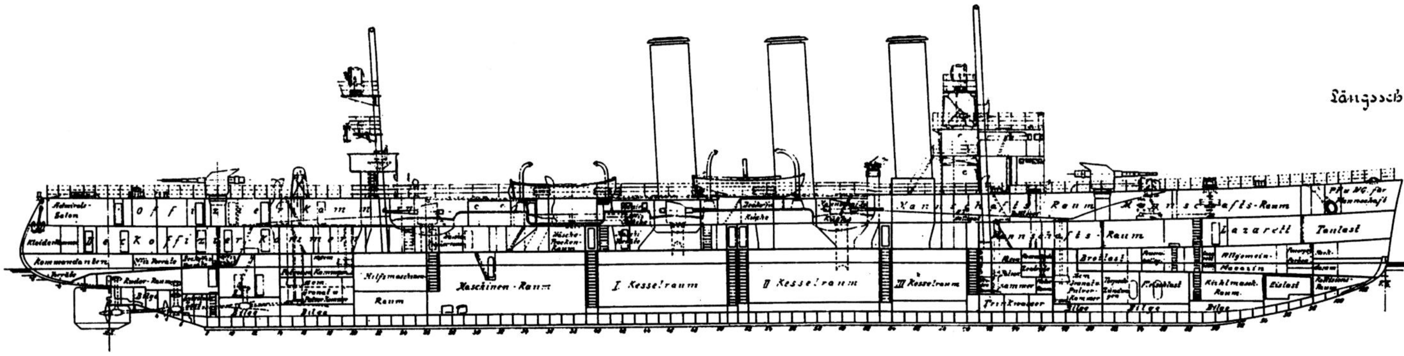

Sectional drawing from *Lübeck*'s booklet of plans, as revised after her reconstruction. *(DN collection)*

Stuttgart working up after her conversion to a seaplane carrier. The canvas screens of her hangar are open, giving a through view, as no planes have yet been embarked. Just visible on the forecastle are the two 8.8cm AA guns, replacing the old 10.5cm weapons. *(DN collection)*

BEYOND JUTLAND[8]

In the wake of the Jutland losses, the II. and IV. SGs were re-organised. The new *Brummer* (commissioned on 2 April 1916, but still on trials at the time of Jutland) joined the II. SG shortly after the battle. In August, *Danzig* rejoined the fleet after refit and was assigned to the IV. SG, alongside *Stettin, München* and *Berlin*. Another mine-victim, *Graudenz*, rejoined the fleet on 13 September, and became flagship of I. LTB, although still attached tactically to the II. SG.

On 18–19 August 1916, the fleet deployed for a bombardment of Sunderland by the Scouting Force, as planned for back in May, although owing to ships being still under repair after Jutland, the I. SG comprised *Moltke, Von der Tann* and the battleships *Bayern, Großer Kurfürst* and *Markgraf*. On the morning of the 19th, the battleship *Westfalen* was torpedoed by HMS/M *E23* and forced to turn back. However, the operation continued, and at one point the HSF and the Grand Fleet (as usual, forewarned by signals intelligence) came within 90nm of each other, but British concerns over the presence of submarines, and German airship reconnaissance sightings, meant that no clash took place. On the other hand, the British light cruisers *Nottingham* and *Falmouth* were sunk by German submarines: for once the 'submarine ambush' strategy accompanying fleet deployments had had some results.

The next sortie was planned for early September, but was cancelled because of unsuitable weather for airship reconnaissance. Appropriate weather for the next deployment not found until the middle of October. This began on the 18th, with *Stralsund* experimentally embarking a seaplane to supplement the eight airships being employed. However, while off the Dogger Bank, *München* was torpedoed by HMS/M *E38* abreast the middle boiler room, taking aboard 500 tonnes of water. This resulted in the salting of her boilers, and meant that she had to be towed by *V73* and *Berlin* until power was restored. Subsequent to her torpedoing, the whole operation was abandoned. Although she safely reached Wilhelmshaven and was repaired, since more modern cruisers were now joining the fleet, *München* was relegated to an accommodation ship for the rest of the war.

München in drydock after having been torpedoed. The torpedo had run quite shallow, thus hitting at about the depth where the armoured deck supported the outer plating. *(DN collection)*

Danzig serving as ice-breaker for a UC II-type submarine in the frozen-over Kaiser-Wilhelm canal. *(DN collection)*

Bremse (commissioned 1 July) joined the II. SG in October, as did the second *Königsberg*, the latter as flagship. A reorganisation of the HSF occurred on 1 December. The II. Sqn of pre-dreadnoughts was withdrawn from the battlefleet and a new IV. Sqn created by splitting the existing III. Sqn. As far as the small cruisers were concerned, *Bremse*, *Brummer* and *Stralsund* were switched from the II. to IV. SG, with the latter relieving *Stettin* as flagship. *Berlin* and *Danzig* moved in the other direction, with *Stuttgart* being decommissioned, producing the following organisation:

II. SG: *Königsberg* (flag); *Berlin*; *Danzig*; *Pillau*.
IV. SG: *Stralsund* (flag); *Bremse*; *Brummer*; *Stettin*.

Berlin and *Danzig* were, however, withdrawn in January and June 1917, respectively, to make way for the new *Karlsruhe* and *Nürnberg*, which joined the II. SG in February and May 1917. *Regensburg* joined the IV. SG in March 1917, when relieved as flagship of II. LTB by the new *Emden*. The latter became flagship of I. LTB on 6 June, when *Graudenz* switched to the II. LTB role. When withdrawn, *Danzig* joined the Submarine Inspectorate as a target for working up submarines, a common employment for some of the older small cruisers during the latter part of the war.

The Scandinavian convoys

During the autumn of 1917, it was decided to expand the ongoing campaign against commerce by using surface units to attack convoys between the UK and Scandinavia, with the supplementary intent of diverting Allied ships from anti-submarine operations in the Atlantic. The ships to be used were *Brummer* and *Bremse*, in view of their high speed, good endurance, and chance of their being mistaken for British light cruisers of the *Arethusa* and *Caroline* classes. To enhance the latter effect, they were repainted in the darker grey used by the Grand Fleet.

The attack took place soon after dawn on 17 October, about 70nm east of Lerwick, against a westbound convoy comprising twelve merchantmen, escorted by the destroyers HMS *Strongbow* and *Mary Rose* and two trawlers. The hoped for uncertainty about the cruisers' identity delayed reaction by the escort, and *Strongbow*, which was leading the convoy, was disabled by *Brummer*'s second salvo, fired from only some 2,800m. *Mary Rose*, to the north of the convoy, was hit in the engine room about an hour later, and was able to achieve one hit in return in the forecastle of *Brummer*, but without significant effect. With both destroyers sinking, the German cruisers then sank nine of the merchant ships, although three, together with the trawlers, escaped. No news of the disaster reached the UK until the surviving ships reached Lerwick, by which time the German cruisers were almost home.

Unknown to the Germans was the amount of luck both vessels had experienced during the operation. On the afternoon of 15 October, the British Admiralty had intercepted a signal from *Brummer* that the execution of the 'most secret order No. 71950' had been postponed until 16 October. It therefore knew had that *something* was about to happen in the North Sea. A further intercept added that both vessels would depart through the 'Nordmann Deep', close to the Danish coast, instead of the ordered 'Weg Blau', which been found to be infested with mines. One hour after this signal had been deciphered, CinC Grand Fleet, Adm Sir David Beatty, received the following message from London: 'Minelayer BRUMMER will proceed northward through Nordmann deep tomorrow the 16 October, presumably for laying mines'. Beatty's light forces were already on short notice for a minelaying operation of their own, and therefore could be rapidly retasked to intercept the German vessel(s).

Beatty thus sent twenty-eight light cruisers and fifty-four destroyers into the North Sea for the hunt, supported by the 15in/18in-armed large light cruisers *Glorious*, *Courageous* and *Furious*. However, owing mainly to strict W/T discipline, and the failure of the convoy escorts to report the attack, *Brummer* and *Bremse* evaded the hunting forces and returned along the same inshore route they had used previously when outbound.

Even if comparisons of colours in monochrome images can be deceptive, there seems to be a strong contrast between the light grey funnels of *Graudenz* in the back and *Brummer*'s darker grey uptakes. *(DN collection)*

Bremse on picket duty somewhere in the North Sea. In contrast to other vessels, both sisters wore the rudder indicator cones on the foremast instead of the stump mainmast. *(DN collection)*

It had been planned that *Bremse* should conduct war on commerce to the west of the British Isles immediately after the successful attack on the convoy. However, as her CO, FKpt Siegfried Westerkamp, later noted in her war diary, due to the high speed maintained during the 'run to the north', the ship now had insufficient supplies of fuel remaining for such an operation. From the point of termination of the convoy battle, enough fuel remained for some 960nm steaming – enough only to take her to the Outer Hebrides, before having to return, allowing additionally for any need for high-speed steaming during the final run back to Germany.

FKpt Max Leonhardi in *Brummer* agreed with Westerkamp's assessment, especially as both ships had been struggling with fuel issues – mainly regarding oil – throughout the operation. On the way home they had to reduce speed from 26 knots to 22 knots because of the constant emission of heavy smoke and large quantities of bright sparks from the funnels. This was mainly caused by the inferior quality of the tar oil, which also tended to constantly clog the oil filters.

Despite the success of the raid, the issues experienced revealed that suggestions *Brummer* and *Bremse* might be deployed to the Atlantic as raiders along with an oiler would be problematic at best – not only because of the lack of experience with oiling at sea and the lack of a suitable oiler, but the aforementioned technical issues revealed during the convoy raid. It is interesting that the pair had been seriously considered for the task in light of the comment quoted on p 193, above, regarding *Brummer*, that '[f]or a further going employment as cruiser the vessel is unsuited'.

Frankfurt at anchor on Schillig Roads. She, *Stralsund* and *Graudenz* were unique in having their forward spotting top mounted below the yards. She has now received AA guns forward of the mainmast. *(DN collection)*

The battles of the minefields: the Second Battle of Heligoland Bight

A key part of British strategy now lay in offensive minelaying to hinder the passage of German submarines from their home bases into the North Sea and beyond. Accordingly, minesweeping and the protection of the vessels undertaking the task was becoming a key role for the HSF. On 16 August 1917, two of the cruisers of the II. SG, *Frankfurt* and *Karlsruhe*, were so-employed, with three boats of the XII. TBHF, in supporting the V., VI. and VIII MSHF in the Heligoland Bight.

The extent of the British minefields meant that the minesweeping was being carried out some distance out to sea and vulnerable to attack – with any minesweeper losses likely to directly impact the German strategic ability to sweep clear channels and thus the ability of submarines to exit home waters. Accordingly, around midday on the 16th, the light cruisers *Centaur*, *Conquest* and *Canterbury*, of the 5th LCS, and sixteen destroyers, attacked, being first sighted by the torpedo boat *A36*. While no minesweepers were sunk, *M4*, *M37* and *M65* were all damaged. As a result of the very restricted visibility and teething troubles in communication between units of the HSF and the more informally commanded minesweepers, the impression arose that the cruisers had done little to protect the minesweepers. This perception led to the senior officer, FKpt Friedrich Rebensburg, CO of *Frankfurt*, being relieved of his command. In fact, this reaction ignored the lessons of 1914, when cruisers hurrying in penny numbers towards the sound of the guns had led to the disaster of the First Battle of Heligoland Bight.

A major clearance operation was to be undertaken on 17 November, carried out by VI. MSHF (*A36*, *M1*, *M3*, *M4*, *M7*, *M53*, *M66* and *T74*) and II. (fishing vessels), IV. (A41, A52, A63, A68, A69 and A74) and VI. (fishing vessels) AuxMSHFs, covered by the whole II. SG (now *Königsberg* [flag], *Frankfurt*, *Pillau* and *Nürnberg*), plus the torpedo boats *S62* and *G87* (VII. TBF), *V43*, *V44* and *V45* (XII. TBHF) and *V83*, *G92* and *G93* (XIV. TBHF). The battleships *Kaiser* and *Kaiserin* were to be in distant support, escorted by *S18* and *S24*. As usual, the British were warned by signals intelligence, having intercepted KAdm von Reuter's order on 16 November (after a one-day postponement due to bad weather) for the II. SG to sortie at 00:30 the following day from Schillig Roads. Accordingly, a raid was planned by the 1st CS (large light cruisers *Courageous* and *Glorious*), the 1st LCS (*Caledon* [flag], *Galatea, Royalist* and *Inconstant*), the 6th LCS (*Cardiff* [flag], *Ceres*, *Calypso* and *Caradoc*), and ten destroyers of the 13th DF, with cover from the 1st BCS, and distant cover by the 1st BS.

Fortunately for the unsuspecting Germans, the

Below: *Königsberg* directly after the 15in hit from HMS *Repulse* on 17 November 1917, which went through her aftermost funnel into a starboard upper coal bunker abreast the forward funnel, with a detail of the entry-hole to the right. The bottom-left photograph shows the starboard forward 15cm mounting in *Pillau*, after being struck by a dud 15in shell at 08.55. The gun, trained aft on the disengaged side, had suffered the loss of one man killed instantly, two thrown overboard and drowned, and the remaining three crew wounded. The gun was, however, provisionally operable again only an hour after the end of the battle. The linoleum deck cladding is visible between the guns. *(DN collection)*

minesweepers were delayed and thus had not advanced so far that they would be cut-off from retreat by the approaching British forces, as originally intended. Sweeping began around 07.00, and the covering forces were alerted at around 08.28, when several vessels could be made out to the west, at least one of them seemingly of a larger kind, closing at high speed. The action began at 08.37 when *Courageous* opened fire, the first shell landing within 200m of *Pillau*. *Glorious*, the light cruisers and the destroyers all began firing soon afterwards, the trawler *Kehdingen* being sunk. The other minesweepers were able to withdraw behind smokescreens, while the VI. MSF and the small torpedo boats of the IV. AuxMSHF exchanged fire with British destroyers; however, the German vessels were able to get away without damage, as did the II. and VI. AuxMSHFs.

The II. SG had now formed a line, following *Königsberg*, which had been detached for a short while, and retreated on a roughly southeasterly course, zigzagging and making smoke. Running before a northwesterly wind, the cruisers' smoke and artificial fog screens were most effective, at times granting them a break from British shooting for some thirty minutes, and thus greatly aiding their escape. However, *Pillau* was struck on the shield of the starboard forward 15cm gun by a 15in shell from *Courageous* at 08.55, with *Königsberg* consistently straddled between 09.05 and 09.31, but not hit. In exchange, *Pillau* hit a destroyer at a distance of about 8,000m at 09.23 and, around 09.50, *Cardiff* was hit three times, possibly by *Königsberg* (the latter's war diary does not mention any observed hits at that time, which may be attributed to the restricted visibility).

Königsberg fired torpedoes at 09.33 and 09.50,[9] both shots using an estimated calculated target range of 8,500m, before her starboard deck-tube was disabled by a splinter from the 15in hit towards the end of the battle. Soon afterwards, at about 10.00, the battlecruiser *Repulse*, from the 1st BCS, joined the action, with the German cruisers frequently straddled. *Nürnberg* was damaged by splinters, *Königsberg* struck by a small-calibre shell on PI gun-shield at 10.00, and *Frankfurt*, which had unsuccessfully fired a torpedo at 10.10, was hit ten minutes later by three 6in shells. One of the latter put number IV gun and the aft rangefinder out of action. At 10.12, the German torpedo boats were ordered to attack, but no successful hits were scored, although *Galatea* may have been struck by a dud.

A hit was scored by either *Pillau* or *Frankfurt* on *Calypso*'s conning tower at 10.41, by which time the two British large light cruisers were out of range owing to the presence of a minefield. The smaller vessels had not been properly briefed regarding this field, which meant that they pressed on for the time being. However, at 10.50, *Kaiser* and *Kaiserin* joined the action, a 30.5cm shell from the latter hitting *Caledon*, albeit causing little damage, but prompted the British to retire, covered by *Repulse*. The II. SG did, nevertheless, initially attempt to follow, but was thwarted when the British battlecruiser hit *Königsberg* with a 15in shell directly from aft that passed the aft two funnels before breaking-up in a starboard upper coal-bunker athwart the forward funnel and caused a bunker fire and reduction in speed; the flag was accordingly transferred to *Pillau*. Reinforcements in the form of the large cruisers *Hindenburg* and *Moltke* arrived around 13.30, followed by *Friedrich der Große* and *König Albert* around 14.00. However, the British were by then long gone, and the German ships turned for their bases at 15.00.

Into the last year of war

Stralsund had spent 7 August to 15 October 1917 under refit at Kiel, in particular to have her centre turbine reinstated (see pp 140-141, above), before being detached to the Baltic for the occupation of the Baltic islands. Back with the fleet, she temporarily acted as flagship of I. LTB between 10 and 20 November 1917, when *Emden* resumed the role. This duty was enhanced on 5 December, when the I. LTB was directly subordinated to the CinC, with the II. LTB reporting to the I. LTB. The first operation under the new regime came on 11–12 December, when IV. TBHF (*B109*, *B110* and *B112*) was deployed off the east coast of England, sinking three ships, while III. TBHF (*G101*, *G103*, *G104* and *V100*) operated off the Norwegian coast, attacking a six-ship convoy escorted by the destroyers HMS *Partridge* and *Pellew*, together with four trawlers, which engaged their attackers while the convoy scattered. *Partridge* was disabled after ten minutes, and later sank after having been hit by a torpedo from either *V100* or *G103*; *Pellew* was badly damaged, while all the merchantmen were destroyed.

Between 10 and 13 March 1918, *Emden* and *Graudenz*, with seventeen torpedo boats from VI. and IX. TBFs, together with *Frankfurt* from II. SG and *Bremse* from the IV. SG, made a sortie against shipping in the Skagerrak and Kattegat. On the 11th, the force divided into four, each group comprising a cruiser and a torpedo boat half-flotilla, but only five merchantmen were stopped during the operation. On 13 April, *Graudenz* accompanied the II. TBF on a similar sortie into the Skagerrak.

Following the successful October and December convoy-raids, British battleships had been detached from the Grand Fleet to provide cover for the convoys. Since this provided the opportunity to pick-off discrete parts of the British fleet in accordance with the long-standing German strategy, it was planned to launch an attack on a convoy using the I. and II. SGs, supported by the II. TBF, with the main battlefleet standing by to engage any British capital ships that might attempt to intervene. It was also hoped that a raid in the north by heavy ships would force British vessels currently based in the

9. The time lapse between the shots can be attributed, inter alia, to the fact that, for reloading, the port deck tube had to be unloaded first and the torpedo transferred to starboard tube. Thus, the second shot actually became a salvo of two, because the starboard submerged tube and the corresponding deck tube would fire simultaneously.

Top: *Stralsund*, a few days before her mining in January 1918, seen in the North Sea from an altitude of 100m. **Bottom:** *Brummer*, photographed on the same occasion, on escort duty off Terschelling. *(DN collection)*

English Channel to be redeployed further north, to the advantage of German submarines and light vessels in that area. The operation was launched at dawn on 23 April 1918, the attack force being followed by the battlefleet, the I., III. and IV. Sqns being supported by the IV. SG and the I., VI., VII. and IX. TBF, the latter led by *Graudenz*. *Stralsund* did not participate: she had been badly damaged by a mine in the North Sea on 2 February 1918 while in company of *Brummer*, covering minesweeping operations. However, in spite of two flooded compartments – the forward boiler room and the former torpedo room (now a magazine) – filled with a total of 650 tonnes of water, she managed to return to Wilhelmshaven, where she was repaired between 4 February and 25 April; she then went to the Baltic for most of the remainder of the war (pp 213-214).

However, at 0600 on 24 April, *Moltke* shed her inner starboard propeller while some 90nm southwest of Bergen. The overspeeding of the connected turbine led to the disintegration of a turbine wheel, its fragments severing several major steam and condenser pipes, leading to the flooding of the central engine room and adjacent compartments with 1,600 tonnes of water. *Moltke* had to be sent back to port. Initially capable of 13 knots, salt water contamination of feedwater brought her to a standstill. *Strassburg* was detached for an initial attempt to take *Moltke* in tow and, after this operation had failed, to stand by while the battleship *Oldenburg* rigged a tow. The operation was cancelled, the ships returning to Wilhelmshaven on 25 April and ending the last significant HSF sortie into the North Sea. Except for *Strassburg*'s assistance of the crippled *Moltke*, the small cruisers' part in the operation was uneventful.

Three weeks later, the penultimate new small cruiser to join the fleet completed her trials and became part of the II. SG. This was *Cöln* (ii), under the command of FKpt Erich Raeder (1876–1960), later CinC of the German navy from 1928 to 1943. The very last cruiser addition to the fleet came on 21 August when *Dresden* (ii) joined the same formation, commanded by FKpt Prince Adalbert of Prussia (1884–1948), the Kaiser's third son, and previously captain of *Danzig*. The new cruisers' employment would be limited to escorting minesweepers and picket duties in the Jade and Ems. No further vessels of their class had been completed by the Armistice, although a number were in a fairly advanced condition (cf pp 162-163, above).

End-game

August 1918 marked the turning point in the war in the west, the German front line being hopelessly broken by the Allied advance by the end of the month. The Grand Offensive, launched on 26 September, broke the Hindenburg Line on 8 October, the rest of the month witnessing a German retreat back towards their own borders. The submarines and torpedo boats deployed to Flanders ports were withdrawn from the end of September, covered by *Emden* and HSF torpedo boats. *Graudenz* was under refit between 6 September and 16 October, during which time *Frankfurt* and *Pillau* were employed in turn as flagship of the II. LTB.

The naval side of the war thus became increasingly dwarfed by the dismal events on shore. The navy's main residual task was to keep the submarine lanes into the North Sea free from mines, something that became increasingly difficult in the face of the continuing mining offensive by the Royal Navy. In view of these external pressures, even the long-overdue reorganisation of the fleet's high command, including the creation of a position of a centralised Leadership of the War at Sea (Seekriegsleitung – SKL) – something that should have been a key task for the Kaiser once war had begun – had little or no effect on the conduct of the naval war for its remaining few months.[10]

On 5 October, the German government put out feelers to President Woodrow Wilson of the USA towards agreeing an armistice. The latter's response required German withdrawal from occupied territory; the ending of the submarine campaign against trade; and the abdication of the Kaiser as preconditions to any agreement.

The end of the submarine campaign against merchant ship-

10. The creation of this centralised command had been Tirpitz's objective since the beginning of the war – with him in the leading role, of course. In view of the Kaiser's complicated personality and the turf wars between the individual bodies with direct access to the Kaiser's attention, its creation was, of course, problematic – until the point of growing desperation in 1918, when it was too late to bear any fruits.

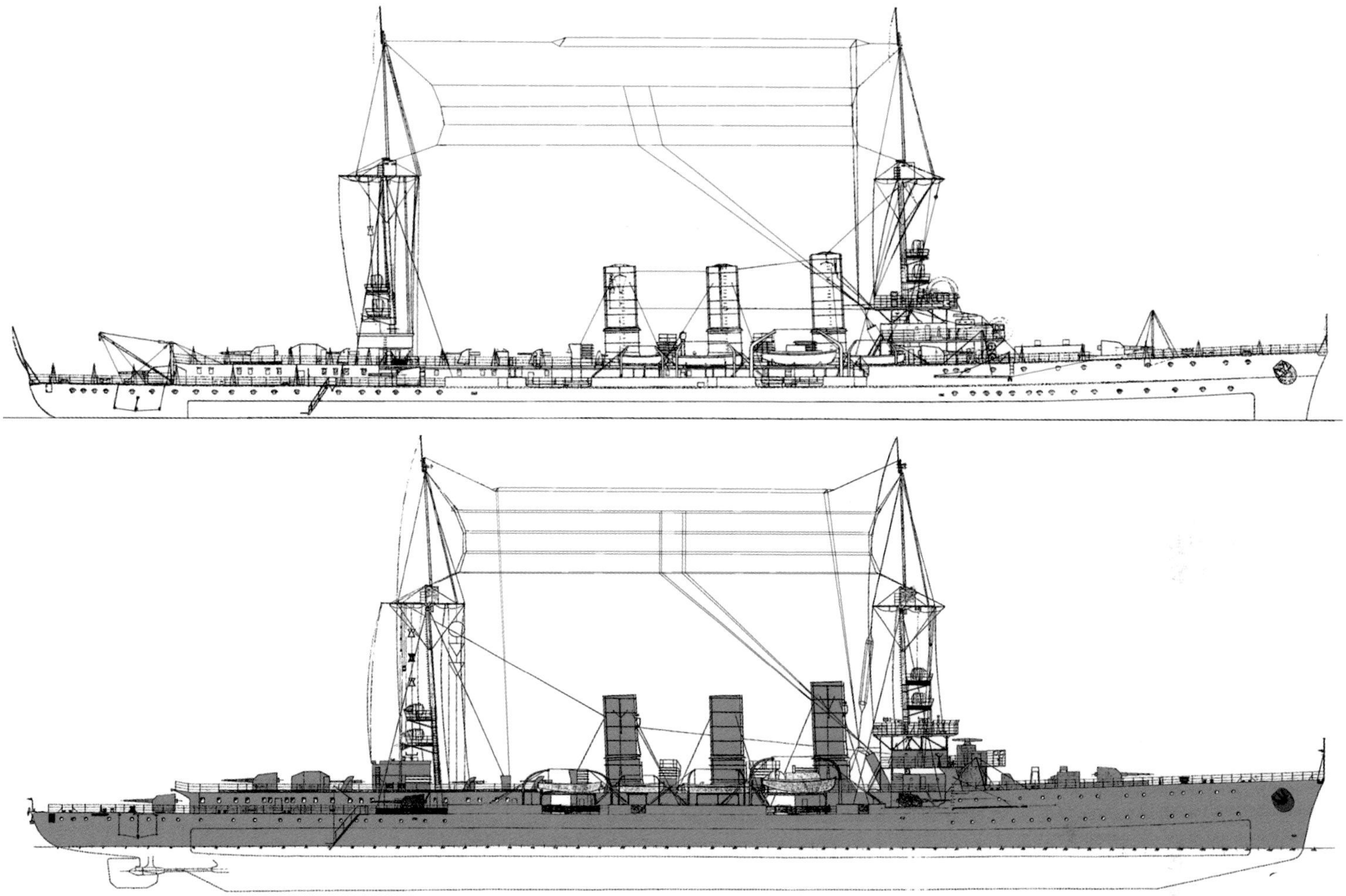

'As fitted' drawings of *Cöln* (ii, top) and *Dresden* (ii), showing the planned full sets of AA guns, one in a rather cramped position aft of the mainmast and two in front. As compared with *Cöln*, the drawing of *Dresden* shows the re-sited forward beam guns, a different position of the mainmast and also changes to the superstructure at the base of the latter. *Dresden*'s drawing is unusual in that the above-water hull and superstructure have been shaded in grey. *(DN collection)*

ping was implemented on 24 October 1918. However, the new availability of submarines for fleet support – and with a wider notion of maintaining the 'honour' of the navy and possibly influencing the peace settlement – the Chief of Staff at the SKL, KAdm Magnus von Levetzow (1871–1939), decided to implement a plan (originally drawn up in 1916) for a fleet-supported raid by small cruisers on the Thames Estuary, with the aim of provoking a final battle with the Grand Fleet.[11] The intention was that the I. SG would penetrate the Thames Estuary, thus supporting *Königsberg*, *Cöln*, *Dresden* and *Pillau*, plus the five torpedo boats of II. TBHF, in attacks on shipping, while the rest of the II. SG, *Graudenz, Karlsruhe* and *Nürnberg*, bombarded targets in Flanders. The remainder of the HSF, the I., III., and IV. Sqns, the IV. SG (acting as minelayers) and forty-three torpedo boats, would deploy in distant support, with a view to engaging the Grand Fleet, drawn south by the Thames attack, off Terschelling. Submarines were deployed to ambush British forces, including *UB116*, sent to penetrate Scapa Flow (which had not, actually, been the Grand Fleet's home base since April; the boat was mined and sunk in the attempt).

The order for the operation was issued on 24 October, with sailing scheduled for the 30th. On the 27th, the IV. SG was ordered to Cuxhaven to load mines, indicating that an operation was imminent; in response, a number of *Strassburg*'s engine room complement temporarily deserted as she was leaving Wilhelmshaven. The flagship *Regensburg* suffered a minor mutiny on the 29th while loading mines.

The same day, while passing through the Wilhelmshaven locks en route to Schillig Roads, two large cruisers lost between 200 and 300 men through desertion – a further concrete manifestation of a widespread concern at taking part in what was seen as a suicidal act, at a time when peace was seemingly in sight. There was also unrest aboard a number of battleships, and that evening the decision was taken to scale back the operation to just the small cruiser raids, which were themselves soon cancelled.

11. For the last weeks of the High Seas Fleet, see D Woodward, *The Collapse of Power: Mutiny in the High Seas Fleet* (London: Arthur Barker, 1973); N Jellicoe, *The Last Days of the High Seas Fleet: From Mutiny to Scapa Flow* (Barnsley: Seaforth, 2019), pp 31–61.

The end of the Imperial navy. Top: *Strassburg* at Stettin in mid-November 1918, after the end of the war. Her boilers are lit, but she does not show any flag, contrary to other ships that flew either a red flag or the civilian ensign. Bottom: *Augsburg* under the revolutionary red flag at Hamburg on 13 November 1918, allegedly having 'carried the revolution' from Cuxhaven to Hamburg on the 9th. *(DN collection)*

The fleet was then dispersed, with the exception of two battleships that had been seized by mutineers and were only regained under threat of one of them being torpedoed. Of the dispersed elements, the III. Sqn was sent to its home port, Kiel, where rebellious sailors from the battleships soon stoked a situation already enflamed by rumours of what had been happening in Wilhelmshaven. *Bremse, Brummer, Regensburg* and *Strassburg* of the IV. SG, plus *Dresden*, arrived at Kiel on 3 November, and on the following day there was a stand-off between *Dresden* and *Markgraf.* The latter trained a turret on the cruiser, in an attempt to stop her sailing for Eckernförde, where she was to become a repeating ship to ameliorate some of the communications difficulties arising from the ongoing unrest. *Dresden* eventually sailed, as did the IV. SG, which made its way to Glücksburg.

The IV. SG (plus *Dresden*) then moved on to Swinemünde, and later upstream to Stettin, as the revolt spread from Kiel, arriving on the 7th. Once there, rumours of an attack by rebel ships from Kiel led to the cruisers being placed out of commission, with their magazines (and, inadvertently, other compartments as well in *Dresden*) flooded and confidential books destroyed.

On the 9th, the cadet training ship (ex-battleship) *Schlesien* arrived from Marstal Roads in Danish territorial waters, where she had briefly taken refuge while waiting for the political situation at home to clarify. By this time work had begun to pump out and dry the ammunition of the four cruisers. The latter were ultimately recommissioned on the 18th.

The Armistice came into effect at 11.00 on 11 November 1918. On that day, the HSF had fourteen light cruisers on its strength: two (*Emden* and *Frankfurt*) deployed as torpedo boat leaders, the rest assigned to the II. (*Königsberg* [F], *Karlsruhe, Pillau, Nürnberg, Cöln* and *Graudenz*) and IV. (*Strassburg* and *Stralsund*) SG; *Regensburg, Bremse, Brummer* and *Dresden* were then temporarily decommissioned. There were also *Stuttgart*, now a seaplane carrier, and the old *Blitz* and *Pfeil* as tenders.

In addition, *Kolberg* was active in the Baltic, with *Berlin* as the local HQ ship, *Hamburg* as the HQ ship for submarines at Wilhelmshaven, and *Augsburg* still at Cuxhaven as flagship of the minesweepers. After Cuxhaven had been surrendered to the revolutionaries on 6 November, *Augsburg* was sent by them to Hamburg on 9 November, to support the local revolutionaries in taking the second largest city of the Reich. *Augsburg* remained at Hamburg for several days with a greatly reduced crew before returning to Cuxhaven and decommissioning there on 17 December 1918.

Deployed in secondary roles were *Thetis* as a gunnery training ship, *Medusa* as accommodation ship and tender to *König Wilhelm* at Flensburg-Mürwik, *Stettin* as a submarine target ship and *Arcona* as wireless relay ship, with a residual minelaying role. *Lübeck* and *Danzig* were both in reserve, the rest of the remaining small cruisers being on disarmed harbour service, as HQ (*Niobe*), mine (*Condor, Gazelle*), accommodation (*Amazone, Gefion, München, Nymphe*) or target (*Schwalbe*) vessels. In addition, a number of long-stricken hulks were also extant around the military harbours of Germany.

Hamburg, rather dirty and unkempt but still with searchlights mounted, laid up in Wilhelmshaven in 1918, but still employed as flagship of Leader of Submarines (as she had been since 1912) and as temporarily accommodation for submarine crews. *(DN collection)*

Under the terms of paragraph 23 of the Armistice:

> German surface warships which shall be designated by the Allies and the United States shall be immediately disarmed and thereafter interned in neutral ports or in default of them in allied ports to be designated by the Allies and the United States. They will there remain under the supervision of the Allies and of the United States, only caretakers being left on board. The following warships are designated by the Allies: six battle cruisers, ten battleships, eight light cruisers (including two minelayers), fifty destroyers of the most modern types.

Königsberg carried KAdm Hugo Meurer (1869–1960) to Rosyth to agree the details of this internment, being met by *Cardiff* and the 6th LCS on 15 November. Following two meetings between Meurer and the British CinC, Adm Beatty, she sailed for Germany on the 17th.[12] The 'eight light cruisers' were originally listed as being the specifically-mentioned *Bremse* and *Brummer*, plus *Cöln*, *Emden*, *Frankfurt*, *Karlsruhe*, *Nürnberg* and *Wiesbaden*. The demand for the latter, still incomplete, reflected Allied intelligence's failure to spot the diversion of resources from major warship construction during the latter part of the war. This was mirrored by a demand that the still-gunless and engineless large cruiser *Mackensen* be included among the interned capital ships.

Thus, the German ships that arrived in the Firth of Forth on 21 November were short of one large cruiser and one small cruiser – with a further battleship (*König*) detained in dockyard hands, and one torpedo boat (*V30*) missing by virtue of having been mined and sunk while leaving the Heligoland Bight.[13] They were also late, sailing having been delayed by condenser problems in *Cöln*, and the large cruiser *Von der Tann* missing orders to raise steam. The small cruisers followed the large cruisers (in the van) and the battleships, under Kdre Victor Harder flying his broad pennant in *Karlsruhe*, with *Emden*, *Frankfurt*, *Nürnberg*, *Brummer*, *Cöln* and *Bremse* in her wake.

Having been met by the Grand Fleet off Rosyth, the German ships were escorted to Scapa Flow over the next few days, beginning with torpedo boats, followed by larger vessels. *Karlsruhe*, *Nürnberg* and *Emden* were transferred to Scapa Flow on the 25/26th, in company with the battleships *Friedrich der Große*, *König Albert*, *Kaiserin*, *Prinzregent Luitpold* and *Kaiser*; *Frankfurt*, *Cöln*, *Bremse and Brummer* followed on the 26/27th, in the company of *Bayern*, *Großer Kurfürst*, *Kronprinz Wilhelm* and *Markgraf*. The large cruisers and torpedo boats had been moved to the Orkneys between the 22nd and the 25th.

To make up numbers, on 4 December *König*, *Dresden* (apparently still suffering leakage following the events of 7 November) and *V129* arrived in the Flow, followed on 9 January 1919 by the fleet flagship *Baden*, substituting for *Mackensen*. *Königsberg* also made a return voyage to Scapa Flow during December 1918, carrying supplies for the interned vessels. *Emden* became flagship of the interned ships in March 1919, following repeated incidents of poor discipline and revolutionary agitation aboard the original flagship, *Friedrich der Große*

Königsberg, flying the flag of KAdm Hugo Meurer, escorted by HMS *Cardiff* and another cruiser of the 6th LCS (top) and on 16 November 1918 in company with HMS *Cassandra* (bottom). One may notice the difference in smoke discharge between the mainly coal-burning Königsberg and the oil-burning British 'C' class vessels. *(DN collection/AD collection)*

12. For this, see Jellicoe, *Last Days*, pp 62–72.

13. On the internment and following events see D Van der Vat, *The Grand Scuttle: the sinking of the German fleet at Scapa Flow in 1919* (London: Hodder & Stoughton, 1982), and now Jellicoe, *Last Days*, pp 73–236.

10 | AFTERGLOW

KOLBERG, *STRALSUND* AND *AUGSBURG* decommissioned on 17 December 1918. Of the handful of cruisers that Germany was permitted to keep operational after the Armistice, *Regensburg* was used to escort the battleship *Hercules*, carrying members of the Allied Control Commission to Wilhelmshaven on 3–5 December. Later, she was to make four return trips to Scapa Flow, from 7 to 12 January 1919 escorting *Baden* and carrying supplies from Germany to the interned ships; *Regensburg* made further runs between 23–28 January, 15 to 19 February, and 25 April–1 May. The destroyer *B98* was similarly employed, *Königsberg* also coming back to Scapa Flow on this duty in mid-May.

In addition to *Regensburg* and *Königsberg*, *Graudenz*, *Strassburg*, *Arcona*, *Hamburg* and *Berlin* were in commission, although only *Regensburg* and *Graudenz* were permitted be retain their full gun armament (torpedo tubes had to be landed from all ships). *Königsberg*, although fully crewed, had to have her guns removed. Where above-water torpedo tubes had been

Arcona remained active during the immediate post-war period, as a support vessel for minesweepers clearing German minefields. *(AD collection)*

removed the gap in the side plating was plated over. The three cruisers now comprised the principal naval force of Germany. In addition, however, the whole German minesweeping force was active in clearing the huge number of mines laid during the war. *Strassburg*, employed as flagship of Baltic Minesweepers, was permitted a single 15cm gun on the forecastle for the destruction of mines. *Arcona* was a parent ship for minesweepers at Wilhelmshaven, while *Hamburg* was initially HQ ship for submarines. However, after the surrender of Germany's submarine fleet, she became HQ for torpedo boats, still at Wilhelmshaven. *Berlin* was now serving as HQ ship for Flag Officer Baltic (the old battleship *Kaiser Wilhelm II* also remained in commission as a stationary HQ ship, now of Flag Officer North Sea). *Pillau*, out of commission, was under refit in dry dock, and had had her AA guns and above-water tubes removed.

Regensburg's activities also included escorting four submarine support vessels destined for surrender in the UK. First, on 15 March 1919, she escorted the tugs *Wendemuth*, *Loewer*, *Enak* and *Roland* towing a pressure test floating dock (Flender yard number 21) from Kiel to Brunsbüttel. However, its departure from the latter for Harwich was delayed by two months, and in the interim the cruiser and the tugs were detailed to deliver the submarine salvage dock ships *Cyclop* and *Vulcan*. These were towed from Brunsbüttel on 4 April, but two days later they ran into a storm, during which *Vulcan* foundered; *Cyclop* nevertheless reached Harwich on 9 April, her crew being repatriated by *Regensburg* two days later.

Next, a second pressure test dock (the unfinished Flender 25) was towed out of Wilhelmshaven on 8 May, but broke tow on the 10th, being recovered shortly afterwards and towed to IJmuiden on the 11th by the Dutch fishing vessels *Gorredijk* and *Liesbeth Betty*. It remained in the Dutch port for some time, being initially taken into Dutch naval custody, but then passing into that of the local civil authorities. During this time, it appears that a payment of 750,000 Marks was made to the Germans, while in the other direction the owners of the trawlers demanded salvage money.

In the meantime, the cruiser and tugs successfully delivered the other dock from Brunsbüttel to Harwich, leaving on 23 May, and arriving at the British port on the 30th. En route, instructions were received to then proceed to IJmuiden to pick up the remaining dock, the German ships departing the UK on the 31st. Further delays ensued when the civil authorities at IJmuiden demurred at handing the dock back to the Dutch navy for transfer back to the Germans, and it was not until 7 June that *Regensburg* and her tugs were able to resume the dock's journey across the North Sea, finally arriving at Harwich on the 9th.[1]

All other cruisers not at Scapa were out of commission, and by the late spring the peace terms emerging from Allied deliberations in Paris (the Germans were not part of the discussions: the terms were to be a *diktat*) envisaged the surrender of all ships now at Scapa, plus (as far as the small cruisers were concerned) *München*, *Lübeck*, *Danzig*, *Stettin*, *Stuttgart*, *Augsburg*, *Kolberg* and *Stralsund*.[2]

Under Article 181 of the prospective treaty, the future German cruiser force could not exceed six light cruisers, Article 190 allowing replacements for these ships on a one-for-one basis once life expired, after twenty years. All other warships had to be disarmed and placed in reserve or devoted to commercial purposes.

Thus, as things stood in the middle of June, five of the six cruisers allowed seemed likely to be the modern cruisers not listed for surrender (*Strassburg, Graudenz, Regensburg, Pillau*[3] and *Königsberg*). The sixth ship would be the best of the older retained ships, the newest of which were *Berlin* and *Hamburg* – launched nearly a decade before any of the modern vessels.

However, all this changed on 21 June 1919, when the Scapa vessels were all scuttled. *Brummer* was the first small cruiser to sink, capsizing to starboard at 13.05, followed *Dresden* (13.32), *Cöln* (13.50), *Bremse* (14.30), and *Karlsruhe* (settled by stern and capsized to port at 15.50).[4] Attempts were made by the British to beach a number of vessels before they sank, with a significant number of destroyers put ashore or sinking in shallow water. Some larger ships were towed by destroyers towards Smoogro Bay at the northern end of the Flow.

These included *Emden*, whose scuttling had been delayed by her being flagship of the interned vessels, with two British drifters and a water tanker alongside when scuttling was ordered. She thus did not begin the process until one hour forty minutes after the order had been signalled to the fleet. Accordingly, when boarded by personnel from the flotilla leader HMS *Shakespeare* soon after 14.00, water had only begun to rise over the floor plates of the machinery spaces; the destroyer, a tug and a trawler were thus able to tow her ashore.

1. The story of the 'IJmuiden' dock has been pieced together from the report of Kaptlt Max Braeutigam, the German officer responsible for the transfers (RM20/277 – quoted in W Göthling, O Lörscher and S Schnetzke, *Ausgeliefert – Die deutschen U-Boote 1918–1920 und ihr Verbleib* [Berlin: digital business and printing 2012], pp 48–49), contemporary Dutch newspapers, and a letter from S C L Reygersberg, UK Vice-Consul at IJmuiden, 20 December 1919, (in TNA ADM 116/1974). The latter states regarding the 750,000 Marks that '[t]his sum, however, did not reach Berlin ? Different people took a piece of the pie'. The narrative given here, which still contains a number of obscurities, differs from that previously published in Dodson and Cant, *Spoils of War*, p 19.

2. For the Paris discussions, see Jellicoe, *Last Days*, pp 118–35.

3. *Pillau* had, of course, been seized from Russia while under construction, but no attempt was made by the Allies to facilitate her return (perhaps plus compensation for the sunken *Elbing*). By now the former Russian Empire was in the grip of a civil war, with the Allies actively intervening against the Red authorities.

4. For a summary of events of the day, see Jellicoe, *Last Days*, pp 155–212, as well as McCartney, *Scapa 1919: the Archaeology of a Scuttled Fleet* (London: Bloomsbury, 2019), pp 30–51.

Nürnberg beached on the island of Cava at Scapa Flow after her attempted scuttling; note the unique vertically-recessed starboard anchor (see pp 157-158). *(Geirr Haar collection)*

Frankfurt was much further along when taken over by boarding parties from the battleship HMS *Royal Sovereign* and the destroyer HMS *Wessex*, but was nevertheless grounded in 3½ fathoms in Smoogro Bay. *Nürnberg*'s anchor chain was parted by men from the destroyer HMS *Walpole* using explosives, allowing her to drift ashore on west side of Cava.

Bremse was towed towards the shore by the destroyer HMS *Venetia*, and her bow put aground. Unfortunately the sea bottom sloped away steeply, leaving her to roll over to starboard and sink, with her stern lying in 73m of water, but the bow above the surface. The drifter HMS *Clonsin* took *Dresden* in tow towards the eastern shore of the island of Cava, but the cruiser's deck was already awash, and she sank suddenly before reaching the shallows.

Emden, *Frankfurt* and *Nürnberg*, plus twenty-one destroyers, were rapidly refloated by the Royal Navy, being declared fit for towing in fine weather on 8 October 1919. *Baden* had already left Scapa at the end of July. However, the majority of the German ships were total losses. Furious at having been deprived of the most important part of their naval spoils, the Allies accordingly insisted that additional materiel would need to be ceded over and above that listed in the Treaty of Versailles signed on 29 June. Thus, on 2 September, a list of ships and equipment to be given up in reparation for the Scapa losses was presented to the Germans; it included the five modern cruisers originally due to be retained.[5]

In an attempt to avoid having to hand over the latter ships, in December 1919 Germany proposed an alternative. This was for Germany to complete five of the incomplete *Coln* (ii) class vessels and hand these over to the Allies instead. France counter-proposed that if this were to be done, the five existing ships should be handed over 'on account', to be returned as the new ships were delivered.

The French view was prompted by the realisation that, if Germany were stripped of her five modern cruisers, she would be left only with *Bremen* and *Gazelle*-class vessels. As these had all be launched between 1899 and 1903, Germany would be allowed to start a replacement programme immediately, potentially giving her a fleet of six brand-new small cruisers by the mid-1920s. However, if Germany were permitted to keep the 'five', only one near-term replacement would be possible, with no further new vessels possible until *Strassburg* became overage in 1931.

However, on 7 January 1920 it was officially determined that such an arrangement would be contrary to Article 181 of the

5. Much of the following material is derived from files of the Naval Inter-Allied Control Commission, now in the UK National Archives, especially file ADM116/1989.

Treaty of Versailles, which required 'the breaking up of all the German surface warships now under construction', no matter that the intent of France's proposed 'relaxation' was ultimately to the detriment of Germany. Accordingly, a protocol finally signed by the Germans on 10 January 1920 provided for the delivery of the five cruisers, together with the harbour equipment that had also been demanded to make up for the scuttled capital ships and destroyers.[6]

Even after signing the protocol, Germany attempted to avoid being left with only antiques as a cruiser force. A letter of 27 January argued that Articles 181 and 190 (which allowed the replacement of ships over twenty years old), when read together, gave Germany the right to have a force of six underage ships. To achieve this, she proposed that the two 2,060-tonne 15cm-armed big destroyers *S113* and *V116* should be reclassified as cruisers and be retained by Germany,[7] which should also be allowed to keep and complete *Wiesbaden*, the most advanced of the nine incomplete light cruisers. This proposal was rapidly rejected by the Allies. It was pointed out that *S113* and *V116* had been listed as torpedo craft in the protocol; the requirements of Article 186 were also cited.

The Article 185 ships were all stricken from the German navy list on 5 November 1919 (but with *Pillau* swapped for *Stralsund*), with *Graudenz*, *Regensburg*, *Strassburg* and *Stralsund* following on 10 March 1920, and finally *Königsberg* on 31 May. All were then 'renamed' with letters, as were also the battleships to be surrendered. Also stricken during 1919 were *Gefion* on 5 November 1919, and the incomplete *Ersatz-Cöln*, *Ersatz-Emden*, *Ersatz-Karlsruhe*, *Frauenlob* (iii), *Leipzig* (iii), *Magdeburg* (ii), *Rostock* (ii) and *Wiesbaden* (ii) on the 17th; *Gazelle* was removed from the list on 28 August 1920.

SURRENDER

The year 1919 had seen months of often bad-tempered wrangling between the Allies over the distribution of surrendered ex-enemy ships, in particular over whether such vessels should be destroyed, or whether some might be incorporated into Allied navies. The French and Italians were particularly keen to keep some ships, neither country having modern (or in the case of France any) light cruisers in service or under construction.[8] Concerns at equal treatment in any share out emerged when the Italians proposed that they take the four Austro-Hungarian plus two German light cruisers, and the French six German ships. The French refused, insisting on having two of the Austro-Hungarian cruisers, even though these were significantly smaller than any of the German ships.

6. For which, see Dodson and Cant, *Spoils of War*, pp 35–37.

7. Substituting these two vessels for two 'conventional' cruisers would make sense in the context of the late-war policy (pp 163-166, above) regarding the abandonment of the use of large 'fleet cruisers' as TB leaders and their replacement by scouts.

8. Cf J Jordan and J Moulin, *French Cruisers 1922–1956* (Barnsley: Seaforth Publishing, 2013), pp 24–25.

This rare image shows *Stralsund* laid up at Kiel Dockyard moored outboard of two unfinished ships. The vessel inboard is the large cruiser *Graf Spee*, towed from Danzig in early 1919, and slowly being stripped of her fittings to meet the terms of the Treaty of Versailles regarding incomplete vessels. In between lies the hull of a small cruiser, lacking its forecastle, although the whole stem-post is in place. This may be the only existing image of *Frauenlob* (iii), launched as the final Imperial cruiser on 16 September 1918. *(DN collection)*

In the end a deal was reached, with three distinct groups of ships identified.[9] The first group comprised 'Propaganda' vessels, for short-term publicity or experimental use before being sunk or broken up within a defined period. Each major power would accordingly receive a battleship, a cruiser (eventually not Italy) and three destroyers. Under this, the UK would get *Nürnberg*, France *Emden*, the USA *Frankfurt* and Japan *Augsburg*.[10]

After these allocations were made, all ships to be surrendered under the Treaties of Versailles, Saint-Germain-en-Laye and Sèvres,[11] or the post-Scapa protocol were put into a single pool. This was then divided between the Allied powers in proportion to their war losses, with the UK taking all ships sunk at Scapa Flow (see further pp 236-237). The remainder of the pool (i.e. ships still afloat) was then divided into two categories: the first group was to be scrapped or sunk within a defined period of time by the receiving power; the second could be put into long-term service if so desired. Under this latter heading, France and Italy were each to receive five cruisers and ten destroyers (France also received ten submarines); a number

9. The following data are derived from UK National Archives ADM116/1992.

10. Allocations in other categories were as follows:

	Battleship	Destroyers
UK	*Baden*	*V44*; *V82*; *V125*
France	*Thüringen*	*V46*; *V100*; *V126*
Italy	*Tegetthoff* (A-H)	Three ex-A-H
Japan	*Oldenburg*	*S60*; *V80*; *V127*
USA	*Ostfriesland*	*V43*; *G102*; *S132*

11. The latter, with Turkey, was never implemented, and annulled as a result of the Turkish War of Independence; the superseding Treaty of Lausanne left all ships in Turkish hands, in contrast to Sèvres, under which almost the entire navy would have been surrendered.

of smaller navies were also to receive ships in this category.[12]

To allow France and Italy to have a proper choice of ships, it was directed that '[a]t least six [German cruisers] from those vessels that are in the best condition are to proceed to a French port, and if after their selection there are any more in a serviceable condition they should also go to France' (only four modern Austro-Hungarian cruisers existed, all of which were to be considered). Fifteen (if possible twenty) German destroyers would accompany them. Then '[r]epresentatives of France and Italy should inspect the German and Austro-Hungarian light cruisers and destroyers and draw up priority lists of their fitness, the two Ministries of Marine subsequently deciding between themselves … which vessels they will incorporate in their respective fleets'. All leftover vessels from this process would be handed over the UK for disposal, to join others to be delivered for that purpose direct to Rosyth.

Cruiser arrivals at Cherbourg (the 'French port') and at Rosyth ran as follows:

Ship	Sailed	Arrived	Place
Kolberg	1 Apr	5 Apr	Cherbourg
Graudenz	28 May	1 Jun	Cherbourg
Regensburg	1 Jun	5 Jun	Cherbourg
München	1 Jul	5 Jul	Rosyth
Königsberg; *Strassburg*; *Pillau*; *Stuttgart*	14 Jul	19/20 Jul	Cherbourg
Stralsund	28 Jul	3 Aug	Cherbourg
Augsburg; *Lübeck*	28 Aug	2 Sep	Rosyth
Danzig; *Stettin*	9/11 Sep	17 Sep	Rosyth

In the event, France took the former *Stralsund*, *Regensburg*, *Königsberg* and *Kolberg*, plus the Austro-Hungarian *Novara*, together with one ex-Austro-Hungarian and nine ex-German destroyers. Italy chose *Graudenz*, *Strassburg* and *Pillau*, plus the Austro-Hungarian *Helgoland* and *Saida*, together with seven ex-Austro-Hungarian and three ex-German destroyers/torpedo boats. The UK thus took the unwanted *Stuttgart*, the Austro-Hungarian *Admiral Spaun* and eight ex-German torpedo boats, plus the remaining Article 185 vessels, including four cruisers. Of them, *Lübeck*, *Stettin* and *Danzig* were soon sold for scrap (as was *Stuttgart*), while *München* was expended in torpedo trials in the Firth of Forth in September 1921.[13]

Making the ex-enemy ships fit for further service under their new flags was by no means straightforward. For example,

Regensburg is towed away from Kiel for the last time, to be handed over to the Allies at Cherbourg. Before she left, considerable effort had to be expended on gathering together all the equipment that had been removed during her lay-up. This also applied to each of her consorts, to meet the demands of the ships' new owners (in this case France), and was a considerable burden for the new German naval administration. *(Author's collection)*

Stralsund had been cannibalised extensively over the nineteen months prior to her delivery to Cherbourg, making it very difficult for the former Imperial Dockyard (now Reichswerft) to put the cruiser into a suitable condition. The French unsurprisingly insisted that she be delivered fitted in accordance with her original equipment tables, meaning that fittings had to retrieved or replaced from scratch. This issue probably applied to all vessels to some extent. The replacement of the ships' armament also presented issues.

SWORDS INTO PLOUGHSHARES?

Under Article 181 of the Treaty, surplus German warships could be devoted to commercial purposes. A large number were listed for conversion, but only a handful were actually rebuilt, most simply having their scrapping delayed. Among the small cruisers, the hulk of *Gefion*, lying at what had now become the Free City of Danzig, was (along with the hulks of the battleship *Brandenburg* and the large cruiser *Victoria Louise*) purchased by the Danziger Hoch- und Tiefbau GmbH for mercantile conversion. In September, Allied authorities had refused permission for the three ships to be taken to the Netherlands for scrapping,[14] but now work was to be undertaken to convert the two cruisers, with the aid of material stripped from the battleship, both to provide employment in the former Danzig Imperial Dockyard and as a symbol of Danziger commerce, work being authorised by the local Allied authorities in May 1920.[15]

12. Brazil: six German torpedo boats (disarmed for police duties); Greece: seven Austro-Hungarian torpedo boats (six for police duties); Poland: six German torpedo boats (police duties); Romania: seven Austro-Hungarian torpedo boats (six for police duties); Serb-Croat-Slovene State: twelve Austro-Hungarian torpedo boats; Portugal: six Austro-Hungarian torpedo boats (police duties); she was also due to receive one Turkish gunboat, not delivered following the annulment of the Treaty of Sèvres. The intent had been that all other ex-Turkish ships should be scrapped by the UK, except for the battleship *Turgut Reis*, to be scrapped by Japan.

13. While standard reference sources list her as also broken up, for her actual fate see http://canmore.org.uk/site/102121/sms-munchen-fidra-firth-of-forth; her wreck lies on its port side at a depth of some 45m and is well preserved (cf M Clark, *Wrecks & Reefs of Southeast Scotland* [Caithness: Whittles Publishing, 2010], pp 23–26).

14. TNA ADM116/1939, dated 9 September 1919.

15. TNA ADM116/1994, dated 7 March 1920.

Most of the surrendered cruisers were allocated to the UK for scrap. Some were broken up in British yards, including *R* (ex-*Danzig*, left) which arrived at Whitby in early 1921, where the scrapping took some years. Others were sold to continental breakers, including *T* (ex-*Stettin*, right), which was purchased by Petersen & Albeck of Copenhagen in February 1921. She is seen here shown passing through one of the bascule bridges of central Copenhagen, bearing her prize-letter on the bow, and the last of the series of experimental camouflage schemes that she had borne during the latter part of the war. *(AD collection/Heidrich collection)*

P (ex-*Lübeck*) was also sold by the British to a Copenhagen breaker, which re-sold her for breaking-up at an under-employed shipyard in the small port of Rødbyhavn. *(Heidrich collection)*

Gefion on her delivery voyage as *Adolf Sommerfeld*. Only the embrasures under the turtleback forecastle give a significant clue to her origins, her former distinctive bronze-forged ram bow having been removed for the value of its metal, although the stern-post was left in place. *(DN collection)*

As with all such conversions, the magazines and most of the machinery spaces were adapted as holds. While *Victoria Louise* (renamed *Flora Sommerfeld*) kept her original centre reciprocating engine, *Gefion* (*Adolf Sommerfeld*) received a pair of 2,400bhp (downrated to 750bhp) MAN diesels from the unfinished submarines *U115* and *U116* (building at Danzig). These were fitted in what had been her after engine room; she also had her valuable bronze stem- and stern-posts replaced in steel. *Adolf Sommerfeld* was completed as a cargo ship in October 1920 but, like all mercantile conversions of warships, she was not wholly satisfactory. Particular issues stemmed from her narrow hull and large number of internal decks – as compared with a 'normal' merchantman of her size – which significantly limited her freight carrying capacity. Thus, both *Adolf Sommerfeld* and *Flora Sommerfeld* went to the breakers as early as the autumn of 1923.[16] *Gazelle* was reported by the Naval Inter-Allied Control Commission (NIACC) in 1921 as having 'been converted into an Ammunition carrier' at Rüstringen but this cannot be confirmed.

Article 186 of the Treaty required 'the breaking up of all the German surface warships now under construction', but on 13 February 1920 the German Foreign Office wrote to the NIACC asking for a ruling on the definition of 'breaking up'. It was proposed that it should be understood as 'so stripping such vessels of their characteristics as war vessels that reconstruction of war vessels would be impossible', so that such vessels could be used as the basis for merchant ships.[17] This was referred to

16. On the other hand, the former coast defence ship *Odin* survived as a car carrier into the 1930s. She, together with *Aegir*, wrecked in 1929, and *Frithjof*, scrapped in 1929, had first been rebuilt as diesel-engined locomotive transporters (see Dodson, *Kaiser's Battlefleet*, p 150), utilising the strength of their armour decks, which now became their upper decks. *Odin* and *Aegir* had been further altered, during 1923/24, as the first housed-over car carriers in the world.

17. Most of this section is based on UK National Archives files ADM116/1994, ADM116/1992 and ADM116/2113.

the Allied Conference of Ambassadors with a recommendation for acceptance, as it achieved the objectives of the clause, also meeting a requirement under Article 189 that material arising from the breaking up of warships must be used for industrial or commercial purposes.

The Germans were required to provide a list of vessels proposed for conversion, which included the unfinished *Cöln*-class light cruisers, as well as the battleships *Sachsen* and *Württemberg*, the *Mackensen*-class large cruisers, and various destroyers. The bigger ships were originally sketched as dry cargo vessels with armour and protective bulkheads and decks removed (where structurally possible – which it was not for the belts of the small cruisers), and magazines and most machinery spaces given over to cargo.[18] Most, including the ex-small cruisers, were to be diesel-powered, the engines coming from incomplete submarines.

By the autumn of 1920, options on the cruisers and big ships had been taken by the Deutsches Petroleumgesellschaft, now with a view to them becoming oil tankers. However, although the plans were approved by the NIACC, nothing was done to implement the conversions. By the spring of 1921 the NIACC was becoming increasingly concerned that not enough was being done in the meantime to gut the ships of their military features. This culminated in a demand that all unfinished warships should have all side armour removed and all machinery, armament, armour decks and torpedo bulkheads destroyed by 31 July 1921, which was indeed carried out.[19] In the event, none of the larger vessels would ever be converted, the hulks all being sold for scrap before the end of 1921, only a few destroyers actually being completed as merchantmen.[20]

TARGETS

Of the Allies' publicity/experimental ships, the Japanese ex-*Augsburg* was never taken up by her new owners, and was scrapped on Japanese orders at Dordrecht in the Netherlands. Of the remaining three, all ex-Scapa and thus with ruined machinery, the Americans' *Frankfurt* was handed over at Rosyth on 11 March 1920. Commissioned on 4 June, she left the Firth of Forth on the 17 June 1920 under the tow of the American minesweepers *Redwing*, *Rail* and *Falcon*, which were also pulling the destroyers *V43*, *G102* and *S132* (all also beached at Scapa Flow). Calling at Brest until 13 July, the convoy then sailed for the United States via the Azores, *Frankfurt* now being towed by the battleship (now-USS) *Ostfriesland*, and the destroyers by the minesweepers; they arrived off Sandy Hook on 9 August.

18. For proposed capital ship conversions, see Dodson, *The Kaiser's Battlefleet*, pp 149–52.

19. See Dodson and Cant, *Spoils of War*, p 78.

20. *S178* and *S179* became four-masted auxiliary schooners under the names *Franziska Kimme* and *Georg Kimme*, while *H186* and *H187* became the coasters *Hansdorf* and *Hoisdorf* (see Dodson, 'Beyond the Kaiser: the Imperial German Navy's destroyers and torpedo boats after 1918', *Warship* [XLI] (2019), pp 136–38).

All were expended as targets in the anti-shipping demonstrations off Cape Henry, Virginia, the following summer. On 18 July 1921, having been prepared at New York Navy Yard by both stripping and also sealing bulkheads to maximise watertight integrity, *Frankfurt* was the target for Army Air Force and Navy aircraft.[21] They began with 250lb (110kg) and 300lb (140kg) bombs, which caused minor damage, and continued with 550lb (250kg) and 600lb (270kg) weapons. Two of the latter, dropped by Army Martin NBS-1 twin-engined bombers, struck the ship between the funnels and the mainmast, a third, abreast the bridge, causing such underwater damage that *Frankfurt* sank at 18.25. Of her compatriots, *V43* had been sunk by the battleship USS *Florida* on the 15th; *Ostrfriesland* would be sunk by bombs on the 21st, *G102* on 13 July and *S132* on 15 July.

Nürnberg was towed to Portsmouth, where she was prepared for target service.[22] For the first trial, on 5 November 1920, she was placed only 400 yards away from the firing ship, the monitor *Terror*, to ensure a maximum number of hits; however, reduced charges were used and the cruiser heeled 10 degrees towards *Terror* by shifting coal, so as to imitate long-range fire (a similar stratagem was used for firing trials against *Baden*).[23] Guns used were a 7.5in weapon on a special proof mounting loaned by the Shoeburyness range, and a 6in, both being part of a battery of guns specially fitted in *Terror* for the series of firing trials carried out against ex-German ships during 1920–21.[24]

A range of shell types for each calibre were used, with specific parts of the ship targeted: the conning tower, light structures, the belt, and the upper deck. During the first series, flooding was caused by one hit, reducing the ship's heel to 7.5 degrees. For the second series, on 8 November, the heel was increased to 20 degrees by also flooding the bunkers. The following year, on 7 July 1922 *Nürnberg* was sunk by gunfire from the battlecruiser *Repulse*, coming to rest on her port side in 62m of water halfway between Poole and Cherbourg. Despite her use for explosive trials, the French *Emden* survived to be scrapped at Caen in 1926.

SALVAGE AT SCAPA

From 1920 onwards, the various wrecks at Scapa Flow, now all formally belonging to the UK, began to be salvaged for scrap.

21. T Wildenberg, *Billy Mitchell's War with the Navy: the Interwar Rivalry Over Naval Air Power* (Annapolis, MD: Naval Institute Press, 2013), pp 73–74, 77.

22. For which see *Royal Navy Gunnery Manual 1921*, pp 100–20.

23. W Schleihauf, 'The Baden Trials', *Warship* XXIX (2007), pp 81–90.

24. See I Buxton, *Big Gun Monitors: Design, Construction and Operations 1914–1945*, 2nd edition (Barnsley: Seaforth, 2008), pp 157–58. Other vessels fired upon were the destroyers *V82* (13 and 15 October 1920) and *V44* (8 December), plus the submarines *UB21* (sunk 30 September 1920) and *U141* (7 October 1920); see Dodson and Cant, *Spoils of War*, pp 49–50.

25. S C George, *Jutland to Junkyard: the raising of the scuttled German High Seas Fleet from Scapa Flow – the greatest salvage operation of all time* (Cambridge: Patrick Stevens Ltd, 1973), pp 87–88; K Heath and M Thomson, *Scapa Flow Underwater Salvage Sites Survey: Phase 2 Report* (University of the Highlands and Islands Archaeology Institute/SULA Diving/Orca Marine, 2019), pp 81–88.

The first cruiser to be sold for salvage was *Bremse*, purchased by the firm of Cox & Danks in December 1925.[25] In spite of still being partly above water, her salvage was by no means straightforward, since she lay at a steep angle. In addition, with two-thirds of her boilers oil-fired, she contained far more liquid fuel than most other HSF wrecks, leading to a number of explosions while being prepared for refloating. This was problematic, and the actual lift took two days. The forward part of the wreck was then burned out by the spread of fires lit to deal with a slick of oil accidentally released from her oil bunkers. In no state to be towed to Rosyth for scrapping, as was usual practice, *Bremse* was accordingly demolished at Lyness over the next eighteen months, where one of her 15cm guns is preserved.

None of the remaining small cruisers were raised, *Karlsruhe*, *Brummer*, *Dresden* and *Cöln* thus remaining on the bottom, together with the battleships *König*, *Markgraf* and *Kronprinz Wilhelm*. The latter had been sold to Metal Industries along with *Derfflinger* in April 1936, as was *Karlsruhe* in 1955, being sold-on to a series of salvagers from the mid-1950s. These removed armour and other valuable material using explosives, but made no attempt to actually raise the wrecks. Salvage rights for *Brummer*, *Dresden* and *Cöln* were also sold during the late 1950s and early 1960s, with similar salvage work carried out.[26] These latter rights having expired on 17 September 1985, the three cruiser wrecks were then sold to the Orkney Islands Council by the Ministry of Defence for the nominal sum of £1; in recognition of the ships' historic importance, all wrecks were scheduled in 2001.[27] However, the formal ownership of *König*, *Markgraf*, *Kronprinz Wilhelm* and *Karlsruhe* was auctioned online via eBay in June 2019, a century on from their sinking; the battleships were sold in July to Middle Eastern interests for £25,000 each, and *Karlsruhe* to a UK private individual for £8,500.

CRUISERS OF THE *REICHSMARINE*

Following the forced deletions of 1919/20, the newest cruisers left to the new German Navy, the Reichsmarine,[28] were *Hamburg* and *Berlin*, and then, in order, *Arcona*, *Medusa*, *Amazone*, *Thetis*, *Nymphe* and *Niobe*. Of these, *Hamburg*, *Berlin* and *Arcona* had remained in commission, albeit in secondary roles, after the end of the war, although they had paid off on 16 August 1919, 10 June 1921 and 19 February 1920, respectively. *Thetis* had decommissioned a month after the end of the war from her role as a gunnery training ship.

26. For their history since 1919, see I McCartney, *Scapa 1919*, pp 147–276, 317–18.

27 Historic Scotland, scheduling document dated 23 March 2001.

28. For an overview of the history of the *Reichsmarine* see G Paloczi-Horvath, 'The German Navy from Versailles to Hitler', *Warship 1997–98*, pp 64–76, although this contains a number of detail errors.

Hamburg, shown at Swinemünde in 1924. Modifications have been limited to the removal of the 'swallows' nest' sponsons under the forecastle, the modernisation of the main battery and the installation of an above-water torpedo tube on each side aft, replacing the submerged tubes. *(DN collection)*

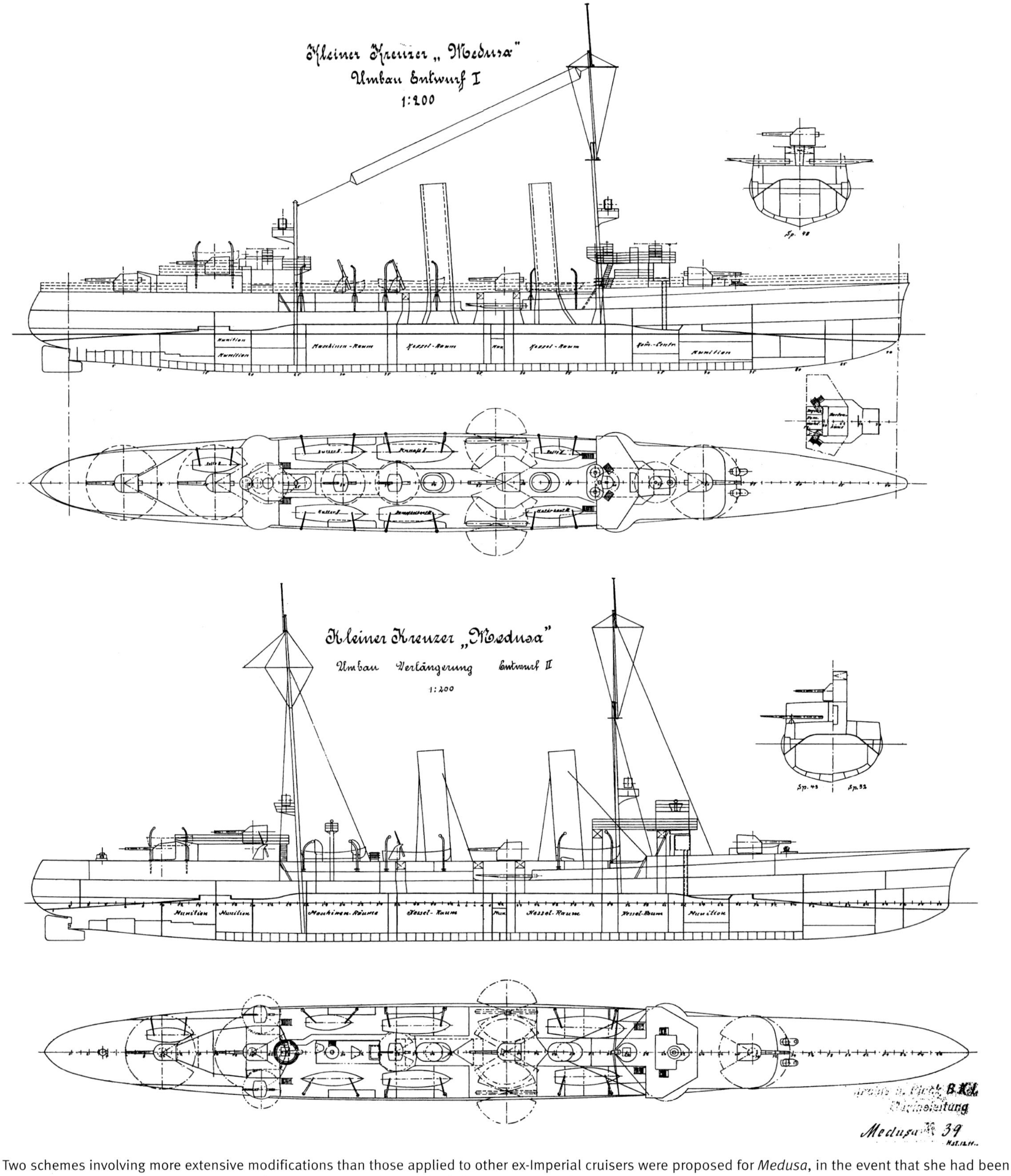

Two schemes involving more extensive modifications than those applied to other ex-Imperial cruisers were proposed for *Medusa*, in the event that she had been given a second stint in commission with the Reichsmarine. These included rearmament with 15cm guns, arranged on the centreline in an arrangement similar to that employed in *Brummer* and *Bremse*. Unsurprisingly, the naval architects from the 1920s faced the same problems as had Tirpitz a quarter of a century before on her limited tonnage. Thus any solution would be sub-optimal even with the fitting of shallow bulges, or further lengthening forward in the case of 'Entwurf II'. The latter also incorporated a third 8.8cm AA gun. *(DN collection)*

In contrast to the earlier refittings, *Berlin, Nymphe* and *Amazone* (shown here) had their bows rebuilt when refitted for Reichsmarine service. *(DN collection)*

Under the Treaty, six could be in commission at any one time. In March 1920 the Allies agreed an allowance for a further pair in reserve, but with guns on board, the reserve pair being then declared as *Niobe* (at Wilhelmshaven) and *Nymphe* (at Kiel).[29] First back in operational service was *Medusa*, which recommissioned in July 1920 as the first major warship of the Reichsmarine and station flagship in the Baltic. Her North Sea opposite number would be *Hamburg*, which re-entered service in September 1920, being joined there by *Arcona* in May 1921. *Thetis* brought Baltic strength up to two when she recommissioned in April 1922. Relieved as station flagship by the battleship *Hannover* on 10 February 1921, *Medusa* continued in service until paid off in September 1924.

At the end of the previous year, in the wake of Germany's improving economic state, it had been considered whether *Medusa*'s life might be extended by a more extensive reconstruction than was being applied to some other ex-Imperial cruisers (see below). She was still in good shape because of her rather brief active career, but in the end it was decided she was too small to adequately oppose current or future opponents; accordingly she was converted to an accommodation hulk at Wilhelmshaven in 1927 and stricken at the end of the decade, when *Ersatz-Medusa* was commissioned as *Karlsruhe* (iii) (see p 240, below). The old ship continued, however, to provide accommodation for destroyer and torpedo boat crews until 1940.

29. Reserve ships had previously been required to be wholly disarmed; an armed reserve pair of battleships (*Preußen* and *Lothringen*, although never armed), four reserve destroyers (*V6, S19, T175* and *T170*) and four torpedo boats (*T89, T88, T86* and *T85*) were agreed at the same time.

In the North Sea, *Hamburg* accompanied a minesweeping group to the Arctic in July 1921, to clear mines laid by the auxiliary cruiser SMS *Meteor* in 1915, before becoming a cadet training ship on 1 April 1925. During the winter of 1921/22, *Arcona* acted as an emergency ice-breaker in the Baltic, suffering hull damage that required dockyard attention.

While *Medusa* had re-entered service little altered, the next three ships had the after superstructure built up and the submerged tubes replaced by heavier-calibre deck tubes (*Hamburg* also received 10.5cm/45 main guns, replacing her original 40-calibre weapons). *Thetis* had her after searchlight moved to the mainmast, with a second added above it. However, the fifth ship to recommission, *Berlin*, was more extensively modified at Wilhelmshaven during 1921/22. Her bow was rebuilt to enclose the former ram in a clipper stem and the set of main armament embrasures abreast the bridge plated in; the number of guns was accordingly reduced to eight, but these were now of the 10.5cm/45 type. She re-entered service as a cadet training ship in July 1922.

Similar modifications (except that the forward pair of embrasures were retained) were applied to *Amazone* at Wilhelmshaven during 1921/23 before the ship recommissioned in December

1923 for service in the North Sea. She relieved *Arcona*, which paid off into reserve. *Nymphe* had been towed from Kiel to Wilhelmshaven on 4 November 1920, where she began her major refit in November 1922 along the same lines as *Amazone*. *Nymphe* recommissioned in November 1924 as flagship of Flag Officer Light Naval Forces Baltic, replacing *Thetis* in the order of battle, the latter being placed in reserve at Wilhelmshaven. *Amazone* was part of the pioneering 1926 fleet cruise along with her sister *Nymphe* and the battleships *Schleswig-Holstein* (flag), *Hannover*, *Elsaß* and *Hessen*; she also participated in the following year's cruise. *Nymphe* took part in the 1928 deployment, during which her steering gear was damaged in a storm in the Bay of Biscay. The year 1928 also saw *Amazone* make visits to Scandinavia; she paid off in January 1930.

The oldest ship, *Niobe*, was never to recommission in German service. Under Article 190 of the Treaty of Versailles, cruisers could be replaced twenty years after their launch. As *Niobe* had entered the water on 18 July 1899, her scheduled replacement date almost coincided with the signing of the Treaty; thus the 1920 budget included 25 million Marks for *Ersatz-Niobe*.[30] On 3 May 1920, before work began, the German authorities approached the Allies seeking permission to utilise the hull of *Magdeburg*, then being dismantled under Article 186 (see above),[31] for reasons of economy. The request was turned down on the 11th by the NIACC as incompatible with terms of the Treaty, but the Germans then appealed to the Commission of Guarantees on the grounds that this decision was economically illogical. The Commission of Guarantees declared itself incompetent in the matter, the issue going to the Allied Conference of Ambassadors in January 1922. The British were in favour of granting the request on economic grounds, but this was opposed by France and Italy on the basis that this would set a precedent for nullifying the letter of the Treaty; the request was thus refused on 22 August.

The Germans had, however, long since given up on the idea, since *Magdeburg*, mutilated beyond recovery following the July 1921 NIACC ultimatum (p 236, above) had been sold for scrap on 28 October 1921. By August 1922, *Ersatz-Niobe* had been on the slipway at Wilhelmshaven for some nine months, and would be launched as *Emden* (iii) on 7 January 1925. The new ship was, nevertheless, in many essentials a unit of the *Cöln* class, with a significantly modified forepart, superfiring guns, a 4:6 coal:oil ratio, geared turbines, 50 per cent greater range and a tubular foremast.

However, this in no way represented an endorsement of a continuation of the principles upon which the 'classic' German small cruiser had been based: indeed, as already noted (pp 163-166, above), these principles had been found partly inappropriate or even 'obsolete' during the war. Rather, this was purely a matter of expediency, since post-war Germany had neither the technical nor financial resources to undertake any substantive development, nor had it yet formulated a new strategic objective for the future role of the small/light cruiser.

Ersatz-Niobe – launched as *Emden* (iii), the first new cruiser for the Reichsmarine, shown as completed. Her masts would later be significantly shortened, mainly for reasons of stability. *(DN collection)*

The one planned substantive innovation had been the fitting of her 15cm main armament in twin mountings, superimposed fore and aft. However, this had been frustrated, partly by the refusal of the victorious powers to agree to such an enhancement, and partly by the location of the intended armament contractor, Rheinmetall, in the French-occupied Rhineland. Thus, when German designers were free to create a design from scratch (albeit tonnage-limited by the Versailles treaty), they produced something very different – the 'K' class (*Königsberg* [iii], *Karlsruhe* [iii] and *Köln* [iii]), with triple turrets and auxiliary diesel propulsion.

Emden commissioned on 15 October 1925, bringing the

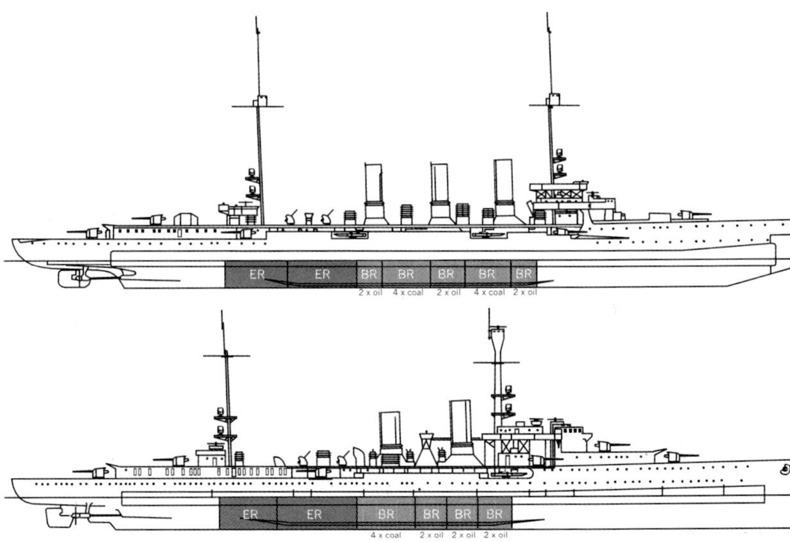

Comparison between *Emden* (iii) and her design predecessors of the later *Coln* (ii) class. *(AD graphic)*

30. Actually the second '*Niobe* replacement': the first had been *Karlsruhe* (ii) – since 1919 rusting on the bed of Scapa Flow.

31. The following account is based on UK National Archives file T 160/102/1.

cruiser force up to five vessels and relieving *Berlin* in her cadet-training role. *Berlin* then transferred to the Baltic command, from which she took part in the 1927 fleet cruise. The number of cadet training ships had, however, been brought up to two when *Hamburg* took on the role in 1925, undertaking a world cruise that lasted from 14 February 1926 until 20 March 1927. On her return, she paid off in June 1927, *Berlin* returning to her former role on 1 October 1927, for a final round-the-world cruise from 1 December 1927 to 7 March 1929. On her return she paid off at Kiel, many of her crew manning *Karlsruhe* (iii – *Ersatz Medusa*), the second of the wholly-new 'K' class, which would be the basis for all later German light cruisers. The first of that class, *Königsberg* (iii – *Ersatz Thetis*), had replaced *Nymphe* as light forces flagship, while the final vessel, *Köln* (iii – *Ersatz Arcona*),[32] superseded *Amazone* in service and took her crew.

Amazone and the new *Köln* moored stern to stern in January 1930, following the latter's commissioning with the old cruiser's crew, marking the end of former Imperial cruisers in German front-line service. The new *Königsberg* class marked a radical break in the conception of the German cruiser. *(AD collection)*

Thetis had been employed since paying off as an accommodation ship, but with the commissioning of new ships she was stricken in March 1929; sold to Blohm und Voss along with the destroyers *V1* and *V6* for a total of 351,000 Marks, all three of them were broken up by Unterelbe AG at the small village of Wewelsfleth in 1930. *Medusa* was stricken on the same day, but was not sold, instead becoming an accommodation ship at Wilhelmshaven; she was left with just masts and with her machinery dismantled. *Arcona* was next to be stricken in January 1930 but, externally little changed, she was retained as

32. After the First World War, German spelling was reformed, so that words hitherto spelled with a 'C' now used a 'K' – including the German name of the city of Cologne.

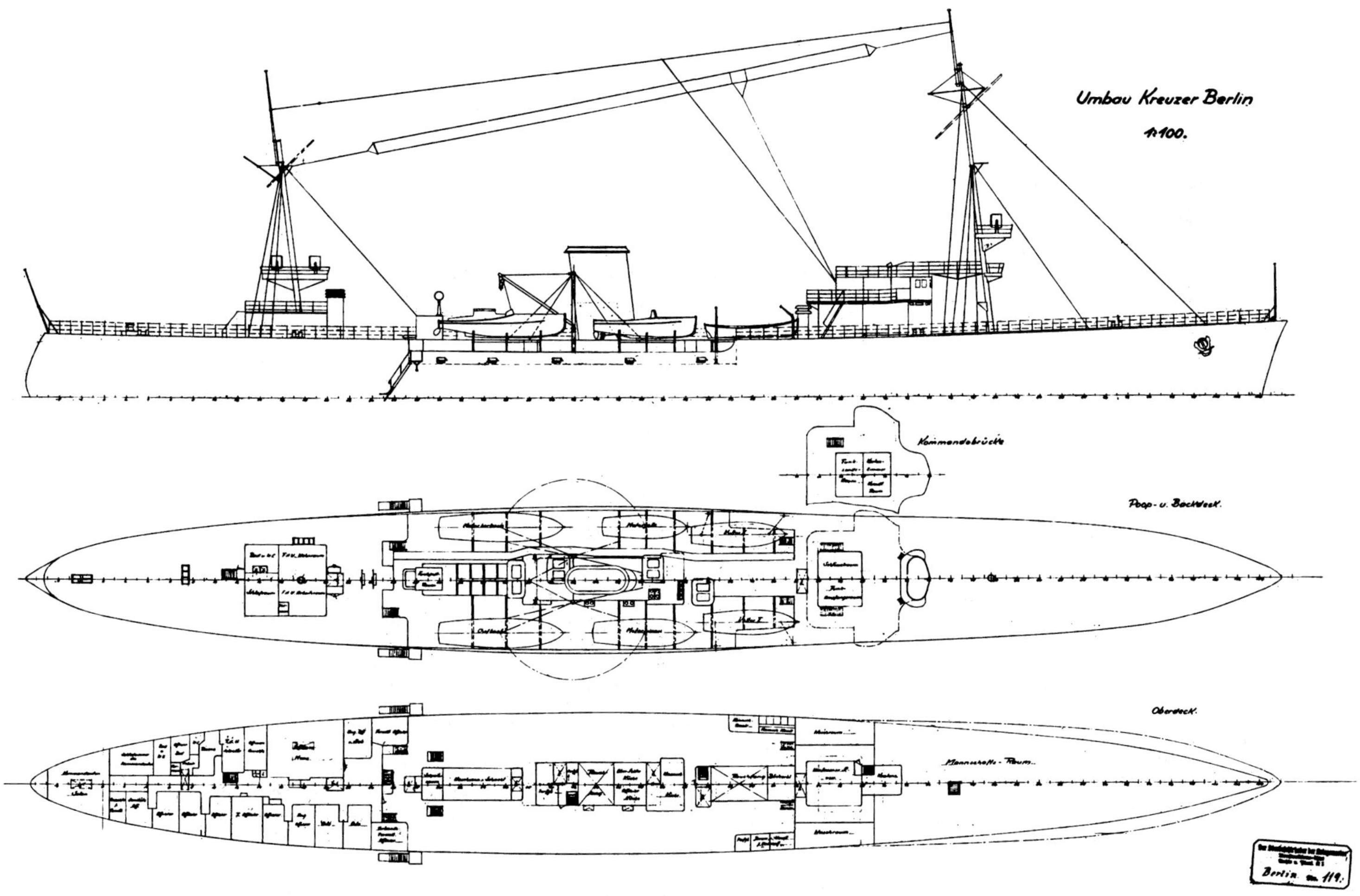

Undated proposal for the conversion of *Berlin* into flagship/HQ ship for the Leader of Submarines. *(DN collection)*

an accommodation hulk, first at Wilhelmshaven, from 1936 at Swinemünde, and from 1938 to 1940 at Kiel.

The day 31 March 1931 saw the deletion from the list of a large block of old ships, not only *Hamburg*, *Amazone* and *Nymphe*, but also the battleships *Braunschweig*, *Elsaß* and *Lothringen*. After brief use as a barracks ship, *Nymphe* was sold for 61,500 Marks and broken up. However, *Hamburg* and *Amazone* were kept as long-term hulks, stripped of superstructure and funnels; both kept their foremasts, *Amazone* her bridge as well. Both had additional accommodation fitted at upper-deck level, *Hamburg* becoming an accommodation ship for submarine personnel at Kiel in 1936, and both becoming accommodation vessels at Kiel.

The last of the old cruisers on the fleet list was *Berlin*, which was not stricken until October 1935, when she also became an accommodation ship at Kiel; she was left externally largely intact, but stripped of guns, searchlights and other fittings. Nevertheless, consideration was given for her further seagoing service as a flagship/tender for FO Submarines. However, it was ultimately decided that new-build tonnage would be more satisfactory, and *Berlin* remained on harbour service for the rest of her career.

At the outbreak of war, the surviving old cruisers in German hands initially remained in their humble roles. However, concerns at the level of protection available to German naval bases led in 1940 to two of the old ships being selected – along with various captured vessels of similar vintage[33] – for conversion to anti-aircraft vessels.[34] *Arcona* was taken in hand at the Deutsche Werke at Kiel during May/June 1940. No attempt was made to put her propulsion machinery – unused for nearly two decades – back into order; the forefunnel was cut down to form the support for a searchlight, although the after funnel was retained. She was first employed in the defence of Swinemünde, before moving to Wilhelmshaven for service with Naval AA Group 282. She later had her armament enhanced and equipment rearranged, the after funnel being cut down to the level of the platform atop the ex-forefunnel, on which was now mounted a radar dish. *Arcona* was mainly moored in Schillig Roads at Wilhelmshaven, until moved to Brunsbüttel in July 1944 to protect its locks against attacks from seaward. Sometime during the six weeks following the German surrender, she was moved back to Wilhelmshaven and the crew discharged. Although most sources state that *Arcona* was scuttled in the II. Entrance at Wilhelmshaven on 3 May 1945, she was certainly afloat opposite the IV. Entrance on 3 September, moored inboard of the ex-Dutch AA battery *Undine* (ex-*IJmuiden*, ex-*Jacob van Heemskerck*: see further below).

Medusa was rebuilt along similar lines (by Rickmers at Wesermünde) although, as a bare hull before conversion, she looked rather different from her sister, with a completely new superstructure and funnel; like *Arcona*, she had her armament enhanced later in the war and her appearance further modified. She was moored in the Vareler Deep, south of Schillig Roads at Wilhelmshaven as part of Naval AA Group 222, being severely damaged in an air raid on 19 April 1945; casualties were forty-one injured and twenty-three killed. She was then shifted into Wilhelmshaven itself and moored at the head of the Wiesbadenbrücke, beyond immediate repair. Four 10.5cm were therefore ordered removed for employment ashore on 22 April, and the remaining two 10.5cm and one quadruple and four twin 20mm on the 25th. Although it was planned to sink *Medusa* as a blockship outside the III. Entrance to the dockyard, this was overtaken by the surrender of Wilhelmshaven, and she remained afloat.

Medusa (top) and *Arcona* at different stages of their careers as anti-aircraft vessels. While *Medusa* is depicted at the very beginning of her career, in October 1940, with a rather simple superstructure, *Arcona* has been more elaborately modified by July 1943, including a 'Würzburg' radar atop the stump of the forward funnel, although its antenna has been touched-out by the wartime censor. *(Heidrich collection/ AD collection)*

33. Four coast defence ships, two Dutch and two Norwegian, were converted, as was one Dutch cruiser; of them, the two ex-Norwegian vessels and the ex-Dutch cruiser were self-propelled. They were seemingly regarded implicitly as sisters to *Arcona* and *Medusa*, all being given the names from the *Gazelle*/*Frauenlob* group: *Ariadne* (ex-*Vlierede*, ex-*Hertog Hendrik*) and *Undine* (ex-*IJmuiden*, ex-*Jacob van Heemskerk*; both ex-Dutch coast defence ships); *Nymphe* (ex-*Tordenskjold*) and *Thetis* (ex-*Harald Haarfagre*; both ex-Norwegian coast defence ships); and *Niobe* (ex-*Gelderland*; ex-Dutch cruiser, not commissioned until after the loss of the original *Niobe* [see below]).

34. F A Greve, *Die Luftverteidigung im Abschnitt Wilhelmshaven 1939–45: 2. Marineflakbrigade* (Jever, 2000) pp 224-46; see also a forthcoming article by Dodson and Nottelmann in *Warship* on the whole group of converted AA-vessels.

The floating AA batteries *Arcona* and *Undine* (ii, ex-Dutch *Jacob van Heemskerck*) in the lock in the III. Entrance at Wilhelmshaven, probably during February 1946: *Undine* arrived back in the Netherlands at the end of that month via Hamburg. *Arcona* still seems to be in good condition, contradicting many published sources that have her scuttled on 3 May 1945. Also in the lock are the Kiel-based tugs *Heros* (1941) and *Enak* (1943). *(DN collection)*

The last of the Imperial cruisers left afloat, *Amazone* is seen here as an accommodation hulk at Bremen in 1946, now in US ownership. *(DN collection)*

The detail of the final fates of the two old ex-cruisers remain problematic. Together with the ex-Dutch *Ariadne* and *Undine*, they are recorded as being moored opposite the IV. Entrance during September 1945, with the two German and ex-Dutch ships moored in 'national' pairs. An aerial photograph of the 3rd of that month has, however, just either *Arcona* or *Medusa* moored inboard of *Ariadne* or *Undine* in that location. From the winter of 1945/46 come photographs of *Arcona* and *Undine* in the lock of the III. Entrance, presumably on the way out: *Undine* arrived back in the Netherlands at the end of February 1946. Beyond this, sources are unclear, with one report having *Medusa* still afloat in the northern part of Wilhelmshaven as late as the mid-1950s. Other sources, however, have both *Medusa* and *Arcona* broken up at the end of the 1940s.

Curiously, the Allies' Trinational Naval Commission (TNC), charged with determining the fates of all German warships during the autumn of 1945,[35] noted both ships as 'wrecks', and placed them in Category C, which meant that they were to be destroyed no later than 15 August 1946. This is, of course, incompatible with them having been broken up around the late 1940s or later, and would imply an exceptional failure of the British (as in control of Wilhelmshaven) to fulfil their inter-Allied obligations to destroy all Category C ships by the deadline.

British scrupulousness on such matters is made clear by the fate of *Berlin*. Although actually still afloat and in fair condition in 1945, and still in use as an accommodation ship, she was erroneously listed as sunk in shallow water by the TNC, and so placed in Category C. Although consideration was given to correcting the error and transferring *Berlin* to the list of UK prizes, this was not done. As it was clear that facilities to scrap the various Category C vessels were insufficient to allow them to be 'destroyed' by the 15 August 1946 deadline, sinking in deep water was the only option to meet the requirement. An area in the Kattegat was therefore chosen, the UK mounting a series of group scuttlings. The third scuttling convoy left Kiel on 16 May, its ships included *Berlin* and a range of smaller vessels; *Berlin* was scuttled that evening, only one charge firing on the first attempt.[36]

UNDER NEW MANAGEMENT

Yugoslavia

Emden (iii) having been launched on 7 January 1925, the old *Niobe* was stricken in June. However, rather than being disposed of for scrap, she was sold to the Kingdom of Serbs, Croats and Slovenes (after 1929 Yugoslavia) for further service as a training cruiser under the name *Dalmacija*.[37] Having failed to obtain any major warships at the dissolution of the Austro-Hungarian Empire,[38] the young nation was keen to obtain suitable vessels, and the old German cruiser was clearly regarded as a useful acquisition.

35. Dodson and Cant, *Spoils of War*, pp 186–88.

36. While most published sources record that the sinking of *Berlin* to be part of the programme of disposal of German chemical weapons by sinking at sea, the surviving official documentation gives no indication of this: all confirmed such scuttlings were of merchantmen, except for one machinery-less unfinished destroyer, and loading significant quantities of munitions into such a vessel would have been problematic. In addition, *Berlin* and accompanying ships were sunk by scuttling charges, rather than by opening seacocks, as appears to have been the protocol with 'chemical munition' sinkings, to avoid any danger of disturbing their deadly cargoes or of dispersing them over a wide area (cf Dodson and Cant, *Spoils of War*, pp 196–97).

37.On ex-*Niobe* in Yugoslav and subsequent service, see Z Freivogel, *Warships of the Royal Yugoslav Navy* (Zagreb: Despot Infinitus, 2020), pp 21–41.

38. Although most of the Austro-Hungarian fleet at Pula was handed over to the National Council of the State of Slovenes, Croats and Serbs on 31 October 1918, this was nullified by Italy (who sank the battleship *Viribus Unitis* on 1 November), which ensured that the whole fleet was surrendered to the Allies; only a few minor vessels were allocated to the new state from those surrendered under Article 139 of the Treaty of Saint-Germain-en-Laye (see Dodson and Cant, *Spoils of War*, pp 24–27, 46–47, 73–74).

Her acquisition was managed by the Dutch Piet van Wienen concern, which also developed and oversaw her reconstruction at the Deutsche Werke at Kiel, a specification laid down by a Yugoslav commission. Work began soon after her deletion from the German navy list, and included the same bow rebuild as in *Amazone* and *Nymphe*. Other changes including the removal of the conning tower, and plating up of the main deck embrasures fore and aft; an additional broadside sponson was installed on each side, where torpedo tubes had been installed in the *Reichsmarine* refits. The machinery was overhauled, the boilers being retubed, and the funnels shortened slightly and caps added. Owing to Versailles Treaty restrictions, no armament was installed at this stage.

Having run trials from 7 August 1926, she arrived at the Tivat arsenal in the Bay of Kotor on 3 September 1927. Over the winter she was armed with six 83.5mm/55 M27 Škoda guns (one fore, one aft, the remainder on the beam), plus four 47mm/44 and two 15mm Zbrojovka AA machine guns (also of Czech origin). She was refitted during 1930/31, receiving a fire-control post in the forward part of the hull, with a control top added to her foremast, which now received support struts, making it into a tripod. Primarily a training ship, making a number of Mediterranean cruises, she was on occasion also used as a flagship, including during the futile struggle against the Axis attack on Yugoslavia in April 1941.

Together with most of the Yugoslav fleet,[40] she fell into Italian hands at Kotor on 17 April. Renamed *Cattaro* (the Italian name for Kotor), she was reclassified as a gunboat and was employed as a training ship by the gunnery school at Pola (Pula). During 1942–43 she was also employed on anti-partisan duties and as a target ship for submarines and aerial torpedoes. On 31 July 1942 she narrowly avoided becoming a real torpedo victim when, while south of Premantura, she was missed by torpedoes from HMS/M *Traveller*.

Italy's surrender found the old cruiser undergoing boiler repairs at Pola, where she was captured by the Germans on 11 September 1943, thus returning the ship to her original owners after almost two decades.[41] There was some debate as to her future name, with the old Austro-Hungarian names of *Zenta* and *Novara* proposed, before a simple reversion to her original name was finally agreed (apparently only two weeks before her loss). Likewise, there was debate as to *Niobe*'s future role, the decision being that she should become a floating AA battery at Pula or Trieste. However, as work on refitting her for further seagoing service had already begun (with the 47mm guns removed and the light AA battery significantly enhanced), she commissioned with a mixed German–Croat crew into the 11th Protection Flotilla.[42] Her appearance was slightly altered by the funnel tops being cut off obliquely, perhaps to give a more 'German' appearance.

She took part in the first part of anti-partisan Operation *Herbstgewitter* on 13 November 1943, and was participating in its second phase in company with the ex-Italian old torpedo boats *TA20* (ex-*Audace*), *TA21* (ex-*Insidioso*) and *TA22* (ex-*Giusseppe Missori*), when a navigational error led to *Niobe* grounding on the south side of the island of Silba around 18.00 on 19 December. Tugs were requested from Pola ninety minutes later, but attempts to get her off were unsuccessful. On the night of 22 December, the British motor torpedo boats

The old *Niobe* as first refitted for service in the Navy of the Kingdom of Serbs, Croats and Slovenes – later Yugoslavia. *(AD collection)*

Niobe, back again in German service, aground on Silba Island soon after being hit by two torpedoes from British motor torpedo boats. *(AD collection)*

40. The destroyer *Zagreb* was scuttled, and a submarine and two MTBs escaped to Egypt.

41. For *Niobe*'s renewed German career, see Freivogel, *Kriegsmarine in der Adria 1941–45: Ex-jugoslawische Kriegsschiffe unter deutscher Flagge – ein Stück weitgehend unbekannter Marine- und Seekriegsgeschichte*, Marine-Arsenal Band 40 (Wölfersheim-Berstadt: Podzun-Pallas-Verlag, 1998), pp 4–8.

42. The statement in many reference books that the ship served in the Croat navy under the name *Znajm/Zniam/Znijam* is in error (the name is meaningless in the Croat language), and may be a confusion resulting from the proposed name *Zenta* and/or the existence of the Yugoslav seaplane tender *Zmaj* (see Freivogel, *Kriegsmarine in der Adria*, p 5).

MTB226[43] and *MTB298*, alerted by local partisans, succeeded in hitting her with two torpedoes, forward and aft, leaving the ship a total loss with seventeen dead and sixteen badly injured; she subsequently broke her back. The tug *Parenzo*, which had been alongside aiding salvage efforts, was hit by a third torpedo and sank.[44]

Niobe's crew were evacuated on 23 November, except for a small party to dismantle guns and other recoverable items, a floating crane being sent from Pola to aid in the work.[45] Blown up by the Germans, the wreck was subsequently cannibalised by Yugoslav partisans, with formal scrapping begun in 1947, the salvage company Brodespas finishing the work in 1952.

Ancona (ex-*Graudenz*) refitted with a forecastle catapult. *(AD collection)*

Italy

All the ex-enemy cruisers ceded to Italy spent considerable time in dockyard hands before becoming operational. *Bari* (ex-*Pillau*) commissioned as a scout at Taranto in January 1924. She was followed by *Ancona* (ex-*Graudenz*) in May 1925 and by *Taranto* (ex-*Strassburg*) in June 1925. All had 76mm AA guns fitted in lieu of their (where-fitted – cf pp 213 n2, 220) 8.8cm German outfit, *Bari* being little otherwise altered. The other two vessels initially had their after superimposed 15cm guns (reclassified as 149mm/43 by the Italian Navy) moved amidships, but then shifted back again in 1926, when a platform for an aircraft (initially a Macchi M.7, later a CANT 25AR) was fitted amidships, handled by a derrick stepped from the mainmast.

Taranto was in the Red Sea as flagship from May 1926 to January 1927, while in 1929 all three ex-German cruisers joined with *Premuda* (ex-*V116*) to form the Scout Division of the 1st Squadron, based at La Spezia; later that year they were reclassified from scouts to cruisers. During 1928/29 *Ancona* had been refitted with a catapult on the forecastle, requiring the stem to be extended forward in a rather odd-looking clipper shape; the intention was to trial this arrangement, which was being incorporated into the new generation of Italian cruisers. However, difficulties were now emerging in the maintenance of the ex-German ships, and following an August 1932 deployment, *Ancona*, judged to be in the poorest condition, was laid up in reserve at Taranto as a source of spares for *Bari* and *Taranto*.

Early in the 1930s, *Bari* had a temporary extension made to the rear of her bridge and the forefunnel cut down to the same height as the remainder, this combination indicating that her six coal-fired forward boilers were no longer in use. They (and the funnel) were removed during a refit during the summer of 1934, the remaining funnels being cut down to the top of their casings. The remaining four oil-fired boilers gave *Bari* 21,000shp, for a speed of 24.5 knots, In September she sailed for the Red Sea, remaining there until relieved by the new sloop *Eritrea*[46] in May 1938.

She was joined there in September 1935 by *Taranto*, which remained in the Red Sea for a year before returning home for refit. During this period, *Taranto* lost her foremost pair of boilers, the uptakes of the remaining pair in the boiler room being trunked back into the second funnel; the fourteen remaining mixed-fired units gave 13,000shp for 21 knots.

Proposals were put forward in 1936 to also refit *Ancona* for colonial service, with her after boilers removed, the remaining two uptakes (now from new oil-fired boilers) trunked into a single funnel and three 76mm/40 guns added. Another option, put forward in April of that year, was to transform her into an anti-aircraft vessel for the defence of emergency bases. This would have involved removing all but six of her boilers, giving a speed of 21 knots and dismantling all the superstructure abaft the first funnel. No fewer than thirteen 100mm/47 twin mountings plus three HA directors (plus a fourth reserve director) would then be installed. The ship would have retained a minelaying capability of 100 mines.[47] However, the cost of the reconstruction was regarded as excessive (17,469,300 Lire, compared to 10 million Lire for an *Oriani*-class destroyer); an alternative scheme, which involved new machinery, giving the ship a fleet escort capability, was even less affordable. The colonial cruiser option was also ruled out on cost grounds, and *Ancona* was stricken on 11 March 1937 (as were the two ex-Austro-Hungarian cruisers, which had served as *Venezia* and *Brindisi*), and broken up the following year.

Following Italy's entry into the Second World War, *Bari* and *Taranto* were based at Taranto for service in the Adriatic and Aegean, including mining and bombardment operations. The two ex-German cruisers were intended to lead the landing force

43. Often misprinted as *MTB276*.

44. Both MTB captains, respectively Lts P H Hyslop and F M A Shore, received the Distinguished Service Cross for the action.

45. British intelligence report in UK National Archives file HW1/2301.

46. See M Cosentino, 'The Colonial Sloop *Eritrea*', *Warship* [XXXVIII] (2016), pp 30–41.

47. E. Bagnasco and E. Cernuschi, 'La Regia Marina e l'incrociatore antiaerei', *Storia Militaire* 40 (1997), pp 24–34.

for the projected occupation of Malta in 1942, while *Bari* was flagship for the Italian landings in Corsica in November 1942.

Both had their light AA batteries enhanced during the war, and both were earmarked for conversion to anti-aircraft cruisers in 1943.[48] Work actually began at Leghorn on rearming *Bari* with eight single 90mm/50, eight 37mm/54 and eight 20mm weapons, but on 28 June 1943 she was sunk by American bombs. Salvage work was interrupted by the Italian armistice, and the wreck was sabotaged to prevent German recovery of the vessel. The hulk was partially demolished by German forces during 1944, the remains (which had been formally stricken on 27 February 1947) being refloated on 13 January 1948 and broken up.

Taranto had transferred to Leghorn on 26 February 1942 as a seagoing training ship, but had then been placed in reserve at La Spezia in December, where she was scuttled on 9 September 1943 following the Italian Armistice. Soon refloated by the Germans, she was sunk again on 23 October 1943 during an Allied air raid, and although refloated yet again during January/April 1944 the hulk was finally sunk by bombs that September and broken up after the war.

48. Cf Bagnasco and Cernuschi, *Storia Militare* 40.

France

The first surrendered vessel commissioned by France was *Metz* (ex-*Königsberg*) in 1920, the remainder of her ships joining the fleet in 1922. Modifications were minimal, principally the fitting of 75mm AA guns, which directly replaced the former German 8.8cm AA guns, except that in *Strasbourg* they replaced the superimposed 15cm gun aft, and in *Colmar* they were installed on a new deckhouse aft of the mainmast. *Metz* was also fitted with two 60cm torpedo tubes, in place of her original four 50cm models (the submerged tubes were deleted).

Colmar (ex-*Kolberg*) sailed for the Far East on 19 June 1922

The oldest and newest ex-German cruisers to join the French navy: *Kolberg* (top), commissioned into the French navy as *Colmar*, the French name of her eponymous Alsatian city, and shown here in 1922; and *Metz* (bottom), the former *Königsberg*. (AD collection)

to become flagship of the *Division Navale de l'Extrême Orient* (DNEO), relieving the armoured cruiser *Montcalm* and arriving on 7 September. In 1923 she was at Vladivostok when the Tokyo earthquake occurred, and proceeded there to provide aid at Yokohama. She left Indochina in November 1924, being relieved on station by the armoured cruisers *Jules Michelet* and *Victor Hugo*, arriving back in France on 11 February 1925. Stricken in 1927 and condemned soon afterwards, *Colmar* was scrapped in 1929.

Metz served in the Atlantic Flying Division from November 1921, before moving to the Mediterranean in the spring of 1922, where she served with *Mulhouse* (ex-*Stralsund*) and *Strasbourg* (ex-*Regensburg*), and also briefly the ex-Austro-Hungarian *Thionville* (ex-*Novara*), in the 3rd Light Division, renamed the 2nd Light Division in December 1926. At first based in the Mediterranean (Toulon), the squadron/division was transferred to the Atlantic (Brest) in August 1928, but all the ex-German ships went into reserve, first at Brest, and then at Landévennec, during 1929/30.[49] The final active pair were *Mulhouse* and *Strasbourg*, which formed the 2nd Light Squadron at Brest, the former doubling as the flagship of the whole Brest (2nd) Squadron, which was generally composed of the older vessels of the French fleet. The withdrawal of the ex-German ships from service coincided with the commissioning of French-built modern cruisers, beginning with the three *Duguay-Trouins* in 1927 and the two big *Duquesnes* in 1929, as well as the second series of large destroyers (*Guépard* class). Of the latter, *Bison* relieved *Mulhouse* as flagship of the 2nd Squadron on 19 November 1930.

With yet more new cruisers joining the fleet as the 1930s progressed, there was soon no need to retain the older ships even in reserve. *Mulhouse* was thus stricken on 15 February 1933, *Metz* on 18 August; they were sold for scrap that November and in August 1934, respectively. Partially dismantled after striking – her after funnels had been cut down and the mainmast removed even prior to being moved to Landévennec – *Metz* caught fire in the scrapyard in December 1934. *Strasbourg* was renamed *Strasbourg II* in early 1934 to free her name for the new battleship, being moved to Landévennec in November. However, on 15 January 1936 she arrived at Lorient under tow to become the depot ship for the 6th Destroyer Division, being stricken in June but retained as a hulk.

As such, she fell into German hands at Lorient in 1940. Although consideration was reportedly given to returning her to service, this was not done and the ship became first an accommodation ship for German submarine crews. Later, she was stripped and her hulk moored opposite the Keroman 3 submarine pen at Lorient, rigged with a number of high masts supporting nets as a protection against aerial torpedoes; scuttled there, probably in 1944, her remains are still to be seen, the very last of the Kaiser's cruisers at least partly still above the surface.

49. *Thionville* remained active as part of the torpedo school until 1 May 1932; she was stricken on 17 August 1933, but retained as a hulk for the gunnery school at Toulon until sold there for scrap on 1 February 1941.

The rusted remains of *Strasbourg II* at Lorient, formerly SMS *Regensburg* and the last German First World War cruiser partly above water. *(Jean Moulin)*

11 RETROSPECT

DURING ITS NEAR-HALF CENTURY OF EXISTENCE, Germany's Imperial Navy commissioned 105 vessels that can be considered 'small cruisers' under the terms of the Fleet Laws, while eight more were left unfinished at its dissolution. Of them, fifteen were lost as a direct result of enemy action,[1] five lost wholly by accident,[2] two scuttled in the face of the enemy after being disabled by accident,[3] one seized while interned[4] and six scuttled to avoid capture or seizure.[5] Many losses had occurred in chronological and geographical clumps, with a dozen coming during the very first months of the First World War. These had been largely the result of the elimination of the German overseas naval forces by the Allies and the carnage at the First Battle of Heligoland Bight, but also included the internal explosion aboard *Karlsruhe*, the torpedoing of *Hela* and the stranding and subsequent scuttling of *Magdeburg*. Underwater threats in the Baltic had done for *Bremen* and *Undine* at the end of 1915 (as well as ending the active career of *Gazelle* at the beginning of that year), with four ships lost during the Battle of Jutland in 1916. One old ship, now on subsidiary duties, would be lost by accidental explosion in 1917, and another, interned in 1914, seized by the USA on joining the war that April. The final operational loss – *Breslau*, serving under the Ottoman flag – would come in 1918, followed by the scuttling of eight vessels interned at Scapa Flow in 1919.

Of the remainder, six were surrendered[6] and one sold[7] after 1918 for further service, while the rest ended their days as targets or in the scrapyard. Six of these had previously passed to foreign powers as war booty,[8] and were joined in this by three vessels scuttled at Scapa, but beached before sinking.[9]

1. *Ariadne* (ii), *Bremen, Breslau, Cöln* (i), *Dresden* (i), *Emden* (i), *Frauenlob* (ii), *Hela, Königsberg* (i), *Leipzig* (ii), *Mainz, Nürnberg* (i), *Rostock* (i), *Undine* (ii) and *Wiesbaden* (i).
2. *Augusta, Gneisenau, Wacht, Karlsruhe* (i) and *Seeadler*.
3. *Magdeburg* (i) and *Elbing*.
4. *Geier*.
5. *Brummer, Bremse, Cöln* (ii), *Cormoran, Karlsruhe* (ii) and *Dresden* (ii).
6. *Kolberg, Graudenz, Regensburg, Königsberg* (ii), *Pillau* and *Strassburg*.
7. *Niobe*, later captured by Germany and lost under its flag during the Second World War.
8. *München, Lübeck, Danzig, Stuttgart, Stettin* and *Augsburg*.
9. *Emden* (ii), *Nürnberg* (ii) and *Frankfurt*.

German industry had also laid down six vessels for foreign customers, of which two were actually completed for and commissioned by the German navy – and are included in the 105 vessels quoted above.

Down to the 1890s these conformed to types found in most major navies of the world: the medium-sized, fully rigged vessel intended for overseas cruising; the smaller, rigged, 'colonial cruiser'; and the unrigged 'scout' or 'aviso' intended for fleet use. The first group, built in iron from the mid-1870s, endured rather longer in most other navies (although France continued building *wooden* ships of the type into the 1880s). These remained the Reich's principal means of overseas power projection into the early 1890s, the first two 'modern' cruisers not being begun until 1886. Only four had joined the fleet before 1895, and even then not all could be regarded as wholly suited for service on distant stations (cf pp 57, 87). The rigged cruisers also played the role of cadet training ships, the last of the breed (recognised as obsolete at completion) taking this function from the very outset – and all survivors reclassified as 'training ships' en bloc in 1893 – although on occasion diverted to take on an ad hoc operational role.

The colonial cruisers were very much enlargements of the gunboats that had previously fulfilled the roles of station-ships abroad, the establishment of formal German colonies during the 1880s requiring larger vessels able to provide landingparties of meaningful size. However, although formally 'cruisers' they were recognised as having a minimal role in any general war, and found themselves ultimately reclassified as gunboats once replaced on the list of 'cruisers' by new construction.

The avisos had begun as a disparate set of vessels of assorted pedigree, including ships that were ultimately yachts for senior officers and royalty. However, by the 1880s the type had become fast vessels capable of both a scouting role and leading flotilla craft. Yet, although *Blitz* and *Pfeil* were a great success, and would remain in fleet service for well over three decades, the *Wacht* and *Meteor* classes suffered from poor sea-keeping and were reduced to subsidiary duties after only a decade. On the other hand, the last of the type to be completed for the German navy would represent an important step towards the general-purpose cruiser.

A sea-change in German cruiser procurement occurred

The last voyage of the cruisers of the Imperial navy: *Nürnberg*, *Cöln*, *Brummer* and *Bremse* steam across the North Sea to internment and self-immolation. *(NHHC NH356)*

during the 1890s. The German navy had hitherto eschewed the oversized cruisers, verging on capital rank, found in the French, Russian and British navies, maintaining the clear division between true capital ships and cruising vessels. Now, the decade saw the construction of the first 'large' German cruisers, soon rivalling battleships in size and gun power and following a strand of development that would lead to what the British and Japanese navies would call 'battlecruisers'. In parallel, the various cruiser roles noted above were swept up into a new 'small' cruiser type whose numbers would, like their 'large' brethren, be henceforth baked into law.

The latter, courtesy of the Fleet Laws, was a somewhat double-edged sword, as while it guaranteed a steady year-on-year construction programme, it resulted in a 'one size fits all' approach based on the progressive evolution from the baseline type (the *Gazelle* class), rather than a regular scrutiny of the actual requirement, other than as regards speed. Radical changes came about with the *Magdeburg* class, but these were simply better technical solutions to addressing the existing basic requirement. The legal nature of the production drum-beat meant that costs were continually a driving force, one result being that the German navy retained the 10.5cm gun as the small cruiser main armament well after the British navy had begun the move to a larger calibre. This closely mirrored the situation with capital ships, where German battleships' gun power was consistently below that of their British counterparts until the *Bayern* class of the 1913 Estimates.

That the small cruisers did not fully meet the requirements of actual combat did not become clear until after the first battles of the First World War, resulting in a crash rearmament programme with the 15cm guns that had belatedly been specified for the last vessels ordered in peacetime. But even this up-gunning was not sufficient, and before the end of the war a fundamental debate was under way that clearly pointed to the fallacy of the 'one size fits all' concept for smaller cruising vessels.

Yet the policy did mean that the German navy was the only fleet – other than the British – to begin the First World War with modern small cruising vessels of the kind that experience would show to be the almost indispensable for day-to-day naval operations, combining seaworthiness and a handy armament with a degree of expendability. Seemingly transfixed by the big cruiser, France had finally decided to build small cruisers only shortly before the outbreak of the First World War, only to have to cancel them, and have to operate oversized armoured cruisers and undersized destroyers in roles that would have been far better undertaken by vessels of the German and British types. Italy, the United States and Austria-Hungary were in almost the same position, with only a handful of small cruisers alongside their forces of big armoured cruisers.

Indeed, after the war, it was German small cruisers (and the Austro-Hungarian scout cruisers) that were – together with modern destroyers – the only vessels seriously coveted by the major powers, France seeing them as the only way to make up for its complete lack of ships in the category. Thus, four German and one Austro-Hungarian ships went to the French navy; to maintain balance between the Mediterranean powers, Italy took three German ships and two Austro-Hungarian ones. Two of the latter German ships (*Strassburg* and *Pillau*) would survive to fight in the Second World War – as would the ancient *Niobe*, sold to Yugoslavia in 1925, captured by Italy in 1941 and by Germany in 1943.

The story of the German cruiser is thus one of many facets, and contains excellent case studies in a wide range of aspects of the development of maritime military technology, its political aspects, and the way that certain individuals were able to turn a navy on to hitherto unimaginable courses. In light of the latter, while the first German cruisers were in many ways organic outgrowths of the German polity that emerged in 1871, later vessels were very much the creatures of Tirpitz and Wilhelm II: truly the Kaiser's cruisers.

Ships of the German Navy

Gefion

SAIL-FRIGATE

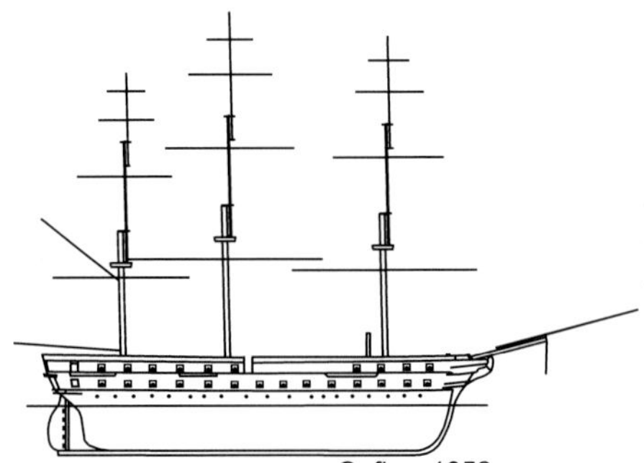

Gefion 1852

Displacement:	1,385 (design), 1,826 (full load tonnes).
Dimensions:	52.4 (wl), 59.4 (oa) x 13.5 x 5.7 metres.
Armament:	Two 60pdr SB, twenty-six 24pdr/long SB, twenty 24pdr/short SB guns; 1867: eighteen 36pdr SB, six 24pdr SB, two 12pdr guns.
Complement:	38+382.

Name	Builder	Laid down	Launch	Comm	Fate
Gefion (i) (ex-*Eckernförde*, ex-*Gefion*)	Copenhagen DYd	1840	27 Sep 43	DK: 6 May 44 NGE: 5 Apr 49 PR: 1 May 52	Stricken 5 May 80; coal hulk; BU Kiel DYd 1891.

Home 6 Apr–30 Nov 49, 11 May–Nov 52; overseas 11 Nov 52–13 Sep 54; overseas (cadet TS) 1 Apr 58–20 Sep 59, 5 Aug 62–21 Nov 63; gunnery TS Jun 65–30 Nov 66; home 12 Jun 67–14 Sep 67, 1 Apr 68–25 May 70; accommodation ship Kiel 1873.

Arcona class (first group)

DECKED-CORVETTES (ex-screw-frigates)

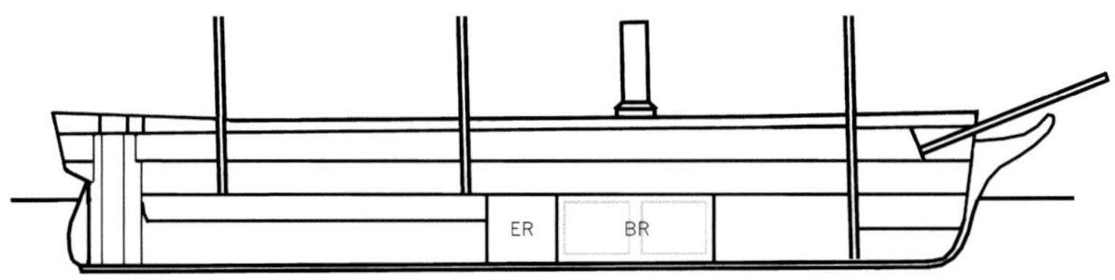

Displacement:	1,928 (design), 2,391 (full load) tonnes.
Dimensions:	63.6 (wl), 71.9 (oa) x 13.0 x 6.4 metres.
Machinery:	Four trunk boilers; one shaft; 2-cyl reciprocating (HSE), IHP 1,365 (*Arcona*)/1,320 (*Gazelle*) = 12 knots; coal 176/229 tonnes; range 1,150nm @ 11 knots.
Armament:	six 68pdr ML, twenty-two 36pdr ML guns; 1865: six (1869: two) 24pdr BL, twenty-two 36pdr ML guns; 1873: eight 15cm/22 BL guns (*Arcona*); six 68pdr ML, twenty-two 36pdr ML guns; 1869: six 15cm/22 BL, twenty-two 36pdr ML guns; 1871: eight 15cm/22 BL guns (*Gazelle*).
Complement:	35+345.

Name	Laid down	Builder	Launch	Comm	Fate	
Arcona (i)	1855	Danzig DYd	8 Nov 55	19 May 58	15 Apr 59	Stricken 18 Mar 84; BU Kiel.
Gazelle (i)	1855	Danzig DYd	3 Dec 55	19 Dec 59	15 May 62	Stricken 8 Jan 84; accommodation ship Wilhelmshaven; BU 1906.

Grille

AVISO

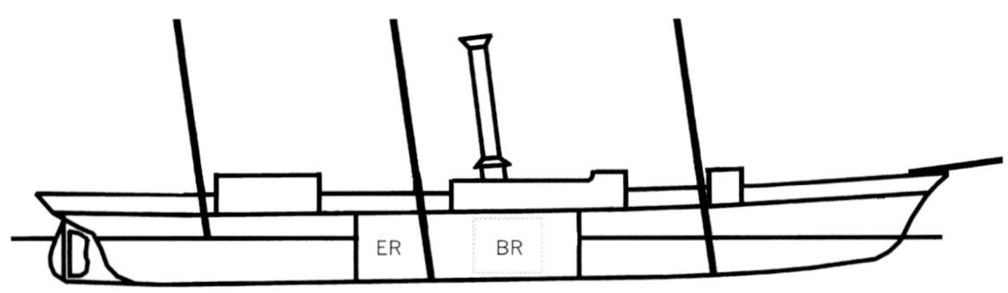

Displacement:	350 (design), 491 (full load) tonnes.
Dimensions:	52.5 (wl), 56.9 (oa) x 7.4 x 3.2 metres.
Machinery:	Two cylindrical boilers; one shaft; 2-cyl reciprocating (HSE; 1,886: HC), IHP 700 (1,886: 750) = 13 knots; coal 65 tonnes; range 3,230nm @ 7 knots.
Armament:	1864, 1870–71: two 12pdr guns. 1871: disarmed; 1879: one 12.5cm/23, two 8cm/23 guns; three 3.7cm MG added in 1882; 1898: six, later reduced to two, 3.7cm MG.
Complement:	5/6+65/72.

Name	Builder	Laid down	Launch	Comm	Fate
Grille	Normand (Le Havre)	1856	9 Sep 57	3 Jun 58	Stricken 7 Jan 20; sold; BU Hamburg-Moorburg.

Thetis

SAIL-FRIGATE

Displacement: 1,508 (design), 1,882 (full load) tonnes.
Dimensions: 50.9 (wl), 60.2 (oa) x 14.1 x 5.8 metres.
Armament: Thirty-eight 68pdr guns.
Complement: 35+345.

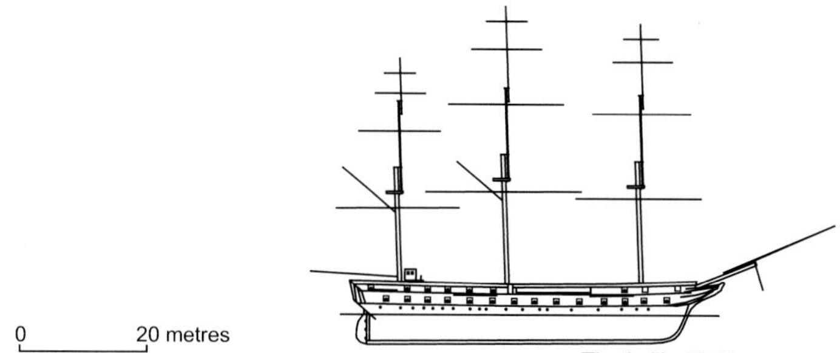

Thetis (i) 1856

Name	Builder	Laid down	Launch	Comm	Fate
Thetis (i)	Devonport DYd	2 Dec 44	21 Aug 48	UK: 30 Dec 46 PR: 12 Jan 55	Stricken 28 Nov 71; coal hulk Wilhelmshaven; sold 1894; BU Kiel 1894–95.

Home 12 Jan 55–26 Oct 55; Americas/home 30 Apr 56–7 Dec 58, overseas 20 May 59–15 Dec 62; gunnery TS 6 Oct 66–30 Oct 69.

Arcona
Overseas Dec 59–May 62; home 10 Dec 63–6 May 67; overseas 15 Feb 69–6 May 71; cadet training ship 1 Oct 73–31 Dec 74; stoker & engineer TS Kiel 15 Mar 76–25 Feb 84.

Gazelle
Overseas 23 Oct 62–3 Jun 65; home 3 Apr–Sep 66; Mediterranean Oct 66–Apr 67; decomm 23 Sep 67; overseas (cadet TS) 1 Jul 71–26 May 73, 2 Jun 74–12 May 76; stoker & engineer TS 6 Nov–16 Dec 76; overseas (cadet TS) 20 Dec 76–20 May 78; stoker & engineer TS 17 Mar 79; TS 15 Mar–6 Jul 81.

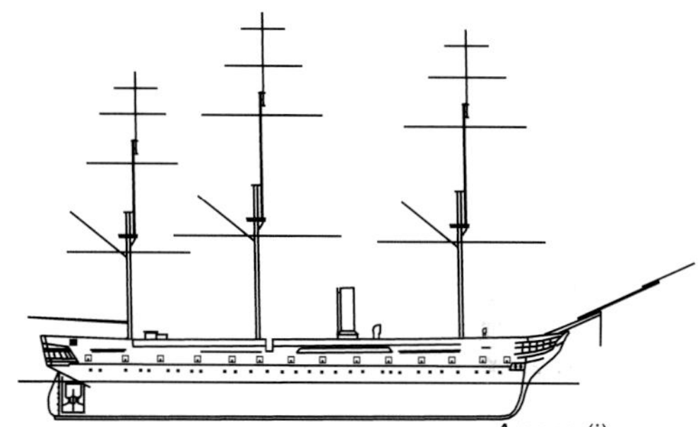

Arcona (i)

0 20 metres

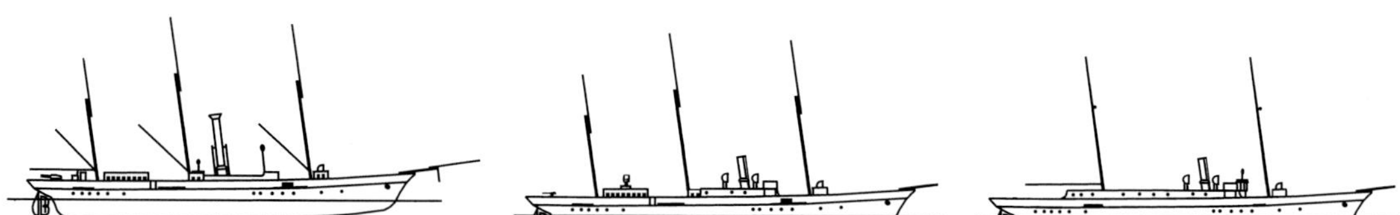

Grille 1864 *Grille* 1890 *Grille* 1898

0 20 metres

Home May 59–25 Oct 60; royal yacht/flagship 16 Jan 62–22 Oct 85; rebuilt Danzig 1885–88; Baltic Reserve Division 1 Oct 88; home 2 Apr–89–Sep 91; TS/yacht 1 Apr 92; tender to *Freya* (ii) 10 Jul 15–7 Dec 18.

UK *Diamond* class

SAIL-FRIGATE

Displacement: 1,270 (design), 1,590 (full load) tonnes.
Dimensions: 43.3 (wl) x 12.8 x 5.4 metres.
Armament: Sixteen 68pdr SB, four 30pdr SB; later: six 15cm/22 BL, six 12cm/23 guns.
Complement: 34+316.

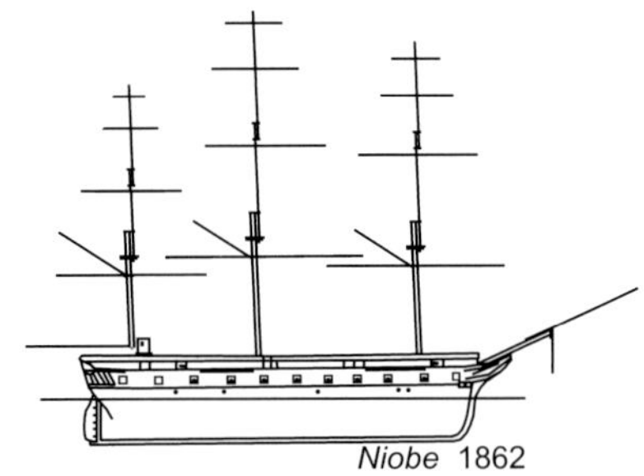

0 20 metres

Niobe 1862

Name	Builder	Laid down	Launch	Comm	Fate
Niobe (i)	Devonport DYd	May 47	18 Sep 49	UK: – PR: 21 Oct 62	Stricken 18 Nov 90; accommodation ship Kiel; Flensburg 1907; Kiel Jan 08; BU Peters (Wewelsfleth) 1919.

Americas (cadet TS) 21 Oct 62–25 Jan 63, 25 Jun 63–30 Jun 67, 1 Aug 67–21 Jun 69, 16 Aug 69–18 Jul 70; accommodation ship; West Indies (cadet TS) 11 May 71–8 Jan 73; Azores (cadet TS) 18 Apr 73–10 Oct 73; North Sea/Baltic (cadet TS) 15 Apr–20 Sep 74, 1 Apr–30 Sep 75, 1 Apr–30 Sep 76, 1 Apr–25 Sep 77, 1 Apr–27 Sep 78, 1 Apr–30 Sep 79, 1 Apr–30 Sep 80, 1 Apr–30 Sep 81, 1 Apr–30 Sep 82, 3 Apr–28 Sep 83, 1 Apr–28 Sep 84, 8 Apr–3 Oct 85, 8 Apr–30 Sep 86, 5 Apr–30 Sep 87, 6 Apr–29 Sep 88, 2 Apr–28 Sep 89, 9 Apr–25 Sep 90.

Nymphe class

FLUSHDECKED-CORVETTES; 1884: CRUISER-CORVETTES

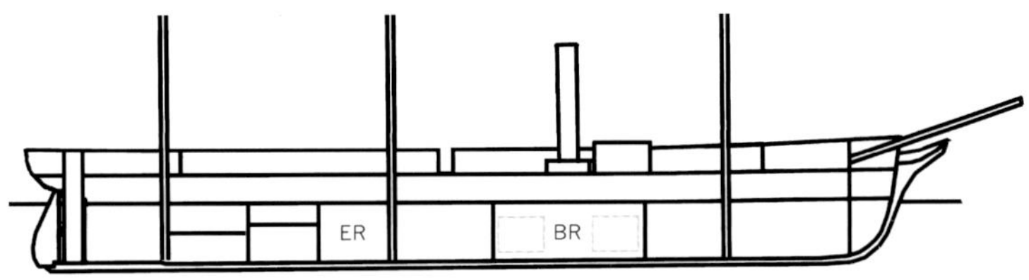

Displacement: 1,085 (design), 1,202 (full load) tonnes.
Dimensions: 58.5 (wl), 64.9 (oa) x 10.2 x 4.5 metres.
Machinery: Two transverse trunk boilers; one shaft; 2-cyl reciprocating (HSE), IHP 800 = 12 knots; coal 126 tonnes; range 1,250nm @ 12 knots.
Armament: Ten 36pdr, six 12pdr guns. 1869: seventeen, later nine, 12cm/23.
Complement: 14+176.

Name	Programme	Builder	Laid down	Launch	Comm	Fate
Nymphe (i)	1859	Danzig DYd	25 Jan 62	15 Apr 63	25 Nov 63	Stricken 21 Jul 87; engineer training hulk Hamburg; sold 1891; BU Hamburg.
Medusa (i)	1859	Danzig DYd	6 Feb 62	20 Oct 64	10 Apr 67	Stricken 5 Apr 81; hulked; sold 1891; BU Danzig.

Nymphe
Home 20 Feb 64–25 Aug 70; overseas 1 Jun 71–20 May 74; home 1 Jun–15 Oct 74; refit Danzig; overseas (cadet TS) 1 Apr 76–27 Sep 77, 1 Apr 78–30 Sep 79; Americas 12 Jul–3 Oct 80; Mediterranean (cadet TS) 1 Apr–6 Sep 82; West Indies 16 Jul 84–7 Oct 85.

Medusa
Mediterranean Sep 67–15 May 68; overseas 20 Oct 68–10 Oct 71; refit Danzig; overseas Aug 75–30 Sep 76; overseas (cadet TS) 27 Jul 77–15 Sep 78; Americas (TS) 15 Jul–30 Sep 79.

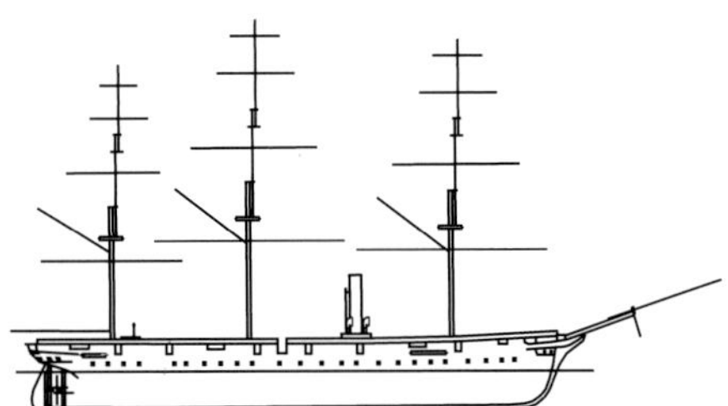

Nymphe (i) 1870

0 20 metres

Arcona class (second group)

DECKED-CORVETTES (ex-screw-frigates)

Displacement: 2,113 (design), 2,504 (full load) tonnes.
Dimensions: 65.5 (wl), 73.3 (oa) x 12.9 x 6.5 metres.
Machinery: Four trunk boilers; one shaft; 2-cyl reciprocating (HSE), IHP 1,580 (*Vineta*)/1,510 (*Hertha*) = 11.5 knots; coal 150/190 tonnes; range 1,350nm @ 11 knots.
Armament: Twenty-eight 68pdr. 1870: seventeen 15cm/22 (*Arcona*), two 12.5cm guns.
Complement: 35+345.

Name	Programme	Builder	Laid down	Launch	Comm	Fate
Vineta	1859	Danzig DYd	17 Sep 60	4 Jun 63	3 Mar 64	Stricken 15 Aug 84; hulked as recruit TS Wilhelmshaven; sold 1897 (55,220M); BU Kiel.
Hertha	1859	Danzig DYd	1 Sep 60	1 Oct 64	1 Nov 65	Stricken 12 Aug 84; coal hulk Kiel-Wik; sold 1902 (45,600M); BU Swinemünde.

Vineta
Home 3 Mar 64–Sep 65; overseas 28 Sep 65–24 Oct 68; refit Kiel 1870–71; overseas 1 Jul 71–5 May 73; home 4 Jun–24 Sep 73; overseas (cadet TS) 11 Oct 75–17 Nov 77; engineer & stoker TS 16 Mar–22 Jul 78; refit Danzig 1878–79; overseas (cadet TS) 14 Oct 79–12 Dec 81; engineer & stoker TS 21 Feb–14 Jul 82, 15 Mar–10 Jul 83, 15 Mar–12 Jul 84.

Hertha
Home Nov 65–6 Oct 66; 10 Apr–Sep 67; Mediterranean 14 Sep 67–15 May 68; overseas (cadet TS) 8 Sep 69–11 Dec 72, 1 Oct 74–19 Jul 78, 1 Oct 80–15 Nov 82.

Augusta class

FLUSHDECKED-CORVETTES

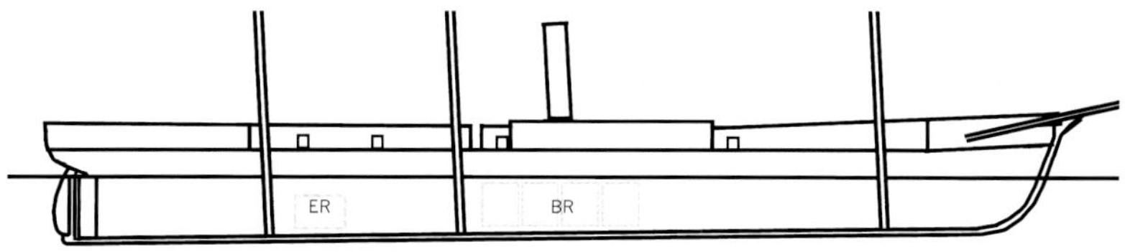

Displacement: 1,827 (design), 2,272 (full load) tonnes.
Dimensions: 75.2 (wl), 81.5 (oa) x 11.1 x 5.6 metres.
Machinery: Four transverse trunk boilers; one shaft; 2-cyl reciprocating (HSE), IHP 1,300 = 12 knots; coal 340 tonnes; range 2,500nm @ 12 knots.
Armament: Eight 24pdr, six 12pdr guns. 1867: six 24pdr, four 12pdr guns. 1872: four 15cm/22, six 12cm/23, one 8cm/23 guns.
Complement: 15+215.

Name	Builder	Laid down	Launch	Comm	Fate
Augusta (ex-*Yeddo*, ex-*Mississippi*)	Arman (Bordeaux)	1863 (purchased 13 May 64)	1864	4 Jul 64	Foundered in hurricane Gulf of Aden (~13° N, 45° E) 2 Jun 85.
Victoria (ex-*Osakka*, ex-*Louisiana*)	Arman (Bordeaux)	1863 (purchased 13 May 64)	1864	14 Sep 64	Stricken 14 Apr 91; sold 1892; BU Hamburg.

Augusta
Home Jul 64–21 Oct 66; overseas 11 Dec 67–7 Sep 68; Atlantic (raiding) 26 Oct 70–24 Apr 71; Americas 1 Mar 74–6 Jan 76; overseas 3 Oct 76–28 Oct 78; refit Aug 79–Dec 81; overseas 14 Apr 85 to loss.

Victoria
Home Oct 64–31 Oct 66; Americas 7 Sep 68–19 Oct 69; home 11 Nov–5 Dec 71; Americas 10 Oct 75–10 Aug 77; overseas 1 Jul 80–4 Jan 82; fishery protection Jul 84, 27 Mar–6 Aug 88, 18 Mar–14 Sep 90.

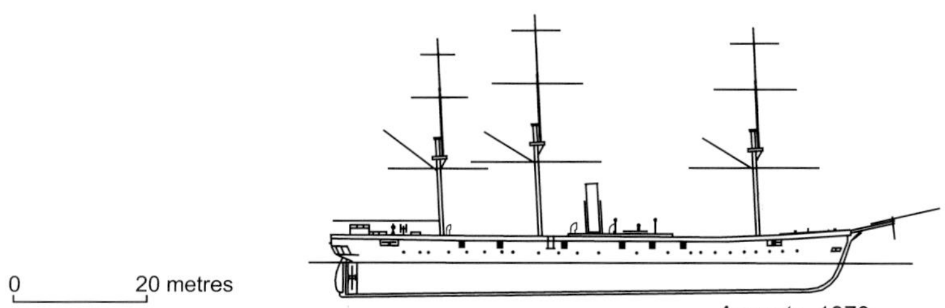

Augusta 1870

Arcona class (third group)

DECKED-CORVETTE (ex-screw-frigate); 1884: Cruiser-Frigate

Displacement: 2,454 (design), 2,912 (full load) tonnes.
Dimensions: 71.5 (wl), 79.3 (oa) x 13.2 x 6.4 metres.
Machinery: Four trunk boilers; one shaft; 2-cyl reciprocating (HSE), IHP 2,440 = 12.1 knots; coal 170/240 tonnes; range 1,900nm @ 10 knots.
Armament: Six 68pdr, twenty 36pdr guns. 1870: seventeen 15cm/22, two 12.5cm guns.
Complement: 35+345.

Name	Programme	Builder	Laid down	Launch	Comm	Fate
Elisabeth	1859	Danzig DYd	1 May 66	18 Oct 68	29 Sep 69	Stricken 20 Sep 87; hulked Kiel as stoker & engineer TS; sold 1904 (83,000M); BU Stettin.

Mediterranean 4 Oct 69–23 Apr 70; home 18 Jul 70–21 Apr 71; overseas (cadet TS) 1 Oct 72–1 May 75, 1 Oct 76–2 Nov 78, 1 Oct 81–13 Oct 83, 16 Apr 84–13 Apr 86; torpedo TS 1 Oct–29 Apr 87.

Ariadne class (first group)

FLUSHDECKED-CORVETTES; 1884: CRUISER-CORVETTES; 1888 (*Ariadne*)/1885 (*Luise*) TRAINING SHIPS

Displacement: 1,692 (design), 2,072 (full load) tonnes.
Dimensions: 65.8 (wl), 68.2 (oa) x 10.8 x 5.7 metres.
Machinery: Four trunk boilers; one shaft; 3-cyl reciprocating (HC), IHP 2,100 = 14 knots; coal 168 tonnes; range 1,340nm @ 10 knots.
Armament: Six 15cm/22, two 12cm/23 guns; four 3.7cm MG (added 1882). As TS: eight 12cm/23 guns.
Complement: 13+220.

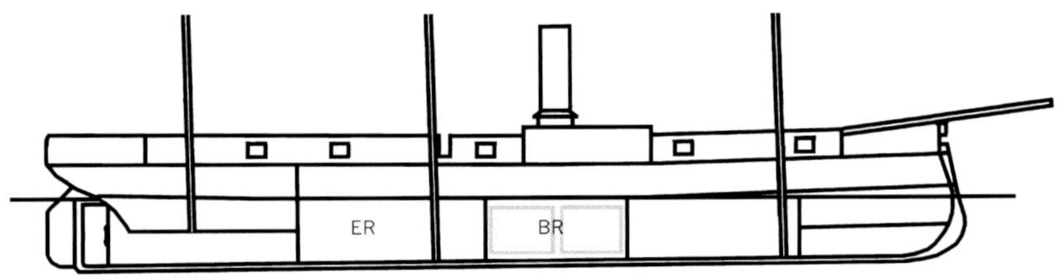

Name	Programme	Builder	Laid down	Launch	Comm	Fate
Ariadne	1867	Danzig DYd	Sep 68	21 Jul 71	23 Nov 72	Stricken 14 Apr 91; sold 6 Oct 91; BU Hamburg.
Luise	1867	Danzig DYd	Jun 71	16 Dec 72	4 Jun 74	Stricken 19 Dec 96; sold 1897 (65,150M); BU Kiel.

Ariadne
Home 13 Apr 73–Sep 74; overseas 5 Oct 74–30 Oct 76, 30 Oct 77–12 Oct 79; refit Wilhelmshaven 1879–80; overseas 1 Apr 80–31 Oct 81; engineer & stoker TS 15 Jul–Sep 84; Africa 30 Oct 84–Mar 85; home/Americas 29 Sep 85–14 Oct 86; home/Americas 1 Apr 87–29 Sep 88; Caribbean/home 16 Apr 89–30 Sep 90.

Luise
Overseas 11 Oct 75–13 Sep 77, 20 Nov 78–20 Nov 80; overseas (TS) 15 Apr 81–25 Sep 82; refit Danzig 1883–85; overseas (TS) 24 Feb 85–15 Sep 87; home 15 Oct 87–30 Sep 91; special service ship 1892; harbour service 1893; torpedo trials ship Kiel 1 Nov 94–16 Apr 95.

0 20 metres

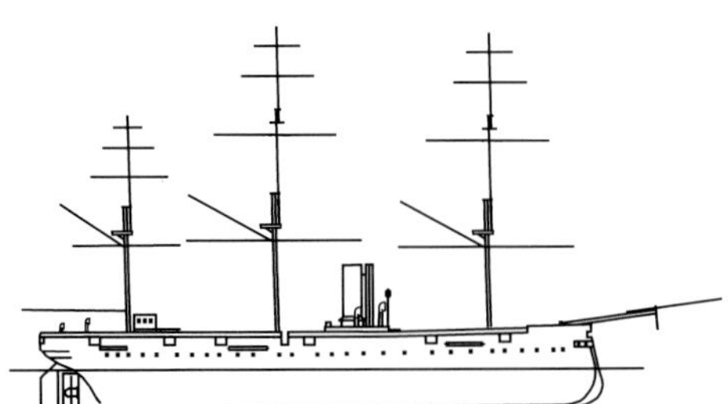

Ariadne (i) 1880

Falke

AVISO

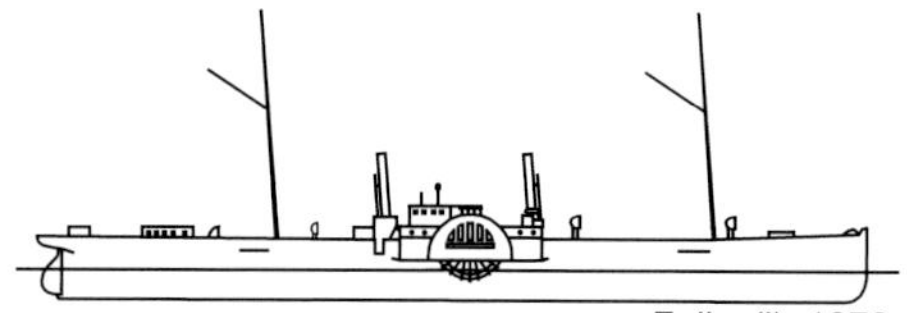

0 20 metres

Falke (i) 1872

Displacement: 1,002 (design), 1,230 (full load) tonnes.
Dimensions: 77.5 (wl), 78.4 (oa) x 11.7 x 2.6 metres.
Machinery: Two trunk boilers; paddle wheels; 2-cyl oscillating (VSE), IHP 1,100 = 12 knots; coal 200 tonnes; range 1,400nm @ 12 knots.
Armament: Two 12cm/23 guns; five 3.7cm MG added in 1880.
Complement: 6+84.

Name	Builder	Laid down	Launch	Completed	Purchased/Comm	Fate
Falke (ex-*Aviso D*, ex-*Heinrich Heister*) = *Emden* (4 Sep 70) = *Falke* (12 Sep 70)	Henderson, Coulborn (Renfrew)	–	1865	1866	25 Aug 70/4 Sep 70	Stricken 18 Nov 90; sold Sep 92 (18,000M); BU.

Home 4 Sep–21 Nov 70; Armoured Exercise Squadron 19 May–10 Oct 75, 7 May–5 Nov 77, 27 May–17 Jul 78; tender to North Sea Naval Station 1 Apr 79–25 Aug 81; refit 1883; fishery protection 24 Mar–30 Sep 86, 29 Mar–30 Sep 87; Admiralty yacht Apr–Sep 88.

Pommerania

AVISO

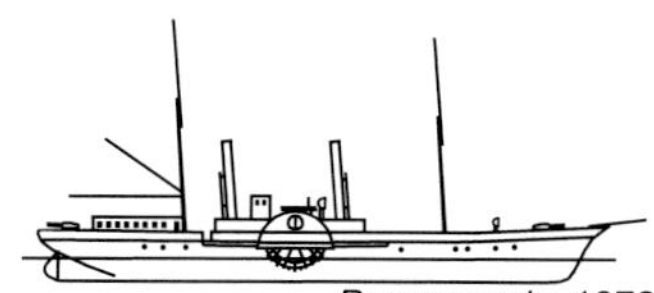

0 20 metres

Pommerania 1872

Displacement: 391 (design), 460 (full load) tonnes.
Dimensions: 50.5 (wl), 55.2 (oa) x 9.7 x 2.4 metres.
Machinery: Two trunk boilers; paddle wheels; 2-cyl oscillating (VSE), IHP 700 = 12 knots; coal 75 tonnes; range 300nm @ 14 knots.
Armament: Two 8cm/23 guns; 1880: two 8.7cm/24 guns; four 3.7cm MG.
Complement: 4+61.

Name	Builder	Laid down	Launch	Completed	Purchased/Comm	Fate
Pommerania = *Adler* (ii) (1892)	AG Vulcan (Stettin)	1864	Sep 64	1 May 65	2 Jul 70/27 Apr 71	Stricken 10 Aug 90; sold mercantile Paulsen & Ivers (Kiel) 1892; foundered in storm North Atlantic (49° 45' N, 12° 48' W) 20 Jan 94.

Fishery research 27 Apr–16 Nov 71, 11 Jul–21 Sep 72, 16 Apr–31 Oct 73; Armoured Exercise Squadron 1 May 76–9 Aug 79; tender to North Sea Naval Station 25 Aug 81–24 May 84; fishery protection 25 Mar–30 Sep 85; survey vessel 8 Apr–16 Oct 89.

Loreley (ii)

PADDLE-AVISO

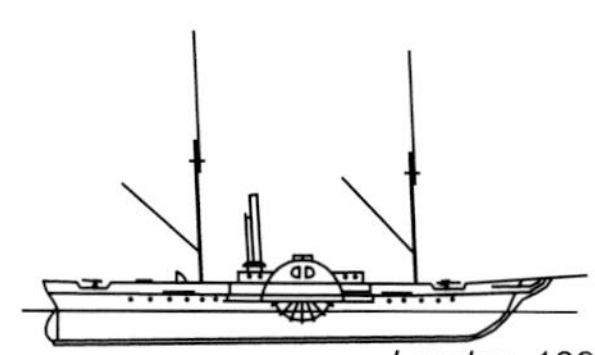

0 20 metres

Loreley 1895

Displacement: 395 (design), 450 (full load) tonnes.
Dimensions: 42.8 (wl), 46.6 (oa) x 6.6 x 3.0 metres.
Machinery: One trunk boiler; paddles; 2-cyl oscillating (VSE), IHP 350 = 10 knots; coal 34 tonnes; range 450nm @ 9 knots.
Armament: One 12.5cm/23, two 8cm/23 guns.
Complement: 4+53.

Name	Builder	Laid down	Launch	Comm	Fate
Loreley (ii)	Wilhelmshaven DYd	1869 [1 Feb 58]	19 Aug 71	16 Apr 73	Stricken 7 Sep 96; sold at ‹stanbul 23 Oct 96. Rebuilt in 1869-73 from Loreley (i), with composite hull; tender to North Sea Naval Station 16 Apr–23 Jan 79; station ship İstanbul 1 Jul 79–7 Sep 96.

Ariadne class (second group)

FLUSHDECKED CORVETTES; 1884: CRUISER-CORVETTES

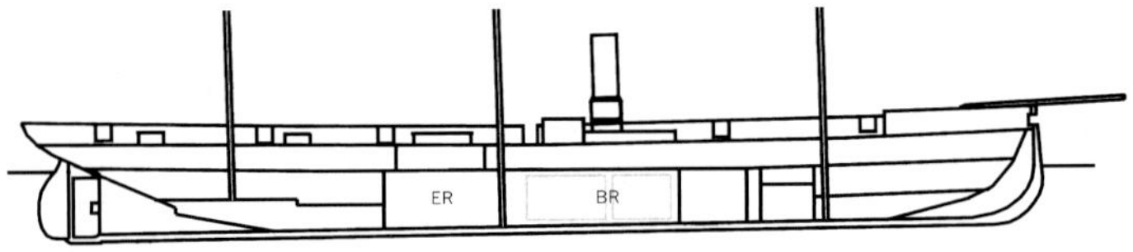

Displacement: 1,997 (design), 2,406 (full load) tonnes.
Dimensions: 83.6 (wl), 85.4 (oa) x 10.8 x 5.6 metres.
Machinery: Four trunk boilers; one shaft; 3-cyl reciprocating (HC), IHP 2,400 = 14.5 knots; coal 264 tonnes; range 2,500nm @ 10 knots.
Armament: Eight/seven 15cm/22 guns; six 3.7cm MG added 1882.
Complement: 14+234.

Name	Programme	Builder	Laid down	Launch	Comm	Fate
Freya (i)	1867	Danzig DYd	Jan 72	29 Dec 74	1 Oct 76	Stricken 14 Dec 96 sold (65,160M); BU Kiel 1897.
Thusnelda	–	Danzig DYd	–	–	–	Reordered as *Leipzig* (i).

Freya
Overseas 1 Nov 77–27 Sep 79, 1 Oct 79–21 Oct 81, 3 Apr 83– 11 Oct 84; home 23 Oct 87–7 Jan 88; harbour service 1893.

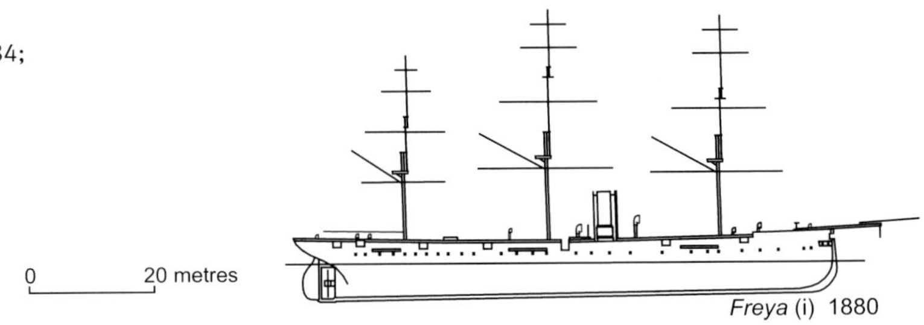

Freya (i) 1880

Leipzig class

DECKED-CORVETTES; 1884: CRUISER-FRIGATES

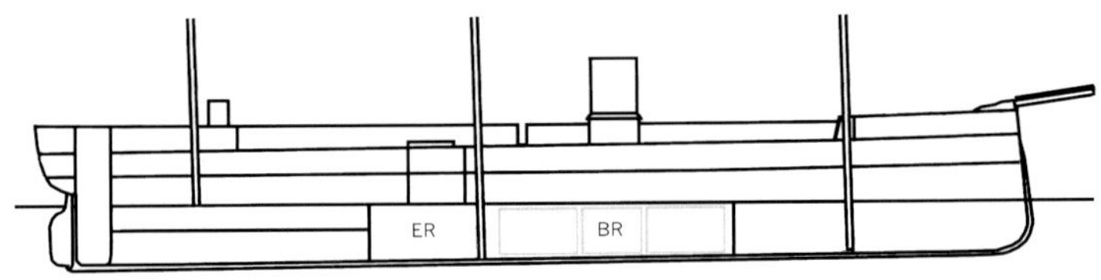

Displacement: 3,980 (design), 4,626 (full load) tonnes.
Dimensions: 87.0 (wl), 87.5 (oa) x 14.0 x 6.9 metres.
Machinery: Six trunk (*Leipzig* 1888: ten cylindrical) boilers; one shaft; 3-cyl reciprocating (HSE), IHP 6,050 = 14 knots; coal 370 tonnes; range 2,330nm @ 10 knots.
Armament: Two 17cm/25, ten 17cm/20 guns; four AW 35cm TT added 1888.
Complement: 39+386.

Name	Prov name	Programme	Builder	Laid down	Launch	Comm	Fate
Leipzig (i)	*Thusnelda*	1873	AG Vulcan (Stettin)	Dec 73	13 Sep 75	1 Jun 77	Stricken 27 Aug 94; hulked Wilhemshaven; foundered Wilhelmshaven 5 Oct 19; salved 1921; sold Hattingen; BU.
Sédan = *Prinz Adalbert* (ii) (1 Sep 78)	*Decked-corvette A*	1873	AG Vulcan (Stettin)	Dec 73	17 Jun 76	28 Aug 77	Stricken 6 May 90; accommodation hulk Wilhelmshaven; sold 7 Jun 07 (131,000M); BU Netherlands.

Leipzig
Overseas 6 Oct 77–18 Oct 79, 3 Oct 82–22 Oct 84; refit Feb 85–Aug 86; overseas 6 Apr 88–2 Jun 93.

Sédan = Prinz Adalbert
Overseas 1 Oct 78–16 Oct 80, 2 Oct 83–4 Jan 86; home 8 Apr–Oct 86; overseas 14 Oct 86–10 Apr 88; TS to 20 Sep 88.

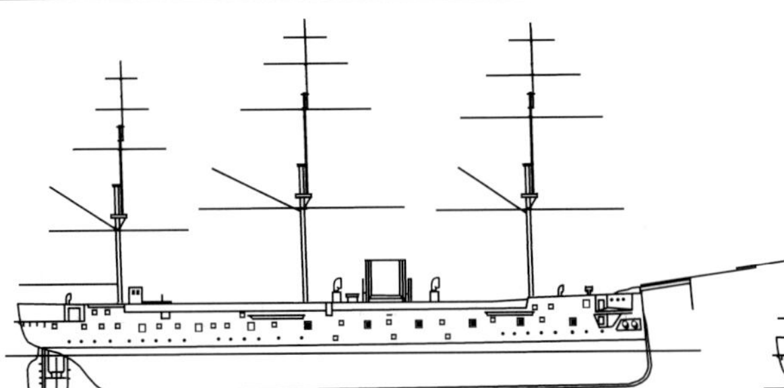
Leipzig 1877

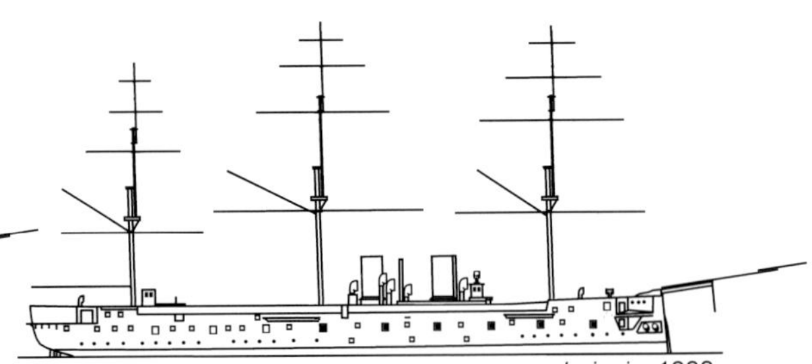
Leipzig 1888

0 20 metres

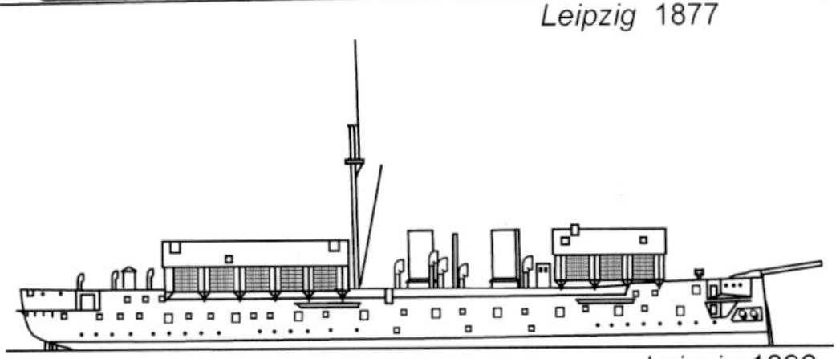
Leipzig 1896

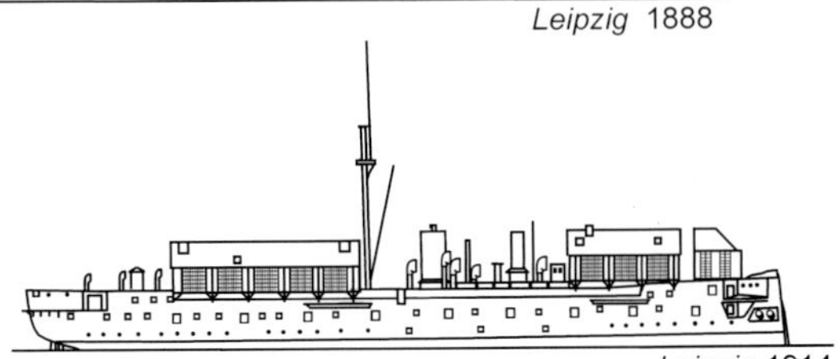
Leipzig 1914

Bismarck class

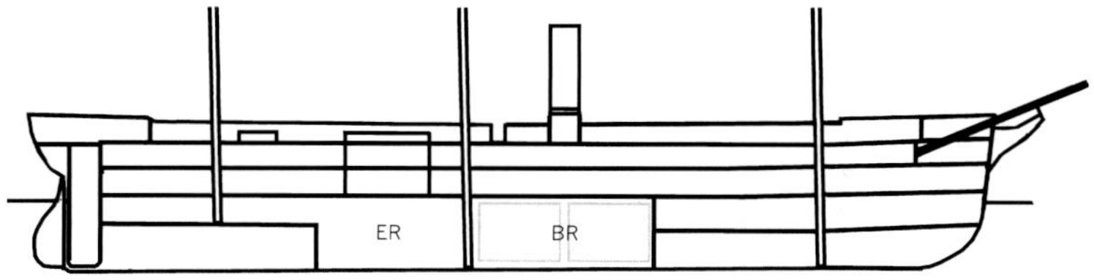

DECKED-CORVETTES; *Blücher* 1880: TORPEDO TRAINING SHIP; others 1884: CRUISER-FRIGATES; 1 Jan 91: TRAINING SHIPS (not *Bismarck* & *Blücher*)

Displacement: 2,857 (design), 2,741 (full load) tonnes (*Blücher*); 2,994/2,980 (full load 1,880/1,900) tonnes (others).
Dimensions: 72.2 (wl), 82.0–82.5 (oa) x 13.7 x 6.2–6.3 metres.
Machinery: Four transverse trunk boilers; one shaft; 3-cyl reciprocating (HSE), IHP 2,500 = 12 knots; coal 270/326 tonnes; range 2,380nm @ 9 knots.
Armament: Sixteen (later *Stosch* & *Moltke*: ten; *Stein*: twelve; *Gneisenau*: fourteen) 15cm/22, two 8.8cm/30 QL (not *Bismarck* & *Blücher*) guns; two 35cm AW TT added in *Bismarck* 1881. *Blücher* 1880: two/four 8cm/25, thirteen MG guns; seven 35cm AW/UW TT.
Complement: 18+386.

Name	Prov name	Programme (Estimates)	Builder	Laid down	Launch	Comm	Fate
Bismarck (i)	*Decked-corvette B*	1873 (1875)	Norddeutsche Schiffbau (Kiel)	Nov 75	25 Jul 77	27 Aug 78	Stricken 21 Sep 91; accommodation hulk Wilhelmshaven; BU Rüstringen 1920.
Moltke (i) = *Acheron* (Oct 11)	*Ersatz-Arcona*	1873 (1875)	Danzig DYd	Jul 75	18 Oct 77	16 Apr 78	Stricken 24 Oct 10; submarine tender Kiel 28 Oct 11; sold 7 Jul 20; BU.
Blücher (i)	*Decked-corvette C*	1873 (1876)	Norddeutsche Schiffbau (Kiel)	Mar 76	20 Sep 77	21 Dec 78	Stricken 29 Feb 08; sold … (Rotterdam) 1908; coal hulk Vigo; fate uncertain.
Stosch	*Ersatz-Gazelle*	1873 (1876)	AG Vulcan (Stettin)	Nov 75	8 Oct 77	3 Dec 77	Stricken 27 May 07; sold; BU.
Gneisenau (i)	*Decked-corvette D*	1873 (1877)	Danzig DYd	Jun 77	4 Sep 79	3 Oct 80	Foundered Malaga (36° 42' N, 04° 26' W) 16 Dec 00 after stranding in hurricane.
Stein	*Ersatz-Hertha*	1873 (1878)	AG Vulcan (Stettin)	Jul 78	14 Sep 79	3 Oct 80	Stricken 21 May 08; accommodation hulk Wilhelmshaven; BU Wilhelmshaven 1920.

Bismarck
Overseas 1 Oct 78–14 Oct 80; refit Wilhelmshaven Jan 81–Aug 83; overseas 4 Oct 84–1 Sep 88.

Moltke
South America 1 Apr 81–23 Oct 83; training voyages home/West Indies/Americas/Mediterranean & annual manoeuvres Apr 85–23 Mar 08.

Blücher
Torpedo trials ship 10 Aug 80–25 Sep 06; training & accommodation hulk Flensburg-Mürwik; boiler explosion 6 Nov 07.

Stosch
Overseas 15 Apr 81–31 Dec 85; refit; Mediterranean 20 Sep 88–27 Apr 89; training ship for cadets & boys 7 Apr 91–3 Apr 07.

Gneisenau
Mediterranean 13 Aug 82–9 Jan 83; overseas 5 Oct 84–14 Oct 86; training voyages home/West Indies/Americas/Mediterranean & annual manoeuvres Apr 87 to loss.

Stein
Overseas 16 Jul 83–6 Jan 84; training voyages home/West Indies/Americas/Mediterranean & annual manoeuvres Apr 85–3 Apr 08.

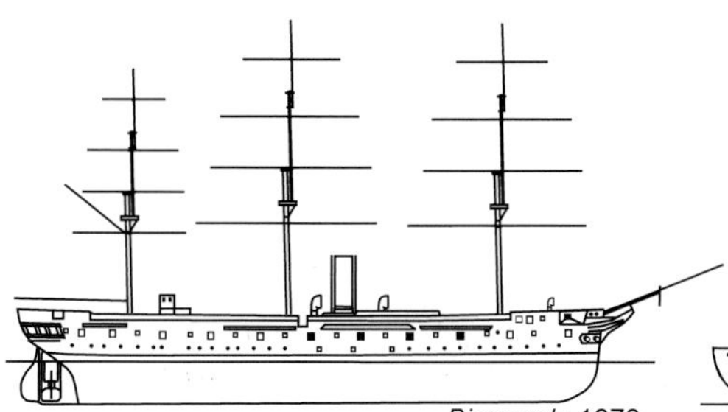
Bismarck 1878

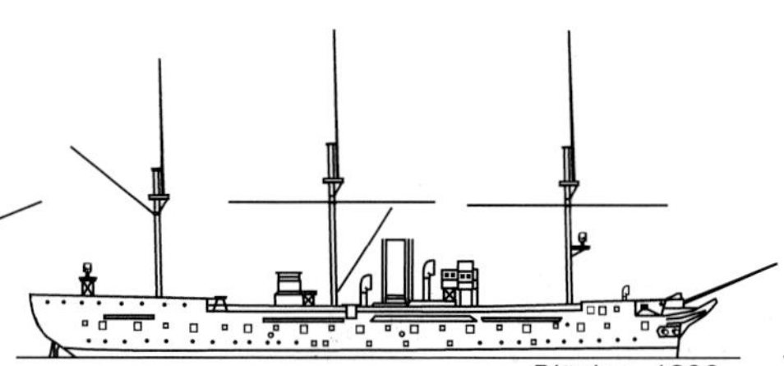
Blücher 1890

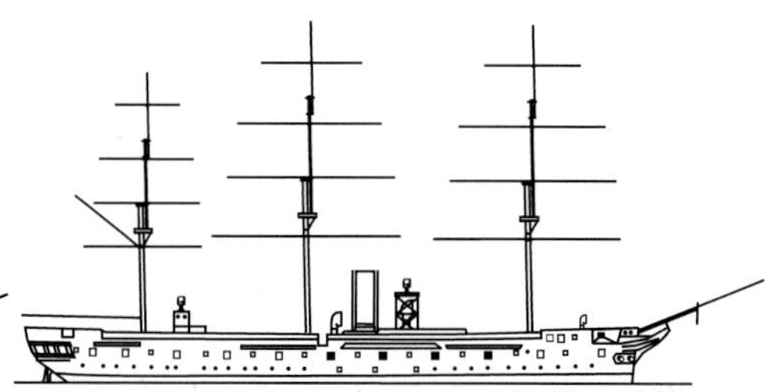
Moltke 1898

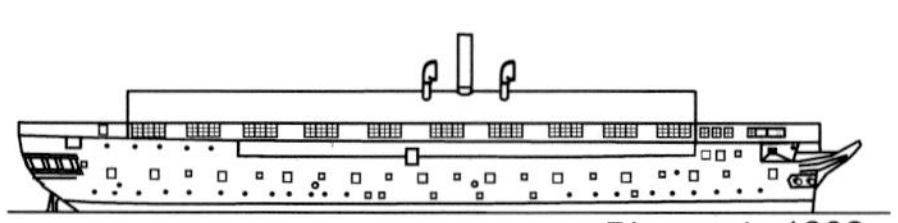
Bismarck 1892

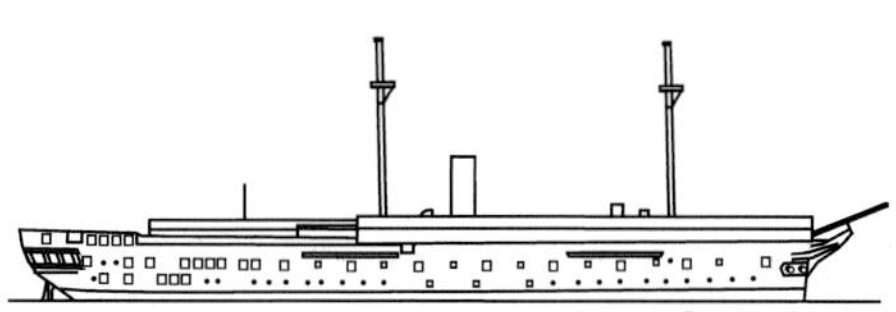
Stein 1910

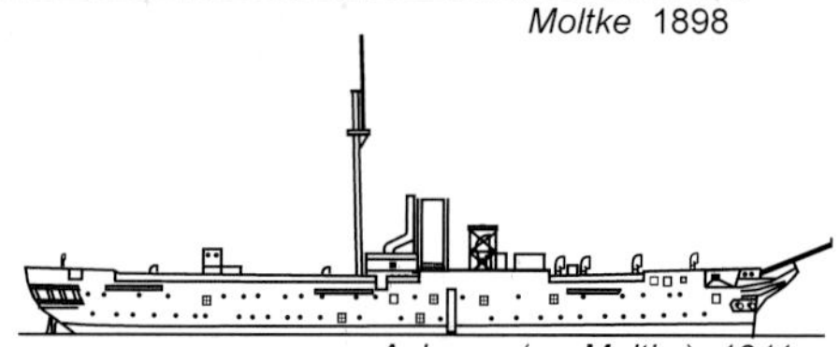
Acheron (ex-*Moltke*) 1911

0 20 metres

Zieten

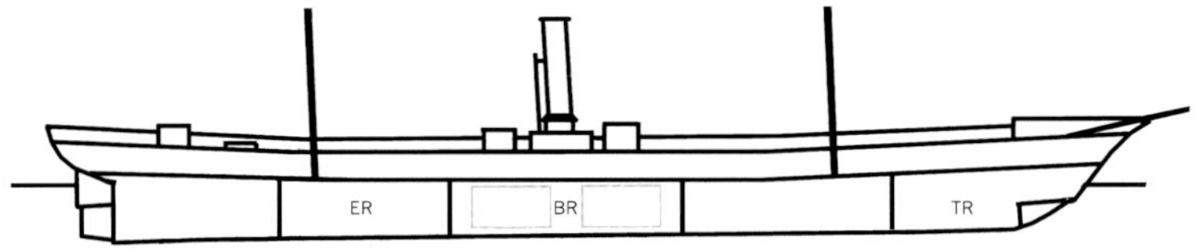

TORPEDO-VESSEL; 1881: AVISO; 1899: SMALL CRUISER; 1904: SPECIAL SHIP

Displacement: 1,001 (design), 1,170 (full load) tonnes.
Dimensions: 69.5 (wl), 79.4 (oa) x 8.6 x 4.6 metres.
Machinery: Six cylindrical boilers; two shafts; 2-cyl reciprocating (HC), IHP 2,000 = 16 knots; coal 129/130 tonnes; range 1,770nm @ 9 knots.
Armament: Four 8.7cm/24 guns; six 3.7cm MG (added 1881); two 38cm UW TT. 1900: six (later four) 5cm/40 QL guns; no TT; 44 mines.
Complement: 6+88; 1900: 7+99–104.

Name	Programme (Estimates)	Builder	Laid down	Launch	Comm	Fate
Zieten	1873 (1875)	Thames Iron Works (Blackwall)	Jul 75	9 Mar 76	1 Aug 76	Stricken 6 Dec 19; sold 18 Apr 21 (655,000M); BU Wilhelmshaven.

Carola class (first group)

FLUSHDECKED-CORVETTES; 1884: CRUISER-CORVETTES;
***Olga, Marie, Sophie* 1893: III. CLASS CRUISERS;**
***Carola* 1893: GUNNERY TS;**
***Olga, Marie, Sophie* 31 Mar 97: TRAINING SHIPS**

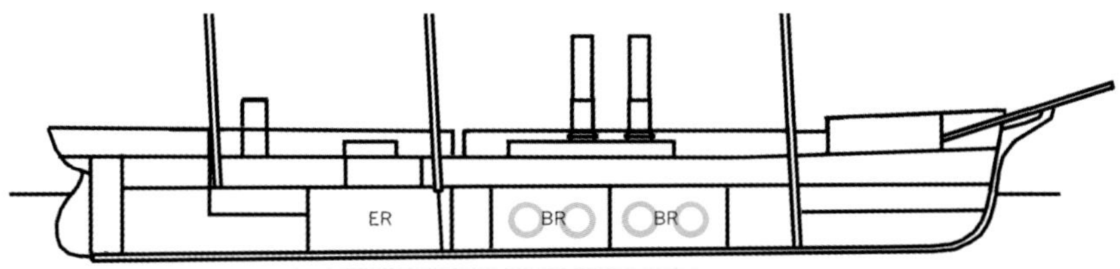

Displacement: 2,147 (design), 2,424 (full load) tonnes.
Dimensions: 70.6 (wl), 76.4 (oa) x 12.5 x 6.1 metres.
Machinery: Eight (*Marie* & *Sophie*: six) cylindrical boilers; one shaft; 3-cyl reciprocating (HC), IHP 2,100 = 13.5 knots; coal 297/350 tonnes; range 3,420nm @ 10 knots.
Armament: Ten 15cm/22, two 8.7cm/24 guns (*Sophie/Marie* 1895: two 8.8cm/30 QL) guns; six (*Sophie/Marie* 1895: ten) 3.7cm MG. *Carola* 1893: six, later four 15cm/22, two 10.5cm/35 QL, eight 8.8cm/30 QL, two 5cm/40 QL; *Olga* 1900: two 8.8cm/30 QL guns; ten 3.7cm MG.
Complement: 25+244.

Name	Prov name	Programme (Estimates)	Builder	Laid down	Launch	Comm	Fate
Carola	*Flushdecked-corvette E*	1873 (1879)	AG Vulcan (Stettin)	Late 1879	27 Nov 80	1 Sep 81	Stricken 4 Oct 05; sold Feb 06 (136,000M); BU Hamburg 1906.
Olga	*Ersatz-Augusta*	1873 (1879)	AG Vulcan (Stettin)	1879	11 Dec 80	10 Sep 81	Stricken 22 Jun 05; sold Mar 06 (136,000M); BU Hamburg 1908.
Marie	*Ersatz-Vineta*	1873 (1880)	Reiherstieg (Hamburg)	1880	20 Aug 81	12 Sep 82	Stricken 29 Oct 04; sold 1909 (116,000M); BU Stettin.
Sophie	*Flushdecked-corvette F*	1873 (1880)	Danzig DYd	Jan 80	10 Nov 81	10 Aug 82	Stricken 21 May 08; accommodation hulk Wilhelmshaven; sold 7 Jul 20; BU 1921.

Carola
Overseas 18 Oct 81–1 Nov 83, 4 May 86–15 Apr 91; refitted as gunnery TS; served as such 20 Mar 93–10 Jan 05.

Olga
East coast South/Central America 1 Oct 82–21 Mar 84; overseas 1 Oct 84–23 Sep 89; refit; manoeuvres 25 Jul–30 Sep 93; fishery protection 29 Mar–30 Nov 98; refitted as gunnery TS 1900; Naval Gunnery Inspectorate 15 Jan 01–29 Mar 05.

Marie
Overseas 1 May 83–22 Feb 86; refit; overseas 1 Dec 92–26 Sep 95; reserve; refit as gunnery TS cancelled.

Sophie
Overseas 2 Oct 83–16 Sep 84, 12 May 85–13 Aug 92; refit as TS; S America as boys' TS 1 Apr 98–7 Apr 99.

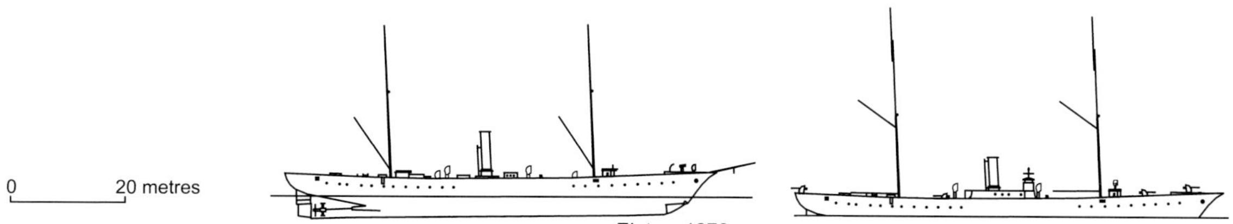

Zieten 1878 *Zieten* 1900

Torpedo experimental vessel Aug 76–15 Oct 80; home 27 Jun–20 Oct 81; Mediterranean 14 Aug–25 Nov 82; home 30 Jun 86–30 Sep 92; fishery protection 16 Mar 97–30 Nov 99; refit 1900; tender 15 Mar 01–Jul 14; Jade/Weser Harbour Flotilla 1 Aug 14–Jun 18; leader Elbe Forward Defence Flotilla Jul–Dec 18; tender Jan–Jul 19.

Carola class (second group)

CRUISER-CORVETTES (ex-flushdecked corvettes); 1893: III. CLASS CRUISERS; 1899: SMALL CRUISERS

Displacement: 2,362 (design), 2,662 (full load) tonnes.
Dimensions: 71.8 (wl), 81.2 (oa) x 12.6 x 6.3 metres.
Machinery: Eight cylindrical boilers; one shaft; two 2-cyl reciprocating (HC), IHP 2,400 = 14 knots; coal 270/340 tonnes; range 4,180nm @ 8.5 knots.
Armament: Ten 15cm/35, four 10.5cm/35 guns; six 3.7cm MG.
Complement: 25+257.

Name	Prov name	Programme (Estimates)	Builder	Laid down	Launch	Comm	Fate
Alexandrine	*Flushdecked-corvette G*	1873 (1881)	Kiel DYd	Feb 82	7 Feb 85	6 Oct 86	Stricken 27 May 07; sold (148,000M); BU Danzig 1907.
Arcona (ii) = *Mercur* (11 Jan 02)	*Ersatz-Nymphe*	1873 (1882)	Danzig DYd	1881	7 May 85	1 Dec 86	Stricken 22 Jun 05; sold Dec 05 (145,000M); BU Danzig 1906.

Alexandrine
Overseas 2 Apr 89–1 Jun 95; harbour service (floating battery) 3 May 04.

Arcona
Overseas 20 Apr 92–6 Jun 99.

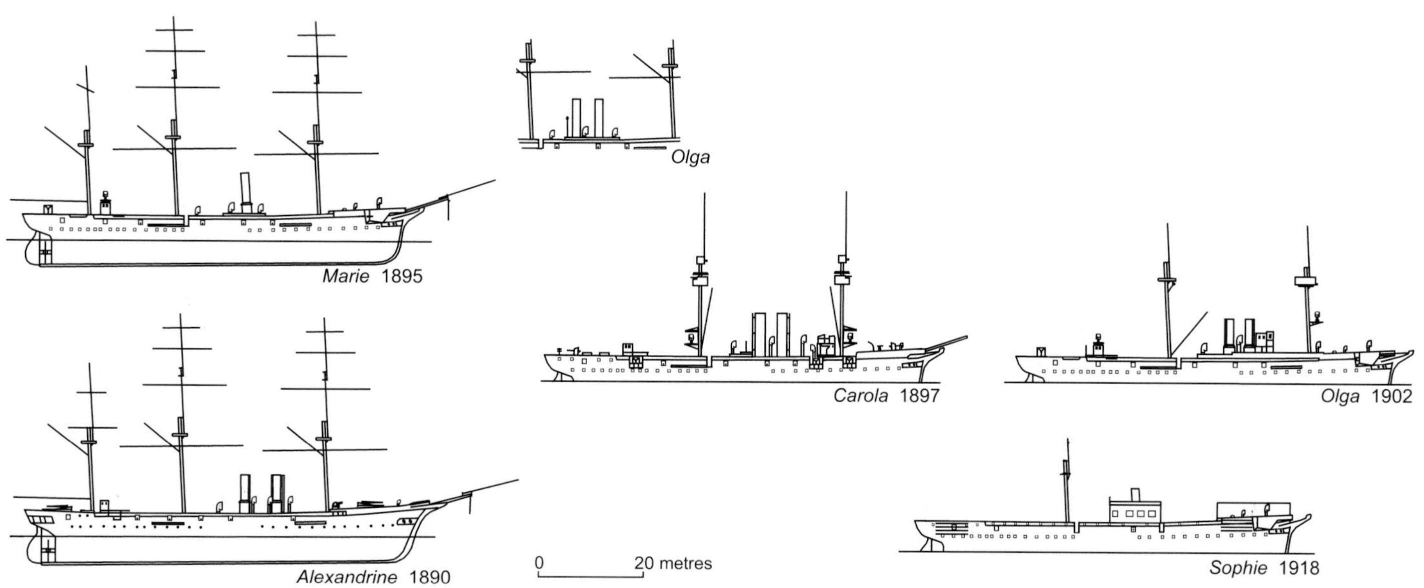

Olga · *Marie* 1895 · *Carola* 1897 · *Olga* 1902 · *Alexandrine* 1890 · *Sophie* 1918

Blitz class

AVISOS; 1899: SMALL CRUISERS; 1910: SPECIAL-DUTY SHIPS

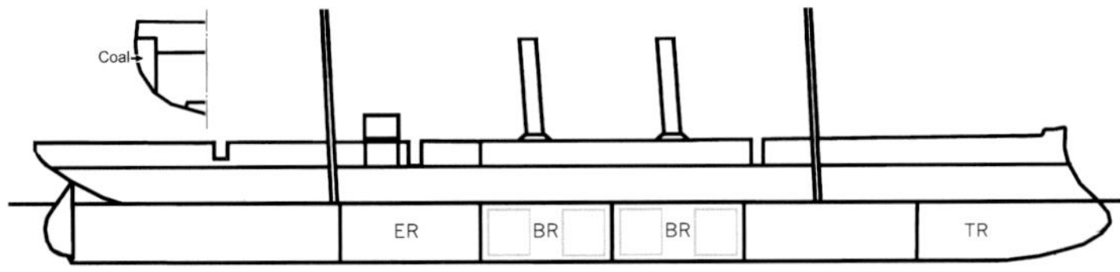

Displacement: 1,381 (design), 1,486 (full load) tonnes.
Dimensions: 75.3 (wl), 78.4 (oa) x 9.9 x 4.4 metres.
Machinery: Eight cylindrical boilers; two shafts; 2-cyl reciprocating (HC), IHP 2,700 = 16 knots; coal 185/220 tonnes; range 2,440nm @ 9 knots.
Armament: One 12.5cm/23, four 8.7cm/24 guns; four 3.7cm MG; one 35cm UW TT. 1892–93: six 8.8cm/30 QL; one 35cm UW, two 35cm AW TT; TT later removed.
Complement: 7/6+127/135; plus 3+16 as flotilla leader.

Name	Prov name	Programme (Estimates)	Builder	Laid down	Launch	Comm	Fate
Blitz	*Aviso D*	1873 (1878)	Norddeutsche Schiffbau (Kiel)	1881	26 Aug 82	28 Mar 83	Stricken 8 Mar 21; sold (520,000M); BU Wilhelmshaven.
Pfeil	*Ersatz-Grille*	1873 (1878)	Wilhelmshaven DYd	1881	16 Sep 82	25 Nov 84	Stricken 16 Feb 22; BU Wilhelmshaven.

Blitz
Summer manoeuvres (inc as TB leader) 8 Jun 83–30 Sep 97; TS/tender 13 Apr–23 Sep 98; Inspectorate of Naval Gunnery 15 Feb–Sep 98; fishery protection 16 Sep–Nov 99; Inspectorate of Naval Gunnery 26 Nov 99; fishery protection early 1900; TB leader 18 Apr 00; scout Aug–22 Sep 00; refit Danzig to early 03; Scouting Force 2 May–Aug 03; fleet tender from 25 Sep 03.

Pfeil
Exercise Squadron 22 Jun–5 Oct 85; Manoeuvre Squadron 3 May–16 Sep 87; East Africa/Mediterranean 12 Nov 88–13 Dec 89; Armoured/Manoeuvre Squadron 1 Apr 90–8 Mar 92; refit; Manoeuvre Squadron 3 Apr 94–18 Dec 95; engineering TS 28 Aug–Sep 97; fishery protection/engineering TS/I. Squadron 21 Sep 97–21 Sep 98; fishery protection/I. Squadron 16 Mar–29 Sep 00; refit Danzig; fleet tender 30 Mar 04–17 Dec 18.

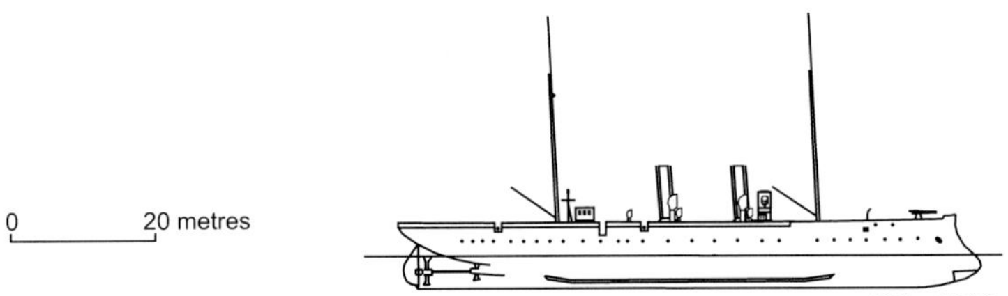

Blitz 1883

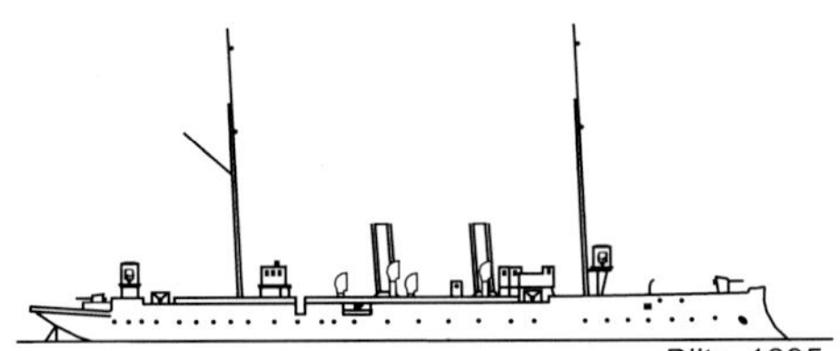

Blitz 1895

Charlotte

CRUISER-FRIGATE (ex-decked-corvette); 1893: TRAINING SHIP

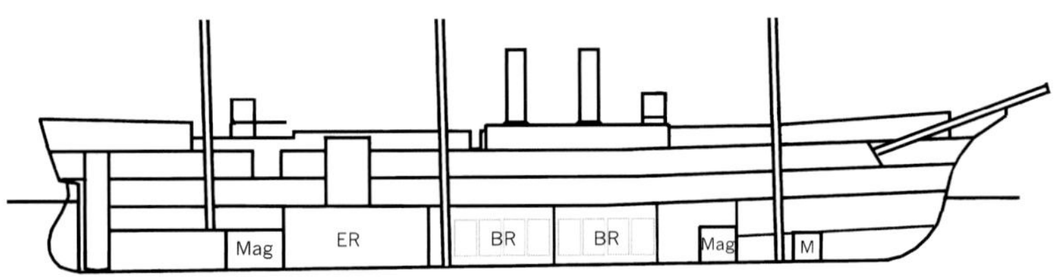

Displacement: 3,288 (design), 3,768 (full load) tonnes.
Dimensions: 76.9 (wl), 83.9 (oa) x 14.6 x 6.9 metres.
Machinery: Eight (1905: six) cylindrical boilers; one shaft; two (1905: one) 2-cyl reciprocating (HC), IHP 3,000 (1905: 1,200) = 13 knots (1905: 11 knots); coal 528 tonnes; range 2,300nm (1905: 4,000nm) @ 11 knots.
Armament: Eighteen 15cm/22 (1890: two 8.8cm/30 QL added) guns; six 3.7cm MG; 1899: twelve 15cm/22, two 10.5cm/35 QL, two 8.8cm/30 QL guns; 1905: sixteen 8.8cm/30 QL guns.
Complement: 20+486.

Name	Prov name	Programme (Estimates)	Builder	Laid down	Launch	Comm	Fate
Charlotte	*Ersatz-Victoria*	1873 (1883)	Wilhelmshaven DYd	Nov 81	5 Sep 85	1 Nov 86	Stricken 26 May 09; accommodation hulk/ tender to *König Wilhelm* Kiel/ Flensburg-Mürwik 1910 (restored to list 20 Oct–4 Nov 14); sold ... (Hamburg) 1921; store hulk.

Mediterranean (cadet & boys' TS) 29 Sep 88–25 Apr 89; home 22 Apr–Sep 97; overseas/home (cadet & boys' TS) 16 Sep 97–2 Apr 03; rebuilt; home/Atlantic (cadet & boys' TS) 1 Apr 05–31 Mar 09.

Nixe

CRUISER-CORVETTE (ex-flushdecked/decked-corvette); 1893: TRAINING SHIP

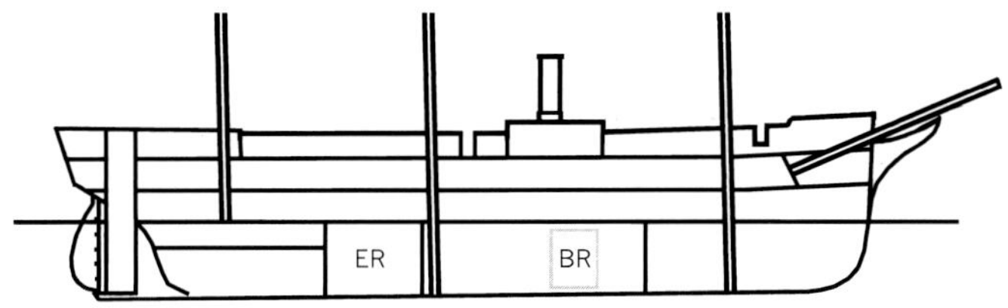

Displacement: 1,781 (design), 1,982 (full load) tonnes.
Dimensions: 54.4 (wl), 63.3 (oa) x 13.2 x 6.4 metres.
Machinery: Two cylindrical boilers; one shaft; 2-cyl reciprocating (HC), IHP 700 = 9 knots; coal 105/125 tonnes; range 1,480nm @ 8 knots.
Armament: Eight (1894: seven, 1895: six) 12.5cm/23 guns; two 8.8cm/30 QL guns, four 3.7cm MG added 1894.
Complement: 27+331.

Name	Prov name	Programme (Estimates)	Builder	Laid down	Launch	Comm	Fate
Nixe = *Hulk C* (1 Apr 23) = *Nixe* (1925)	*Ersatz-Medusa*	1873 (1883)	Danzig DYd	Aug 83	23 Jul 85	1 Apr 86	Stricken 24 Jun 11; accommodation hulk Kiel; sold Emil Retzlaff (Stettin) 1925; lighter; BU Wewelsfleth 1930.

Overseas (boys' TS) 15 Jun 86–25 Jul 87; manoeuvres 6–28 Aug 87; guardship Wilhelmshaven 17 Sep 87–17 Apr 88; West Indies/Americas 4 Jun 88–9 Sep 89, 9 Apr 90–25 Aug 91; manoeuvres 18–30 Sep 91; Mediterranean 1 Apr–Sep 92; West Indies 23 Sep 92–15 Mar 94; refit Danzig; West Indies 1 Apr 97–19 Mar 98; Americas 15 Aug 98–1 Apr 99, May 99–26 Mar 00; home 25 May–11 Aug 00; refit 1902–3; HQ ship High Seas Fleet 1 Nov 06–18 May 1910.

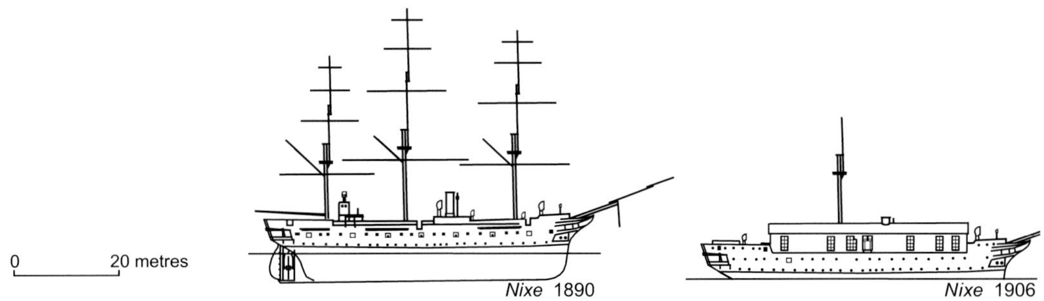

Nixe 1890 *Nixe* 1906

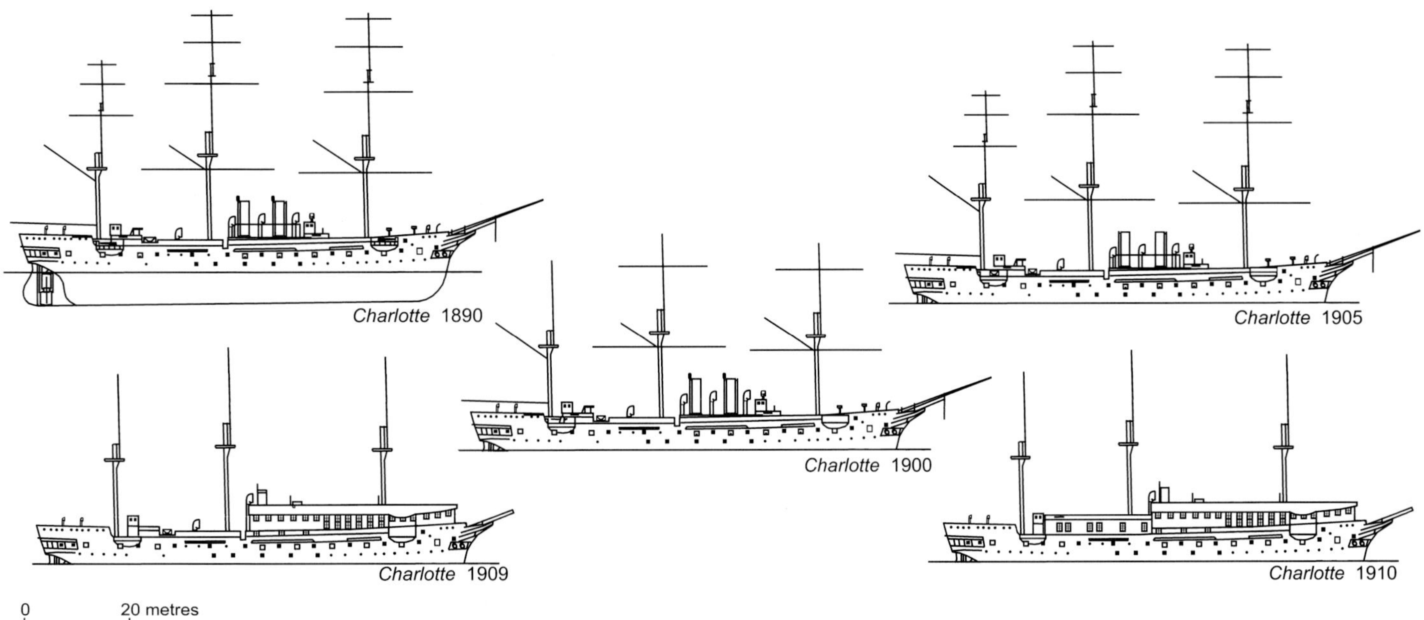

Charlotte 1890 *Charlotte* 1905 *Charlotte* 1900 *Charlotte* 1909 *Charlotte* 1910

Greif

AVISO; 1899: SMALL CRUISER

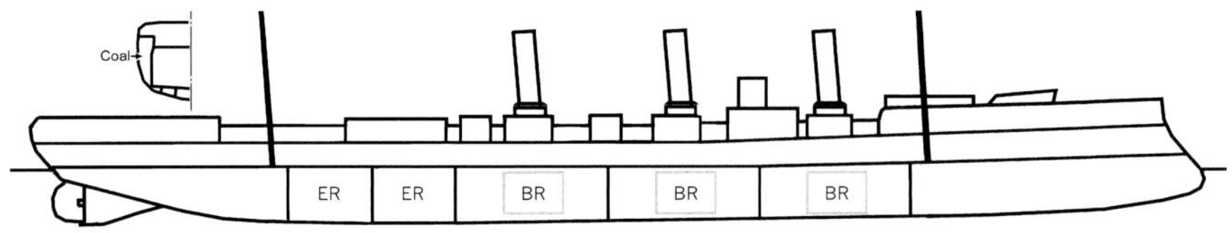

Displacement: 2,050 (design), 2,266 (full load) tonnes.
Dimensions: 99.5 (wl), 102.6 (oa) x 9.8 x 4.3 metres.
Machinery: Six (1901: eight) cylindrical boilers; two shafts; 2-cyl reciprocating (HC), IHP 5,400 = 18 knots; coal 330/350 (1901: 436) tonnes; range 2,180nm @ 12 knots (1906: range 3,960nm @ 10 knots).
Armament: Two 10.5cm/35 guns; ten 3.7cm MG. 1891: eight (later six) 8.8cm/30 QL guns; six (later four) 3.7cm MG.
Complement: 7+163.

Name	Prov name	Programme	Builder	Laid down	Launch	Comm	Fate
Greif	*Ersatz-Loreley*	1885	Germania (Kiel)	Oct 85	29 Jul 86	9 Jul 87	Stricken 25 Oct 12; hulked Kiel; sold 1921; BU Hamburg.

Home 19 Mar–30 Sep 89, 1 Nov 90–17 Apr 93; refit 17 Apr–2 Oct 93; torpedo experimental vessel 3 Oct 93–31 Oct 94; fleet scout/repeating ship 5 May 97–22 Sep 00; refit 1901; special duty vessel 21 Jun 11.

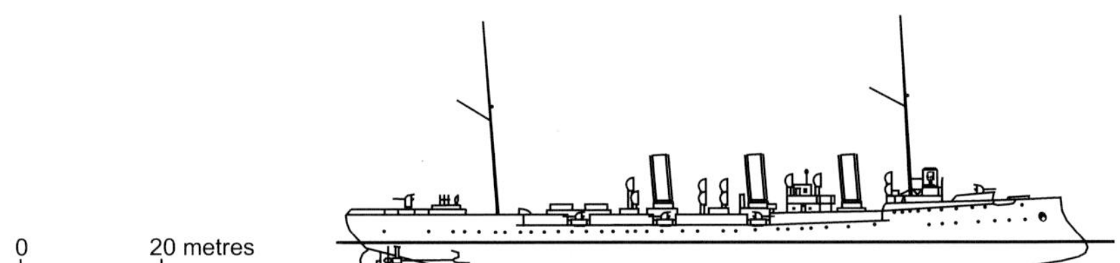

Greif 1891

Irene class

II. CLASS CRUISERS; 1899: SMALL CRUISERS

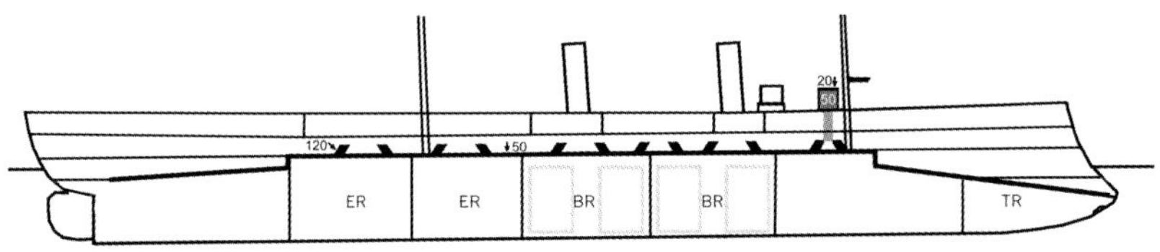

Displacement: 4,271 (design), 5,027 (full load) tonnes.
Dimensions: 98.9 (wl), 103.7 (oa) x 14.2 x 7.6 metres.
Machinery: Four cylindrical double boilers; two shafts; reciprocating (HC), IHP 8,000 = 18 knots; coal 400/550 tonnes; range 2,490nm @ 9 knots.
Armament: Four 15cm/30, ten 15cm/22 guns; six 3.7cm MG (1893: four 15cm/30, eight 10.5cm/35 QL, six 5cm/40 QL guns; six 3.7cm MG); three (1 x UW, 2 x AW) 35cm TT
Protection: Deck 20+30mm/20+55mm; CT 20mm (roof)-55mm (sides).
Complement: 28+337 (1893: 17+357).

Name	Prov name	Estimates	Builder	Laid down	Launch	Comm	Fate
Irene	*Ersatz-Elisabeth*	1885/86	AG Vulcan (Stettin)	May 86	23 Jul 87	25 May 88	Stricken 17 Feb 14; submarine tender Kiel/1916 Wilhelmshaven; sold 26 Nov 21 (909,000M); BU Wilhelmshaven 1922.
Prinzeß Wilhelm	*Ersatz-Ariadne*	188687	Germania (Kiel)	May 86	22 Sep 87	13 Nov 89	Stricken 17 Feb 14; mine hulk Danzig/Kiel/ Wilhelmshaven; sold 26 Nov 21 (909,000M); BU Wilhelmshaven 1922.
–	*Cruiser-corvette H*	1888/89	–	–	–	–	Cancelled; re-ordered as II. class cruiser (to be *Kaiserin Augusta*).

Irene
Active service 25 May–26 Nov 88, 1 Apr 89–24 Sep 90 (Mediterranean Sep–Nov 89); refit 1893; Far East 1 Nov 94–1 Oct 01; Wilhelmshaven refit 1903–05; accommodation ship for Kiel submarines Dec 13.

Prinzeß Wilhelm
Active service 19 Nov 89–25 Mar 90, 16 Apr 91–14 Nov 92 (Mediterranean Aug–Nov 92); refit 1893; active service 10 Oct 93–22 Jul 99 (Far East Apr 95–Apr 99); Wilhelmshaven refit 1899–1902; towed to Danzig 11 Oct 12.

Wacht class

AVISO; 1899: SMALL CRUISER

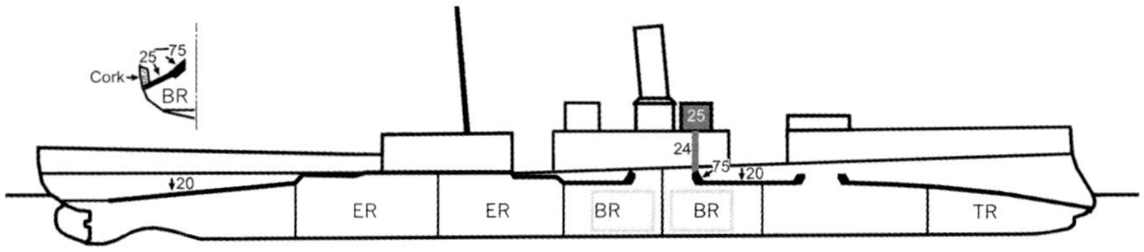

Displacement: 1,246 (design), 1,499 (full load) tonnes.
Dimensions: 84.0 (wl), 85.5 (oa) x 9.7 x 4.7 metres.
Machinery: Four locomotive boilers; two shafts; 3-cyl (OTE), IHP 4,000 = 19 knots; coal 100/230 tonnes; range 2,860nm @ 10 knots.
Armament: Three 10.5cm/35 (1891: four 8.8cm/30 QL) guns; ten (removed 1891) 3.7cm MG; three 35cm (1 x UW, 2 x AW) TT.
Protection: Deck 20/25mm; CT 25mm.
Complement: 7+134.

Name	Prov name	Estimates	Builder	Laid down	Launch	Comm	Fate
Wacht	*Aviso E*	1886/87	AG Weser (Bremen)	Nov 86	27 Aug 87	9 Aug 88	Collision SMS *Sachsen* Baltic (54° 41' N, 13° 31' E) 4 Sep 01.
Jagd	*Ersatz-Pommerania*	1887/88	AG Weser (Bremen)	Oct 87	7 Jul 88	25 Jun 89	Stricken 14 May 10; hulked as torpedo-firing platform Friedrichsort; BU Rüstringen 1920.

Wacht

Manoeuvre/Exercise Squadron 1 May 89–6 Mar 90; refit; Manoeuvre Squadron 6 Oct 91–12 Oct 92; engineer & stoker TS 13 Jan–Apr 93; I. TB Flotilla 25 Apr–11 Oct 93; Manoeuvre Squadron 3 Apr–8 Dec 94, 18 Mar 96–4 May 97; fleet scout 6 Apr–27 Sep 99; I. SG 11 Aug 01 to loss.

Jagd

Imperial yacht escort/Kiel guardship 15 Apr–3 Oct 90; rearmed; Imperial yacht escort/ Wilhelmshaven guardship/repeating ship for manoeuvres 21 Apr 91–5 Oct 91; Wilhelmshaven guardship 13 Oct 92–30 Sep 93; reboilered Wilhelmshaven 1893–94; Manoeuvre Squadron 8 Mar–19 Dec 95; I. Squadron/fleet 18 Mar 96–8 Mar 98; fleet/fishery protection 25 Sep 99–11 Aug 01; harbour service 3 May 04.

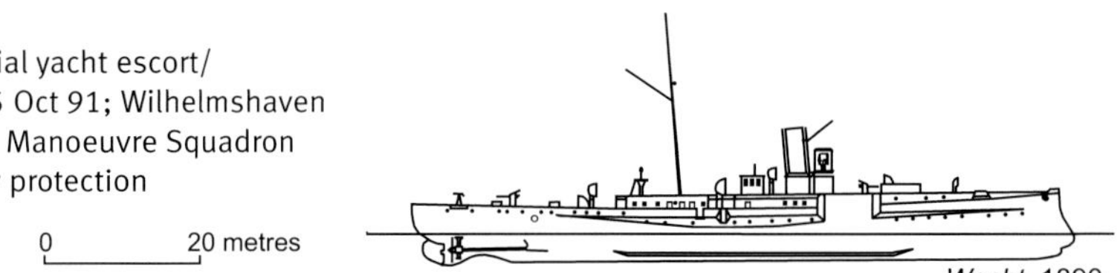

Wacht 1890

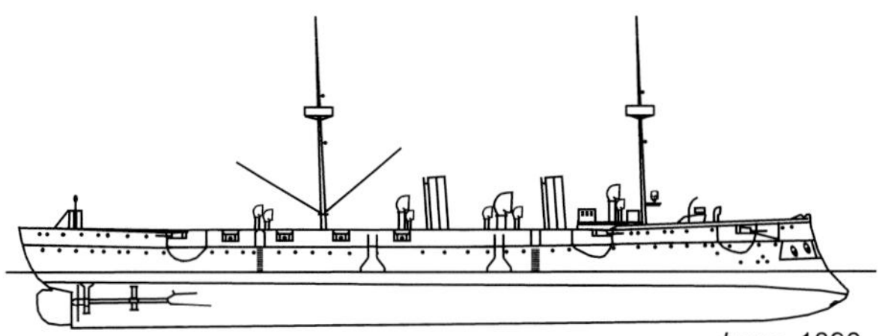

Irene 1890

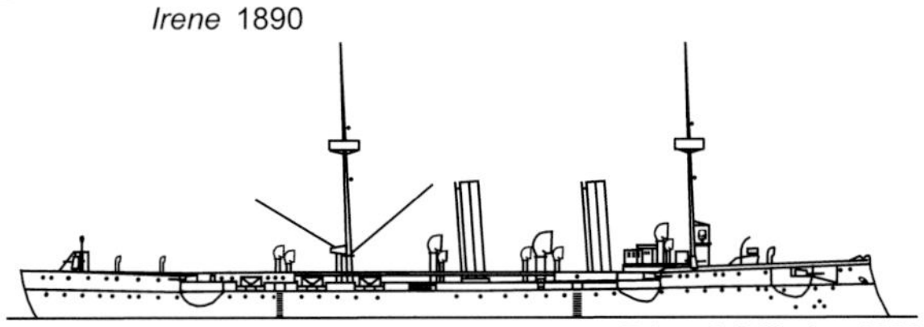

Prinzeß Wilhelm 1893

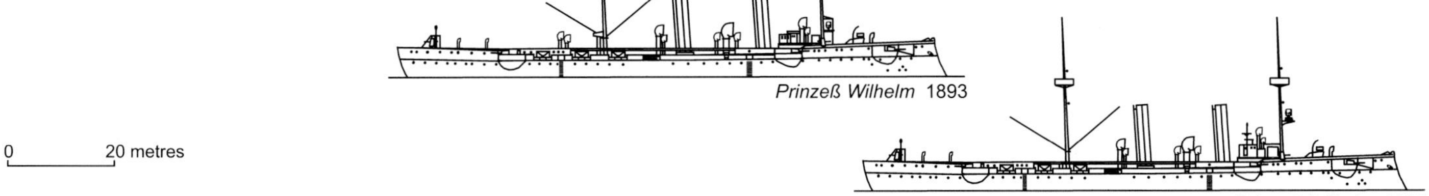

Prinzeß Wilhelm 1902

Schwalbe class

CRUISERS; 1893: IV.CLASS CRUISERS; 1899: SMALL CRUISERS; 1911: GUNBOAT (*Sperber*); SPECIAL-DUTY SHIP (*Schwalbe*)

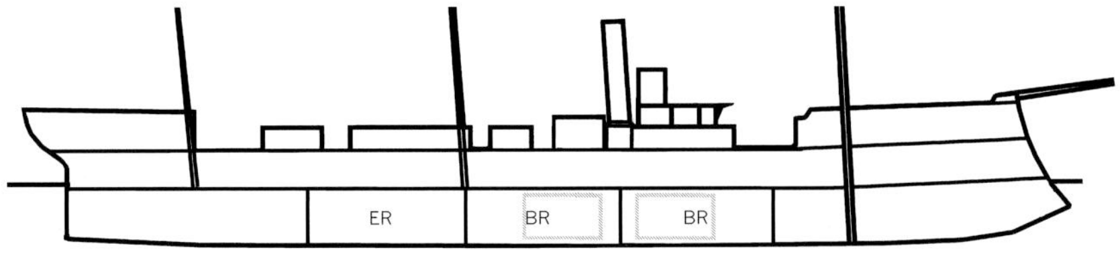

Displacement:	1,111 (design), 1,359 (full load) tonnes.
Dimensions:	62.6 (wl), 66.9 (oa) x 9.4 x 4.7 metres.
Machinery:	Four cylindrical boilers; two shafts; 2-cyl reciprocating (HC), IHP 1,500 = 13.5 knots; coal 150/240 tonnes; range 3,290nm @ 10 knots.
Armament:	Eight 10.5cm/35 guns; five 3.7cm MG; one 35cm TT (AW).
Complement:	9+108.

Name	Prov name	Estimates (Programme)	Builder	Laid down	Launch	Comm	Fate
Schwalbe	*Cruiser A*	188687	Wilhemshaven DYd	Apr 86	16 Aug 87	4 May 88	Stricken 6 Dec 19; sold ... (Cuxhaven) 7 Aug 20; BU Hamburg-Moorburg 1922.
Sperber	*Cruiser B*	1887/88	Wilhemshaven DYd	Sep 87	23 Aug 88	2 Apr 89	Stricken 16 Mar 12; target hulk; sold ... (Cux-haven) 7 Aug 20; BU Hamburg-Moorburg 1922.

Schwalbe
East Africa 20 Nov 88–25 Aug 93; refit Kiel; East/South Africa 20 Apr 98–5 Jul 00; Far East Jul 00–13 Dec 02; refit; special service vessel 26 Oct 11; target ship; refit as TS vice *Grille* cancelled Aug 14; hulked Kiel; target hulk 1918.

Sperber
Overseas 20 Aug 89–7 Dec 96; refit Jan 97–Aug 98; overseas 16 Dec 02–6 Jul 11.

0 20 metres

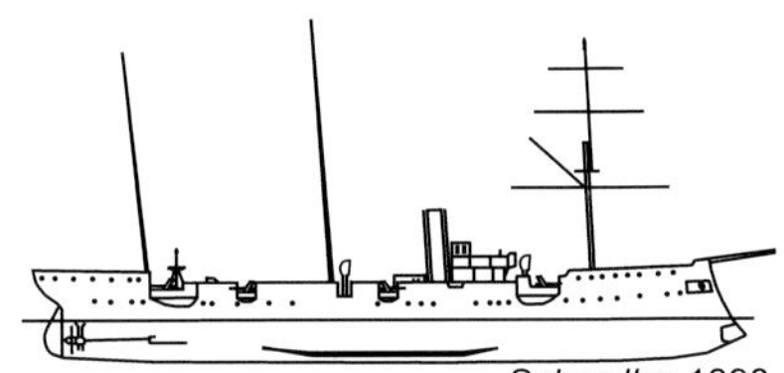

Schwalbe 1898

Bussard class

IV.-CLASS CRUISERS; 1899: SMALL CRUISERS; *Condor* 8 Jan 13, *Cormoran* 24 Feb 13, *Seeadler*, *Geier* 6 May 14: GUNBOATS

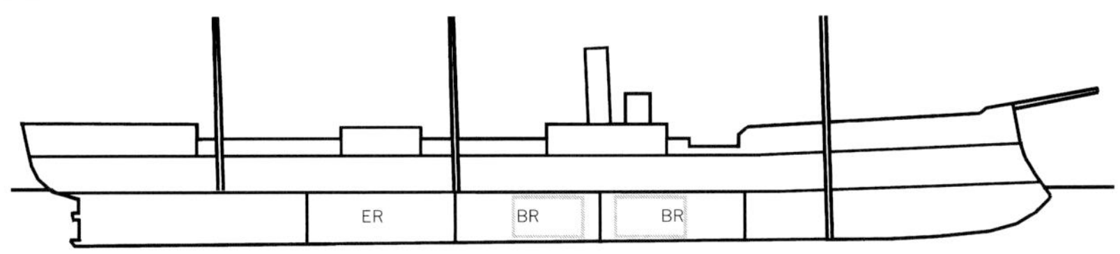

Displacement:	1,559–1,612 (design), 1,864–1,918 (full load) tonnes.
Dimensions:	79.2 (wl), 82.6/83.9 [*Geier*] (oa) x 10.2–10.6 x 5.2–5.6 metres.
Machinery:	Four cylindrical boilers; two shafts; 3-cyl reciprocating (HTE), IHP 2,800 (*Geier*: 2,880) = 15.5 knots; coal 180–205/305–320 tonnes; range 2,950–3,610nm @ 9 knots.
Armament:	Eight 10.5cm/35 (*Bussard*)/10.5cm/35 QL (others) guns; five 3.7cm MG; two 35cm (*Geier*: 45cm) AW TT.
Complement:	9+152.

Name	Prov name	Estimates (Programme)	Builder	Laid down	Launch	Comm	Fate
Bussard	*Cruiser C*	1888–89	Danzig DYd	Aug 88	23 Jan 90	7 Oct 90	Stricken 7 Oct 12; sold Neugebauer (Lemwerder), BU Hamburg 1913.
Falke (ii)	*Cruiser D*	1889/90 (ex-1892/93)	Kiel DYd	Jan 90	4 Apr 91	14 Sep 91	Stricken 25 Oct 12; BU Danzig DYd 1913.
Kaiseradler = Seeadler (17 Aug 92)	*Ersatz-Adler*	1890/91	Danzig DYd	Sep 90	2 Feb 92	27 Jun 92	Mine hulk autumn 14; internal explosion off Wilhelmshaven (53° 28' N, 08° 12' E) 19 Apr 17.
Cormoran	*Cruiser E*	1890/91 (ex-1893/94)	Danzig DYd	Nov 90	17 May 92	25 Jul 93	Scuttled Tsingtau (36° 03' N, 120° 16' E) 28 Sep 14.
Condor	*Ersatz-Eber*	1890/91	Blohm & Voss (Hamburg)	Jun 91	23 Feb 92	9 Dec 94	Mine hulk Kiel-Friedrichsort 1916; stricken 18 Nov 20; sold 8 Apr 21; BU Hamburg 1921.
Geier = Schurz (9 Jun 17)	*Cruiser F*	1893/94	Wilhelmshaven DYd	2 Nov 93	18 Oct 94	24 Oct 95	Seized USA 7 Apr 17; US commission 15 Sep 17; collision SS *Florida* off Cape Look-out (34° 11' 13.08" N, 76° 36' 7.62" W).

Meteor class

AVISO; 1899: SMALL CRUISER

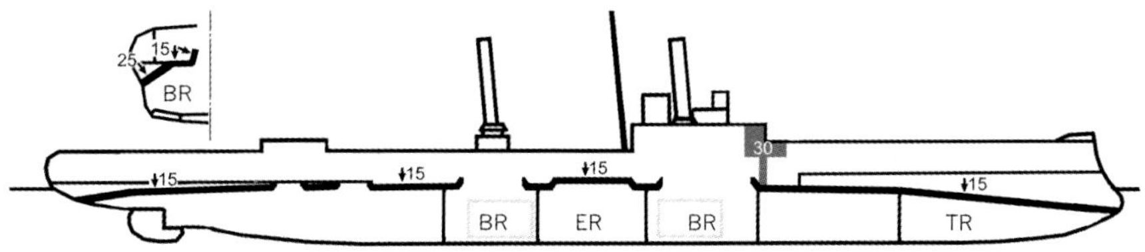

Displacement:	961 [*Meteor*]–992 [*Comet*] (design), 1,078/1,117 (full load) tonnes.
Dimensions:	78.5/78.7 (wl), 79.9 (oa) x 9.6 x 4.5 metres.
Machinery:	Four locomotive boilers; two shafts; 3-cyl reciprocating (VTE), IHP 4,500/5,000 = 19/19.5 knots; coal 60/120–147 tonnes; range 960nm @ 9 knots.
Armament:	Four 8.8cm/30 QL guns; three 35cm (2 x AW, 1 x UW) TT.
Protection:	Deck 15mm/25mm; CT 15mm (roof)-30mm (sides).
Complement:	7–8+108–110.

Name	Prov name	Estimates	Builder	Laid down	Launch	Comm	Fate
Meteor (ii)	*Aviso F*	1888/89	Germania (Kiel)	Dec 88	20 Jan 90	15 May 91	Stricken 24 Jun 11; accommodation hulk Kiel; sold 1919; BU Rendsburg-Audorf.
Comet	*Aviso G*	1890/91	AG Vulcan (Stettin)	Nov 91	15 Nov 92	29 Apr 93	Stricken 24 Jun 11; mine hulk Emden 1913; BU Hamburg 1921.

Meteor

TB leader for manoeuvres 29 Sep 92; Manoeuvre Fleet 1 May–29 Sep 93; imperial yacht escort 30 Jun–30 Sep 94; fishery protection 19 Mar–27 Aug 95; Manoeuvre Fleet 28 Aug–24 Sep 95; fishery protection/engineer & stoker TS 18 Mar–4 Oct 96; harbour service 3 May 03.

Comet

Trials only.

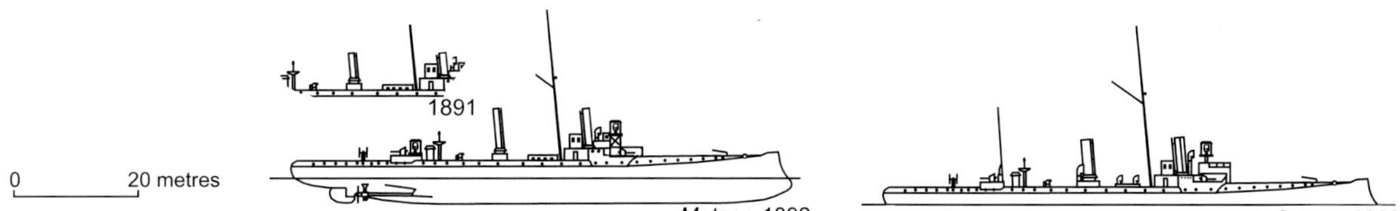

Meteor 1892

Comet 1893

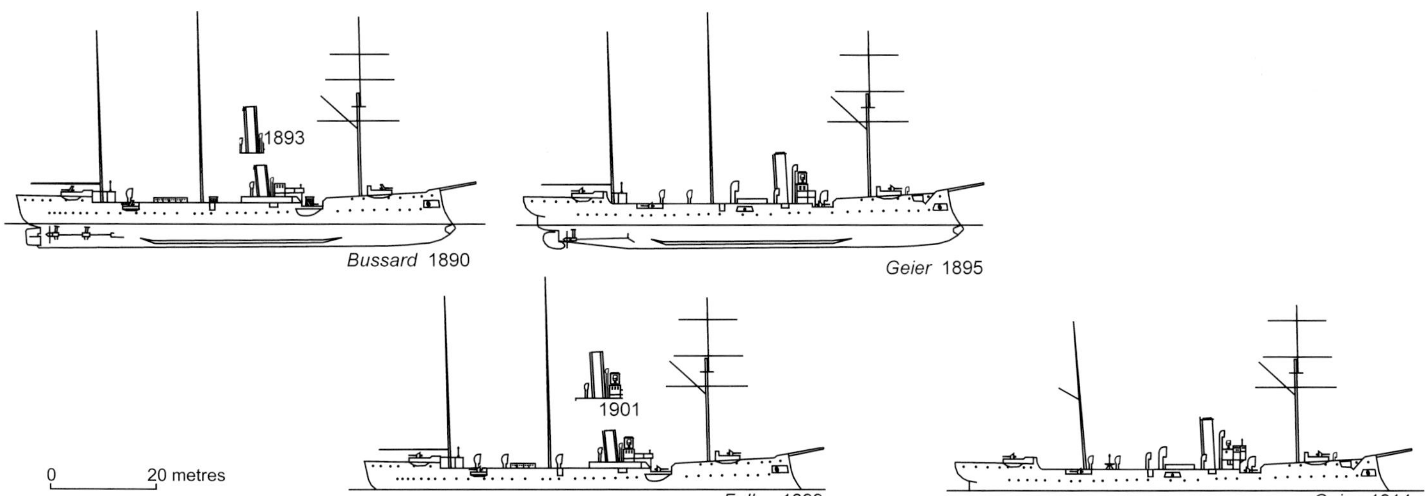

Bussard 1890

Geier 1895

Falke 1899

Geier 1914

Bussard

Overseas 1 May 91–20 Apr 99; refit Danzig; overseas 26 Jun 00–12 Mar 10.

Falke

Overseas 16 Oct 92–3 Nov 99; refit Danzig; overseas 2 Oct 01–20 Apr 07.

Seeadler

Overseas 15 Mar 93–9 Jul 98; refit Danzig; overseas 3 Oct 99–30 Mar 14.

Condor

Africa 2 Oct 94–23 Mar 01; overseas 1 Apr 03–30 Mar 14.

Cormoran

Overseas 2 Oct 94–23 Sep 03; refit; overseas 1 May 09–6 Aug 14 (decommissioned & stripped).

Geier

Overseas 1 Dec 97–29 Mar 05; refit 1909/10; overseas 28 Apr 11 until interned Honolulu 7 Nov 14.

Gefion (ii)

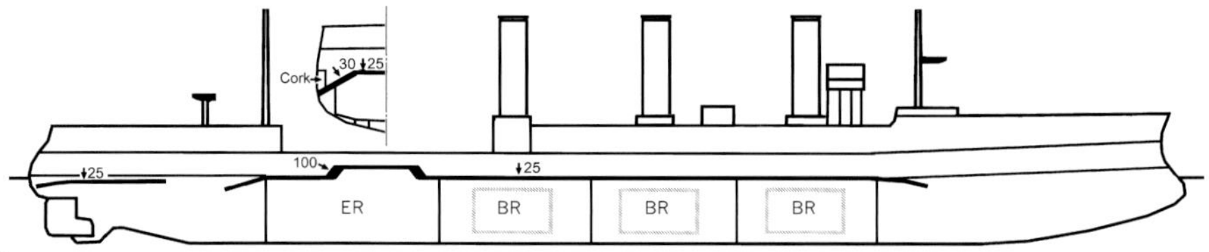

CRUISER-CORVETTE; 1893: III. CLASS CRUISER; 1899: SMALL CRUISER

Displacement: 3,746 (design), 4,275 (full load) tonnes.
Dimensions: 109.2 (wl), 110.4 (oa) x 13.2 x 6.5 metres.
Machinery: Six cylindrical boilers; two shafts; 3-cyl reciprocating (VTE), IHP 9,000 = 19 knots; coal 400/860 tonnes; range 3,500nm @ 12 knots.
Armament: Ten 10.5cm/35 QL, six 5cm/40 QL guns; two 45cm AW TT.
Protection: Deck 25-0-25mm/30mm-0; coaming 40mm; ER glacis 100mm.
Complement: 13+289.

Name	Prov name	Estimates (Programme)	Builder	Laid down	Launch	Comm	Fate
Gefion (ii) = *Adolf Sommerfeld*	*Cruiser-corvette/ III. Class cruiser J*	1890/91 (Oct 20)	Schichau (Danzig)	28 Mar 92	31 May 93	27 Jun 94	Stricken 5 Nov 19; sold Norddeutsche Tiefbaugesellschaft (Berlin) 1919; sold Danziger Hoch- & Tiefbau (Danzig) 1919 (freighter); BU Danzig or Hamburg 1923.

Home 5 Jun 95–22 Sep 97; refit Kiel; Far East 16 Dec 97–1 Oct 01; refit Wilhelmshaven 1901–4; laid up; accommodation ship Danzig 1916.

Hela

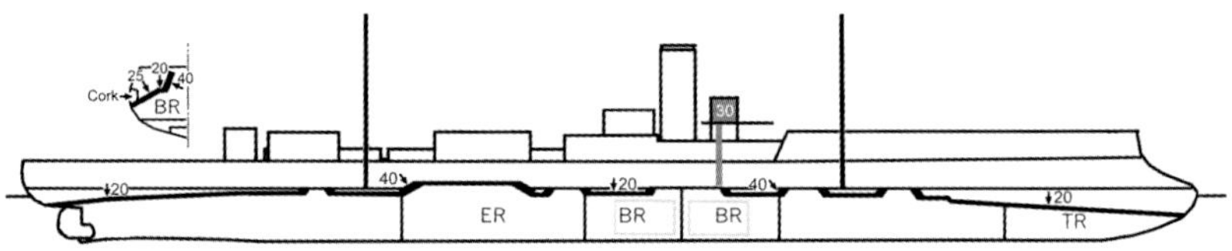

AVISO; 1899: SMALL CRUISER

Displacement: 2,027 (design), 2,082 (full load) tonnes.
Dimensions: 104.6 (wl), 105.0 (oa) x 11.0 x 4.6 metres.
Machinery: Six locomotive (1905: eight Navy) boilers; two shafts; 3-cyl reciprocating (VTE), IHP 6,000 = 20 knots; coal 340 (1906: 412) tonnes; range 3,000nm @ 12 knots.
Armament: Four (1910: two; Aug 14: three) 8.8cm/30 QL, six (1910: four) 5cm/40 QL guns; three 45cm (2 x AW, 1 x UW) TT.
Protection: Deck 20mm/25mm; coaming 40mm; CT 30mm (sides).
Complement: 7+171 (1906: 8/187).

Name	Prov name	Estimates	Builder	Laid down	Launch	Comm	Fate
Hela	*Aviso H*	1893/94	AG Weser (Bremen)	Dec 93	28 May 95	3 May 96	Torpedoed HMS/M *E9* Heligoland Bight (54° 03' N, 07° 55' E) 13 Sep 14.

I. Squadron 10 Mar 98–Jun 00; Far East 9 Jul 00–11 Aug 01; home Aug 01–25 Apr 03; refit Danzig to 1906/1910; fleet tender 1 Oct 10–Aug 14; IV. SG Aug 14 to loss.

Gazelle class (first group)

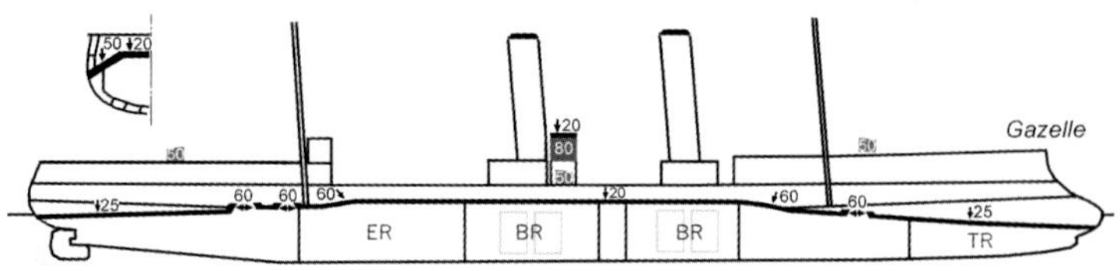

SMALL CRUISER

Displacement: 2,643 (design), 2,963 (full load) tonnes.
Dimensions: 104.4 (wl), 105.0 (oa) x 11.8 x 5.5 metres.
Machinery: Eight Niclausse (1907: Navy) boilers; two shafts;
4-cyl reciprocating (VTE), IHP 6,000 = 19.5 knots; coal 300/500 tonnes; range 3,570nm @ 10 knots.
Armament: Ten 10.5cm/40 QL guns; fourteen 3.7cm MG (removed 1912); three (1 x UW, 2 x AW) 45 cm TT; 1916 disarmed.
Protection: Deck 25-20-25mm/50mm; coaming 60mm; CT 20mm (roof)-70mm (sides); shields 50mm.
Complement: 12+423.

Name	Prov name	Estimates	Builder	Laid down	Launch	Comm	Fate
Gazelle (ii)	*IV. class cruiser G*	1896/97	Germania (Kiel)	Apr 97	31 Mar 98	23 Nov 98	Stricken 28 Aug 20; BU Wilhelmshaven.

West Indies Feb 02–03 Aug 04; reboilered Danzig 1905–07; laid up 1907–14; Baltic 4 Aug 14; mined off Cape Arcona 25 Jan 15; decommissioned 22 Feb 15; mine hulk Cuxhaven/Wilhelmshaven 1916.

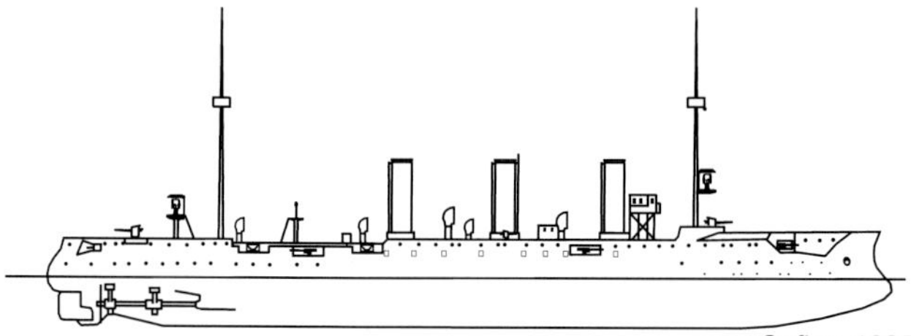

Gefion 1895

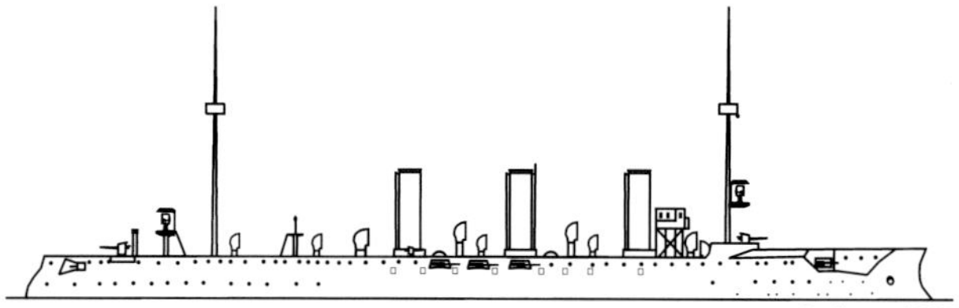

Gefion 1905

0 20 metres

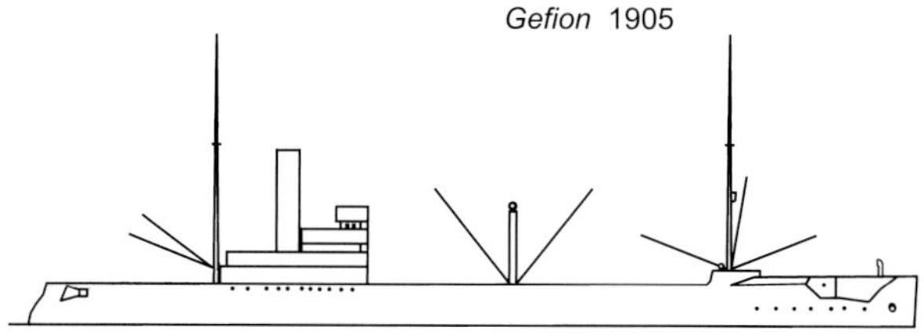

Adolf Sommerfeld (ex-*Gefion*) 1921

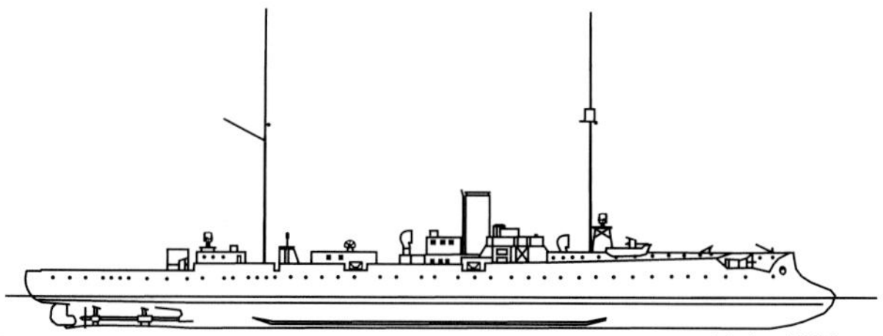

0 20 metres

Hela 1899

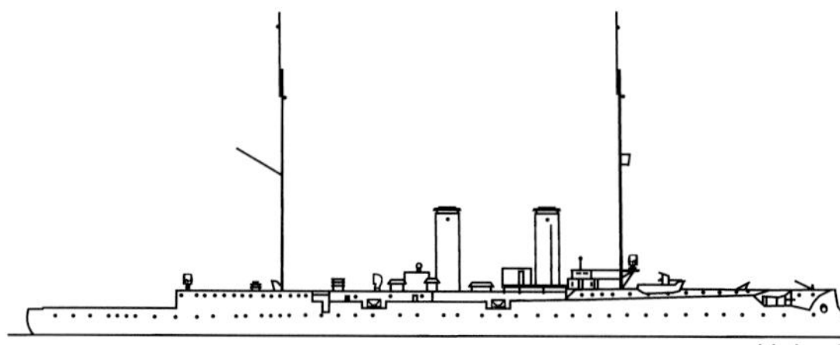

Hela 1914

Gazelle class (second group)

SMALL CRUISER

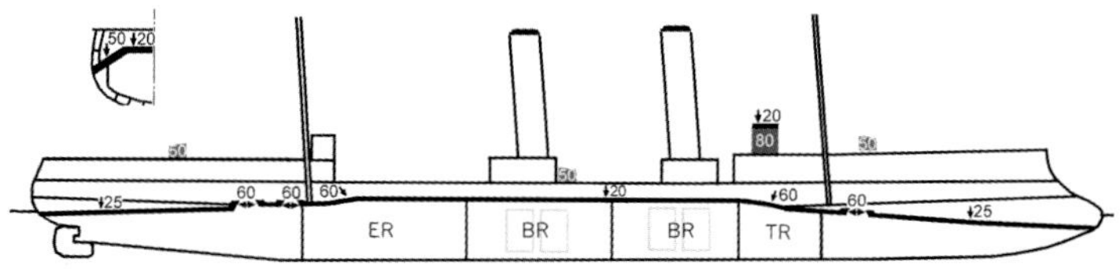

Displacement: 2,643 (design), 2,963 (full load) tonnes.
Dimensions: 104.4 (wl), 105.0 (oa) x 11.8 x 5.5 metres.
Machinery: Eight Thornycroft boilers; two shafts; 4-cyl reciprocating (VTE), IHP 8,000 = 21.5 knots; coal 300/500 tonnes; range 3,570nm @ 10 knots.
Armament: Ten 10.5cm/40 QL guns; fourteen 3.7cm MG (removed 1912); two (2 x UW) 45 cm TT; 1925 – six 8.4cm/55 guns; 1943 – six 8.4cm/55, four 4.7cm AA, thirty 2cm AA guns.
Protection: Deck 25-20-25mm/50mm; coaming 60mm; CT 20mm (roof)-70mm (sides); shields 50mm.
Complement: 12+423.

Name	Prov name	Estimates	Builder	Laid down	Launch	Comm	Fate
Niobe (ii) = *Dalmacija* (1925) = *Cattaro* (Apr 41) = *Niobe* (Sep 43)	*Small Cruiser B*	1898/99	AG Weser (Bremen)	30 Aug 98	18 Jul 99	25 Jan 00	Stricken 26 Jun 25; YU; IT 17 Apr 41; GE 11 Sep 43 (commission 8 Nov 43); stranded Silba Island (44° 21' N, 14° 42' E) 19 Dec 43; torpedoed HM *MTB226* & *MTB298* 22 Dec 43; BU 1947–49.

I. TB Flotilla 11 Apr 01–28 Feb 03; I. SG 1 Mar 03–28 Sep 04; Far East 19 Jun 06–31 Mar 09; laid up 1909–14; cost defence Jade/Weser 2 Aug 14–Sep 15; HQ ship 8 Sep 15–3 Feb 19.

Gazelle class (third group)

SMALL CRUISERS

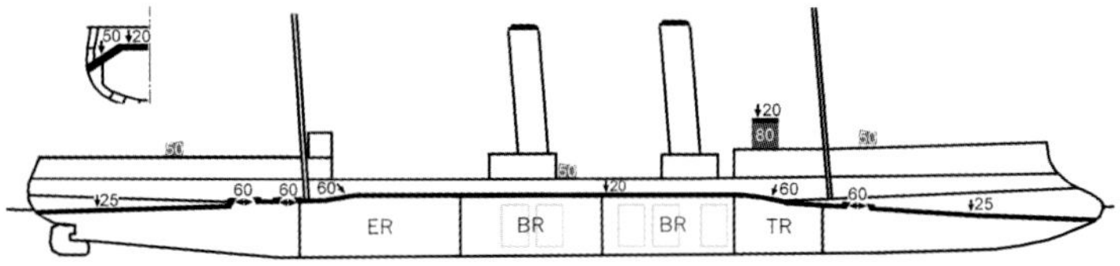

Displacement: 2,659 (design), 2,972–3,017 (full load) tonnes.
Amazone 1923, *Nymphe* 1925 – 2,654 (design), 3,139 (full load) tonnes.

Dimensions: 104.1 (wl), 105.1 (oa) x 11.8 x 5.4 metres.
Amazone 1923, *Nymphe* 1925 – 104.4 (wl), 108.7 (oa) x 11.8 x 5.4 metres.

Machinery: Five (*Nymphe*)/nine (others) Navy boilers; two shafts; 4-cyl (*Ariadne*, *Medusa* & *Amazone* 3-cyl) reciprocating (VTE), IHP 8,000 = 21.5 knots; coal 380/560 tonnes; range 3,560nm @ 12 knots (others).

Armament: Ten 10.5cm/40 QL guns; fourteen 3.7cm Mk (removed 1912); two (2 x UW) 45 cm TT.
Nymphe 1907–09 – six 10.5cm/40 QL, four 8.8cm QL, two 5.2in QL guns.
Medusa 1916 – ten 10.5cm/40 QL guns.
Thetis 1917 – nine 10.5cm/45 QL guns.
Others 1916 – disarmed.
Thetis 1922, *Amazone* 1923, *Nymphe* 1925 – ten 10.5cm/45 QL guns; two 50cm AW TT.
Medusa 1940 – Four (1941: five, 1943: six) 10.5cm/45 AA, one, later two, 3.7cm AA, four 2cm AA guns.

Protection: Deck 25-20-25mm/50mm; coaming 80mm (*Nymphe*: 60mm); CT 20mm (roof)-80mm (sides)(*Nymphe: 70mm*); shields 50mm.

Complement: 12+423.

Name	Prov name	Estimates	Builder	Laid down	Launch	Comm	Fate
Nymphe (ii)	*Small Cruiser A*	1898/99	Germania (Kiel)	Nov 98	21 Nov 99	20 Sep 00	Stricken 31 Mar 31; sold 29 Aug 31 (61,500M); BU Hamburg 1932.
Thetis (ii)	*Small Cruiser C*	1899/00	Danzig DYd	2 Sep 99	3 Jul 00	14 Sep 01	Stricken 27 Mar 29; sold Blohm & Voss; resold Unterelbe AG; BU Wewelsfleth 1930.
Ariadne (ii)	*Small Cruiser D*	1899/00	AG Weser (Bremen)	14 Dec 99	10 Aug 00	18 May 01	Gunfire UK surface vessels N of Norderney (54° 08' 36" N, 06° 58' 57" E) 28 Aug 14.
Medusa (ii)	*Small Cruiser E*	1900	AG Weser (Bremen)	22 Jun 00	5 Dec 00	26 Jul 01	Stricken 27 Mar 29; accommodation ship; AA battery Jul 40; decommissioned Wilhelmshaven 19 April 45; BU 1948–50.
Amazone (ii)	*Small Cruiser F*	1900	Germania (Kiel)	1 Dec 99	6 Oct 00	15 Nov 01	Stricken 31 Mar 31; accommodation hulk Kiel; to US 1945; accommodation ship Bremen 1946–54; BU Hamburg 1954.

Nymphe
Imperial yacht escort/Torpedo Inspectorate/TS Jan 01–19 Sep 07; light gunnery TS 23 May 08–15 Feb 09; laid up 1909–14; leader, Elbe Port Flotilla 8 Aug 14–Aug 15; Torpedo Inspectorate 1 Sep 15–1 Nov 16; accommodation ship for Torpedo Inspectorate; rebuilt Wilhelmshaven Nov 22–Nov 24; fleet 30 Nov 24–16 Apr 29.

Thetis
Far East/East Africa 1 Dec 01–18 Jun 06; laid up 1906–14; Baltic 4 Aug 14–3 Sep 15; gunnery TS 19 Oct 17–19 Dec 18; fleet 2 Apr 22–30 Nov 28.

Ariadne
I. Squadron 22 Oct 02–Feb 03; Scouting Force 1 Mar 03–22 Sep 06; laid up 1906–14; Jade/Weser Port Flotilla 2 Aug 14 to loss.

Medusa
Scouting Force 1 Apr 03–Sep 07; light gunnery TS 15 Sep 07–23 May 08; laid up 1908–14; Elbe Port Flotilla 4 Aug 14–13 Sep 15; Baltic 1 Dec 15–18 Dec 16; tender to *König Wilhelm*, Flensburg-Mürwik; fleet 17 Jul 20–26 Sep 24.

Amazone
Fleet 21 Dec 01–Feb 03; Scouting Force 1 Mar 03–28 Sep 05; laid up 1905–14; Baltic 2 Aug 14–Mar 16; submarine target Mar 16–14 Mar 17; Torpedo-Inspectorate accommodation ship; rebuilt Wilhelmshaven 1921–23; fleet 1 Dec 23–15 Jan 30.

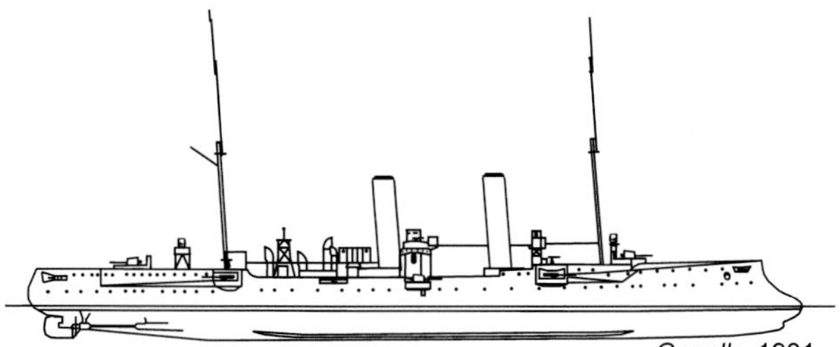

Gazelle 1901

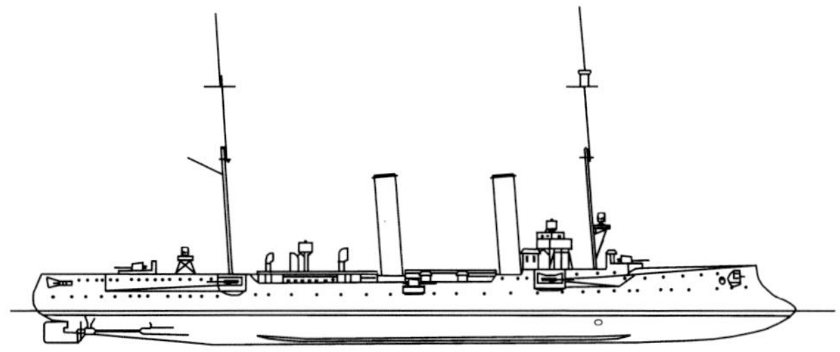

Nymphe 1914

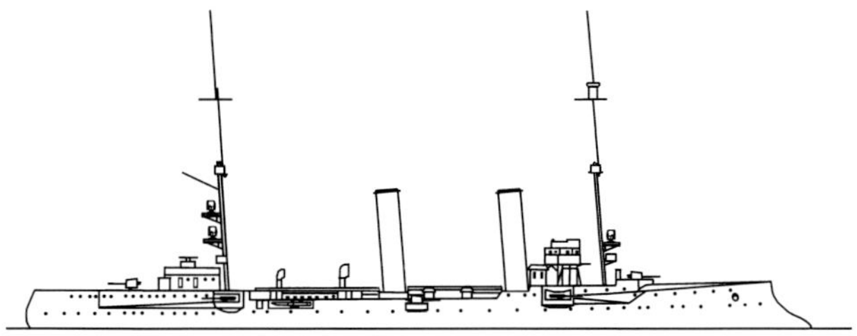

Thetis 1922

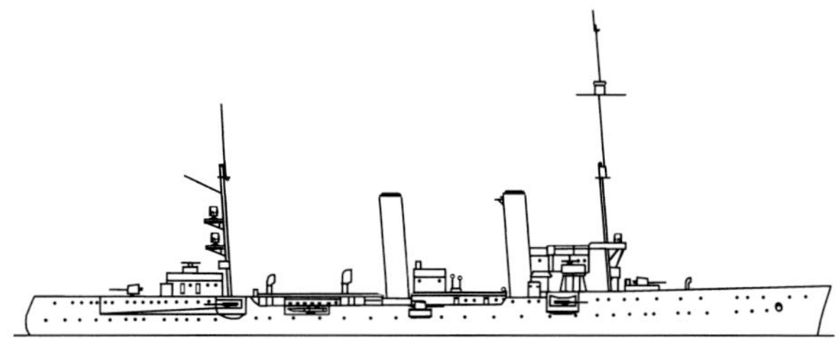

Nymphe 1925

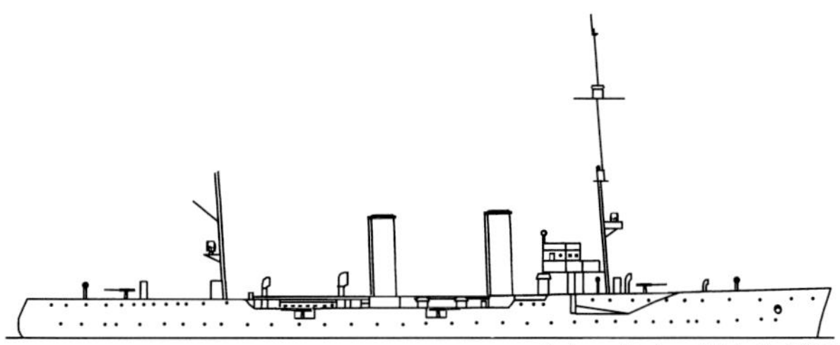

Dalmacija (ex-*Niobe*) 1928

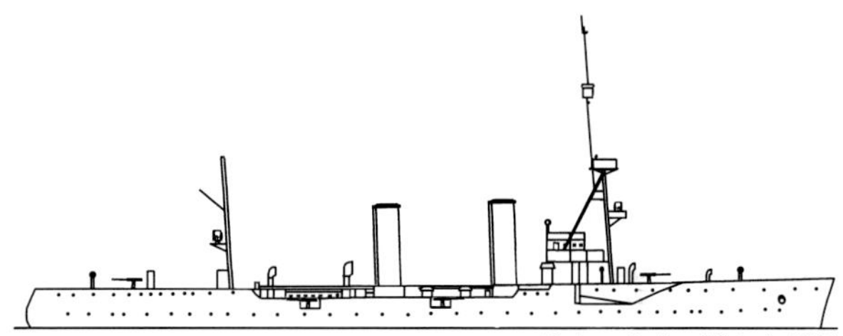

Dalmacija (ex-*Niobe*) 1931

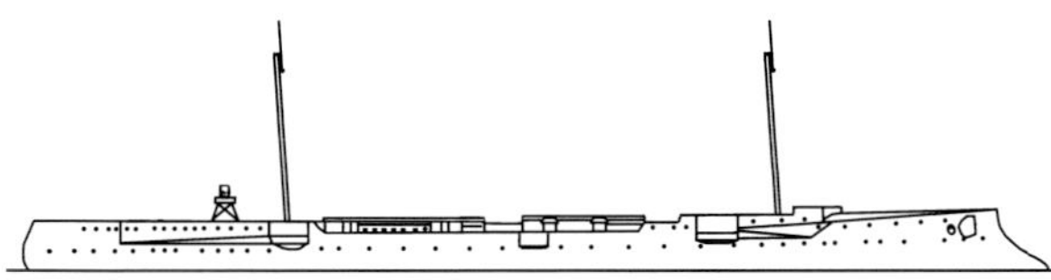

Medusa 1937

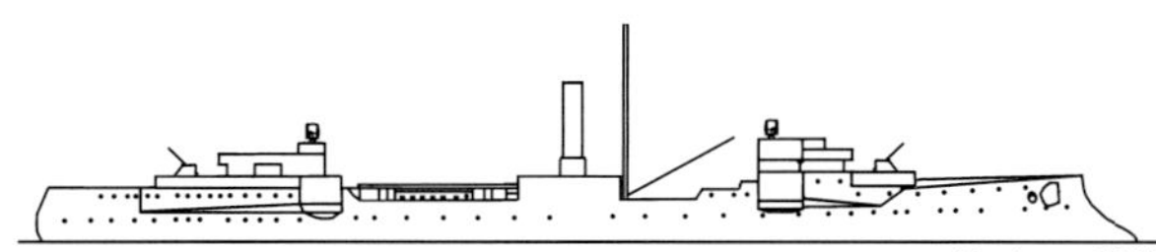

Medusa 1940

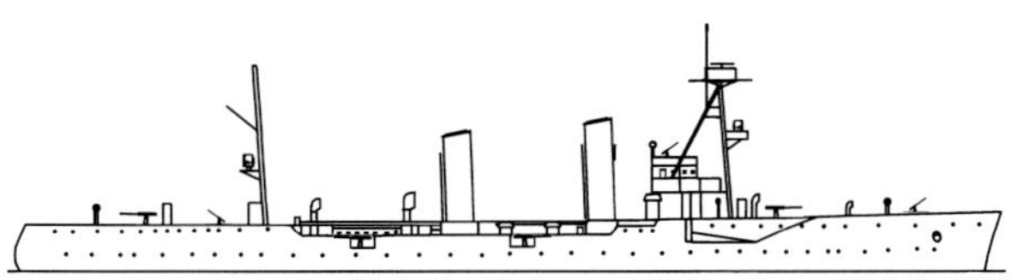

Niobe (ex-*Cattaro*, ex-*Dalmacija*, ex-*Niobe*) 1943

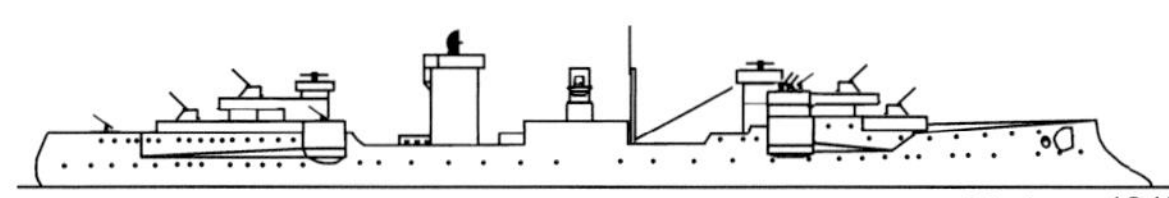

Medusa 1945

0 20 metres

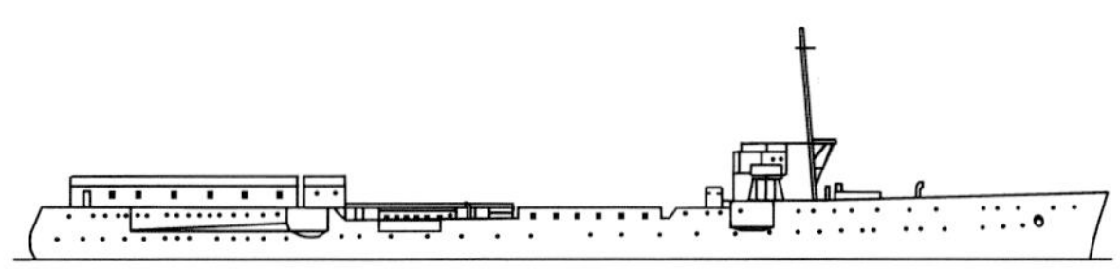

Amazone 1946

Frauenlob class

SMALL CRUISER

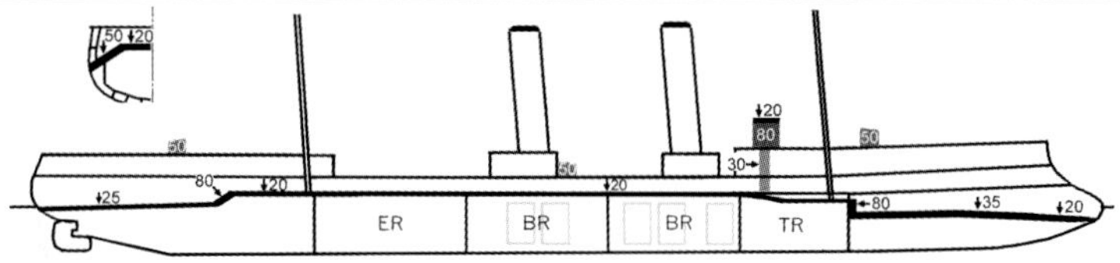

Displacement: 2,706 (design), 3,112–3,158 (full load) tonnes.
Dimensions: 104.4 (wl), 105.0 (oa) x 12.3 x 5.6 metres.
Machinery: Nine Navy boilers; two shafts; 3-cyl reciprocating (VTE), IHP 8,000 = 21.5 knots; coal 380/700 tonnes; range 4,400nm @ 12 knots.
Armament: Ten (*Arcona* 1912–14: eight; *Frauenlob* 1913–14: eight) 10.5cm/40 QL guns; ten 3.7cm MG (removed 1912); two 45cm UW (*Arcona* 1916: 50cm AW) TT; *Arcona*, *Frauenlob* 1912–13: 200 mines.
Arcona 1940: four (1941: five, 1943: six) 10.5cm/45 AA, two 4cm AA, six 2cm AA guns.
Protection: Deck 25-20-35-25mm/50mm; coaming 80mm; CT 20mm (roof)-80mm (sides); shields 50mm.
Complement: 14+256.

Name	Prov name	Estimates	Builder	Laid down	Launch	Comm	Fate
Frauenlob (ii)	*Small Cruiser G*	1901	AG Weser (Bremen)	8 Jul 01	22 Mar 02	17 Feb 03	Torpedoed HMS *Southampton* North Sea 31 May 16.
Arcona (iii)	*Small Cruiser H*	1901	AG Weser (Bremen)	Jun 01	22 Apr 02	13 May 03	Stricken 15 Jan 30; accommodation ship; AA battery May 40; surrendered Brunsbüttel 3 May 45; BU Wilhelmshaven 1948–49.
Undine (ii)	*Small Cruiser J*	1901	Howaldt (Kiel)	28 Sep 01	11 Dec 02	5 Jan 04	Torpedoed HMS/M *E19* off Cape Arcona (54° 59' N, 13° 51' E) 7 Nov 15.

Frauenlob
I. Squadron 17 Feb 03; Scouting Force 1 Mar 03–19 Jan 08; refit 1912–13; IV. SG 2 Aug 14 to loss.

Arcona
Scouting Force 12 May 03–4 Apr 07; Far East 27 Aug 07–30 Mar 10; refit as minelayer 1911–12; Inspectorate of Coastal Artillery and Mining 31 Oct 12–Aug 14; Ems Coast Defence/Forward Defence Flotilla Aug 14–Nov 18; minesweeper depot ship Jan 19–19 Feb 20; refit; fleet 25 May 21–1 Dec 23.

Bremen class (first group)

SMALL CRUISERS

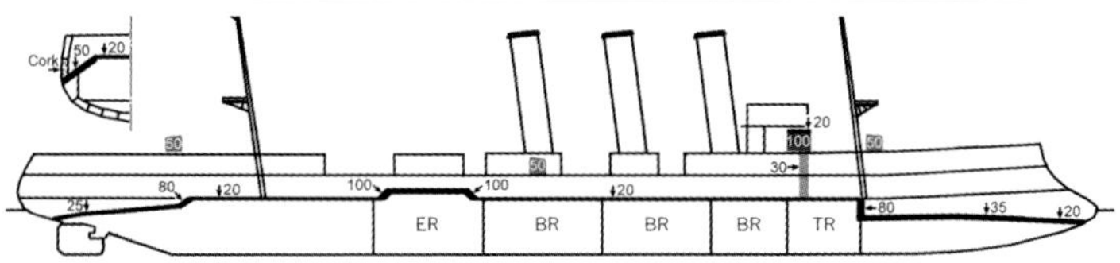

Displacement: 3,278 (design), 3,661–3,797 (full load) tonnes.
Dimensions: 110.6 (wl), 111.1 [*Berlin* 1922: 113.8] (oa) x 13.3 x 5.4–5.5 metres.
Machinery: Ten Navy boilers; two/four [*Lübeck*] shafts; 3-cyl reciprocating (VTE), IHP 10,000/Parsons turbines, SHP 11,500 [*Lübeck*] = 22.0/22.5 knots; coal 400/860 tonnes; range 4,270/3,800[*Lübeck*]nm @ 12 knots.
Armament: Ten 10.5cm/40 QL guns; ten 3.7cm MG (removed 1912); two 45cm UW TT.
Bremen & *Lübeck* 1915/16: two 15cm/45 QL, six 10.5cm/40 QL guns; two 45cm UW (*Bremen*)/two 50cm AW (*Lübeck*) TT.
Berlin & *München* 1916: disarmed.
Hamburg 1916: six 10.5cm/40 QL guns; 1917 disarmed.
Hamburg 1920: ten 10.5cm/45 QL guns; two 50cm AW TT.
Berlin 1922: eight 10.5cm/45 QL guns; two 50cm AW TT.
Protection: Deck 25-20-35-20mm/50mm; glacis 100mm; coaming 80mm; CT 20mm (roof)-100mm (sides); shields 50mm.
Complement: 14+274–287.

Name	Prov name	Estimates	Builder	Laid down	Launch	Comm	Fate
Bremen	*Small Cruiser L*	1902	AG Weser (Bremen)	1 Aug 02	9 Jul 03	19 May 04	Mined near Spon Bank (N Baltic – 57° 31' N, 20° 24' E) 17 Dec 15.
Berlin	*Ersatz-Zieten*	1902	Danzig DYd	Aug 02	22 Sep 03	4 Apr 05	Stricken 1 Oct 35; accommodation ship; scuttled Skagerrak (58° 08' 09" N, 10° 48' 51" E) 30 May 46.
Hamburg	*Small Cruiser K*	1902	AG Vulcan (Stettin)	1 Aug 02	25 Jul 03	8 Mar 04	Stricken 31 Mar 31; accommodation ship; bombed Hamburg 1944; BU 1949–56.
München = *Q* (1920)	*Small Cruiser M*	1903	AG Weser (Bremen)	18 Aug 03	30 Apr 04	10 Jan 05	Stricken 5 Nov 19; surrendered Rosyth 5 Jul 20; to UK Sep 20; expended as torpedo target Firth of Forth (56° 07' 00" N, 02° 45' 50" W) 28 Oct 21.
Lübeck = *P* (1920)	*Ersatz-Mercur*	1903	AG Vulcan (Stettin)	12 May 03	26 Mar 04	26 Apr 05	Stricken 5 Nov 19; surrendered Rosyth 3 Sep 20; to UK Sep 20; sold Anders J. Anderson 12 Mar 21 (£4,600); resold; BU Rødbyhavn.

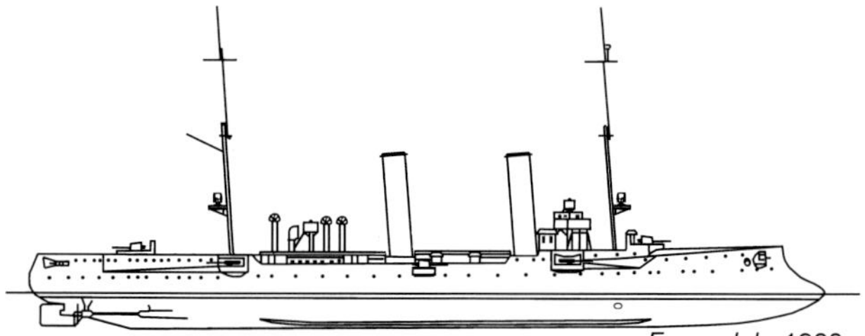
Frauenlob 1903

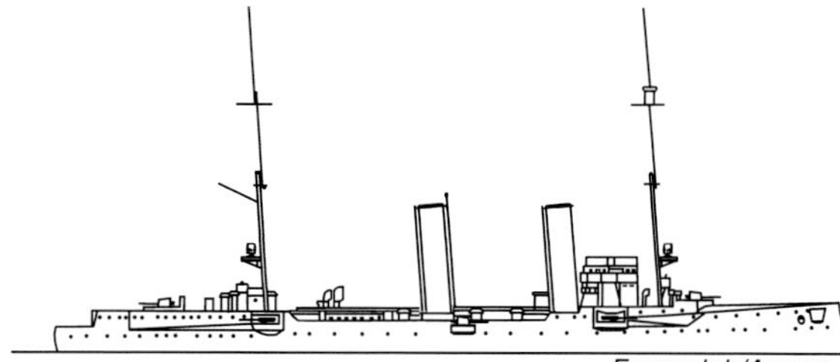
Frauenlob/Arcona 1914

Frauenlob 1916

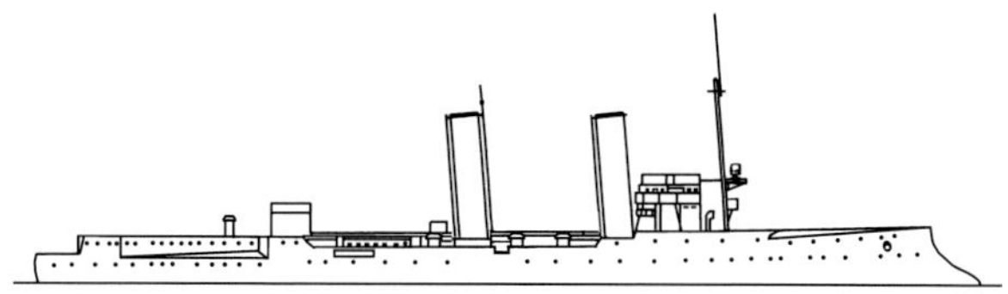
Arcona 1936

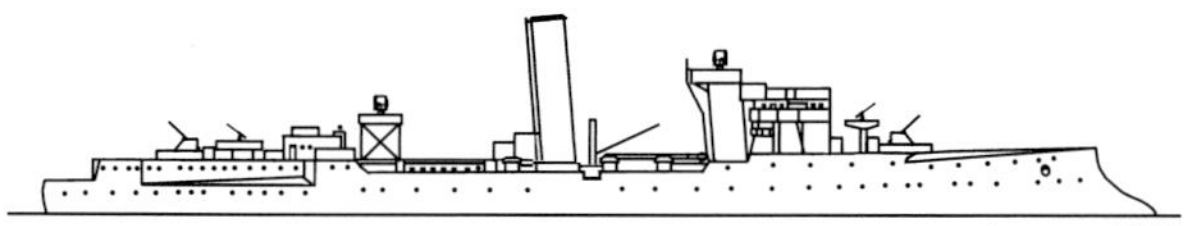
Arcona 1940

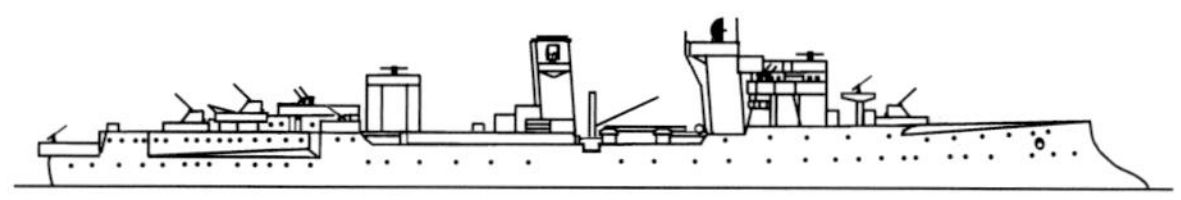
Arcona 1945

0 20 metres

Undine

Gunnery TS (vice *Carola*) 10 Jan 05–12 Jul 12; Baltic 4 Aug 14 to loss.

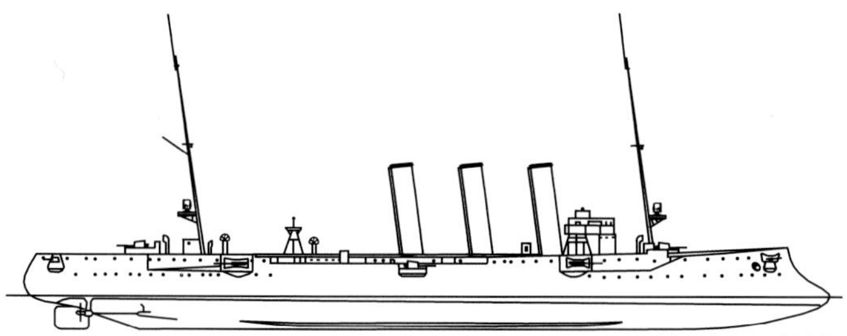
Hamburg 1904

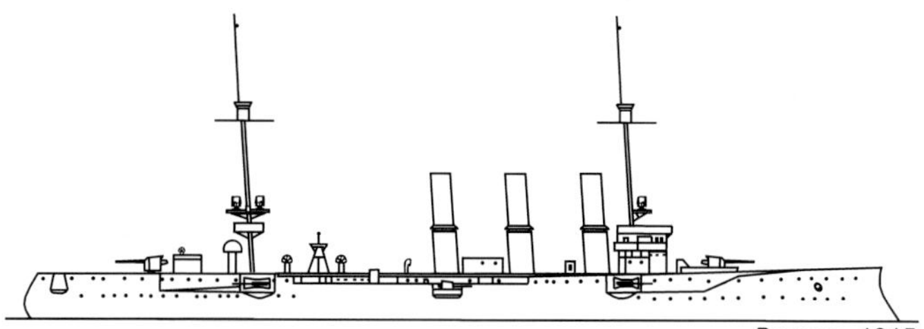
Bremen 1915

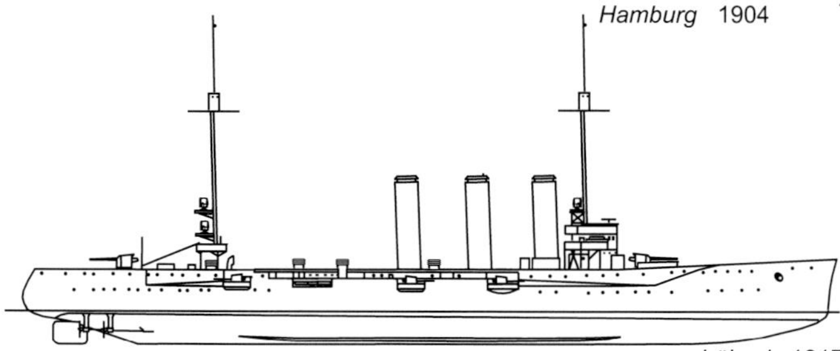
Lübeck 1917

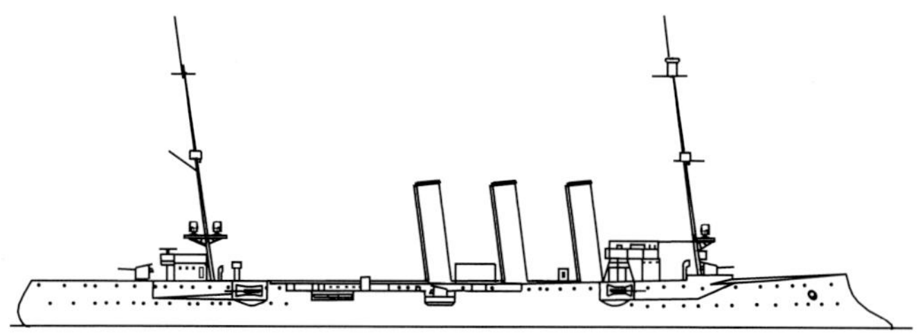
Hamburg 1922

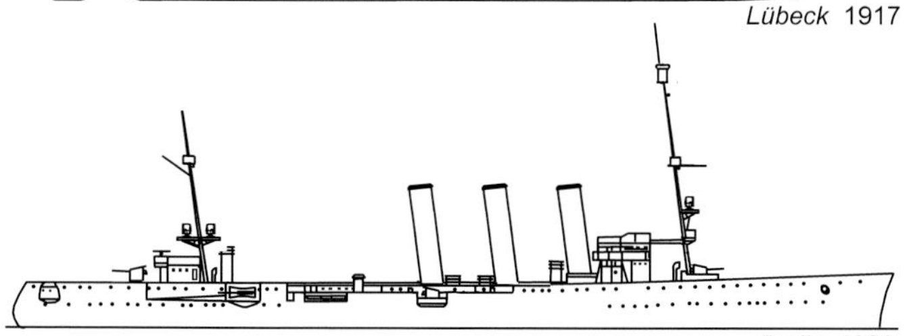
Berlin 1928

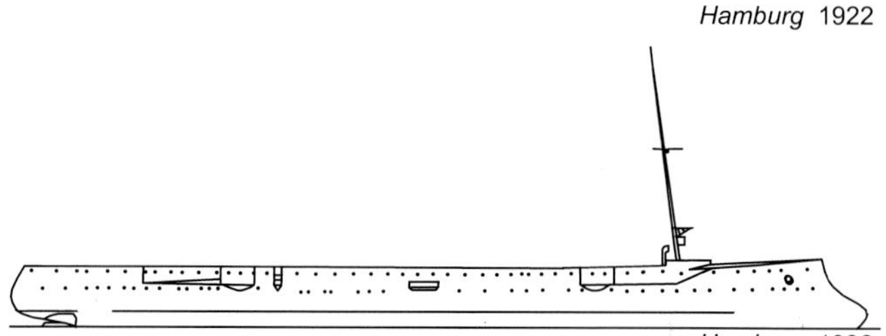
Hamburg 1936

Bremen

Americas 27 Aug 04–27 Mar 14; refit Apr 14–May 15; Baltic 27 May 15 to loss.

Continued overleaf

Bremen class continued

Berlin
Home 15 June 05–29 Oct 12; Baltic 17 Aug 14–Oct 15; IV. SG 24 Oct 15–Dec 16; II. SG Dec 16–14 Jan 17; HQ ship Kiel 26 Apr 18–Jun 21; rebuilt Wilhelmshaven 1921–22; cadet TS 2 Jul 22–15 Oct 25; home Oct 25–Sep 27; cadet TS 1 Oct 27–7 Mar 29.

Hamburg
Imperial yacht escort Jun–Aug 04; Scouting Force 28 Sep 04–15 Sep 09; submarine flagship (I. SMF)/HQ ship 2 Jul 12–3 Jan 19; TB HQ ship Feb 19–16 Aug 19; fleet 7 Sep 20–Mar 25; cadet TS 1 Apr 25–30 Jun 27.

München
Torpedo Inspectorate 10 Jan 05–Aug 14; III/IV. SG 2 Aug 14–15 Nov 16 (torpedoed HMS/M *E38* 19 Oct 16); II. Reserve; accommodation ship for Sound guardships 1918.

Lübeck
Scouting Force 22 Sep 06–10 Oct 11; Baltic 12 Aug 14–28 Jan 16 (mined 13 Jan 16); rebuilt Stettin Feb–Dec 16; submarine TS/target 17 Mar 17–8 Mar 18.

Königsberg class (first group)

SMALL CRUISER

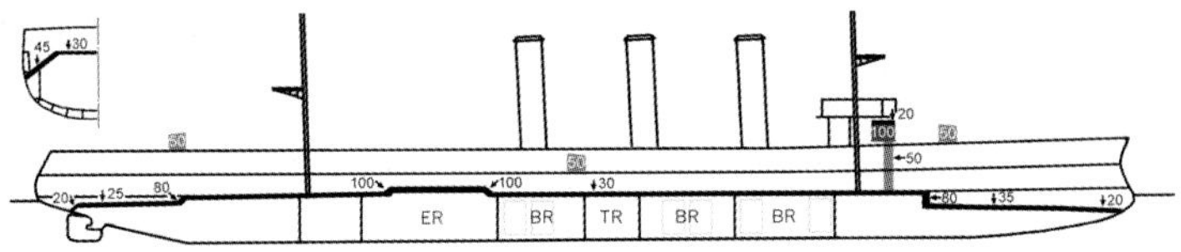

Displacement: 3,390 (design), 3,814 (full load) tonnes.
Dimensions: 114.8 (wl), 115.3 (oa) x 13.2 x 5.3 metres.
Machinery: Eleven Navy boilers; two shafts; 3-cyl reciprocating (VTE), IHP 13,200 = 23 knots; coal 400/820 tonnes; range 5,750nm @ 12 knots.
Armament: Ten 10.5cm/40 QL, eight 5.2cm/55 QL (removed 1911) guns; two 45cm UW TT.
Protection: Deck 25-20-35-20mm/50mm; glacis 100mm; coaming 80mm; CT 20mm (roof)-100mm (sides); shields 50mm.
Complement: 14+308.

Name	Prov name	Estimates	Builder	Laid down	Launch	Comm	Fate
Königsberg (i)	*Ersatz-Meteor*	1904	Kiel DYd	12 Jan 05	12 Dec 05	6 Apr 07	Gunfire HMS *Severn* & *Mersey* Rufiji Delta (07° 52' 06" S, 39° 14' 24" E) 11 Jul 15; partly BU to 1966.

Scouting Force 5 Nov 07–10 Jun 11; fleet 22 Jan–19 Jun 13; East Africa 1 Apr 14 to loss.

Königsberg 1910

Königsberg class (second group)

SMALL CRUISER

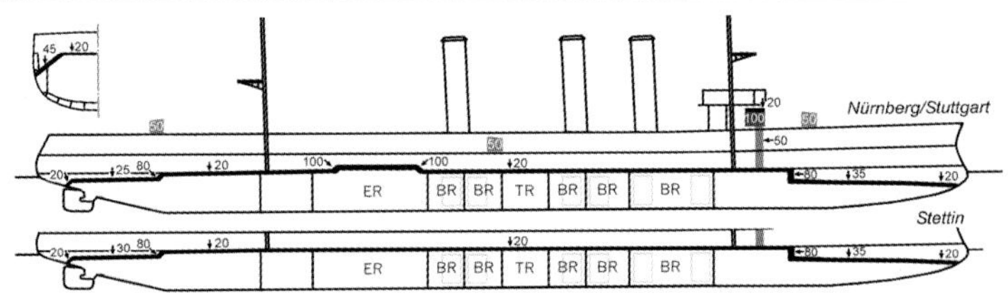

Displacement: 3,469 (design), 3,822–4,002 (full load) tonnes.
Dimensions: 116.8 (wl), 117.4 (oa) x 13.3 x 5.3 metres.
Machinery: Eleven Navy boilers; two/four [*Stettin*] shafts; 3-cyl reciprocating (VTE), IHP 13,200/Parsons turbines, SHP 13,500 [*Stettin*] = 23.0/24 knots; coal 400/860 tonnes; range 4,120nm @ 12 knots.
Armament: Ten 10.5cm/40 QL, eight 5.2cm/55 (removed 1912) guns; two 45cm UW TT. *Stuttgart* 1918: four 10.5cm/40 QL, two 8.8cm/45 AA guns; two 45cm UW TT; three aircraft.
Protection: Deck 25-20-35-20mm/50mm (*Stettin*: 30-20-35-20mm/50mm); glacis 100mm; coaming 80mm; CT 20mm (roof)–100mm (sides); shields 50mm.
Complement: 14+308.

Name	Prov name	Estimates	Builder	Laid down	Launch	Comm	Fate
Nürnberg (i)	*Ersatz-Blitz*	1905	Kiel DYd	16 Jan 06	28 Aug 06	10 Apr 08	Gunfire HMS *Kent* off Falklands (53° 28' S, 55° 04' W) 8 Dec 14.
Stettin = *T* (1920)	*Ersatz-Wacht*	1905	AG Vulcan (Stettin)	22 Mar 06	7 Mar 07	29 Oct 07	Stricken 5 Nov 19; surrendered Rosyth 15 Sep 20; to UK Sep 20; sold Petersen & Albeck 15 Feb 21 (£6,350); BU Copenhagen.
Stuttgart = *S* (1920)	*Small Cruiser O*	1905	Danzig DYd	1 Nov 05	22 Sep 06	1 Feb 08	Stricken 5 Nov 19; surrendered Cherbourg 20 Jul 20; to UK Sep 20; sold Channel Shipbreaking Company (Teignmouth) 22 Oct 20 (£9,500); BU Dartmouth to 1922.

Bremen class (second group)

SMALL CRUISERS

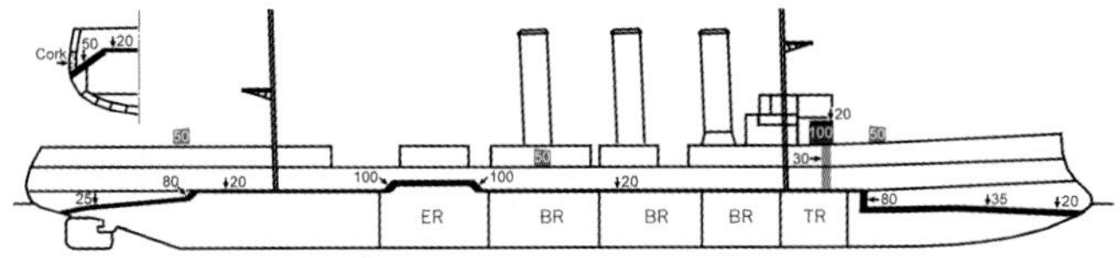

Displacement: 3,278 (design), 3,783–3,816 (full load) tonnes.
Dimensions: 110.6 (wl), 111.1 (oa) x 13.3 x 5.6 metres.
Machinery: Ten Navy boilers; two shafts; 3-cyl reciprocating (VTE), IHP 10,000 = 22 knots; coal 400/860 tonnes; range 4,690nm @ 12 knots.
Armament: Ten 10.5cm/40 QL guns; ten 3.7cm MG (removed 1912); two 45cm UW TT.
Protection: Deck 25-20-35-20mm/50mm; glacis 100mm; coaming 80mm; CT 20mm (roof)-100mm (sides); shields 50mm.
Complement: 14+287.

Name	Prov name	Estimates	Builder	Laid down	Launch	Comm	Fate
Danzig (ii) = *R* (1920)	*Ersatz-Alexandrine*	1904	Danzig DYd	23 Jul 04	23 Sep 05	1 Feb 07	Stricken 5 Nov 19; surrendered Rosyth 15 Sep 20; to UK; sold George Clarkson 17 Feb 21 (£5,525); BU Whitby 1921–28.
Leipzig (ii)	*Small Cruiser N*	1904	AG Weser (Bremen)	12 Jul 04	21 Mar 05	20 Apr 06	Gunfire HMS *Cornwall* & *Glasgow* off Falklands (53° 55' S, 55° 55' W) 8 Dec 14.

Danzig
Scouting Force Apr 08–Jun 10; gunnery TS 5 Jun 10–Aug 14; III/IV. SG 1 Aug–11 Nov 15; Baltic 13 Nov–16 Dec 15; refit Bremen 27 Jan–12 Jul 16; IV. SG 4 Aug–11 Dec 16; II. SG 11 Dec 16–10 June 17; submarine target ship 11 Jun 17–25 Mar 18.

Leipzig
Far East/Pacific 19 Aug 06 to loss.

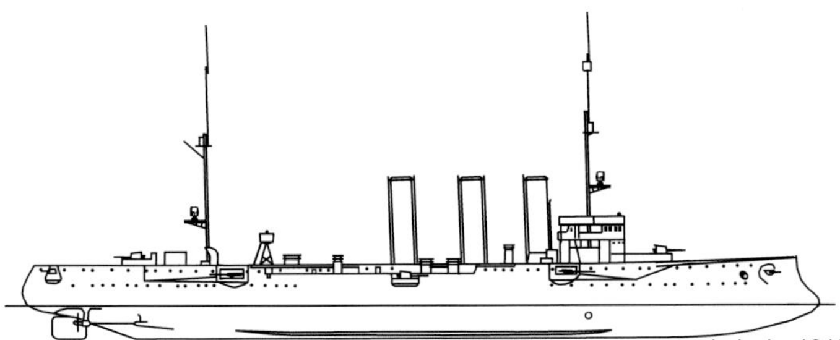

Leipzig 1910

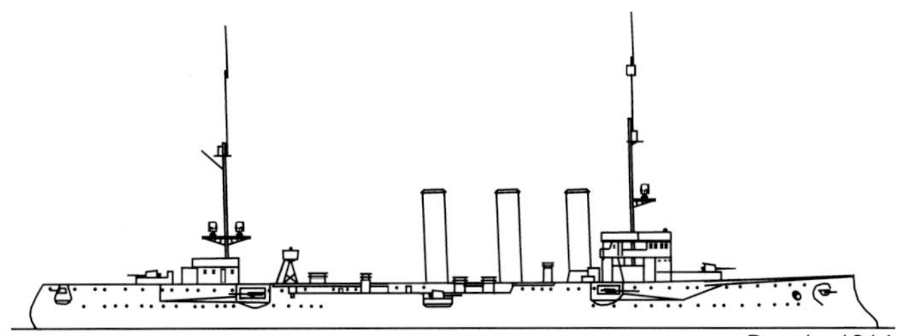

Danzig 1914

0 20 metres

Nürnberg
Far East/Pacific 1 Feb 10 to loss.

Stettin
Scouting Force 20 Jan 08–4 Feb 14; submarine flagship (II. SMF) 1 Jul 14–Jan 15; IV. SG 26 Jan 15–Aug 17; FO Baltic Defence 10 Sep–8 Dec 17; Submarine Inspectorate Feb–May 18; Minesweeping force 13 May–20 Jul 18; Submarine Inspectorate Jul–10 Dec 18.

Stuttgart
Gunnery TS 16 Feb 09–Aug 14; III/IV. SG 7 Aug 14–15 Dec 16; rebuilt as seaplane carrier Feb–May 18; fleet 16 May–17 Dec 18.

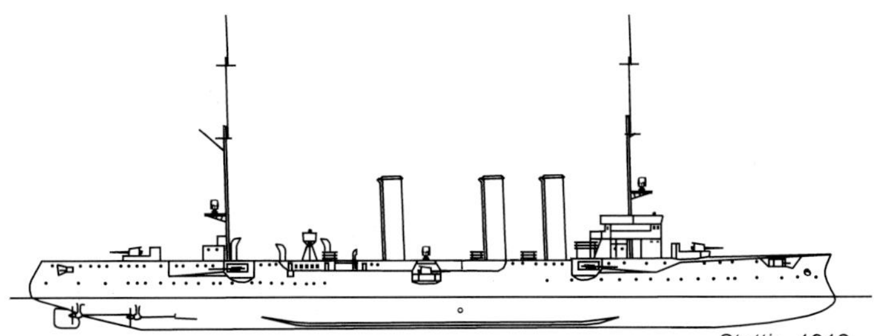

Stettin 1912

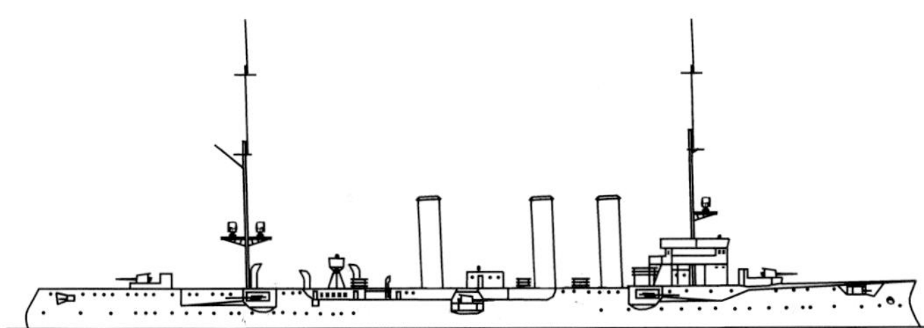

Nürnberg 1914

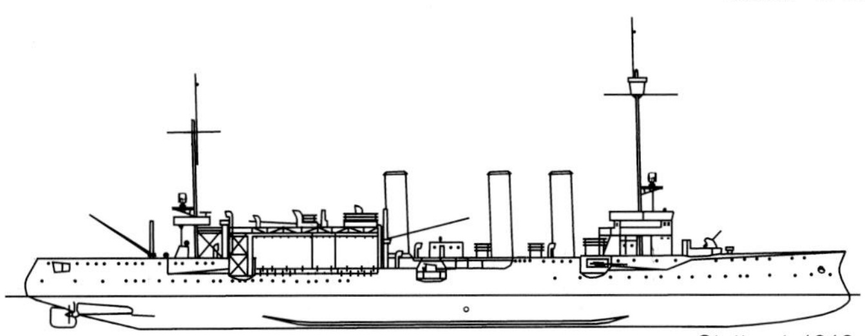

Stuttgart 1918

0 20 metres

Nautilus

MINE-STEAMER[1]

Displacement: 1,975 (design), 2,330 (full load) tonnes.
Dimensions: 90.2 (wl), 98.2 [1910: 100.9] (oa) x 11.2 x 4.5 metres.
Machinery: Four Navy boilers; two shafts; 3-cyl reciprocating (VTE), IHP 6,600 = 20 knots; coal 200/490 tonnes; range 3,530nm @ 9 knots.
Armament: Eight 8.8cm/35 QL (1918: four 2cm AA) guns; 200 mines.
Complement: 10+191.

Name	Prov name	Estimates	Builder	Laid down	Launch	Comm	Fate
Nautilus = *Hulk I* (1 Jan 23) = *Hulk A* (26 Feb 23)	*Mine-steamer A*	1905	AG Weser (Bremen)	19 Dec 05	20 Aug 06	19 Mar 07	Stricken 21 Mar 19; store hulk Kiel; sold Didia (Bremen) 1921; sold 18 Aug 28 (180,000M); BU Copenhagen.

Mine Experimental Commission 19 Mar 07–26 Oct 08; rebuilt Kiel 1909–10; fleet/Mine Experimental Commission 15 Jan 10–30 Oct 12; fleet 5 Jun 14–Apr 16; Baltic Apr 16–10 Dec 18.

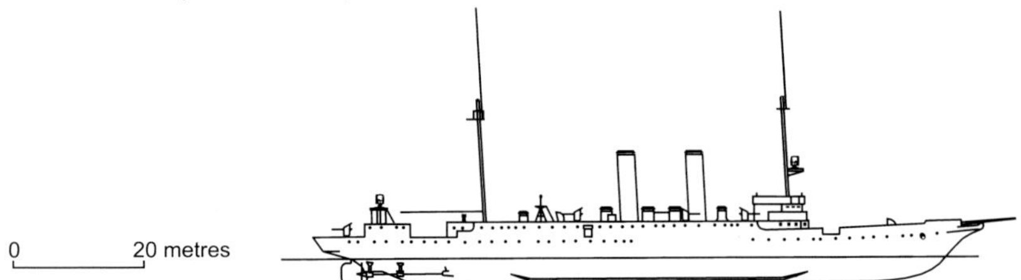

Nautilus 1907

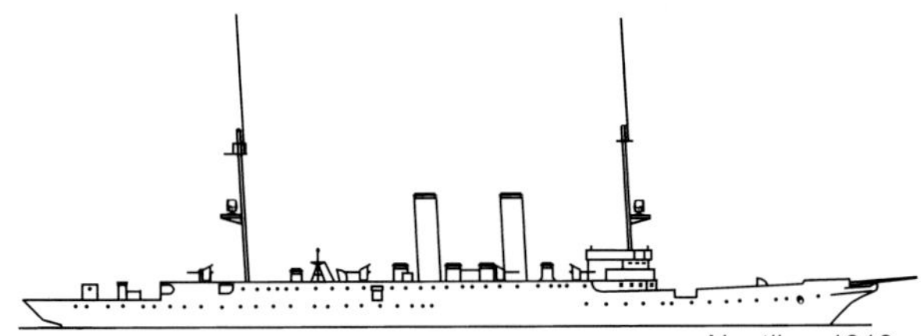
Nautilus 1910

[1] A reported reclassification of *Nautilus* and *Albatross* as 'mine cruisers' in 1914 cannot be verified (cf p 185 n1).

Dresden class

SMALL CRUISERS

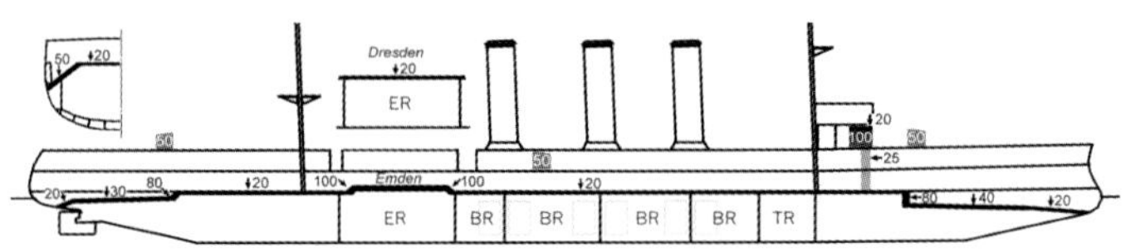

Displacement: 3,664 (design), 4,268 (full load) tonnes.
Dimensions: 117.9 (wl), 118.3 (oa) x 13.5 x 5.5 metres.
Machinery: Twelve Navy boilers; two [*Emden*]/four [*Dresden*] shafts; 3-cyl reciprocating (VTE), IHP 13,500 [*Emden*]/Parsons turbines, SHP 15,000 [*Dresden*] = 23.5/24 knots; coal 400/790–860 tonnes; range 3,760nm @ 12 knots [*Emden*]/3,600nm @ 14 knots.
Armament: Ten 10.5cm/40 QL, eight 5.2cm/55 QL (removed 1912) guns; two 45cm UW TT.
Protection: Deck 30-20-40-20mm/50mm; glacis 100mm (only *Emden*); coaming 80mm; CT 20mm (roof)-100mm (sides); shields 50mm.
Complement: 18+343.

Name	Prov name	Estimates	Builder	Laid down	Launch	Comm	Fate
Dresden (i)	*Ersatz-Comet*	1906	Blohm & Voss (Hamburg)	2 Mar 07	5 Oct 07	14 Nov 08	Scuttled Más a Tierra (33° 36' 6" S, 78° 49' 30" W) 14 Mar 15 after gunfire HMS *Kent* & *Glasgow*.
Emden (i)	*Ersatz-Pfeil*	1906	Danzig DYd	1 Nov 06	26 May 08	10 Jul 09	Stranded Cocos Islands (11° 49' 60" S, 96° 49' 0" E) 9 Nov 14 after gunfire HMAS *Sydney*.

Dresden
Scouting Force 22 Oct 09–Apr 13; Mediterranean Division 6 Apr–29 Sep 13; Americas 27 Dec 13 to loss.

Emden
Overseas 1 Apr 10 to loss.

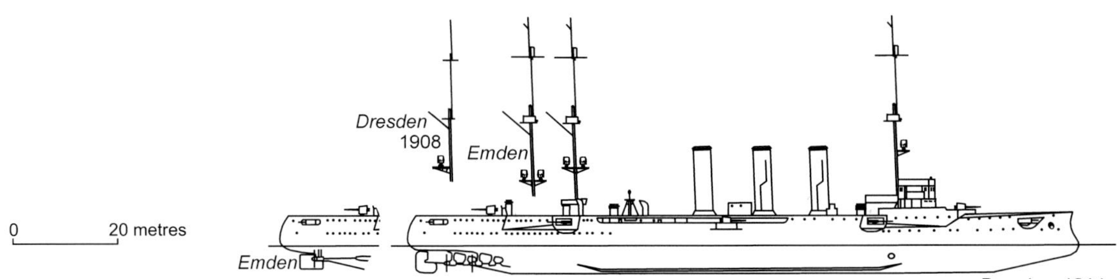

Dresden 1914

Albatross

MINE-STEAMER

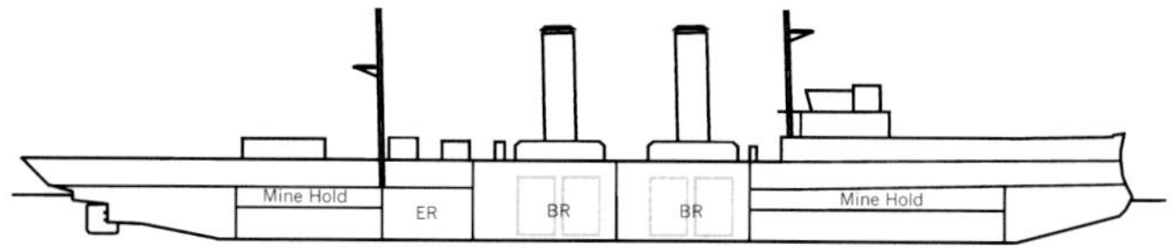

Displacement: 2,208 (design), 2,506 (full load) tonnes.
Dimensions: 96.6 (wl), 100.9 (oa) x 11.5 x 4.6 metres.
Machinery: Four Navy boilers; two shafts; 3-cyl reciprocating (VTE), IHP 6,600 = 20 knots; coal 200/526 tonnes; range 3,680nm @ 9 knots.
Armament: Eight 8.8cm/35 QL guns; 200 mines.
Complement: 11+197.

Name	Prov name	Estimates	Builder	Laid down	Launch	Comm	Fate
Albatross	*Mine-steamer B*	1906	AG Weser (Bremen)	24 May 07	23 Oct 07	19 May 08	Stranded off Gotland (57° 25' N, 18° 57' E) 2 Jul 15 after gunfire Russian *Admiral Makarov, Bayan, Bogatyr* & *Oleg*; salved; interned Oskarshamn 1 Oct 15; to Kiel Jan 19; stricken 21 Mar 21; sold (900,000M) 1921; BU Hamburg.

Fleet/mine warfare TS 19 May 08–14 Jan 10; refit Kiel 1910–11; fleet/mine warfare TS 7 Apr 11 to loss.

Albatross 1908

Kolberg class

SMALL CRUISERS

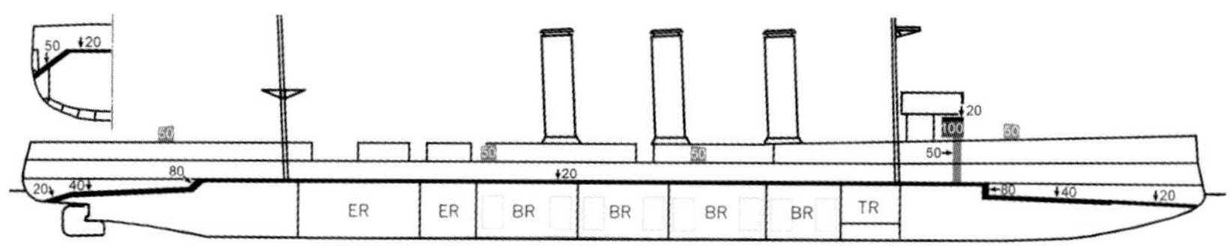

Displacement: 4,362 (design), 4,864–4,915 (full load) tonnes.
Dimensions: 130.0 (wl), 130.5 (oa) x 14.0 x 5.6 metres.
Machinery: Fifteen Navy boilers; two [*Mainz*]/four [others] shafts; Melms & Pfenniger [*Kolberg*]/AEG-Curtiss [*Mainz*]/Zoelly (1911: Germania) [*Cöln*]/Parsons [*Augsburg*] turbines, SHP 19,000/20,200 [*Mainz*] = 25.5/26 knots; coal 400–970–1,010 tonnes; range 3,250–3,630nm @ 14 knots.
Armament: Twelve 10.5cm/45 QL, four 5.2in/55 QL (removed 1912) guns; two 45cm UW TT.
Kolberg & *Augsburg* 1917: six 15cm/45 QL guns; two 45cm UW TT; two 50cm AW TT added 1918.
Protection: Deck 40-20-40-20/50mm; coaming 80mm; CT 20mm (roof)-100mm (sides); shields 50mm.
Complement: 18+349.

Name	Prov name	Estimates	Builder	Laid down	Launch	Comm	Fate
Kolberg = *W* (1920) = *Colmar* (1920)	*Ersatz-Greif*	1907	Schichau (Danzig)	15 Jan 08	14 Nov 08	21 Jun 10	Stricken 5 Nov 19; surrendered Cherbourg 25 Apr 20; to FR Sep 20; FR comm 1922; stricken 21 Jul 27; BU 1929.
Mainz	*Ersatz-Jagd*	1907	AG Vulcan (Stettin)	4 Dec 07	23 Jan 09	1 Oct 09	Gunfire British cruisers & destroyers Heligoland Bight (53° 58' N, 06° 42' E) 28 Aug 14.
Augsburg = *Y* (1920)	*Ersatz-Sperber*	1908	Kiel DYd	22 Aug 08	10 Jul 09	1 Oct 10	Stricken 5 Nov 19; surrendered Rosyth 3 Sep 20; to JP Sep 20; BU Dordrecht 1922.
Cöln (i)	*Ersatz-Schwalbe*	1908	Germania (Kiel)	25 May 08	5 Jun 09	16 Jun 11	Gunfire British cruisers Heligoland Bight (53° 13' N, 06° 54' E) 28 Aug 14.

Kolberg
II. SG 7 Aug 11–Jan 16; VI. SG Feb–Dec 16; refit Kiel 16 Dec 16–26 Apr 17; VI. SG 7 Jun–26 Dec 17; refit 1 Jan–17 Mar 18; Baltic Mar–17 Dec 18.

Mainz
Scouting Force 6 Jun 10–Jun 12; II. SG Jun 12 to loss.

Continued overleaf

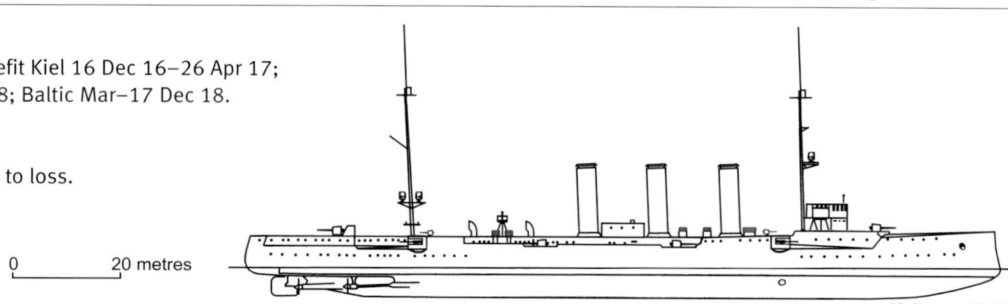

Kolberg 1910

Kolberg class continued

Augsburg
Torpedo trials ship 24 Feb 11–Jul 12; gunnery TS Jul 12–Aug 14; Baltic Aug 14–17 Dec 18.

Cöln
II. SG 10 Oct 11–loss.

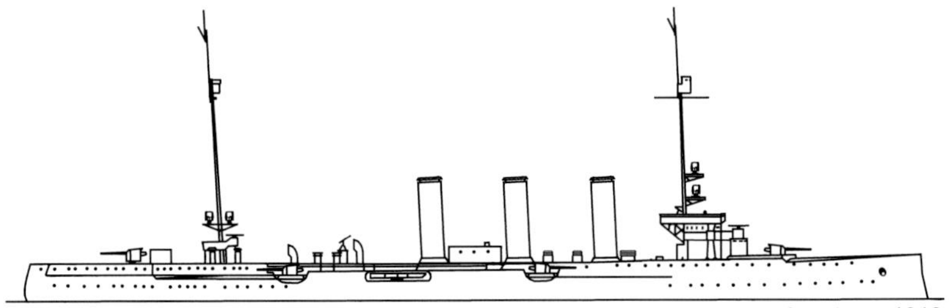

Augsburg 1918

Magdeburg class

SMALL CRUISERS

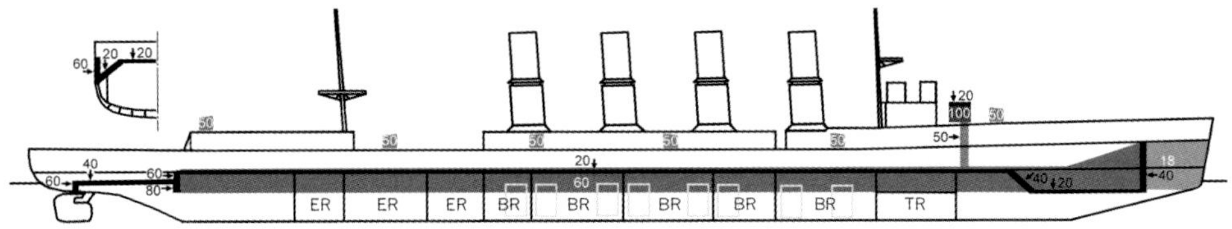

Displacement: 4,535 [*Magdeburg*]/4570 [*Stralsund*]/4,564 [others] (design), 4,570/5,587/5,281 (full load) tonnes.
Dimensions: 136.0 (wl), 138.7 (oa) x 13.5 x 5.1–5.7 metres.
Machinery: Sixteen Navy boilers; two [*Strassburg*; *Magdeburg* 1914; *Stralsund* 1916–17]/four [*Breslau*]/three [others] shafts; AEG-Vulcan [*Breslau*]/Navy [*Strassburg*]/Bergmann [others] turbines, SHP 25,000 = 27 knots; coal 450/1200 tonnes; range 5,820nm @ 12 knots.
Armament: Twelve 10.5cm/45 QL guns; two 50cm UW TT.
Magdeburg 1913/14: ten 10.5cm/45 QL guns; four 50cm TT (2 x UW, 2 x AW).
Straßburg 1915: seven 15cm/45 QL guns; four 50cm TT (2 x UW, 2 x AW).
Stralsund 1916: seven 15cm/45 QL guns; two 50cm TT (2 x AW).
Midilli May 15: ten 10.5cm/45 QL guns; two 50cm UW TT.
Midilli Jan 16: two 15cm/45 QL, ten 10.5cm/45 QL guns; two 50cm UW TT.
Midilli Apr 17: eight 15cm/45 QL guns; two 50cm UW TT.
Taranto: seven 15cm/45 QL, two 7.6cm/40 AA guns; eight 2cm/65 AA added 1941/42.
Mulhouse: seven 15cm/45 QL, two 7.5cm/ AA guns; two 50cm TT (2 x AW).
Protection: Belt 0-60-18mm; deck 40-20mm/20mm; CT 20mm (roof)-100mm (sides); shields 50mm.
Complement: 18+336.

Name	Prov name	Estimates	Builder	Laid down	Launch	Comm	Fate
Magdeburg (i)	*Ersatz-Bussard*	1909	AG Weser (Bremen)	Apr 10	13 May 11	20 Aug 12	Scuttled after stranding Odensholm (59° 18' N, 23° 21' E) 26 Aug 14;
Breslau = *Midilli* (Aug 14)	*Ersatz-Falke*	1909	AG Vulcan (Stettin)	May 10	16 May 11	10 May 12	To Turkey 16 Aug 14; mined off Imbros (40° 05' N, 26° 02' E) 20 Jan 18.
Stralsund = *Z* (1920) = *Mulhouse* (1920)	*Ersatz-Cormoran*	1910	AG Weser (Bremen)	Sep 10	4 Nov 11	10 Dec 12	Stricken 10 Mar 20; surrendered Cherbourg 3 Aug 20; to FR Sep 20; FR commission 3 Aug 22; stricken 15 Feb 33; condemned Jun 33; sold to BU 2 Nov 33; BU Brest.
Strassburg = *O* (1920) = *Taranto* (1920)	*Ersatz-Condor*	1910	Wilhelmshaven DYd	Oct 10	24 Aug 11	9 Oct 12	Stricken 10 May 20; surrendered Cherbourg 20 Jul 20; to IT Sep 20; IT comm 26 Jun 25; scuttled La Spezia 9 Sep 43; salved; bombed 23 Oct 43; salved 13 Apr 44; bombed 23 Sep 44; BU from 1945.

Magdeburg
Torpedo trials ship 1 Dec 12–Jul 14; Baltic 2 Aug 14 to loss.

Breslau
Mediterranean 3 Nov 12–16 Aug 14.

Stralsund
II. SG 15 Feb 13–19 Feb 16; refit Kiel 21 Feb–17 Jun 16; II. SG 6 Jul–2 Dec 16; IV. SG 3 Dec 16–17 Dec 18.

Strassburg
II. SG 23 Dec 12–Jul 15; refit Kiel 14 Jul–18 Oct 15; II. SG 20 Oct 15–18 Mar 16; VI. SG 20 Mar 16–10 Jan 18; IV. SG 8 Apr–Dec 18; Baltic Minesweeping Force 24 Mar 19–4 Jun 20.

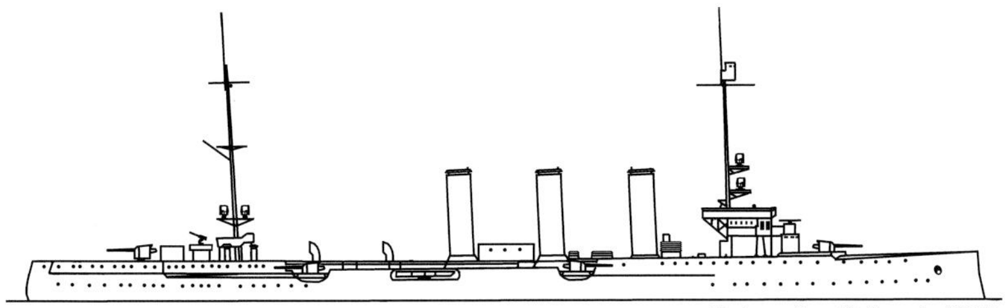

Colmar (ex-*Kolberg*) 1925

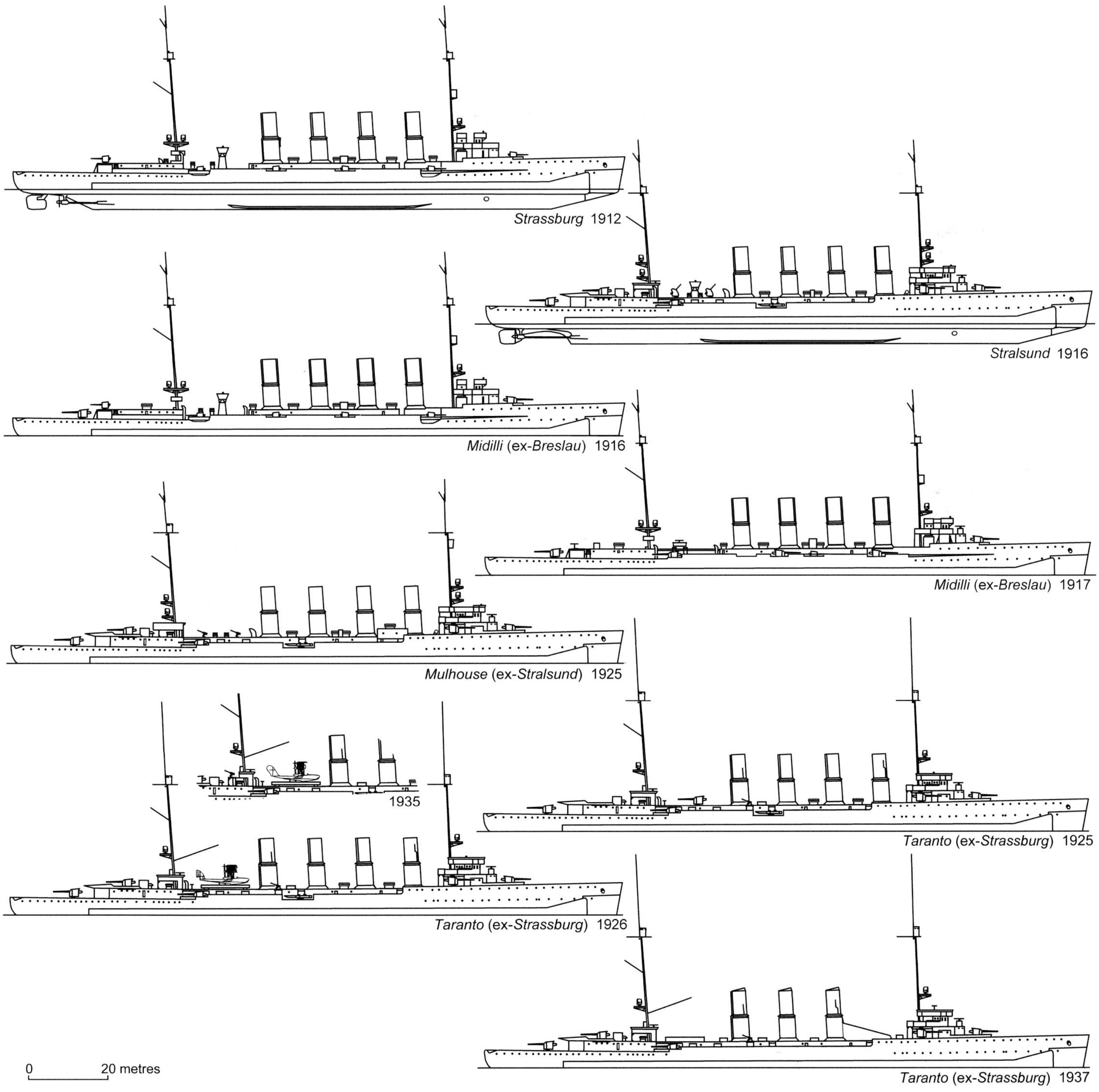

Karlsruhe class

SMALL CRUISERS

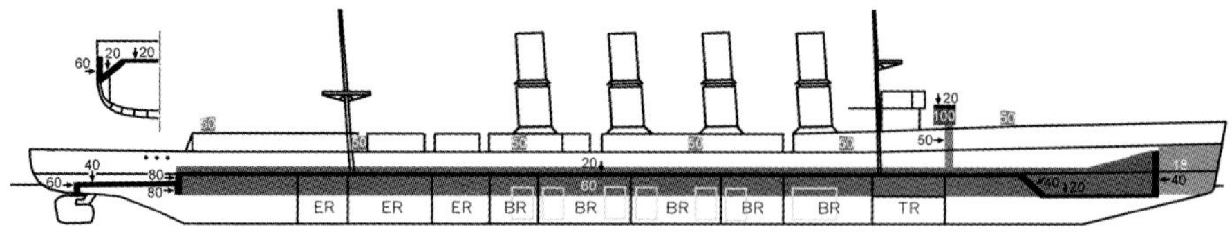

Displacement: 4,900 (design), 6,191 (full load) tonnes.
Dimensions: 139.0 (wl), 142.2 (oa) x 13.7 x 6.2 metres.
Machinery: Twelve Navy boilers; two shafts; Navy turbines, SHP 26,000 = 27.8 knots; coal 400/1,300 + oil 70/200 tonnes; range 5,000nm @ 12 knots.
Armament: Twelve 10.5cm/45 QL guns; two 50cm UW TT.
Protection: Belt 0-60-18mm; deck 40-20mm/20mm; CT 20mm (roof)-100mm (sides); shields 50mm.
Complement: 18+355.

Name	Prov name	Estimates	Builder	Laid down	Launch	Comm	Fate
Karlsruhe (i)	*Ersatz-Seeadler*	1911	Germania (Kiel)	21 Sep 11	11 Nov 12	15 Jan 14	Internal explosion West Indies (11° 07' N, 55° 25' W) 4 Nov 14.
Rostock (i)	*Ersatz-Geier*	1911	AG Weser (Bremen)	13 May 11	12 Nov 12	5 Feb 14	Scuttled torpedoes SMS *V71* & *V73* after torpedo UK destroyer North Sea 1 Jun 16.

Karlsruhe
East Coast America 14 Jun 14 to loss.

Rostock
Scouting Force May 14; torpedo boat leader 31 Jul 14 to loss.

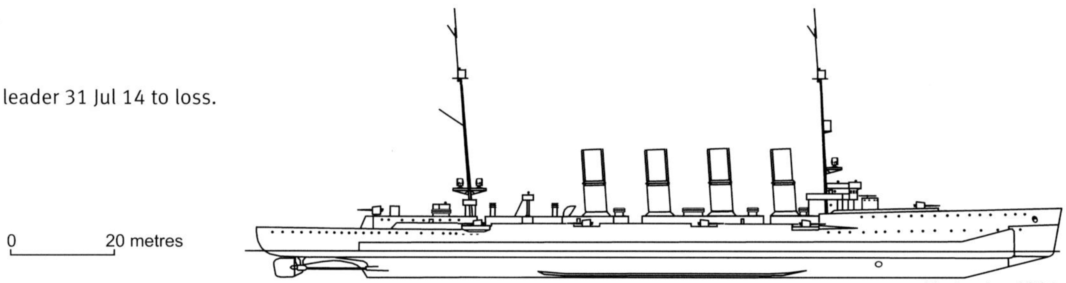

Karlsruhe 1914

Regensburg class

SMALL CRUISERS

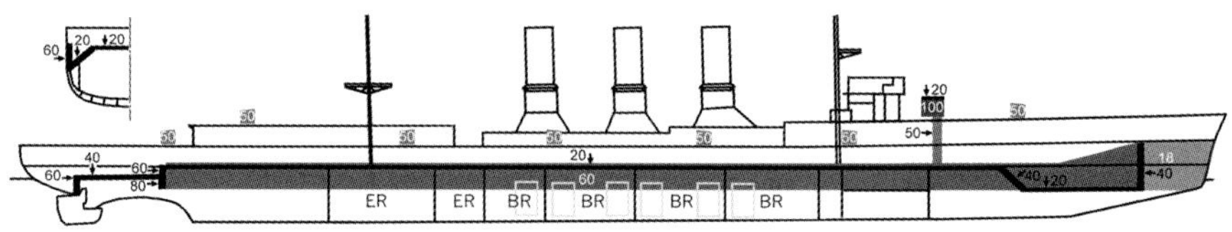

Displacement: 4,912 (design), 6,382 (full load) tonnes.
Dimensions: 139.0 (wl), 142.7 (oa) x 13.8 x 6.1 metres.
Machinery: Twelve Navy boilers (ten coal, two oil); two shafts; Navy turbines, SHP 26,000 = 27.5 knots; coal 380/1,280 + oil 100/375 tonnes; range 5,500nm @ 12 knots.
Armament: Twelve 10.5cm/45 QL guns; two 50cm UW TT.
Graudenz 1915: seven 15cm/45 QL guns; four 50cm TT (2 x UW, 2 x AW).
Regensburg 1917: seven 15cm/45 QL guns; four AW 50cm TT; 120 mines.
Ancona: seven 15cm/45 QL, two 7.6cm/40 AA guns.
Strasbourg: seven 15cm/45 QL, two 7.5cm AA guns; four AW 50cm TT.
Protection: Belt 0-60-18mm; deck 40-20mm/20mm; CT 20mm (roof)-100mm (sides); shields 50mm.
Complement: 21+363 (24+378 as flag).

Name	Prov name	Estimates	Builder	Laid down	Launch	Comm	Fate
Graudenz = *E* (1920) = *Ancona* (1920)	*Ersatz-Prinzeß Wilhelm*	1912	Kiel DYd	Oct 12	25 Oct 13	10 Aug 14	Stricken 10 Mar 20; surrendered Cherbourg 1 Jun 20; to IT Sep 20; IT comm 6 May 25; stricken 11 Mar 37; BU 1938.
Regensburg = *J* (1920) = *Strasbourg*	*Ersatz-Irene*	1912	Kiel DYd	13 Nov 12	25 Apr 14	3 Jan 15	Stricken 10 Mar 20; surrendered Cherbourg 4 Jun 20; to FR Sep 20; FR comm May 22; stricken 14 Jun 36; hulked Lorient; GE 1940; sunk Lorient 1944.

Graudenz
II. SG 27 Nov 14–22 Apr 16; I. LTB 13 Sep 16–5 Jun 17; II. LTB 6 Jun–8 Dec 18; North Sea Jan 19–10 Mar 20.

Regensburg
II. SG 10 Mar 15–Apr 16; II. LTB Apr 16–Mar 17; IV. SG 14 Mar 17–7 Nov 18; out of commission 7–17 Nov 18; North Sea 2 Dec 19–19 May 20.

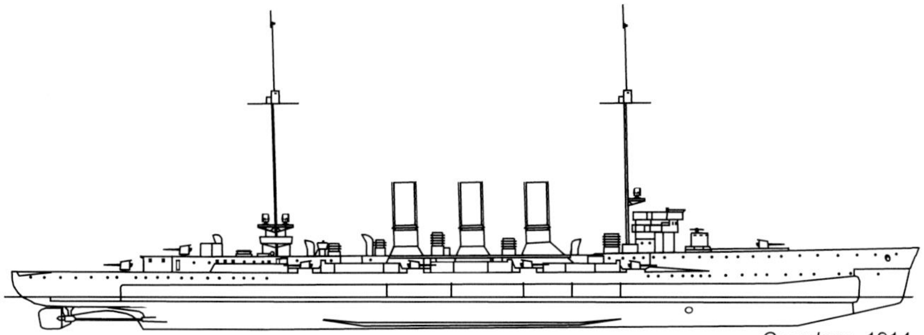

Graudenz 1914

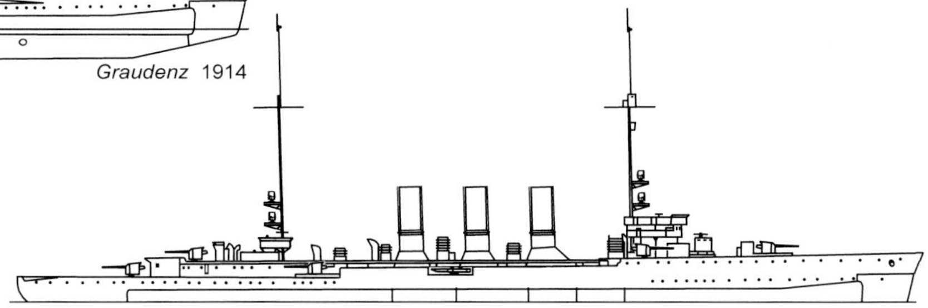

Graudenz 1918

Regensburg 1918

Strasbourg (ex-*Regensburg*) 1922

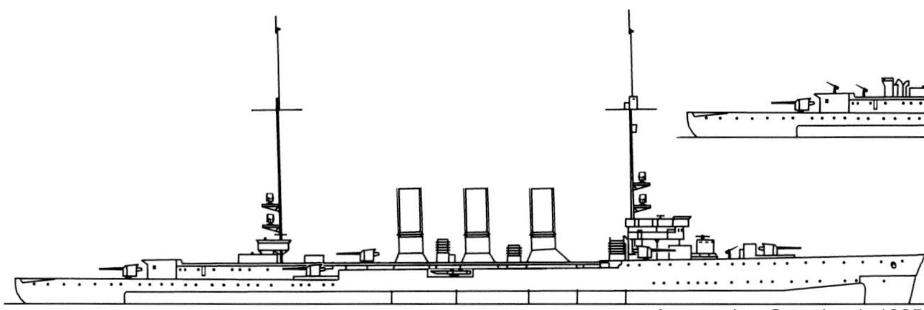

Ancona (ex-*Graudenz*) 1925

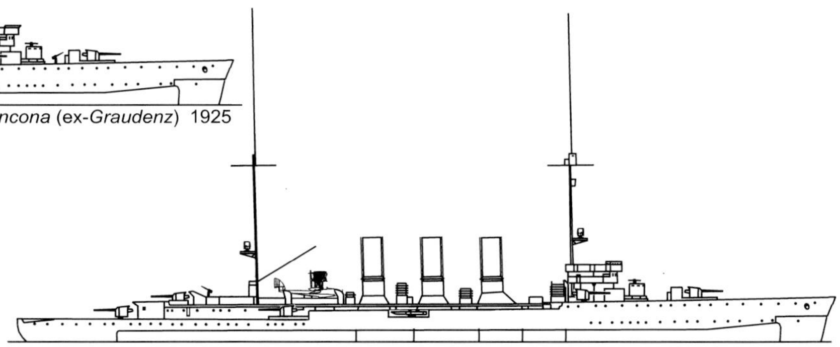

Ancona (ex-*Graudenz*) 1926

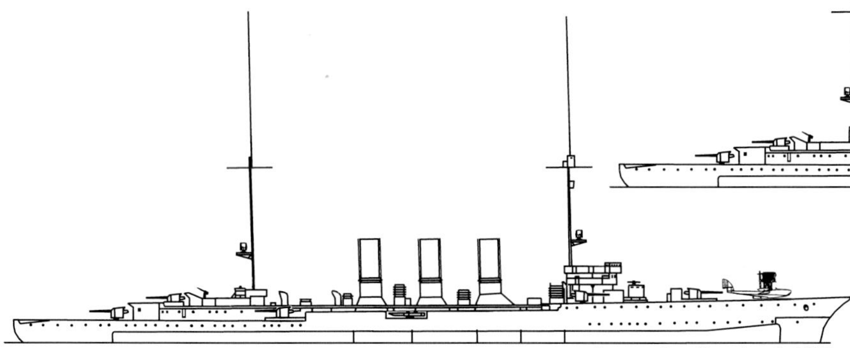

Ancona (ex-*Graudenz*) 1929

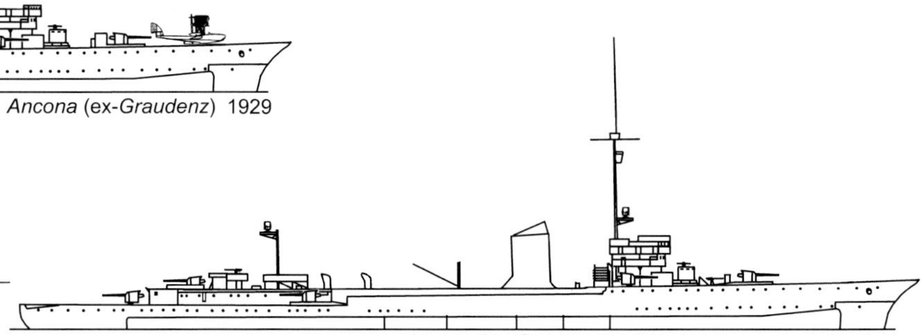

Ancona (ex-*Graudenz*) 1936 sketch as colonial cruiser

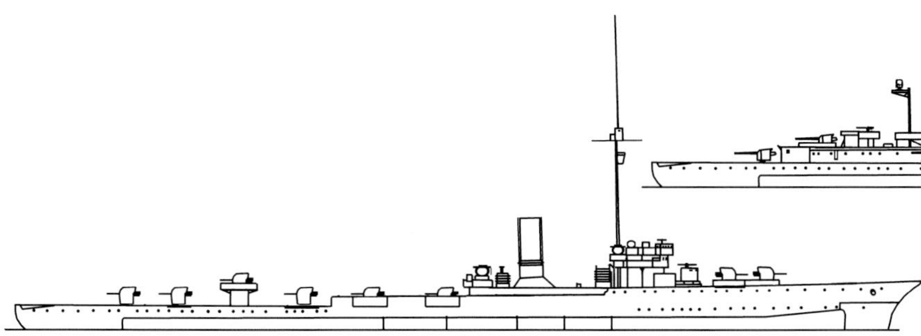

Ancona (ex-*Graudenz*) 1936 sketch as AA cruiser

0 20 metres

Wiesbaden class

SMALL CRUISERS

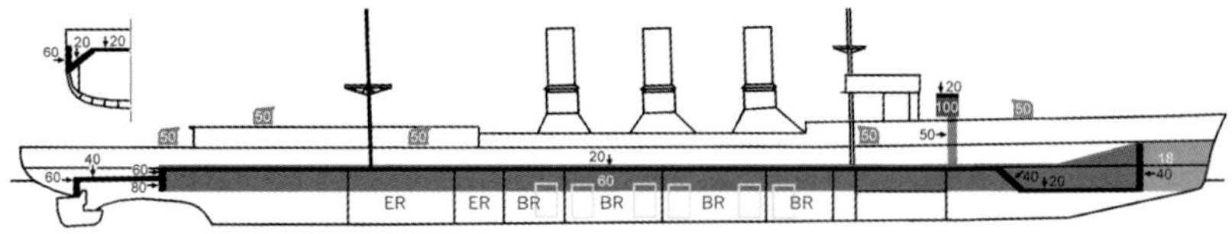

Displacement: 5,180 (design), 6,601 (full load) tonnes.
Dimensions: 141.7 (wl), 145.3 (oa) x 13.9 x 6.1 metres.
Machinery: Twelve Navy boilers (ten coal, two oil); two shafts; Navy turbines (*Wiesbaden*: with Föttinger transmission), SHP 31,000 = 27.5 knots; coal 380/1,280 + oil 150/470 tonnes; range 4,800nm @ 12 knots.
Armament: Eight 15cm/45 QL, two 8.8cm/45 AA (since 1916) guns; four 50cm TT (2 x UW, 2 x AW).
Protection: Belt 0-60-18mm; deck 40-20mm/20mm; CT 20mm (roof)-100mm (sides); shields 50mm.
Complement: 17+457.

Name	Prov name	Estimates	Builder	Laid down	Launch	Comm	Fate
Wiesbaden (i)	*Ersatz-Gefion*	1913	AG Vulcan (Stettin)	10 Nov 13	20 Jan 15	1 Sep 15	Gunfire and torpedo UK forces North Sea (57° 01' N, 05° 53' E) 1 Jun 16.
Frankfurt	*Ersatz-Hela*	1913	Kiel DYd	1 Dec 13	20 Mar 15	20 Aug 15	Scuttled Scapa Flow 21 Jun 19; beached Smoogro Bay; salved 12 Jul 19; to US; comm 4 Jun 20; expended as aircraft bombing target off Cape Henry, VA, 18 Jun 21.

Brummer class

MINE-STEAMERS

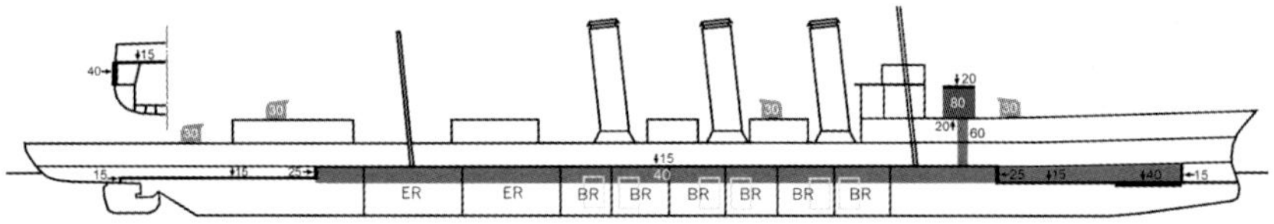

Displacement: 4,385 (design), 5,856 (full load) tonnes.
Dimensions: 135.0 (wl), 140.4 (oa) x 13.2 x 6.0 metres.
Machinery: Six Navy (four oil, two coal) boilers; two shafts; AEG-Vulcan turbines, SHP 33,000 = 28 knots; coal 300/600, oil 500/1,000 tonnes; range 5,800nm @ 12 knots.
Armament: Four 15cm/45 QL, two 8.8cm/45 AA guns; two 50cm AW TT; 400 mines.
Protection: Belt 0-40-0mm; deck 15mm; CT 20mm (roof)-80mm (sides); shields 50mm.
Complement: 16+293.

Name	Prov name	Estimates	Builder	Laid down	Launch	Comm	Fate
Bremse	*Mine-steamer D*	War	AG Vulcan (Stettin)	27 Apr 15	11 Mar 16	1 Jul 16	Scuttled Scapa Flow 21 Jun 19; sold Cox & Danks 28 Oct 25; salved 27 Nov 29; arrived Lyness 30 Nov 29; BU to May 31.
Brummer	*Mine-steamer C*	War	AG Vulcan (Stettin)	24 Apr 15	11 Dec 15	2 Apr 16	Scuttled Scapa Flow 21 Jun 19; salvage rights sold Nundy Marine Metals (£200) 6 Nov 62; salvage work Sep/Oct 70; rights sold Scapa Flow Salvage Ltd 21 Oct 77; rights sold Undersea Associates 1978; leased Clark Diving Services. 20 Nov 81; reverted to MoD transferred Orkney Islands Council Sep 85; scheduled monument 23 Mar 2001.

Bremse
II. SG Oct–Nov 16; IV. SG 1 Dec 16–7 Nov 18; out of commission 7–17 Nov 18; interned Scapa Flow 26 Nov 18.

Brummer
II. SG Jun–Nov 16; IV. SG 1 Dec 16–7 Nov 18; out of commission 7–17 Nov 18; interned Scapa Flow 26 Nov 18.

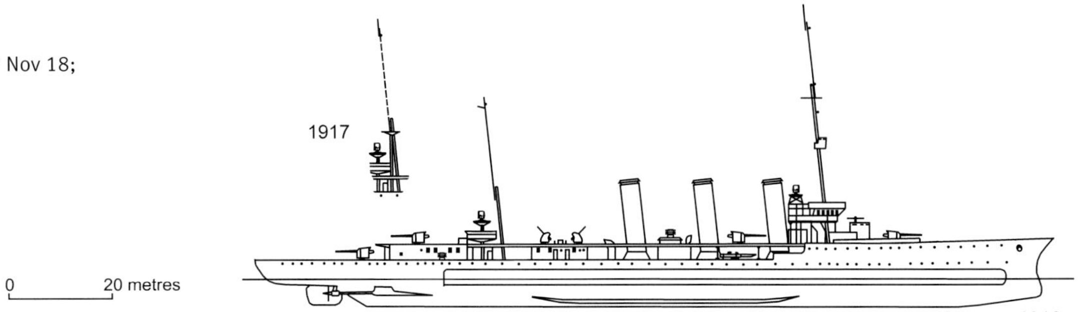

Bremse 1916

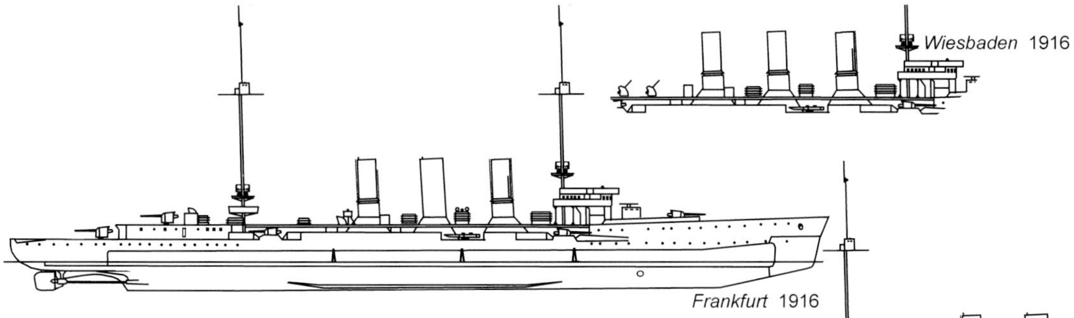

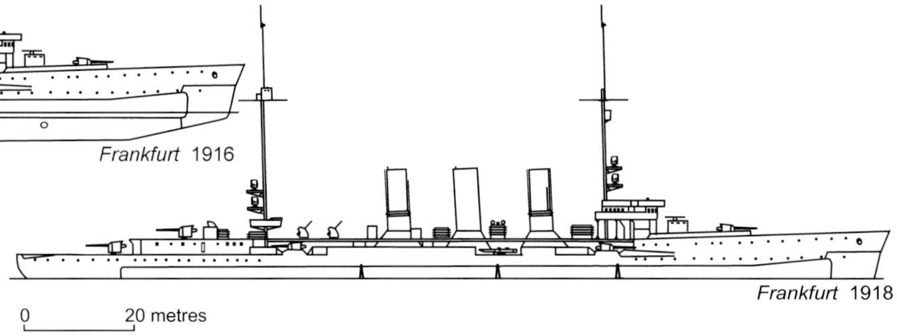

Wiesbaden
II. SG 23 Oct 15 to loss.

Frankfurt
II. SG 12 Oct 15–18 Nov 18; interned Scapa Flow 26 Nov 18.

Königsberg (ii) class

SMALL CRUISERS

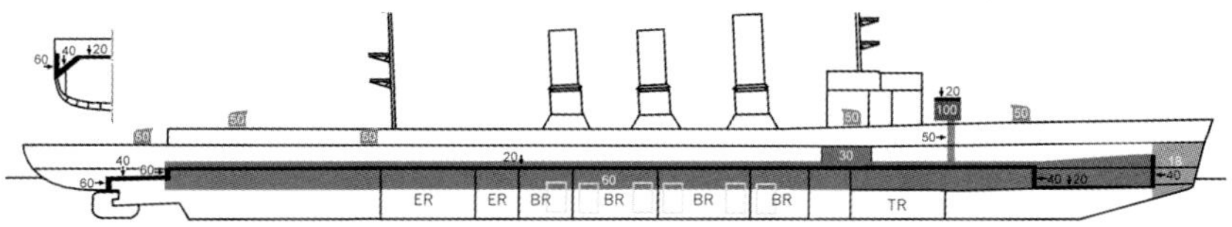

Displacement: 5,440 (design), 7,125 (full load) tonnes.
Dimensions: 145.8 (wl), 151.4 (oa) x 14.2 x 6.3 metres.
Machinery: Twelve Navy boilers (ten coal, two oil); two shafts; Navy turbines (*Karlsruhe*: geared), SHP 31,000 = 27.5 knots; coal 350/1,340 + oil 150/500 tonnes; range 4,850nm @ 12 knots.
Armament: Eight 15cm/45 QL, two 8.8cm/45 AA guns; four 50cm TT (2 x UW, 2 x AW).
Metz: seven 15cm/45 QL, two 7.5cm AA guns; four 50cm TT (2 x UW, 2 x AW).
Protection: Belt 0-60-18mm; deck 20-40mm/20mm; aux. engine room[2] deck 28mm, sides 30-25mm; CT 20mm (roof)–100mm (sides); shields 50mm.
Complement: 17+458 (23+478 as flag).

Name	Prov name	Estimates	Builder	Laid down	Launch	Comm	Fate
Königsberg (ii) = *A* (1920) = *Metz* (1920)	*Ersatz-Gazelle*	1914	AG Weser (Bremen)	22 Aug 14	18 Dec 15	12 Aug 16	Stricken 31 May 20; to FR Sep 20; FR commission 6 Sep 20; stricken 18 Aug 33; condemned Jan 34; sold Aug 34; BU Brest.
Karlsruhe (ii)	*Ersatz-Niobe*	1914	Wilhelmshaven DYd	5 May 15	31 Jan 16	23 Dec 16	Scuttled Scapa Flow 21 Jun 19; salvage rights sold Metal Industries 1955 (£100); salvage rights sold Nundy Marine Metals 1968; resold Scapa Flow Salvage Ltd 21 Oct 77; sold Undersea Associates 1978; sold Clark Diving Services. 20 Nov 81; scheduled monument 23 Mar 2001; sold UK interests 9 Jul 2019 (£8,500).
Emden (ii)	*Ersatz-Nymphe*	1915	AG Weser (Bremen)	2 Dec 14	1 Feb 16	16 Dec 16	Scuttled Scapa Flow 21 Jun 19; beached Smoogro Bay; salved 28 Jun 19; to FR 11 Mar 20; BU Caen 1926.
Nürnberg (ii)	*Ersatz-Thetis*	1915	Howaldt (Kiel)	8 May 15	14 Apr 16	15 Feb 17	Scuttled Scapa Flow 21 Jun 19; beached off Cava; salved 3 Jul 19; target 5 Nov 20; gunfire target HMS *Repulse* S of Poole (50° 08.172' N, 01°41.738' W) 7 Jul 22.

2 This room has – inexplicably – been dubbed 'mine hold' in the various editions of Gröner's *Deutschen Kriegsschiffe*. In fact, it was to hold the starboard diesel generator, for which no other location could be found except above the armour deck; as a consequence it received some extra splinter protection.

Königsberg
II. SG 30 Oct 16–7 Dec 18; North Sea 17 Dec 18–31 May 20; surrendered Cherbourg 20 Jul 20.

Karlsruhe
II. SG 22 Feb 17–18 Nov 18; interned Scapa Flow 26 Nov 18.

Emden
HSF TB leader 12 Mar 17–18 Nov 18; interned Scapa Flow 26 Nov 18.

Nürnberg
II. SG 1 May 17–18 Nov 18; interned Scapa Flow 26 Nov 18.

Continued overleaf

Königsberg class continued

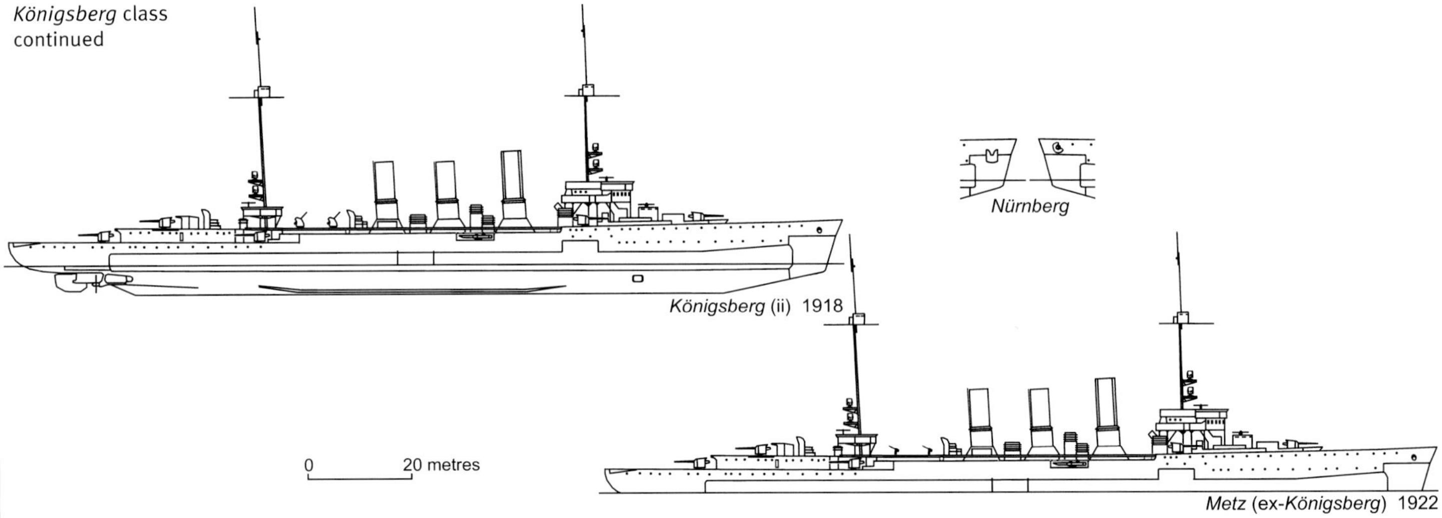

Russian *Muravev-Amurskiy*

SMALL CRUISERS

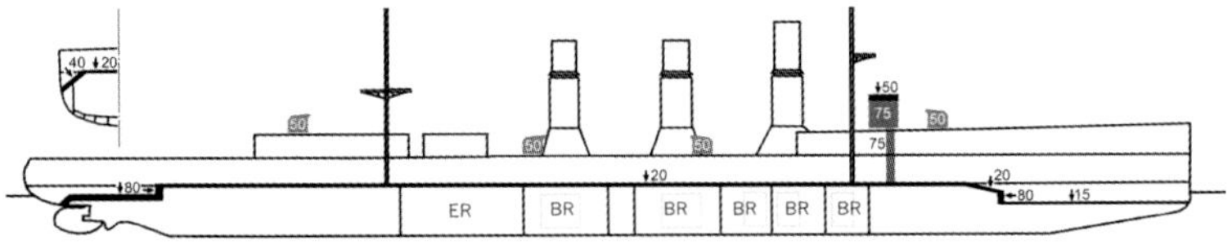

Displacement: 4,390 (design), 5,252 (full load) tonnes.
Dimensions: 128 (pp), 134.4 (wl) 135.3 (oa) x 13.6 x 6 metres.
Machinery: Ten Yarrow boilers (six mixed; four oil); two shafts; Schichau turbines, SHP 27,400 = 27.5 knots; coal 80/620; oil 250/580 tonnes; range 4,300nm @ 12 knots.
Armament: Eight 15cm/45 QL [13cm/55 RU], four (*Pillau*) 5.2cm/55 (from 1915/16 two 8.8cm/45) AA [four 6.35cm RU]; two 50cm TT [none RU]; 120 mines.
Bari: Eight 15cm/45 QL, three 7.6cm/40 AA; six 2cm/65 AA added 1935, six 2cm/65 AA added 1941.
Bari 1942: Eight 15cm/45 QL, nineteen 2cm/65 AA.
Protection: Deck 80-20-15mm/40mm; shields 50mm; CT 50mm (roof)-75mm (sides).
Complement: 21+421.

Name	Builder	Laid down (acquired)	Launch	Comm	Fate
Elbing (ex-*Admiral Nevelskoi*, ex-*Nevelskoi*)	Schichau (Danzig)	21 May 13 (21 Nov 14)	21 Nov 14	4 Sep 15	Scuttled 1 Jun 16 North Sea (55° 49' N, 05° 45'), after collision SMS *Posen*.
Pillau (ex-*Muravev-Amurskiy*) = *U* (1920) = *Bari* (1920)	Schichau (Danzig)	12 Apr 13 (27 Aug 14)	11 Apr 14	14 Dec 14	Stricken 5 Nov 19; surrendered Cherbourg 20 Jul 20; to IT Sep 20; IT commission 23 Jan 24; bombed Leghorn 28 Sep 43; BU 1944–48.

Cöln class

SMALL CRUISERS

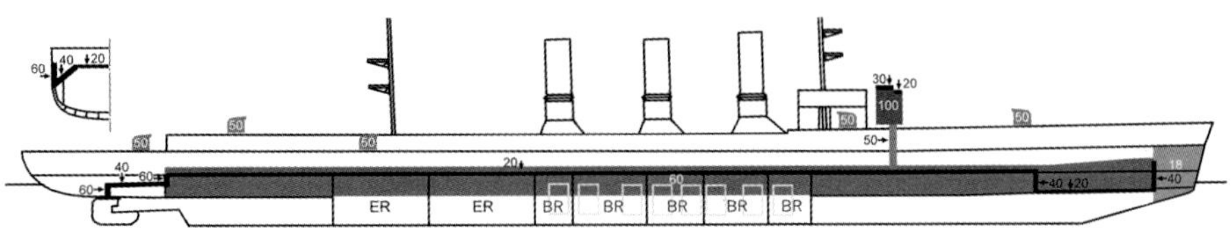

Displacement: 5,620 (design), 7,486 (full load) tonnes.
Dimensions: 149.8 (wl), 155.5 (oa) x 14.2 x 6.4 metres.
Machinery: Fourteen Navy boilers (eight coal, six oil); two shafts; Navy turbines, SHP 31,000 = 27.5 knots; coal 300/1,100 + oil 200/800 (*Cöln*: 1,050) tonnes; range 5,400nm @ 12 knots.
Armament: Eight 15cm/45 QL, three (1918: two) 8.8cm/45 AA guns; four 60cm AW TT; 200 mines.
Protection: Belt 0-60-18mm; deck 40-20mm/20mm; CT 30mm (roof)-100mm (sides); shields 50mm.
Complement: 17+542.

Elbing
II. SG 16 Nov 15 to loss.

Pillau
II. SG 16 Mar 15–7 Dec 18.

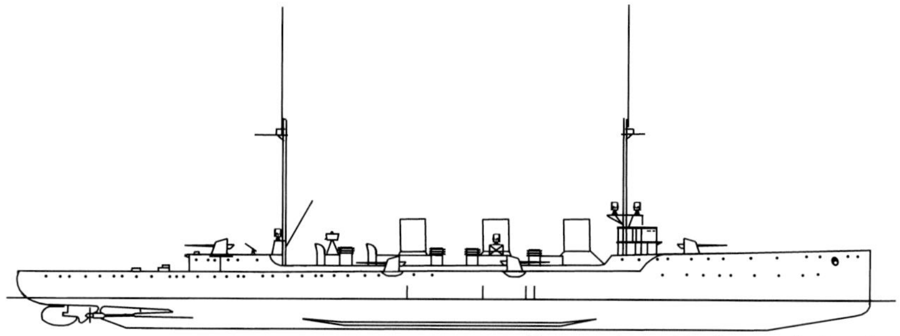
Muravev-Amurskiy class as designed

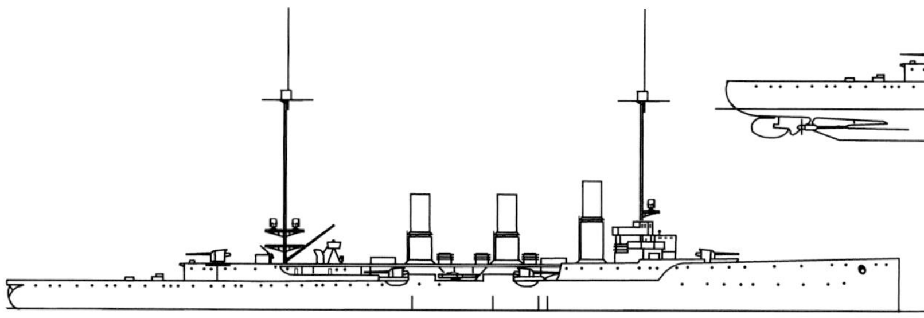
Elbing 1916

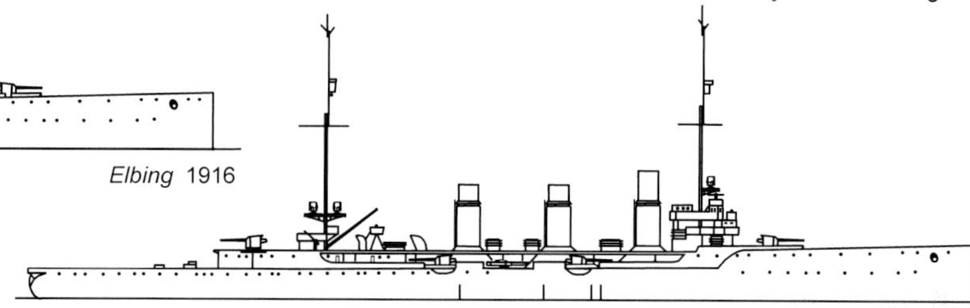
Pillau 1918

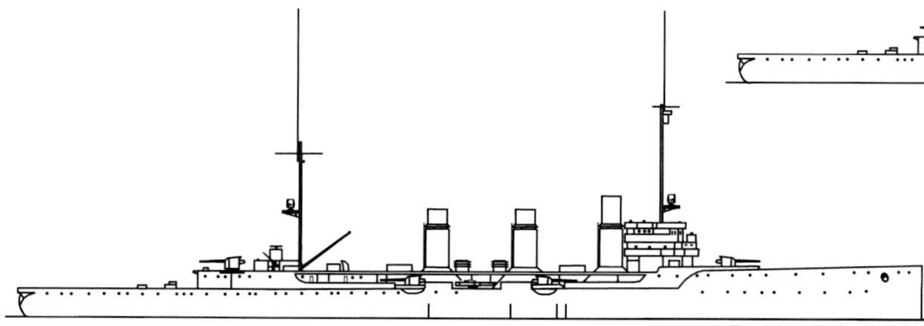
Bari (ex-*Pillau*) 1930

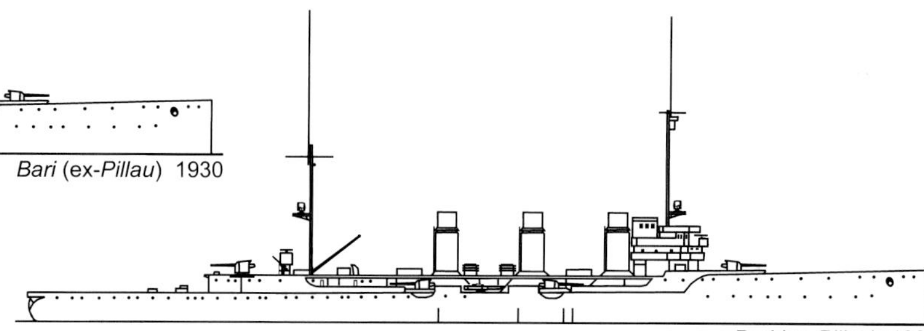
Bari (ex-*Pillau*) 1933

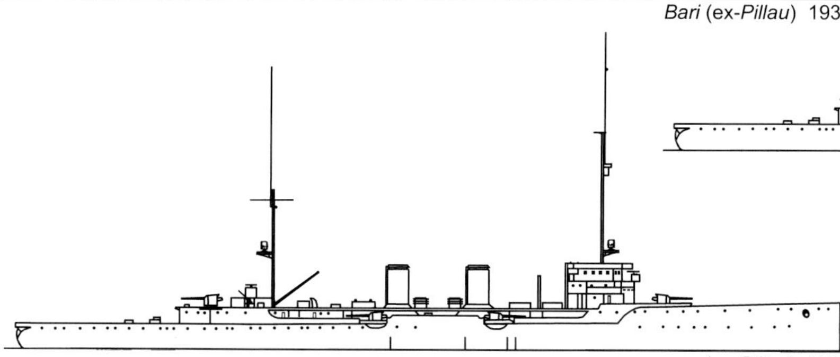
(ex-*Pillau*) 1935

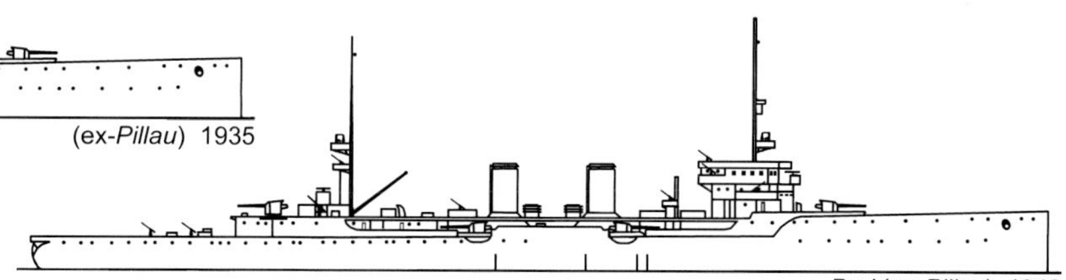
Bari (ex-*Pillau*) 1942

0 20 metres

Name	Prov name	Programme	Builder	Laid down	Launch	Comm	Fate
Cöln (ii)	*Ersatz-Ariadne*	War	Blohm & Voss (Hamburg)	Aug 15	5 Oct 16	17 Jan 18	Scuttled Scapa Flow 21 Jun 19; salvage rights sold Nundy Marine Metals (£200) 6 Nov 62; salvage work Sep/Oct 70; rights sold Scapa Flow Salvage Ltd 21 Oct 77; rights sold Undersea Associates 1978; leased Clark Diving Services. 20 Nov 81; reverted to MoD transferred Orkney Islands Council Sep 85; scheduled monument 23 Mar 2001.
Leipzig (iii)	*Ersatz-Leipzig*	War	AG Weser (Bremen)	Aug 15	28 Jan 18	–	Stricken 17 Nov 19; sold Neugebauer (Lemwerder) 21 Jun 21; BU Hamburg 1921.
–	*Ersatz-Cöln*	War	AG Weser (Bremen)	Aug 15	c.Nov 19	–	Stricken 17 Nov 19; sold Neugebauer (Lemwerder) 21 Jun 21 (~400,000M); BU Hamburg-Köhlbrandwerft.

Continued overleaf

Cöln class continued

Name	Prov name	Programme	Builder	Laid down	Launch	Comm	Fate
–	*Ersatz-Emden*	War	AG Weser (Bremen)	Aug 15	c.Nov 19	–	Stricken 17 Nov 19; sold 25 Jun 21 (~400,000M); BU Hamburg-Altenwärder by P Berendsohn.
Wiesbaden (ii)	*Ersatz-Nürnberg*	War	AG Vulcan (Stettin)	Oct 15	3 Mar 17	–	Stricken 17 Nov 19; stripped Lübeck; BU 1921.
Rostock (ii)	*Ersatz-Mainz*	War	AG Vulcan (Stettin)	Nov 15	6 Apr 18	–	Stricken 17 Nov 19; stripped Lübeck; sold 1921; BU Hamburg.
Frauenlob (ii)	*Ersatz-Königsberg*	War	Kiel DYd	Dec 15	26 Sep 18	–	Stricken 17 Nov 19; BU Deutsche Werke Kiel 1921.
Dresden (ii)	*Ersatz-Dresden*	War)	Howaldt (Kiel)	May 16	25 Apr 17	28 Mar 18	Scuttled Scapa Flow 21 Jun 19; salvage rights sold Nundy Marine Metals (£200) 6 Nov 62; salvage work Sep/Oct 70; rights sold Scapa Flow Salvage Ltd 21 Oct 77; rights sold Undersea Associates 1978; leased Clark Diving Services. 20 Nov 81; reverted to MoD transferred Orkney Islands Council Sep 85; scheduled monument 23 Mar 2001.
Magdeburg (ii)	*Ersatz-Magdeburg*	War	Howaldt (Kiel)	Jun 16	17 Nov 17	–	Stricken 17 Nov 19; sold 28 Oct 21 (1,300,000M); BU Kiel-Nordmole 1922.
–	*Ersatz-A*	War	Kiel DYd	Sep 16	–	–	Stricken 17 Nov 19; BU on slip 1920.

Cöln

II. SG 13 May–18 Nov 18; interned Scapa Flow 23 Nov 18.

Dresden

II. SG Aug–7 Nov 18; out of commission 7–17 Nov 18; interned Scapa Flow 16 Dec 18.

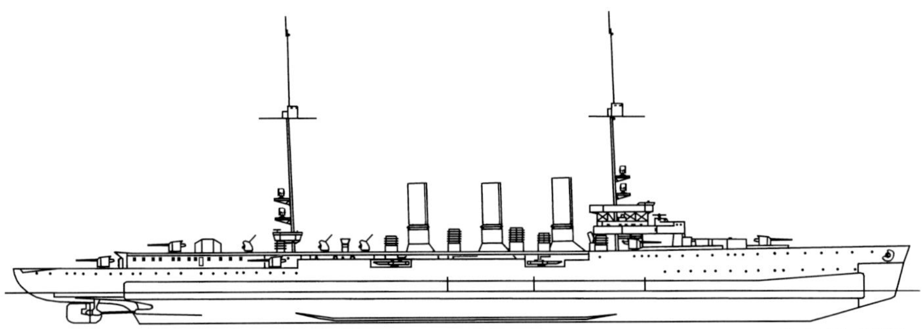

Coln (ii) 1918

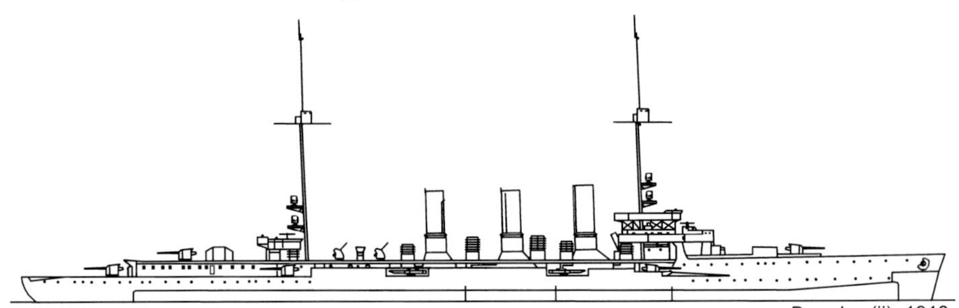

Dresden (ii) 1918

0 20 metres

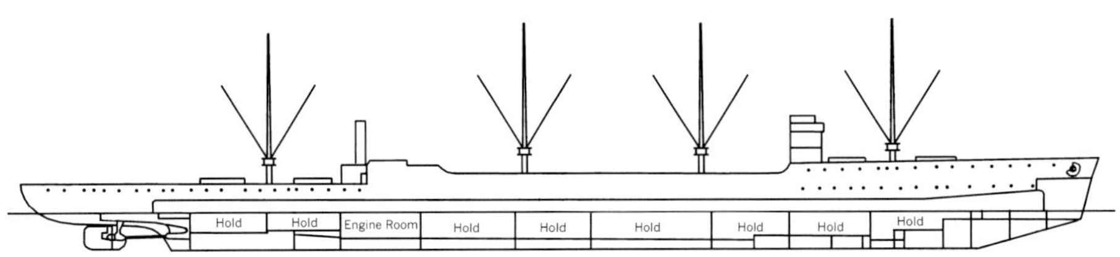

Cöln class - sketch as dry-cargo vessel 1920

Summary of Small Cruiser Authorisations

Programme	New-build designation	Launch name
1855	–	*Arcona* (i)
1855	–	*Gazelle* (i)
1859	–	*Vineta* (i)
1859	–	*Hertha* (i)
1859	–	*Nymphe* (i)
1859	–	*Medusa* (i)
1859	–	*Elisabeth*
1867	–	*Ariadne* (i)
1867	–	*Luise*
1867	–	*Freya*
Programme/Estimates (first instalment)		
1873	–	*Leipzig* (i)
1873	*Decked-corvette A*	*Sédan*
1873/1875	*Decked-corvette B*	*Bismarck* (i)
1873/1875	*Ersatz-Arcona*	*Moltke* (i)
1873/1875	–	*Zieten*
1873/1876	*Decked-corvette C*	*Blücher* (i)
1873/1876	*Ersatz-Gazelle*	*Stosch*
1873/1877	*Decked-corvette D*	*Gneisenau* (i)
1873/1878	*Ersatz-Hertha*	*Stein*
1873/1879	*Flushdecked-corvette E*	*Carola*
1873/1879	*Ersatz-Augusta*	*Olga*
1873/1880	*Flushdecked-corvette F*	*Sophie*
1873/1880	*Ersatz-Vineta*	*Marie*
1873/1882	*Ersatz-Nymphe*	*Arcona* (ii)
1873/1878	*Ersatz-Grille*	*Pfeil*
1873/1878	*Aviso D*	*Blitz*
1873/1881	*Flushdecked-corvette G*	*Alexandrine*
1873/1883	*Ersatz-Victoria*	*Charlotte*
1873/1883	*Ersatz-Medusa*	*Nixe*
Estimates		
1885/86	*Ersatz-Loreley*	*Greif*
1885/86	*Ersatz-Elisabeth*	*Irene*
1886/87	*Ersatz-Ariadne*	*Prinzeß Wilhelm*
1886/87	*Aviso E*	*Wacht*
1886/87	*Cruiser A*	*Schwalbe*
1887/88	*Cruiser B*	*Sperber*
1887/88	*Ersatz-Pommerania*	*Jagd*
1887/88	*Aviso F*	*Meteor*
1888/89	*Cruiser-corvette H*	(*Kaiserin Augusta*)
1888/89	*Cruiser C*	*Bussard*
1889/90 (ex-1892/93)	*Cruiser D*	*Falke* (ii)
1890/91	*Aviso G*	*Comet*
1890/91	*Aviso H*	Rejected by Reichtag
1890/91	*Ersatz-Adler*	*Kaiseradler/Seeadler*
1890/91	*Ersatz-Eber*	*Condor*
1890/91 (ex-1893/94)	*Cruiser E*	*Cormoran*
1890/91	*Cruiser-corvette/ III. Class cruiser J*	*Gefion* (ii)
1891/92, 1892/93	*Cruiser F*	Rejected by Reichtag
1892/93	*Aviso H*	Rejected by Reichtag
1893/94	*Cruiser F*	*Geier*
1893/94	*Ersatz-Möwe*	Rejected by Reichtag
1893/94	*Aviso H*	*Hela*

Estimates	New-build designation	Launch name
1893/94, 1894/95, 1897/98	*Ersatz-Falke*	Rejected by Reichtag
1896/97	*IV. class Cruiser G*	*Gazelle* (ii)
1898	*Small Cruiser A*	*Nymphe* (ii)
1898	*Small Cruiser B*	*Niobe* (ii)
1899	*Small Cruiser C*	*Thetis* (ii)
1899	*Small Cruiser D*	*Ariadne* (ii)
1900	*Small Cruiser F*	*Amazone* (ii)
1900	*Small Cruiser E*	*Medusa* (ii)
1901	*Small Cruiser G*	*Frauenlob* (ii)
1901	*Small Cruiser H*	*Arcona* (iii)
1901	*Small Cruiser J*	*Undine* (ii)
1902	*Small Cruiser K*	*Hamburg*
1902	*Small Cruiser L*	*Bremen*
1902	*Ersatz-Zieten*	*Berlin*
1903	*Small Cruiser M*	*München*
1903	*Ersatz-Mercur*	*Lübeck*
1904	*Small Cruiser N*	*Leipzig* (ii)
1904	*Ersatz-Alexandrine*	*Danzig* (ii)
1904	*Ersatz-Meteor*	*Königsberg* (i)
1905	*Ersatz-Blitz*	*Nürnberg* (i)
1905	*Ersatz-Wacht*	*Stettin*
1905	*Small Cruiser O*	*Stuttgart*
1905	*Mine-steamer A*	*Nautilus*
1906	*Mine-steamer B*	*Albatross*
1906	*Ersatz-Comet*	*Dresden* (i)
1906	*Ersatz-Pfeil*	*Emden* (i)
1907	*Ersatz-Greif*	*Kolberg*
1907	*Ersatz-Jagd*	*Mainz*
1908	*Ersatz-Sperber*	*Augsburg*
1908	*Ersatz-Schwalbe*	*Cöln* (i)
1909	*Ersatz-Bussard*	*Magdeburg* (i)
1909	*Ersatz-Falke*	*Breslau*
1910	*Ersatz-Cormoran*	*Stralsund*
1910	*Ersatz-Condor*	*Strassburg*
1911	*Ersatz-Seeadler*	*Karlsruhe* (i)
1911	*Ersatz-Geier*	*Rostock* (i)
1912	*Ersatz-Prinzeß Wilhelm*	*Graudenz*
1912	*Ersatz-Irene*	*Regensburg*
1913	*Ersatz-Gefion*	*Wiesbaden* (i)
1913	*Ersatz-Hela*	*Frankfurt*
1914	*Ersatz-Gazelle*	*Königsberg* (ii)
1914	*Ersatz-Niobe*	*Karlsruhe* (ii)
1915	*Ersatz-Nymphe*	*Emden* (ii)
1915	*Ersatz-Thetis*	*Nürnberg* (ii)
War	*Mine-steamer C*	*Brummer*
War	*Mine-steamer D*	*Bremse*
War	*Ersatz-Ariadne*	*Cöln* (ii)
War	*Ersatz-Cöln*	–
War	*Ersatz-Dresden*	*Dresden* (ii)
War	*Ersatz-Emden*	–
War	*Ersatz-Königsberg*	*Frauenlob* (ii)
War	*Ersatz-Leipzig*	*Leipzig* (iii)
War	*Ersatz-Mainz*	*Rostock* (ii)
War	*Ersatz-Magdeburg*	*Magdeburg* (ii)
War	*Ersatz-Nürnberg*	*Wiesbaden* (ii)
War	*Ersatz-A*	–

Ships for Export

Chinese *Tsi Yuen*

ARMOUR DECK CORVETTE

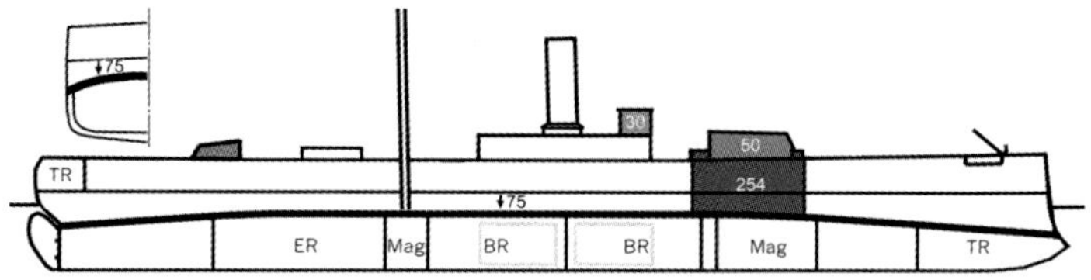

Displacement: 2,337 tonnes.
Dimensions: 71.9 (wl) x 10.5 x 5.2 metres.
Machinery: Six cylindrical boilers (coal); two shafts; reciprocating (HC), IHP 2,800 = 15 knots.
Armament: 1886: two 21cm/35 (1 x 2), 1 x 15cm/35 guns; six 3.7cm MG; four 38.1cm TT (1 x UW, 3 x AW).
1894: two 21cm/35 (1 x 2), 1 x 15cm/35, four 7.0cm, two 4.7cm guns; nine 3.7cm MG; four 38.1cm TT (1 x UW, 3 x AW).
Protection: Deck 75mm; barbette 250mm; CT 30mm; shields 50mm.
Complement: 180.

Name	Builder	Laid down	Launch	Comp	Fate
Tsi Yuen = *Saiyen* (16 Mar 95)	AG Vulcan (Stettin)	16 Jan 83	1 Dec 83	Aug 84	JP 16 Mar 95; mined off Port Arthur 30 Nov 04.

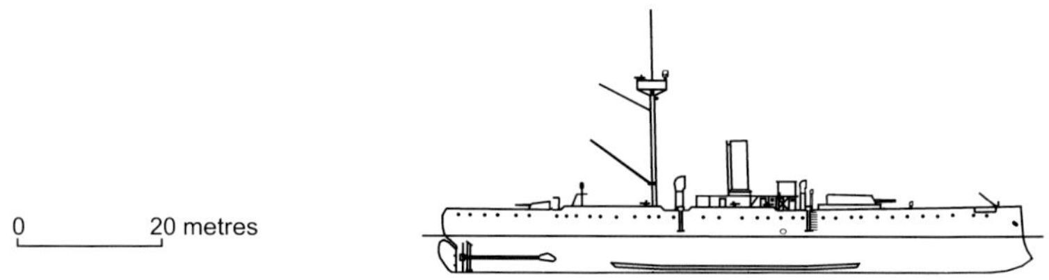

Tsi Yuen

Chinese *King Yuen* class

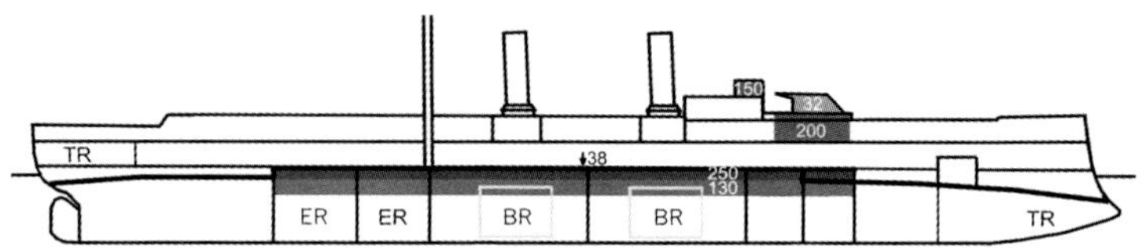

Displacement: 2,900 tonnes.
Dimensions: 82.4 (lwl) x 13 x 5.1 metres.
Machinery: Four cylindrical boilers; two shafts; reciprocating (HC), IHP 3,400/4,400 = 15.5 knots; coal 320 tonnes.
Armament: 1887: two 21cm/35 (1 x 2), two 15cm/35 guns; seven 3.7cm MG; four 35.6cm TT (1 x UW, 3 x AW).
1894: two 21cm/35 (1 x 2), two 15cm/35, one 4.0cm guns; two 4.7cm MG, five 3.7cm MG; four 35.6cm TT (1 x UW, 3 x AW).
Protection: Belt 240mm; armour deck 75-40-75mm; barbette 203mm; conning tower 160mm.
Complement: 202–270.

Name	Builder	Laid down	Launch	Comp	Fate
King Yuen	AG Vulcan (Stettin)	Late 1885	3 Jan 87	Jul 87	Gunfire Battle of Yalu 17 Sep 94.
Lai Yuen	AG Vulcan (Stettin)	Late 1885	25 Mar 87	Jul 87	Torpedoed Japanese torpedo boat *Kotaka*, Weihaiwei, 5 Feb 95.

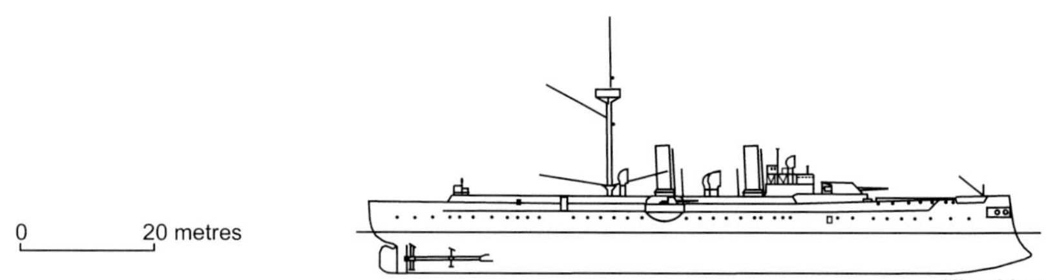

King Yuen

Chinese *Nan Thin* class

CRUISER

Displacement: 2,200 tonnes.
Dimensions: 77.1 (pp), 85.9 (oa) x 11.0 x 5.5 metres.
Machinery: Eight cylindrical boilers (coal); one shaft; HC, IHP 2,400 = 14.5 knots; coal 600 tonnes.
Armament: Two 20.3cm, eight 12.7cm guns; two 3.7cm MG.
Complement: 250.

Name	Builder	Laid down	Launch	Comp	Fate
Nan Thin	Howaldt (Kiel)	1883	12 Dec 83	Mar 84	Hulked; BU 1919.
Nan Shui	Howaldt (Kiel)	1883	8 Jan 84	Mar 84	Decommissioned 1903; sold to BU 1906.

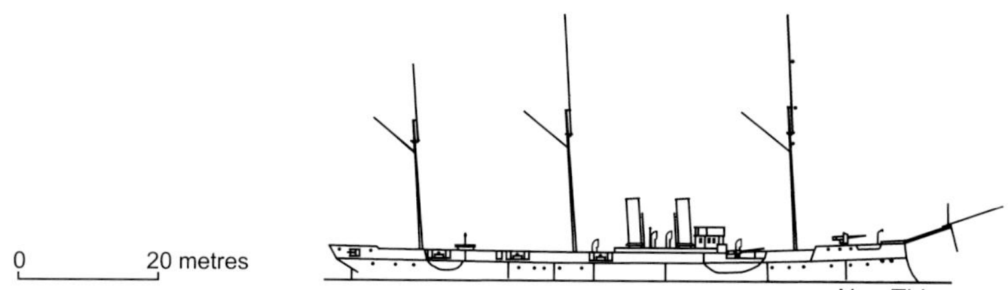

Nan Thin

Chinese *Hai Yung* class

PROTECTED CRUISER

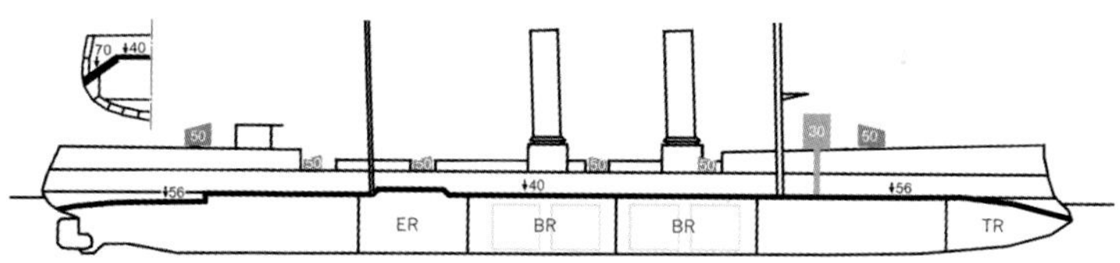

Displacement: 2,965 (full load) tonnes.
Dimensions: 100 (wl) x 12.5 x 5 metres.
Machinery: Eight cylindrical boilers (coal); two shafts; VTE, IHP 7,500 = 19.5 knots; coal 200/800 tonnes.
Armament: Three 15cm/40, eight 10.5cm/40 guns; six 3.7cm MG; four 45cm TT (1 x UW, 3 x AW).
Protection: Deck 56-40-56/70mm; shields 50mm; CT 30mm.
Complement: 244*.

Name	Builder	Laid down	Launch	Comp	Fate
Hai Yung	AG Vulcan (Stettin)	1896	15 Sep 97	Apr 98	Scuttled Yangtze 25 Sep 1937; salved 25 Apr 59; BU Luojiaqiao.
Hai Shew	AG Vulcan (Stettin)	1896	11 Dec 97	Jun 98	Scuttled Yangtze 25 Sep 1937; salved 1960; BU Changshanjlao.
Hai Chen	AG Vulcan (Stettin)	1896	12 Feb 98	Jul 98	Scuttled Yangtze 25 Sep 1937; salved 1964; BU Changshanjlao.

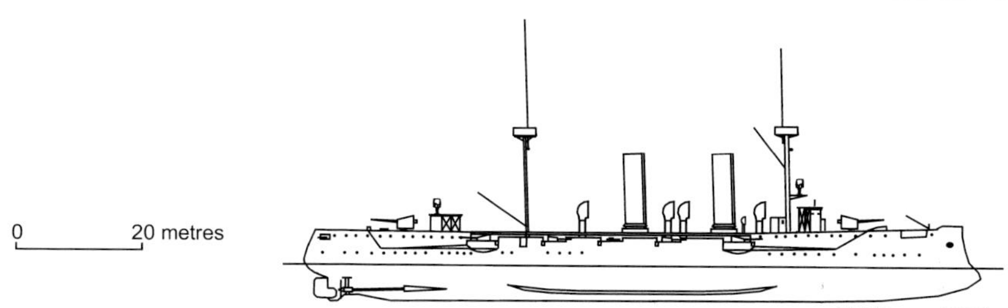

Hai Yung 1900

Russian *Bogatyr*

FIRST-CLASS CRUISER; CRUISER (10 Oct 07)

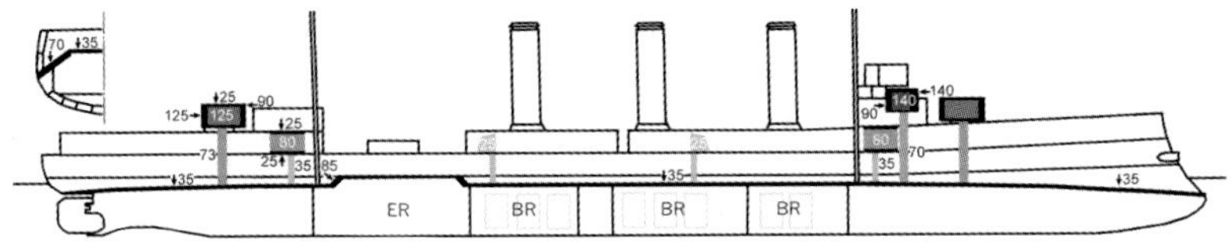

Displacement: 6,410 (design), 7,428 (full load) tons.
Dimensions: 127 (pp), 132.4 (wl), 134.1 (oa) x 16.6 x 6.3 metres.
Machinery: Sixteen Normand boilers (coal); two shafts; 4-cyl reciprocating (VTE), IHP 19,500 = 23 knots; coal 720/1,220 tonnes; range 4,900nm @ 10 knots.
Armament: Twelve 15.2cm/45 (2 x 2, 8 x 1), twelve 7.5cm/50 (12 x 1) guns; eight 4.7cm/43, two 3.7cm/23, two 7.62mm MG; four 38.1cm (2 x AW, 2 x UW) TT.
Protection: Deck 35mm/70mm; glacis 80mm; CT 140mm (sides); turrets 125 (front) 90mm (rear); casemates 19–80mm; shields 25mm.
Complement: 30+550.

Name	Builder	Laid down	Launch	Comp	Fate
Bogatyr	AG Vulcan (Stettin)	21 Dec 99	30 Jan 01	20 Aug 02	Sold Derumetall 1 Jul 22; BU Bremen from late 1922; stricken 21 Nov 25.

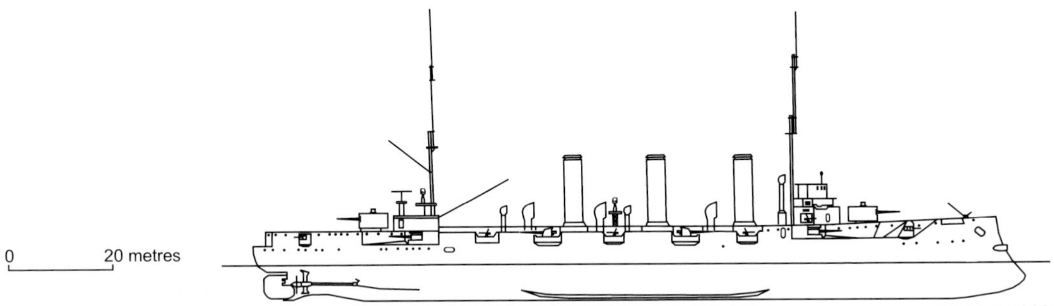

Bogatyr 1903

Russian *Askold*

FIRST-CLASS CRUISER; CRUISER (10 Oct 07)

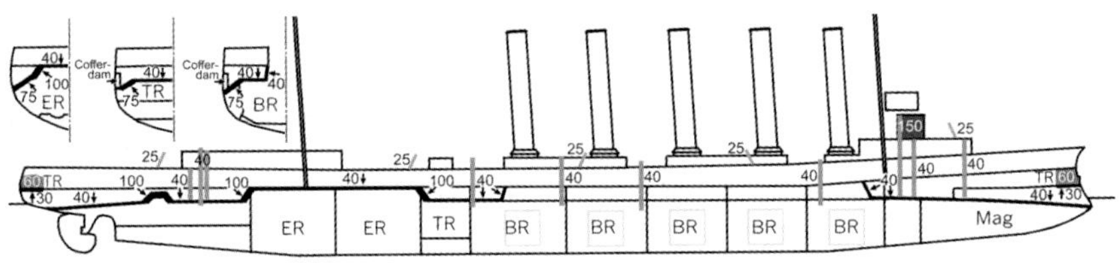

Displacement: 6,135 (normal) tons.
Dimensions: 123.3 (pp), 130 (wl), 131.2 (oa) x 16.87 x 6.3 metres.
Machinery: Nine Schultz-Thorneycroft boilers (coal); three shafts; 4-cyl reciprocating (VTE), IHP 19,000 = 23 knots; coal 720/1,250 tons; range 4,100nm @ 10 knots.
Armament: Twelve 15.2cm/45, twelve 7.5cm/50 guns; eight 4.7cm/43, two 3.7cm/23, two 7.62mm MG; six (1912: two) 38.1cm (4 x AW, 2 x UW; 1912: UW only) TT; thirty-five mines.
Protection: Deck 40mm/40–75mm; glacis 102mm; CT 30mm (roof), 150mm (sides); shields 25mm; TT 37–63mm.
Complement: 30+550.

Name	Builder	Laid down	Launch	Comp	Fate
Askold = *Glory IV* (3 Aug 18)	Germania (Kiel)	20 Jul 99	15 Mar 00	21 Sep 01	Sold Derumetall 1922; BU Hamburg.

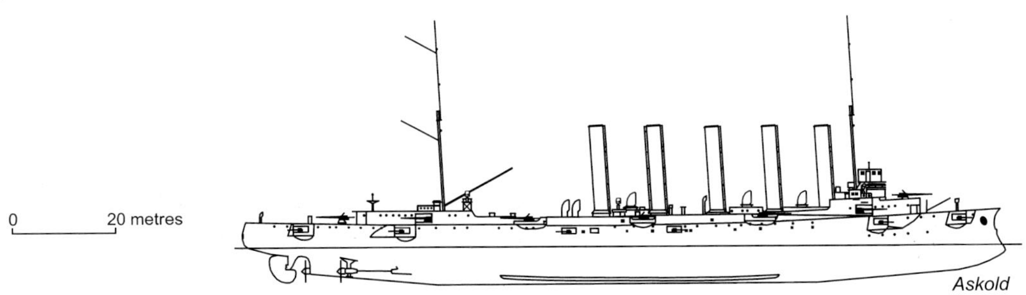

Askold

Russian *Novik*

SECOND-CLASS CRUISER; CRUISER (10 Oct 07)

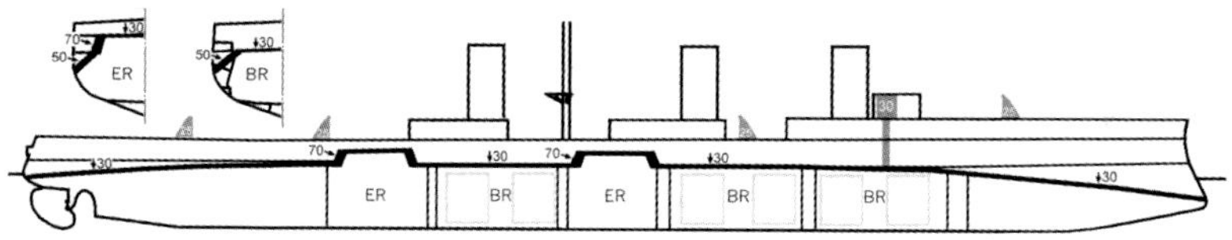

Displacement:	3,027 (full load) tons.
Dimensions:	106 (pp), 110.1 (wl) 111 (oa) x 12.2 x 5 metres.
Machinery:	Twelve Schichau-Thornycroft (1908: eight Miyabara) boilers (coal); three shafts; reciprocating (4-cyl VTE), IHP 17,000 = 25 knots; coal 360/509 tons; range 3,500nm @ 10 knots.
Armament:	Six 12cm/45, six 4.7cm/40 guns; five 38.1cm AW TT; 12 mines. 1908: two 15.2cm/50, four 12cm/40 guns; five 38.1cm AW TT. Dec 1908: two 12cm/40, four 7.8cm/40 guns; five 38.1cm AW TT.
Protection:	Deck 30/50mm; engine glacis 70mm; shields 25mm; CT 30mm.
Complement:	12+316.

Name	Builder	Laid down	Launch	Comp	Fate
Novik = *Suzuya* (1906)	Schichau (Danzig)	13 Mar 00	15 Aug 00	17 Dec 01	Scuttled Korsakovsk 20 Aug 04; salved 16 July 1906; JP commission Dec 08; stricken 1 Apr 13; BU.

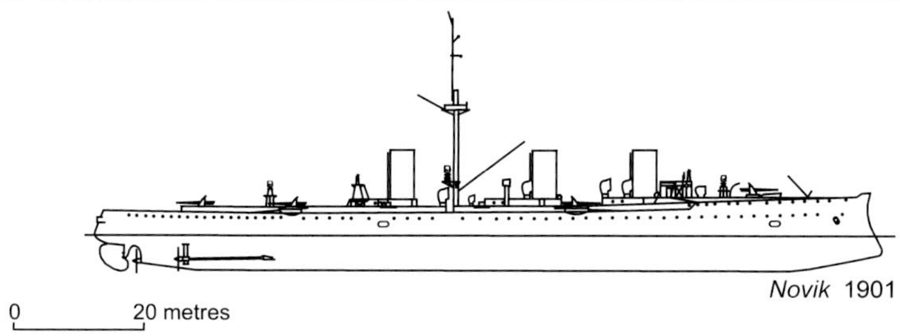

Novik 1901

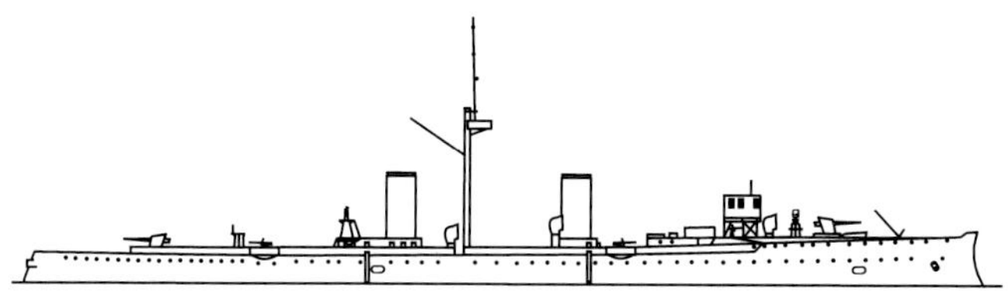

Suzuya (ex-*Novik*) 1908

Russian *Muravev-Amurskiy* class

CRUISERS

See pp 282-283, above.

Uruguayan *Uruguay*

CRUISER

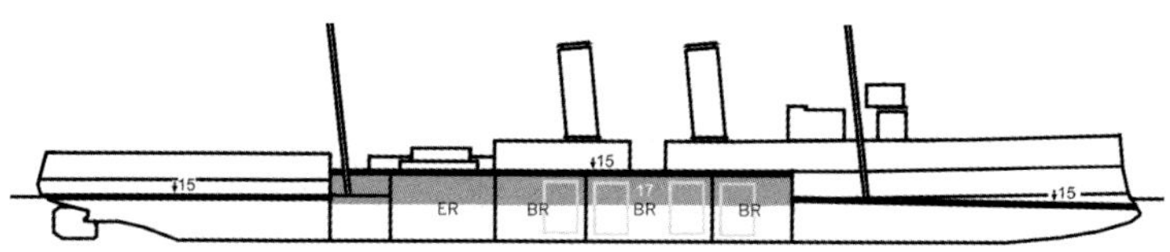

Displacement:	1,400 (normal) tonnes.
Dimensions:	85.0 (pp) x 9.4 x 3.6 metres.
Machinery:	Four Normand boilers (coal); two shafts; reciprocating (4-cyl VTE), IHP 8,250 = 25 knots; coal 210 tonnes; range 3,000nm @ 12 knots.
Armament:	Two 12cm/45, four 7.6cm/40, six 3.7cm/40 guns; two 45cm AW TT.
Protection:	Belt 17mm; deck 15mm.
Complement:	125.

Name	Builder	Laid down	Launch	Comp	Fate
Uruguay	Vulcan (Stettin)	1908	12 Apr 10	23 Jul 10	Stricken May 51; BU 1962.

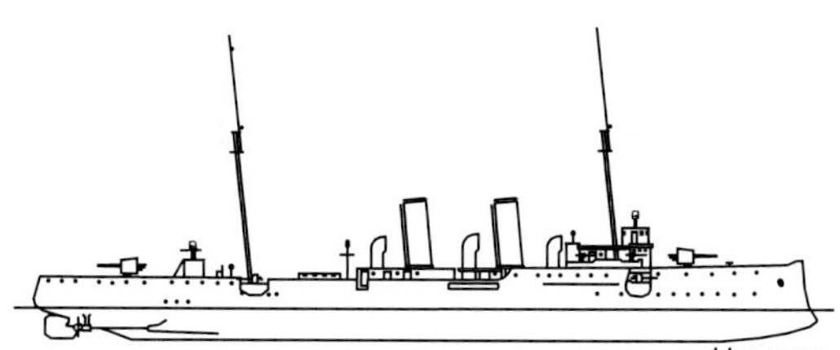

Uruguay

APPENDIX 1. THE FLEET LAWS

LAW, CONCERNING THE GERMAN FLEET, 10 APRIL 1898.[1]

I. Ship Strength.

§.1.

1. The ship strength of the German fleet, excluding torpedo vessels, training ships, special ships and gunboats, shall be:

a) ready for service:

1 fleet flagship,
2 squadrons of 8 battleships each,
2 divisions of 4 coastal armoured ships each,

6 large cruisers 16 small cruisers	as scouting ships of the home battlefleet,
3 large cruisers 10 small cruisers	for the overseas service;

b) as material reserve:

2 battleships,
3 large cruisers,
4 small cruisers.

2. Of the vessels existing and under construction on 1 April 1898, this target strength is classified:

as battleships	12,
as coastal armoured ships	8,
as large cruisers	10,
as small cruisers	23.

3. The provision of funds for the construction of new construction necessary for the achievement of the target strength is subject to the annual fixing of the Reich Budget with the proviso that the completion of the legal strength of ships will be carried out at the end of the financial year 1903 provided that sufficient funds are provided under §.7.

§.2.

The provision of funds for necessary replacement construction is subject to the annual Reich budget, to replace

battleships and coastal armoured vessels after 25 years,
large cruisers after 20 years,
small cruisers after 15 years

The periods run from the year of granting the first instalment of the ship to be replaced to the granting of the first instalment of the replacement ship.
An extension to the replacement period requires case-by-case consent of the Bundesrat, shortening of that of the Reichstag. Any authorisations of replacement construction before expiry of the legal lifetime – *force majeure*, such as the sinking of a ship, excluded – are to be settled within a period to be agreed with the Reichstag by deferring other replacement construction.

II. Implementation.

§.3.

The provision of appropriations for the home battlefleet is subject to the annual budget of the Reich, provided that there can be kept in service:

a) for the establishment of active formations:
9 battleships,
2 large cruisers,
6 small cruisers;

b) as parent ships of reserve formations:
4 battleships,
4 coastal armoured vessels,
2 large cruisers,
5 small cruisers;

c) to activate as a reserve formation for the duration of two months:
2 battleships or coastal armoured vessels.

III. Manpower.

§.4.

Deck officers, petty officers and ordinary seamen, shipyard divisions and torpedo divisions should comprise:

1. one and a half times the crews for ships overseas;
2. full crews for
the ships belonging to active formations of the home battlefleet,
half of the torpedo vessels,
the training ships,
the special-service ships;

3. nucleus crews (two-thirds engineering personnel, remaining personnel half of full crews) for

[1 *Deutsches Reichsgesetzblatt* 1898/15, pp 165-68.]

the ships belonging to reserve formations of the home battlefleet,
the second half of the torpedo vessels;

4. the required shore support;
5. a supplement of five percent of the total requirements.

§.5.

The budgets of the seamen divisions, shipyard divisions and torpedo divisions required by these principles are subject to the annual budget of the Reich.

IV. Other expenditure.

§.6.

All ongoing and one-off expenses of the navy budget, for which no provision is made in this law, are subject to the annual budget process as required.

V. Costs.

§.7.

During the next six financial years (1898–1903) the Reichstag is not obliged to provide more than 408,900,000 marks for the total one-off expenditure items in the naval budget, specifically no more than 356,700,000 marks for shipbuilding and armaments, and for the other one-off expenditure no more than 52,200,000 marks. Additionally, it will not be obliged to provide more than the average increase of 4,900,000 marks for the annual ongoing expenditure on the naval budget.
In the event that the law cannot be carried out by the end of the financial year 1903 its execution will be deferred beyond the year 1903.

§.8.

In the event that the sum of the ongoing and one-off expenditure of the regular budget for naval administration exceed the total of 117,525,494 Marks in a single budget year, and the revenues available to the Reich are insufficient to cover the shortfall, that shortfall may not be covered by raising or increasing indirect Reich taxes on mass consumption.

LAW, CONCERNING THE GERMAN FLEET, 14 JUNE 1900.[2]

I. Ship strength.

§.1.

It should consist of:

1. the battlefleet:

comprising 2 fleet flagships,
4 squadrons of 8 battleships each,

8 large cruisers }
24 small cruisers } as scouting ships of the home battlefleet;

2. the overseas fleet:

comprising 3 large cruisers,
10 small cruisers;

3. the material reserve:

comprising 4 battleships,
3 large cruisers,
4 small cruisers.

At the time of adoption of this Law, the ships listed in Annex A will be included in this target strength.

§.2.

Except for ship losses, replacements will be made:
battleships after 25 years,
cruisers after 20 years.

The periods run from the year of granting the first instalment of the ship to be replaced to the granting of the first instalment of the replacement ship.
For the period from 1901 to 1917 replacement construction will be regulated by Annex B.

II. Implementation.

§.3.

Regarding the maintenance of the battlefleet in service, the following principles apply:

1. the I. and II. Squadrons form the active battlefleet, the III. and IV. Squadron form the reserve battlefleet.
2. The active battlefleet and half of the battleships and cruisers of the reserve fleet shall be kept permanently in service.
3. For manoeuvres, individual out-of-service vessels of the reserve battlefleet shall be temporarily put into service.

III. Manpower.

§.4.

Deck Officers, non-commissioned officers, and ordinary seamen, shipyard divisions, and torpedo divisions should be available for:

1. full crews for the vessels belonging to the active battlefleet, for half of the torpedo boats, the training ships and the special-service vessels,
2. crews (machinery personnel 2/3, remaining crew ? of full crews) for the vessels belonging to the reserve

[[2] *Deutsches Reichsgesetzblatt* 1900/21, pp 255-59.]

battlefleet and for the second half of the torpedo boats,
3. 1½ times crews for ships abroad,
4. the required shore resources,
5. a supplement of 5 percent to the total requirement.

IV. Costs.

§.5.

The provision of the resources required to implement this Law is subject to the annual budget of the Reich.

§.6.

In the case that the excess requirement of the ongoing and one-off expenditure of the regular budget for naval administration from 1901 exceeds the excess revenue of the Reich stamp-duty by more than of 53,708,000 marks, and the shortfall cannot be covered by the Reich's other income, then the shortfall may not be covered by raising or increasing indirect Reich taxes on mass consumption.

Annex A. Ships included in the target strength at the time of this Law.

27 Battleships

1. *Bayern*
2. *Sachsen*
3. *Württemberg*
4. *Baden*
5. *Oldenburg*
6. *Brandenburg*
7. *Kurfürst Friedrich Wilhelm*
8. *Weißenburg*
9. *Wörth*
10. *Kaiser Friedrich III*
11. *Kaiser Wilhelm II*
12. *Kaiser Wilhelm der Große*
13. *Kaiser Barbarossa*
14. *Kaiser Karl der Große*
15. *C*
16. *D*
17. *E*
18. *F*
19. *G*
20. *Siegfried*
21. *Beowulf*
22. *Frithjof*
23. *Hildebrand*
24. *Heimdall*
25. *Hagen*
26. *Aegir*
27. *Odin*

12 large cruisers

1. *König Wilhelm*
2. *Kaiser*
3. *Deutschland*
4. *Kaiserin Augusta*
5. *Hertha*
6. *Victoria Louise*
7. *Freya*
8. *Hansa*
9. *Vineta*
10. *Fürst Bismarck*
11. *Prinz Heinrich*
12. *B*

29 small cruisers

1. *Zieten*
2. *Blitz*
3. *Pfeil*
4. *Arcona*
5. *Alexandrine*
6. *Greif*
7. *Irene*
8. *Prinzeß Wilhelm*
9. *Schwalbe*
10. *Wacht*
11. *Jagd*
12. *Sperber*
13. *Bussard*
14. *Meteor*
15. *Falke*
16. *Comet*
17. *Cormoran*
18. *Condor*
19. *Seeadler*
20. *Gefion*
21. *Geier*
22. *Hela*
23. *Gazelle*
24. *Niobe*
25. *Nymphe*
26. *C*
27. *D*
28. *E*
29. *F*

Completed as a IV. class cruiser, *Seeadler* became a small cruiser under the terms of the Fleet Laws. She is shown here on 18 March 1914, approaching her buoy at Kiel, and wearing her 'home pennant' denoting 13 years abroad. On 6 May she was reclassified as a gunboat, her 'legal' replacement, *Karlsruhe* (i) having been in commission since 15 January that year. *(DN collection)*

Annex B. Distribution of the replacement construction to be carried out during the years 1901 to 1917.

Replacement year	Battleships	Large cruisers	Small cruisers
1901	–	1	–
1902	–	1	1
1903	–	1	1
1904	–	–	2
1905	–	–	2
1906	2	–	2
1907	2	–	2
1908	2	–	2
1909	2	–	2
1910	1	1	2
1911	1	1	2
1912	1	1	2
1913	1	1	2
1914	1	1	2
1915	1	1	2
1916	1	1	2
1917	2	–	1
Totals	**17**	**10**	**29**

AMENDMENT TO THE LAW, CONCERNING THE GERMAN FLEET, OF 14 JUNE 1900, OF 5 JUNE 1906.

The strength of ships specified in §.1 of the Law, Concerning the German Fleet, of 14 June 1900 is increased:

1. in the overseas fleet by 5 large cruisers;
2. in the material reserve by 1 large cruiser.

AMENDMENT TO THE LAW, CONCERNING THE GERMAN FLEET, OF 14 JUNE 1900, OF 6 APRIL 1908.

§.2.

Except for ship losses, battleships and cruisers will be replaced after 20 years.

The period runs from the year of granting the first instalment of the ship to be replaced to the granting of the first instalment of the replacement ship.

For the period from 1908 to 1917 replacement construction will be regulated by Annex B.

AMENDMENT TO THE LAW CONCERNING THE GERMAN FLEET OF 14 JUNE 1900, OF 14 JUNE 1912.

Article I.

In place of §.1 of the Law Concerning the German Fleet of 14 June 1900 and the Amendment to this Law of 5 June 1906, insert the following

§.1. It should consist of:

1. the battlefleet:
   comprising 1 fleet flagship,
   5 squadrons of 8 battleships each,
   12 large cruisers, 30 small cruisers } as scouting ships;

2. the overseas fleet:
   comprising 8 large cruisers,
   10 small cruisers;

3. the material reserve:
   comprising 4 battleships,
   3 large cruisers,
   4 small cruisers.

Article II.

In place of paragraphs 1 and 2 of §.3 of the Law, insert the following.

1. 1 fleet flagship,
   3 battleship squadrons,
   8 large cruisers and
   18 small cruisers
   forming the active battlefleet
   2 battleship squadrons,
   4 large cruisers and
   12 small cruisers
   forming the reserve battlefleet.

2. In addition to the active battlefleet, a quarter of the battleships and cruisers of the reserve fleet shall be kept permanently in service.

Article III.
In place of the introduction and paragraphs 1 and 2 of §.4 of the Law Concerning the German Fleet of 14 June 1900 insert the following.

Except for ship losses, battleships and cruisers will be replaced after 20 years.
The period runs from the year of granting the first instalment of the ship to be replaced to the granting of the first instalment of the replacement ship.
For the period from 1908 to 1917 replacement construction will be regulated by the table.

II. Implementation

§.3

Regarding the maintenance of the battlefleet, the following principles apply:

1. 1 fleet flagship,
   3 battleship squadrons,
   8 large cruisers and
   18 small cruisers
   form the active battlefleet;
   2 battleship squadrons,
   8 large cruisers and
   18 small cruisers
   form the reserve battlefleet;
2. In addition to the active battlefleet, a quarter of the battleships and cruisers of the reserve fleet shall be kept permanently in service.
3. For manoeuvres, individual out-of-service vessels of the reserve battlefleet shall be temporarily put into service.

III. Manpower

§.4

Deck Officers, petty officers, and ordinary seamen, shipyard divisions, and torpedo divisions should be available for:
1. full crews for the vessels belonging to the active battlefleet, for half of the torpedo boats, the training ships and the special-service vessels,
2. nucleus crews (machinery personnel ⅓, remaining crew ¼ of full crews) for the vessels belonging to the reserve battlefleet and for the second half of the torpedo boats,
3. 1½ times crews for ships abroad,
4. the required shore resources,
5. a supplement of 5 percent to the total requirement.

Dresden and the large cruisers *Victoria Louise* and *Hertha* at New York for the Hudson-Fulton celebration, 24 September-9 October 1909. *(Library of Congress 04281)*

APPENDIX 2: ORGANISATION OF CAPITAL SHIPS AND CRUISERS FROM 1884

Prior to 1914, these comprise the organisation for that year's summer manoeuvres.

1884

I. Division	**II. Division**	**III. (Training) Division**
Baden (F)	*Grille* (F)	*Sophie*
Württemberg	*Hummel*	*Nymphe*
Bayern	*Camaeleon*	*Niobe*
Sachsen	*Crocodill*	*Undine*
Hansa	*Biene*	*Rover*

1885

Armoured Division	**Unarmoured Division**
Friedrich Carl	*Stein*
Bayern	*Olga*
Hansa	*Sophie*
Pfeil	

1886

I. Division	**II. (Training) Division**	**III. (Gunboat) Division**
Baden (F)	*Stein* (F)	*Mücke* (F)
Sachsen	*Moltke*	*Camaeleon*
Württemberg	*Prinz Adalbert*	*Viper*
Oldenburg	*Sophie*	*Salamander*
Zieten	*Hansa*	

1887

I. Division	**II. (Training) Division**	**III. (Gunboat) Division**	**Baltic Squadron**
König Wilhelm (F)	*Stein* (F)	*Mücke* (F)	*Friedrich Carl* (F)
Kaiser	*Gneisenau*	*Camaeleon*	*Sachsen*
Oldenburg	*Moltke*	*Viper*	*Hansa*
Pfeil	*Prinz Adalbert*	*Salamander*	*Nixe*
			Rhein

1888

I. Division	**II. (Training) Division**
Baden (F)	*Stein*
Bayern	*Gneisenau*
Kaiser	*Moltke*
Friedrich der Große	*Prinz Adalbert*
Zieten	

1889

I. Division	**II. (Training) Division**
Baden (F)	*Kaiser* (F)
Sachsen	*Deutschland*
Oldenburg	*Preußen*
Irene	*Friedrich der Große*
Wacht	*Zieten*

1890

I. Division	II. (Training) Division
Baden (F)	*Kaiser* (F)
Bayern	*Deutschland*
Württemberg	*Friedrich der Große*
Oldenburg	*Irene*
Zieten	*Pfeil*

1891

I. Division	II. (Training) Division
Baden (F)	*Kaiser/Friedrich Carl* (F)
Bayern	*Deutschland/Kronprinz*
Siegfried	*Preußen*
Oldenburg	*Friedrich Carl/Prinzeß Wilhelm*
Zieten	*Pfeil*

1892

I. Division	II. (Training) Division	Scouting Group
Baden (F)	*Friedrich Carl* (F)	*Pelikan*
Bayern	*Deutschland*	*Siegfried*
Oldenburg	*Kronprinz*	
Zieten	*Friedrich der Große*	
	Wacht	

1893

I. Division	II. Division	III. Division
Baden (F)	*König Wilhelm* (F)	*Stein* (F)
Bayern	*Deutschland*	*Gneisenau*
Beowulf	*Friedrich der Große*	*Moltke*
Württemberg	*Frithjof*	*Stosch*
Meteor		

1894

Fleet flag: *Wörth*

I. Division	II. Division	III. Division	IV. Division	Scouting Force
Baden/Bayern/Kurfürst Friedrich Wilhelm (F)	*König Wilhelm* (F)	*Stein* (F)	*Hildebrand* (F)	*Prinzeß Wilhelm*
Bayern	*Deutschland*	*Stosch*	*Frithjof*	*Pelikan*
Württemberg	*Friedrich der Große*	*Moltke*	*Beowulf*	*Brummer*
Pfeil	*Brandenburg*	*Gneisenau*		

1895

I. Division	II. Division	III. Division	IV. Division	Scouting Force
Kurfürst Friedrich Wilhelm (F)	*Baden* (F)	*Stein* (F)	*Hildebrand* (F)	*Kaiserin Augusta*
Brandenburg	*Bayern*	*Stosch*	*Frithjof*	*Gefion*
Weißenburg	*Württemberg*	*Moltke*	*Beowulf*	*Meteor*
Wörth	*Sachsen*	*Gneisenau*	*Siegfried*	*Grille*
Jagd	*Pfeil*			*Pelikan*
				Carola
				Hagen

1896

I. Squadron		II. Squadron		
I. Division	**II. Division**	**III. Division**	**IV. Division**	**Scouting Force**
Kurfürst Friedrich Wilhelm (F)	*König Wilhelm* (F)	*Stein* (F)	*Hildebrand* (F)	*Kaiserin Augusta*
Brandenburg	*Sachsen*	*Stosch*	*Siegfried*	*Gefion*
Weißenburg	*Württemberg*	*Moltke*	*Beowulf*	*Carola*
Wörth	*Wacht*	*Gneisenau*	*Frithjof*	*Hagen*
Jagd				*Meteor*
				Grille

1897

I. Squadron		II. Squadron		
I. Division	**II. Division**	**III. Division**	**IV. Division**	**Scouting Force**
Kurfürst Friedrich Wilhelm (F)	*König Wilhelm* (F)	*Hildebrand* (F)	*Frithjof* (F)	*Charlotte*
Brandenburg	*Sachsen*	*Siegfried*	*Hagen*	*Stein*
Weißenburg	*Württemberg*	*Beowulf*	*Heimdall*	*Carola*
Wörth	*Greif*			*Gefion*
Jagd				*Blitz*
				Pfeil

1898

I. Squadron			II. Squadron		
I. Division	**II. Division**	**I. Scouting Group**	**III. Division**	**IV. Division**	**II. Scouting Group**
Kurfürst Friedrich Wilhelm (F)	*Baden* (F)	*Greif*	*Aegir* (F)	*Frithjof* (F)	*Blitz*
Brandenburg	*Bayern*	*Pelikan*	*Odin*	*Beowulf*	*Pfeil*
Weißenburg	*Oldenburg*	*Hela*	*Hagen*	*Heimdall*	
Wörth					

1899

I. Squadron		II. Squadron		
I. Division	**II. Division**	**III. Division**	**IV. Division**	**Scouting Force**
Kurfürst Friedrich Wilhelm (F)	*Baden* (F)	*Hildebrand* (F)	*Aegir* (F)	*Hela*
Brandenburg	*Bayern*	*Siegfried*	*Odin*	*Greif*
Weißenburg	*Sachsen*	*Beowulf*	*Frithjof*	*Wacht*
Wörth				*Blitz*
				Zeiten
				Pelikan
				Grille

1900

I. Squadron	II. Squadron		
II. Division	**III. Division**	**IV. Division**	**Scouting Force**
Kaiser Wilhelm II (F & FF)	*Hildebrand* (F)	*Aegir* (2F)	*Blitz*
Kaiser Friedrich III (2F)	*Siegfried*	*Odin*	*Greif*
Sachsen	*Heimdall*	*Frithjof*	*Grille*
Württemberg			*Jagd*

1901

Fleet flag: *Kaiser Wilhelm II*

I. Squadron

Kaiser Wilhelm der Große (F)
Kaiser Barbarossa
Kurfürst Friedrich Wilhelm (2F)
Brandenburg
Weißenburg
Wörth

II. Squadron

Baden (F)
Sachsen
Württemberg
Aegir (2F)
Siegfried
Hagen
Odin

I. Scouting Group

Victoria Louise
Hela
Jagd/Wacht

II. Scouting Group

Nymphe
Gazelle
Niobe

1902

Fleet flag: *Kaiser Wilhelm II*

I. Squadron

Kaiser Friedrich III (F)
Kaiser Barbarossa
Kaiser Wilhelm der Große
Kaiser Karl der Große
Kurfürst Friedrich Wilhelm (2F)
Brandenburg
Weißenburg

II. Squadron

Baden (F)
Württemberg
Beowulf
Hagen
Heimdall
Hildebrand (2F)

I. Scouting Group

Victoria Louise
Amazone
Hela

II. Scouting Group

Prinz Heinrich
Niobe
Nymphe

1903

Active Battefleet

Fleet flag: *Kaiser Wilhelm II*

I. Squadron

Kaiser Friedrich III (F)
Kaiser Wilhelm der Große
Kaiser Barbarossa
Kaiser Karl der Große
Zähringen
Wittelsbach (2F)
Wettin

II. Squadron

Baden (F)
Württemberg
Hildebrand (F)
Frithjof
Odin
Beowulf

Scouting Force

Prinz Heinrich
Victoria Louise
Amazone
Ariadne
Frauenlob
Niobe
Medusa
Arcona
Hela
Blitz

1904

Fleet flag: *Kaiser Wilhelm II*

I. Squadron

Wittelsbach (F)
Zähringen
Wettin
Mecklenburg
Kaiser Karl der Große

II. Squadron

Kaiser Friedrich III (F)
Kaiser Wilhelm der Große
Wörth (2F)
Weißenburg
Elsaß
Braunschweig

Scouting Force

Prinz Heinrich (F)
Frauenlob
Arcona
Hamburg
Ariadne
Amazone
Medusa
Niobe

1905

Fleet flag: *Kaiser Wilhelm II*

I. Squadron
Wittelsbach (F)
Zähringen
Wettin
Mecklenburg
Kaiser Wilhelm der Große
Kaiser Karl der Große
Kaiser Friedrich III (2F)

II. Squadron
Preußen (F)
Braunschweig (2F)
Brandenburg
Weißenburg
Wörth

I. Scouting Group
Friedrich Carl (F)
Arcona
Medusa
Hamburg

II. Scouting Group
Prinz Heinrich (2F)
Frauenlob
Ariadne
Berlin

1906

Fleet flag: *Deutschland*

I. Squadron
Wittelsbach (F)
Zähringen
Wettin
Mecklenburg
Kaiser Wilhelm der Große
Kaiser Karl der Große
Kaiser Wilhelm II
Kaiser Friedrich III (2F)

II. Squadron
Preußen (F)
Hessen
Elsaß
Braunschweig
Lothringen
Brandenburg
Kurfürst Friedrich Wilhelm (2F)

Scouting Force
Yorck (F)
Roon
Lübeck
Hamburg
Berlin
Friedrich Carl (2F)
Medusa
Frauenlob
Arcona

1908

Fleet flag: *Deutschland*

I. Squadron
Wittelsbach (F)
Zähringen
Wettin
Mecklenburg
Kaiser Wilhelm der Große
Kaiser Karl der Große
Kaiser Wilhelm II
Kaiser Friedrich III (2F)

II. Squadron
Preußen (F)
Hessen
Elsaß
Braunschweig
Lothringen
Brandenburg

Scouting Force
Yorck (F)
Roon
Lübeck
Hamburg
Berlin
Friedrich Carl (2F)
Medusa

Exercise Squadron (temp.)
Kurfürst Friedrich Wilhelm
Frithjof
Aegir
Albatross
Nautilus
Blitz
Pfeil
Frauenlob
Zieten
Arcona

1909

Fleet flag: *Deutschland*

High Seas Fleet

I. Squadron
Hannover (F)
Schliesen
Mecklenburg
Zähringen
Kaiser Karl der Große
Kaiser Barbarossa
Wettin
Wittelsbach (2F)

II. Squadron
Preußen (F)
Hessen
Elsaß
Pommern
Lothringen
Braunschweig (2F)

Scouting Force
Yorck (F)
Gneisenau
Danzig
Königsberg
Hamburg
Roon (2F)
Berlin
Lübeck
Stettin

Reserve Fleet

III. Squadron
Hildebrand (F)
Frithjof
Siegfried
Beowulf
Heimdall
Odin
Hagen
Aegir (2F)

VII. Division
Schwaben (F & FF)
Kurfürst Friedrich Wilhelm
Weißenburg

III. Scouting Group
Prinz Adalbert (F)
Friedrich Carl
Stuttgart
München
Undine

1912

Fleet flag: *Deutschland*

High Seas Fleet

I. Squadron
Ostfriesland
Thüringen
Helgoland
Westfalen
Nassau
Posen
Rheinland
Elsaß

II. Squadron
Preußen (F)
Schleswig-Holstein
Hessen
Lothringen
Pommern
Braunschweig (2F)
Hannover
Schlesien

Scouting Force
Moltke (FO)
Von der Tann
Yorck (2F)
Mainz
Kolberg
Dresden
Berlin
Cöln
Stettin
Hela

Reserve Fleet

North Sea Division
Wittelsbach
Zähringen
Mecklenburg
Schwaben

Baltic Division
Kaiser Wilhelm II
Kaiser Friedrich III
Kaiser Barbarossa
Kaiser Wilhelm der Große

August 1914

Fleet flag: *Friedrich der Große*

I. Squadron
Ostfriesland (F)
Thüringen
Helgoland
Oldenburg
Posen (2F)
Rheinland
Nassau
Westfalen

II. Squadron
Preußen (F)
Schlesien
Hessen
Lothringen
Hannover (2F)
Schleswig-Holstein
Pommern
Deutschland

III. Squadron
Prinzregent Luitpold (F)
Kaiserin
Kaiser
König Albert
Großer Kurfürst

IV. Squadron
Wittelsbach (F)
Wettin
Zähringen
Schwaben
Mecklenburg
Braunschweig (2F)
Elsaß

V. Squadron
Kaiser Wilhelm II (F)
Kaiser Wilhelm der Große
Kaiser Barbarossa
Kaiser Friedrich III (2F)
Kaiser Karl der Große
Wörth
Brandenburg

VI. Squadron
Hildebrand (F)
Heimdall
Hagen
Frithjof
Odin
Beowulf
Siegfried
Aegir (2F)

I. Scouting Group
Seydlitz (F)
Moltke
Blücher
Von der Tann (2F)
Derfflinger

II. Scouting Group
Cöln (F)
Mainz
Stralsund
Kolberg
Rostock
Strassburg
Graudenz

III. (ex-IV.) Scouting Group
Roon (F)
Yorck
Prinz Adalbert
Prinz Heinrich

IV. (ex-III.) Scouting Group
München (F)
Danzig
Stuttgart
Frauenlob
Hela

V. Scouting Group
Hansa (F)
Vineta
Victoria Louise
Hertha

Ems Coast Defence Division
Arcona

Jade/Weser Coast Defence Division
Ariadne
Berlin
Niobe
Blitz

Elbe Coast Defence Division
Nymphe
Medusa
Pfeil

Baltic Coast Defence Division
Amazone
Augsburg
Freya
Magdeburg
Lübeck
Thetis
Gazelle
Undine

East Asiatic Squadron
Scharnhorst (F)
Gneisenau
Emden
Leipzig
Nürnberg
Iltis
Tiger
Luchs
Jaguar

Mediterranean Division
Goeben (flag)
Breslau

East American Station	East African Station	South Seas Station
Dresden	*Königsberg*	*Geier*
Karlsruhe		

May 1916

Fleet flag: *Friedrich der Große*

I. Squadron	II. Squadron	III. Squadron	I. Scouting Group	II. Scouting Group	IV. Scouting Group
Ostfriesland (F)	*Deutschland* (F)	*König* (F)	*Lützow* (F)	*Frankfurt* (F)	*Stettin* (F)
Helgoland	*Pommern*	*Großer Kurfürst*	*Derfflinger*	*Pillau*	*München*
Thüringen	*Schlesien*	*Markgraf*	*Seydlitz*	*Elbing*	*Frauenlob*
Oldenburg	*Hannover* (2F)	*Kronprinz*	*Moltke*	*Wiesbaden*	*Stuttgart*
Posen (2F)	*Schleswig-Holstein*	*Kaiser* (2F)	*Von der Tann*		*Hamburg*
Rheinland	*Hessen*	*Kaiserin*			
Nassau		*Prinzregent Luitpold*			**LTB**
Westfalen		*König Albert*			*Rostock*

November 1918

Fleet Flagship: *Baden*

I. Squadron	III. Squadron	IV. Squadron	I. Scouting Group	II. Scouting Group	IV. Scouting Group
Ostfriesland (F)	*König* (F)	*Friedrich der Grosse* (F)	*Hindenburg* (F)	*Königsberg* (F)	*Regensburg* (F)
Thüringen	*Bayern*	*König Albert*	*Derfflinger*	*Karlsruhe*	*Bremse*
Posen	*Großer Kurfürst*	*Kaiserin*	*Moltke*	*Pillau*	*Brummer*
Nassau	*Kronprinz Wilhelm*	*Prinzregent Luitpold*	*Von der Tann*	*Nürnberg*	*Strassburg*
Oldenburg	*Markgraf*	*Kaiser*	*Seydlitz*	*Cöln*	*Stralsund*
Westfalen (TS)				*Graudenz*	
Helgoland				*Dresden*	**LTB**
					Emden

WEST AFRICAN CRUISER SQUADRON

Bismarck (F)	Sep 84–Jul 85
Ariadne	Oct 84
Gneisenau	Oct–Dec 84
Olga	Oct 84–Apr 85

EAST AFRICAN CRUISER SQUADRON

Stosch (F)	Jul–Aug 85
Bismarck (F)	Aug 85–Jan 86
Prinz Adalbert	May 79–Sep 85
Elisabeth	Apr 84–Oct 85
Gneisenau	Oct 84–Jun 86
Möwe	Apr 84–Aug 89

CRUISER SQUADRON

Bismarck (F)	Dec 86–Apr 87
Leipzig (F)	Jul 88–Mar 93
Olga	to Sep 89
Carola	to Apr 91
Sophie	Nov 86–Jun 92
Alexandrine	Jul 89–Mar 93
Arcona	Mar 92–Mar 93
Marie	Jan–Mar 93
Schwalbe	Dec 88–May 93, Mar–May 92, Feb–Mar 93
Pfeil	Nov 88–Sep 89
Sperber	Oct 89–Apr 90 (attached)
Möwe	Aug 85–Aug 89, Mar–May 92, Feb–Mar 93
Hyäne	(intermittent)
Adler	(intermittent)

EAST ASIATIC DIVISION/SQUADRON

East Asiatic Division

1859–61

Arcona (i)
Thetis (i)
Frauenlob (i)

1874–81

Vineta (i) (F)	Jun–Aug 76; Aug 76–Jan 77
Hertha (i)	Mar 74–Jun 76
Ariadne (i)	Jan 75–Jun 76
Luise	Jul 76–May 77
Cyclop	Aug 75–Jan 81
Nautilus	Sep 76–May 81

July	1881	1882	1883	1884	1885	1886	1887
Flag	–	*Stosch*	*Stosch*	*Stosch*	*Stosch*	*Bismarck*	*Bismarck*
	Stosch	*Hertha* (i)	*Wolf*	*Leipzig* (i)	*Iltis* (i)	*Olga*	*Carola*
	Wolf	*Elisabeth*	*Iltis* (i)	*Prinz Adalbert*	*Nautilus*	*Iltis* (i)	*Sophie*
	Iltis (i)	*Wolf*		*Wolf*	*Wolf*	*Wolf*	*Iltis* (i)
		Iltis (i)		*Iltis* (i)			*Nautilus*
							Wolf
							Adler

July	1888	1889	1890	1891	1892	1893
Flag	*Bismarck*	*Leipzig* (i)	*Leipzig* (i)	*Leipzig* (i)	*Leipzig* (i)	*Leipzig* (i)
	Carola	*Sophie*	*Sophie*	*Alexandrine*	*Alexandrine*	*Alexandrine*
	Sophie	*Iltis* (i)	*Iltis* (i)	*Sophie*	*Iltis* (i)	*Arcona* (i)
	Iltis (i)	*Wolf*	*Wolf*	*Iltis* (i)	*Wolf*	*Iltis* (i)
	Wolf	*Eber*		*Wolf*		*Wolf*
	Adler	*Adler*				

	East Asiatic Cruiser Division			**East Asiatic Cruiser Squadron**			
July	1894	1895	1896	1897	1898	1899	1900
Flag	*Arcona* (ii) (Oct)	*Irene/Kaiser*	*Kaiser*	*Kaiser*	*Kaiser*	*Deutschland*	*Hertha* (ii)
	Wolf	*Arcona* (ii)	*Arcona* (ii)	*Arcona* (ii)	*Arcona* (ii)	*Irene*	*Irene*
		Prinzeß	*Irene*	*Irene*	*Irene*	*Prinzeß*	*Hansa* (ii)
		Wilhelm	*Prinzeß*	*Prinzeß*	*Prinzeß*	*Wilhelm*	*Kaiserin*
			Wilhelm	*Wilhelm*	*Wilhelm*	*Kaiserin*	*Augusta*
			Cormoran	*Cormoran*	*Kaiserin*	*Augusta*	*Gefion* (ii)
					Augusta	*Gefion* (ii)	*Iltis* (ii)
					Cormoran	*Iltis* (ii)	*Jaguar*
					Gefion	*Jaguar*	*Tiger*

July	1901	1902	1903	1905	1906	1907	1904
Flag	*Fürst Bismarck*	*Fürst Bismarck*	*Fürst Bismarck*	*Fürst Bismarck*	*Fürst Bismarck*	*Fürst Bismarck*	*Fürst Bismarck*
	Hertha (ii)	*Hertha* (ii)	*Hertha* (ii)	*Hansa* (ii)	*Hansa* (ii)	*Leipzig* (ii)	*Hertha* (ii)
	Hansa (ii)	*Hansa* (ii)	*Hansa* (ii)	*Thetis* (ii)	*Niobe* (ii)	*Niobe* (ii)	*Hansa* (ii)
	Kaiserin Augusta	*Thetis* (ii)	*Thetis* (ii)	*Iltis*	*Iltis*	*Iltis*	*Thetis* (ii)
	Iltis (ii)	*Iltis* (ii)	*Iltis* (ii)	*Jaguar*	*Jaguar*	*Jaguar*	*Iltis* (ii)
	Jaguar	*Jaguar*	*Jaguar*	*Tiger*	*Tiger*	*Tiger*	*Sperber*
	Tiger	*Tiger*	*Tiger*	*Luchs*	*Luchs*	*Luchs*	*Jaguar*
	Luchs	*Luchs*	*Luchs*				*Tiger*

July	1908	1909	1910	1911	1912	1913	1914
Flag	*Fürst Bismarck*	*Scharnhorst*	*Scharnhorst*	*Scharnhorst*	*Scharnhorst*	*Scharnhorst*	*Scharnhorst*
	Leipzig (ii)	*Leipzig* (ii)	*Leipzig* (ii)	*Gneisenau* (ii)	*Gneisenau* (ii)	*Gneisenau* (ii)	*Gneisenau* (ii)
	Niobe (ii)	*Arcona* (iii)	*Nürnberg*	*Nürnberg*	*Nürnberg*	*Nürnberg*	*Nürnberg*
	Arcona (ii)	*Iltis*	*Emden*	*Emden*	*Emden*	*Emden*	*Emden*
	Iltis	*Jaguar*	*Iltis*	*Iltis*	*Iltis*	*Iltis*	*Iltis*
	Jaguar	*Tiger*	*Jaguar*	*Jaguar*	*Jaguar*	*Jaguar*	*Jaguar*
	Tiger	*Luchs*	*Tiger*	*Tiger*	*Tiger*	*Tiger*	*Tiger*
	Luchs		*Luchs*	*Luchs*	*Luchs*	*Luchs*	*Luchs*

EAST AMERICAN CRUISER DIVISION

Vineta (ii) (F)	Jun 00–Mar 05
Moltke (i)	Sep–Dec 01
Stein	Oct 01–Jan 02
Falke (ii)	Nov 01–Mar 05
Gazelle (ii)	Feb 02–Jun 04
Charlotte	Nov 02–Jan 03
Stosch	Nov 02–Jan 03
Sperber	Feb–Mar 03
Panther	Aug 02–Mar 05

Nürnberg, *Dresden* and *Frankfurt*, members of the II. SG, at their buoys off the Kiel waterfront during the summer of 1918. In the lower right is the disarmed battleship *Schleswig-Holstein*, laid up after completing her previous duty as a submarine tender at Bremerhaven. *(DN collection)*

APPENDIX 3. PRINCIPAL GUNS MOUNTED IN GERMAN SMALL CRUISERS

Official designation	Calibre in inches	Muzzle velocity m/sec	Ships
15cm SK L/45 C/16	5.87	835	*Lübeck* (rearmed)
			Cöln (ii) class
15cm SK L/45 C/14	5.87	835	*Königsberg* (ii) class
			Kolberg (rearmed)
			Augsburg (rearmed)
			Strassburg (rearmed)
			Graudenz (rearmed)
			Pillau class
			Wiesbaden class
			Brummer class
15cm RK L/30 C/82	5.87	495	*Carola* class (2nd group)
			Irene class
15cm RK L/22 C/77	5.87	446	*Bismarck* class
			Carola class (1st group)
			Charlotte
			Irene class
15cm RK L/22 C/68	5.87	446	*Bismarck* class
12.5cm RK L/23 C/84	4.92	471	*Nixe*
12.5cm RK L/23 C/78			*Blitz* class
			Loreley
10.5cm SK L/45 C/12	4.134	710	*Graudenz* class
10.5cm SK L/45 C/06	4.134	710	*Kolberg* class
			Magdeburg class
			Karlsruhe class
10.5cm SK L/40 C/04	4.134	710	*München, Lübeck, Danzig, Leipzig*
			Königsberg class
			Dresden class
10.5cm SK L/40 C/97	4.134	715	*Gazelle* (ii) class
			Frauenlob class
			Bremen, Hamburg, Berlin
10.5cm SK L/35 C/91	4.134	600	*Falke, Seeadler, Cormoran, Condor, Geier*
			Irene class
			Gefion (ii)
10.5cm RK L/35 C/86	4.134	600	*Carola* class (2nd group)
			Bussard
			Jagd class
			Schwalbe class
			Greif
8.8cm SK L/45 C/13	3.46	750	AA gun
8.8cm SK L/30 C/89	3.46	590	*Charlotte*
			Hela
			Jagd class
			Meteor class

Official designation	Calibre in inches	Muzzle velocity m/sec	Ships
8.7cm RK L/24 C/73	3.43	471	*Blitz* class *Pommerania* *Carola* class (1st group)
5.2cm SK L/55 C/03	2.05	850	*Nymphe* 1907–09 *Königsberg* (i) class *Dresden* class *Kolberg* class *Pillau*
5cm SK L/40 C/90	1.97	656	*Gefion* (ii) *Hela*

Top left: *Irene*'s maindeck as completed, showing three of her original short-barrelled 15cm RK L/22 C/77 weapons. **Middle left:** an unshielded 10.5cm SK L/40, mounted in the 'first generation' of modern small cruisers. **Bottom left:** the (in)famous 5.2cm L/55 QL gun. After being unshipped from most vessels in 1911, there was a brief attempt to revive it an AA-weapon (see pp 152, 155). Its main use proved to be as armament of various auxiliary vessels during the First World War. **Above:** an 8.8cm SK L/45 anti-aircraft gun, the German navy's standard such weapon into the 1930s. *(DN collection)*

APPENDIX 4. SHIPYARDS RESPONSIBLE FOR SMALL CRUISER CONSTRUCTION

Yard	Yard – full form	Ships	Year of launch
Arman (Bordeaux)	Chantiers l'Arman Fréres, Bordeaux, FR	*Augusta*	1864
		Victoria	1864
Blohm & Voss (Hamburg)	Blohm & Voss, Hamburg	*Condor*	1892
		Dresden (i)	1907
		Cöln (ii)	1916
Copenhagen DYd	Orlogsværftet, Copenhagen, DK	*Gefion* (i)	1843
Danzig DYd	Kaiserliche Werft Danzig	*Arcona* (i)	1858
		Gazelle (i)	1859
		Nymphe (i)	1863
		Vineta (i)	1863
		Hertha (i)	1864
		Medusa (i)	1864
		Elisabeth	1868
		Ariadne (i)	1871
		Luise	1872
		Freya (i)	1874
		Moltke (i)	1877
		Gneisenau (i)	1879
		Sophie	1881
		Arcona (ii)	1885
		Nixe	1885
		Bussard	1890
		Cormoran	1892
		Kaiseradler	1892
		Thetis (ii)	1900
		Berlin	1903
		Danzig (ii)	1905
		Stuttgart	1906
		Emden (i)	1908
Devonport DYd	HM Dockyard, Devonport, UK	*Thetis* (i)	1846
		Niobe (i)	1849
Germania (Kiel)	Schiff- und Maschinenbau-AG „Germania"; from 1902: Friedrich Krupp Germaniawerft AG Kiel	*Greif*	1886
		Prinzeß Wilhelm	1887
		Meteor	1890
		Gazelle (ii)	1898
		Nymphe (ii)	1899
		Amazone (ii)	1900
		Askold (RU)	1900
		Cöln (i)	1909
		Karlsruhe (i)	1912

Yard	Yard – full form	Ships	Year of launch
Henderson, Coulborn (Renfrew)	Henderson, Coulborn & Co., Renfrew, UK	*Falke* (i)	1866
Howaldt (Kiel)	Howaldtswerke AG, Kiel	*Nan Thin* (CN)	1883
		Nan Shui (CN)	1884
		Undine (ii)	1902
		Nürnberg (ii)	1916
		Dresden (ii)	1917
		Magdeburg (ii)	1917
Kiel DYd	Kaiserliche Werft, Kiel	*Alexandrine*	1885
		Falke (ii)	1891
		Königsberg (i)	1905
		Nürnberg (i)	1906
		Augsburg	1909
		Graudenz	1913
		Regensburg	1914
		Frankfurt	1915
		Frauenlob (iii)	1918
		Ersatz A	-
Norddeutsche Schiffbau (Kiel)	Norddeutsche Schiffbau-Schiffbau Gesellschaft; from 1882: Schiff- und Maschinenbau-AG „Germania", Kiel	*Bismarck* (i)	1877
		Blücher (i)	1877
		Blitz	1882
Normand (Le Havre)	Chantiers et Ateliers Augustin Normand, Le Havre	*Grille* (i)	1857
Reiherstieg (Hamburg)	Reiherstieg Schiffwerft, Hamburg	*Marie*	1881
Schichau (Danzig)	F(erdinand) Schichau, Danzig	*Gefion* (ii)	1893
		Novik (RU)	1900
		Kolberg	1908
		Elbing (ex-RU)	1914
		Pillau (ex-RU)	1914
Thames Iron Works (Blackwall)	Thames Ironworks & Shipbuilding Company, Ltd, Blackwall, UK	*Zieten*	1876
AG Vulcan (Stettin)	Stettiner Machinenbau AG „Vulcan", Stettin	*Pommerania*	1865
		Leipzig (i)	1875
		Sédan	1876
		Stosch	1877
		Stein	1879
		Carola	1880
		Olga	1880

Yard	Yard – full form	Ships	Year of launch
AG Vulcan (continued)		*Tsi Yuen* (CN)	1883
		Irene	1887
		King Yuen (CN)	1887
		Lai Yuen (CN)	1887
		Comet	1892
		Hai Shew (CN)	1897
		Hai Yung (CN)	1897
		Hai Chen (CN)	1898
		Bogatyr (RU)	1901
		Hamburg	1903
		Lübeck	1904
		Stettin	1907
		Mainz	1909
		Uruguay (UR)	1910
		Breslau	1911
		Brummer	1915
		Wiesbaden (i)	1915
		Bremse	1916
		Wiesbaden (ii)	1917
		Rostock (ii)	1918
AG Weser (Bremen)	AG „Weser", Bremen	*Wacht*	1887
		Jagd	1888
		Hela	1895
		Niobe (ii)	1899
		Ariadne (ii)	1900
		Medusa (ii)	1900
		Arcona (iii)	1902
		Frauenlob (ii)	1902
		Bremen	1903
		München	1904
		Leipzig (ii)	1905
		Nautilus	1906
		Albatross	1907
		Magdeburg (i)	1911
		Stralsund	1911
		Rostock (i)	1912
		Königsberg (ii)	1915
		Emden (ii)	1916
		Leipzig (iii)	1918
		Ersatz-Cöln	1919
		Ersatz-Emden	1919
Wilhelmshaven DYd	Kaiserliche Werft Wilhelmshaven	*Loreley* (ii)	1871
		Pfeil	1882
		Charlotte	1885
		Schwalbe	1887
		Sperber	1888
		Geier	1894
		Strassburg	1911
		Karlsruhe (ii)	1916

SUMMARY

Yard	Arman	Blohm & Voss	Copenhagen DYd	Danzig DYd	Devonport DYd	Germania	Henderson	Howaldt	Kiel DYd	Norddeutsche	Normand	Reiherstieg	Schichau	Thames Iron Works	Vulcan	Weser	Wilhelmshaven DYd	Total
Germany	2	3	1	23	2	8	1	4	10	3	1	1	2	1	20	21	8	111
Export						1		2							3*			6*

* Two taken over and commissioned into German navy

The launch of *Falke* at Kiel Dockyard on 4 April 1891. *(DN collection)*

Also at Kiel Dockyard, *Graudenz* lies ready for launching in October 1913. *(DN collection)*

APPENDIX 5. LOSSES

TOTAL LOSSES BY CAUSE TO 1920

Surface Gunfire/ torpedo	Submarine torpedo	Mine	Scuttled	Internal explosion	Collision	Stranded	Foundered	Captured	Surrendered under Treaty & Protocol
10+1*	2	2	9	2	1+1*	1+1*	1	1	13
Ariadne (ii)	*Hela*	*Bremen*	*Cormoran*	*Karlsruhe* (i)	*Wacht*	*Gneisenau*	*Augusta*	*Geier****	*München*
Mainz	*Undine*	*Breslau*	*Brummer*	*Seeadler*	*Elbing**	*Magdeburg* (i)*			*Lübeck*
Cöln (i)			*Bremse*						*Danzig*
Emden (i)			*Cöln* (ii)						*Stuttgart*
Nürnberg (i)			*Karlsruhe* (ii)						*Stettin*
Leipzig (ii)			*Dresden* (ii)						*Kolberg****
Dresden (i)			*Frankfurt***						*Augsburg*
Königsberg (i)			*Emden* (ii)**						*Strassburg****
Wiesbaden (i)			*Nürnberg* (ii)**						*Stralsund****
Frauenlob (ii)									*Graudenz****
Rostock (i)*									*Regensburg****
									*Pillau****
									Königsberg (ii)***

* Final destruction by scuttling
** Salved and ceded to Allies
*** Further service under foreign flag

Wreck of *Emden* ashore following her defeat at the Cocos Islands by HMAS *Sydney* on 9 November 1914. *(AD collection)*

TOTAL LOSSES BY YEAR TO 1920

1885	1900	1901	1914	1915	1916	1917	1918	1919	1920
1	1	1	10	4	4	2	1	8	13
Augusta	*Gneisenau*	*Wacht*	*Magdeburg* (i)	*Dresden* (i)	*Wiesbaden* (i)	*Geier*	*Breslau*	*Brummer*	*München*
			Cormoran	*Königsberg* (i)	*Frauenlob* (ii)	*Seeadler*		*Bremse*	*Lübeck*
			Ariadne (ii)	*Undine*	*Rostock* (i)			*Cöln* (ii)	*Danzig*
			Mainz	*Bremen*	*Elbing*			*Karlsruhe* (ii)	*Stuttgart*
			Cöln (i)					*Dresden* (ii)	*Stettin*
			Hela					*Frankfurt*	*Kolberg*
			Karlsruhe (i)					*Emden* (ii)	*Augsburg*
			Emden (i)					*Nürnberg* (ii)	*Strassburg*
			Nürnberg (i)						*Stralsund*
			Leipzig (ii)						*Graudenz*
									Regensburg
									Pillau
									Königsberg (ii)

The former *Graudenz* (nearest the camera [now *E*]), *Stralsund* (ahead [*Z*]) and *Kolberg* (right [*W*]) at Cherbourg in 1920, following their surrender there (respectively on 1 June, 3 August and 25 April that year). The ships may be seen to be in poor condition, especially *Kolberg*, which also lacks topmasts and searchlights. She had been, like *Stralsund*, out of commission since the end of 1918 (cf p 234), unlike *Graudenz*, which had remained in service until March 1920. *Graudenz* went to Italy, while the other two vessels were taken over by the French. *(DN collection)*

BIBLIOGRAPHY

Afonin, N N, 'Kreisery "Murav'ev-Amurskii" i "Admiral Nevel'skoi"', *Sudostroenie*, 1989/2, pp 49–52.

Afonin, N N, 'Malye kreisery "Murav'ev-Amurskii" i "Admiral Nevel'skoi"', *Gangut* 26 (2001), pp 31–42.

Bagnasco, E and Cernuschi, E, 'La Regia Marina e l'incrociatore antiaerei', *Storia Militaire* 40 (1997), pp 24–34.

Bauer, G, 'Über moderne Turbinenanlagen für Kriegsschiffe', *Jahrbuch der Schiffbautechnischen Gesellschaft* 10 (1909), pp 301–51.

Berghahn, V R and Deist, W, *Rüstung im Zeichen der wilhemi-nischen Weltpolitik: Grundlegende Dokumente 1890–1914* (Düsseldorf: Droste, 1988).

Besteck, E, *Die trügerische 'First Line of Defence'* (Freiburg: Rombach Verlag 2006), pp 193–195.

Blechschmidt, F., *Nachrichten über den Kriegsschiffbau - Leichte Kreuzer.* (Werft-Reederei-Hafen, 1931).

Blohm & Voss, *Planbuch Kl. Kr. Ersatz-Ariadne*, (Hamburg: Blohm & Voss, 1916).

Boveri, W., 'Die Verwendung der Parsons-Turbine als Schiffsmaschine', *Jahrbuch der Schiffbautechnischen Gesellschaft* 8 (1907), pp 85–129.

Brysch, T, *Marinepolitik im preußischen Abgeordnetenhaus und Deutschen Reichstag 1850–1888* (Hamburg, Mittler, 1996).

Brown, D K, 'Seamanship and Steel: HMS *Calliope* at Samoa 15–16 March 1889', *Warship* XII/48 (1988), 30–36.

Busley, C, *Die Schiffsmaschine: ihre Construction, Wirkungsweise und Bedienung* (Kiel: Lipsius und Tischer, 1885).

Buxton, I, *Big Gun Monitors: Design, Construction and Operations 1914–1945*, 2nd edition (Barnsley: Seaforth, 2008).

Chen Yue, 中國軍艦圖誌 1855-1911 [*Zhōngguó jūnjiàn tú zhì/ Chinese Warships Atlas 1855-1911*] (Hong Kong: The Commercial Press, 2013).

Chunxiao, J, *Mit Barbaren gegen Barbaren: Die chinesische Selbststärkungsbewegung und das deutsche Rüstungsgeschäft im späten 19. Jahrhundert* (Berlin: Lit Verlag, 2002).

Clark, M, *Wrecks & Reefs of Southeast Scotland* (Caithness: Whittles Publishing, 2010).

Cosentino, M, 'The Colonial Sloop *Eritrea*', *Warship* [XXXVIII] (2016), pp 30–41.

Dodson, A, *The Kaiser's Battlefleet: German capital ships 1871–1918* (Barnsley: Seaforth, 2016).

——, *Before the Battlecruiser: the big cruiser in the world's navies 1865–1910* (Barnsley: Seaforth, 2018), pp 30–67.

-----, 'Beyond the Kaiser: the Imperial German Navy's destroyers and torpedo boats after 1918', *Warship* [XLI] (2019), pp 129–44.

Dodson, A, and Cant, S, *Spoils of War: the fate of enemy fleets after the two World Wars* (Barnsley: Seaforth, 2020), pp 89–90.

Eger, C L, 'Hudson-Fulton Naval Celebration', *Warship International* 49/2 (2012), pp 123–51.

Foerster, R, *Politische Geschichte der Preußischen und Deutschen Flotte bis zum ersten Flottengesetz von 1898* (Dresden, Limpert, 1928).

Föttinger, H, 'Die hydrodynamische Arbeitsübertragung besonders durch Transformatoren, ein Rückblick und Ausblick', *Jahrbuch der Schiffbautechnischen Gesellschaft* 31 (1930), pp 171–214.

Freivogel, *Kriegsmarine in der Adria 1941–45: Ex-jugoslawische Kriegsschiffe unter deutscher Flagge – ein Stück weitgehend unbekannter Marine- und Seekriegsgeschichte*, Marine-Arsenal Band 40 (Wölfersheim-Berstadt: Podzun-Pallas-Verlag, 1998).

——, *Warships of the Royal Yugoslav Navy* (Zagreb: Despot Infinitus, 2020).

Friedman, N, *British Cruisers: Two World Wars and After* (Barnsley: Seaforth, 2010).

——, *British Cruisers of the Victorian Era* (Barnsley: Seaforth, 2012).

Friedman, N (ed.), *German Warships of World War I: The Royal Navy's Official Guide to the Capital Ships, Cruisers, Destroyers, Submarines and Small Craft, 1914–1918* (London: Greenhill Books, 1992).

Gardiner, R, Chesneau, R, and Kolesnik, E M (eds), *Conway's All the World's Fighting Ships 1860–1905* (London: Conway Maritime Press, 1979).

George, S C, *Jutland to Junkyard: the raising of the scuttled German High Seas Fleet from Scapa Flow – the greatest salvage operation of all time* (Cambridge: Patrick Stevens Ltd, 1973).

Goldrick, J, *Before Jutland: the naval war in northern European waters, August 1914–February 1915* (Annapolis, MD: Naval Institute Press, 2015).

——, *After Jutland: The Naval War in Northern European Waters, June 1916–November 1918* (Barnsley: Seaforth, 2018).

Göthling, W, Lörscher, O, and Schnetzke, S, *Ausgeliefert – Die deutschen U-Boote 1918–1920 und ihr Verbleib* (Berlin: digital business and printing 2012).

Greve, F A, *Die Luftverteidigung im Abschnitt Wilhelmshaven 1939–45: 2. Marineflakbrigade* (Jever, 2000)

Grießmer, A, *Große Kreuzer der Kaiserlichen Marine 1906–1918: Konstruktionen und Entwürfe im Zeichen des Tirpitz-Planes* (Bonn: Bernard & Graefe, 1996).

——, *Linienschiffe der Kaiserlichen Marine 1906–1918: Konstruktionen zwischen Rüstungskonkurrenz und Flottengesetz* (Bonn: Bernard & Graefe, 1999).

Gröner, E, *Die deutschen Kriegsschiffe 1815–1936* (Munich/Berlin: J F Lehmanns Verlag, 1937).

Groos, O (ed), *Der Krieg zur See – der Krieg in der Nordsee,* vol 1, (Berlin: Mittler, 1920)

Haack, R, 'Ueber die in Deutschland gebauten chinesischen Panzerschiffe', in *Sitzungsberichte des Vereins zur Beförderung des Gewerbefleisses* 1896, pp 53–83.

Hänisch, O, *Entwurf der Turbinenanlage für einen Kleinen Kreuzer* (Wilhelmshaven: 1 November 1910).

Hallmann, H, *Der Weg zum deutschen Schlachtflottenbau* (Stuttgart: Kohlhammer Verlag, 1933).

Heath, K and Thomson, M, *Scapa Flow Underwater Salvage Sites Survey: Phase 2 Report* (University of the Highlands and Islands Archaeology Institute/SULA Diving/Orca Marine, 2019).

Hepper, D J, *British Warship Losses in the Ironclad Era 1860–1919* (London: Greenhill Books, 2007).

Herold, H, *Reichsgewalt bedeutet Seegewalt: Die Kreuzergeschwader der Kaiserlichen Marine als Instrument der deutschen Kolonial- und Weltpolitik 1885 bis 1901* (Munich: Oldenbourg, 2013).

Hildebrand, H H, Röhr, A, and Steinmetz, H-O, *Die Deutschen Kriegsschiffe: Biographien – ein Spiegel der Marinegeschichte von 1815 bis zur Gegenwart,* 10 volumes ([Ratingen]: Mundus Verlag, [1997]).

Höft, M, *Der Vulcan in Stettin und Hamburg,* III: *Der Kriegsschiff-, Lokomotiv- und Eisenbahnbau,* (Rotenburg/W: Edition Falkenberg, 2017).

Hubatsch, W, *Kaiserliche Marine* (Munich: J F Lehmanns Verlag 1975).

Jacobsen, H, *Die Entwicklung der Schiesskunst in der Kaiserlich Deutschen Marine* (Berlin: Reichswehrministerium, 1928).

Jakobsen, K, *Die Seeschlacht vor dem Skagerrak* (Thyborøn: Sea War Museum Jutland, 2018).

Jane, F T (ed.), *All the World's Fighting Ships 1900* (London: Sampson Low, Marston, 1900).

Jellicoe, N, *The Last Days of the HSF: From Mutiny to Scapa Flow* (Barnsley: Seaforth, 2019).

Johow, H, *Hilfsbuch für den Schiffbau* (Berlin: J Springer, 1884).

——, *Die Kreuzer-Korvette „Problem" – eine nautisch-technische Studie* (Kiel and Leipzig, 1889; reprinted Saarbrücken: Fines Mundi, 2009).

Jordan, J and Moulin, J, *French Cruisers 1922–1956* (Barnsley: Seaforth Publishing, 2013).

Jungmann, E, *Eckernförde und der 5. April 1849 – Eine artilleristische Studie aus dem Deutsch-Dänischen Kriege* (Hamburg: Perthes, 1852).

Koop, G, 'The Imperial German Navy and the Hurricane at Samoa', *Warship* XII/48 (1988), pp 36–42.

Krest'ianinov, V Ia, *Kreisera Rossiiskogo imperatorskogo flota 1856–1917 gody,* 2 volumes (St Petersburg: Galeia Print, 2009).

Kronenfels, J F von, *Das schwimmende Flottenmaterial der Seemächte* (Vienna: Hartleben, 1881; reprinted Munich: Schmidt, 1976).

Lambi, I N, *The Navy and German Power Politics, 1862–1914* (Boston: Allen & Unwin, 1984).

Langensiepen, B, Nottelmann, D and Krüsmann, J, *Halbmond und Kaiseradler: 'Breslau' und 'Goeben' am Bosporus 1914–18* (Hamburg: Mittler, 1999).

Lengerer, H, 'The Genesis of the Six-Six Fleet', *Warship* [XLI] (2019), pp 46–57.

Lyon, D, 'The First Town Class 1908–31', *Warship* I/1 (1977), pp 48–58, I/2 (1977), pp 54–61, I/3, pp 46–51.

Mach, A, 'The Chinese Battleships', *Warship* VIII (1984), pp 9–18.

McCartney, I, *Jutland 1916: the archaeology of a naval battlefield* (London: Conway, 2016).

——, *Scapa 1919: the Archaeology of a Scuttled Fleet* (London: Bloomsbury, 2019).

McLaughlin, S, 'Retvisan: An American Battleship for the Tsar', *Warship* XXIII (2000), pp 48–66.

——, *Russian & Soviet Battleships* (Annapolis: Naval Institute Press, 2003).

——, *Russian and Soviet Cruisers to 1960* (Barnsley: Seaforth, in preparation).

Mulder, J and Ruygrok, W F, *De Nederlandsche Zeemacht - Pantserschepen, Pantserdekschepen, Monitors* (Emmen: Lanasta, 2004).

'Nauticus', 'Die deutsche Kriegsmarine im Jahre 1904/05', *Nauticus: Jahrbuch für Deutschlands Seeinteressen* 1905, pp 18–53.

N N, *75 Jahre Marinewerft Wilhelmshaven* (Oldenburg, G. Stalling, 1931).

Nottelmann, D, 'From Ironclads to Dreadnoughts: The Development of the German Navy 1864–1918', *Warship International* 48/3 (2011), pp 241–73; 49/1 (2012), pp 54–84; 49/4 (2012), pp 317–55; 50/3 (2013), pp 209–49; 51/1 (2014), pp 43–90; 52/2 (2015), pp 137–74; 52/4 (2015), pp 304–21; 53/2 (2016), pp 122–66; 54/3 (2017), pp 199–247; 55/4 (2018), pp 281–332, 56/4 (2019), pp 287–333; 57/1 (2020), pp 49–55.

——, 'Das Kanonenboot *Iltis* (II)', *Das logbuch* 19 (2018), p 98.

——, *Die Brandenburg-Klasse: Höhepunkt des deutschen Panzerschiffbaus* (Hamburg: E S Mittler, 2002).

Paloczi-Horvath, G, 'The German Navy from Versailles to Hitler', *Warship 1997–98*, pp 64–76.

Pinl, H, *Deutsch-russischer Schiffbau vor 1914* (Langenhagen: BoD, 2002).

Rahardt, O, *Schiff Profile: SMS „Charlotte" – Segelschiff der Kaiserlichen Marine* (Stengelheim: UNITEC-Medienvertrieb, 2018).

Reichs-Marine-Amt, *Bauvorschrift für den Schiffskörper des Kleinen Kreuzers 'Ersatz ~~Leipzig~~ Nürnberg, Mainz'*, S (Berlin, 1915).

——, *Bauvorschrift für die Hauptmaschinen (zwei Turbinensätze auf zwei Wellen) und Kessel mit zugehörigen Hilfsmaschinen, Zubehör und Inventar des Kleinen Kreuzers 'Ersatz Dresden' – M Teil I*, (Berlin, 1915).

——, *Bauvorschrift für die Hauptmaschinen (zwei Turbo-Transformatorsätze auf zwei Wellen) und Kessel mit zugehörigen Hilfsmaschinen, Zubehör und Inventar des Kleinen Kreuzers 'Ersatz Gefion', M Teil I – Hauptmaschinen* (Berlin, 1913).

——, *Endgültige Bauvorschrift für die komplette Maschinenanlage (Dampfturbinen-Antrieb) nebst Zubehör für den Kleinen Kreuzer 'Ersatz Merkur'* (Berlin, 1903).

——, *Deutsche Kriegsflotte, IV: Kleine Kreuzer* (Berlin, 1907–1915).

——, *Marine-Verordnungsblatt* 24/20 (1893), pp 233–36.

——, *Nachweisung sämtlicher Seereisen S M Schiffe und der Ablösungskommandos (Seedienstnachweisung) mit Nachträgen.* (Berlin: RMA, 1906, 1913).

——, *Neubauten und Neuentwürfe S.M. Schiffe – Abgeschlossen Ende 1917* (Berlin, 1918).

Schleihauf, W, 'The Baden Trials', *Warship* XXIX (2007), 81–90.

Schulz, B, *Die Ölfeuerung* (Halle/S: W. Knapp, 1925).

Sondhaus, L, *Preparing for Weltpolitik: German sea power before the Tirpitz era* (Annapolis: Naval Institute Press, 1997).

Spasskii, I D (ed.), *Istoriia otechestvennogo sudostroeniia*, III (St Petersburg: Sudostroenie, 1995).

Sullivan, D M, 'Phantom Fleet: The Confederacy's Unclaimed European-Built Warships', *Warship International* 24/1 (1987), pp 12–32.

Tirpitz, A von, *Erinnerungen* (Leipzig/Berlin: Koehler, 1942).

Trubitsyn, S B, 'Kreisery "Elbing" i "Pillau"', *Gangut*, 26 (2001), pp 42–48.

Van der Vat, D, *The Grand Scuttle: the sinking of the German fleet at Scapa Flow in 1919* (London: Hodder & Stoughton, 1982).

Vulcan-Werke, *Projekt Nr. 1612/31, S.M. Kleiner Kreuzer "Ersatz Gazelle" Anlage mit Turbo-Transformatoren* (Hamburg/Stettin, 1914).

Wildenberg, T, *Billy Mitchell's War with the Navy: the Interwar Rivalry Over Naval Air Power* (Annapolis, MD: Naval Institute Press, 2013).

Woodward, D, *The Collapse of Power: Mutiny in the HSF* (London: Arthur Barker, 1973).

Wright, R N J, 'The Peiyang and Nanyang Cruisers of the 1880s', *Warship* XX (1996), pp 95–110.

——, *The Chinese Steam Navy, 1862–1945* (London: Chatham Publishing, 2000).

I. Werftdivision, *Neuerungen im Schiffsmaschinenbetrieb – Anhang zum Leitfaden für Maschinenkunde an den Divisionsschulen der Kaiserl. Marine* (Kiel: Kaiserliche Werft, 1917).

ARCHIVAL MATERIAL

UK National Archives, Kew

ADM116/1939
ADM116/1989.
ADM116/1992
ADM116/1994
ADM116/2113
HW1/2301

Bundesarchiv-Militärarchiv, Freiburg

Ma 473
N 253/3
N 253/4
RM2/1583
RM2/1613
RM2/1614
RM3/2
RM3/348
RM3/360
RM3/361
RM3/362
RM3/374
RM3/384
RM3/836
RM3/848
RM3/862
RM3/865
RM3/871
RM3/2526
RM3/3481
RM3/3602
RM3/3681
RM3/3682
RM3/3684
RM3/3685
RM3/3697
RM3/3698
RM3/6690
RM3/23005
RM3/23039
RM3/23148
RM92/2265
RM92/2279

US National Archives

NARA-Roll T1022-494 PG-67388-NID
NARA-Roll T1022-497 PG-67448-NID
NARA-Roll T1022-510 PG-66707-NID
NARA-Roll T1022-1109 PG-69202-NID
NARA-Roll T1022-1303 PG-77649-NID
NARA-Roll T1022-1559 PG-66033-NID
NARA-Roll T1022-1659 PG-77733-NID

INDEX

Ships

All dates are of launch, except: ld = laid down; proj = projected

Images and data-pages are shown in **bold**

Non-German naval vessels are coded as follows:

AU = Australia
BR = Brazil
CL = Chile
CN = China
CSA = Confederate States of America
DK = Denmark
FR = France
HT = Haiti
JP = Japan
PE = Peru
RU = Russia
SE = Sweden
SP = Spain
TU = Ottoman Empire
UK = United Kingdom
US = United States
UY = Uruguay
VE = Venezuela
YU = Yugoslavia

People

Geographical

Ship timelines

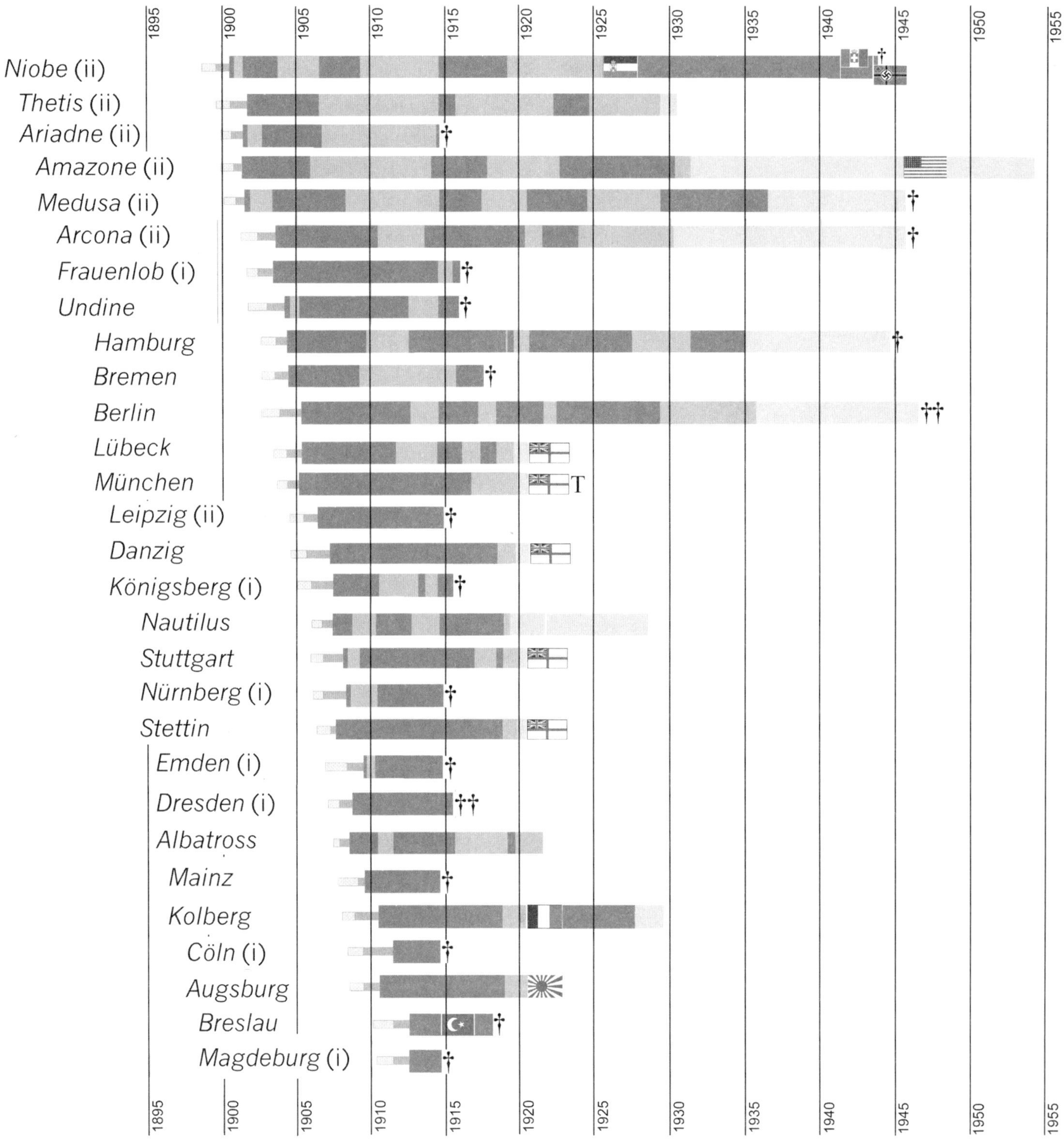

Key

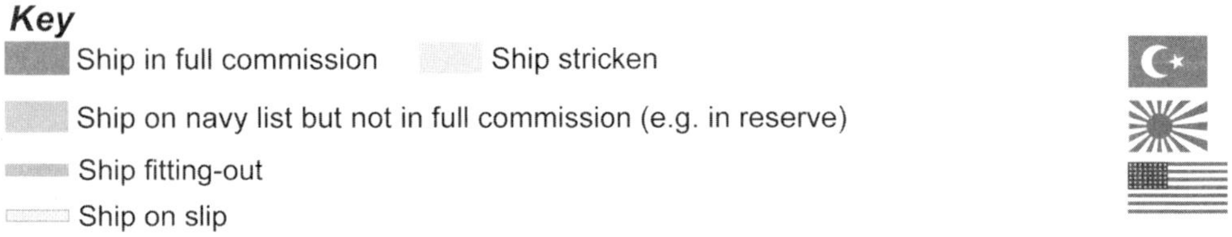

Ship in full commission

Ship stricken

Ship on navy list but not in full commission (e.g. in reserve)

Ship fitting-out

Ship on slip

Ship transferred to Ottoman Navy

Ship ceded to Japan

Ship ceded to/seized by USA